Nelson Appleton Miles

Harper's Pictorial History of the War With Spain

Nelson Appleton Miles

Harper's Pictorial History of the War With Spain

ISBN/EAN: 9783744748230

Printed in Europe, USA, Canada, Australia, Japan

Cover: Foto ©ninafisch / pixelio.de

More available books at **www.hansebooks.com**

HARPER'S

PICTORIAL HISTORY

OF THE

WAR WITH SPAIN

WITH AN INTRODUCTION BY

MAJ.-GEN. NELSON A. MILES

COMMANDING UNITED STATES ARMY

IN TWO VOLUMES

VOLUME II.

NEW YORK AND LONDON

HARPER & BROTHERS PUBLISHERS

1899

U. S. Gunboat *Nashville* Small Boats Cutting Cables U. S. Auxiliary Gunboat *Windom* U. S. Cruiser *Marblehead*

CUTTING THE TELEGRAPH CABLES AT CIENFUEGOS, UNDER FIRE OF SPANISH BATTERIES.—DRAWN BY S. H. NEALY

OPERATIONS IN THE WEST INDIES

FOLLOWING a comprehensive scheme of general attack, powerful forces were assembled, as has been seen, at various points on the Atlantic and Gulf coasts of the United States, to invade the Spanish possessions in the West Indies. Meanwhile, naval demonstrations were made at several exposed points, particularly at Cardenas, Matanzas, and Cabanas on the north coast of Cuba, Cienfuegos on its south coast, and San Juan, the capital of Puerto Rico. Some of these demonstrations were incidental, either to the general maintenance of the blockade, the cutting of ocean cables, the prevention of the erection of fortifications by the enemy, or the search for a hostile fleet that was known to have left Europe for American waters; and all were influenced by a spirit of humanity and forbearance, as it was still hoped at the national capital that Spain would recognize the futility of a war with the United States and sue for peace.

On Wednesday, the 4th of May, one week after the shelling of the defences of Matanzas, Admiral Sampson sailed eastward in search of the Spanish fleet; and on Friday Commodore Watson took command of the blockading squadron. On Thursday, the 5th, the torpedo-boat *Dupont*, cruising off Matanzas, observed, on the point near Matanzas light, a number of Spaniards engaged in raising the red-and-yellow flag; and it was conjectured that the construction of batteries was still going on in spite of the lesson of the 27th of April. On the afternoon of the following day, therefore, the *Dupont* and the auxiliary cruiser *Hornet*—two of the smallest vessels in the navy of the United States—scouted close in-shore, and were received with a storm of bullets from the rifles of a body of Spanish cavalry. The little vessels opened fire with their quick-firing guns, driving the cavalry to cover and demolishing three block-houses. One of the Matanzas batteries now fired an 8-inch shell at the *Dupont*, but it fell short. Not a man on either boat was hit by the bullets of the Spanish cavalry. On the morning of the 7th the *Dupont* and *Hornet* resumed the bombardment, but failed to elicit a reply. The little *Dupont* then decked herself with her gayest flags and took the news to Key West, where she was received by the troopship *Panther* with "a burst of cheers and applause that was heard well into the town."

At Cienfuegos, on the south coast, south-east of Matanzas, and Cardenas, on the north coast, east of Matanzas, occurred, on Wednesday, the 11th of May, the first tragedies of the war. On the forenoon of that day boats from the *Marblehead* and *Nashville* cut two cables off Cienfuegos under a heavy infantry fire, during which they were supported by the guns of the *Marblehead* and *Nashville*, and, later, the *Windom*. In this action one man was killed and eleven men were wounded. On the afternoon of the same date the *Machias*, *Wilmington*, *Winslow*, and the revenue-cutter *Hudson* were engaged at Cardenas. The *Winslow*, when well within the harbor, suddenly found herself under the fire of masked shore batteries. Many of the enemy's shells struck her, disabling her port main engine, forward boiler, and steering engine, and setting one compartment on fire. Ensign Worth Bagley, her executive officer, and four of her crew were killed. Her commanding officer was wounded, and the vessel, with the rest of the crew, was only saved from entire destruction by the gallant action of the commanding officer of the *Hudson*, who took his vessel in under a severe fire and towed the *Winslow* out. In connection with the same expedition, a force was landed on Diana Cay, in Cardenas Bay, to explode the harbor mines, which were understood to be controlled from a station on that cay. The station having been hurriedly abandoned, the American flag was hoisted over it. "This," said the Secretary of the Navy in his report, "so far as the records of the Navy Department show, was the first raising of the American flag in Cuba during the war."

The first land fight of the war took place near Cabanas on Thursday, the 12th of May, when a detachment of the First Regular Infantry, under Captain Joseph H. Dorst, of the Fourth Cavalry, landed from the steamship *Gussie* at Point Arbolitos with couriers and supplies for the Cubans. The Spanish garrison was routed with loss, and the Americans, having seen the couriers safely mounted and well on their way westward, re-embarked without casualty under cover of the guns of the *Manning* and the *Wasp*.

On the morning of Thursday, May 12, while the *Gussie* was steaming towards Cabanas, Admiral Sampson, looking for the Spanish fleet, was bombarding the defences of San Juan de Puerto Rico. On April 29 a fleet, composed of the Spanish armored cruisers *Cristobal Colon*, *Vizcaya*, *Almirante Oquendo*, and *Infanta Maria Teresa*, and the torpedo-

THE CASTLE AT CIENFUEGOS

gunboats *Furor*, *Terror*, and *Pluton*, had sailed from the Cape de Verde Islands, under command of Admiral Cervera. As the destination of this fleet was uncertain, Admiral Sampson sailed east with a portion of the fleet under his command for the purpose of observation. He left Key West on the 4th of May on the flag-ship *New York*, and off Havana picked up the *Iowa*, *Indiana*, and *Detroit*. On the way east he was afterwards joined by the monitors *Terror* and *Amphitrite*, and the *Montgomery*, *Porter*, *Wompatuck*, and collier *Niagara*.

Continuing eastward in the hope of finding the enemy at San Juan, Puerto Rico, he found it necessary, on account of the small coal supply of the monitors, to take them in tow, and the squadron did not arrive off San Juan until the morning of the 12th. A bombardment of that place followed for two hours and a half, but as there was no land force to hold it in case of its surrender, and as the Spanish fleet was not there, it was determined to return to Havana, where it was possible Cervera might have gone.

While the squadron was on its return the following despatch was received from the Navy Department:

"The Spanish fleet from Cape Verde Islands off Coraçao, West Indies, May 14. Flying Squadron *en route* to Key West, Florida. Proceed with all possible despatch to Key West."

CUTTING CABLES OFF CIENFUEGOS

Commander McCalla's Account

Having found out the location of the cables leading from the south and west into the cable house, near the light-house at the entrance to Cienfuegos Harbor, I prepared to cut them.

The arrival of the collier *Saturn*, with the *Windom*, and the departure of the steamer *Adula* with refugees from Cienfuegos on the 10th of May, placed me in a position where I could make the attempt to cut the cable, severing communication with Havana.

For this purpose Lieutenant Southerland was directed to leave the station off Cienfuegos with the *Eagle* sometime during the night of the 10th and steam to the westward, where the cable was laid in shallow water near the light-ship off Diego Perez Key. He was directed to cut the cable, burn the light-ship mentioned above, and destroy the light-house off Piedras Key.

Lieutenant C. McR. Winslow was placed in command of the steam-launches and sailing-launches from the *Nashville* and *Marblehead*, with Lieutenant E. A. Anderson second in command and Ensign Magruder having charge of the steam-launches. The four boats were to be used to drag for and to cut the cables off Cienfuegos under the protection of the guns of the *Nashville* and *Marblehead*.

The details were carefully explained to Commander Maynard and Lieutenant Winslow, and the attempt was made on the morning of the 11th.

An infantry and cavalry force posted about the cable house was driven from their position by the guns of the *Nashville* and *Marblehead*, and the four launches then dragged for and succeeded in cutting the cables leading to the south and to the west. The cable house was destroyed by the guns.

Two cables were cut and a small one was found inshore, but before this could be cut the fire from the infantry with, evidently, a Maxim gun was so severe as to compel the boats to withdraw, as they were within 150 yards of the enemy.

The enemy was so sheltered towards the last by the gullies and ravines that the fire from the ships could not keep down their fire entirely.

The enemy, having concealed themselves in the light-house and opened fire on the boats, the light-house was destroyed.

I cannot speak in too high terms of the officers and men engaged in the four boats in cutting the cables. Their work was performed with the utmost coolness and intrepidity under most trying circumstances.

Account by Lieutenant Anderson, of the *Marblehead*

Having been placed in charge of the steam and sailing launches of the *Marblehead*, under the command of Lieutenant Cameron McR. Winslow, who was also in command of the steam and sailing launches of the *Nashville*, I reported to that officer about 6.30 A.M. on the 11th, and was directed by him to keep off his starboard hand while going in.

In the steam-launch, in addition to the regular crew of five men, there was a crew of three men in charge of a 1-pounder Hotchkiss gun mounted on the forecastle; also six men of the marine guard, armed with rifles and selected for their proficiency in marksmanship. This boat was intended to cover the sailing-launch while at work.

In the sailing-launch, which was used to pick up and cut the cable, in addition to crew of twelve men and coxswain, were the chief carpenter's mate and blacksmith. These men were armed with rifles and revolvers. I took immediate charge of this boat.

After the beach had been shelled by the *Marblehead* and *Nashville* and the cable house and barracks destroyed, the boats approached the shore in tow of the steam-launches. When opposite the cable house the sailing-launches were cast off, and the steam-launches, in charge of Ensign Magruder, took position about 150 to 200 yards from the beach and kept up a fire directed on the supposed position of the enemy.

A 6-inch armored cable was quickly picked up by the launch from the *Marblehead*, and, assisted by the *Nashville's* launch, was under-

CIENFUEGOS, FROM THE HARBOR

run out to 12¾ fathoms of water, and there a section the length of the boat was cut from the cable. This cable led in about an east-southeast direction from the cable house. Ranges were taken and sketches made to recover the end of the cable if desired.

A second 6-inch armored cable was found by the *Nashville's* launch, leading in a southerly direction from the cable house. This cable was also picked up by the *Marblehead's* launch about thirty yards from the beach, and, after having been cut by us, was again cut by the *Nashville's* launch in about 5½ fathoms, and the section of about 100 feet coiled down in the *Marblehead's* launch.

While the work of cutting the second cable was going on the enemy opened a slow fire on us, which was returned by such men in the launch as were not actually engaged in cutting the cable. This fire, assisted by the steam-launches, silenced the fire of the enemy for a time.

A small cable was seen leading parallel and close to the second large cable. An effort was made while cutting the large cable to pick up the small one, but the grapnel fouled the bottom and was lost.

In searching for the small cable, after cutting the second large one, either a third large cable or a section of the second cable nearer the cable house was found. This cable had been lifted within a foot of the rail of the stern of the launch, when the enemy, who had taken a position within about 150 yards of the water, opened on the boats with volley firing. One man in the launch was badly wounded at the first volley, and, having been ordered by Lieutenant Winslow to cast off, the cable was slipped and the launch started to return.

The enemy, who were evidently in force, fired very rapidly at the boats with rifles, machine-guns, and, from some shells that fell near the launch, I should judge with 1-pounder guns.

The cockswain having been wounded just as the launch got started, I steered the boat off and directed the crew to keep down between the thwarts as much as possible. In spite of this precaution, three more men were wounded, the bullets penetrating the sides of the boat. Owing to the bullet holes in the launch, she was making water freely while going off, requiring constant bailing.

A heavy ground-swell made the work of lifting the cable difficult, and towards the end a fresh onshore breeze sprang up, causing the launch to ship some water after the weight of the cable came on it, and made the work of running off very slow.

The conduct of the men was worthy of all praise. They worked intelligently and cheerfully at the exhausting labor of picking up and cutting the heavy cables, and, when under a heavy fire and one of the crew badly wounded, continued to work, without confusion, until ordered to stop. Where every one did his whole duty it is difficult to specify particular instances, but I think the following worthy of mention: J. J. Doran, boatswain's mate, after having received a very painful wound, encouraged the rest of the crew and the wounded by his cheerful manner and talk. J. H. Bennett, boatswain's mate, and A. Sundquist, chief carpenter's mate, particularly distinguished themselves by the intelligence and great energy they displayed in the work. In the steam-launch, F. Gill, gunner's mate, and L. Chadwick, apprentice, remained exposed on the forecastle of the launch under a very heavy fire, and served the 1-pounder gun until ordered by me to cease firing.

ENSIGN WORTH BAGLEY, U. S. N.

Executive Officer of Torpedo-boat Winslow. Killed in Action in Cardenas Harbor, May 11

BRINGING ASHORE THE BODY OF ENSIGN WORTH BAGLEY AT FORT TAMPA, MAY 13.—Drawn by Clyde D. V. Hunt

LIEUTENANT JOHN B. BERNADOU, U. S. N.

Commanding Torpedo-boat Winslow. Wounded in Action in Cardenas Harbor, May 11

Commander Maynard's Account

At 6.46 A.M. the steam and sailing launches of the *Marblehead* and *Nashville*, armed and prepared for grappling and cutting cables, under command of Lieutenant C. McR. Winslow, left their respective ships and stood in for the reefs of Colorados Point under cover of the guns of the *Nashville*. The latter, after bringing the light-house to bear northwest, headed in for the point, and, when within 1200 yards of the cable house to the eastward of the light-house, at 7.45 A.M. opened fire with the starboard battery on that building and a number of the enemy's soldiers who were seen in a small earthwork near that house.

The *Marblehead* took position to the westward, at the entrance of the port, and opened fire, and in a few minutes the cable house was destroyed and the enemy's troops had disappeared, after firing a few rounds from their small-arms. The *Nashville* continued to stand in towards the point until within from 600 to 800 yards from shore, firing continuously into the woods and bushes to the right of the light-house. The enemy not returning the fire, the launches proceeded in close to the shore and soon grappled and raised two cables, which they underran and cut.

The *Nashville* continued to fire rapidly until 8.18 A.M., after which time, as there was no response from the enemy, a slow fire from the rapid-fire guns was maintained.

Considerable difficulty was experienced in keeping the ship in position off the cable-house point, owing to the wind, which was blowing directly on shore, and also to a moderate swell. Aiming was much interfered with by the smoke of our guns, as it hung between the ship and the shore.

At about 9.45 A.M. the enemy, evidently much reinforced, suddenly opened a scattering rifle-fire, which increased to a heavy fire by 10 A.M., on our boats just as they had grappled a third cable. The enemy were firing from the light-house and from cover and bluffs to the right of it. At 10.10 the boats retreated towards their ships, while the *Nashville* steamed in between them and the enemy, and at the same time opened up a rapid fire on the light-house and wherever else the enemy appeared to be.

In obedience to Commander McCalla's signal and previous order, we had been careful not to hit the light-house, but at this time, when it was seen that the enemy were using it as a cover, I directed the fire of the guns of the *Nashville* against it in order to drive them out.

The boats having been secured alongside of the ship, on the side away from the enemy, the *Nashville* stood out of range, and after discharging boats hoisted them at 11 A.M.

The *Nashville* was struck by many rifle bullets, but no damage was done except cutting some boat falls and running-gear. Several persons on board were struck, but not seriously injured.

In the sailing-launch of the *Nashville* Robert Volz, seaman, was seriously wounded, and Lieutenant Winslow was shot through the fingers of his left hand. The boats received several bullets through them, but were not much injured.

I cannot praise too highly the coolness and good behavior of all on board, officers and men. Lieutenant A. C. Dillingham, the executive officer, deserved great credit for his coolness and good judgment throughout the affair, and especially towards the close of the engagement, when, the commanding officer being temporarily disabled by a shock, caused by being struck over the heart by a rifle bullet, he handled the ship and boats admirably.

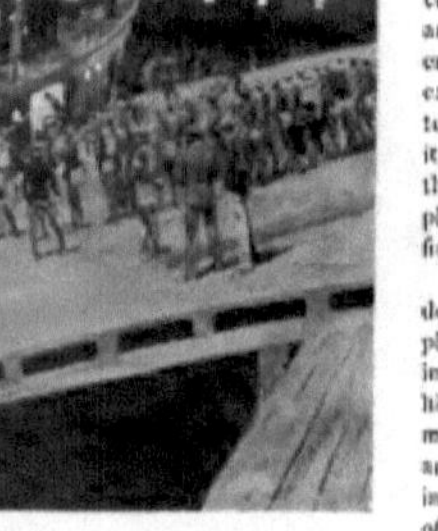

THE *GUSSIE* EXPEDITION—FIRST EMBARKATION OF UNITED STATES TROOPS FOR CUBA, AT PORT TAMPA, MAY 11.—DRAWN BY FREDERIC REMINGTON

ACCOUNT BY LIEUTENANT WINSLOW, OF THE *NASHVILLE*

UNDER verbal orders from Commander McCalla, I proceeded about 7 A.M. with the steam-cutter and sailing-launch of the *Nashville* and the steam-cutter and sailing-launch of the *Marblehead* to execute the duty assigned me. After the ships had demolished the cable house and had apparently dislodged the enemy from the chaparral, hills, and rifle-pits, I proceeded with the boats under my command directly for the cable house, opening fire from the Colt's automatic gun in the bow of the *Nashville's* steam-cutter and from the 1-pounder cannon in the bow of the *Marblehead's* steam-cutter, also from the sharp-shooters in both steam-cutters. We cast the sailing-launches off from the steam-cutters when about 300 yards from the beach. I was in the sailing-launch of the *Nashville*; Lieutenant E. A. Anderson, of the *Marblehead*, in the *Marblehead's* sailing-launch. Ensign T. P. Magruder was left in command of both steam-cutters, with orders to keep up a fire on the hills and chaparral. The fire from these two boats was kept up incessantly while we were engaged in the work of cutting the cables. The cable going to the eastward was first grappled, and was underrun by both sailing-launches, and a section about 24 fathoms in length was cut out of this cable, the sea end being cut in about 13 fathoms of water. The section of this cable cut out was brought to the *Nashville* on the return of the sailing-launch. After cutting the first cable we proceeded in both sailing-launches to the southwestward of the demolished cable house and grappled within 60 feet of the beach for the cable leading westward.

After about one-half hour's work we succeeded in grappling this cable. Great difficulty was experienced in lifting it, and we were only able to underrun 15 fathoms of it. We cut a section out of this cable about 15 fathoms long and threw it overboard in deep water, leaving the sea end of the cable in from 6 to 10 fathoms of water. While working with the second cable, we discovered a third cable, much smaller than the other two, parallel to the cable leading to the westward. After cutting the second cable we proceeded to grapple this third cable.

Up to this time the enemy had from time to time opened fire upon us, but we were able to silence his fire by the fire from our steam-cutters and the continuous heavy fire maintained by the *Marblehead* and the *Nashville*. While grappling the third cable, the enemy apparently greatly increased his force and opened a deadly fire on our boats. Believing that we had cut the two important cables, and knowing that we could not endure the terrific fire of the enemy, I ordered the sailing-launches to let go the third cable, and ordered the steam-cutters to take the sailing-launches in tow. We manned the oars of the sailing-launches to keep the boats clear of the breakers until the steam-cutters could take them in tow.

At the same time we opened fire from the men in the sailing-launches not at the oars, the steam-cutters keeping up their fire. We continued firing while in retreat, under a very heavy fire from the enemy, our men displaying great coolness. Shortly after my launch was taken in tow, while I was reaching for a fresh rifle, I was struck in my left hand by an enemy's ball, but was not crippled, and I was able to continue in command. We steamed as rapidly as possible against a head sea for the *Marblehead* and the *Nashville*, keeping up our fire as we retreated. One man in my boat, Robert Volz, seaman, was shot in the head and badly injured. The *Marblehead's* boats, though farther from the beach than the *Nashville's*, suffered more loss.

No one in the *Nashville's* steam-cutter was injured.

The work, owing to the heavy armored cables used, 1¾ inches in diameter, and the heavy swell rolling in, was extremely difficult. The water being clear, we were able to see the cables at a great depth. Had it not been possible to see the cables, it would have been extremely difficult, if not impossible, to grapple them, as the uneven formation of the coral bottom continually caught our grapples.

The boats were splendidly supported by the heavy fire of the *Marblehead* and the *Nashville*. Towards the end of the action the *Nashville* took a position to the eastward and close in on the reefs, and admirably covered our retreat, crossing her fire with that of the *Marblehead*, and passing quickly between our boats and the enemy. Owing to the fact that the enemy had excellent cover in the hills and chaparral, and to the fact that they used smokeless powder, it was impossible accurately to locate them. At the last part of the engagement, just at the completion of our work, judging from the very hot fire, the enemy must have been in large force.

I was ably supported by Ensign T. P. Magruder, in command of the steam-cutters, who displayed great coolness, bravery, and promptness in carrying out my orders and in protecting his men. Lieutenant E. A. Anderson commanded the sailing-launch of the *Marblehead*, and did his work with coolness, bravery, and intelligence, continuing the work, regardless of the hot fire to which he was exposed, until ordered by me to desist.

LIEUTENANT SOUTHERLAND'S ACCOUNT

THE *Eagle* reached the light-ship off Diego Perez Island at 7 A.M., and at once commenced a search for the submarine cable connecting Batabano with Cienfuegos.

A boat was sent to the light-ship and the keeper's services secured to aid in the search.

Six lines were carefully run at varying depths between the light-ship and a point of the shoal to the eastward that was marked by a wreck, the bottom being visible most of the time. The *Eagle* and two of her boats performed this duty, but without a satisfactory result. The strong wind and rough sea, the pilot's assurance that no good holding-ground could be found for an anchorage, the evident fact that the chart was extremely unreliable, and the positive statement of the light-ship keeper that no one had overhauled the cable in that vicinity for over three years determined me to abandon the search at 4 P.M. as fruitless, it being more than probable that the cable was buried deep in the sand of the reefs.

THE *GUSSIE* EXPEDITION—LANDING HORSES THROUGH THE SURF UNDER FIRE FROM THE SHORE.—DRAWN BY R. F. ZOGBAUM

In accordance with the division commander's order, the light-ship was then set on fire and was burning fiercely when the *Eagle* left. Her keeper expressing a desire to go to Cienfuegos, we took him on board the *Eagle* with his personal effects and his own small boat. This action on my part was principally due to the fact that the sea was too rough for him to get ashore unaided. He stated that he was a Cuban and had not received his salary from the government for seven months.

We reached Piedras Cay at sunset. Sent an armed crew on shore and destroyed the lighting apparatus and what pertained thereto. Two men were in charge of the light, and with them a small boy. These we found in a starving condition, in consequence of which it became necessary to bring them on board for removal from the island. They had been eight months without pay, three weeks without any communication with the outside, and five days without food.

THE ACTION AT CARDENAS

Commander Merry's Account

Having for some time conceived a plan to attack and cut out the three small gunboats inside, but not having suitable ships, the arrival of the *Wilmington* and *Winslow* on the morning of May 11th induced me to confer with Commander Todd, of the *Wilmington*, on the subject. He was anxious to participate.

The *Machias*, *Wilmington*, *Hudson*, and *Winslow* proceeded in as far as the obstructions would allow. The *Machias* took up position about 2100 yards northeast of Diana Cay. The *Wilmington*, with the *Hudson* and *Winslow*, proceeded to enter the inner harbor between Romero and Blanco cays, where I felt quite certain there were no mines, the depth of water by chart being $1\frac{3}{4}$ fathoms. The three vessels found no trouble in entering, and were soon steaming into Cardenas Bay. I opened fire on Diana Cay signal-station and sent the launch, with Ensign Willard in charge, to take possession of the station and find the wires and explode the mines, if possible, or cut them. No wires were found, however, although strict search was made for them on the island and by dredging around it.

Mr. Willard accomplished the work in a very excellent manner, destroying the station and all government property, which had been abandoned in a very hurried manner; and, as a signal of his success, hoisted the American flag on the signal-station, and brought on board the Spanish flag, together with the station's signal apparatus.

At 1.40 P.M. fire opened from the *Wilmington* and *Hudson* and *Winslow*, and was continued until 3 P.M., when the three vessels commenced the return to the outer anchorage.

Serious casualties occurred. I sent the *Hudson* to Key West with the dead and wounded.

Commander Todd's Account

Upon the arrival of the *Wilmington* off Cardenas on the morning of May 11, to relieve the *Machias*, three Spanish gunboats were observed inside of what were believed to be mines. Soon after the arrival of the *Wilmington* the torpedo-boat *Winslow*, Lieutenant J. B. Bernadou commanding, appeared, the revenue-cutter *Hudson* being already at the station.

A careful study of the chart showed that the *Wilmington* could get inside the bay through another channel. With the approval of the senior officer, the *Wilmington*, the torpedo-boat *Winslow*, and the *Hudson* proceeded inside the bay, in off the city of Cardenas, to capture these boats if possible. It was not possible for the *Wilmington* to approach the wharves nearer than 2000 yards or more, on account of the depth of the water, the pilot being on board. The gunboats could not be made out from the *Wilmington*, and the *Winslow* was directed to go closer in, to see if she could determine where they were lying. She had proceeded probably 700 or 800 yards inside of the *Wilmington*, when a gun was fired from on shore, apparently from the bow of a gunboat moored. The fire was at once returned from the *Wilmington* and the *Winslow*, the *Hudson* not yet being within range. A rapid fire was kept up on this and other guns, the location of which could not be determined, whether they were on board vessels or not; but it was believed that there was a battery behind some of the shipping lying along the water front.

After a rapid exchange of shots for about fifteen or twenty minutes, it was evident that the *Winslow* could not steer. In the meantime the *Hudson* had come up and opened fire, and the *Winslow* asked to be towed out, as her steering-gear had been disabled. The fire from the *Wilmington* was continued until the *Winslow* was out of the range of the shore guns. The torpedo-boat seemed to be the main target at which the enemy fired, for she was struck several times, one engine disabled, steering-gear shot away, and one boiler disabled. Her commanding officer, Lieutenant Bernadou, was wounded, but not seriously. Ensign Worth Bagley was fatally wounded, and died before he could be brought on board the *Wilmington*. Two enlisted men, John Varveres, oiler, and John Deneefe, fireman, first class, were killed on board the *Winslow*; two other men were fatally wounded, one of them, J. V. Meek, fireman, first class, died in a boat while being transferred to the *Wilmington*; the other, Josiah Tunell, ship's cook, first class, died on the *Wilmington* after having been brought on board. One other man of the *Winslow*, W. J. Patterson, fireman, first class, was brought on board the *Wilmington* seriously but not fatally wounded.

Lieutenant Bernadou's Account

The *Winslow* arrived off Cardenas from Matanzas at 9 A.M. on the 11th, having left her station on the blockade off Matanzas to obtain an additional supply of coal, the amount of fuel in her bunkers being reduced to five tons. The *Machias* and *Wilmington* were found at Piedras Cay. Upon making application to Captain Merry, the senior officer present, I was directed to apply to Captain Todd, commanding the *Wilmington*, for necessary supplies.

On boarding the *Wilmington* I was informed by her commanding officer of his intention to enter Cardenas Harbor on the afternoon of that day. Of the three channels leading through the cays, two were believed to be mined. There remained unexplored a third channel, between Romero and Blanco cays, over which the minimum depth of water, as shown by the chart, was $1\frac{3}{4}$ fathoms. As the rise of tide at this place was about $1\frac{1}{2}$ feet, and as the *Wilmington* drew scant 10 feet, I was directed to receive on board a Cuban pilot, Santos, to take with me the revenue-cutter *Hudson* to sound this channel, and, in company with the *Hudson*, to sweep the channel for torpedoes. This work I completed by noon, except the sweeping of the channel, which could not be done on account of the grounding of the *Hudson*. That vessel touched lightly, but managed to work off without injury. The *Winslow*, therefore, dragged the channel with grapnels and returned to the *Wilmington*, reporting to Captain Todd upon the practicability of the entrance.

The entrance was begun at 12.30, high tide, the *Hudson*, on the starboard side, and the *Winslow*, on the port side of the *Wilmington*, assisting in marking out shoal water. No vessels were in sight on entering Cardenas Bay save two square-rigged merchantmen with sails unbent, anchored directly off the town. As it was thought possible that gunboats might attempt to escape, the *Hudson* was sent along the western side and the *Winslow* along the eastern side of the bay to intercept them in event of such movement: not finding them, the three vessels met off the town at a distance of about 3500 yards. When in this position, the *Winslow* was signalled to approach the *Wilmington* within hail, and I was directed by Captain Todd to go in and investigate a small gunboat then observed for the first time, painted gray, with black smoke-stack, apparently not under steam, and moored to a wharf, to the left of which arose a compact mass of buildings close to the water front. Torpedoes were set for surface runs, the fans upon the war-noses were run up so as to provide for explosion at short range for use alongside of the gunboat, and all preparations were made for immediate action.

At a distance of about 1500 yards, at which time the *Winslow* was advancing at about twelve knots, which seemed to be her maximum speed in quite shoal water, the first gun of the engagement was fired from the bow of the Spanish gunboat, marked by a clear puff of white smoke. This shot, which passed over the *Winslow*, was at once replied to by that ship, and was the signal for the commencement from the beach of a rapidly sustained fire, characterized primarily by a total absence of smoke. At the commencement of this firing I received a flesh wound in the left thigh. As the action advanced a cloud of haze collected on shore at the location of this battery; and, when closest, I detected one or two gun flashes from among the buildings, but at no time could I detect the exact position of the guns. My uncertainty as to the position of the enemy was attested by the commanding officer of the *Hudson* and by officers commanding gun divisions on the *Wilmington*, who inquired of me shortly after the action what I made out to be the enemy's exact position.

At this time the wind was blowing from the ships towards the shore. The first shot that pierced the *Winslow* rendered her steam and hand-steering gear inoperative and damaged them beyond repair. Efforts to work the

BEFORE THE BOMBARDMENT OF SAN JUAN—ADMIRAL SAMPSON TRANSFERS HIS FLAG TO THE *IOWA*, MAY 11, 5.10 P.M., SAN JUAN BEARING S.S.E. ABOUT SEVENTY MILES

DRAWN BY CARLTON T. CHAPMAN

Sr Carlos Batteries

RICO, MAY 12, 1898.—DRAWN BY CARLTON T. CHAPMAN

THE BOMBARDMENT OF SAN JUAN DE PUERTO RICO, MAY 12, 1898.—DRAWN BY CARLTON T. CHAPMAN

hand steering-gear from aft were frustrated by the wrecking of that mechanism and the rupture of both wheel ropes; relieving tackles failed to operate the rudder. For a short time the vessel was held in her bows on position by use of her propellers. She then swung broadside to the enemy. A shot now pierced her engine-room, rendering one engine inoperative. I directed my attention to maintaining fire from her 1-pounder guns, to keeping the vessel constantly in movement, so as to reduce the chances of her being hit, to endeavoring to withdraw from close range, and to keeping clear of the line of fire of the *Wilmington* and *Hudson*. The use of the remaining engine, however, had the effect of throwing her stern towards the enemy upon backing, while going ahead threw her bow in the same direction. Under the heavy fire of the *Wilmington* the fire of the enemy slackened. The Spanish gunboat was silenced and put out of action early in the engagement. The 1-pounder guns of the *Winslow* were constantly in action throughout the fight. Torpedoes were ready, but there was no chance to employ them.

The *Winslow* now being practically disabled, I signalled to the *Hudson* to tow us out of action. She very gallantly approached us, and we succeeded in getting a line to her. Previous to this, the alternate rapid backing and steaming ahead of the *Winslow* had had the effect of working her out from under the enemy's batteries, and in this way a distance of about 300 yards was gained. Finding that we were working out in this manner, I directed Ensign Bagley to concentrate his attention upon the movement of the *Winslow*, watching the vessel so as to keep her out of the *Wilmington's* way, and to direct the movements of the man at the reversing gear, mechanical communication from deck to engine-room being impracticable. This necessitated Mr. Bagley making repeated short trips from the deck to the foot of the engine-room ladder while directing the vessel's course, and at the moment of being on deck he stood abreast of the starboard gun close to a group of men who had been stationed below, but who had been sent on deck from the disabled machinery. A shell hitting, I believe, a hose-reel, exploded instantly, killing Ensign Bagley and two others and mortally wounding two. This accident, which occurred at the close of the action, was virtually its end; the enemy fired a few more shots, but was soon completely silenced by the heavy fire of the *Wilmington*. The conduct of Ensign Bagley and the men with him, as well as that of the crew who survived the fight, was beyond commendation. After seeing the dead and wounded removed from the *Winslow* and conveyed on board the *Wilmington*, I turned over the command of the ship to Gunner's Mate G. P. Brady, my own injury preventing me from performing active duty for the time being.

—

LIEUTENANT NEWCOMB'S ACCOUNT

At 11.30 A.M., while off the main entrance to Cardenas Bay, the *Hudson* was ordered by the senior officer present to accompany the *Wilmington* and the torpedo-boat *Winslow* inside. All three vessels started immediately, and after some preliminary soundings to determine the best water, passed through Blanco Channel into the bay and headed for Cardenas. About 1 P.M., when abreast of Corajal Point, the *Hudson* was ordered by the commanding officer of the *Wilmington* to "go out and look at small craft." Steamed over towards Diana Cay, and skirted the western shore of the bay. Discovered no vessels, and, observing that the *Wilmington* and *Winslow* were nearing Cardenas, at 1.35 P.M. steamed towards them at full speed. At 1.45, when a little over a mile distant from our vessels, saw firing commence from the shore, which was immediately returned by our ships. At 1.50, when within range of the shore guns, the *Hudson* opened fire upon them with her two 6-pounders. Observing that the *Winslow* was quite close inshore and exposed to the full strength of the enemy's guns, ran up alongside of the *Wilmington* and asked if we should go to the assistance of the *Winslow*. Received the answer "Yes," and immediately steamed in to the immediate vicinity of the *Winslow*, keeping up a constant and rapid fire from the *Hudson's* battery upon the enemy's guns on shore. At 2.20 the commanding officer of the *Winslow* reported his vessel totally disabled and requested to be towed out of range. Owing to the shoal water and the rapid drift towards shore of the *Winslow* (the wind was on shore), it was fully thirty minutes before the *Hudson* succeeded in making a line fast from the *Winslow* and starting ahead with her. The enemy kept up a constant fire during this time, which appeared to be especially directed towards the *Winslow*, which was returned at every opportunity by the *Winslow* and *Hudson*. The *Winslow* was towed alongside the *Wilmington*, from which vessel a boat was sent with a medical officer, who transferred the dead and wounded from the *Winslow* to the *Wilmington*. Finally, at about 3.30 P.M., all three vessels steamed out of the bay, the *Winslow* in tow of the *Hudson*. At about dark I joined the *Machias* outside, when the *Winslow* was anchored.

At 9.15 P.M. the *Hudson* started for Key West with despatches for the senior officer commanding that station, and carrying the dead and wounded from the *Winslow*. I reported to the senior officer commanding at Key West at 7.10 on the morning of the 12th instant. The only damage resulting to the *Hudson* during the engagement were a few slight marks from small projectiles upon two of the fire-room ventilators, and a few bullet marks upon the outside of the pilot-house plating. One hundred and thirty-five shells were fired from the two 6-pounders during the action.

I testify to the remarkable bravery displayed by Lieutenant Bernadou and the men of the *Winslow*, and consider it as one of the greatest privileges of my life to have been an eye-witness of their conduct at a time when many men would have felt justified in abandoning all hope.

THE *GUSSIE* EXPEDITION

By R. F. Zogbaum

It was well on in the afternoon as we neared the entrance to Cabañas Bay, and it was decided to attempt a landing on Arbolitos, the point on the western side. Sounding constantly, the big red bulk of the *Gussie* crept closer and closer in towards the reef. With a roar of chain and upward splash of spray the anchor took the ground, and we swung slowly abreast the beach—in sea parlance, "close enough to shy a biscuit on shore." The gunboat *Manning*, with gentle, easy dip and roll, lay just off our quarter; a little farther out to sea the graceful lines of a diminutive cruiser, the United States gunboat *Wasp*, showed up in a gray mass on the unbroken surface of the sea. The *Gussie* was short-handed, and it took some time to lower the boats. Amid some confusion two of the boats were filled and manned by the soldiers, the boat first "shoved off" moving up the reef, as if seeking an opening, the second pulling direct for the shore. As it neared the reef the swell began to lift it, sending it in quick-succeeding leaps rapidly forward, until in a burst and smother of foam it plunged right into the surf, almost disappearing from view. For a moment we on the ship held our breath in anxious expectation; then, as we saw one blue-clad form after the other boldly plunge overboard and rush through the water, stumbling, falling full length, picking themselves up again, in eager emulation to reach the land, while others grabbed the gunwales of the boat on either side, and, shoving it along between them, carried it bodily up on the strand, an enthusiastic shout burst out, as cheer on cheer went up for the first American soldiers to set foot on Cuban soil.

Meanwhile the first boat seemed to be hard and fast on the reef, teetering up and down in the swell like the *Gussie's* walking-beam; but the fine athletic fellows were out of her in a jiffy, and soon, strung out in long skirmish line on the beach alongside their comrades, moved forward into the bush. The Cubans were quickly landed, and the task of setting the horses ashore began. The great port, opening at the side from the deck where the stalls were placed, was swung wide, a line made fast to the halter of the horse was passed to men in a small boat alongside, and the startled animal was pushed and driven to the opening, until with a desperate leap he plunged into the water. Guided by the man in the stern, while his companion headed the boat for the shore, the horse, snorting in alarm, but swimming easily, reached the reef, and, finding foothold, scrambled through the surf, making for the shore, where he was soon standing tethered to a tree, and apparently none the worse for his experience. The second horse gave less trouble; or perhaps the men who took him ashore had benefited by the experience of the first landing; and soon the third animal was well on his way towards the beach. On the hurricane-deck of the ship, lined up under cover of the hay-bales, the men who formed the covering party had been watching the proceedings with anxious interest. Suddenly, some way up the beach, right on the edge of the brush, we saw something moving. Two or three blue figures emerged partly, and were running forward, arms at a trail; one dropped on knee; with quick, jerky movement up went rifle to shoulder, and we saw the flash of the discharge. "By God, they're attacked!" speaks a voice at my side, and simultaneously the air about us is filled with a whirring, humming sound, followed by a distant pattering

THE *DETROIT* SILENCES CAÑUELA BATTERY—Drawn by Carlton T. Chapman

noise, like fire-crackers on Independence day. Zip! hum! buzz! the angry bullets come flying, and a thin blue haze floats over the brush just beyond where one of the boats has been hauled up on the shore. "Ten shun!" The hardy figures behind the hay-bales become rigid. "With magazines, load!" A momentary rattling and clicking of steel on steel. "Aim just to the right of the boat on the shore! Steady! Fire!" and like the discharge of a single piece the volley hits back at the attacking enemy. Again and again, quietly and as on drill, the men respond to the orders. The fire on shore rolls here and there, now falling, now rising again, slacking finally to a few scattering shots, then dying away. The enemy's attack is repulsed, and he has retired, leaving behind him the bodies of an officer and two soldiers, victims of the first encounter between American and Spanish soldiers on Cuban shores. But, victorious as were our men for the time being, their position on shore was exceedingly precarious. Our morning's work had shown us that the country was swarming with Spanish soldiery. Cabañas was not far distant, the enemy knew our force, and it would not be long before he could confront us in overwhelming numbers. We must try to make the woods too hot to hold him, and so word was sent to our friends of the gunboats with request to shell and drive him away, while dispositions were made to re-embark.

THE *PORTER* ENGAGING THE BATTERIES OFF SAN JUAN

It was a pretty sight to witness as the two gunboats moved slowly broadside to the beach. Their fire swept the entire length of the jungle, and the boom of the guns, the whir of the projectiles, and the sharp burst of the shells as they plunged in among the trees mingled in one continuous roar, and were added to by the rumble of the storm over the land. Time was pressing, the afternoon was waning, the tide was falling, and the roar of the surf struck heavier and heavier on the ear. Captain Dorst, the officer in command of the expedition—his boat upset on landing, casting him and all its occupants into the sea—stood with the Cubans by the trees where the horses were.

Word had been brought off to the ship that our allies, alarmed by the presence of the enemy, hesitated to carry out the mission for which they had been put ashore; but now we saw them saddling the horses, and soon they had mounted and were riding off up the shore, picturesque figures in their wide-brimmed hats and loose cotton garments. Our men had gone forward into the bush again, ready to repel the enemy should he renew the attack, but now the bugle sounded the recall, and we saw them emerging from the trees and gathering in squads on the beach. It was going to be more difficult to re-embark even than it had been to land. The boats had to be shoved out to the reef, where the water deepened abruptly, and the surf was angry and growing more violent every moment as the swells ran in from the open sea. The men waded into the water, pushing the boat before them, until the reef was reached, and scrambled in; some, up to their necks in the water, threw their rifles into the boat, and, clinging to the gunwales as the light craft was driven out over the swells, were dragged in by their comrades. A boat from the *Manning*, as close in to the reef as it could get, lay on its oars waiting to take Dorst off, and I own to a grateful feeling of relief when, after struggling neck-deep through the surf, I saw him safe in the stern-sheets of the *Manning's* boat, the last to leave the shore.

THE BOMBARDMENT OF SAN JUAN

BY CARLTON T. CHAPMAN

AT 3 A.M. the fleet was off San Juan, the light showing for a time, but about 3.30 going out suddenly. With a glass the lights of the town could be plainly seen, and low in the sky a waning moon shed its pale glow over the rough sea and looming masses of the ships. The single red light showing only from the rear told the fleet the position of the flag-ship, the *Iowa*. Not a single light showed from any other ship, nor was there a sound, except the swash of the water and the piping wind that whistled through the rigging. The moon, hidden at times behind dark masses of clouds, gave the scene a weird and romantic aspect. Soon the first streaks of dawn lighted up the gloomy hills, and made the position of our ships and the harbor and forts plain enough. We were right off the entrance of the harbor, and in advance and close in were the *Wompatuck*, *Porter*, and *Detroit*, followed by the *Iowa*. The *Wompatuck* seemed to be cautiously approaching the entrance to the port. She had gone in to put down stake-boats as steering-guides. The monitors *Terror* and *Amphitrite* were close on the port side of the despatch-boat at this time, and we crossed the bows of the *Terror* to get to windward and be in position for a better view of what might follow. The ships were lined up in fighting order, but perfectly silent, and no flag or sign of activity on any of them. The *Wompatuck* disappeared for a time under the shadow of the land, and then reappeared to our sight, steaming slowly about. At this moment the *Iowa* broke out a large American flag at the fore, followed immediately by all the other ships, and in an instant or two afterwards the dull boom of a gun sounded across the water. It was from the *Iowa*. Then the *Detroit*, farther in and right under the guns of Morro, burst into flames and smoke. It seemed a minute or two before any reply came from the fort, but it was probably much less. A flash and puff of white smoke from Morro, and the engagement was on, and flash and heavy thunder of guns, reverberating among the hills, followed rapidly. The first shots from the *Iowa* and *Indiana* fell short, sending up spurts of water immediately under the fort. The *New York*, following, seemed to have the range better, and clouds of heavy yellow dust hung over the spots where her 8-inch guns had struck.

At this time the *Detroit* was pouring in a perfect fury of fire, her guns making a continuous flare and roar, so it became impossible to distinguish the monitors and the *Montgomery*, which had come into action. All this time the torpedo-boat *Porter* was lying close in, her flags flying out defiantly, and occasionally taking a shot with her small guns. The big ships drawing out of action at this time, she became a mark for the fire of all three batteries, and the water spurted up in jets all about her; but Fremont seemed to enjoy it, and did not budge an inch. The *Iowa*, *Indiana*, *New York*, and the monitors having gone out of range, the fire of Morro and San Cristobal batteries was concentrated on the *Detroit*, which lay quite close in off the Cañuela water battery, which the *Detroit* completely silenced after a time. The *Montgomery* during this first attack lay astern of the *Detroit*, and directed her fire against Cañuela. She was signalled, however, to drop out of the line of fire, to give the heavier ships a better chance. So, to their sorrow, the *Montgomery* people did not have all the opportunity they wanted to distinguish themselves.

At eight minutes past six the *Iowa*, having made a wide circle, came back to the attack, followed closely by the *Indiana* and *New York*, and, reserving her fire till close in front of Morro, began with her forward 12-inch guns. The first two shots struck fair and square on the top of the hill and among the buildings of Morro, sending up a vast cloud of sickly yellow dust, that hung there for some minutes; this was followed by her broadside battery, which for the time seemed to silence the fire of Morro completely, San Cristobal and San Geronimo keeping up a continuous fire, however. The *Indiana* followed quickly the *Iowa*, the heavy roar of her 13-inch guns reverberating like the heaviest thunder, and the flash of fire followed by the thick yellow smoke completely obscured her for the instant; from the *New York* came the thunder of her 8-inch guns, and from the two monitors the deep roar of their 10-inch turret guns. The scene at this time was grand and awe-inspiring. The crest of the high hill on which San Juan is situated was wreathed in circles of pale smoke hanging in curious forms about the guns, and relieved by the blue mountains beyond. Glimpses of the buildings of the town, fort, and barracks could be seen at times, while the flash and roar of the guns came steadily from all the batteries. Close in under the shore, which is backed to the west of the harbor by high ranges of hills, lay the ships, flame and smoke bursting from their sides; all around them, over, and short of them fell the fire of the forts' shells from the old guns of Morro, bursting in the air, and jets of white water showing where solid shot had struck. Every instant or two the deeper roar of a 13-inch gun would swell the chorus, and along the top of the hill, and particularly about Morro, hung a heavy mass of dust and débris, spreading out and sinking slowly, and telling where the shots were falling. Still the forts were not silenced, though their fire slackened perceptibly during this attack. We were lying at this time to the windward of the fleet and about three or four miles off San Geronimo, making a fair target for their modern 8-inch guns, which had been well served, and had kept up a continuous fire; not being in range of the fleet, they had not suffered, and while the ships were drawn off to form for the third attack, they paid us the compliment of firing at us. The first shot was wide of the mark, but the second whistled unpleasantly near overhead, while the third came so near that had there been a fraction of an inch less elevation to that gun we would certainly have been struck; as it was, it passed over our heads and struck the water 100 yards beyond.

At 7.22 the *Iowa* again returned off the fort, firing slowly and with accuracy, and followed by the *Indiana* and *New York*. The *Iowa* fired only once from her forward turret guns this time, but remained for some minutes under the fire of the fort, a shell from Morro bursting over her and splintering one of her whale-boats, injuring three men stationed at the secondary battery. The *Porter* had been signalled to leave her dangerous position, and moved over near the *Iowa*. At least a dozen shots fell in the water about them, sending up spurts of foam but doing no harm. The *Indiana* and *New York* remained in front of the forts nearly half an hour, pouring in a slow but careful fire, that at times covered the hills with dust and obscured the ships in their own smoke. When they drew off, as they did at a few minutes past eight o'clock, the *Terror* and *Amphitrite* remained, and the latter continued for some time to pour a heavy fire into the forts, whose reply was now coming slowly and at intervals, San Cristobal and San Geronimo alone keeping up a regular fire.

While the firing was at its height smoke and flames came from the buildings on the hill, and at one time the whole place seemed to be ablaze. From the opening of the engagement the entire city of San Juan was in a state of dreadful panic. It was known three days before, by cable from Cape Haiti, that Sampson's fleet was on its way to Puerto Rico, and many of the inhabitants had fled inland; but when the opening guns announced the arrival of the enemy the rush to get out of town became a panic, people paying any price for carriages to drive ten miles into the country. San Juan lies on the inner side of a high hill, the northern side of which is crowned by the fortifications. Owing to the heavy swell and consequent uncertainty of elevation, many shots from the ships fell into the town, destroying buildings, public and private, with a loss of life that is not known to us at present.

In the harbor were a number of neutral vessels. Among them the French steam-frigate *Amiral Rigault de Genouilly*. This vessel arrived at St. Thomas the next day, and we learned from her that many shots had fallen about her, but, fortunately, had not struck near enough to do any damage.

Soon after eight o'clock the firing ceased entirely, except for an occasional shot from the forts that did no harm.

By 8.30 o'clock the fleet had been drawn off out of danger, and then we learned that the *New York* had also been struck by a shell, that burst over the port 8-inch broadside gun, killing one man, able seaman Frank Wildmark, and injuring Samuel Feltman (leg broken), ordinary seaman, and Michael Murphy, William Rupp, and Michael Spron slightly.

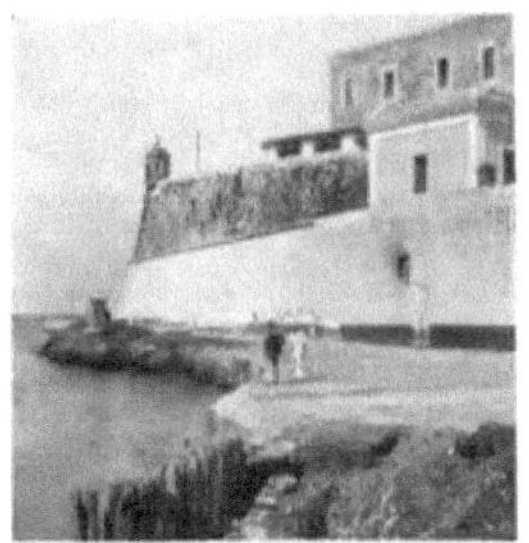

THE FORTIFICATIONS OF SAN JUAN

Rear-Admiral Sampson's Account

Upon approaching San Juan it was seen that none of the Spanish vessels were in the harbor. I was therefore considerably in doubt whether they had reached San Juan and again departed for some unknown destination, or whether they had not arrived. As their capture was the object of the expedition, and as it was essential that they should not pass to the westward, I determined to attack the batteries defending the port, in order to develop their positions and strength, and then, without waiting to reduce the city or subject it to a regular bombardment—which would require due notice—turn to the westward.

Our progress had been so much slower than I had reason to anticipate, from Key West to Puerto Rico, owing to the frequent breakdowns of the two monitors, which made it necessary to tow them both the whole distance, and also to the disabled condition of the *Indiana*, that eight days had been consumed instead of five, as I had estimated.

I commenced the attack as soon as it was good daylight. This lasted about three hours, when the signal was made to discontinue the firing, and the squadron stood to the northeast until out of sight of San Juan, when the course was laid for the westward, with the view of communicating with the department at Port Plata to learn if the department had obtained information as to the movements of the Spanish vessels.

At Cape Haytien I received word from the department that the Spanish vessels had been sighted off Curaçao on the 14th instant, and I was directed to return with all despatch to Key West.

As stated in my telegram, no serious injury was done to any of the ships, and only one man was killed and seven wounded slightly.

The following notes were taken during the attack:

Weather fair; very light breeze; long swell from northward and westward.

3.30: Breakfast.

4: Call "All hands" to complete clearing for action. Squadron standing in for San Juan, the lights of the town being plainly visible. *Detroit* leading; *Wompatuck* on starboard bow to anchor boat for turning stake as provided in my "Order of battle"—second plan of action; the other ships in column as follows: *Iowa*, *Indiana*, *New York*, *Amphitrite*, *Terror*, and *Montgomery*. Speed, 4 knots.

4.58: *Detroit* inshore, standing across harbor entrance. In this passage across the front of the harbor, and very close to the town, the *Detroit* received no fire at all. No Spanish flag was flying on the Morro or elsewhere. No Spanish vessels could be seen in the harbor. There was one merchant steamer in the inner harbor.

5: Sounded "General quarters."

5.16: *Iowa* began firing on the Morro with forward 6-pounder, and then with all starboard battery. Smoke hanging over the ship made firing slow.

5.24: First return shot from the shore batteries.

5.30: *Iowa* turned from the batteries, circling to the westward.

5.59: Made signal "Form column."

6.09: Made telegraphic signal "Use only large guns." The smoke from the smaller guns had been interfering with the fire of the heavier guns. The column was headed in for the batteries in the same line of attack as in the first round.

6.15: *Detroit* seen standing away from the Morro, with the *Montgomery* not far off her port beam. From the time when the shore batteries began firing (5.24) until this time (6.15) the *Detroit* had been lying close inshore, between the line followed by the squadron and the Morro, and she had been subjected to what seemed a concentrated fire of all the shore batteries for all this time, she in the meanwhile pouring in broadsides from her own rapid-fire battery.

6.30: Made signal to *Detroit* and *Montgomery* not to follow battle-ships. By this time all the shore batteries had been developed, and they were more numerous than the information received had led me to suspect.

6.35: *Iowa* began firing at Morro on the second round; range, 1500 yards.

6.40: *Iowa* ceased firing. Almost calm; smoke hanging over the shore fortifications, pretty effectually screening them.

7.12: *Amphitrite* signalled "After turret disabled for to-day."

SAN JUAN—WATER-FRONT AND HARBOR

7.16: *Iowa* began firing on the third round.

7.38: Signalled to *Detroit* and *Montgomery* "Report casualties." Received replies as follows: *Detroit*, "0;" *Montgomery*, "0."

7.43: *Iowa* sounded "Secure."

7.45: Made signal "Form column, course northwest," and hauled down the signal at 8.01.

8.12: Made signal "Report casualties."

8.15: The *Terror*, which had been lying close inshore engaged with the fortifications, ceased firing.

8.47: *New York* reported "1 killed, 4 wounded." All other ships reported no casualties, except the *Amphitrite*, which reported the death of one gunner's mate from the effects of heat.

Captain Evans's Account

FOLLOWING the instructions contained in the commander-in-chief's order of battle, the *Iowa* entered the firing-line at 5.15 A.M.

The crews of the port secondary battery were sent below in the casemate.

At 5.17 two shots were fired from the 6-pounder on the starboard forward bridge and one shot from the starboard 8-inch turret. After this the entire starboard battery became engaged.

The fire was directed against Morro battery.

The speed maintained while passing over the firing-line, about 1500 yards in length, was from four to five knots; and the fire was continued for about eight minutes, until 5.25.

The ranges varied from 2300 to 1100 yards.

The commander-in-chief having ordered the discontinuance of the use of the light battery, all the crews of the starboard battery were now, about 5.30, ordered below, within the casemate.

The ship was then hauled off shore, in accordance with instructions, and stood slowly to the northwest; turned again to the eastward, re-entered the firing-line, and, followed by the squadron, made two more runs, three in all, over the firing-line, firing principally at the Morro, but during the last run some shots were fired at the eastern battery.

While on the return course, steering northwest after the second run, a shell of 6 or 8 inch caliber (estimated from the base plug and fragments found) exploded at the after-port skid frames, beneath the boats. The fragments of this shell wounded three men and injured the first whale-boat, sailing-launch, joiner-work about the bridge, and inflicted other slight damages. This shell was probably fired from the eastern battery, the most important of all the batteries at San Juan.

It was noticeable that all shots striking, or striking near, vessels were made when the vessels were on the outer or return course, and the greater part of these were fired by the eastern battery.

At 7.25 the *Iowa* completed its third run, and, after steaming to the northwest, the battery was secured, as ordered by the commander-in-chief, and the action discontinued.

I consider that this engagement has demonstrated the efficient condition of the battery of the *Iowa* under service conditions and the admirable spirit of the officers and men.

The smoke hanging about the ship and about the batteries during the engagement so obscured the latter that the fire of this vessel was rendered very slow. The breeze was extremely light, force about 1.

There was a long ground-swell setting to the southward.

The battery of the *Iowa* was in all respects ready for immediate service after the engagement.

Commander Dayton's Account

AFTER receiving the order from the torpedo-boat *Porter* to precede the flag-ship, taking soundings, the *Detroit* stood in until I judged her to be about one-half mile from the reef; she then stood east until Fort Cañuela and the western end of Cabras Island were in range, when she was headed east by south. Shortly afterwards 10¼ fathoms was obtained, and from the appearance of the rollers I judged myself too far in and headed off to east by north until abreast the eastern end of Cabras Island, when she was again brought to east by south. When the western batteries of Morro were screened, the ship was turned short around and headed towards the entrance of the harbor. By stadiometer measurement on the light-house she was found to be 1100 yards from the Morro. In this position further developments were awaited—the crew at quarters, the guns loaded but breech-blocks open.

Very few signs of life were observed on shore. Signals were being made at the semaphore station, and a few men were seen hurrying about the Morro, apparently carrying rammers and sponges. With the light as it was it was difficult to determine accurately the position of the guns.

At 5.15, the *Iowa* having commenced firing, the *Detroit* opened fire with the port battery on the northern face of Morro; frequent pauses were made to allow the smoke, which was very dense, to clear. As the *Iowa* approached our quarter, "Cease firing" was sounded, in order not to obscure her view. At this time guns were seen to be firing from the eastern forts, the shot dropping outside of us. When the *Iowa* was clear the firing from the *Detroit* was recommenced, a portion of it being directed at the eastern forts. This was continued until the fleet passed, "Cease firing" being sounded whenever it was judged our smoke would interfere with the fire of other vessels. After the *Terror* passed, the *Detroit* was turned and followed her out. By this time shot were dropping on all sides of us, but at long intervals. They appeared to be the result of chance, and not of accurate aim. The ship was not struck and no casualties occurred. During the remainder of the engagement the *Detroit* remained out of range, in obedience to a signal not to follow the flag-ship.

The behavior of every one on board was excellent. The only fault I found was a tendency to fire more rapidly than the circumstances justified. From this cause and the ground-swell a considerable amount of ammunition was wasted. There being no junior officers on board, Passed Assistant Paymaster Arms volunteered to take charge of the after powder division, and Paymaster's Clerk Iglehart to act as my aid on the bridge.

The battery was practically in the same condition after as before the engagement.

Captain Ludlow's Account

AT 4 A.M., weather clear and pleasant, wind light, easterly, and the sea smooth, the *Terror* was in her position in column, at distance in accordance with the plan of battle. The lights of the city of San Juan de Puerto Rico were in sight on the port bow, the course being S. S. E. ¼ E., magnetic. At daybreak we sighted high land on the starboard bow. I called all hands, cleared ship for action, and we went to general quarters. At about 4.50 the flag-ship *Iowa*, leading the column, opened fire on the batteries, heading east by south. The other vessels in column opened fire as soon as range was obtained, the *Montgomery* and *Detroit* firing, the former from a position outside of Fort Cañuelo, the latter lying under the Morro. The forts and batteries replied briskly to the fire of the squadron. The *Terror* opened fire at 5.13 from starboard 6-pounder, immediately followed by the forward turret and then the after turret, as soon as guns could be brought to bear. The smoke was so thick under the Morro Hill and in the harbor that I ceased firing for several minutes and stopped the ship to await a clear chance. I was obliged, however, to keep station, and proceeded. Our first shots were fired into the inner harbor in hopes of striking any vessels anchored there, the smoke being so thick I could see nothing. When the air cleared a little I could see that the harbor was unoccupied, and fired no more shots in that direction.

The *Terror* made the circuit three times, each time approaching closer to the batteries, and during the third round stopped, with both turrets on starboard beam, and fired at a battery which seemed to be the most vicious, situated a short distance to the south of the Morro. I saw one shell from the right gun, forward turret, explode in this battery. I threw several shells across the neck of land, hoping to strike any vessel in the inner harbor. The flag-ship made signal at about 5.45 to use only the large guns. The secondary battery then ceased firing, and the men were ordered to take cover behind the turrets or below the armored deck.

I had no idea of the amount of damage done to the batteries, but at about 6.30 I observed a very noticeable diminution of their fire. When the *Terror* came out, at 8.45, the batteries pitched shell after her quite rapidly out as far as about 6000 yards. The *Terror* came away at a speed of about four knots, in obedience to signal from the flag-ship. Not a projectile struck the *Terror* at any time, although a fuse and some small pieces of shell were picked up about the decks.

I am most gratified to report that the conduct of every officer and man under my command was everything that could be desired. The forward turret division, Lieutenant Coffman in charge, was more especially under my observation all the time, and all hands were cool, alert, and full of enthusiasm. Lieutenant-Commander Garst took especial charge of the after end of the ship, with Lieutenant Dunn in charge of after turret. Ensign Terhune, in charge of the secondary battery, assisted Lieutenant Qualtrough in signals after fire from that battery was discontinued. Lieutenant Hubbard had charge of the berth-deck division. The engines responded promptly to every signal made, and everything connected with them worked well.

Absolutely no damage was done to the *Terror* by the enemy's fire, with the exception of the loss of part of the leadsman's apron, port side, which was carried away by a shell passing near it.

Captain Chadwick's Account

All hands on the *New York* were called at 3 A.M., and the crew went to breakfast at 3.30, at 4.36 went to quarters, and stood in, third in column, as by the order of battle laid down by the commander-in-chief, the *New York* following the movements of the *Iowa* and *Indiana* and making a circuit of the batteries three times.

The following are the times: First circuit, commenced firing at 5.27 A.M., ceased 5.45; second circuit, commenced firing at 6.55 A.M., ceased 7.11; third circuit, commenced firing at 7.29 A.M., ceased 7.46.

Time from open fire to cease fire, two hours and nineteen minutes; time engaged in firing, fifty-one minutes. During the whole period, from 5.27, when we began firing, until 7.46—namely, two hours and nineteen minutes—the ship was under the fire of the enemy, which at times was very heavy.

A great number of projectiles struck in the vicinity of the *New York*, chiefly passing beyond, but the ship itself was struck but once, namely, by a 6-inch shell, which came aboard about six feet above the after end of the superstructure deck, taking off the top of the after stanchion on that deck, exploded, killing one seaman and wounding four at the port waist 8-inch gun, totally destroying the fourth cutter and the port search-light, piercing the ventilators and smoke-pipes in many places, and making a number of small holes in other boats. This shot struck about 7.40, as the ship was making her third circuit and was headed out from the batteries. It was supposed to have been fired from the eastern battery, then about 3000 yards distant.

Everything worked well on board the ships, except that considerable difficulty was experienced from the jamming of primers in the vents of the 8-inch guns, causing the lock extractors to break, and in the after turret the locking-catch on the face-plate of the right-hand gun jammed and had to be repaired, causing considerable delay in the firing of the gun. The conduct of the officers and men was most commendable.

The efficiency of fire was no doubt somewhat less than it ought to have been on account of a very heavy swell setting in from the north-northwest, evidently the effect of a heavy gale to the northward.

The only injuries to the ship, excepting those named as occurring through the explosion of the 6-inch shell, were from the concussion of firing the 8-inch guns, by which the flooring on the starboard side of the forward bridge was started and partially blown away, the wings of the after bridge stowed on edge alongside the superstructure shattered, as also the starboard waist search-light; the starboard life-buoy was also blown away.

This slightness of injury was extraordinary, considering the incessant fire to which the ship was subjected for so prolonged a period.

Captain Taylor's Account

During the night of May 11 the *Detroit* made final preparations for battle, and at daylight, following the movements of the *Iowa*, which carried the Admiral's flag, I approached the entrance to the harbor, opening fire upon the Morro at about 4500 yards, and continued a gradual approach east by south until within 1300 yards, at which point the *Indiana* turned in the wake of the *Iowa* and returned to the starting-point. This round was made a second and third time under practically similar conditions, except that in the second and third rounds the *Indiana* stopped for a longer period in making the turn in order to keep her starboard broadside bearing longer. It was necessary to cease firing frequently while the smoke from the fleet and the batteries obscured the enemy's positions. The total number of projectiles expended was 187.

The *Detroit* was not struck, and there were no casualties.

The turrets, guns, and mounts remained in good condition and unaffected by the firing.

I am glad to be able to commend the executive officer, Lieutenant-Commander J. A. Rodgers, and all officers and men for the good order and absence of confusion which prevailed.

THE CITY OF SAN JUAN, FROM THE SEA-WALL

Lieutenant Fremont's Account

[Written for Harper's Magazine]

April 22 found the torpedo-boats tuned up to the highest pitch and anxious for a chance to try themselves, and it was with great hopes and unlimited enthusiasm that we started across to Havana that memorable morning.

It was rough—rough even for the Gulf Stream—and that day and night showed us that the life on board the *Porter* was going to be a struggle with nature, a test of physical endurance. The *Porter's* motion in such a sharp sea as nearly all the time runs off the coast of Cuba was, to say the least, uncomfortable. The roll was from 30 to 45 degrees each way, and twenty-five times a minute, with occasionally an extra roll thrown in, which was beyond the registering limit of the indicators, and made you wonder why she took the trouble to come back, it seemed so much easier just to go on all the way round.

To rest and sleep in such conditions is very difficult, and is only possible when physical exhaustion overcomes every other feeling; and then the sleep is so broken that it ill fits one to renew the exacting duties of handling the delicate mechanisms of the boats, or exercise the cool judgment and instant decision demanded by the service.

In addition to this, the heat below was such that no one went there except on duty. The life was on deck: those on duty at their posts were on their feet; the remainder, if not struggling with their very simple meals, were trying to get some sleep, stretched out and wedged in between torpedo-tubes and rail, or in some place that prevented their sliding round.

In spite of its apparent severity, this open-air life proved most healthful, for whenever the boat went into port for a day or two, or had comparatively smooth water, every one at once recovered his energy and good temper. The absence of routine and routine drills, the constant excitement of the rapid motion, the frequent accidents to the machinery, and the struggle to repair the latter and at the same time keep the boat going—all kept up a feeling of excitement and expectation which reconciled us to every hardship, and made us feel that we were right where we wanted to be; and all we asked for was a chance—something that never came for the torpedo-boats during the war.

Hopes that our chance had come were high on the *Porter* the first day off Havana. A man-of-war was sighted under the land, and the *New York*, *Marblehead*, *Wilmington*, and *Porter* started in for her; but it turned out to be an Italian, and the only guns used were those fired in salute. Immediately afterwards the *Porter's* sorrow at the lost opportunity was partly assuaged by the capture of a schooner within range of the guns of the eastern batteries of Havana. When the crew of the schooner found they were not to be murdered at once, as they had been led to believe, they were not only reconciled to their fate, but voluntarily gave us information of more sugar-laden vessels due the next day. The roughness and tedium of that day were easily endured in the hope of more prizes on the morrow. The hopes were realized; daylight found the *Porter* steaming slowly for the flag-ship to report, with a 200-ton-schooner load of sugar in tow.

This ended the first forty-eight hours of the war. No one in the *Porter* had slept a half-hour at a time, and every one was looking hollow-eyed and worn out. Fortunately the next few days were the smoothest seen off Havana, and regular blockading duties were taken up, the *Porter's* station being on the inside line, as near the Morro as possible. The nights were spent in working in as closely as we could, waiting for a chance at anything that might attempt to get out of Havana, to capture it if a merchantman, to torpedo it if a man-of-war.

Frequently, in the anxiety to discover whether the strange craft were friend or foe without betraying her own presence, a torpedo-boat was fired on by her own friends. The blockading squadron were taking no chances of any kind of approaching dark little craft, and used the Western method of shooting first and inquiring afterwards. In the excitement consequent on the signal "Enemy's torpedo-boat sighted," even torpedo-boats engaged each other. This happened one of the first nights off Havana. The moment the signal was made, all the scouting vessels in that vicinity converged at full speed towards the point where the signal stars had been seen. Suddenly out of the gloom of night, and right across the bows of the *Porter* rushed a dark object, the sparks from its funnels and the dim outline marking it distinctly as a torpedo-boat. No questions were asked by the *Porter*, for we knew no other torpedo-boat of ours was on that section of the blockade. There was a heavy sea, and dense clouds of black smoke were sweeping down between us from our low funnels. This fortunately caused the first shots to go wild, and instantly, in answer to our fire, the night signal was shown. It was one of our own boats that had come from Cardenas with despatches, and she was looking for the flagship. A joking apology and a hearty laugh from us all ended our little encounter, and the two boats parted, not to meet again for weeks—not until the *Porter*, returning to Key West from her cruise to Puerto Rico, found the *Winslow* battle-scarred and torn by the enemy's shell, her captain wounded, and her executive and five of her crew dead. It was no laughing matter this time; but, with all its horror, the uppermost feeling in us was that of pride in the gallant fight they had made in all but hopeless circumstances—circumstances that would have proved fatal to all on board had it not been for the gallantry of American sailors—the crew of the *Hudson*, who, literally fighting with one hand and helping the wounded with the other, remained under fire until they could pull the disabled *Winslow* out to safety.

About two o'clock one morning a steamer was reported running towards Havana. It was an ideal night for torpedo attack, dark, with a strong wind blowing and occasional light rain-squalls. She was allowed to pass, but nothing definite could be made out, and, as the *Porter* was well off to the eastward of Havana, the supposition was that it could not be one of the blockaders.

Dropping into her wake, our speed was increased, all hands were called to their stations, and every preparation made for attack. The *Porter* was now closing rapidly in, and through the smoke we could make out that the vessel ahead was a man-of-war, and a large one. At this time the whereabouts of the Spanish armored cruisers was unknown, and from what we then could see of the vessel ahead she answered their description perfectly. More steam was put on, and the *Porter* rushed up close on the quarter of the chase, well within torpedo distance and still undiscovered. Being now so close that, even if discovered, we could not be stopped before the torpedo was discharged, and wishing to make no mistake, the night signal was made for an instant and then turned off. It brought no answer.

Excitement on the *Porter* was at fever-heat, and the enforced silence and the nervous tension were hard to bear. That we had found the enemy, and that we had him all to ourselves, and had him where there was no possibility of his getting away, was such an unhoped-for opportunity that nothing short of firing and cheering would express what we felt, and the effort to express these was most difficult. To make assurance doubly sure, the night signal was again made, and the forward gun fired, immediately followed by a second. That we were now discovered was evident, and in a moment signal-lights were shown and a gun fired at us. The signal-lights shown were the *wrong ones* for that night, and only served to strengthen our conviction that the chase was an enemy. Full speed was rung on the *Porter*, and the final rush to torpedo was made, when, just in the nick of time, the identity of the ship was recognized, and, amidst shouting of orders to cease firing and hails through the megaphone demanding explanations, the vessels were brought to a standstill within 100 yards of each other, and mutual explanations made.

Blockading duty settled down into a steady, monotonous routine, and we welcomed the orders that sent us to communicate with the shore after dark and try and get a messenger from Havana. Though unsuccessful, this led to the *Porter's* being sent off 200 miles along the enemy's coast, away from all our blockade-line, and directly into the haunt of the enemy's gunboats, to land messengers to General Gomez. We found the enemy's gunboats at the entrance of the very bay we were ordered into, and in the morning had the pleasure of driving three of them before us. They returned in the afternoon, reinforced by two larger vessels, and nearly closed the exit from the bay to us before we could get out. We expected more trouble with these vessels on our proposed return to pick up the messengers, but we never went back, as we found orders awaiting us at Key West to join the flag-ship in the expedition to Puerto Rico.

There had been no real fighting up to this time, and we started with pleasant anticipations of seeing some. The cruise proved to be the hardest and longest ever made by a torpedo-boat. It lasted three weeks, during which 2800 miles was run by the *Porter*, some of it at high speed; and while no breaks or accidents occurred that could not be remedied by the crew, it proved one continuous struggle, with small but incessantly occurring breakages, due to the strain of constant running in a heavy sea, and allowed but little rest for the vessel's mechanics. Running, as the squadron did, without lights, it required the most ceaseless vigilance to keep in position and not run into some vessel. For the torpedo-boats this was especially hard, as there were but two officers to a boat, and one of these had to be on watch night and day. This severe duty, taken in connection with the fact that what rest we got was of a very unsatisfactory kind, made the duty extremely wearing. Had the weather been as hot as that which the *Porter* experienced later on the south coast of Cuba, it is probable that the crew would have succumbed. As it was, we went through in fairly good state, only two men giving out on the cruise.

At the bombardment of San Juan the *Porter* took a more prominent part than was either intended or desired, but, fortunately, escaped without harm. The apparently safe position assigned to the *Porter* was taken, and the first round of the attacking vessels was completed, when the wall that was supposed to be without guns developed a strong and active battery. As the attacking ships were then making the turn out at sea preparatory to returning for the second round, the little *Porter* occupied a position of undue prominence, and in consequence received the entire attention of this battery, directly under which she lay. It is hard to understand how such a storm of projectiles could all have missed her; but it was not a chance to be risked a second time, and before the battery could fire again the *Porter* was turning out at full speed, firing back with her 1-pounders, and swallowed up in a cloud of black smoke from her own funnels. It was a narrow escape, and it was evident that our report of "no damage and no casualties" was received by the flag-ship with much relief.

Cervera's fleet was now reported as being behind us, and the squadron started at once back towards Key West, the *Porter* keeping up connection through the cable stations at the various ports along the homeward track. It was tough service, for high speed had to be made, however rough the water or however thick the weather. Unknown ports must be entered, as often as not at night, without pilotage; and on that coast a mistake means in all probability the loss of the vessel, for the sea is always heavy and the shore is a net-work of coral reefs. Good-luck, however, attended the *Porter*, and when she did finally strike a reef it was inside a harbor and in smooth water, and she escaped with slight damage—so little, in fact, that she was able to steam to Mobile and repair damages, joining the flag-ship again on the sixth day, just in time to accompany the *New York* and *Oregon* to Santiago.

MAJOR-GENERAL WESLEY MERRITT, U. S. A.—BY T. DE THULSTRUP

THE MILITARY EXPEDITION TO THE PHILIPPINES

UPON the receipt at Washington of news of Dewey's victory in the Far East, reinforcements were hurried to Manila under the command of Major-General Merritt and firmly established within sight of the capital, which lay helpless before the guns of the American squadron.

BRIG.-GENERAL THOMAS M. ANDERSON
Formerly Colonel 14th Infantry

On the 7th day of May the government of the United States was advised officially of the victory at Manila, and at once inquired of the commander of the fleet what troops would be required. The information was received on the 15th day of May, and the first army expedition sailed May 25th and arrived off Manila June 30th. Other expeditions, as already related, soon followed, the total force, during the period of hostilities with Spain, consisting of 641 officers and 15,058 enlisted men.

"Only reluctance to cause needless loss of life and property," said the President of the United States, "prevented the early storming and capture of the city, and therewith the absolute military occupancy of the whole group. The insurgents meanwhile had resumed the active hostilities suspended by the uncompleted truce of December, 1897. Their forces invested Manila from the northern and eastern side, but were constrained by Admiral Dewey and General Merritt from attempting an assault. It was fitting that whatever was to be done in the way of decisive operations in that quarter should be accomplished by the strong arm of the United States alone. Obeying the stern precept of war which enjoins the overcoming of the adversary and the extinction of his power wherever assailable as the speedy and sure means to win a peace, divided victory was not permissible, for no partition of the rights and responsibilities attending the enforcement of a just and advantageous peace could be thought of."

The insurrectionary movement here referred to by the President was one of the frequent rebellions which had occurred in the Philippines while under Spanish rule. A conspiracy of the Filipinos had developed into open rebellion during 1896, and General Primo Rivera, who was appointed Governor in the latter part of 1897, had been charged by the Spanish government with instructions to carry out a scheme of reforms. In December of that year terms were arrived at with the insurgent general Aguinaldo and other leaders for their submission. A number of these leaders were deported and went to Hong-Kong; and, despite a small rising against the taxes in March, 1898, a semblance of peace was maintained until the appearance of the American Asiatic Squadron in the Bay of Manila. Then, to use the words of an English writer, "the rebels came again to the fore." Aguinaldo and other leaders crossed the China Sea, took the field, and were engaged in the investment of Manila from the land side upon the arrival of the American troops that were sent from San Francisco at the call of Admiral Dewey.

OFF FOR MANILA

BY OSCAR KING DAVIS

As I sat in front of the hotel at Fort Monroe, the telegraph-operator came across the street with this message in his hand:

"Go to Washington with all haste. Get army passes and passports, and hurry to San Francisco to go to Philippines."

Half an hour to pack up and catch a train. The first expedition was due to leave San Francisco in five days. By the closest work it could be caught. A frantic rush about the departments in Washington the next morning—War, Navy, and State—and then across the continent.

How peaceful it was at the start! As we whizzed through the little stations the farmers were bringing in their milk-cans, just as if no guns were waiting to roar about Cuba and no soldiers were getting in shape to sail for Manila. Market-gardeners with crates of berries and garden-truck were loading up the platforms here and there as we shot along. Rows of 'buses stood idly waiting in the sunshine at the stations where we stopped. Then the limited, and no war at all. Business men dictating business letters to the train stenographer, the last magazines, the latest novels, idle gossip about the scenery and the backward spring, and the peaceful calm over all.

Thus for a day and a night, and another day and another night, and then Omaha and soldiers and the outward and visible signs of warlike preparations again. Now straight out through Nebraska. Somewhere troops are on the move to-day for the rendezvous at San Francisco. They are going over this road, and the people are beginning to turn out to cheer them on. Here a little company with a flag. There a band of school-children with flowers. Then a whole town full of flags, and now a band. At last Grand Island and a long wait, and here the soldiers catch us—the first battalion of the First Regiment of Nebraska Volunteers. The town throbs with excitement. It pours itself into the open space about the station, and cheers itself black in the face as the troop-train rolls in. There are Grand Island boys in the blue-uniformed crowd in the train, and Grand Island shouts aloud in pride. The soldiers lean out of the windows, and the Grand Island girls run along beside the cars and grasp their hands and kiss their faces and throw them flowers and give them good things to eat, and everybody is laughing and shouting and cheering in hysterical happiness. Oh, war is grand now! The boys are brave and young and sturdy, and very fine in their uniforms, and all the trouble and the heart-breaking weariness and toil and the danger are far away. So it's cheer again, and laugh and shout, and one cheer more as the train pulls out, and then back home again, where the boy's room is vacant, to the long, sober, quiet realization of the side that shows no glamour.

On with the train through the night, and in the morning the flat, desolate, barren, bunch-grass country, and Cheyenne. It's very early, but the crowds are out already. The troop-train rolls in, the soldiers swarm out for a bit of a run to limber up after the cramped night in a day coach. There's hot coffee aplenty here, and more girls to kiss and give buttons to; and before there's been half a chance to go around the bugles are singing out the "assembly," and it's rush back for your car or disgrace your regiment by being left behind.

Now the mountains and snow and cold, raw wind. Up through the clear morning, over the blinding snow; clouds in the valley below us, black and sullen; but above, the bright sunshine and bracing breeze. Cities, towns, and villages all left behind now—just an occasional section-house, or a ranch, but at nearly every one a flag, and somebody—often only a child, but always some one—to cheer as the soldiers pass. Then Laramie, and more coffee—no, it was ordered for the third division, and we can't have it. So on to Rawlings; and here Indians have joined the crowd waiting at the station—stolid, wrinkled-faced old bucks, and squaws in gaudy blankets. Some one shoots a gun by way of making more noise than he can get out of his throat. Instantly half a hundred others follow suit, and the boys hear the first volley of the war—fired by friends. Then Rock Springs, and a holiday.

BRIG.-GENERAL FRANCIS V. GREENE
Formerly Colonel 71st New York Volunteers

Schools dismissed, shops closed, mines shut down, and children, shopkeepers, miners, and band, with all the anvils from the blacksmith-shops adding their ear-cracking roar to the general din of shouts and cheers and blare of brass horns. The train rolls in to the accompaniment of the E-flat tuba, booming out above all the frightful racket a steadfast and undisturbed bass to "The Star-spangled Banner." Purple-faced from his exertion, with eyes starting out of their sockets, but with triumphant determination in his soul, the E-flat tuba bellows away, the conquering hero of that chaos of sound.

Then Green River and supper, and a chance to fall in by platoons and run about for ten minutes to warm up and stir the blood and ease the stiffened legs. And then night again. But no let-up to the noisy welcome. It remains for Evanston to fit the capstone to the riot-making by turning loose a fiendish chorus of steam-whistles at midnight, and adding their dreadful din to the wild tumult of cheers and horns that wake the tired soldiers and keep their eyes open hours after Evanston was miles behind. That was the climax of the noise-makers' art. The fondest dreams of Hallowe'en or Fourth of July night never stirred the breast of any boy with thought of such noise as Evanston called a welcome to sleepy soldiers.

CALIFORNIA, COLORADO, NEBRASKA, AND KANSAS REGIMENTS IN CAMP AT BAY DISTRICT, SAN FRANCISCO.—Photograph by Edwin R. Jackson

Day again, and the Nevada desert. Providence had been good to the boys, and rain that fell in sheets kept down the dust that usually makes travel across the desert so uncomfortable. But big towns and little towns, villages, and solitary houses turned out to cheer. One more night, and then California. And if the other States had welcomed the Nebraska soldiers, what of California? It was holiday all along the road. Women and children swarmed about the train at every stop, and while the men and boys split their throats the women and girls scattered flowers and fruit among the soldiers. It was a procession of triumph clear to their camp out back of San Francisco, not the least part of which was the march up through the streets of that city.

But it was not until May 23 that San Francisco turned out in force. On that morning the First California Volunteers marched from their camp at the Presidio to the mail dock and boarded the transport *City of Peking*. They started out in heavy marching order—blankets, knapsacks, and all on their backs—forty pounds or more to the man. It was a long tramp over wretched cobblestone pavements, and the last two miles of it was not a march in company formation, but a single-handed fight through a mob. They started at seven o'clock, and it was noon when they reached the shelter of the pier shed. The police were utterly powerless to clear the streets. Mounted men cleared a path no longer than their horses. On the instant as they passed the crowds that filled the streets swarmed back across the path of the soldiers.

It was a glorious day. The sun rode through a sky of unspotted blue, and a fresh breeze from the west cracked the myriad banners that floated from the house-tops like whips. Scarcely a window along the line that did not show at least one flag. The crowds in the street bore flowers by the armful—wreaths of great long-stemmed American Beauties, sweet-peas, carnations, violets, pansies, geraniums—blossoms of all the thousand kinds that teem in the Golden State. They threw them at the men and over their necks, hung them on their shoulders, piled them on their knapsacks, tossed them over their guns, and, for want of other ways of demonstration, threw them on the ground for a carpet for the soldiers. Thousands of small flags added to the brilliancy of color. They were pinned to the soldiers' hats, stuck in their rifle-barrels, jammed into their knapsacks or blanket-rolls—any place where they would stick. So the First California marched away, the first United States soldiers to make attack on a foreign land oversea.

Only two airs marked the departure. The bands that marched with the regiment played one of them. Over and over again they played it, and always the same—"The girl I left behind me." And all along the line the crowd responded in a booming chorus of

"John Brown's knapsack is strapped upon his back,
And his soul goes marching on."

So down to the pier. And then form up again out of the straggling mass, surrounded by and mixed up with friends. Now good-byes are over. The trooper is just ahead. Make-believe is ended, war begins.

"Wheel! Oh, keep your touch; we're goin' round a corner.
Time! Mark time, an' let the men be'ind us close.
Lord! the transport's full, an' 'alf our lot not on 'er—
Cheer, oh, cheer! We're goin' off where no one knows.

"Front! The faces of the women in the 'ouses
Ain't the sort o' things to take aboard the ship."

More impressive than the great spectacle of General Grant's return from the Orient was the farewell which San Francisco gave to the first Philippine expedition. The bay was alive with steamers, tugs, yachts, launches, and row-boats, and when the three great steamers weighed anchor and moved down the bay and out towards the Golden Gate the sight was one long to be remembered. Hundreds of whistles sounded their shrill note, cannon boomed, and cheers of thousands on the water and on neighboring hills almost drowned other sounds of God-speed and good-bye. The *City of Peking* sailed first; behind her came the *Australia* and the *City of Sydney*. Only a few minutes were required to bring the steamships out opposite the Presidio. Then against the rays of the setting sun they showed out as clear as an etching, every rope and spar fine and sharp, as their prows were pointed due west over the ocean that a Spaniard first saw from the heights of Darien.

AT HONOLULU

By Oscar King Davis

The two days spent in Honolulu by the soldiers of General Anderson's brigade of General Merritt's Philippine army were a most decided change from the lazy life of the days aboard the transports. Loafing on the hurricane-deck, watching the flying-fish, and speculating on the end of man, in particular the man who went to the Philippines as a private soldier, gave place to positive, emphatic things to do, most desirable things too, in a most delightful city. Honolulu had developed for herself lately a Hawaiian version of "There'll be a hot time in the old town to-night." They said it very briefly, but for two days they had been saying it a great many times. "*Wele ke mau*," they said, and you heard it everywhere. They had been living up to it, too. There had been a hot time—such a hot time as even Honolulu, noted for hospitality, had not seen before. It began when the three troop-ships, *City of Peking*, *Australia*, and *City of Sydney* were sighted on Wednesday afternoon, and there had been scarcely a moment's cessation since. The whole city turned out to welcome the transports in. The wharves were thronged, and there were constant volleys of cheers, until even after the ships were in their berths. As soon as gang-planks were down the serious business began. There were receptions at once at the clubs for the officers, and they were not over until early in the morning.

Kapiolani, the dowager queen, had taken the opportunity of the arrival at Honolulu of the *Charleston* to arrange for the presentation of a beautiful silk flag to the ship which brought home the body of her husband, King Kalakaua, who died in San Francisco. The formal presentation occurred on the morning after the troopers got to Honolulu, being delayed for that purpose. All the officers were present, and the United States diplomatic representatives. The presentation was made by Kapiolani's nephews, Prince Cupid and Prince David, who made the address. Afterwards there was a luncheon on the ship. President Dole received the officers the same afternoon. The men were permitted to go ashore, half a company at a time, and they did have such a good time. They wandered about the streets, staring at the curious shops, and they swarmed on the beach at Waikiki and went swimming in the surf. The Kapiolani Park was open for them, and the government and Hawaiian bands gave a concert.

Friday, June 3, was the great day—it was feast-day for the boys. Arrangements had been made to give every soldier in the brigade a "square meal." All the city had contributed. Tables were set up under the trees in the grounds about the government buildings, and spread with everything that even a hungry soldier who had had nothing but government rations for seven days could name as part of a "square meal." The government band was there to accompany the great feast with sweet music. At 9.30 in the morning the soldiers left their ships and marched up by companies. They filed into the government grounds, and attacked the tables in battalion front.

Every man in the expedition, except the unlucky chaps who had been detailed to sentry duty, was in the hungry army. Every man got what he wanted. There was a great quantity of soda and mineral water, and 3500 quarts of water that had been boiled and then cooled. The boys strolled about the grounds after the feast was over, and in the afternoon went out to Waikiki for surf-bathing. Every soldier in town was decorated with wreaths of flowers, and many of them were half concealed by the leis.

In the morning Chief-Justice Judd, on behalf of the Sons of the Revolution resident in Honolulu, delivered a formal address of welcome to General Anderson. The general, in reply, hoped that annexation would soon be an accomplished fact.

President Dole held an informal reception in the government building for the soldiers who were feasting in the grounds. Little groups of them were presented to him constantly.

The hospitality of Honolulu was remarkable; the exhibition of it on the last two days was something no man who witnessed it would ever forget. But through it all this curious feature had struck the soldiers with especial force: the flags that greeted the arrival of the transports, fluttering from a forest of tall poles, from every prominent building, and from scores of residences, that waved in hundreds in the streets, were the stars and stripes. Yet over the government buildings there floated a strange flag—the banner of the Hawaiian Republic. The gentlemen and ladies who so royally extended their hospitality were Americans. The language they spoke was English. The men we dealt with in the shops were Americans; we bought goods made in the United States, and we paid for them with United States money; we rode about in carriages built in the United States and pulled by American horses; we were at home, and our own flag waved over our heads constantly. But over the government buildings the strange flag still floated—Hawaii was still a foreign land.

CALIFORNIA VOLUNTEERS SAYING GOOD-BYE, ON THE WHARF AT SAN FRANCISCO, BEFORE EMBARKING.—Drawn by J. A. Cahill, San Francisco

THE TAKING OF GUAM

By Oscar King Davis

Observation taken June 27 showed us to be in latitude 17° 9′ north, longitude 126° 26′ east. Three days more, perhaps only two, and we should see the flags waving over Dewey's ships in Manila Bay. It had been a long, hard trip, broken only twice—at Honolulu and at San Luis d'Apra—but each was a memorable occasion. It was the day after we left Honolulu that we first heard of Guam. That day Captain Glass, of the *Charleston*, which convoyed the troop-ships from the Hawaiian Islands, opened the sealed orders which he had been instructed to read when out of sight of land after leaving Honolulu. These orders directed him to call at Guam, one of the Mariana, or Ladrone, Islands, capture the governor and all officials and soldiers, and destroy any fortifications at Agaña, the capital, or in the harbor of San Luis d'Apra, the port of Agaña.

The message from Captain Glass wigwagged to the transports, making public these orders, stirred up a lot of enthusiasm among the soldiers. Straightway charts and Pacific directories were hauled out and studied for information about the Ladrones and Guam. But it quickly became apparent that most of our information would be obtained by personal contact, for the directories knew precious little. The ships held a steady and uninterrupted course towards the little island, unbroken by the sight of a single sail, and varied only by the occasional target practice of the *Charleston*, until the afternoon of June 15, when there was a time. The practice of the cruiser had been particularly interesting, as it indicated—or we thought it did, and that served as well—that Captain Glass expected to have to use his guns in capturing Guam. But this afternoon it was not subcaliber at boxes tossed over from the *Peking* and floating by, but regular practice with the big guns and service charges, at a regular pyramidal cloth target set adrift from the cruiser herself. This surely was preliminary to fort-destruction. Besides this practice, there was a conference of all the captains and General Anderson on the *Australia*, and arrangements for the attack on Guam were completed.

Considering the fact that the *Charleston's* crew was composed largely of green men, the shooting was very good. The range was about two miles, and every shot would have struck a ship, except possibly the first. Two rounds were fired from each of the 6-inch guns in the port and starboard broadside batteries, and from the bow and stern 8-inch rifles. Captain Glass was greatly pleased with the practice.

Early on the morning of Monday, June 20, land was seen. The convoy had come to the westward of the island of Guam, thereby avoiding the signal station at Point Ritidian, and caught sight first of the rocky shore north of Agaña Bay. The *Charleston* cleared for action, and with the men at general quarters went into Agaña Bay to look around. The morning was thick with frequent rain squalls, which blotted out everything even at a short distance from the ship. The *Charleston* went boldly into the harbor, and as close to the shore line as the dangerous coral reefs would allow, but the bay was empty. Then down past Devil's Point and Apepas Island she steamed, with the transports trailing behind and half a mile or more farther out to sea.

As the cruiser passed Apepas Island her officers made out, over the low-lying rock, the spars of a vessel at anchor in the bay of San Luis d'Apra. Apepas Island cleared, the vessel showed full and white, and Captain Glass thought he had a Spanish gunboat, but she set the Japanese flag as soon as she made out the war-ship, and proved to be the copra-trading brigantine *Minatogawa*, of Tokio. The cruiser went on past Luminan Reefs, and turned in by Point Orote, along the north shore of the little peninsula. The cliffs rise sharp out of the water, like the Palisades of the Hudson, and against them the *Charleston*, in war-paint, was hardly visible. Old Fort Santiago, on the point, dismantled long ago, made no opposition to the cruiser's advance, but as she rounded the next point, and saw Fort Santa Cruz ahead, hope revived in the hearts of the silent men at the guns. Then Captain Glass gave the order to try out the old fort with the 3-pounders, and the men were happy. The firing began at 3000 yards, and for four minutes the little shells burst in and around Fort Santa Cruz in a fashion which made the solitary Chamorro setting his fish-traps behind the fort row for his life to get out of range. Thirteen shells were fired, the last at 2600 yards, and, there being no response, the action of Guam ended. The troop-ships could see but not hear the shooting, and every shell got a round of wild cheers.

The shelling of Santa Cruz brought a fairly prompt response in the persons of Lieutenant Garcia Gutierrez, of the Spanish navy, captain of the port of San Luis d'Apra, and Dr. Romero, of the Spanish army, health officer, who rowed out in their boats, flying the Spanish flag, to see if the health of the *Charleston* were good, and to promise to return Captain Glass's salute as soon as they could borrow some powder for a couple of old guns they had ashore. They were thunderstruck on being informed of the real situation, and when told that Manila was in Dewey's hands, practically, the Spanish fleet destroyed, and that they were prisoners of war, they were most unhappy. Francis Portusac, a native of Guam and an Agaña merchant, who was naturalized in Chicago in 1888, was with the officials to act as interpreter; but Captain Glass used him more as a bureau of information about the island. Finally the captain paroled the Spaniards for the day, and sent them away in their boats with a verbal message to the Governor, Lieutenant-Colonel Don José Marina y Vega, to hurry up and pay his official call. That evening Governor Marina sent Captain Glass a message to the effect that the military regulations of Spain forbade him to set foot on a foreign vessel, but he would be pleased to see the captain at his office in the morning. Captain Glass replied that he would see the Governor himself, or send an officer to represent him.

The next morning Lieutenant William Braunersreuther, the navigator of the *Charleston*, with Ensign Waldo Evans and five men, went ashore. Lieutenant Braunersreuther carried a formal note to the Governor from Captain Glass, which gave him thirty minutes in which to surrender unconditionally. The guns of the *Charleston* were ready to enforce the demands. Lieutenant Braunersreuther met the Governor at the landing-place at the native village of Piti. With the Governor were Captain Duarte, of the Spanish army, his secretary, the port captain, Lieutenant Gutierrez, and Dr. Romero. In presenting the note from Captain Glass, Lieutenant Braunersreuther said, in Spanish:

"I have the honor to present a communication from my commandant. I am authorized to wait one half-hour for your reply. In presenting this communication I call your attention to the fact that we have, as you see, three large ships in the harbor, and a fourth [the *Sydney* had remained outside] outside ready to come in. One of these ships is a modern war-vessel of high power, with large guns. The others are transports full of soldiers. We have a large force here. I call your attention to these facts in order that you may not make any hasty or ill-considered reply to the note of my commandant."

Governor Marina bowed and thanked Lieutenant Braunersreuther, took the note, and retired with his staff into his office. From its window, if he chanced to look out, he could see the steam-launch of the *Charleston* towing a string of boats full of men up towards

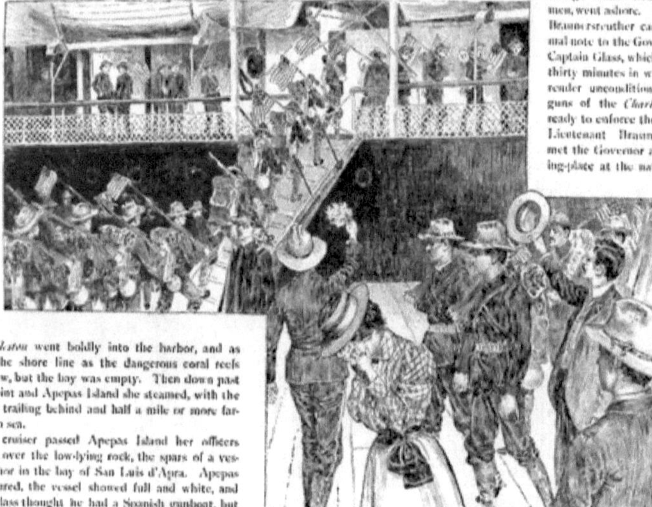

VOLUNTEERS EMBARKING ON THE *CITY OF PEKING*.—Drawn by J. A. Cahill

THE *CITY OF PEKING* PULLING OUT FROM THE WHARF, SAN FRANCISCO, MAY 26

DRAWN BY T. DE THULSTRUP AFTER A PHOTOGRAPH BY WEIDNER

the landing-place. In the boats were Lieutenant Myers, of the United States Marine Corps, from the *Charleston*, with forty marines from the ship, and part of Company A, Second Oregon, Captain H. L. Heath, from the *Australia*. This was the first detachment of the landing-force which General Anderson and Captain Glass had agreed on the night before. The rest of Company A, and Company D, Captain A. T. Prescott, were waiting on the *Australia* for the launch to return and tow them to land. To their intense disgust, not a man of them set foot on land. The first detachment tied up to the Japanese brigantine while the launch went back for the rest, and before it came back the work had all been done.

For twenty-nine minutes Lieutenant Braunersreuther waited, watch in hand, for the reply. Then Governor Marina came out of his office with a sealed letter addressed to Captain Glass. "It is for your commandant," he said, as Lieutenant Braunersreuther broke it open. "I represent my commandant here," was the reply. Governor Marina had written:

"SIR,—In the absence of any notification from my government concerning the relations of war between the United States and Spain, and without any means of defence, or the possibility of defence in the face of such a large opposing force, I feel compelled, in the interests of humanity and to save life, to make a complete surrender of all under my jurisdiction. Trusting to your mercy and justice,

"I have the honor to be," etc., etc.

So Guam was surrendered, with all the Mariana Islands. The unhappy Governor had no notion that the force which had threatened him was intended really for Manila, and thought that it had been sent out solely against the Mariana group. He had but fifty-four Spanish regulars and a company of Chamorros, and was, as he said, quite without means of making a defence. Lieutenant Braunersreuther required him to write an order to Lieutenant Ramos, in command of the troops at Agaña, to have them on the pier at Piti, with all arms, accoutrements, and ammunition, and the four Spanish flags on the island, at four o'clock that afternoon. That done, the Governor wrote a long farewell to his wife, telling her to send his clothing and personal effects to Piti at once. He offered the letter to Lieutenant Braunersreuther to read, as he had done the order to Lieutenant Ramos. The *Charleston's* officer waved the letter away, and said,

"No, no; that is not for me."

Apparently that courtesy was more than the Governor had expected. He put his head down on his desk and fairly broke down and cried. When he regained his composure, he and his staff took places in the *Charleston's* boat, and were taken aboard the cruiser. On the way the boat passed the two detachments of the landing-party, and ordered them back to the *Australia*.

ON BOARD THE *CHINA*—THE LAST VIEW OF HOME

Soon after the arrival of the prisoners on the *Charleston*, Captain Glass took a large United States flag and went in his barge to Fort Santa Cruz, where he hoisted the stars and stripes on the old Spanish staff. As the first broad red stripe rose over the ruined battlements, the 6-inch rifles of the *Charleston* roared out the national salute. Formal possession had been taken of Guam. At the same time the bands on the *Australia* and *Peking* played the "Star-spangled Banner," and the soldiers and sailors on the troop-ships and cruiser gave three times three for Uncle Sam's new island.

"THE LAST MAN ABOARD"—AN INCIDENT OF THE SAILING OF THE *CITY OF PEKING*

The *Sydney* had been ordered to come in from outside the reef, and as soon as Captain Glass got back from raising the flag over Santa Cruz he made arrangements with Captain Pillsbury, with General Anderson's permission, to quarter his prisoners on the transport. Lieutenant Braunersreuther then took the *Charleston's* marines, under Lieutenant Myers, and with Ensign Evans and Dr. Farenholt went into Piti to receive the surrender of the Spanish soldiers. The troops were waiting for him in the boat-house at the landing-place. With Lieutenant Ramos in command was Lieutenant Berruezo, both of the Spanish naval infantry. The company of regulars was drawn up in line on one side of the boat-house, and on the other side, facing them, were the fifty-four Chamorros. The regulars were armed with '96 model Mausers, and had two great boxes of ammunition. The natives carried Remington 45-90's, and had about two bushels of cartridges loose in a big box.

Lieutenant Myers took his marines through the boat-house and formed them in line facing the water. The left of the line moved forward left oblique, turning the flank of the boat-house, and the Spaniards were helpless in a trap, if they had cherished any notion of making a last stand. But they had not. At Lieutenant Braunersreuther's command the regulars stepped forward, man by man, to Ensign Evans, who stood near the landing-stage, broke open their rifles, and showed them to be not loaded, then handed them to him. As Ensign Evans passed the guns on to blue-jackets, who stowed them in one of the *Charleston's* boats, the soldiers passed over their belts, bayonets, and other accoutrements. When the regulars had been thus disarmed and had reformed in line, the natives went through the same form.

Then Lieutenant Braunersreuther stepped out in front of the marines, followed by the two Spanish officers. The marines presented arms, and the Spaniards gave their swords and their revolvers to Lieutenant Braunersreuther.

Then the Spanish regulars learned for the first time that they were to be held as prisoners. Lieutenant Braunersreuther told them that they might say good-bye to the Chamorros. There was a great outcry and much embracing. The natives could hardly repress the evidences of their satisfaction, and as soon as they were sure that they were to be set free from the Spanish yoke, they began ripping the Spanish buttons off their uniforms and the little insignia of their service from their collars. Buttons and collar marks they threw away by handfuls, and the *Charleston's* marines and blue-jackets picked them up as souvenirs. The Chamorros took the farewell messages of their old comrades and scattered. Then the Spaniards were put in a big barge and taken out to the *Charleston*. The two officers and the four Spanish flags went in Lieutenant Braunersreuther's boat. The *Sydney* had anchored near the *Charleston* by this time, and all the prisoners were put aboard her at once. The officers were put two in a state-room and the men were sent below. Armed guards watched them while the ship was in the harbor, but they all had plenty of freedom to move about. The officers' baggage came out to the ship the next morning, and some of the clothing of the men. The captured arms consisted of fifty-four Mauser and fifty-four Remington rifles, with belts, cartridge-boxes, and bayonets, 7500 rounds of Mauser ammunition, and about as much for the Remingtons.

While this was going on the *Charleston* had been taking coal from the *Peking*. It was put in sacks in the *Peking's* bunkers, hoisted into a boat, and towed over to the cruiser. There the sacks were hoisted on board and dumped into the bunkers, and then they were sent back for more. Working constantly for two days, the cruiser got 125 tons from the troop-ship, and on the morning of Wednesday, June 22, four weeks from the day we left San Francisco, we were ready to leave Guam on the last stretch of the road to Manila.

WITH GENERAL GREENE

BY JOHN F. BASS

IT was a long time since San Francisco had seen so many brass buttons, and under the excitement of preparations for the invasion of the Philippine Islands the city was exclusively given up to things military. Whenever new detachments of troops arrived the crowd choked the streets, and all traffic along the line of march was stopped. In skirting the edge of this crowd and feeling its pulse, one could only come to the conclusion that their pleasure in the swing and dash of martial display came of a light-hearted pride that at last they had an army like other countries, rather than from any deep appreciation of what war really meant.

However, the people of San Francisco deserved the greatest praise for the generous hospitality they had shown. The Red Cross had been especially active. Arriving troops were marched into a long hall, where the Red Cross gave them a hearty meal. Some of the leading society women waited on the tables. This kind treatment was thoroughly appreciated by the men. One day one of the Volunteers handed his waitress, a daughter of a California millionaire, a tip of ten cents, with the assurance that he had not had so good a meal since he left his home in Pennsylvania.

Between two hills, in the outskirts of the city, lay Camp Merritt. At one end of the camp began the Golden Gate Park, with its thick masses of bright foliage, its smooth greensward, and well-kept winding roads. Here and on the hill-side above the camp squads drilled daily. The sandy ground of the camp was separated by wooden fences into lots, each reserved for one regiment. Around the barriers, eager to talk to the soldiers, visitors gathered. Women predominated, and they nearly all begged the soldiers for buttons. I saw one soldier, on arriving in San Francisco, deliberately cut all the buttons from the front of his coat and throw them among the crowd. This fad of button-collecting had become such a nuisance that officers jokingly declared that unless the troops moved on soon the army of occupation in the Philippines would have to rely on pins.

The twelve thousand troops then at Camp Merritt, coming as they did from every part of the Union, differed materially in preparation and equipment. Some of the States would not allow the militia to take their uniforms with them, and the men came in a very ragged condition. Luckily the Red Cross had furnished many of these soldiers with shoes and other articles of clothing. It was noticeable that these same troops were the least efficient in their drill. Other regiments, such as the Tenth Pennsylvania, were well equipped and smart, and made an excellent showing by the side of the Regulars on the drill-ground. Indeed, if there was any delay in sending off the second expedition for Manila, it was not that a sufficient number of trained men was lacking, but because the steamship companies were slow in fitting up the transports, and the government seemed unable to turn out rapidly the required number of duck uniforms which were necessary for a campaign in a tropical climate.

For all the apparent delay in getting off troops, the wonder was, considering our inexperience, that preparations were so near complete.

The days of Lexington were over, when a farmer could take down his old gun and go potting the enemy on his own account. The soldier of 1898 must know something of the intricate tactics of modern warfare. The non-commissioned officer, "the backbone of every army," must be formed. In European armies it took a year to bring men up to the ordinary duties of a soldier from the time of individual drill to the grand manœuvres, and this when all the officers were trained to their profession. The hardy mountaineers of Greece, who had carried rifles all their lives, found that a knowledge of field tactics limited to lying on mountain ridges and shooting at Turks was not sufficient for the requirements of modern war. There is no occupation in which the accurate and instinctive knowledge of details is more essential than in that of the soldier. In battle the coolest man may lose his head; he must then depend on habit—and military habit was very foreign to our country, where every man was accustomed to act independently.

To add to these difficulties the campaign in hand was one of foreign conquest, and the expedition which went to the Philippines must be efficient in itself. The difficulties were thoroughly appreciated. One of the most experienced officers at headquarters said to me, "The details of the expedition are all experimental with us; every question that comes up is new."

The difficulties were lightened, however, in the splendid material with which the officers had to deal. None of the troops, it is true, came up to European standards in finish; but they were learning rapidly, and they brought to the task an unlimited supply of good-will and energy. In comparing them with Continental troops, the superior determination and life of the men immediately struck one. They marched as if they were going somewhere and meant to get there. I understood that excessive finish in drilling was not aimed at in our army, as it was supposed to make mere machines out of the men. According to this standard, the "painfully perfect" company was not looked upon with favor.

On the 15th of June Market Street was packed with pushing, eager spectators. Way up above the people, on the sky-pointing *Call* Building, a little cannon pounded its monotonous salute to the troops who were marching down from Camp Merritt to embark on their long journey to the Philippines. On opposite corners of the street two noisy bands, proudly testifying to the patriotism of advertising agents, drowned each other in a hurly-burly of chaotic dissonance. The street-cars, blocked, began to stretch out in a broken line of yellow, green, and red. Then the crowd opened in the middle of the street and crushed back to the sidewalks. With guidon flying, the Utah Light Battery came swinging around the corner, in the lead. The people cheered, and pushed out again close to the marching line. A tall girl flapped a highly scented handkerchief close to the soldiers' faces in odoriferous farewell.

The boys had already marched some miles under the hot sun; their brown, manly faces were streaked with dirt. They were heavily loaded with knapsacks and ammunition, and over the shoulder was strapped in hot bulk the blue-gray blanket. Some men had engaged the willing services of the street arabs to carry extra rifles, bags, and other impedimenta. These small citizens, proud to help the nation's warriors, stretched their short legs in a vain endeavor to keep step. The spectators pressed so closely about the marching troops that one soldier shouted out, "Give us more air!"

About the docks those who could not get inside stood around envying the more fortunate personal friends of the soldiers who were allowed to pass inside of the cordon. The regiments were stretched along the dock, seated on their unrolled blankets, while good angels from the Red Cross, with bright-colored dress and dishevelled hair, hurried about, pitcher and basket in hand, administering to the soldiers' wants. There was a decided smell of bread-and-butter about the place. Friends squatted around the volunteers in

THE *CITY OF PEKING*, *AUSTRALIA*, AND *CITY OF SYDNEY* PASSING OUT OF THE GOLDEN GATE, MAY 25, 1898.—PHOTOGRAPH BY WEIDNER

AN INCIDENT OF THE VOYAGE TO THE PHILIPPINES—GENERAL MERRITT RESPONDING TO THE TOAST

Drawn from Life by G. W. Peters on Bo

R COUNTRY AND OUR PRESIDENT" AT THE INDEPENDENCE DAY DINNER ON THE STEAMER *NEWPORT*
THE UNITED STATES TRANSPORT *NEWPORT*

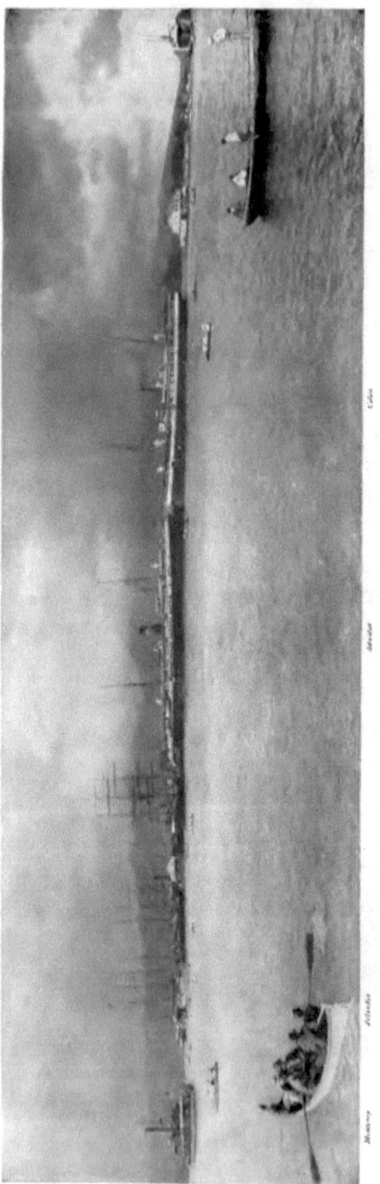

THE MONITOR *MONTEREY* AND TROOP-SHIPS IN THE HARBOR OF HONOLULU ON THEIR WAY TO MANILA

groups. The good-looking soldier had a girl on each side, and was weighted down with flowers and good things.

All day the ships were loading. Cannon swung in the air, bumped against the ship's side, and finally landed on the deck. At last every man was on board, and amidst great shouting and blowing of whistles the boats moved into the bay and anchored.

The night was very warm, and every one was uncomfortable, but happy in the thought that he was among those chosen to start. The men had not been assigned to their bunks yet, and they were packed about like sardines on the deck. A concert was organized, and all joined boisterously in the chorus. At last taps were sounded and lights were out, and the men tried to find a soft place on the smooth boards. On the deck above, the officers paced up and down, smoking and telling yarns, while the ship swung lazily in the tide.

Next morning the ships woke up with the first gray of dawning. "Jimmy Green" drank his coffee and chewed his hardtack. The sun came up, and soon the decks were sweltering hot, with no wind blowing. The soldier threw off his coat, and sought every convenient shelter to write his farewell letter home.

At noon a great tug-boat came puffing up alongside, bringing a crowd of enthusiastic Red Cross girls waving flags and throwing flowers. The quizzical old captain at my side whispered in my ear, "The women are having the time of their life, but they have done lots of good."

The soldiers ran up in the rigging and crowded to the edge of the boat as the tug bumped up against our side. The girls threw flowers and packages of good things among us. Other tugs and pleasure boats came out and surrounded us, until we were the centre of a little fleet. On board the various boats the bands played the "Star-spangled Banner" and "Marching Through Georgia." The excitement grew, and amid waving flags the crowd on board the Red Cross tug broke out into old familiar airs. The high voices of the women floated over to us in soft, melancholy good-bye. It was a sight not to be forgotten.

We were to stop at Honolulu, there stay some days, awaiting orders which were to come to us from the *Belgic*, sailing from San Francisco on Saturday, the 18th. There was no cable to Honolulu. Rumor had it that our delay there meant that we would be expected to take possession of Hawaii in the name of Uncle Sam. If we should see the annexation *de facto* it would be a glorious sight.

Brigadier-General Greene came on board with his orders. The ship shouted him an enthusiastic welcome. The signal was given, and at last we started, the *China* leading, followed by the *Zelandia*, *Senator*, and *Colon*. I counted fifty excursion-boats, all blowing whistles and flying flags. Crowds lined the docks, and the forts gave us the brigadier salute. We were off for Manila.

On the 22d, at sunrise, we saw the green hills above Honolulu, and very welcome was the sight to our sea-wearied eyes. A heavy mist hung over the city, which slowly lifted as we entered the harbor. At the wharf a few people with a brass band had already gathered to meet us, but most of Honolulu was still asleep. Gradually it awoke and came down to the wharf. The soldiers were not allowed to leave the ship; and the people expressed disappointment, for they wished to take the soldier and regale him with the best they had, and prove that they were really worthy of annexation. Later the men were marched down a long dusty road to the sea-shore, where they all had a good swim. Between the sand-bar, half a mile out, and the shore one thousand soldiers plunged as in a huge bath-tub. All were afterwards refreshed with a good meal along great tables in the palm-filled garden of the palace, under the green canopy of lofty trees. The girls of Honolulu, in their best frocks of white muslin and bright ribbons, pounced upon the soldiers and strung wreaths of flowers about their necks. Watching the scene, I turned to an old citizen of Honolulu and asked him: "Why do you wish for annexation? You seem perfectly happy without it." He tucked his arm under mine and led me up to lunch at the Officers' Club, which had opened its heart and its doors wide to the American officers. He stopped me before the club door and pointed out to me a long line of polished quick-firing guns.

"Have you noticed those Maxims? The childlike native sometimes wakes up. We never know when it is coming."

On Fourth of July, with the peep of dawn, we, nearest of all Americans to the 190th degree of longitude, had the honor, in all probability, of beginning the celebration. Where they came from I do not know, but a few fire-crackers were fired before the officer of the day put an end to this innocent but dangerous amusement.

Down on the horizon a long white line pops up, and the shouts of "Land! land!" break from our ship-weary hearts.

"Wake Island, a coral atoll 19° 11' north, by 166° 33' east," shouts down the captain from the bridge. As we draw near, two open boats are lowered, and General Greene celebrates the Fourth in earnest by raising the American flag on the island. A dreary sun-beaten spot we find it, glistening with white coral and shells, and covered with a sickly growth of low shrubs. This barren waste stretches along for twenty miles. An oblong lagoon, cut from the sea by shallow reefs, over which the waves constantly break, eats its way into the heart of the island. Perhaps this heretofore unclaimed island may some day be used as a telegraph post, or even a coaling station. It lies well on the way to Manila, and therefore has been visited only by a few exploring expeditions and unfortunate castaways. Leaving the stars and stripes to be torn to pieces by indignant gulls, who in flocks fearlessly swept down upon us and pecked at our hats, we returned to the *China*.

LANDING PARTY UNDER GENERAL GREENE WHICH HOISTED THE AMERICAN FLAG ON WAKE ISLAND, JULY 4, 1898

Photograph by [illegible]

At Guam Island we had expected to meet one

GUAM ISLAND

of the American gunboats sent out to join us; and the absence of the expected convoy caused uneasiness, which finally ended about midnight in a scare. Like the rush of water through an open lock the rumor spread through the ship that a Spanish gunboat was sighted off our starboard bow. I rushed up the companion-way, and as I passed between the decks a tall, lanky Volunteer stuck his head through a door and called out in a hoarse whisper, "Cheese it! we're pinched!" Could it be that I was not on the Pacific, but really on the Bowery? However, we met no Spanish gunboat, and steamed safely and jubilantly on to the Bay of Manila and up alongside of our brave little fleet at Cavité. The tars gave us a rousing cheer, which we answered with a will, and a few of us who did not wear uniforms jumped into boats and put for the shore.

Cavité seemed to us a paradise indeed, with its great shade trees, its quaint buildings, and the very little natives, with very little clothing, who crowded curiously about. It would take about five able-bodied Filipinos to make one Jimmy Green, of Troy, New York; and yet the quartermaster assured me that five of these thin dwarfs would do as much work as twenty-five of our brawny soldiers.

On the 16th Lieutenant Lazelle, of the Eighteenth Infantry, who died on the *Colon*, was buried in the old fort. A more appropriate grave for a soldier could not well be imagined. Overlooking the sea, in a space one hundred yards square, surrounded with ancient battered walls, with old dismounted guns and cannon-balls lying about, the grave was dug. Native men, women, and children in rags of variegated hues crowded the walls. Slowly, with muffled beat of drums, the funeral passed in through the old stone gate. The officers crowded close about the grave, feeling, over their first dead among these strange surroundings, the strong need of standing side by side. Three volleys, and then the trumpeter steps to the open grave and blows for the last time "taps" for his officer.

WITH GENERAL MERRITT

BY F. D. MILLET

THE departure of the *Newport* on the morning of the 29th of June was accompanied by the display of fervent patriotic enthusiasm which the emotional people of San Francisco had not restrained on the occasion of the sailing of other detachments of the Philippine expedition. But the departure of the *Newport* with General Merritt, his personal and department staff, together with about five hundred picked troops, caused a degree and quality of excitement which was most gratifying to witness. Scarcely had we turned our thoughts from the friends we were leaving to the consideration of personal comfort, scarcely had we time to note the vanishing of the bold outlines of the noble headlands of the Golden Gate into the gray veil of summer mist, before we were headed and lashed by the advance gusts of a severe gale, which soon compelled the steamer to lie to and hammer the vicious sea for seventeen long hours. The transport was fortunately not crowded beyond the measure of comparative comfort, although the lower deck, where the men were berthed in five rows of double banks three tiers high, cannot be said to have offered the most sumptuous accommodations. The chief subject of complaint had been the lack of mess-room for eating, and the men found it at times very difficult to manage their mess-tins and their cups of soup or coffee without any available table-room to balance them on.

General Merritt, however, at considerable discomfort to himself and to his officers, did not restrict the movements of the men on the decks, and they wandered at will at all times of the day and night all over the ship, except, of course, in the saloon and social hall, where the officers were quartered in comfortable, airy state-rooms. On the lower deck, admirably ventilated through a large forward hatch, and several small ones with wind-sails, the Astor Battery was quartered forward, K Battery of the Third Regular Heavy Artillery in the waist of the ship, and H Battery near the stern. After the storm was over and we were able to stand away on our true course again, the men were not slow to crawl out from their quarters, and the decks were covered by a chattering, happy crowd, apparently devoting the larger part of their time to the consumption of food. Many of them produced tins of preserves and other delicacies to tempt their appetites, jaded by the turmoil of the past days. The chronic grumblers found the bill of fare too solid and heavy for any human being to eat; they even went so far as to criticise the liberality with which the rations were dispensed. But the grumblers we have always with us, although they found on this boat few active supporters and plenty of philosophical opponents.

Fourth of July, fortunately, turned out a perfect day. Certain crude luxuries, like apple-duff, were added to the bill of fare of the soldiers, and an impromptu entertainment was managed on the upper deck. Father Doherty, the chaplain of the expedition, followed the reading of the Declaration of Independence by Colonel Whipple with a vigorous and inspiring though brief oration, and the glee club of the Astor Battery sang the usual patriotic songs. As there was no band aboard, the popular music of the day, often sung to words written by a witty member of the coterie, furnished the only entertainment of a musical

POSITION OF AMERICAN FLEET AT THE SURRENDER OF GUAM

order possible aboard. In the saloon, after luncheon, a short list of toasts was drunk in punch strong enough to satisfy a Russian, and thus we, with no cloud over our spirits, without a thought of the uncertainties of the future, which, it must be confessed, come to all of us at times, cheered by the companionship of sympathetic friends, and unconsciously exalted by the ineffaceable memories of the festival at home, picked off a red-letter day in our calendar. Who could tell when and where we should put another indelible mark to record an event to be remembered in the history we were helping to make?

A slight accident to the machinery on the afternoon of the 5th stopped the revolution of the screw for five hours and more. The teeming life on the boat seemed suspended for a moment at the sudden pause in the forward motion, and then took a new and more active start. Sharks were seen in great numbers, and several were hauled up the side, but each one succeeded in breaking away just as the men with cheers and laughter had hauled his vicious head up to the rail. This pastime was perforce suspended as soon as the screw began to churn the water again and the monotony of the trip, if that can be called monotony which was a succession of amusing human incidents. Then naturally all thoughts were turned towards Honolulu. The last day before reaching port was the happiest day of the week on the water. Eager to have a run on shore, and anticipating pleasures which did not fully materialize, imagining prospective beauty of tropical scenery which was more than realized, the whole ship's company were in a state of mild exaltation. The quartermasters issued shore-going suits of tan-colored linen, with thin underwear, and the non-commissioned officers made up their squads for landing. The excitement of trying on the new clothes and the occupation of the letter-writing made the day seem all too short. The officers appeared shy as school-boys at first in suits of gray linen with blue or red trimmings. Helmets of unexpected shape and startling size were produced, and, but for the knowledge that this was to be only a brief pause in our voyage, we should all have felt much as the passengers on an Atlantic liner do when Queenstown is passed or the Lizard sighted. The hazy outlines of Molokai shimmered in the distant horizon to the south just before sunset.

When we landed, early in the morning, the little town was already given over to peaceful military occupation. Soldiers everywhere, most of them, following the pleasant custom of the island, decorated with wreaths of pinks and garlands of fragrant leaves and flowers. In the shade of great trees and palm-thatched bowers in the grounds of the old palace tables were laid, heavy with tropical fruits and more solid food; and already, long before noon, hundreds of ladies had assembled to welcome the soldiers, and, after the feast was over, Mrs. Dole, wife of the President of the Hawaiian Republic, and her friends held an informal reception on the green. Hawaiian hospitality has unique and fascinating elements of grace and picturesqueness in it which make such a festival as I have briefly alluded to the most perfect in the world. Nor were the men who enjoyed it unworthy of it or unappreciative of its rare qualities. Marshal Brown, who was at the head of the police force of the island, informed me that up to that date not a single arrest of a soldier had been made, and not a disturbance of the peace of any kind had been reported to him. This, with all restraints of discipline temporarily suspended, with all the excitement of novel surroundings and the temptations of abundant hospitality, proved the temper of the men, and was worth as much to the cause they were fighting for as a victory in the field.

The five other steamers of our fleet were already nearly all coaled when we reached Honolulu on the 7th, and in the evening they were, with one exception, sent outside the reef, to free the little harbor, already much overcrowded, there to await the *Newport*, and to start on the long voyage together. We were ordered to be on board at eleven o'clock the next morning—an hour which promised to come far too quickly for even the most unemotional among us—and the brief period which was allowed us on shore was improved with almost hysterical activity. General Merritt was met, on landing, by Consul-General Haywood, who proved to be a most efficient and energetic guide; the courtesies of the Pacific Club were tendered to the General and his staff, and the forenoon was spent in a pleasant visit to Minister Sewall, in a call upon President Dole and his cabinet, and in other formalities. The chief embarrassment to both officers and men was the lavishness, and, withal, the kindly urgency, of the hospitality. Nothing could be too good for a soldier; almost every man was decorated with wreaths of pinks and fragrant tropical blossoms, twined around his hat and hung around his neck and across his shoulders.

Every one wore a badge with eagle and crossed flags, and the motto "Aloha nui to our Boys in Blue"—an expression of loving welcome, suggesting in its phraseology a kinship of sentiment, if not of blood, anticipating, indeed, a union of interests which the long-desired annexation would confirm and establish. The spectacle of great, brown, hardy soldiers from the Northwest running about the town like so many children on a picnic, with wreaths and flowers and tropical fruits, sometimes accompanied by happy natives, sometimes driving with the ladies of society in sumptuous equipages, sometimes lounging on the shady lawns of the bungalows under palm and pepper trees, sometimes dashing along on bicycles, all as careless as school-boys

THE OUTER GATE OF THE ARSENAL YARD, CAVITÉ—SPANISH WRECKS IN THE DISTANCE

DRAWN BY CHARLES BROUGHTON AFTER A SKETCH BY JOHN T. MCCUTCHEON

UNITED STATES SOLDIERS DRILLING ON THE PARADE-GROUND AT CAVITÉ

Drawn by Charles Broughton after a Sketch by John T. McCutcheon

—this spectacle, forsooth, is not to be described, and can never be forgotten. Reluctantly the soldiers boarded the crowded transports again; still more reluctantly did those whose foresight secured for them the enjoyment of a clean, airy room in the hotel, and who were able to enjoy something of the unique Hawaiian hospitality, break away from the fascinating place, whose irresistible delights were only beginning to unfold themselves when the cruel moment of departure arrived.

A rumor that the Cadiz fleet had passed through the Suez Canal reached Honolulu by our boat, and was partly confirmed by newspapers brought by a quick steamer which left Victoria two days after we sailed from San Francisco. This rumor caused a certain anxiety at Honolulu, for the story of the Spanish occupation of Ponapi in the Carolines, in 1888, and the consequent interruption of successful mission-work, was still vividly remembered there; and, besides, the citizens were hyper-conscious of their position as avowed friends of the United States in the present crisis, and naturally considered the voyage of Spanish cruisers for revenge and conquest quite within the range of possibility. The departure of General Merritt and his fleet caused, therefore, a lively exhibition of sentimental and patriotic interest, and the wharf was crowded with our new-found friends long before the hour of sailing. Officers and men on the *Newport* were adorned as for a carnival festivity, some of them, in fact, almost smothered with flowers.

The citizens sent as an escort the fine Hawaiian band, which played patriotic airs as we slowly steamed along the narrow channel in the reef towards the distant group of steamers awaiting our arrival before starting on the long voyage. It was found, on reaching them, that one of the vessels was slightly disabled, and therefore, after an hour of busy signal-work, General Merritt, to the satisfaction of every one on the *Newport*, decided to lay the course of his transport straight to the Philippines by way of Farallon de Pajaros, the most northerly island of the Ladrones, and to leave the rest of the fleet to follow the plan originally decided upon, namely, to make first for the island of Guam in the Ladrones, where, it was believed, the monitor *Monterey* would be overtaken, and then to steer for the general line of rendezvous, beginning at a point 600 miles due east from Cape Engaño, the northeastern point

BARRACKS OF SPANISH MARINES, NEAR MAIN GATE OF ARSENAL.—Drawn by Charles Broughton after a Sketch by John T. McCutcheon

of the island of Luzon. Farallon de Pajaros is 450 miles north of Guam, and the route to Manila taken by the *Newport* would be about 1970 miles, as against almost 5100 miles on the course followed by the other vessels. The convoy of the monitor was certainly desirable, but the delay caused by the increased mileage and the reduction of speed necessary to keep in sight of the other ships would have caused the *Newport* to lose three days at least. Some-where on the line of rendezvous it was expected that a vessel sent by Admiral Dewey would meet us to escort us into port, or at least to give us news of the situation there for our guidance.

REBEL LEADERS, AND SPANISH OFFICERS IN CHARGE OF THEIR DEPORTATION FROM THE ISLANDS

For ten whole days we ran at an average of about 310 miles, in weather absolutely perfect, and with a thermometer standing between 80° and 85° day and night. A following trade-wind of about the same speed as we were making made the heat seem much more oppressive than these figures indicate; but an occasional shower apparently cooled the air, although the mercury scarcely ever fell a degree.

For ten days not an object broke the horizon, and the monotony of its sharp line was only varied by the slanting dashes of small showers as they slowly moved across the water. For ten days we saw nothing on the ocean more interesting than great schools of flying-fish and an occasional gull or albatross. The busy, teeming life on the steamer was a continuous entertainment, and the ten days, which would otherwise have been deadly monotonous, passed with extraordinary rapidity. The men's quarters were cramped enough below, but the ventilation was good, the temperature at least a degree and a half lower than in the saloon, and the troop-deck was kept scrupulously clean. The bunks were, however, fixed and stationary, and, unlike the hammocks and folding-bunks in use on the English troopships, could not be removed to make room for mess-tables. They accommodated more men in a given area, but the system compelled the occupants to eat their food and perform the manifold minor duties of soldier life wherever and whenever they could find a place on the crowded boat. It was therefore necessary to allow the men free run of all the decks, except a small space reserved for the officers between the deck-houses.

The Astor Battery preempted the roof of the saloon deck-house, and many of them bivouacked there among the life-rafts and spars, and the sound of music and merriment was often heard above the awnings until late at night. K Battery, of the Third Regular Heavy Artillery, swarmed all over the bow; H Battery gathered on the stern, and stragglers from all three batteries were found at night stretched all over the hurricane-deck. After leaving Honolulu a system of squad drills in calisthenics and the manual of arms was carried on with great regularity, for the weather seldom interfered with these exercises, and there was no sea-sickness. There was no deck-room for parade, and the regulations about dress were not strictly enforced. Indeed, there was almost full liberty given to the men in this respect, and some of the officers themselves wore tennis suits and other civilian clothes for a larger part of the voyage. As for occupations and pastimes, they were so numerous that the days were all too short to exhaust the programme. Officers and men spent a great deal of time in the study of Spanish, and little groups busy over the same book occupied every retired corner at certain times of the day. Perhaps there was some indifference to the music of pure Castilian, and surely a wide ignorance of it prevailed, but a useful vocabulary was rapidly acquired, and even some fluency in speaking the language might be credited to some earnest students. Boxing was indulged in by the men every evening, and impromptu conversaziones were organized by the officers, and at twilight nearly every evening some officer related an interesting experience. Colonel Brainard's story of the Greely expedition will long remain in the memory of those who gathered around him in the warm evening air, and, dressed in the lightest possible garments, listened to the dramatic tale of life in the ice and snow of the far North. General Merritt gave a vivid but brief picture of an incident in the Civil War; Major Thompson, of the signal corps, told of the Custer massacre; Surgeon Woodruff turned our thoughts to the disturbing theories of degeneracy; the Astor Battery furnished a well-equipped variety troupe on more than one occasion, and so the evenings succeeded each other with pleasant entertainment.

We ran into Spanish waters on the evening of the tenth day from the Hawaiian Islands, and then the real object of our voyage, lost sight of but not forgotten in the diversions of the trip, came strongly to our minds again, and the fertile imaginations pictured all sorts of adventures to be in store for us before we should reach Manila, if, indeed, we got there at all. It was with a sense of appreciation of the possible uncertainties of the situation in these waters that we had gayly sailed away from Honolulu, but all anxiety was soothed away as we quietly went along, and no one seemed to think very much about anything. But at four o'clock on the afternoon of the 19th (we had lost a day at the 180th meridian, it must be remembered) the great pyramid of the island volcano Assumption was discovered looming up boldly to the southwest. A few moments later, on the distant horizon, directly in our path, a tiny white wreath of smoke made a bright spot against the gray of the low clouds, and we rapidly ran up in the mirage the symmetrical cone of the Farallon de Pajaros, with its immense plume of sulphur steam drifting far away to the northeast, puffing up in huge rounded masses many hundreds of feet above the summit. A most gorgeous and dramatic sunset, with the great active volcano and its cloud of steam strong in contrast against a kaleidoscopic sky, kept every one watching its rapid transformations, until all the light went out of the west and Venus blazed brightly in our path. The volcano is over a thousand feet in height, and rises directly out of the ocean in the form of a slightly depressed cone, with a small rugged promontory jutting out to the southward. The crater is apparently about two hundred and fifty feet across, and, judging from the strong reflection on the steam-cloud, it is full of molten lava. We had the mountain abeam and about four miles distant at a quarter past eight, only six minutes later than Captain Saunders had promised ten days before. Our course was slightly changed to the southward, and in an hour the red light of the crater had disappeared astern.

Time now began to drag a little, as it always does towards the end of a long voyage, and the soldiers no longer talked of their present discomforts, but of the probable future operations. The wise words of the veterans were listened to with earnestness and attention, and discussions on the field operations, the new system of formation, the use of the weapons, and on kindred topics were heard on all sides. The non-coms., too, began to have a more paternal authority over the men, and even to a casual observer there were signs of awakened interest in the soldier's trade. The six-hundred-mile point was passed at one o'clock on the morning of the 22d, and we began to look for signs of vessels to the westward. The sea was almost without a ripple, for the trade-wind had died away altogether, and the horizon-line was clear and sharp. The heat rose gradually to 87°, where it remained without perceptible variation day and night, and threatening clouds hung over the western sky. Late in the afternoon of the 24th we saw through the veil of mist and between the distant showers of rain the headlands of Cape Engaño, and before midnight were well in the middle of the narrow strait between that point and the Babuyan Islands. At daybreak Sunday morning we entered the China Sea, and shortly after, passing a large steamer a dozen miles to the northward, which went on its course without so much as showing a flag, we stood away to the southward, towards the entrance to Manila Bay, less than three hundred miles distant.

Heavy rains and wind-squalls made our last night disagreeable and very uncomfortable for everybody. At ten o'clock on the morning of Monday, the 26th, we passed the luxuriantly wooded and beautiful islands at the entrance of the harbor, and in a few moments saw in the distance the towering masts of a man-of-war off Cavité and a forest of smaller spars beyond. Shortly after eleven o'clock the *Concord* steamed out to meet us, and an officer came aboard, bringing the news of the fall of Santiago, the destruction of the Spanish fleet in Cuban waters, and the annexation of Hawaii. Admiral Dewey visited General Merritt after the steamer had dropped her anchor.

FIRST COLORADO VOLUNTEERS LANDING ON THE BEACH NEAR CAMP TAMBO—CRUISER *BOSTON* IN REAR OF *ISABEL*

SKETCHED BY JOHN T. MCCUTCHEON

IN THE INSURGENTS' TRENCHES

BY JOHN F. BASS

To get through the American lines and into the insurgents' trenches it was necessary to have two passes. One was easily obtained at General Anderson's headquarters; the other was a matter of long diplomatic negotiations at the headquarters of General Aguinaldo, President of the revolutionary government of the Philippines.

We made our way along the wharves of the arsenal, past the machine-shop—left intact by the Spaniards, and now noisily worked by the American workmen—down the long walk shaded with luxuriant trees and lined with low flat barracks, where the American soldier slept, cooked, and hung out his washing. Everywhere the grounds were crowded with ragged, stolid, silent natives, some working, some standing about, some begging, their whole attitude that of indifference. An occasional leper dragged himself along. Down in one corner of the wharves had settled a regular colony of dark-skinned Filipinos, employed in transporting troops and stores on their long bamboo-covered casco-boats. Their emaciated little children played about, and their women appeared to be constantly employed in washing their rags and scouring their primitive pots and kettles. A very cleanly lot they seemed, considering their resources.

Well in the middle of the grounds stood General Anderson's headquarters. As we went up the steps a tall man rather shabbily dressed preceded us. We noticed his military bearing, and were told that he was the captain of one of the Spanish men-of-war which lay with projecting spars at the bottom of Cavité Harbor. Following his footsteps, we of necessity overheard what he said to the general's aide:

"Señor, I borrowed, some time ago, two hundred dollars from Admiral Dewey to pay off my men. I have come to repay the debt."

He turned his profile towards us, and we noticed how thin he looked. He must have starved himself to collect the money. With a very straight back he counted out the Spanish bills, and turned to go.

"Will you not take a receipt?" asked the aide of General Anderson.

"Never from an officer," answered the gray-haired old gentleman, with a courtly, old-fashioned bow.

Here, at least, was a true Spanish *caballero*.

Leaving the arsenal, we walked through the narrow streets of Cavité, crowded with nut-brown natives in loose garments of bright colors.

At the wharf outside the town we got into our long dug-out, dignified by the name of *Harper's Weekly Despatch-boat*, which, under the steady strokes of our four silent boatmen, took us to Bacoor, to which place General Aguinaldo had moved from Cavité.

We were entertained by the secretary of Aguinaldo, who, in the reflected grandeur of his master, was also a very great man. He was very polite, but never allowed himself to show anything like interest in what was going on about him. With inscrutable face he discussed the political situation, after the fashion of a man of the world who is rather bored. nightfall four of us started on the muddy road which led direct to Manila; our fat interpreter, the quondam keeper of a sailors' boarding-house in the capital, showed symptoms of turning tail.

"It is very dangerous," he ventured, after an animated conversation with some natives.

"Very well; you go ahead, Ruis, and ward off danger." This plan did not seem to please Ruis, for he very soon dropped behind, saying that he would see that no one took us by surprise from the rear.

About a mile out we came to our own outposts; the men were having a good time, singing "Marching Through Georgia."

"Not much like the English army in the field," remarked our Yorkshire man, who had seen twelve years of British service. "No in the darkness. In the insurgents' trenches along the road ragged Filipinos, rifle in hand, lay stretched in the rain, watching for the enemy. On our right a desultory firing began, and we asked to be taken to the place where they were fighting. Ruis consulted with the leaders, and after many protests that it would be most dangerous, a guide was given us, who led us through swamps and bogs towards the firing-line. For some reason, tramp as we would, we did not seem to get there. At last we reached another barricade, only a short distance from the fighting. The commandant of this position informed us that the insurgent lines at this point were so scattered that the soldiers had orders to fire on any one approaching during the night. They were evidently afraid of a flank movement on the part of the Spaniards. Much against our will

BRINGING IN A WOUNDED INSURGENT FROM THE TRENCHES.—SKETCHED BY JOHN T. McCUTCHEON

For all his society airs, he put us some rather difficult questions. "The Americans have, of course, come to give independence to the Philippines?" "Do we not find the people as worthy of self-government as the Cubans?" "Why will General Anderson not recognize the government of President Aguinaldo?" To all these questions we made answer as best we could, and after an hour's delay in getting our passes we rose to go, with a feeling that it was really we who had been interviewed. A very clever young man, this secretary of the President. One thing, however, we were given to understand—that only so long as the Americans favored the independence of the islands might they expect friendly treatment from the insurgents.

An hour's row brought us to Camp Dewey, where, wishing to see the fighting in the insurgents' trenches after dark, we waited. At man on outpost duty is even allowed to light a cigarette."

A short distance ahead we ran upon the last American picket.

The road became more muddy and rough. It might have been possible to get cannon along those paths, but, once at the front, it would have been impossible to move them back again in a hurry. We floundered about in the blackness, and, to add to our discomforts, it began to rain. Not as it rains in America, but as if some one were throwing buckets of water on the particular spot where you happened to be. Two miles from camp we stumbled over the first insurgent barricade, a rude structure of bamboo and dirt thrown across the road. Passing this, we finally reached the fighting-line of the insurgents. Here two muzzle-loading cannon threatened the Spanish lines, some two hundred yards ahead we were obliged to accept the hospitality of the commandant, and spend the night in an improvised hut fifteen feet square, where we were crowded with twenty-five insurgents and a large population of vermin.

With the first light we went into the insurgents' trenches, and were much impressed with the strength of the Spanish earthworks. With block-houses at regular intervals, only about two hundred yards separated the insurgent and Spanish lines. While we were in the trenches a fusillade was opened on both sides, apparently for our benefit. Much ammunition was wasted and no harm done. Farther on we ran across a Krupp gun which the insurgents had taken from the arsenal and brought into position. So far as we could judge, both sides confined themselves to lying behind their earth-works and firing at each other—a method of campaign likely to be dragged on indefinitely without any result.

ASSISTANT NAVAL-CONSTRUCTOR HOBSON'S HEROIC EXPLOIT IN BLOWING UP THE COLLIER *MERRIMAC* AT THE ENTRANCE TO SANTIAGO HARBOR.—BY T. DART WALKER

THE RUNNING-DOWN OF THE SPANISH FLEET

ADMIRAL SAMPSON having arrived off San Juan on the morning of May 12, the bombardment of that place ensued, as already related, and it was seen that Cervera's squadron was not in the port. It was clear that the Americans would have had little difficulty in forcing the surrender of the place; but the fact that they would have been held several days in completing arrangements for holding it, that part of their force would have to be left to await the arrival of troops to garrison it, that the movements of the Spanish fleet were still unknown, that the Flying Squadron was still at Hampton Roads, and that Havana was thus open to possible entry by Cervera while the American naval forces were a thousand miles distant, made an immediate movement towards the Cuban capital imperative. Reluctantly, therefore, Sampson left San Juan and stood westward for Havana. While on the way, he was notified of the presence of the Spanish fleet off Curaçao, and was instructed to proceed quickly to Key West, whither also the Flying Squadron had been ordered.

Meanwhile the *St. Louis*, which had joined the squadron under Admiral Sampson, was ordered to proceed to Santiago and Guantanamo for the purpose of cutting cables; to Ponce, Puerto Rico, for the same purpose, and thence to St. Thomas to await orders. This work was bravely done under exposure to the enemy's fire. "Captain Goodrich," said Sampson, "from the first rendered valuable assistance in severing telegraphic communication between Cuba and the outside world. This was difficult, because the Cubans had placed dummy cables so that it was impossible to learn when a cable was cut."

On the morning of the 17th of May the flagship left the squadron in the Bahama Channel and proceeded to Key West. That afternoon the *Dupont* was met with a despatch from Washington stating that the Spanish fleet had munitions of war destined for the defence of Havana, and was under imperative orders to reach Havana, Cienfuegos, or a port connected with Havana by rail, and that as Cienfuegos appeared to be the only port fulfilling the conditions, the Flying Squadron would be instructed upon arrival at Key West to proceed to Cienfuegos. Instructions were at the same time given to Admiral Sampson to increase the Flying Squadron by such armored ships as he might deem desirable.

On the 19th the Flying Squadron, composed of the *Brooklyn*, *Texas*, *Massachusetts*, and *Scorpion*, sailed from Key West for Cienfuegos with instructions to establish a blockade at that place as soon as possible. On the 20th, the *Iowa*, *Castine*, and the collier *Merrimac* sailed to join Commodore Schley's squadron off Cienfuegos. On the same day the Navy Department informed Admiral Sampson of a report that Cervera's squadron was at Santiago de Cuba, and advised him to order Commodore Schley to proceed off that port with the vessels under his command.

Sampson left Key West for the Havana blockade on the 21st, having previously sent the *Dupont* with despatches to Schley and ordered the *Marblehead* and *Eagle* to join the Flying Squadron. By the *Marblehead* orders were sent to Schley advising him that the Spanish squadron was probably at

DON PASQUALE DE CERVERA Y TOPETE

Conde de Jerez and Marqués de Santa Ana, Rear Admiral, Spanish Navy

Santiago de Cuba, and directing him, if he were satisfied that it was not at Cienfuegos, to proceed with all despatch to Santiago, and upon arrival there to establish communication with some of the inhabitants and ascertain definitely whether the ships were in port or not. The *Hawk* followed with duplicate despatches, which were delivered to Schley on the 23d.

On the 22d Sampson received a despatch from Key West stating that Cervera's squadron was in the harbor of Santiago on the morning of the 21st; also a telegram from Washington stating that it was expected to visit San Juan, Puerto Rico, and if Schley found that it had left Santiago he should follow it.

At 8 A.M. on the morning of the 23d Admiral Sampson left off Havana, sailing eastward, with a view to occupying St. Nicholas Channel in such manner as to prevent the approach of the Spanish squadron in that direction. The *Montgomery* joined him on the 24th, with despatches stating that information had been received to the effect that Cervera's squadron had not left Santiago. On the 26th Admiral Sampson received from Commodore Schley a letter dated May 23, stating that he was by no means satisfied that the Spanish squadron was not at Cienfuegos, and that he would, therefore, remain off that port with his squadron. The *Wasp* was sent on May 27 to carry advices to Commodore Schley, informing him that daily confidential reports received at Key West from Havana stated that the Spanish squadron had been in Santiago from the 19th to the 25th, inclusive, and directing him to proceed with all possible despatch to that port. At this time two telegrams dated Cienfuegos, May 24, were received by Admiral Sampson from Commodore Schley, stating that coaling off that port was very uncertain; that he had ascertained that the Spanish fleet was not in Cienfuegos, and would go eastward on the next day, the 25th, but that on account of short coal supply in ships he could not blockade if the Spanish squadron was in Santiago, but would proceed to the vicinity of Mole St. Nicholas, on the western coast of Haiti, from which point he would communicate.

Upon the receipt of this information Sampson decided to go to Key West for coal, and, if authorized by the Navy Department, to proceed to Santiago in person. The *New Orleans* was instructed on this same day, May 27, to proceed as rapidly as possible to that port in company with the collier *Sterling*, and with orders to Commodore Schley "to remain on the blockade at Santiago at all hazards, assuming that the Spanish vessels are in that port." This order further directed that the collier *Sterling* should be used to obstruct the channel leading into the harbor, and that in the meantime the utmost care should be exercised that none of the Spanish vessels in that port be allowed to escape. Admiral Sampson arrived at Key West on May 28 and cabled to Commodore Schley, advising him that the *New Orleans* would meet him off Santiago on May 29 with important despatches, and further emphasizing the importance of immediate communication with persons ashore, in order to ascertain definitely whether or not Cervera's squadron was in the port of Santiago.

Commodore Schley left Cienfuegos on the evening of the 24th, and at 5.30 P.M. on the 26th reached a point twenty miles or more to the southward and eastward of Santiago, where the squadron stopped while repairs were made to the collier *Merrimac*. At 7.30 P.M. he signalled to the squadron: "Destination Key West, *via* south side of Cuba and Yucatan Channel, as soon as collier is ready. Speed, 9 knots." About 9 P.M. the squadron got under way, and, after steaming to the westward until 11.20 P.M., stopped to make repairs to the *Yale*. On the morning of the 27th the *Harvard*, from Mole St. Nicholas, delivered to Commodore Schley the following despatch from Washington: "Proceed at once and inform Schley and also the senior officer present off Santiago as follows: All department's information indicates Spanish division is still at Santiago. The department looks to you to ascertain facts, and that the enemy, if therein, does not leave without a decisive action. Cubans familiar with Santiago say that there

THE SPANISH SQUADRON AT THE CAPE VERDE ISLANDS

From a Photograph [illegible]

are landing-places five or six nautical miles west from the mouth of harbor, and that there insurgents probably will be found and not the Spanish. From the surrounding heights can see every vessel in port. As soon as ascertained notify the department whether enemy is there. Could not squadron and also the *Harvard* coal from *Merrimac* leeward off Cape Cruz, Gonaives Channel, or Mole, Haiti? The department will send coal immediately to Mole. Report without delay situation at Santiago de Cuba." At 11 o'clock of the same day Commodore Schley signalled to the squadron, "Can you fetch into the port of Key West with coal remaining? Report by signal." At noon the *Harvard* left, carrying this reply to the despatch received from Washington: "*Merrimac* engines disabled; is heavy; am obliged to have towed to Key West. Have been unable absolutely to coal the *Texas*, *Marblehead*, *Vixen*, *Brooklyn* from collier, all owing to very rough sea. Bad weather since leaving Key West. The *Brooklyn* alone has more than sufficient coal to proceed to Key West; cannot remain off Santiago present state squadron coal account. Impossible to coal leeward Cape Cruz in the summer, all owing to southwesterly winds. . . . Much to be regretted, cannot obey orders of department. Have striven earnestly; forced to proceed for coal to Key West by way of Yucatan Passage. Cannot ascertain anything respecting enemy positive. . . . Very difficult to tow collier, to get cable to hold."

Later in the day, the squadron meantime having again moved westward, the signal "Stop" was made to the Flying Squadron, after which the *Texas* and *Marblehead* went alongside the *Merrimac* and coaled. The squadron was at that time distant about forty miles to the southward and westward of Santiago. The Flying Squadron remained here until 1.12 P.M. of the 28th, when signal was made to return in the direction of Santiago. This course was kept until a little after dark, when the squadron stopped for the night about ten miles to the southward of Santiago, with the *Marblehead* scouting two miles inside the squadron. Early on the morning of the 29th a Spanish man-of-war, the *Cristobal Colon*, was seen lying at anchor inside the harbor entrance, and later a second man-of-war and two smaller vessels. At 10 A.M. Commodore Schley cabled that Cervera's squadron was at Santiago. On the morning of the 31st, with the *Massachusetts*, *Iowa*, and *New Orleans*, he exchanged fire with the ships inside the harbor and the forts at a range of about seven thousand yards.

On June 1 Admiral Sampson arrived off Santiago and found Commodore Schley's squadron in column to the westward of the mouth of the harbor. Immediately upon the concentration of these two forces at Santiago a close and efficient blockade was established, Admiral Sampson in command. The harbor was closely guarded day and night by the American ships in a semicircle. Powerful search-lights were thrown upon its entrance during the night. A plan of attack, by which the American vessels were to close in at once upon any of Cervera's ships coming out, was provided for in standing orders.

"The next act in the war," wrote the President of the United States, "thrilled not alone the hearts of our countrymen, but the world, by its exceptional heroism. On the night of June 3, Lieutenant Hobson, aided by seven devoted volunteers, blocked the narrow outlet from Santiago harbor by sinking the collier *Merrimac* in the channel, under a fierce fire from the shore batteries, escaping with their lives as by a miracle, but falling into the hands of the Spaniards. It was a most gratifying incident of the war that the bravery of this little band of heroes was cordially appreciated by the Spanish Admiral, who sent a flag of truce to notify Admiral Sampson of their safety and to compliment them on their daring act. They were subsequently exchanged July 7." "This attempt," said the Secretary of the Navy in his report, "though unsuccessful in its object, was daringly executed. It is now one of the well-known historic marvels of naval adventure and enterprise, in which Naval Constructor Hobson and his men won undying fame."

Another hero whose intrepidity was at this time called into action by the exigencies of the situation was Lieutenant Victor Blue, of the *Suwanee*, who on two occasions, at the request of Admiral Sampson, undertook to locate the position of the Spanish fleet in the harbor of Santiago. To accomplish this it was necessary to travel on the first occasion,

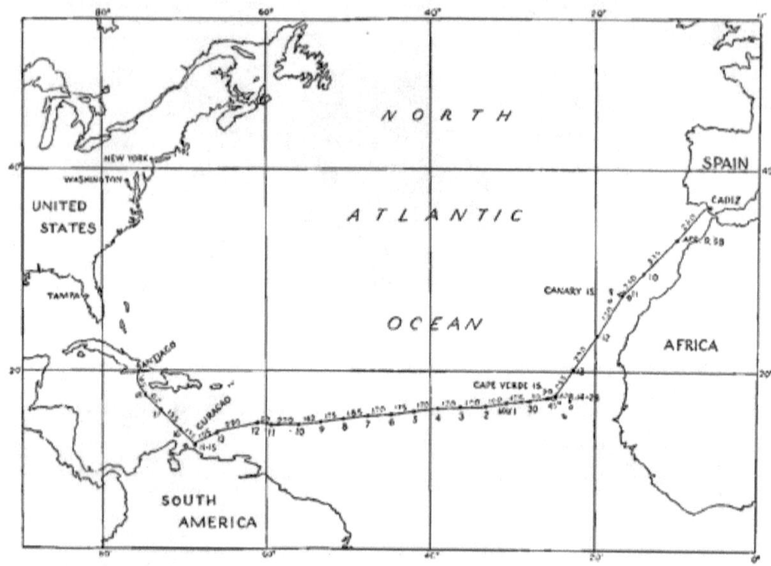

DAILY POSITIONS OF THE SPANISH SQUADRON UNDER ADMIRAL CERVERA, ACCORDING TO THE LOG-BOOK OF THE *CRISTOBAL COLON*

(The figures between the dates indicate distance in nautical miles)

June 11, over a distance of seventy-three miles, and on the latter, June 25, a distance of sixty miles, mostly through territory occupied by the intrenchments of the Spanish army.

"By June 7," said the President, "the cutting of the last Cuban cable isolated the island. Thereafter the invasion was vigorously prosecuted." On June 7 the *Marblehead* and *Yankee* took possession of the lower bay of Guantanamo as a harbor of refuge for the American fleet, and on June 10 the first battalion of marines was landed there and went into camp. For three days and nights these men, supported by the *Marblehead* and *Dolphin*, fought almost constantly. The position which they defended was a most important one for the fleet, as it was necessary to have near at hand a harbor in which ships could be coaled and repaired in safety. The following official recognition of the work of the Marine Corps was published by the Navy Department at the close of hostilities: "The First Marine Battalion, composed of six companies, one of which was an artillery company, was organized at New York, under Lieutenant-Colonel Huntington, and equipped for service in Cuba. The command numbered 24 commissioned officers and 623 enlisted men, and under instructions from the department sailed for Key West on April 22 on board the transport *Panther*. On June 7 the *Panther* left Key West for Guantanamo Bay, Cuba, where she arrived on the 10th, and the battalion landed and went into camp. This was the first permanent landing by our forces on Cuban soil. On the following day the camp was attacked by a force of Spaniards, and from that time until the 14th was constantly under fire. Assistant Surgeon John Blair Gibbs and five enlisted men were killed. Too much praise cannot be given these officers and men for the gallantry and discipline displayed under the trying conditions which confronted them almost immediately upon landing on Cuban soil. For three days and nights they were compelled to remain constantly under arms, repelling the Spanish attacks, and this, too, in a semitropical country, where the dense undergrowth afforded shelter to the sharpshooters of the enemy. This command remained in camp at Guantanamo from the 10th of June to the 5th of August, and did not lose a man by disease, while the cases of sickness was only 2 per cent. This speaks for the careful preparation of the battalion for the service which devolved upon it, and for the vigilance and care of those intrusted with the health and comfort of the men. But praise is not alone due to those officers and men of the Marine Corps who served with the First Marine Battalion. The records are full of incidents in which conspicuous and gallant service was rendered."

On the 15th of June the *Texas*, *Marblehead*, and *Suwanee* proceeded into Guantanamo Harbor, and, after engaging and silencing the adjacent fort and battery, took possession of that harbor. The *Yankee* had successfully engaged a gunboat and batteries off Cienfuegos on the 13th; and on the 29th the *Eagle* and *Yankee* had an engagement with a force of Spanish cavalry off the mouth of the Rio Hondo, Cuba. On the 30th the *Hist*, *Wompatuck*, and *Hornet*, while making a reconnaissance between Cape Cruz and Manzanillo, were engaged with the enemy's vessels, field batteries, and infantry at Manzanillo. The *Hornet* was struck many times, and had her main steam-pipe cut, being thereby absolutely disabled. The *Wompatuck* gallantly towed the *Hornet* out of danger. Another action occurred at Manzanillo on July 1, in which the same Spanish gunboats were engaged on one side and the *Scorpion* and *Osceola* on the other.

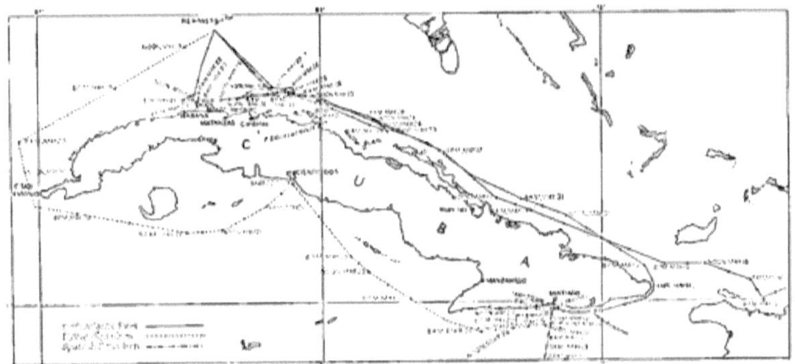

CHART SHOWING DAILY POSITIONS OF AMERICAN FLEET IN CAMPAIGN AGAINST SPANISH SQUADRON UNDER ADMIRAL CERVERA

(The positions shown are those of the flag-ship in each case, except that the Spanish positions are those taken from the log of the Cristobal Colon)

OPERATIONS OF THE FLYING SQUADRON

As Told by Commodore Schley

The squadron sailed from Key West on the morning of the 19th of May for Cienfuegos, Cuba, in obedience to orders from Rear-Admiral Sampson. In company with the *Brooklyn* (flag-ship) were the *Massachusetts*, *Texas*, and *Scorpion*. *En route*, passed the *Marblehead*, *Nashville*, and *Wasp*, communicating with the last-named vessel. Off Cape San Antonio communicated with the *Cincinnati* and *Vesuvius*, scouting.

On the morning of the 22d of May the squadron stood in for the entrance of Cienfuegos Harbor to reconnoitre, and later in the day passed the entrance twice, close in. As I had heard the firing of guns on the previous afternoon in the direction of the port, and as there was considerable smoke observed in the harbor, I was led to believe that the Spanish squadron might have arrived there. That day the *Dupont* joined me with despatches from Admiral Sampson, directing that the blockade of Cienfuegos be preserved and that the *Scorpion* be sent to communicate with the *Minneapolis* and *Harvard*, off Santiago. Also on this day the *Iowa* joined the squadron.

A line of blockade was established about four miles off-shore, and at night an inshore line was maintained, consisting variously of the *Scorpion*, *Dupont*, and *Castine*, the last-named vessel arriving on the 23d, convoying the *Merrimac*.

Also, on the 23d, the *Hawk* arrived with despatches from Admiral Sampson, directing me to move eastward with the squadron to Santiago, if satisfied that the enemy's vessels were not in Cienfuegos. Not being satisfied at this time that they were not there, I held my position, being further strengthened in my opinion by the fact that I was informed by the captain of the British steamer *Adula* that when he left Kingston a cablegram had been received, on the Thursday preceding my arrival off Cienfuegos, stating that the Spanish squadron had sailed from Santiago.

The *Iowa*, *Castine*, and *Dupont* took coal from the collier on that day, the *Iowa* particularly needing coal, as she had sailed from Key West to join the squadron before completely coaling, and consequently was considerably short.

On the 24th the *Marblehead*, *Vixen*, and *Eagle* joined the squadron, and the *Marblehead* and *Eagle* were immediately sent to communicate with the insurgents to the westward of Cienfuegos, and to furnish them with ammunition, clothing, and dynamite. Upon Commander McCalla's return, in the course of the afternoon, he reported to me that he had obtained information that the Spanish squadron was not in Cienfuegos. Despatches were at once sent by the *Dupont* to Admiral Sampson and to Commodore Remey for the Navy Department, indicating that the squadron would move towards Santiago de Cuba.

Great difficulty was experienced in coaling the *Texas*, on account of her projecting sponsons, in any seaway whatever, and only under the most favorable conditions could she go alongside a collier. In anything more unfavorable than absolutely smooth water there was great danger of injury either to the *Texas* herself or to the collier. In this connection the advantage of a tumblehome to the side was very marked, insuring great freedom from accidents due to projections on the ship's side.

After dark on the evening of the 24th the squadron stood to sea, to the eastward, with the *Brooklyn*, *Massachusetts*, *Iowa*, and the *Texas* in column natural order; the *Marblehead*, *Vixen*, and *Eagle* on the outer flank, and the collier inshore of the battle-ships. The *Castine* was left at Cienfuegos to notify the *Scorpion* on her return, should she not be sighted by us, to proceed to Key West in company.

OLD FORT AT SANTIAGO DE CUBA

The run to Santiago was marked by rain and rough weather to such an extent that the *Eagle* was unable to keep up a speed of 7.5 to 8.5 knots, and fell behind so much as seriously to delay the squadron, which was forced to slow to a speed of from 4 to 5 knots for her to regain and hold her position. As this rough head-sea continued, with no apparent prospect of abating, and as the *Eagle's* coal supply was becoming dangerously low, she was sent to Port Antonio, Jamaica, for coal, with directions to make the best of her way back to Key West.

On arriving off Santiago de Cuba, the collier *Merrimac* was disabled by the breaking of her intermediate pressure-valve stem and the cracking of the stuffing-box. This served as a further embarrassment to the squadron and a source of considerable anxiety, as, with the weather conditions that had prevailed since leaving Cienfuegos, it appeared absolutely necessary to abandon the position off Santiago and seek a place where the vessels could be coaled and the collier's machinery repaired.

Off Santiago the *St. Paul*, *Yale*, and *Minneapolis* were sighted and communicated with. The *Minneapolis* reported that she only had sufficient coal to reach Key West, and that her machinery was in bad condition. The coal supply of the two other scouts was also much reduced. Arrangements were at once made whereby the *Yale* was to tow the collier, and, as the prospect did not seem favorable for replenishing the meagre coal supply of the other vessels, the squadron stood to the westward, towing the collier. The operation of taking the collier in tow proved to be quite difficult, owing to the size and weight of the two ships and the repeated parting of the tow-lines. Finally, however, after twenty-four hours' unremitting exertions, the collier's chain cable was gotten to the *Yale* and the squadron proceeded. The *St. Paul* was ordered to remain off Santiago until her coal supply would no longer permit of further delay.

After standing to the westward for about three hours, or about twenty-five miles, the conditions became less unfavorable and the squadron stopped. The *Texas* and *Marblehead* were sent alongside the collier, whose injury had been temporarily repaired, and coaled during the night.

Inasmuch as it was known that, in case the Spanish squadron had reached Santiago, Admiral Sampson was able to block any movement of the enemy through the Bahama Channel, my intention in standing to the westward was, should it become necessary, to bar any effort of the enemy to reach Havana by a dash through the Yucatan Passage.

On the 28th instant continued coaling the *Texas* and *Marblehead*, and later the *Vixen*. In the afternoon, having managed to get sufficient coal into these vessels to enable them to remain with the squadron, shaped course for Santiago, off which port we arrived about dusk. Established an inner picket-line consisting of the *Vixen* and *Marblehead*, the remainder of the squadron lying to off the entrance of the port, about four to five miles out.

The next morning, the 29th, steamed in to examine the entrance to the harbor, and sighted the *Cristobal Colon*, apparently moored, head and stern, across the western channel around Cay Smith; also one of the vessels of the *Vizcaya* or *Infanta Maria Teresa* class moored in the eastern channel, and two small torpedo-boats. Later in the day made out the military tops of a third vessel farther up the harbor.

A close blockade of the harbor was maintained, and no vessels entered or left after our arrival. On the morning of the 29th H.M.S. *Indefatigable* came up to the line of blockade and made signal "Request permission to communicate with the Commodore," which was, of course, granted. A boarding officer came on board the flag-ship with a letter from the commanding officer, Captain L. A. Primrose, requesting permission for his vessel to pass the line of blockade in order to communicate with her Majesty's consul at this port. My reply was that there could not be the slightest objection to his doing so. Instead, however, of availing himself of the permission, the *Indefatigable* at once steamed off in the direction from whence she came, signalling "No harm done for courtesy." It may have been that his learning that the Spanish fleet was in this port was of more importance than her Majesty's consul, and he may have desired first to communicate with his government from Jamaica.

On the 30th the *New Orleans* arrived, convoying the collier *Sterling*.

On the 31st of May, as the *Brooklyn*, *Texas*, and *Marblehead* were coaling, I shifted my broad pennant to the *Massachusetts*, and, together with the *Iowa* and *New Orleans*, steamed in from a position about five miles southwest of the entrance. At 12.45 made signal, "Clear for action," and at 1.05 the signal for "General quarters." The speed was set at ten knots, with the three vessels in column at distance, the *Massachusetts* leading and the *Iowa* following the *New Orleans*.

I stood in with port helm heading gradually to about N.E., then easing to E.N.E. The distance having decreased to about 7000 yards, I headed east, and at 2, the *Colon* having been opened out in the entrance, we commenced firing with our port batteries, using the guns of greatest range on the *Colon* and the smaller ones against the fortifications.

Our fire was at once returned by the ships inside the harbor (firing at random over the land) and by the forts to the eastward and westward of the entrance and on Cay Smith; also by the *Colon*. At 2.10 ceased firing, turned with port helm to W. by S., and slowed. Headed offshore at 2.23 and stood out of range. The shore batteries and the *Colon* continued firing until about 3 P.M.

None of our vessels was struck, although the shots fell over and around them. I learned from insurgent sources that the *Reina Mercedes* was struck by a shell and eight men were killed; also that a number of shots struck the Morro.

The reconnaissance developed the fact that

the Spanish vessels were in the harbor and that the fortifications were well provided with long-range guns of large caliber. They used smokeless powder almost exclusively, with the exception of the batteries to the westward of the entrance.

CABLE-CUTTING BY THE *ST. LOUIS*

As Told by Captain Goodrich

On the night of May 16 I made an attempt to cut the Santiago-Jamaica cables, going myself in the *Wompatuck*. Unluckily, we were discovered by a patrol-boat, and, not knowing what might be the resources of the defence in guns and search-lights, I deemed it prudent to withdraw.

I took with me Lieutenant Catlin and eight marines, Chief Officer Segrave, Third Officer Smith, Second Engineer Preston, and several men from the *St. Louis* ship's company, under Mr. Segrave's orders, for the purpose of picking up the cable.

It is a pleasure, as well as a duty, to report in commendatory terms the conduct of Lieutenant Carl W. Jungen, commanding the *Wompatuck*.

Mr. Segrave and his associates were volunteers, yet they did not hesitate to incur great risks and to expose their lives to an attack from an unseen foe in the dark.

On the 18th, at daylight, being then some seven miles off Santiago light and the Morro Castle, I steamed with the *St. Louis* on various courses, gradually approaching the fortifications. The water is so deep close to, that with the meagre and improvised appliances at my command I was obliged to come within 1.3 miles of the Castle. I had no sooner hooked the cable in over five hundred fathoms of water than I was fired upon from the Morro, and from a new work to the westward of the harbor, and, most formidable of all, from a mortar battery on Casper Point. Of course, with the very modest broadside of the *St. Louis*, aided by the one 3-pounder of the *Wompatuck*, which joined me just as the firing began, it was impossible to do much execution on the fortifications. Nevertheless, we silenced the one gun on the Morro which was placing its shot dangerously close, both over and short of us; the crew, as could be plainly seen, running away from their piece. Similarly our fire silenced the western battery. From the mortar battery above mentioned the projectiles came with singularly good aim, both as to direction and distance, falling close aboard, some not one hundred feet away, and rendering our position extremely uncomfortable. The damage of which one of their shells was capable might have been serious, even to wrecking or completely crippling this fine and costly vessel. Our position was now extremely uncomfortable, but we held firmly on to the cable, firing all the time, and steamed slowly out of range, where we could pick up the cable at leisure. We cut out quite a length. It may be said with absolute exactness that we not only succeeded in our undertaking, but had to fight for our success in a ship entirely unsuited to fighting.

The action, which took place at 2500 to 3000 yards, lasted forty-one minutes. There were no injuries to either ship and no casualties among the officers or men.

Lieutenant Carl W. Jungen, in his little vessel, the *Wompatuck*, added a most praiseworthy display of coolness and pluck in battle to his uniformly zealous and intelligent co-operation with me previously.

My thanks are due to Ensign U. S. Payne and to Lieutenant A. W. Catlin for their faithful labors in preparing a set of raw recruits for battle and for coolness and courage under fire.

The officers were not appointed in the navy nor were the men enlisted, yet greater bravery in action or more devotion to their flag than theirs could not have been shown. With shells whistling over their heads, the gang of men who, under Chief Officer Segrave, were employed on the forecastle in the dangerous task of heaving up the telegraph cable, never flinched, but stuck to their posts to the end.

I regret my failure to cut the French cable at Guantanamo on the morning of the 19th. The port was guarded by a Spanish gunboat, carrying heavier guns than the 6-pounders of the *St. Louis*; she was commanded by an officer who did not hesitate to attack us. Doubtless he had been informed from Santiago de Cuba of the light nature of our batteries, and had been warned to be on the lookout for us. In addition, there was a small gun on shore.

I sent the *Wompatuck* into the mouth of the harbor to drag for the wire, while I lay just outside. She caught the cable shortly before the action. It was only after a hot engagement of forty minutes, in which both ships took part, that the necessity of abandoning my enterprise in that locality was forced upon me. To have remained longer might have cost the loss of the ship, for she was very vulnerable.

Again it is my agreeable duty to speak highly of Lieutenant Jungen in battle. He obeyed my signal to withdraw with great reluctance after a very pretty fight. Also Chief Officer T. J. Segrave deserves recognition for faithful work under the enemy's fire.

On the morning of May 20, and outside the marine league off Mole St. Nicholas, I broke the French cable to Cuba; and on the morning of the 22d, at daylight, I commenced grappling for the cable to the westward of Ponce, Puerto Rico. The bottom along the south shore of that island is very irregular and rocky, requiring special apparatus, which I did not possess. After opening out my last two grapnels I abandoned the attempt for the present, in the expectation of obtaining more definite information as to favorable points at which to attack this cable, and of providing myself with

WATER-BATTERY AT ENTRANCE TO HARBOR OF SANTIAGO DE CUBA

COMMODORE SCHLEY'S DIVISION FIRING AT THE DEFENCES OF SANTIAGO, JUNE 6.—Drawn by Carlton T. Chapman

suitable appliances. The evidence of uncharted dangers to navigation were but too manifest, and I felt that it would be unwise to risk the ship in such places.

I hoped that on my return I might be given the *Mangrove*, with her grappling outfit, and a cruiser to drive off the smaller vessels of the enemy, which, armed with better guns than mine, were able to interrupt the work. Cable grappling is a very slow and tedious operation, often necessitating repeated drives over the same ground. The good-fortune which attended our efforts was, I was told, quite exceptional in cable practice, and was due, in my opinion, to the unusual skill of Chief Officer Segrave.

THE SINKING OF THE *MERRIMAC*

Admiral Sampson's Account

I decided to make the harbor entrance secure against the possibility of egress of the Spanish ships by obstructing the narrow part of the entrance by sinking a collier at that point. Upon calling upon Mr. Hobson for his professional opinion as to a sure method of sinking the ship, he manifested a most lively interest in the problem. After several days' consideration he presented a solution which he considered would insure the immediate sinking of the ship when she had reached the desired point in the channel. This plan we prepared before we reached Santiago. The plan included ten electric torpedoes on the outside of the ship, each of 78 pounds of gunpowder, sinking the ship partially before going in, cutting the sea-valves, and opening the cargo ports. The plan contemplated a crew of only seven men and Mr. Hobson, who begged that it might be intrusted to him. The anchor-chains were ranged on deck for both the anchors, forward and aft, the plan including the anchoring of the ship almost automatically.

As soon as I reached Santiago and had the collier to work upon, the details were commenced and diligently prosecuted, hoping to complete them in one day, as the moon and tide served best the first night after our arrival. Notwithstanding every effort, the hour of four o'clock in the morning arrived and the preparations were scarcely completed. After a careful inspection of the final preparations I was forced to relinquish the plan for that morning, as dawn was breaking. Mr. Hobson begged to try it at all hazards.

The morning of June 3 proved more propitious, as a prompt start could be made. Nothing could have been more gallantly executed. We waited impatiently after the firing by the Spaniards had ceased. When they did not reappear from the harbor at six o'clock I feared they had all perished. A steam-launch, which had been sent in charge of Naval Cadet Powell to rescue the men, appeared at this time, coming out under a persistent fire from the batteries, but brought none of the crew. A careful inspection of the harbor from the *New York* showed that the *Merrimac* had been sunk in the channel somewhat farther in than had been intended.

In the afternoon the chief of staff of Admiral Cervera came out under a flag of truce with a letter from the Admiral extolling the bravery of the crew in an unusual manner.

I could not myself too earnestly express my appreciation of the conduct of Mr. Hobson and his gallant crew. I venture to say that a more brave and daring thing has not been done since Cushing blew up the *Albemarle*.

Commander J. M. Miller relinquished his command of the *Merrimac* with the very greatest reluctance, believing he should retain his command under all circumstances. He was, however, finally convinced that the attempt of another person to carry out the multitude of details which had been in preparation by Mr. Hobson might endanger its proper execution. I therefore took the liberty to relieve him for this reason only. There were hundreds of volunteers in the squadron who were anxious to participate. There were 150 from the *Iowa*, nearly as many from the *New York*, and large numbers from all the other ships, officers and men alike.

As Told by Senator Lodge

(In Harper's Magazine)

The first movement of Admiral Sampson was to obstruct the narrow channel. He did not hope to block it permanently, for he knew that any obstruction could sooner or later be removed by dynamite. But he believed, and with reason, that he could obstruct it temporarily, and his object was to gain time for the arrival of the troops, whose coming was already announced, and whose presence would be absolutely necessary to enable him to get at the Spaniards, either by forcing Cervera to leave the harbor or by obtaining control of and clearing the mine-fields so that he could himself enter and attack. To attain this object he decided to sink a collier in the channel, and gave orders to that effect to Captain Folger when he sent him off on May 27 to Santiago. On the 29th he opened the subject to Lieutenant Richmond Pearson Hobson, a young naval constructor of marked ability and energy, and by the time the fleet reached Santiago, on June 1, Hobson had prepared his plans, which were so thorough and excellent that the Admiral decided to place the perilous and important work wholly in the hands of the young officer. Thus far nothing had been done towards closely locking Cervera up in his retreat, but as soon as Admiral Sampson arrived the *Merrimac* was selected to be sunk in the channel, and the work of stripping her and making ready the anchors which were to hold her, and the torpedoes which were to shatter her bottom, went forward with hot haste under the direction of Lieutenant Hobson. The call for volunteers was made by signal, and hundreds of the sailors came forward. Men begged to be taken, implored Hobson to choose them, and turned away utterly miserable because they could not go on a desperate undertaking, which every one believed meant certain death. Here was a very fine and noble spirit, telling what the American navy was, and why it was soon to be victorious—something here quite worthy of the consideration of Spain, which had so insisted upon senseless war.

Hobson finally selected from the crowd of applicants, Phillips, Kelly, Mullen, and Deignan, of the *Merrimac*, because they were familiar with the ship; then he took Charette, a gunner's mate, and Montague, chief master-at-arms, from the *New York*, and thus completed his little crew. Commander Miller, of the *Merrimac*, was bitterly disappointed when the Admiral told him he could not go, but that did not prevent him from giving every advice and help to the men who were going on his ship. The preparations, although pushed with such intense energy, were so many, that it was difficult to get them finished, and the night was far gone when all was done. At last the ship started, and then there was more delay in trying to tow the launch, which was to run in as near as possible, and wait to rescue any survivors after the ship had sunk. When they finally set forth there was already a streak of light in the east, and as the *Merrimac* was steaming to the harbor entrance, the torpedo-boat *Fremont* dashed up with an order of recall from the Admiral. Back went the *Merrimac*, and a day of waiting and suspense followed, not easy to bear when men's nerves are strung to such work as lay before Hobson and his crew. Mullen, utterly exhausted by his labors in preparing the ship, gave out, and his place was taken by Murphy, a cockswain on the *Iowa*. Robert Crank, the assistant engineer of the ship, with bitter disappointment, was ordered away at the last moment and not allowed to go. Finally the long day passed, night came, and at half past three in the morning the *Merrimac* started again, this time with an additional man, Clausen, who was cockswain of the barge, and had come on board with Ensign Powell. He asked permission to go, and was accepted by Hobson, thus getting his chance at the great prize of death in battle. This time there was no recall; on she went, every man at his post, the young lieutenant standing upright and alone on the bridge, Deignan at the wheel, steering coolly and taking every order with absolute correctness, and not a sailor moving except at the word of command. Nearer and nearer the doomed ship went, with gradually slackening speed. Then the Spaniards saw her, and there came a storm of shot and shell, fierce, resistless, like a torrent. Still on the ship steered, still slackening in speed—goes too far, as the event proved, her steering-gear having been shot away, and the lashings of Montague's anchor, which dropped too soon—and then, torn by her own torpedoes and by those of the enemy, sinks far up in the channel. The parting of the anchors, the loss of the steering-gear, and consequent running in too far, the sweep of the current, combine, and she goes to the bottom, lying lengthwise, and not across. The crew, every task performed, lie at the appointed place upon the deck in the

ADMIRAL SAMPSON'S EASTERN DIVISION FIRING AT THE DEFENCES OF SANTIAGO, JUNE 6.—Drawn by Carlton T. Chapman

ASSISTANT NAVAL-CONSTRUCTOR RICHMOND PEARSON HOBSON

storm of projectiles, the torpedoes exploding beneath, and go down with the reeling ship into the whirl of dark waters. They have done their duty. The *Merrimac*, as she lies now, makes the entrance perhaps a little more difficult, but does not block it. So far the attempt fails, but the brave deed does not fail, for such gallantry is never a failure. It rouses and uplifts the American people, for these men are theirs; it appeals to the lovers of daring the world over; it is a shining and splendid feat of arms; it tells to all what the American navy is; it ranks Hobson with Cushing when he pushed his torpedo against the *Albemarle*, with Decatur when he fired the *Philadelphia*. And the men who did the deed cling, chilled and spent in the water, to the raft which is fast to the sunken ship, and in the darkness are not hit or found, but in the morning are taken off by Admiral Cervera, who greets them as "valiente." On the American side, brave young Powell, creeping about with his launch, in the midst of a heavy fire from the batteries, on the chance of rescuing Hobson and his men, comes out at last, much fired at, but with no one of the *Merrimac* crew on board; and when he closes his report, saying simply, "and no one came back, sir," the fleet fear the worst, and believe that the gallant deed has been paid for with eight lives. But later in the day comes out a Spanish boat, with a flag from Admiral Cervera, to announce that Hobson and his sailors are prisoners, alive and well, and little hurt. It is sad that for the sake of Spain they could not have remained with Admiral Cervera—a brave man facing inevitable ruin with courage—but they were turned over to the military authorities on land, who placed them and kept them for some days in the Morro Castle, in range of the American bombardment.

Lieutenant Hobson's Story

I swam away from the ship as soon as I struck the water, but I could feel the eddies drawing me backward in spite of all I could do. That did not last very long, however, and, as soon as I felt the tugging cease, I turned and struck out for the float, which I could see dimly, bobbing up and down over the sunken hull.

The *Merrimac's* masts were plainly visible, and I could see the heads of my seven men as they followed my example and made for the float also. We had expected, of course, that the Spaniards would investigate the wreck, but we had no idea that they would be at it as quickly as they were. Before we could get to the float, several row-boats and launches came around the bluff from inside the harbor. They had officers on board and armed marines as well, and they searched that passage, rowing backward and forward, until the next morning. It was only by good-luck that we got to the float at all, for they were upon us so quickly that we had barely concealed ourselves when a boat with quite a large party on board was right beside us.

Unfortunately, we thought then, but it turned out afterwards that nothing more fortunate than that could have happened to us, the rope with which we had secured the float to the ship was too short to allow it to swing free, and when we reached it we found that one of the pontoons was entirely out of the water and the other one was submerged. Had the raft lain flat on the water we could not have got under it, and would have

CADET JOSEPH WRIGHT POWELL

had to climb up on it, to be an excellent target for the first party of marines that arrived. As it was, we could get under the raft, and, by putting our hands through the crevices between the slats which formed its deck, we could hold our heads out of water and still be unseen. That is what we did, and all night long we stayed there with our noses and mouths barely out of the water.

None of us expected to get out of the affair alive, but luckily the Spaniards did not think of the apparently damaged, half-sunken raft floating about beside the wreck. They came to within a cable's length of us at intervals of only a few minutes all night. We could hear their words distinctly, and even in the darkness could distinguish an occasional glint of light on the rifle-barrels of the marines and on the lace of the officers' uniforms. We were afraid to speak above a whisper, and for a good while, in fact whenever they were near us, we breathed as easily as we could. I ordered my men not to speak unless to address me, and with one exception they obeyed.

After we had been there an hour or two the water, which we found rather warm at first, began to get cold, and my fingers ached where the wood was pressing into them. The clouds, which were running before a pretty stiff breeze when we went in, blew over, and then by the starlight we could see the boats when they came out of the shadows of the cliffs on either side, and even when we could not see them we knew that they were still near, because we could hear very plainly the splash of the oars and the grinding of the oarlocks.

Our teeth began to chatter before very long, and I was in constant fear that the Spaniards would hear us when they came close. It was so still that the chattering sound seemed to us as loud as a hammer, but the Spaniards' ears were not sharp enough to hear it. We could hear sounds from the shore almost as distinctly as if we had been there, we were so close to the surface of the water, which is an excellent conductor, and the voices of the men in the boats sounded as clear as a bell. My men tried to keep their teeth still, but it was hard work, and not attended with any great success at the best.

We all knew that we would be shot if discovered by an ordinary seaman or a marine, and I ordered my men not to stir, as the boats having officers on board kept well in the distance. One of my men disobeyed orders and started to swim ashore, and I had to call him back. He obeyed at once, but my voice seemed to create some commotion among the boats, and several of them appeared close beside us before the disturbance in the water made by the man swimming had disappeared. We thought it was all up with us then, but the boats went away into the shadows again.

There was much speculation among the Spaniards as to what the ship was and what we intended to do next. I could understand many of the words, and gathered from what I heard that the officers had taken in the situation at once, but were astounded at the audacity of the thing. The boats, I also learned, were from the fleet, and I felt better, because I had more faith in a Spanish sailor than I had in a Spanish soldier.

When daylight came a steam-launch full of officers and marines came out from behind the cliff that hid the fleet and harbor and advanced towards us. All the men on board were looking curiously in our direction. They did not see us. Knowing that some one of rank must be on board, I waited until the launch was quite close and hailed her.

My voice produced the utmost consternation on board. Every one sprang up, the marines crowded to the bow, and the launch's

LIEUTENANT VICTOR BLUE

engines were reversed. She not only stopped, but she backed off until nearly a quarter of a mile away, where she stayed. The marines stood ready to fire at the word of command when we clambered out from under the float. There were ten of the marines, and they would have fired in a minute had they not been restrained.

I swam towards the launch and then she started towards me. I called out in Spanish: "Is there an officer on board?" An officer answered in the affirmative, and then I shouted in Spanish again: "I have seven men to surrender." I continued swimming, and was seized and pulled out of the water.

As I looked up when they were dragging me into the launch, I saw that it was Admiral Cervera himself who had hold of me. He looked at me rather dubiously at first, because I had been down in the engine-room of the *Merrimac*, where I got covered with oil, and that, with the soot and coal-dust, made my appearance most disreputable. I had put on my officer's belt before sinking the *Merrimac*, as a means of identification, no matter what happened to me, and when I pointed to it in the launch the Admiral understood and seemed satisfied. The first words he said to me when he learned who I was were, "Bienvenido se usted," which means "You are welcome." My treatment by the naval officers and that of my men also, was courteous all the time that I was a prisoner.

A Spanish Account

At 3.30 on the morning of June 3 gunshots were heard towards the mouth of the harbor, and the firing became very lively. At 4 o'clock it was learned at the Comandancia de Marina that a merchant vessel had come very close to the mouth of the channel, that the batteries had fired at her and she had not answered, and at that moment she was inside; shortly after, she passed by the bow of the *Reina Mercedes*, which was moored between the Zocapa and Cay Smith, with her bow towards the channel which she was defending with her two 16-cm. Hontoria guns and Whitehead torpedoes. By 4.20 the firing, which had been very violent, ceased. At 4.30 it was learned that the hostile ship had gone down in the mouth of the channel, close to Punta Soldado, but without obstructing it. At 5.30, it now being daylight, very slow firing was again heard, which ceased at 6. At 5.30 the Commandant of Marine went to the mouth of the harbor in the steam-launch. When he returned, we learned that one of the merchant vessels forming part of the American fleet, called the *Merrimac*, with two masts and one smoke-stack, larger than the *Mejico*, had forced the entrance at 3.30; that she had been sunk in the channel close to Punta Soldado by the guns of the *Mercedes* and the rapid-fire guns of the battery below the Zocapa, and was lying in the direction of the Socapa, without obstructing the entrance or preventing our ships from going out, and that one lieutenant and seven sailors, forming her crew, had been captured and were on board the *Mercedes*. During the day the officer and seven men of the *Merrimac* were transferred to the Morro.

MAP OF SANTIAGO HARBOR

Showing the Location of the sunken Collier *Merrimac*, and of the Vessels of Admiral Cervera's Squadron: revised by Lieutenant R. P. Hobson

On the 4th of June, at 10.30 A.M., the present writer, Lieutenant José Müller y Tejeiro, second in command of the naval forces of the province of Santiago de Cuba, as judge, accompanied by the aid of the Captain of the Port, Señor Leguina, as secretary, and the government interpreter, Señor Isidoro Agostini, went to the Morro in the steam-launch of the Captain of the Port, for the purpose of taking the depositions of the lieutenant and seven men who had been taken prisoners.

The former, Mr. Hobson, twenty-seven years old, born in the State of Alabama, was a lieutenant in the corps of naval constructors, who, in the United States, study in the naval college, and those first promoted are assigned to that corps. I state this so that it may not seem strange that he commanded the *Merrimac*; for, as they were officers of the navy, they could build and command ships.

Upon learning the object of the visit, the prisoner, from whose room a great extent of the sea and part of the blockading fleet could be seen, asked why the British Consul, who was in charge of the United States Consulate, was not present when his deposition was to be taken; and he wanted to know whether I belonged to the army or the navy, what might be the consequences of his statements, and by whose authority he was being examined; and he stated that, since he had been taken prisoner by Admiral Cervera himself in his own boat (as was true), it was his understanding that he could and should answer only Admiral Cervera, or some one delegated by him. And although all this was said in the very best form and with a thousand protestations of his respect and deference for me, it did not prevent our positions from being reversed, and, far from my asking the prisoner any questions, it was he, on the contrary, who asked them of me. I told him so, asking him through the interpreter to state categorically whether he was disposed to answer. He replied he was ready to answer the questions which he thought he ought to answer, but not those which he deemed untimely. Therefore, and in order not to lose time, I at once asked him one question which I knew beforehand he would refuse to answer—namely, by whose order and for what purpose he entered the harbor. He replied: "By order of Admiral Sampson; the second part I cannot answer." I then deemed my mission at an end and had the fact set down.

A few days later this officer was transferred to quarters on the *Reina Mercedes* that had been prepared for him, and the seven men to other quarters on the vessel, where they remained until they were released.

LOCATING CERVERA'S VESSELS

Lieutenant Blue's Experience

On the 11th of June I left the *Suwanee* off Aserraderos Point and proceeded to the camp of the insurgent forces, about one mile inland, finding General Rabí in command. On explaining to him that I was under orders from Lieutenant-Commander Delehanty to proceed to a good point of observation near the Bay of Santiago de Cuba for the purpose of observing unmistakably the enemy's fleet, he gladly furnished me with a trustworthy guide and a good mule. In company with the guide, Major Francisco H. Masaba y Reyes, I left the camp about 10.30 A.M. of the 11th, and, taking generally a northerly course, arrived late in the afternoon at a Cuban outpost, about fifteen or twenty miles to the northward and westward of Santiago. The commander of this outpost furnished me with three additional guides to take me through the Spanish lines. After going through the Spanish lines and travelling an hour after nightfall, the guides concluded that it was dangerous to proceed any farther until next morning, whereupon we camped at the house of a Cuban sympathizer. The next morning we proceeded about twelve miles farther to a point on a hill-top a little to the westward of the north end of the bay and about three miles distant from it. From this point I had an almost unobstructed view of the entire bay except the part south of Smith Cay. In the bay I counted five large vessels that were unmistakably men-of-war. Three of these answered the descriptions of vessels of Admiral Cervera's squadron. One could not be seen sufficiently well to describe definitely anything more about her than that she was a large vessel and had one smoke-pipe. The fifth was a large white vessel anchored near the city, and was said by the Cubans to be old and useless. Another large vessel was anchored near the city, but whether a man-of-war or merchant vessel I was unable to make out on account of the poor background.

LIEUT.-COL. ROBERT W. HUNTINGTON
Commanding First Battalion of Marines

Anchored near the city were also three smaller men-of-war, one of about 1500 tons displacement, one of about 800, and the last was what I made out to be a small gunboat.

Near the entrance to the bay was a vessel under way, which, judging from her relative dimensions, I took to be a destroyer. Two other vessels resembled torpedo-boats, but I was unable to state positively their character.

Two launches and a larger vessel were in the channel near the position of the *Merrimac*.

I remained at the place of observation about an hour and a half, and then started back on the return trip. I was fully satisfied from my own knowledge that the vessels I saw were those of Cervera's squadron.

The point of observation was in plain view of a Spanish garrison about 1000 to 1200 yards away. On our return, Cuban sympathizers informed us that the road we passed over the day before was occupied by the Spanish troops. This necessitated our taking another route. Different people along the road would inform us how to proceed to keep clear of the Spaniards.

On the 11th considerable firing could be heard at various places along the route, and the smoke at Spanish camps could occasionally be seen a mile or two away.

I arrived at the headquarters of General Rabí on the night of the 12th, and joined the ship off Aserraderos Point the next morning.

SHELLING THE SPANIARDS OUT OF CAIMANERA.—Drawn by Carlton T. Chapman

LANDING A FUNERAL PARTY AT CAMP McCALLA.—DRAWN BY CARLTON T. CHAPMAN

SECOND TOUR OF LIEUTENANT BLUE

IN obedience to orders to proceed inland to a good point of observation for the purpose of locating the positions of the enemy's ships in the harbor of Santiago de Cuba, I landed on shore about 6 P.M. of the 25th of June. I happened to meet General Garcia's chief of staff, who was about to embark on one of the transports that were taking troops to Altares. On explaining to him my mission, he gave orders to have me taken to the Cuban front, where I would be furnished with a necessary guard for going through the Spanish lines. I reached Colonel Cebreco's camp at midnight, and learned that his troops had been engaged in fighting the Spaniards all that day. This camp was about one mile inland from Point Cocal and about twenty-four miles from Aserraderos Point, where I landed.

After reading the letter sent by Garcia's chief of staff, for him to furnish me with a suitable guard, the colonel appeared very much displeased, as he was reluctant to send his men through the lines. However, he gave the necessary orders, and early the next morning I set out from his camp with six soldiers. Going to the northward and eastward for several miles, I reached the outer picket-line of the Cuban forces. This line was posted on a hill and fronting a Spanish intrenchment 600 to 700 yards away. At this place it was necessary to leave the mules and to proceed the rest of the way on foot. In order to reach a good point for observation of the harbor, it was necessary to go on the eastern end of the same hill on which the enemy was intrenched, and in so doing pass near another intrenchment to the northward. In order to avoid the enemy's pickets we had to proceed very cautiously, at one time creeping through long grass and at another climbing the steep side of a mountain. In going up this mountain it was necessary to cross the main road from the Spanish camps to the city several times. In doing so, scouts and flankers were thrown out to watch the turns in the road and signal the rest of the party if the way was clear. By proceeding step by step in this manner we managed to reach the point of observation, two miles inside the lines, after four hours' time. After passing through a field where sugar-cane and sweet-potatoes were growing in abundance, I came to the conclusion that the Spanish soldiers in that section could not be in want of food. In fact, we subsisted that day on sugar-cane and mangoes, which I thought were very palatable indeed.

ASSISTANT-SURGEON JOHN BLAIR GIBBS
Killed in the Spanish attack on Camp McCalla, Guantanamo Bay

Although at times it was necessary to pass through open places, yet for the greater part of the time we were screened by the thick foliage of the undergrowth on the mountain.

From the trunk of a tree that projected beyond the dense growth on the mountain-side I obtained an almost perfect view of the entire harbor. The channels on the east and west of Smith Cay were the only parts shut out from view.

Eight men-of-war were observed, four of them being the armored cruisers of Cervera's squadron. None of these vessels, as far as I could discover, had steam up. Two small vessels were also seen south of Smith Cay: one, which I thought to be a destroyer, steamed to the south side of Smith Cay; the other, which I could not clearly make out, was lying close to the land east of the channel.

After staying about an hour at the place of observation I set out on the return trip, and reached the Cuban picket-line shortly after dark without incident during the day.

As far as I could learn from the Cubans, several thousand Spanish troops had been concentrated in that section to repel the advance of any Americans that might be landed west of Santiago. They were intrenched on hills in strong positions that commanded the roads leading to Santiago. There were at least four of these intrenchments.

OPERATIONS AT GUANTANAMO

By Carlton T. Chapman

The coast of Cuba along the south side of the province of Santiago is one succession of desolate hills, rising smoothly from the sea in most places, but dropping off now and then in steep cliffs of limestone or granite rock. In the face of these sea-walls are many caves, hollowed out by the action of the waves, and around them and into them the waters boil and fret, set on by the ground-swell and urged by the almost constant wind. Beyond this first range of rocky hills, covered with low and scraggly gray-green vegetation, is a series of steep and forbidding ranges, backed by mountains that loom blue and distant or hang near by over the lower hills. Precipitous and gashed with deep ravines, they offer no sign of human life or comfort, and on many of their ridged sides the foot of man rarely if ever treads. This is the kind of coast that extends westward from Cape Maisi two hundred miles, and, with the exception of tiny coves where small boats may land, there are no harbors that offer protection to vessels of any size, save two only—one where the hills sweep northward around the plateau in which is set the snug, landlocked harbor of Santiago de Cuba, and the other the beautiful Bahia de Guantanamo, thirty-nine miles to the eastward. Eight miles east of Santiago there are a small town and cove in which an American company has built a large iron pier to which vessels come to load with iron ore, and where it was purposed to land troops to march on Santiago. A refuge for the fleet and a coaling-station being necessary on this coast, Guantanamo was selected as an available spot, and accordingly, on Tuesday, June 7, the *Marblehead*, accompanied by the *St. Louis* and *Yankee*, steamed up there from the fleet, the *Marblehead* and *Yankee* going in and throwing a few shots into the block-house on the hill and the houses along the beach on the inside of Windward Point, and looking about to note the possibilities of the place.

A cable line ran from Santiago to Kingston, another to Guantanamo, and from there to Mole St. Nicholas, Haiti. There was a perfect net-work of wires running out of Santiago, and on Monday, the 6th, after the bombardment in the morning, the *St. Louis* and cable steamer *Adria* got to work and cut the last one, as they supposed. Off Guantanamo the *St. Louis* immediately began grappling for the cable to Mole St. Nicholas, and found and cut it in short order, the *Marblehead* and *Yankee* remaining inside in plain sight of the fort at Caimanera; at dusk the fort fired some shots, and a Spanish gunboat mounting seven 4.7-inch guns came out and gave them battle for a few minutes, and then hastily retired. There were mines in the channel farther on, which alone prevented the two ships from going up and settling matters at once. A collier was sent up from the fleet on Wednesday, with the *Dolphin* and *Vixen*, and when we steamed into the beautiful bay on Thursday we found the *Marblehead* on guard, and the little cruiser *Vixen* coaling from the *Sterling*. Over the point of land the Spanish flag waved above the fort, but the stars and stripes flew in the harbor and had come to stay. The calm water and white beach, shining in the sun, with the rich foliage along the wooded shores and high, blue hills beyond, made the place extremely peaceful and attractive after the rugged hills and tumbling water that we had known outside. The bay was once called Cumberland Harbor, and now, I thought, would be a good time to rename it.

On board the *Marblehead* the lookouts never ceased to watch the fort and the gunboat, whose mast and funnel we could see over the low point which hid the deeper bay beyond. The loaded guns gave out on all sides their warning, and, though a thousand eyes watched the scene from the thicket-hidden shores, no sound of gun disturbed the peace of the day.

Friday morning the transport *Panther*, in company with the *Yosemite*, arrived with the United States marine battalion, six hundred and fifty men, under command of Lieutenant-Colonel Huntington. They anchored close in off the beach, and, after shelling the place and setting fire to the shanties and remains of the block-house on the low hill, the marines went ashore. The cable station, a one-story corrugated-iron affair, was shot full of holes, but left standing. The fishermen's houses were burned down, for fear of contagion. Taking possession of the hill-top, they immediately began clearing away the wreckage, throwing up intrenchments, and setting up tents and camp equipage at the foot of the hill, among the palms and bushes. On the highest point a tall staff was raised, and for the first time the American flag floated in possession of the soil of Cuba.

Sad, dirty soil it was to the tired men who toiled all day in the heat and lay on their arms at night, eaten by mosquitoes, and in expectation of attack at any moment. From the very first the marine battalion had behaved splendidly. The transport *Panther* had been fitted out with remarkable expedition—her stores "broken out," as sailors say, from the navy storehouse at the New York Navy-yard and put aboard in twenty-four hours. Jammed into narrow quarters on the *Panther*, the men

THE AUXILIARY CRUISER *YANKEE*

had to suffer great inconvenience, and when finally landed and camped on the sand-spit called Camp Sampson at Key West they were not much better off, and suffered from heat, flies, and mosquitoes as much as they would have suffered in Cuba; but their fine appearance and the good behavior of the men, as well as their quick and efficient readiness for instant work, spoke volumes for the officers and men of the marine corps.

Friday night and Saturday passed in constant work, getting camp and intrenchments ready, and the men were worn out with loss of sleep and severe labor when darkness came down on Saturday.

Late in the afternoon two pickets, who were posted some two miles away from the camp, were eating a bite of supper and taking a rest under some trees, lulled into carelessness by the quiet that had so far reigned. These two men, privates Dunphy and McColgan, were shot and instantly killed by a Spanish lieutenant and his men, who had crept unobserved through the woods and fired at close range.

At 7 o'clock the Spaniards began firing from all sides and at close quarters. From the hills and black shadow of the trees came the sharp crack of the rifles, the bullets thudding on the ground, whirring through the air, chipping off branches and leaves of trees, and falling in a hail in the water. There were several boats near the shore, and three war-ships lying quietly at anchor in the still bay. The *Marblehead* fired several shots, but, as its fire would have been as dangerous to friend as to foe, it could do little.

The marines had quickly formed, and from their position on the low hill came a steady return fire, checking the attack, and driving it back after a time. All night the shots were popping, now rising in furious volleys and again sinking away to scattered reports. One of the first to fall was Assistant-Surgeon Gibbs, who was shot in his tent door, having just remarked, when the firing began, that he did "not want to be killed in such a place."

On Sunday morning the *Texas* came in, and sent ashore two Colt automatic guns, which were dragged up and set in position at the top of the hill.

In the Saturday-night attack Sergeant Smith was killed, and early in the morning Lieutenant Neville with a platoon of men went out to find his body and bring it in. They were attacked by a strong force, and had to fall back. The bodies of McColgan and Dunphy were recovered, and, with that of Dr. Gibbs, were buried at ten o'clock on the southern slope of the hill, the enemy firing so heavily that the funeral-party had to take to their guns, and the salutes that were fired over the graves were solid shot that whistled in among the Spaniards.

Sunday night the firing began again in heavy volleys, and the war-ships took a hand, word being passed by megaphone where to fire, when the *Marblehead* sent shell after shell among the enemy; one, by request, as close as one hundred feet east of the little hill which the marines were holding. The Spaniards were very much afraid of the ships, as they had learned by experience how much execution they could do.

Monday remained fairly quiet, occasional shots being exchanged, and the men lying by their guns in readiness for an alarm. Sergeant Smith was buried to-day, with Sergeant-Major Good, a splendid soldier, who had spent many years in the service, and who was devoted to his duty.

Tuesday morning, about seven o'clock, while half the marines were at breakfast in the camp at the foot of the hill, the Spanish began firing from the woods to the eastward. The men at breakfast, having stacked their guns at the top of the hill, broke out fresh boxes and rallied, driving back the attacking party. The *Marblehead's* launch, coming in-shore at this time, opened fire on the Spaniards, chasing them along the beach with her rapid-fire 1-pounder.

It was then determined to clean the enemy out of the woods, and an attacking force under Captain Elliott was sent out. Spicer's and Elliott's companies, C and D, with Company A, divided into platoons under Lieutenants Ingate and Magill. Divided among the commands were about forty Cubans.

COMMANDER WILLARD H. BROWNSON
Of the *Yankee*

Ingate's column was misled by his guide, who was then disarmed and brought back under arrest. The platoon of Company A, under Lieutenant Magill, went around to the eastward and drove the enemy back towards their camp and block-house near the shore on the south side of the point, where were Elliott's and Spicer's commands, having followed the shore to westward, driving the Spaniards before them; and between the two fires they were completely whipped and driven off, their block-house and water-supply destroyed, and heliograph-signal outfit captured. The enemy's loss in killed and wounded exceeded the entire number of the attacking party. Several of the Cubans were killed or wounded, and many of the marines were so utterly exhausted that but for the timely aid of the *Dolphin*, which had steamed around the coast and sent in her boats to bring off the wounded, many would have dropped from sheer exhaustion.

The still water and air of quiet that prevailed on Wednesday, the 15th, were in great contrast with the turmoil and battle of Tuesday—the voices of men, the whir of a steam-launch, or plash of oars came in subdued notes across the broad surface of the beautiful bay.

The *Abarenda*, big and black, loaded with coal, and armed with 6-pounder guns, lay near us, and had on board the seventeen prisoners captured on Tuesday. They were much averse to climbing up the slim rope ladder that reached to her deck, but at least have had enough to eat by this time. They all looked half-starved, and reported scarcity of food, though every one and all the men found dead in the woods were loaded down with ammunition. The captured lieutenant was taken on board the *Marblehead*, and I saw him sitting at the hospitable wardroom table and making himself quite at home. Over towards the western shore the *Panther*, *Yosemite*, and *Sterling* were lying in a bunch together. The *Porter* lay alongside the *Abarenda*—small, spirited, and tireless. The *Dolphin* and *Marblehead* swung clear of the other ships, with their guns ready for instant service. On shore the flag floated over the hill, the white tents, and swarming marines, who looked like big brown ants moving about on the fresh red earth of their intrenchments. Tents were going up on the hill, and at the foot, near the mess-tents and hospital, the Cuban forces were setting up shacks built of palms, cleverly put together with the Indian-like wood-lore of these people.

The sun blazed hot on the hill, and the flag drooped in the faint breeze; the green rounded slopes beyond simmered in the glaring light and were still, with big black birds hovering over and dipping in among the trees.

The roughly built landing was surrounded with boats. Distilled water from the *Panther* came in, in large barrels loaded into a cutter, and a sergeant superintended dealing it out to the men, who filled their canteens and supplied their mess-kettles—good, pure water, if it was rather warm. Earlier in the day every man who could was splashing about in the cooling sea, having a good swim and getting the kinks out of his tired limbs. All day, in fact, except at high noon, men were in the water, washing the red dirt of Cuba out of their systems and scrubbing their clothes, after five days of incessant toil and fighting. The clean deep sea-water, clear as crystal, and washing the sands within ten feet of their mess-tents, was a great blessing to the men, and they enjoyed it, even if sharks were lurking farther out. The Cubans alone seemed to despise such trifles, and, once they swung their hammocks under the palm tents, they stuck to them until they were turned out for duty.

About 10.30 o'clock a procession of boats left the *Marblehead* and moved in to the landing—a cutter first, with officers and armed men, and then a steam-launch towing a boat with men in bow and stern, and midship a silent figure covered with a flag—a Cuban who had been wounded the day before and had died on the ship. The boats landed at the little pier. A bugler sounds a few notes of the Dead March, and the column moves slowly up the brown hill. Flags are half-masted, and the soldier who had died bravely for "Cuba libre" is laid to rest beside the others who had given their lives for his cause as well as for their own starry flag; a silence for a time, and then a volley which marked the end, and the bugles blow a quicker step.

On board the *Dolphin*, in the great cool wardroom, now shorn of its luxurious fittings, lay three other poor Cubans, one very badly wounded, but being cared for by the good doctor. A fine-looking black fellow, done up in bandages and lying patiently on the long divan, opened his eyes as I gazed sympathetically at him for a minute, and then smiled in a proud way, as a soldier should who knew he had done his duty.

About one o'clock the *Texas* came steaming rapidly into the bay, and, signalling the *Marblehead* to follow, swung around the low point of land which marks the entrance to the upper bay, at the head of which are the town and fort of Caimanera. The channel was known to be full of mines, and for several nights the *Marblehead's* launch had tried in vain to locate them or drag up the wires; but the *Texas* had orders to destroy the fort and drive out the thousand or more soldiers stationed there. So on she went, regardless, and the *Marblehead* quickly followed, and took position some distance beyond the *Texas* and to the left. It was a very pretty sight, and the *Texas* seemed to be calling by special invitation on the Dons. She swung up as close to the forts as she could go, dropped her anchor, and immediately opened fire from her port 12-inch and 6-inch guns. The *Marblehead* was close behind, and her 5-inch guns flashed and roared amid the deeper thunder of the battle-ship's big turret-guns. The *Suwanee* had come from the fleet to take a hand in the proceedings, and she now took position to the right, and as near the shore as she could get, firing with her 4-inch and 6-pounder guns. The *St. Paul* had come in during the morning, and lay farther out in the bay. Men crowded her rigging and swarmed at the mast-head and from every lofty perch on the *Dolphin* and all the vessels in the harbor. It was like a grand-stand view. Over the low shore they could see it all—the ships, the red-tiled roofs of town and fort, and where the shells struck and sent up the dust in thick clouds. The marines on their hill-top had even a better view, and lined up, watching it all with the greatest interest. The high hills in the background had been veiled in rain half the time during the past week, though not a drop had fallen down our way, and now the dark-blue thunder-cloud lowering in the background made a fine setting for the ships and the wreathing smoke that floated across the bay and melted into the distance.

We of the despatch-boat had followed up after the ships, and lay as near as we could get to the *Suwanee*. The *Marblehead's* launch with a boat in tow was out looking for mines. They suspended their work temporarily and drew out of the way.

The *Texas* opened fire at forty-five minutes past one, and her shots followed one after the other with great deliberation and accuracy. Cheers burst frequently from the men watching as a shell from the 12-inch gun struck the fort, sending up a great cloud of yellow dust, followed by the tremendous roar of the big gun. The flash of the discharge and the effect of the exploding shell seemed to be instantaneous; the eye could not note the difference; then came the smoke rolling and swelling out in a vast cloud, and the shock of explosion reverberating and ringing in our ears.

Awe-inspiring as a thunder-storm is, the rapid firing of these big guns was even more so, and as one watched the dirt and dust spreading out in a thick cloud the force seemed greater than it really was.

As only half the men on the *Texas* were engaged at the guns, her decks aft were crowded with men; officers on the bridge watched with glasses the effect of the shots, and Jackies, no less interested, climbed up anywhere to get a better view. The hose was kept playing to cool the ship, and a stream of water was running off the deck the entire time. We had the ship silhouetted by her own smoke most of the time, standing out in bold relief against the smoke and flame one instant, and the next enveloped in a thick haze.

Except for a few shots from the fort in the early part of the action, there was no reply to all this; its fire was badly aimed, as usual, and as ours became hotter, no doubt the garrison

CAPTAIN CASPAR F. GOODRICH
Of the *St. Louis*

skedaddled. The *Marblehead* fired a number of shots into the barracks in the town, and after an hour and a quarter the firing ceased and the *Texas* withdrew. Having been in close enough to stick her nose into the mud, she left a trail of roiled water behind her. The *Marblehead*, in getting into position in the midst of the work, fouled a mine with her propeller blades; the ship was stopped, the wire hauled on board, and Lieutenant John Nickels, executive officer, calmly sawed off the connection. They afterwards pulled the thing on board, and we saw it on the poop-deck when the ship got back to her anchorage—a small can-buoy it looked, painted red, and with a lot of small barnacles sticking to it; it was dated 1896. Lieutenant Noel took off the war-head and dissected it. Inside was an iron can containing one hundred pounds of gun-cotton, and, had the contact been struck, it is probable that the *Marblehead* would have been destroyed. The launch tarried behind after the ships went back to their station, and continued dragging for mines. They found one after a while, and were getting it up when a lot of Spanish troops on shore opened fire on them. The bullets struck the launch and fell in the water all about the two boats. The 1-pounder rapid-fire gun was quickly turned on, and the men grabbed their rifles and returned the fire vigorously. The 1-pounder was banging away at a great rate, when the mounting got loose, and the gun jumped clear overboard.

Hearing the firing, the *Suwanee* hurried back and began shelling the bushes with her 6-pounders, and, turning two Colt automatics loose on the hidden enemy, soon drove them off. The quick ping! ping! ping! of the little automatic's "lead squirts," as the sailors called them, had a mighty comfortable sound when you were behind them. The launch got the mine and towed it alongside the ship, from where it was taken ashore.

Wednesday night and Thursday passed uneventfully, the war-ships turning their search-lights on the shore at night and keeping a close watch for trouble. On Friday morning the *Oregon* came in for coal, and soon had two big colliers on either side of her. As the bushes and trees on the north shore of the bay were still full of Spaniards, who only waited for an opportunity to pick off a man or two, the *Marblehead, Dolphin, Suwanee*, and *St. Paul* began shelling them out about ten o'clock, and fired for half an hour. The *St. Paul*, astern and slightly outside of us, made music with her shells that whistled through the air at a great rate. In the afternoon the *Oregon*, after coaling, fired a few shots at the railroad station and telegraph offices in Caimanera; a train was standing on the track, and at the first shot stood not on the order of its going, but went shrieking up the line.

On the morning of Saturday, the 18th, about six o'clock, we saw a white flag waving on the shore where Friday's firing took place. The *Porter* went in and sent a boat to bring off a man who claimed to be a Cuban; he was taken on board the *Marblehead* and given a suit of clothes and a square meal, and sent ashore to the Cubans armed with a Lee rifle and cartridge-belt with U.S.N. on it; later in the day it was reported that he had decamped, proving to be a spy. Notices had been posted up in the woods to the effect that men who wanted to surrender would be well treated; the Spanish officers had told their men that they would be killed if captured. One man came in with three Mauser rifles and a knapsack full of cartridges; he said that he had been in Cuba eleven months, had fine things promised him, but had never received any pay, and had had nothing to eat for three days; under the circumstances, he had decided to become an American if they would let him. A party of Cubans on this Saturday afternoon explored the strip of woods shelled on Friday, and found over fifty dead Spaniards as a result of the firing.

About noon the *Marblehead's* launch, with Lieutenant Anderson in command, went up to Caimanera with a flag of truce to arrange an exchange of prisoners, with a view to getting Hobson and his men out of Morro. Nothing was accomplished, but the launch people reported that the fort, though badly damaged, was being repaired and new guns set up, and that the gunboat looked spick and span and ready for business still. All were well ashore except some of the Cubans, who were suffering from overeating and tight shoes, having never, many of them, worn shoes before in their lives. They had a bright new Cuban flag over their camp, and for them the prospects were brightening considerably. There was no doubt of their loyalty or courage, the last words of many of those who were killed being "Viva Cuba libre!"

ENGAGEMENT OF THE *YANKEE* OFF CIENFUEGOS

As Told by Commander Brownson

On Monday, June 13, while lying eight to ten miles southwestward from San Juan Peak, a steamer was seen close inshore to the eastward of the entrance to Cienfuegos, heading to the eastward.

The *Yankee* was immediately cleared for action and headed for the entrance, with the crew at quarters, when the steamer turned to the westward, and, after lying dead in the water for some time near Colorado Point, turned towards us.

We had by this time made her out to be a low steamer, about two hundred feet in length, flying the Spanish colors, with one smoke-stack, one mast between pilot-house and stack, and a bridge over the pilot-house. Her awnings were spread over the pilot-house and over the gangways abreast of it.

When the steamer turned towards us we were running directly towards the mouth of the harbor at full speed. When we had approached within two thousand yards, being at the time within about five thousand yards of the batteries at the entrance and approaching them rapidly, I put the helm aport, hoisted our colors for the first time, and opened fire with the port forecastle 5-inch gun, followed at once by all the port battery, whenever they could see the enemy. This fire was immediately and spiritedly returned by the gunboat. The wind was very light at the time, and she was almost constantly shut out, either by the smoke of our guns or of her own. This was notably the case after the first fire from the forecastle gun.

As soon as our helm was put aport the gunboat made the same move, but turned at once towards the harbor, going very fast. We ran to the northward and eastward, with all the port battery bearing on and firing at him, until he was well under the forts to the westward of the entrance.

The battery to the eastward of the entrance of the harbor, near the ruins of the light-house, opened on us as soon as the gunboat sheered out of range, we being at the time within four thousand yards of it. As the steamer was gradually drawing too far abaft the beam to use our port guns, the helm was put hard aport and the ship swung around to the northward and westward, heading towards the gunboat again, which was lying close under the land near the entrance, and also towards the battery on the hill back of Sabanilla Point.

The two batteries and the gunboat, assisted by another smaller boat which had come out early in the action, kept up an incessant fire on us until we approached within from four thousand to five thousand yards of the Sabanilla batteries, when I swung her again with the starboard helm so as to bring all our starboard guns to bear on the steamers again, and we soon drove both of the enemy's vessels into the harbor.

I am of the opinion that, had it not been for the serious interference of the smoke with the fire of our guns, we would have destroyed the larger gunboat, notwithstanding the fire of the batteries. But the wind was light from the southward, and it was impossible to manœuvre the ship so that the smoke did not hang close under our lee, not only shutting out the object, but also preventing our gun pointers from seeing the fall of their shot.

Notwithstanding the large number of shells which dropped near the ship, both from the batteries and from the gunboats, there was only one casualty — that of S. P. Kennedy, landsman, who was struck by a piece of shell which entered the port of No. 8 gun, striking him in the shoulder and inflicting a serious wound.

From the firing of the larger vessel it could be seen that she had at least four guns in broadside—one forward, one aft, and two in waist. The battery on Sabanilla Point apparently had five or six guns.

The last shots we fired, after the steamers

LIEUTENANT JAMES M. HELM
Of the *Hornet*

had disappeared up the harbor, were directed at the Sabanilla battery, and one of them landed directly in it. From a large volume of smoke that rose a few minutes later, when there was no evidence of a gun having been fired, it was thought that some explosion had taken place in the battery.

THE *EAGLE*, *YANKTON*, AND *DIXIE* OFF RIO HONDO

As Told by Lieutenant Southerland

At six o'clock on the morning of June 29 the *Eagle* arrived off the mouth of the Rio Hondo, about twenty-three miles to the southward and eastward of Cienfuegos light-house, for the purpose of landing a captain and two privates of the Cuban army, by order of Commander C. H. Davis, commanding the *Dixie* and senior officer present.

At 8.30, while cruising back and forth near the river's mouth, awaiting the appearance of a Cuban force in answer to our steam-whistle signals, shots from the shore were heard and projectiles were seen to strike the water short of us. No signs of an enemy could be seen for about ten minutes, several shots in the meantime having struck the water within fifty yards of us, when a large force of cavalry was sighted on a plateau back of the beach. The *Eagle* immediately opened fire with her starboard forward and after 6-pounders and Colt's automatic. The first shot fell in the midst of a large group of the enemy and must have done considerable execution. It caused them to mount and proceed at full speed towards the interior.

In the meantime the *Yankton*, which was passing outside of the *Eagle*, bound to Trinidad, was signalled as to what was going on. She joined the *Eagle* and opened fire, making very good shooting.

The fire was continued from both vessels until the enemy disappeared over a ridge some five thousand yards distant.

Shortly after our fire ceased the *Dixie* came near and I reported all the circumstances to Commander Davis, and also that we had just seen another body of men some distance back of the beach.

He then directed me to land the Cubans at a point thirteen miles to the westward of Cienfuegos, for which place the *Eagle* was immediately headed.

Shortly after leaving the *Dixie* she opened fire on the shore, from which I presume another body of the enemy had appeared.

Eighty-six 6-pounder A. P. shells were fired during the action.

ENGAGEMENTS AT MANZANILLO

Lieutenant Young's Account

In obedience to orders from the commander-in-chief, I proceeded with the *Hist* to Cape Cruz, south of Cuba, arriving there early on the morning of June 30. The *Wompatuck*, under the command of Lieutenant Jungen, arrived about the same time. The *Hornet*, under the command of Lieutenant Helm, was cruising off the cape.

Finding I was the senior officer present, I opened the Admiral's communication in regard to the stopping of the inside traffic west of Cape Cruz and in Manzanillo, and to make a reconnaissance as early as possible.

With an excellent Cuban pilot on board, I immediately made plans accordingly, and, after sending the *Hornet* to take possession of a schooner that was trying to make her way inside, the three vessels were formed in column at half-distance, with the *Hist* leading and the *Hornet* in the rear, a formation that was maintained throughout the day, except as hereinafter mentioned.

The schooner was anchored, and was found to be the *Nickerson*, said to be English, but she was loaded with provisions and had four Spanish subjects on board in addition to her crew.

The *Hornet* being short of officers and men, Ensign McDougall and one man from this ship and one from the *Wompatuck*, all armed, were placed on board to relieve those from the *Hornet*.

Ensign McDougall was given instructions to take possession of her log and papers, and hold all on board, as well as the vessel, until the arrival of another of our ships, or until our return.

In the meantime Lieutenant Purcell, in the *Osceola*, had been given instructions to proceed to and watch the entrance to the Quatros Reales Channel to prevent any vessel from escaping. The column then, at 8.15 A.M., entered the Azuraga Pass at a uniform speed of ten knots. Upon turning the point that opened out into Niguero Bay, I made out a Spanish gunboat at anchor under the block-houses of the army on shore. There not being enough water for the *Wompatuck* to enter the bay, she was directed to remain in the channel to prevent the gunboat's escaping behind the key. The *Hornet* was directed to follow this vessel at close distance, and we headed in.

The gunboat made an effort to hide behind the point that we afterwards found to be alive with soldiers, our approach evidently having been signalled from the heliograph on the West Cay.

With the aid of the pilot and the lead, we succeeded in getting well into the bay and uncovered the gunboat. We immediately opened fire, which was returned by a machine-gun aft and a 3-pounder in the bow of the gunboat, at a distance of 1500 yards. The *Hist* got aground close in, as did the *Hornet*, which at first interfered with the range of the *Hornet's* guns, but they soon got afloat.

The third shot from the 3-pounder of the *Hist* struck the gunboat's stern and silenced the machine-gun aft. By this time a perfect fusillade of small-arms opened on us from the wooded point, at a distance of not more than 400 yards, but they were soon silenced by the Maxim 37-millimeter and a few well-directed shots from the 3 and 6 pounders.

The gunboat, finding that she could not make her escape in that direction, steamed deliberately across the harbor, under cover of the shore and shoal water, keeping up a continuous fire from her 3-pounder. She was hit by both of our vessels repeatedly, and, in a crippled condition, got in behind one of the smaller keys, which, however, did not conceal her, and a shot from the 3-pounder of the *Hist* striking her amidships, she blew up.

The fire of the gunboat was too high, but during the action both of our vessels were repeatedly struck by the small-arm fire from the ambuscade. We had no casualties.

Having completed the destruction of this vessel, the column reformed, and, after passing through Balandras Channel, headed for Manzanillo. The heliograph tower on the key was shelled in passing. On the way up, a sloop with soldiers on board was discovered close inshore, and a few shells drove them on shore and to the bush.

Passing to the left of Giva Keys, we headed in and opened up the harbor of Manzanillo. Upon a nearer approach, we discovered that instead of four small gunboats, as mentioned in the Admiral's instructions, we found a crescent formation of nine vessels stretched across the harbor, close inshore—a large torpedo-boat on the right in entering, and a good-sized gunboat on the left, with three smaller gunboats in the middle, all armed with machine-guns and 3 and 6 pounders. On the right the line was flanked by a big smooth-bore gun on Caimanera Point, and on the left by four large pontoons, armed with 6-inch smooth-bore guns that did effective work in the fight which followed.

To the rear the line was supported by a heavy battery of field-artillery on the water front and several big guns in a fort on the hill, while the shore line for over two miles in length was lined with soldiers, who kept up a fusillade of small-arms during the entire fight.

I rounded Caimanera Point and headed directly into the harbor, and when within 1000 yards of the large torpedo-boat I opened the fight with the bow 3-pounder, and, putting the helm astarboard, and just turning over, brought the broadside guns into action, and, followed by the other two vessels, passed along the entire front.

We commenced action at 3.20 P.M. and came out at 5, thus being under a heavy fire from the enemy for one hour and forty minutes. Most of the enemy's shot passed over, while ours had a tendency to fall short. However, they had our range very accurately, and succeeded in striking this vessel eleven times, one shot passing clear through the engine-room hatch and another exploding inside the hatch, both taking effect within a few inches of the main steam-pipe, which certainly would have been damaged had it not been well protected by bales of waste and a lot of cork fenders.

LIEUTENANT JOHN L. PURCELL
Of the *Osceola*

Another shot ploughed up the deck of the bridge.

The *Hornet* was struck a number of times, one shot cutting the main steam-pipe shortly after going into action, disabling her. Notwithstanding this accident, she gallantly kept up an uninterrupted fire after and during the time she was being towed out by the *Wompatuck*. In this crippled condition she succeeded in sinking one gunboat and a sloop loaded with soldiers. The *Wompatuck* was struck several times, one shot, near the water-line, going clean through her.

As soon as I saw the steam escaping from the *Hornet* I signalled the *Wompatuck*, which was close to her, to take her in tow, and Lieutenant Jungen deserves great credit for the cool manner in which he handled his vessel under a galling fire as he came to the rescue.

The *Hist* backed down to render assistance, and was signalled "No further aid needed," whereupon she was headed in for the large pontoon that was doing serious work with the old 6-inch smooth-bore guns, and in a short time we landed a shell that set fire to the old pontoon and burned her.

With the exception of the above-mentioned damages, we suffered no further, and the only casualties were three men scalded by escaping steam on the *Hornet;* the enemy lost one gunboat, a sloop loaded with soldiers, and a pontoon, with the large torpedo-boat disabled and several gunboats seriously injured, and without doubt sustained quite a loss of life.

THE SECOND DAY'S ENGAGEMENT

As Related by Lieutenant-Commander Marix

At 4 P.M., July 1, and immediately after our arrival off the port of Manzanillo, the *Scorpion* and *Osceola* entered the harbor to attack the four Spanish gunboats that were seen inside.

After entering the harbor between the second and third southernmost of the Manzanillo cays, we went ahead full speed; and when about 2000 yards from their vessels and about 1400 yards from the shore abreast of us, five vessels, five shore batteries, and musketry all along the shore opened fire upon us simultaneously, and kept up an incessant fire throughout the whole engagement. They seemed to have plenty of ammunition.

The firing of the enemy was good throughout; too high at first, but rapidly improving. After we had been under fire about twenty minutes they had evidently got our range, and shot and shell struck all around and between both vessels. At this time I decided to turn around and steam out. We were then less than 1000 yards from the shore, and the Gatling gun of the *Osceola* was doing good work to keep down the musketry fire.

Our firing was deliberate, and must have done considerable damage; but we could not get at the gunboats because they kept in shoal water and carefully kept bows on, presenting very small targets. One of our 5-inch shells was seen to strike the receiving-ship square in the bows. I regretted that we could not steam right past the city and endeavor to sink the gunboats as we went along; but we knew nothing about the channels and had to return by the one we had found by the use of the lead and the appearance of the water.

We were opposed by five vessels—viz., one receiving-ship, housed over, with guns forward, one gunboat of about 1000 tons, two of from 300 to 400 tons, and one very small gunboat—and on shore by five batteries, the principal one being above the city, about half-way up the hill. This was the only one we made out before we entered the harbor. Three other batteries were along the water front between us and the city, and the fifth one abreast of our entrance. I did not believe that they had any modern guns of large caliber, but they certainly had some large guns and quite a number of smaller modern guns.

It was remarkable that no one was struck and neither ship hurt. The *Scorpion* was struck on the outside, slightly, in twelve places; the nose of a shell entered the galley, and the deck was torn in several places by pieces of shell.

After leaving the harbor we remained outside, close to the entrance, until dark, but they did not come out.

OUR WAR-SHIPS OFF THE COAST NEAR SANTIAGO DE CUBA, JUNE 3, 1898.—DRAWN BY CARLTON T. CHAPMAN

SANTIAGO'S MORRO CASTLE, AT THE HARBOR ENTRANCE

OPERATIONS ON THE BLOCKADE

THE more prominent incidents connected with the blockade of the Spanish ports of Cuba have been described in detail. A general view of the blockade of Santiago is presented below in Admiral Sampson's account. On the 19th of June the *St. Paul* left the squadron and proceeded to institute a blockade of San Juan de Puerto Rico, whither she was followed by the *Yosemite*. On the 22d the *St. Paul* engaged off San Juan the torpedo-boat *Terror*, supported by the gunboat *Isabel II.*, and drove them both into port, the former being so seriously injured that she had to be run on shore when inside. Another fight occurred off San Juan on the 28th, when the *Yosemite*, manned by the Michigan Naval Militia under Commander William H. Emory, successfully engaged the Spanish batteries, two cruisers, and the torpedo-boat destroyer *Terror*, and wrecked the transport *Antonio Lopez*, loaded with supplies for the town. Captain Bartlett, Chief of the Auxiliary Naval Force, writing of the work of the Naval Militia, said:

"The department called upon the States of New York, Massachusetts, Michigan, and Maryland to furnish officers and men for the merchant steamers purchased for the war and renamed the *Yankee*, *Prairie*, *Yosemite*, and *Dixie*. This was in accordance with the suggestion that some of the older organizations of Naval Militia were competent to furnish officers and men for sea-going vessels. This call was one which taxed to the utmost the resources of the Naval Militia organizations, coming closely as it did upon that for volunteers to man the monitors, but it was responded to with most gratifying alacrity. To fill the complement of these vessels, each organization called upon contributed about two hundred and fifty men. As examples of the promptness with which the call was met, the contingent from the First Naval Battalion, New York, reported uniformed, armed, equipped, and ready for duty in six hours after receiving notice; and the contingent from the Massachusetts Naval Brigade, which was notified at 1 o'clock on a Saturday afternoon, arrived at the New York Navy-Yard, fully prepared for service on the *Prairie*, at 9 o'clock the next morning. For the first time in the history of the navy, professional men, business men, and men of leisure and of the highest education were brought into the lower ratings, and served with great intelligence and enthusiasm; and after a short experience made good men-of-war's-men, although they had had little or no training as sea-going sailors, and exhibited some of the lack of knowledge of the care of property and themselves that is common to all volunteers."

THE BLOCKADE OF SANTIAGO

ADMIRAL SAMPSON'S ACCOUNT

IMMEDIATELY on arrival, on the morning of June 1, I steamed down past the entrance to Santiago Harbor, and saw, lying close within, the *Cristobal Colon* and one of the *Vizcaya* class. Both of these got up steam and moved up into the harbor out of sight.

Preparations were at once made for sinking the collier *Merrimac* in the entrance, the port watch of the *New York* being sent on board. The night of this day was particularly favorable for the enterprise, the tide, the time of setting of the moon, etc., all conjoining most favorably. Unfortunately the preparations were not completed before daylight of the 2d, and the expedition had to be postponed to the next night, when, at 3.30 A.M., June 3, she went in and was sunk. She did not sink until she was much higher in the channel than was intended. This was owing to the failure of her steering-gear, and to a partial failure of the torpedoes arranged along her side to explode. On June 2 the following order of battle was issued:

"The fleet off Santiago de Cuba will be organized during the operations against that port and the Spanish squadron as follows:

"First squadron (under the personal command of the Commander-in-Chief). — *New York*, *Iowa*, *Oregon*, *New Orleans*, *Mayflower*, *Porter*.

"Second squadron (Commodore Schley). — *Brooklyn*, *Massachusetts*, *Texas*, *Marblehead*, *Vixen*.

"Vessels joining subsequently will be assigned by the Commander-in-Chief. The vessels will blockade Santiago de Cuba closely, keeping about six miles from the Morro in the daytime, and closing in at night, the lighter vessels well in shore. The first squadron will blockade on the east side of the port, and the second squadron on the west side. If the enemy tries to escape, the ships must close and engage as soon as possible, and endeavor to sink his vessels or force them to run ashore in the channel. It is not considered that the shore batteries are of sufficient power to do any material injury to battle-ships.

"In smooth weather the vessels will coal on station. If withdrawn to coal elsewhere, or for other duty, the blockading vessels on either side will cover the angle thus left vacant."

On June 3, about 3 P.M., the Spanish tug *Colon* came out of Santiago Harbor flying a flag of truce, and the *Vixen* was sent to meet her. The Spanish fleet-captain, Bustamente, came on board with a letter from Admiral Cervera to Admiral Sampson announcing the safety of the *Merrimac's* crew. Towards midnight the *Mayflower* left for Key West, *via* Mole St. Nicholas, taking the following telegrams to the Secretary of the Navy:

"Some observations made to-day by a reliable Cuban, in accordance with my instructions, make four Spanish armored vessels and two Spanish torpedo-boat destroyers in Santiago at that time. Repairs and more coal needed by them."

"Have received reliable information from Cuban officers that the Spanish force in the vicinity of Santiago consists of 7000 men, intrenched in Juraguacito and Daiquiri; 5000 men in Santiago de Cuba; in Morro de Cuba, 400 men; at other points in the bay, 100 men, with small rapid-fire gun and submarine mines at various points. With superior force and insurgent force, which is ready, though mostly needing arms, Santiago de Cuba must fall, with ships in port, which cannot be entered against obstructions and mines."

On the 4th the following order of battle was issued:

"The *Texas*, *Massachusetts*, *Iowa*, and the *Oregon* will take positions 4000 yards from Estrella Point and opposite the entrance to the port of Santiago in the order named from west to east in such position as to be able to observe the wreck of the *Merrimac*, and will fire upon any parties which may be seen working about it. If the fire be opened by the batteries, it will be returned and an endeavor made to destroy them.

"The senior officer of the above-named ships will have charge of carrying out these instructions.

"In case of opening fire upon the batteries, the *Brooklyn*, *Marblehead*, and the *Vixen* will take an enfilading position 4000 yards to the westward of the entrance and well inshore, and the *New York*, *New Orleans*, and the *Yankee* a similar position to the eastward, and will engage the batteries at the same time with the battle-ships.

"Firing directly upon Morro Castle will be avoided, as our men from the *Merrimac* are confined there.

"The battle-ships will take the above positions when signalled to do so by the Commander-in-Chief, and will occupy them until signalled to withdraw, when blockading stations will be resumed."

On the 5th I issued the following battle order and plan for proposed attack on batteries June 6:

"Preparations will be made to engage the

batteries Monday morning, June 6, at 7 o'clock. The men should be given their breakfast at 5.30, and the divisions ready to form at 6 o'clock.

"When preparatory signal is made ships will form south of the Morro as follows:

"Western column (heading north).—*Brooklyn, Marblehead, Texas, Massachusetts.*

"Eastern column (heading north).—*New York, Yankee, New Orleans, Oregon, Iowa.*

"When signal of execution is made, the columns will move ahead. The commander of each division will make such signals as may be necessary to bring his division into position, forming circles drawn at 3000 yards from the eastern and western batteries, one column heading in a northwesterly and the other in a northeasterly direction. This will be best accomplished by changing direction of columns, the easterly column to the northeastward and the westerly column to the northwestward, running in these directions until south of the indicated positions, then heading all vessels of the division north simultaneously, turning again into column when the distance of 3000 yards has been reached. Vessels will be 400 yards apart and will retain their positions, the westerly column using the starboard battery and the easterly column the port battery.

"On signal from the Commander-in-Chief both columns will open fire, or fire will be opened in case the enemy begins.

"Bearings will be taken carefully, and distances obtained with all practicable accuracy.

"The *Dolphin* will take position to the eastward and the *Suwanee* and *Vixen* to the westward, for the purpose of looking after any musketry fire from shore.

"The fire will be deliberate and continued until the batteries are silenced, or an order to cease firing has been made."

About 6.30 A.M. of the 6th the vessels formed two columns, as per order of battle issued previous date. At 6.43 called to general quarters, ships standing in towards the batteries. At 7.38 made signal "Commence firing." At 7.41 opened fire, the flag-ship aiming at the battery east of the Morro at 6000 yards. At 8.05 hoisted "Cease firing," when general firing was discontinued, but individual firing at slower rate of speed was continued until 9.40. The *New York* had worked in to within 2000 yards of the Morro batteries and engaged in deliberate firing. At 10.08 made signal "Resume blockading station." At 10.20 flag-ship sounded "Secure."

In the afternoon I sent the following despatch to the Secretary of the Navy by one of the newspaper tugs going to St. Nicholas Mole:

"Bombarded forts at Santiago to-day at 7.30 A.M. to 10 A.M., and have silenced works quickly without injury of any kind, though stationed within 2000 yards. If 10,000 men were here city and fleet would be ours within forty-eight hours. Every consideration demands immediate army movement; if delayed, city will be defended more strongly by guns taken from fleet."

About midnight the *Marblehead* and *Yankee* left for Guantanamo.

On the 7th the following memorandum was issued regarding methods of blockade:

"After careful consideration of the various schemes of maintaining an effective blockade of Santiago de Cuba at night which have been advanced, I have decided upon the following, which will be maintained until further orders:

"The weather permitting, three picket-launches, detailed from the ships of the squadron each evening, will occupy position one mile from the Morro—one to the eastward, one to the westward, and one to the southward of the harbor entrance. On a circle drawn with a radius of two miles from the Morro will be stationed three vessels, the *Vixen* to the westward, from one-half mile to one mile from the shore, the *Suwanee* south of the Morro, and the *Dolphin* to the eastward, between one-half mile and one mile from the shore. The remaining vessels will retain the positions already occupied, but they will take especial care to keep within a four-mile circle.

"All vessels may turn their engines whenever desirable, to keep them in readiness for immediate use, and while so doing may turn in a small circle, but without losing proper bearing or distance.

"I again call attention to the absolute necessity of a close blockade of this port, especially at night and in bad weather. In the daytime,

LIEUTENANT JOHN C. FREMONT
Of the *Porter*

if clear, the distance shall not be greater than six miles; at night, or in thick weather, not more than four miles. The end to be attained justifies the risk of torpedo attack, and that risk must be taken. The escape of the Spanish vessels at this juncture would be a serious blow to our prestige and to a speedy end of the war."

On the 8th I issued the following memorandum regarding the use of search-lights. This was undoubtedly one of the most important elements in making the blockade successful, in that it made it impossible, as was afterwards stated on board the *New York* by the captain of the *Colon*, for the Spanish squadron to leave at night. The entrance was by this means brilliantly lighted, so that the movements of the smallest boat could be seen within. A later modification kept a second battle-ship close to the illuminating ship, so that the first of these two should be able to use her guns without disturbing the illumination.

"During the dark hours of the night search-lights will be used as follows:

"The *Iowa, Oregon,* and the *Massachusetts* will take turns of two hours each—*i.e.*, from dark to 8 P.M., from 8 P.M. to 10 P.M.—in keeping one search-light directly on the harbor entrance, maintaining carefully during that time their blockading positions. Should a vessel's lights fail, the next in order will at once take up the duty.

"The picket-launch and vedette stationed south of the Morro will move to one side or the other sufficiently to get clear of the beam of light.

"The vessel on each flank, the *Brooklyn* and the *Texas* on the western side, the *New York* and *New Orleans* on the eastern side, will take two-hour turns in using one search-light from time to time on the coast-line, swinging it towards the Morro, but avoiding the illumination of the flanking vedettes on the inside line. The light should never be turned off more than five minutes at a time. From time to time the horizon outside will be swept.

"Attention is called to bad and careless handling of search-lights. Last night some of the lights were kept high in the air and were again swept rapidly from side to side. Under such circumstances a search-light is worse than useless.

"The beams must be directed to the horizon and must be moved very steadily and slowly. Not less than three minutes should be employed in sweeping through an arc of 90 degrees.

"The best way to discover a torpedo-boat is by its smoke, and even this will not be seen unless the light is very well handled."

The *Yankee* was sent on this date to St. Nicholas Mole with the following despatch to the Secretary of the Navy:

"Yesterday morning sent from the blockade the *Marblehead* and the *Yankee* to arrive at Guantanamo early daylight. They entered harbor, taking possession of lower bay immediately after their arrival, and small gunboat, defending position, retreated without delay to the upper bay, which is connected with the lower bay by a narrow passage defended by eleven mines. Their instructions were not to enter the upper portion of the bay, but to hold lower bay for the accommodation of our ships, and this was successfully accomplished. The crew of cable-steamer *Adria* spent several days searching for Jamaica cable from Santiago, and destroyed second cable, the *St. Louis* having cut first. But the crew of the *Adria* has refused to do any more work, on grounds that work required of them is illegal. Therefore cable from Santiago to Cienfuegos has not been cut, but all communication between Cuba and outside world has been cut off. As there is some doubt that both Jamaica cables have been cut, suggest that department make inquiry into this subject. I suggest further that as the crew of the *Adria* has failed in their contract, they should not receive compensation after the time at which they refused to do duty. As soon as possible I hope to have communication by telegraph between Guantanamo and the United States through French cables, and will inform the department as soon as it has been established. Under these circumstances, again I urge upon the department to expedite the arrival of troops for Santiago de Cuba, the difficulty of blockading the Spanish ships daily increasing; and as dark and stormy nights approach, difficulty must be increased greatly. Army should be here now. The Spanish force on north side of Cuba is insignificant absolute-

GUARDING THE ENTRANCE TO THE HARBOR OF SANTIAGO, JUNE 3, 1898.—Drawn by Carlton T. Chapman

ly, and can offer no impediment whatever. One cruiser could look after the whole. *Yankee* will wait until one for answer. The *Marblehead* will remain at Guantanamo. I request that you send *Vesuvius* at once to Santiago."

About 1 P.M. of the 9th the *Dolphin* returned from Mole St. Nicholas with the following despatch from Key West:

"Tuesday, 9 P.M., fifteen nautical miles north one-half east Bahia de Cadiz Light, *Eagle* sighted north-northwest. Signal exchanged among * * * Pursued about three nautical miles without bringing vessels in sight. At 9.45 P.M. sighted stern-light armored cruiser N. ½ E. Showed private signal twice. Armored cruiser flashed truck-light. Protected vessel, two torpedo-destroyers, fleet formation answered. *Eagle* scouted abreast until character Spanish vessel was ascertained. Communicated immediately with *Lebanon*, at Piedras Cay, suggesting to her captain to send this news to fleet off Havana. *Eagle* then proceeded with all despatch to Key West. One deep-sea torpedo-vessel chased *Eagle* for a short time. Except stern-light and occasional signal, four vessels total darkness. *Panther* left last night to join *Yosemite*, off Havana, for convoy. *Nashville*, with Watson, left here about same time: supposed they know the news. *Resolute* confirms it."

I placed no confidence whatever in this information, though so specific. During the next morning the *Yosemite*, *Panther*, *Armeria*, *Scorpion*, and *Supply* arrived, the *Panther* bringing the First Marine Battalion and the *Armeria* a supply of ammunition. The *Yankee* also arrived from Mole St. Nicholas, and reported having passed a squadron of eight vessels, one of which was a battleship.

The arrival of the ships mentioned explained the squadron seen by the *Yankee*. The *Yankee* had been observed by them, and the *Scorpion*, which was acting as convoy to the *Armeria* and *Supply*, had fired upon her, taking her for a torpedo-boat, but the *Yankee* was so distant that these reports had not been heard, and the flashes were taken for signals. This still further convinced me of the error of the *Eagle's* report, and showed how easily the most experienced may be deceived at night at sea.

On the 10th the following despatch of the 8th was received from Washington:

"The Spanish armored cruiser, first-class, torpedo-destroyers are reported by *Eagle* and *Resolute* yesterday and last night, and therefore the army expedition is stopped temporarily; convoy is distributed to scour the straits and reinforce the blockade of Cuba; send two of your fastest armored vessels to search through Nicholas Channel, Cuba. * * * at Key West, and thence reinforce convoy too. We mean to start this as soon as convoy is strong enough, the delay being only temporary. Are you sure all four Spanish armored cruisers are at Santiago? Six hundred marines, *Panther*, started for you last evening, convoyed by auxiliary No. 306 (*Yosemite*)."

The following memorandum was issued on the 10th:

"The use of the search-lights during the dark hours of last night clearly indicates that the lights can be used with the greatest efficiency if sufficient care is taken for this purpose. It is absolutely necessary that the beam of light should be held steadily up the channel into the harbor.

"Under these circumstances it is believed to be practically impossible for a vessel to escape detection in any attempt to come out. I therefore enjoin the commanding officers of the *Iowa*, the *Oregon*, and the *Massachusetts* to move forward into their positions, not more than two miles from the entrance, with the entrance bearing north by east; the *Iowa*, arriving first, at 7.30, will place her light squarely up the entrance into the harbor and hold it steadily, except during the time required to change from one search-light to another, as may be required. At the end of two hours from 7.30 P.M. she will be relieved by the *Massachusetts*, each of these vessels going back to her blockading position, three miles from the entrance.

"It is most important that the lights should be held as nearly stationary as possible, and that no discrimination be left to the person manipulating the light. It is believed that this method of using the search-light will prove to be all that is necessary or advantageous in blockading the harbor."

LIEUTENANT NATHANIEL R. USHER
Of the *Ericsson*

The *Yankee* went to St. Nicholas with the following despatch:

"Have no confidence in the report of *Eagle* as to nationality or character of the vessels, and consider very unwise to suspend operations on this account; but even if it is found correct, there is sufficient force to furnish convoy. Armored vessel was probably *Talbot*, which was sighted Thursday, at 9 A.M., by the *Scorpion* standing to the east; am confident no large ship could have escaped from here. Am endeavoring to obtain information from Santiago as to what vessels are inside to-day. Delay seems to me most unfortunate. Marine battalion arrived this morning and will land at Guantanamo to-day."

The *Panther* was sent on the same day to Guantanamo in company with the *Yosemite*. The marine battalion was there landed and established in camp.

On the 11th of June the *St. Louis* arrived with the British steamer *Twickenham* (collier), which she had captured off Jamaica. The *Twickenham* was sent into Key West.

The following despatches to the Secretary of the Navy were sent to Mole St. Nicholas by the *St. Louis*:

"Upon receiving department's authority to exchange prisoners, sent immediately these proposals under flag of truce to the Spanish Admiral: To exchange for Hobson and his seven men First Lieutenant Pius Giner Gastaminza, of Sixth Battalion Lower Peninsular, one second lieutenant, name unknown, one sergeant, five privates. The Spanish Admiral informed me Hobson and his men have been delivered to General commanding the territorial division of Cuba, at Santiago, and that the latter had reported the case to General-in-Chief, resident at Havana, and therefore all arrangements in case must be dealt with through latter. Therefore request that department take the necessary steps to effect this directly through authorities at Havana, as desired results can probably be effected more quickly than to have negotiations carried on from Santiago. My letter to the Spanish Admiral proposed exchange should be accomplished after an agreement by delivering prisoners confined at Atlanta, Ga., to the Spanish authorities at Havana, and that we would receive Hobson and his associates from them at Santiago. Department would perhaps do well to follow same plan of exchange in these negotiations."

"The following is a *résumé* of a letter from General Garcia to Miles, which I send thus as the only means of its reaching him. Miles's letter received through Colonel Hernandez on June 6. Garcia regards his wishes and suggestions as orders, and will immediately take measures to concentrate forces at the point indicated, but cannot do so as early as desired on account of his expedition to Port Banes, Cuba, but he will march without delay. All his subordinates are ordered to assist to disembark the United States troops and to place themselves under orders. Santiago well fortified with advanced intrenchments, but he believes positions for artillery can be taken as Miles desires—approximately, 12,000 regulars and 3000 militia, between Santiago and Guantanamo. He has sent forces in order to prevent aid getting to Santiago from Holquin. Repeats every assurance of good-will and desire to second plans."

"The vessels seen by the *Eagle* were the *Armeria*, *Scorpion*, and *Supply*. They were in just that position at time named. The number is unimportant, as the *Yankee*, coming from Mole, Haiti, Thursday, at 11 P.M., mistook the five vessels arriving yesterday for eight or nine vessels under convoy battleship. In the morning the battleship resolved itself into the *Scorpion*. General Rabi at Aceraderos with 500 men; Garcia expected there to-day."

The following memorandum was issued on the 11th:

"Until further orders, the battleships *Iowa*, *Oregon*, and the *Massachusetts* will employ their search-lights in the manner so successfully employed during the last two nights. Care will be taken, however, to go in close enough to make the light wholly effective for the purpose desired. The picket-boats report that the lights at times are too weak because of the distance of the ships. The lights will be employed from 7.30 till daylight as follows:

"The sequence of ships will be *Iowa*, *Oregon*, *Massachusetts*. To-night, June 11, the *Massachusetts* will begin at 7.30 and continue until 9.30, the *Iowa* from 9.30 to 11.30, the *Oregon*

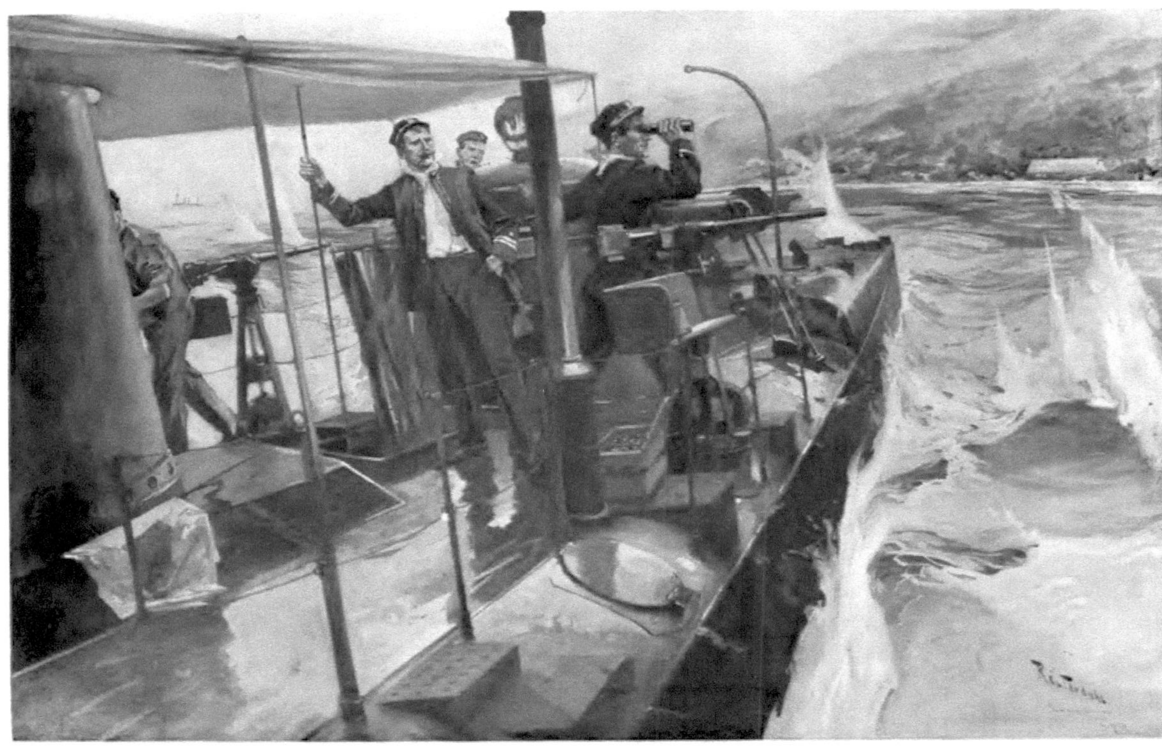

THE TORPEDO-BOAT *ERICSSON* RECONNOITRING OFF SANTIAGO HARBOR TO OBSERVE THE ERECTION OF SPANISH BATTERIES.—Drawn by H. Reuterdahl

from 11.30 to 1.30, the *Massachusetts* from 1.30 to 3.30, and the *Iowa* from 3.30 to daylight.

"On June 12 the *Iowa* will begin at 7.30, on June 13 the *Oregon*, and on June 14 the *Massachusetts* again, and so on.

"The vessel using the light shall keep the entrance of the harbor bearing north by east. The instructions of my memorandum of June 10, 1898, will be followed.

"Regard must be had for the state of the atmosphere. If it is hazy, an effective illumination of the harbor entrance will require a closer approach."

On the 12th the torpedo-boat *Porter* arrived from Guantanamo and brought Commander McCalla's report that "yesterday a scouting-party of one sergeant and two privates from the marine camp were killed and their remains mutilated by a party of regular Spanish soldiery or guerillas in their employ. Dr. Gibbs was killed about 1 A.M. this morning in the camp, and Corporal Glass accidentally shot himself through the hand. It is possible that Dr. Gibbs may have been killed accidentally by one of our own men during the fire which took place about that time."

The *Yankee* was sent to Cienfuegos and the *Yosemite* to the west end of Jamaica to look for the Spanish steamer *Purisima Concepcion*.

The *Vesuvius* arrived on the 13th from scouting in the Old Bahama Channel, the *St. Paul* from New York, and the *St. Louis* from Mole St. Nicholas with despatches, whither she at once returned. The collier *Scindia* arrived at Guantanamo Bay.

Received the following despatches from Washington:

"On account of the army expedition, it is most essential to know positively if all of Cervera's armored vessels are actually at Santiago de Cuba. Inform the department as soon as possible."

"After you have a suitable base on shore, could we authorize to allow the repair and operation of the French cable between your base and Mole, Haiti?"

"The department considers you should have a cruiser off San Juan, Puerto Rico, to observe the port."

"Army expedition starts this afternoon from Tampa, Fla., for Santiago de Cuba."

The following despatch was sent by the *St. Louis* to the Secretary of the Navy:

"Lieutenant Blue has just returned, after a détour of seventy miles, to observe inside Santiago Harbor; reports Spanish squadron all there. Spanish made vigorous attack on Guantanamo camp. An outpost of four marines killed and their bodies were most barbarously mutilated. Surgeon Gibbs killed, apparently accidentally, by our own men. (The report of mutilation arose from the effect of the Mauser bullets, and was later corrected.)"

LIEUT.-COMMANDER JOHN E. PILLSBURY
Of the *Vesuvius*

SANTIAGO, FROM THE HARBOR

CAPTAIN WILLIAM M. FOLGER
Of the *New Orleans*

During the night the *Vesuvius* went in close to shore and fired three shots—two at the western battery and one into the channel, between Cay Smith and the mainland.

During the morning watch, just after daylight of the 14th, the *New Orleans* was ordered in and engaged the battery to the east of the Morro, with the idea of preventing a continuation of work and the replacing of guns which might have been dismounted. She soon became actively engaged with both batteries, and fired with accuracy and effectiveness for about twenty minutes. Though a number of shells fell near the *New Orleans* and flag-ship, neither was struck.

Sent the following despatch to the Secretary of the Navy by the *Gloucester*, with orders to send it from Guantanamo, if possible; if not, from Mole St. Nicholas:

"Affairs at Guantanamo much more satisfactory. Our forces have been reinforced by fifty Cubans, who are reported by Commander McCalla as of greatest assistance. Five hundred more are expected, who need Springfield rifles. Fleet will supply clothing and food as far as possible. Fleet needs supply of both."

On the 14th a force of marines and Cubans attacked the enemy, who was routed. Forty bodies were found. One lieutenant, one corporal, and fifteen privates captured. The block-house was partially destroyed, the well from which they got their supply of water destroyed, and the heliograph apparatus captured. Our loss was two Cubans killed and four wounded, two marines wounded. Twenty-three marines were overcome by heat, but all recovered. The *Dolphin* accompanied the force on the sea-front and shelled the enemy. The force of the enemy was stated by the lieutenant captured at two hundred, by the privates at about four hundred and fifty. The enemy was reinforced by troops from Caimanera, and the *Texas* and *Suwanee* were consequently sent to destroy the fort and capture the gunboat used in transporting men.

The following order of battle was issued on the 15th; also memorandum and addendum to order of battle:

"An examination indicates that the Spaniards have been adding to the defences to the east and west of the entrance. Apparently there are mounted on the left of the western battery two ship's guns, and on the right hand of the same battery two or three old guns. On the eastern battery, to the right of the light-house, are mounted three old guns and possibly several smaller rapid-fire guns.

"The squadron will be prepared to-morrow morning at early daylight to shell both of these batteries.

BIRD'S-EYE VIEW OF SANTIAGO AND SURROUNDING COUNTRY.—Drawn by Charles Graham

"There will be no special formation for this purpose, but vessels will at early dawn carefully adjust their positions and blockading distances of three miles, and go quietly to general quarters, the men having been called early enough to have had their early coffee. The *New York* and the *New Orleans* will exchange blockading positions.

"When signal is made, vessels will move towards the harbor entrance at a speed of five knots. Arrived at a distance of 3000 yards, each ship will stop and turn to present her broadside, the *New York*, *New Orleans*, *Oregon*, and *Iowa* turning with port helm, and the *Brooklyn*, *Texas*, and the *Massachusetts* with starboard helm. This stopping and turning will be done without signal, but all vessels should endeavor to arrive on the firing-line at the same moment. After turning, distance should be closed to 400 yards, using the engines again if needed. The vessels will retain the positions thus taken as nearly as possible, moving in closer, if necessary, in order to see their targets and render their fire effective.

"On signal from the Commander-in-Chief, all vessels will open fire, or fire will be opened in case the enemy begins.

"Bearings will be taken carefully and distances obtained with all practicable accuracy.

"The *Vixen* will take position inshore on the western side and the *Scorpion* on the eastern side, and look out for the musketry fire from shore. They will be slightly outside the flank ship, and where they can enfilade any infantry fire directed upon the ships.

"The fire will be deliberate, and, after the batteries are silenced, will be carefully directed to their destruction. Ammunition will not be thrown away. Careful instructions will be given to gun captains not to fire unless they can see their mark, which in this case will be the enemy's guns.

"The *Vesuvius* and the *Porter* will remain on the east side out of range of the batteries."

"*Memorandum*

"The Commander-in-Chief desires again to call the attention of commanding officers to the positions occupied by the blockading fleet, especially during the daytime, and it is now directed that all ships keep within a distance of the entrance to Santiago of four miles, and this distance must not be exceeded.

"If the vessel is coaling, or is otherwise restricted in her movements, she must nevertheless keep within this distance.

"If at any time the flag-ship makes signal which is not visible to any vessel, such vessel must at once approach the flag-ship or repeating vessel to a point where she can read the signal.

"Disregard of the directions which have already been given on this head has led to endless confusion. Many times during the day the fleet is so scattered that it would be perfectly possible for the enemy to come out of the harbor and meet with very little opposition.

"The Commander-in-Chief hopes that strict attention will be given to this order."

"*Addendum to Order of Battle*

"Reduced charges will be used in all guns of 8-inch caliber and above, with the corresponding sight-marks to increase the angle of fall of the projectiles and the probability of destroying the batteries."

THE *GLOUCESTER* BRINGING CAPTAIN CHADWICK TO SEE GENERAL SHAFTER

The fort in Guantanamo Bay was destroyed on this day by the *Texas* and *Marblehead* and *Suwanee*. One torpedo was picked up by the *Marblehead's* screw. There was no serious fighting reported ashore during the 14th.

On the 16th, following the order of battle of the 15th, the batteries were bombarded at early dawn. They were quickly silenced and the fire was continued half an hour, and probably did much damage, as no shots were fired at the ships as they withdrew.

The following telegram from Washington, dated the 14th, was received *via* Mole St. Nicholas on the 17th:

"From very reliable source it is learned that five small Spanish unprotected vessels and one armed transport at San Juan, Puerto Rico, no more (?). Army supply is nearly out of provisions. Twenty-two thousand tons of coal there and only three hours' supply of shell at their fort, but would be well not to trust too much statement about shell. Department advises you blockade at once cruiser and transport at San Juan, Puerto Rico, and prevent escape. Is *Terror* one of them? Our army and convoy are leaving Tampa."

The following telegram was sent *via* Mole St. Nicholas by the *Scorpion* to the Secretary of the Navy:

"Bombarded the batteries on June 16 for forty-two minutes, firing very accurate. The batteries were silenced completely. Fleet not injured. We are providing Cubans as far as possible with clothing, food, arms. These and supplies of all kinds much needed by fleet. Cubans much assistance at Guantanamo, where everything is now reported quiet. Intercepted letter from Guantanamo to Spanish commanding army officer at Santiago reports there is only a small quantity of food, not more than sufficient for this month, half-rations. Deserter from the *Reina Mercedes* states *Merrimac* does not block up channel; she is too far in the harbor. There is no possibility, however, of anything coming out without our knowledge; a battle-ship is every night at a distance of one mile from entrance illuminating the channel most clearly. I again urge earnestly army move with all possible celerity. Fine weather may end any day."

On the 19th of June I sent the following telegram to the Secretary of the Navy:

"Cienfuegos blockaded by *Yankee*, Cape Cruz and vicinity by *Dixie*. When some of the light-draft vessels arrive, they will be sent to cruise in the vicinity of Manzanillo, Cuba, and Isle of Pines. The President may declare immediately the blockade of whole southern coast. Auxiliaries Nos. 557, 596 are on the way to blockade San Juan, Puerto Rico. Will send back to north coast of Cuba all vessels constituting convoy as soon as they arrive. A part will go by Cape Maysi and part Cape San Antonio, so as to blockade temporarily the whole coast of Cuba. Rifles enough. Request 500,000 rounds of Springfield rifle ammunition, .45 caliber. All foreign cables have been cut by Goodrich; last one on 18th. Recommend that isolation be made complete between Key West and Havana. Any communication sure to furnish Blanco information."

My chief of staff went down to Aserraderos in the *Vixen* to examine the facilities for landing at that point and the points between there and Santiago de Cuba. He returned, bringing with him General Calixto Garcia, General of Division Lora, and several officers of their staffs. General Garcia had about 4000 men back in the country, probably forty-five miles by road from Santiago de Cuba—two days' march. He had left behind him 3000 men, who were engaged in observing the Spanish forces, numbering about 8000 or 10,000, at Holguin, in order to prevent their moving south to the relief of Santiago. All of these 7000 men were well armed and supplied with ammunition, the Florida expedition which landed at Banes having supplied all deficiencies.

The fleet of transports of the Fifth Army Corps and its convoys arrived at a point fifteen miles to the southward at noon of June 20. I at once sent my chief of staff in the *Gloucester* to communicate with General Shafter. The general came up to the blockading line in the *Seguranca*, and I proceeded with him to Aserraderos, where we had an interview with General Garcia, and a landing was arranged for at Daiquiri, 3000 of Garcia's troops to be brought up from Aserraderos and landed as soon as possible.

On the 21st the cable at Guantanamo was connected with that at Mole St. Nicholas, and an office opened there for general telegraphic

THE *ST. PAUL* ON SCOUT DUTY—A SUSPICIOUS CRAFT SIGHTED—PREPARING TO FOLLOW A BLANK CARTRIDGE WITH SOLID SHOT.—Drawn by T. de Thulstrup, after a Sketch by Howard F. Sprague

use. On the same day I issued the following order of battle:

"The army corps will land to-morrow morning, the entire force landing at Daiquiri. The landing will begin at daylight, or as soon thereafter as practicable. General Castillo, with 1000 men, coming from the eastward of Daiquiri, will assist in clearing the way for an unopposed landing by flanking out the Spanish forces at that point.

"Simultaneously with the shelling of the beach and block-houses at Daiquiri, the Ensenada de los Altares and Aguadores, both to the eastward of Santiago, and the small bay of Cabanas, about two and a half miles to the westward of Santiago, will be shelled by the ships stationed there for the purpose.

"A feint in force of landing at Cabanas will be made, about ten of the transports, the last to disembark their forces at Daiquiri, remaining during the day or greater part of the day about two miles to the southward of Cabanas, lowering boats and making apparent preparations for disembarking a large body of troops. At the same time General Rabi, with 500 Cuban troops, will make a demonstration on the west side of Cabanas.

"The following vessels are assigned to bombard the four points mentioned above: At Cabanas, the *Scorpion*, *Vixen*, and *Texas*. At

Aguadores, the *Eagle* and *Gloucester*. At Ensenada de los Altares, the *Hornet*, *Helena*, and *Bancroft*. At Daiquiri, the *Detroit*, *Castine*, *Wasp*, and *New Orleans*—the *Detroit* and *Castine* on the western flank, the *Wasp* and *New Orleans* on the eastern flank. All the vessels named will be in their position at daylight.

"Great care will be taken to avoid the wasteful expenditure of ammunition. The firing at Daiquiri will begin on signal from the *New Orleans*.

"At Cabanas it is probable that after a few minutes, unless the firing is returned, occasional dropping of shots from the smaller vessels will be sufficient, but the semblance of covering a landing should be maintained, the ships keeping close in.

"At Aguadores and Ensenada de los Altares the same rule should prevail. At Daiquiri, the point of actual landing, vessels will, of course, use their artillery until they have reason to believe that the landing is clear. They will take care to make the firing deliberate and effective. As General Castillo's column, approaching from the eastward, is likely to come within range of the guns, sharp-eyed quartermasters with good glasses will be stationed to look out for the Cuban flag, and care will be taken not to direct the fire towards any point where that flag is shown.

"The *Texas* and *Brooklyn* will exchange blockading stations, the *Texas* going inside, to be near Cabanas. The *Brooklyn*, *Massachusetts*, *Iowa*, and *Oregon* will retain their blockading positions, and will keep a vigilant watch on the harbor mouth. The *Indiana* will take the *New Orleans'* position in the blockading-line east of Santiago and between the flag-ship *New York* and the shore. This is only a temporary assignment for the *Indiana* to strengthen the blockading-line during the landing and to avoid any possibility of the enemy breaking through should he attempt to get out of the port.

"The *Suwanee*, *Osceola*, and *Wompatuck* will be prepared to tow boats. Each will be provided with two 5 or 6 inch lines, one on each quarter, each long enough to take in tow a dozen or more boats.

"These vessels will report at the *New York* at 3 A.M. on June 22, prepared to take in tow the ship's boats, which are to assist in the landing of troops, and convey them to Daiquiri.

"The *Texas*, *Brooklyn*, *Massachusetts*, *Iowa*, *Oregon*, *New York*, and *Indiana* will send all their steam-cutters and all their pulling boats, with the exception of one retained on board each ship, to assist in the landing. These boats will report at the *New York* at 3 A.M.

"Each boat, whale-boat, and cutter will have three men, each launch five men, and each steam-cutter its full crew and an officer for their own management. In addition to these men each boat will carry five men, including one man capable of acting as cockswain, to manage and direct the transports' boats. Each steam-launch will be in charge of an officer, who will report to Captain Goodrich. Care will be taken in the selection of boat-keepers and cockswains to take no men who are gun-pointers or who occupy positions of special importance at the battery.

"Unnecessary oars and impedimenta should be removed from the pulling boats for the greater convenience of the transportation of troops, but each boat should retain its anchor and chain.

"Captain C. F. Goodrich, commanding the *St. Louis*, will have, on the part of the navy, general charge of the landing.

"The *New Orleans* will send her boats to report to Captain Goodrich upon her arrival at Daiquiri.

"The attention of commanding officers of all vessels engaged in blockading Santiago de Cuba is earnestly called to the necessity of the utmost vigilance from this time forward, both as to maintaining stations and readiness for action, and as to keeping a close watch upon the harbor mouth. If the Spanish Admiral ever intends to attempt to escape, that attempt will be made soon."

On the 22d I received the following letter from General Shafter:

"HEADQUARTERS FIFTH ARMY CORPS,
"On board S.S. *Seguranca*,
"At Sea, *June 22, 1898*.

"SIR,—I shall commence landing this morning. It is my intention to proceed from Daiquiri to Santiago as rapidly as I can and take some of my land transportation. The animals are in absolute need of some rest, and for that reason I may not get very far to-day.

"I request you to keep in touch during the advance and be prepared to receive any message I may wish to transmit from along the bluffs or any of the small towns, and to render any assistance necessary.

"Very respectfully,
"W. R. SHAFTER,
"Major-General, U. S. V., Commanding.

"Admiral SAMPSON,
"Commanding U. S. Fleet off Santiago de Cuba."

THE *PORTER* WITH THE SQUADRON, AWAITING THE ADMIRAL'S ORDERS

ENGAGEMENT BETWEEN THE *ST. PAUL* AND THE *TERROR*

As Related by Captain Sigsbee

ON June 19 the *St. Paul*, having transferred many of her own stores and some arms and ammunition to other vessels, parted company with our squadron off Santiago de Cuba. Under orders from the Commander-in-Chief, I proceeded to San Juan, Puerto Rico, to institute a blockade of that port. My orders included the information that the *Yosemite*, Commander W. H. Emory, would soon join

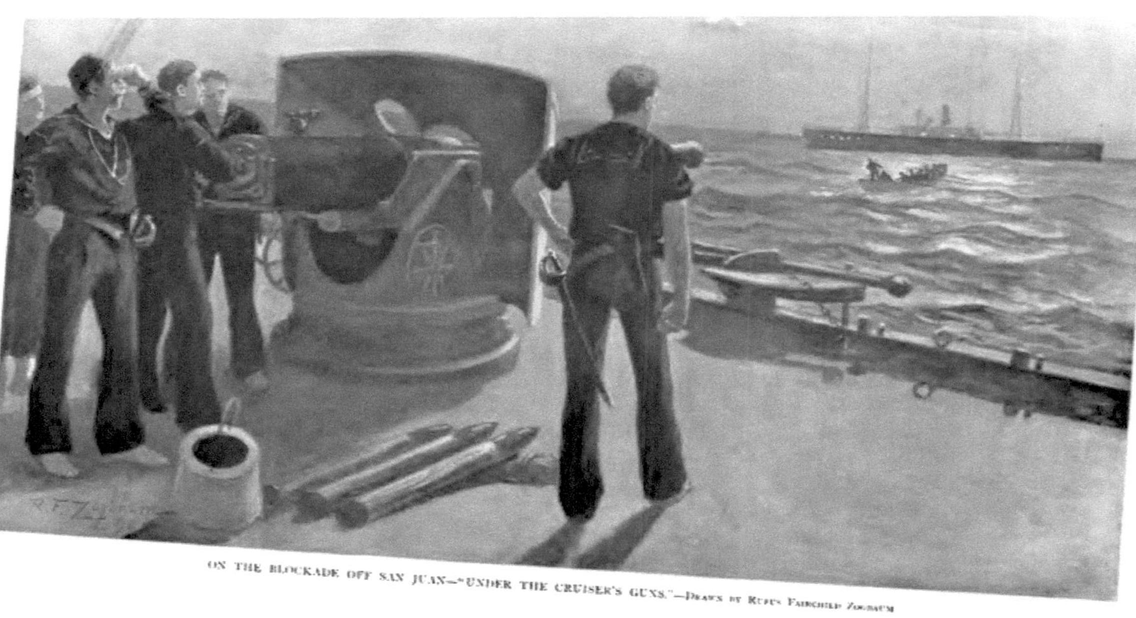

ON THE BLOCKADE OFF SAN JUAN—"UNDER THE CRUISER'S GUNS."—Drawn by Rufus Fairchild Zogbaum

the *St. Paul* off San Juan, thus enabling me to proceed to New York for coal, the necessity for which would soon arise. The *St. Paul*, with a view of intercepting Spanish vessels, proceeded at a moderate speed by the route south of Haiti and through the Mona Passage. She was unsuccessful in her search, and arrived off San Juan at 8 A.M., Wednesday, June 22, at which time the weather was clear, a strong trade-wind was blowing, and the sea was moderately rough.

At 12.40 P.M. of that day our emergency signal for manning the guns was sounded by direction of the officer of the deck, Lieutenant J. A. Pattson. I went at once to the bridge, where I was shown a bark-rigged Spanish cruiser making slowly out of the entrance of San Juan, with her head to the eastward. She was either the *Infanta Isabel* or *Isabel II.*, which were sister-ships of the *Don Juan de Austria*, sunk at Manila. The *St. Paul* was lying without headway, head to the wind, which was east. She held her position, while the Spanish cruiser steamed slowly seaward, manœuvred, and opened fire at long range, under close protection of the shore batteries, which mounted a large number of modern 8-inch and 10-inch guns. None of the Spaniard's shot reached us on direct fire, although several may have passed over us on ricochet. The *St. Paul* replied only by an occasional shell to test the range; nevertheless, the Spanish cruiser continued her ineffective fire.

At 1 P.M. a torpedo-boat destroyer, having the characteristic marks of the *Terror* and believed to be that vessel, came out of the harbor and steamed around the Morro to the eastward. The *St. Paul* then steamed very slowly to the eastward, parallel to the shore-line of the city, keeping the *Terror* on such a bearing that in making a dash at the *St. Paul* she would be obliged to proceed in the trough of the sea. Our manœuvre had the further object of throwing the Spanish cruiser completely out of range to the southward and westward while we engaged the *Terror*. About 1.20 P.M. the *Terror*, then nearly in reach of our heavier guns, the fire of which I was reserving, suddenly opened fire and steamed for us at high speed, with the evident intention of making a dash to torpedo the *St. Paul*. The *St. Paul* held her position practically without headway, head to the eastward, and awaited the attack. When the *Terror* was 5400 yards distant the *St. Paul* opened fire, the accuracy and volume of which were admirable. Although the distance was great, it was apparent that our heavier shells were falling rapidly around the *Terror* and close to her. Suddenly that vessel headed up into the wind, broadside to the *St. Paul*, as if injured, but kept up a fire from her battery, her shot falling short. I was looking at her from the upper bridge with binocular glasses of great power, and at this time I saw a shell explode, apparently against her hull abaft the after smoke-stack. She immediately turned with port helm and stood in for the harbor at considerable speed, her behavior giving evidence of damage. Instead of standing in through the channel close to the Morro, whence she had issued to begin her attack, she fell a long distance to leeward. When down towards Cabras Island, she rounded to and stood to the southward and eastward towards the harbor, apparently not under good management. The Spanish cruiser showed concern by standing in after her.

I was afterwards informed from different sources that the *Terror* was taken in tow by two tugs on her arrival in the harbor, and that she was in a sinking condition. One informant said that she was grounded for safety and her crew sent ashore, and pumps sent to her assistance. All accounts agree that she was struck three times, and that one of her engineers and one of her crew were killed. I was also informed that others of her crew were wounded, that much damage was done, and that repairs were immediately begun and were continuing day and night. One shot was said to have raked her deck and another to have gone through her side into her after engine-room. Her rudder or steering-gear was said to have been injured. Although my information came from persons who saw the exterior of the vessel after her return to the harbor, I was naturally not able to get a technical description of her internal injuries. A large number of people were assembled on the high bluff of San Juan to see the engagement.

After the *Terror* had reached the harbor, the cruiser reappeared outside accompanied by a gunboat. Both stood round the Morro and continued slowly for a considerable distance to the eastward, well inshore and far beyond the range of the *St. Paul's* guns. So well within the range of the San Juan batteries were they that I could see no reason for their manœuvre except to decoy the *St. Paul* within fire of the batteries. At this time the *St. Paul* was heading west, practically in her former position, but occasionally gathering slight headway to maintain the wind and sea directly astern. At 4.45 P.M. the *St. Paul* was turned and headed east, on a course nearly parallel to that which the Spanish vessels were apparently steering. Those vessels immediately turned and then retired to the harbor. During the entire affair the *St. Paul* maintained her position near the city. She was not hit.

The rapid and accurate fire brought to bear on the *Terror* by the *St. Paul*, whose crew had been under drill less than one month and a half against adverse conditions, reflected great credit on the executive officer, Lieutenant Commander Wm. H. Driggs, and on the divisional officers, Lieutenants J. M. Poyer, R. Osborn, Geo. Young, H. Dixon, and Ensigns C. S. Bookwalter, W. V. N. Powelson, and A. L. Cowell. The *St. Paul*, by reason of her great complexity of arrangement and the remoteness of many of her parts from the bridge, was a difficult and trying command in that sphere of action. It therefore gratified me greatly to find that her discipline and skill had been demonstrated to be good in emergency.

The following gentlemen were on the bridge with me at the time, in readiness for service, and their bearing was entirely admirable: Lieutenant J. C. Gillmore, U. S. N., navigator; Lieutenant S. Nicholson Kane, U. S. N., captain's aid and signal officer; Ensign O. P. Jackson, U. S. N., assistant navigator.

Chief Engineer John Hunter, U. S. N., whose position was one of great prospective responsibility under the circumstances, should also be mentioned most favorably.

Although the *St. Paul* was an enormous ship, she had not a great battery. At the time of the action she underwent the novel experience of receiving and accepting the dash of the torpedo-boat destroyer.

EXTRACT FROM "THE WAR BUDGET"

(A periodical printed on the *St. Paul*)

WE came off the port early on the 22d. The weather was fair, the trade-wind blowing fresh from the eastward and raising somewhat of a sea. At about 12.30 the third-class cruiser *Isabel II.*, or one of her class, came out and, steaming under the Morro until she was abreast of the batteries, commenced edging out towards us, firing at such a long range that her shots were ineffective. As her purpose evidently was to put us within fire of the batteries, we took but little notice of her, lying still and occasionally sending in our largest shell at her to try the range. Soon afterwards she dropped to the westward, and the torpedo-boat destroyer *Terror*, or it may have been her sister-ship the *Furor*, was sighted steaming along shore under the batteries. Captain Sigsbee watched her for a while and worked along with her in order to separate her from the cruiser and keep her in the trough of the sea if she came for us. She then circled to get up speed and headed for us, firing straight as far as direction went, but her shots fell short. When within range of our guns the signal "Commence firing" was made, and for several minutes we let fly our starboard battery at her at from fifty-five hundred to six thousand yards, the shells striking all around her. This stopped her; she turned her broadside to us, and her fire soon ceased. She then headed inshore to the southward and westward, going slow, and it was evident to all on board that she was crippled, drifting well leeward of the main harbor entrance. Off the Morro she flashed some signals to the shore, and afterwards a tug came out and towed her into the harbor.

All this time the cruiser was firing at us, and some of her shots and those of the *Terror* fell pretty close. The cruiser followed the *Terror* back towards the port, and soon afterwards was joined by a gunboat, and the two steamed under the batteries to the eastward. But when the *St. Paul*, making an inshore turn, seemed to be going for them, they returned to the harbor and we saw no more of them.

The Spaniards seemed to have settled this whole matter in advance as they wished to have it, for the towns-people came out on the bluffs to see the Yankee driven off or sunk, and the cruiser flew an ensign at her gaff almost as big as a maintopsail.

The *Isabel* is bark-rigged and carries four 4.7-inch breech-loading rifles, four 2.5-inch breech-loading rifles, eight machine-guns, and two torpedo-tubes. The *Terror* has two 14-pounders, rapid fire; two 6-pounders, rapid fire; two 1-pounders, automatic Maxims, and two torpedo-tubes. Length, 220 feet; estimated speed, 28 knots.

We know that the *Terror* was struck three times, and that one shot, entering the engine-room, killed an engineer and a fireman. And from what we regard as trustworthy information, we are inclined to think that she was seriously damaged, requiring the assistance of tugs to keep her afloat.

THE *YOSEMITE* AT SAN JUAN

By Gunner's Mate Edwin Denby

On the 13th day of April, 1898, the United States auxiliary cruiser *Yosemite*, prior to that

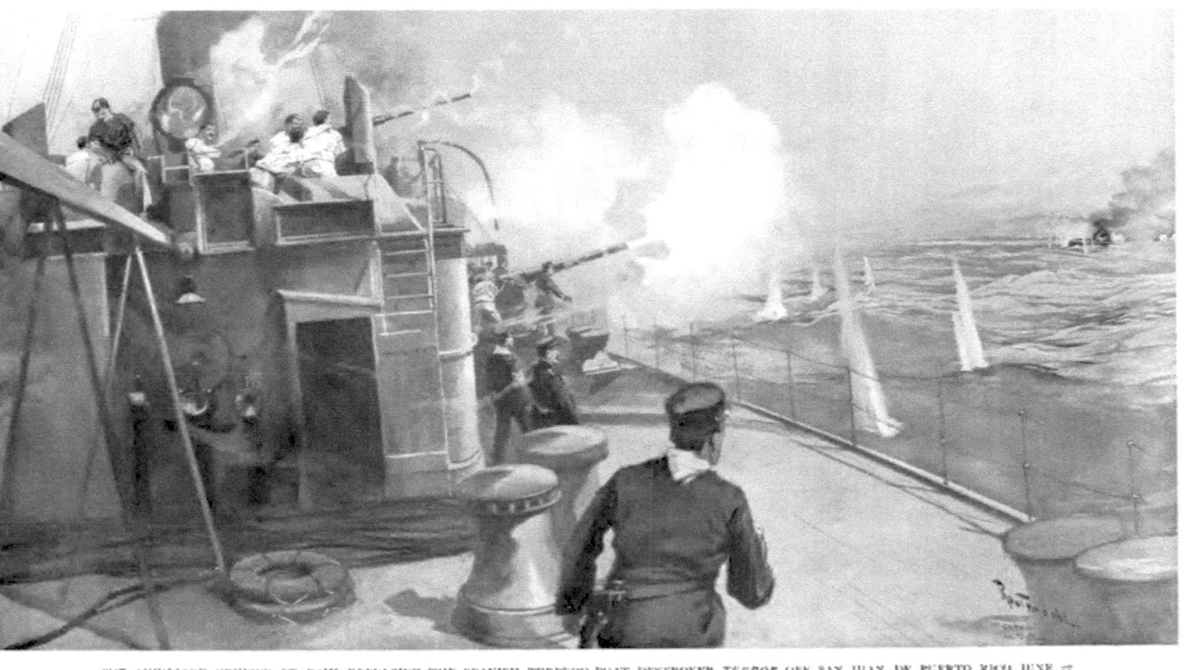

THE AUXILIARY CRUISER *ST. PAUL* REPULSING THE SPANISH TORPEDO-BOAT DESTROYER *TERROR* OFF SAN JUAN DE PUERTO RICO, JUNE 22

Drawn by H. Reuterdahl from Descriptions and Sketches by Captain Sigsbee, Commanding the *St. Paul*

time *El Sud*, of the Morgan line of freighters, was put into commission in the government service.

She was a steel steamer, 408 feet in length, single screw, 15 knots speed. She was built in 1895, and was stanch from stem to stern. The work of converting her went on rapidly.

It may be of interest to recite briefly what it means to convert a vessel of the merchant marine into a fighting ship of war. There was no armor put upon the *Yosemite*, the only attempt at protection being the storing of several hundred bags of coal around the engines on the berth-deck. Three magazines were built in the hold, from which steam ammunition-hoists—little steel boxes running in ways of steel—led to the decks above. Numbered hooks for the hammocks of the crew were put in the deck beams.

Ten 5-inch, six 6-pounder rapid-fire guns, and two Colt's automatic machine-guns, formed her armament.

On May 7th her crew, consisting of the Michigan State Naval Brigade, were received aboard and assisted the yard workmen in the alterations and additions indicated. These were completed on May 17th. On that day the ship, which had gone into dock a dirty merchantman, fresh from a trading venture, came out a spotless gray man-of-war, ready for whatever service her country might demand. It may be noted in passing that the vessels of the navy had begun to receive their "war paint" as early as the month of March, in accordance with the following circular letter dated the 27th: "All vessels except torpedo-boats will be painted lead-color. Commanding officers can obtain a sample color by sending to flag-ship if not otherwise supplied. Boats, guns, hand-rails will not be painted at present. The order applies to hull, superstructures, masts, and smoke-stacks, etc."

The *Yosemite* was manned by 239 men, of whom all but captain, executive officer, navigator, one ensign, lieutenant of marines, and marine guard of forty men were members of the Naval Brigade, recruited mainly in the cities of Detroit and Saginaw.

Ship and crew were therefore well matched, both fresh from the walks of peace.

Except in actual battle the crew had but one opportunity for target practice with service ammunition, and that was on the occasion of trying the guns, when thirty-one 5-inch common, and eighteen 6-pound A. P. shells were expended.

The deeds of the *Yosemite* rendered her position an eminent one in the naval history of the war. She was on the Havana and Santiago blockades. She convoyed the *Panther* from Havana to Guantanamo, and assisted with her boats and under her guns in the landing of the marines. These marines there effected the first successful American footing on Cuban soil during the war. Their gallant seventy-two hours' fight against odds will forever reflect honor upon the corps. And here also occurred, on June 10th, one of those simple deeds of bravery that seem to come so naturally to our sailors, volunteer or regular, that mention of them is scarcely necessary.

The steam-launches of the *Yosemite*, *Marblehead*, and *Scorpion* were sent up the river towards Caimanera, and there patrolled throughout the night, in constant danger from the enemy's mines, under the guns of his fort and in range of his Mausers. Their purpose was to watch for attempts by the Spaniards at torpedoing our vessels. A noise, a spark, a betrayal by the enemy's patrols, and they were lost; but morning came, and with it they returned in safety.

The *Yosemite's* crowning achievement was the victorious battle which she waged against heavy odds, 700 miles from the nearest assistance.

At 2 o'clock P.M. on June 25th the *Yosemite* arrived off the harbor of San Juan de Puerto Rico. She found there the great auxiliary cruiser *St. Paul* maintaining a blockade of the port.

The *St. Paul* stated that two days before she had had a battle with the torpedo-boat destroyer *Terror*, and that one of her batteries was out of order. The two ships took station on either side of the San Juan Harbor mouth and there spent the night. The next day the *St. Paul* ranged alongside the *Yosemite*, within hailing distance, and Captain Sigsbee said, through his megaphone, that he was short of coal, and one of his batteries was out of order, and that he would sail at once for New York; he added that the *Yosemite* was in a very dangerous position, as he had heard from the captain of a vessel overhauled that the *Terror* was being repaired and would be out again in a few days. He stated that her captain was a very brave man, and that the *Yosemite* might surely expect an attack. He would telegraph Admiral Sampson for immediate reinforcements, as one ship was entirely inadequate for the work at San Juan. Repeating that the *Yosemite* was in a very dangerous position and admonishing the utmost caution, Captain Sigsbee steamed away.

Consider the situation: An absolutely unprotected auxiliary cruiser left alone in front of the strongest fortress in the Spanish West Indies, where also lay at least two cruisers, each of a strength almost equal to her own, besides the notorious torpedo-boat destroyer *Terror*—and the nearest help 700 miles away!

However, with brazen impudence she took up her station and began the blockade with vigor. It must have appeared like a joke to the Spaniards. The Supreme Court of the United States has taken that view of it, or at least has declared that such a blockade was "no blockade." But at the time the joke was on the Yellow and Red, and a decidedly practical one it proved.

The *Yosemite* passed to and fro during the day just out of range of the guns of the Morro, overhauling every sail that appeared in sight. At night she would put to sea some miles and keep moving to elude the enemy's torpedo-boats, which there was strong reason to suppose came out on several occasions to find her. Then as dawn approached she would return to her station off San Juan.

On the morning of the 28th day of June, just as the shaggy cloud-fringed dawn was giving place to daylight, the *Yosemite* arrived north of the Morro, about eight miles to sea. She was enveloped in a rain-storm, and a black cloud rolled over her. As the cloud passed away there was seen stealing towards the harbor from the west a large three-masted steamer, about twelve miles distant, which was subsequently learned to have been the *Antonio Lopez*. In order to intercept her the *Yosemite* must cross the zone of Morro's fire. This she started to do at full speed, making for a point some distance ahead of the blockade-runner.

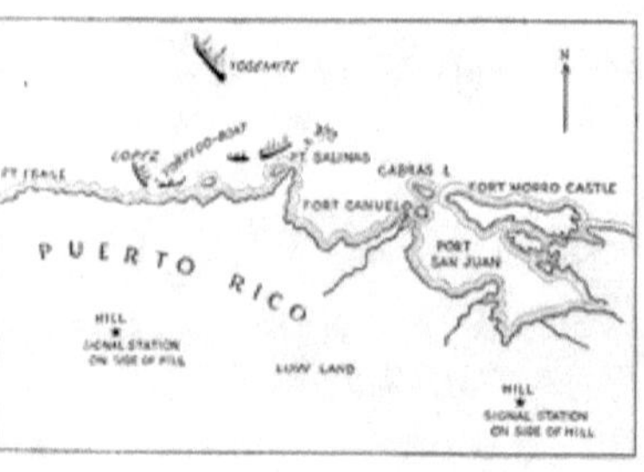

SAN JUAN HARBOR—POSITION OF VESSELS, JUNE 28

As soon as it was practicable a shot from one of the *Yosemite's* bow guns was fired across the bow of the stranger, and a second in rapid succession. The answer was a cloud of black smoke from the stack of the enemy. She was running for it in full earnest, and only quick work could stop her.

The *Yosemite* needed all her speed. As soon as it became clear that it was to be a fight instead of a capture, the order to fire on the stranger was given, and 6-pound shells flew like flies from the starboard battery.

At almost the same moment the *Lopez*, evidently becoming convinced that she could not make the harbor, turned and dashed ashore full speed at a point about six miles west of the Morro.

The *Yosemite* then approached within about four miles of the stranded vessel and proceeded to pour shells into her. Her crew put ashore very hastily in the small boats. In the meantime, over the face of the distant gun-pierced cliff a white cloud suddenly obtruded, and the roar of a great gun told that the Morro had opened. Thirty-five seconds after the appearance of the smoke, a huge projectile dropped into the sea in perfect line, and distant from the *Yosemite* not more than one hundred yards. Morro continued to fire with vicious frequency and accuracy during the entire engagement.

The guns of the American vessel could not reach the far larger-caliber battery on the hill. So she continued manœuvring rapidly to avoid being struck, firing meanwhile into the *Lopez*. And then, having completed the destruction of the *Lopez*, and as the fire from the Morro was becoming uncomfortably close, she retired out of range, and the ship's company went to breakfast.

ENGAGEMENT BETWEEN THE *YOSEMITE* AND THE SPANISH FORTS AND WAR-VESSELS AT SAN JUAN, JUNE 28

In half an hour the *Yosemite* returned to the attack. In the meantime the protected cruiser *Alfonso XIII.*, the cruiser *Isabel II.*, the gunboat *General Concha*, and a torpedo-boat had emerged from the harbor and were making for the stranded steamer. They opened fire immediately upon the *Yosemite* and were reinforced, as before, by the Morro.

Their guns, as well as those of the fort, were of larger caliber than the 5-inch rapid-fires of the American. But this was a disadvantage easily remedied. Whirling fiercely upon the enemy, she dashed at them in the teeth of a heavy fire. As soon as she came within range a perfect whirlwind of fire swept from the five 5-inch and three 6-pounders composing her broadside batteries, first port and then starboard, as she changed position to allow the guns to cool. The guns were served with terrible rapidity. The ship was enveloped in smoke from stem to stern. The roar of the 5-inch and the bark of the 6-pounder guns seemed almost continuous. From the Morro and the enemy's vessels came the steady thunder of their great ordnance. But the American fire was too rapid and accurate to be long withstood. The Spanish vessels ceased to advance, and presently the smaller of the two, taking a heavy list to port, turned and staggered back into the harbor, while the cruiser retired near to the mouth of the harbor and discontinued the engagement.

COMMANDER WILLIAM H. EMORY
Of the *Yosemite*

But the little torpedo vessel, with the intrepidity usually associated with vessels of her type, came down the coast in a shower of projectiles and hid behind the *Lopez*. Then she stuck her nose out and spat at the *Yosemite* with a small-caliber rapid-fire gun.

Victorious and unscathed, the *Yosemite* then withdrew out of range of the Morro, firing a few more shots at the *Lopez* in passing. For the rest of the day she strutted up and down with battle-flags flying and a chip on her shoulder, waiting for the Spaniards to come out and renew the engagement. Once it seemed they would gratify her. They started to move down the coast, but, noticing a significant movement of the American vessel, they again withdrew.

What execution was done upon the enemy it is impossible to say. The American vessel was not touched, though at least fifteen shots fell within less than half a ship's length, and several fell so close that they splashed water upon her decks.

She expended in this action two hundred and fifty-one 5-inch shells, common and armor-piercing, twenty-three shrapnel, and fifty-six 6-pounders.

The action was in every sense an American victory, and the Spaniards, greatly superior in force though they were, made no attempt again to molest the *Yosemite*.

On the 4th of July the American vessel, lying as usual just out of range of the Morro, ran up her flags and fired a national salute at high noon.

The *Yosemite* remained alone at San Juan, overhauling many vessels but making no capt-

COMMANDER CHARLES H. DAVIS
Of the *Dixie*

LIEUTENANT SPENCER S. WOOD
Of the *Dupont*

ures, until July 14th, when she was relieved by the *New Orleans*, and her men heard for the first time the story of Cervera's defeat. She was attached to Watson's squadron for Spain, but the squadron never sailed. Her crew was discharged August 22d, and was received in Detroit upon its return with the most tremendous demonstration which the city had ever seen.

After the close of hostilities between the United States and Spain the *Yosemite* was again converted, this time into a sumptuous man-of-war yacht to convey the new Governor of Guam to his station, and to serve thereafter as his war-vessel and headquarters. She was admirably adapted to her new service.

THE CUBANS AT SANTIAGO

As Related by General Miles

Lieutenant Rowan, returning from his journey to Cuba, brought with him to Washington Brigadier-General Collazo and Lieutenant-Colonel Hernandez, of General Garcia's staff. He also brought very important information concerning the active operations of the Cubans against the Spanish troops, and the location and strength of the Spanish forces in the eastern part of Cuba, numbering at that time some 31,000 men. The two Cuban officers mentioned accompanied me to Tampa, and Colonel Hernandez, having received permission from the Navy Department to be conveyed by a United States vessel to the harbor of Banes, carried the following letter from me to General Garcia:

"Dear General,—I am very glad to have received your officers, General Enrique Collazo and Lieutenant-Colonel Carlos Hernandez, the latter of whom returns to-night with our best wishes for your success.

"It would be a very great assistance if you could have as large a force as possible in the vicinity of the harbor of Santiago de Cuba, and communicate any information by signals, which Colonel Hernandez will explain to you, either to our navy or to our army on its arrival, which we hope will be before many days.

"It would also assist us very much if you could drive in and harass any Spanish troops near or in Santiago de Cuba, threatening or attacking them at all points, and preventing, by every means, any possible reinforcement coming to that garrison. While this is being done, and before the arrival of our army, if you can seize and hold any commanding positions to the east or west of Santiago de Cuba, or both, that would be advantageous for the use of our artillery, it will be exceedingly gratifying to us.

"With great respect and best wishes, I remain, very respectfully,

"Nelson A. Miles,
"*Major-General, Commanding United States Army.*"

COMMANDER CHARLES J. TRAIN
Of the *Prairie*

This letter was sent in anticipation of the movement of the command under General Shafter, which sailed twelve days later. Colonel Hernandez left Key West with it June 2; General Garcia received it June 6, and I received his reply by cable June 9, of which the following is a copy:

"Will take measures at once to carry out your recommendation, but concentration of force will require some time. Roads bad and Cubans scattered. Will march without delay. Santiago de Cuba well fortified with advanced intrenchments, but believe good artillery position can be taken. Spanish force approximate 12,000 between Santiago de Cuba and Guantanamo; 3000 militia. Will maintain a Cuban force near Holguin to prevent sending reinforcements to Santiago."

Also, the following is an extract from a cablegram from Admiral Sampson to the Secretary of the Navy, which was repeated to me at Tampa, June 12, for my information:

"General Miles's letter received through Colonel Hernandez on June 6. Garcia regards his wishes and suggestions as orders, and immediately will take measures to concentrate forces at the points indicated, but he is unable to do so as early as desired on account of his expedition to Banes Port, Cuba, but he will march without delay. All of his subordinates are ordered to assist to disembark the United States troops and to place themselves under orders. Santiago de Cuba well fortified, with advanced intrenchments, but he believes position for artillery can be taken as Miles desires. (Approximate) twelve thousand (12,000) regulars and three thousand (3000) militia between Santiago and Guantanamo. He has sent force in order to prevent aid going to Santiago from Holguin. Repeats every assurance of good-will, and desires to second plans."

It will be observed that General Garcia regarded my requests as his orders, and promptly took steps to execute the plan of operations. He sent 3000 men to check any movement of the 12,000 Spaniards stationed at Holguin. A portion of this latter force started to the relief of the garrison at Santiago, but was successfully checked and turned back by the Cuban forces under General Feria. General Garcia also sent 2000 men, under Perez, to oppose the 6000 Spaniards at Guantanamo, and they were successful in their object. He also sent 1000 men, under General Rios, against the 6000 men at Manzanillo. Of this garrison, 3500 started to reinforce the garrison at Santiago, and were engaged in no less than thirty combats with the Cubans on their way before reaching Santiago. With an additional force of 5000 men General Garcia besieged the garrison of Santiago, taking up a strong position on the west side and in close proximity to the harbor, and he afterwards received General Shafter and Admiral Sampson at his camp near that place. He had troops in the rear, as well as on both sides, of the garrison at Santiago before the arrival of our troops.

SOLDIERS OF THE CUBAN ARMY
From a Photograph taken at the time of the landing of the American army

GENERAL GARCIA AND BRIG.-GENERAL LUDLOW
Taken during their conference at the time of the landing of the American army

GENERAL SHAFTER AND ADMIRAL SAMPSON LANDING ON THE BEACH AT ASERRADERO, JUNE 20, TO CONFER WITH GENERAL GARCIA.—By T. de Thulstrup

MAJOR-GENERAL WILLIAM R. SHAFTER, COMMANDING THE FIFTH ARMY CORPS, DIRECTING THE EMBARKATION OF TROOPS AT PORT TAMPA.—Drawn by T. de Thulstrup

THE INVASION OF CUBA

IN the month of May the Navy Department advised Admiral Sampson of the intention of the War Department to send about thirty transports with troops from Tampa to Santiago, and instructed him to provide a suitable convoy.

On June 4, in reply to a telegram from the Navy Department asking if the convoy was ready, the commandant of the naval base at Key West stated, "Vessels all ready."

On June 8 information was received at Tampa, through the naval base at Key West, from two different sources, indicating the possible presence of a force of Spanish vessels in St. Nicholas Channel. The War Department was informed of this news, and orders were issued to Admiral Sampson to reinforce the convoying squadron by two armored vessels. On the next day the expedition was directed to proceed without regard to this information, as it was discredited both by Admiral Sampson and the department, and the following telegram was sent:

"The expedition will proceed without reference to the Spaniards. Department will inform Commander-in-Chief North Atlantic Station and the War Department of this."

A suitable convoy was retained at Tampa until the transports were ready. The army expedition finally left Tampa on the 14th, the

Navy Department having rendezvoused additional vessels off Rebecca Shoals, where the transports arrived at 8 P.M. June 15, and thence proceeded to Santiago.

Upon arrival of the convoy off Santiago Admiral Sampson sent his chief of staff to communicate with General Shafter. The chief of staff took with him a chart of Santiago Harbor, and explained to General Shafter that, in order to enable the vessels of the navy to enter, it was necessary that the positions occupied by the eastern and western batteries of the enemy should be carried. The possession of these points insured the destruction of the mines, the entrance of the naval vessels, and an attack upon Admiral Cervera's squadron. To this plan General Shafter gave cordial assent. The landing-place on which he finally decided was Daiquiri.

TRANSFERRING STORES FROM TRAIN TO TRANSPORTS
Photograph by James Burton

General Shafter reported to Admiral Sampson on June 22 his intention to commence the landing of troops, and Admiral Sampson put an officer in charge of the disembarkation, which was begun during the forenoon of the 22d by means of the steam-launches and cutters from the ships of the squadron. The naval vessels shelled the coast about Daiquiri, and a demonstration was made at Cabañas to engage the attention of the enemy. All the troops were successfully landed by the boats of the navy, and the joint operations of the army and navy began, which finally resulted in the surrender of Santiago.

THE EXPEDITION TO SANTIAGO

As Related by General Shafter

The expedition was undertaken in compliance with telegraphic instructions of May 30, 1898, from Headquarters of the Army, in which it was stated: "Admiral Schley reports that two cruisers and two torpedo-boats have been seen in the harbor of Santiago. Go with your force to capture garrison at Santiago, and assist in capturing harbor and fleet."

On this date there were a large number of transports in Port Tampa Bay, which had been collected for the purpose of an expedition which it had been previously contemplated I should command, and for such other emergencies as might arise. Orders were immediately given for loading aboard those transports the necessary subsistence and quartermaster's supplies, and for the embarkation of the authorized number of troops and their material. General orders from headquarters, indicating the organizations it was at first proposed to take, were as follows:

"The following troops will hold themselves in readiness to move immediately on board transports upon notification from these headquarters:

"1. The Fifth Army Corps.

"2. The Battalion of Engineers.

"3. The detachment of the Signal Corps.

"4. Five squadrons of cavalry, to be selected by the commanding general of the cavalry division, in accordance with instructions previously given.

"5. Four batteries of light artillery, to be commanded by a major to be selected by the commanding officer of the Light Artillery Brigade.

"6. Two batteries of heavy artillery, to be selected by the commanding officer of the siege artillery battalion, with eight siege guns and eight field mortars.

"7. The Battalion of Engineers, the infantry and cavalry, will be supplied with five hundred rounds of ammunition per man.

"8. All troops will carry, in addition to the fourteen days' field rations now on hand, ten days' travel rations.

"9. The minimum allowance of tentage and baggage, as prescribed in General Orders 54, Adjutant-General's Office, current series, will be taken.

"10. In addition to the rations specified in paragraph 8 of this order, the chief commissary will provide sixty days' field rations for the entire command.

"11. All recruits' and extra baggage, the latter to be stored, carefully piled and covered, will be left in camp, in charge of a commissioned officer, to be selected by the regimental commander. Where there are no recruits available, the necessary guard only will be left.

"12. Travel rations will be drawn at once by the several commands, as indicated in paragraph 8."

This order was afterwards changed to include twelve squadrons of cavalry, all of which were dismounted because of lack of transportation for the animals, and because it was believed from the best sources of information obtainable that mounted cavalry could not operate efficiently in the neighborhood of Santiago. This was found subsequently to be correct.

The facilities at Tampa and Port Tampa for embarking the troops and the large amount of supplies required were inadequate, and with the utmost effort it was not possible to accomplish this work as quickly as I hoped and desired.

On the evening of June 7 I received orders to sail without delay, but not with less than 10,000 men.

The orders referred to caused one division

HOW THE ROUGH RIDERS RODE ROUGHLY TO PORT TAMPA—Photograph by James Burton

composed of volunteer troops—commanded by Brigadier-General Snyder, and which it had been intended to include in my command—to be left behind. I was joined, however, by Brigadier-General Bates, who had already arrived on transports from Mobile with the Third and Twentieth Infantry, and one squadron of the Second Cavalry, with their horses—the latter being the only mounted troops in my command.

After some of the transports had already reached the lower bay, telegraphic instructions were received from the Secretary of War directing that the sailing of the expedition be delayed waiting further orders. This delay was occasioned by the navy reporting that a Spanish war-vessel had been sighted in the St. Nicholas Channel. The ships in the lower bay were immediately recalled. On the next day, in compliance with instructions from the Adjutant-General of the Army, the necessary steps were taken to increase the command to the full capacity of the transports, and the expedition sailed on June 14 with 813 officers and 16,072 enlisted men.

The passage to Santiago was generally smooth and uneventful. The health of the command remained remarkably good, notwithstanding the fact that the conveniences on many of the transports, in the nature of sleeping accommodations, space for exercise, and closet accommodations, were not all that could have been desired. While commenting upon this subject, it is appropriate to add that the opinion was general throughout the army that the travel ration should include tomatoes, beginning with the first day, and that a small quantity of canned fruit would prove to be a most welcome addition while travelling at sea in the tropics; if the future policy of our government requires much transportation for the military forces by sea, definite arrangements should be determined upon to provide the necessary hammock accommodations for sleeping. Hammocks interfere immeasurably less than bunks with the proper ventilation of the ships, and during the day can be easily removed, thus greatly increasing space for exercise; moreover, they greatly diminish the danger of fire.

While passing along the north coast of Cuba, one of the two barges we had in tow broke away during the night, and was not recovered. This loss proved to be very serious, for it delayed and embarrassed the disembarkation of the army. On the morning of June 20 we arrived off Guantanamo Bay, and about noon reached the vicinity of Santiago, where Admiral Sampson came on board my headquarters transport. It was arranged between us to visit in the afternoon the Cuban general, Garcia, at Aserraderos, about eighteen miles to the west of the Morro. During the interview General Garcia offered the services of his troops, comprising about 4000 men in the vicinity of Aserraderos, and about 500 under General Castillo at the little town of Cujababo, a few miles east of Daiquiri. I accepted his offer, impressing it upon him that I could exercise no military control over him except such as he would concede, and as long as he served under me I would furnish him rations and ammunition.

Ever since the receipt of my orders I had made a study of the terrain surrounding Santiago, gathering information mainly from former residents of the city, several of whom were on the transports with me. At this interview all the possible points of attack were for the last time carefully weighed, and then, for the information and guidance of Admiral Sampson and General Garcia, I outlined the plan of campaign, which was as follows:

With the assistance of the small boats of the navy, the disembarkation was to commence on the morning of the 22d at Daiquiri. On the 21st 500 insurgent troops were to be transferred from Aserraderos to Cujababo, increasing the force already there to 1000 men. This force under General Castillo was to attack the Spanish force at Daiquiri in the rear at the time of disembarkation. This movement was successfully made. To mislead the enemy as to the real point of our intended landing, I requested General Garcia to send a small force, about 500 men, under General Rabi, to attack the little town of Cabanas, situated on the coast a few miles to the west of the entrance to Santiago Harbor, and where it was reported the

OFF TO SANTIAGO—ON THE DOCK AT PORT TAMPA—LOADING THE TRANSPORTS.—Photograph by James Burton

enemy had several hundred men intrenched, and from which a trail led around the west side of the bay to Santiago.

I also requested Admiral Sampson to send several of his war-ships, with a number of my transports, opposite this town for the purpose of making a show of disembarking there. In addition I asked the Admiral to cause a bombardment to be made at Cabañas, and also at the forts around the Morro, and at the towns of Aguadores, Siboney, and Daiquiri. The troops under General Garcia remaining at Aserradetos were to be transferred to Daiquiri or Siboney on the 24th. This was successfully accomplished at Siboney.

SECOND MASSACHUSETTS VOLUNTEERS WAITING TO GO ABOARD TRANSPORT.—Photograph by James Burton

These movements committed me to approaching Santiago from the east over a narrow road, at first in some places not better than a trail, running from Daiquiri through Siboney and Sevilla, and making attack from that quarter. This, in my judgment, was the only feasible plan, and subsequent information and results confirmed my judgment.

On the morning of the 22d the army commenced to disembark at Daiquiri. The following general order indicates the manner in which the troops left the transports, and the amount of supplies carried immediately with them:

"1. Under instructions to be communicated to the proper commanders, troops will disembark in the following order:

"First. The Second Division, Fifth Corps (Lawton's). The Gatling-gun detachment will accompany this division.

"Second. General Bates's brigade. This brigade will form as a reserve to the Second Division, Fifth Corps.

"Third. The dismounted cavalry division (Wheeler's).

"Fourth. The First Division, Fifth Corps (Kent's).

"Fifth. The squadron of the Second Cavalry (Rafferty's).

"Sixth. If the enemy in force vigorously resist the landing, the light artillery, or part of it, will be disembarked by the battalion commander and brought to the assistance of the troops engaged. If no serious opposition be offered, this artillery will be unloaded after the mounted squadron.

"2. All troops will carry on the person the blanket roll (with shelter tent and poncho), three days' field rations (with coffee ground), canteens filled, and 100 rounds of ammunition per man. Additional ammunition, already issued to the troops, tentage, baggage, and company cooking utensils will be left under charge of the regimental quartermaster, with one non-commissioned officer and two privates from each company.

"3. All persons not immediately on duty with, and constituting a part of, the organizations mentioned in the foregoing paragraphs will remain aboard ship until the landing be accomplished, and until notified they can land.

"4. The chief quartermaster of the expedition will control all small boats, and will distribute them to the best advantage to disembark the troops in the order indicated in paragraph 1.

"5. The ordnance officer, Second Lieutenant Brooke, Fourth Infantry, will put on shore, at once, 100 rounds of ammunition per man, and have it ready for distribution on the firing-line.

"6. The commanding general wishes to impress officers and men with the crushing effect a well-directed fire will have upon the Spanish troops. All officers concerned will rigidly enforce fire discipline, and will caution their men to fire only when they can see the enemy."

THE MORNING BATH—SOLDIERS SWIMMING BY THE SIDE OF A TROOP-SHIP

The small boats belonging to the navy and to the transports, together with a number of steam-launches furnished by the navy, were brought alongside and loaded with troops as prescribed in the order just quoted. When General Lawton's division was fairly loaded in the small boats, the latter were towed in long lines by the steam-launches towards the shore. The sea was somewhat rough, but by the exercise of caution and good judgment the beach was reached and the troops disembarked satisfactorily. As a precaution against a possible attack upon the part of any Spaniards who might have been hidden in the adjacent block-houses and woods, the navy opened a furious cannonade on these places while the troops were moving towards the shore. It was learned afterwards that the Spanish garrison had retired in the direction of Siboney soon after daylight.

By night about 6000 troops were on shore. General Lawton was ordered to push down a strong force to seize and hold Siboney.

On the 23d the disembarkation was continued and about 6000 more men landed. Early on this date General Lawton's advance reached Siboney, the Spanish garrison of about 600 men retiring as he came up, and offering no opposition except a few scattering shots at long range. Some of the Cuban troops pursued the retreating Spaniards and skirmished with them. During the afternoon of this date the disembarkation of Kent's division was commenced at Siboney, which enabled me to establish a base eight miles nearer Santiago, and to continue the unloading of troops and supplies at both points.

The disembarkation was continued throughout the night of the 23d and 24th, and by the evening of the 24th the disembarkation of my command was practically completed.

THE ARMY OF INVASION

The Inspector-General's Account

Port Tampa was selected as the place for the embarkation of the first expedition for the invasion of Cuba, the army of invasion being under the command of Major-General William R. Shafter, U.S.V. Port Tampa is at the head of Tampa Bay, and about thirty miles from the bar. It could be easily protected—from such small Spanish vessels as could threaten it—by two or three small vessels of our navy. The distance from Port Tampa to Cuba is shorter than from any other port of our mainland. From the city of Tampa to the port is about ten miles. The country is flat and sandy, covered with an open pine forest. The docking facilities at Port Tampa were for steamship lines running from this point to the various points in the Gulf of Mexico. The railway facilities consisted of a single line of a single-track railroad, connected with the Northern and Eastern roads near Jacksonville, some 200 miles from Tampa. Great congestion occurred on this road, and, consequently, delay in bringing troops and supplies. Whether this could have been remedied, in part at least, by special management under military authority, or otherwise, or by adopting another point of departure, was a matter worthy of inquiry and consideration.

The troops were encamped in the vicinity of Tampa for several weeks before actually going on board ship, during which time their facilities for drill, target practice, or military exercises were limited. The health of the troops was generally good, though the climate was hot—much hotter than most of the troops were accustomed to. Good potable water was not to be found in the vicinity, but was brought from a distance. The transports employed were those engaged, for the most part, in trade between the United States, the West Indies, and Central America. Some of the transports were freight steamers, and were fitted up between decks with temporary berths for the accommodation of the troops. As a rule, these berths were quite narrow, and in tiers of three. Ventilation was not good. In some cases temporary structures were made on the upper decks to accommodate the officers, there not being sufficient cabin room on the ships. Animals were as a rule carried on steamers built for that purpose. After the transports were loaded it was found that some were overcrowded, and it was feared that fevers might break out from the unsanitary condition resulting from crowding. Other transports were brought in and the number of troops on the crowded vessels was reduced. It may be stated here that there was very little sickness among the troops on the journey, although it was a longer one than was contemplated when the troops were put aboard. It was necessary to tow lighters and water-carrying vessels, which resulted in reducing the speed of the fleet much below that of the ordinary speed of the slowest vessel in the fleet. One of the scows bought at Tampa was lost *en route*, and the landing facilities were far from adequate; so that both the embarkation and debarkation were most laborious, though conducted by men of the utmost energy

After passing the bar the transport fleet was formed up in three columns, the columns being about 1000 yards from each other, and the distance between the vessels in the same column being about 400 yards. It was found that during the night the column would string out to a much greater length than during the daytime, and several instances occurred of vessels having barges in tow being obliged to fall entirely behind the column; and one lighter was completely lost, and one steamer ordered to accompany the fleet failed to do so.

The convoy consisted of five small naval vessels until the fleet reached a point between the Dry Tortugas and Key West, where ten more naval vessels, one of them being the battleship *Indiana*, joined the fleet, making a convoy of some fifteen vessels along the northern coast of Cuba. The weather was fine from the time the fleet started from Tampa until it reached the southern coast of Cuba, the only rough water encountered being that in the Windward Passage. Only a few animals died *en route*. The fleet sailed from Port Tampa on June 14, and arrived off Santiago de Cuba June 20.

The coast of Cuba in the vicinity of Santiago Bay is steep and rocky, with few good landing-places. There was at Daiquiri an iron pier, used by a railroad company for unloading iron-ore, and also a part of a wharf was still standing. The beach, while having considerable surf, was still not too rough to permit of the landing of horses and mules by swimming ashore. On the 20th a reconnaissance was made east and west of Santiago Bay, and the commanding general went ashore at Aserraderos, about eighteen miles west of Santiago. This point was in the hands of the Cubans, and the landing was made for the purpose of a conference with General Garcia, the Cuban leader. On June 21 plans for landing were made out and transmitted to the various commanders. On the 22d the navy bombarded all the villages along the coast in the vicinity of Santiago, and under the cover of this fire an unopposed landing was made by our troops at Daiquiri. As the water in the small bay was not deep enough for ships to come alongside the wharf, it was necessary to make the landing in small boats belonging to the transports and to the navy. The navy furnished the steam launches to tow these boats back and forth between the shore and transports. The distance required of some appeared excessive, and communications between vessels habitually slow.

As soon as landed, the troops formed and moved inland, taking up positions along the banks of the Daiquiri River, and extending to a distance of about three miles from the village of Daiquiri. A number of Cubans who had been landed the night previous at a point east of Daiquiri marched westward and entered Daiquiri from the land side at about the same time our first troops landed. Under the circumstances the landing of our troops was necessarily slow. No horses were landed on the first day, and less than one division of soldiers succeeded in getting ashore. On the 23d the landing of troops continued, and the advance pushed on to Siboney, a coast village about nine miles distant from Daiquiri. Horses and mules were landed by swimming, and in the afternoon we began to land troops at Siboney, where the beach, though not extensive, was much smoother than at Daiquiri. There was no wharf at Siboney, but later on a small one was built by the engineers from timbers found in a sawmill near by, belonging to the Juragua Mining Company. Perhaps a battalion would have been captured at Siboney if a single staff officer had had a horse to carry the order.

On the 24th the landing of troops continued; the advance, early in the morning, reached the point Las Guasimas, about four miles west of Siboney, where a skirmish had occurred the day before between Cubans and Spaniards, in which one Cuban was killed and eight wounded. Here our advance met a portion of the enemy, posted behind stone walls on a very high and steep hill, and facing a point in the road which it was necessary for our troops to pass on marching from a sunken road into the open space. Here occurred what has since been called the action of Las Guasimas.

SEVENTY-FIRST NEW YORK VOLUNTEERS GOING ABOARD TRANSPORT *VIGILANCIA* AT PORT TAMPA

GOING ASHORE AT DAIQUIRI.—PHOTOGRAPH BY JAMES BURTON

CONVOYING THE TROOPS TO CUBA

CAPTAIN TAYLOR'S ACCOUNT

IN obedience to the orders of Commodore George C. Remey, commanding naval base, Key West, I proceeded in the *Indiana*, with the *Detroit*, *Castine*, *Manning*, *Wasp*, *Eagle*, *Wompatuck*, and *Osceola*, on June 14, 1898, at 5.30 P.M., to the rendezvous off Rebecca Shoal light, to await the arrival of the transports from Tampa.

We remained that night at the rendezvous, and at daylight sent a scout ahead to meet the convoy. The scout returned, reporting nothing seen. The *Ericsson* joined the convoy. I sent ahead another scout in the afternoon, which returned in company with the *Hornet*. The commanding officer reported transports approaching at seven knots speed and straggling, owing to the slowness of those towing lighters.

At 8.30 P.M., June 15, the transports were sighted. Formed column of our force and steamed on the right flank of the main body till daylight, June 16, when made signal, "Take order of cruising"; also signalled speed, "Eight knots." At 8 A.M. fired a salute of thirteen guns in honor of Major-General Shafter. Communicated with him by the *Wasp*, and on her return left the *Indiana* and paid official visit to him on board the transport *Segurança*. Had great trouble in keeping the transports closed up. The torpedo-boat *Rodgers* joined the squadron, and the *Indiana* took her in tow.

At 1.30 sighted the *Montgomery* standing over from Cuban coast flying the flag of Commodore Watson, and fired a salute of eleven guns, which was returned by seven guns from the *Montgomery*. The *Montgomery* remained ahead and inshore of the convoy during the day and night.

At daylight on the 17th found the column very much strung out. At 7.10 the *Annapolis* signalled "Shoal water." Changed course to S.S.E., to bring the left flank into the channel. At 8.40 sighted Paredon Grande light-house. The *Eagle* brought message from the General requesting that the column be stopped to allow the rear vessels to close up. This I regarded as impracticable, as we were approaching the narrow part of Old Bahama Channel, and the General was informed that we would stop as

LANDING AT THE PIER, DAIQUIRI.—PHOTOGRAPH BY JAMES BURTON

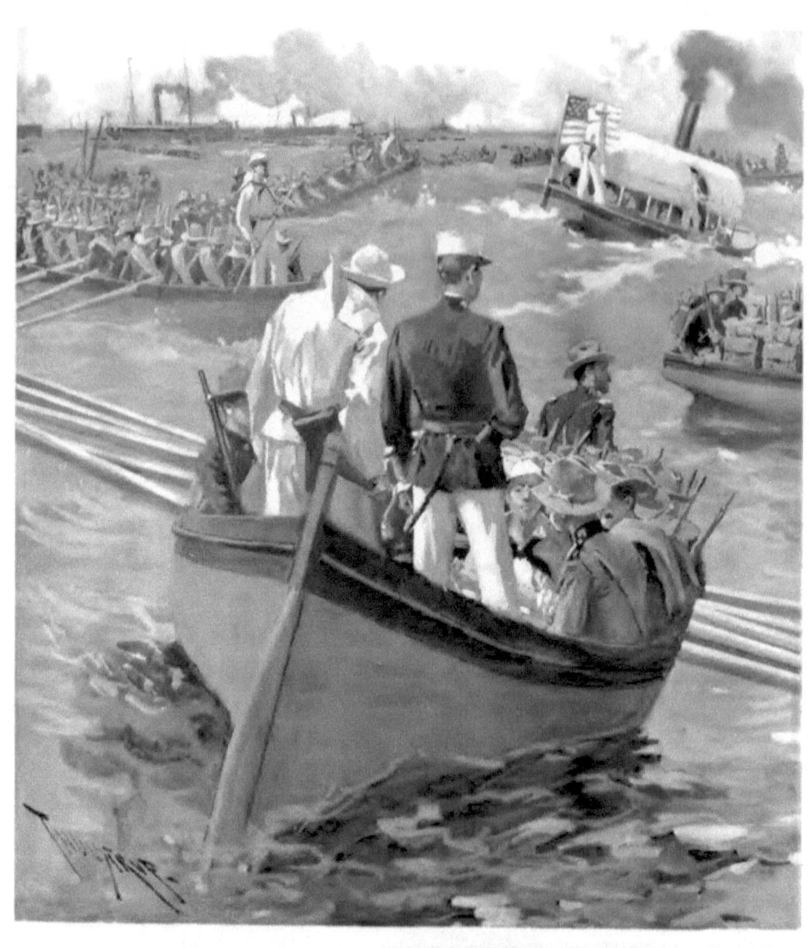

TROOPS OF GENERAL SHAFTER'S COMMAND LANDING I

TRANSPORTS AT DAIQUIRI.—DRAWN BY T. DE THULSTRUP

LANDING TROOPS UNDER DIFFICULTIES IN A HEAVY SEA

soon as we were through this channel. About noon sent the *Helena* in to scout along the shore, and to rejoin at 7 P.M.

At 3 P.M. slowed to six knots, as the column was straggling badly. Detailed the *Bancroft* to look out for stragglers and to remain by them, *Wasp* to assist. *Detroit* was given charge of the rear division. Sighted the *Armeria* standing to the westward. On June 18, about 7.30 A.M., stopped the convoy and signalled "Close up." Coaled the *Rodgers* while waiting for the column to close up. At 11 A.M. all the fleet and transports in sight went ahead at six knots, *Annapolis* guide. About noon sent the *Helena* inshore to scout till 7 P.M., when to take station. Again ordered the *Bancroft* to remain in rear of all transports, and to protect any stragglers. Received a message from General Shafter that the *Gussie* needed water for her cargo of mules. Attempted to keep column closed at seven knots, but found it impossible, so reduced speed again to six knots at 8 P.M.

At 6 A.M. on the 19th sent *Wompatuck* down the columns to find out what ships were straggling. Sent *Helena* in chase of a steamer standing to the southward across the head of the column. *Helena* returned, reporting it an English steamer bound for Morant Point, Jamaica. At 7 A.M. made Great Inagua Island ahead. Sent *Helena* to convoy the *Gussie* to Matthew Town for water. At request of the General the *Olivette* was sent in to Matthew Town to water the *Gussie*, pending the arrival of the water-schooner, which was ordered there. Sent *Osceola* to rear to find *Bancroft*, and order her to take the *City of Washington* and schooner to Matthew Town to water the *Gussie*, and then bring them all to the Commander-in-Chief at Santiago de Cuba. Sent *Wompatuck* ahead to inform the Commander-in-Chief of our approach.

The *Rodgers*, in attempting to take a line from the *Indiana*, had a man knocked overboard, and, although a diligent search was made for him, he was not found.

At 6.30 A.M. on the 20th sent the *Ericsson* ahead to communicate with the fleet off Santiago. Sent the *Rodgers* in to Guantanamo. At 9.45 A.M. sighted the Morro of Santiago and the ships of the fleet. The *Gloucester*, with the chief of staff on board, came out from the fleet and communicated with the headquarters ship, which went in towards the fleet. The column was stopped about fifteen miles offshore. During the afternoon the *Bancroft* and *Wasp* arrived with the two straggling transports, making the entire number. Before dark got the convoy in formation, heading offshore, and remained stopped until 7 A.M. on the 21st.

SWIMMING HORSES ASHORE

The *St. Louis* came out from the fleet, and, upon invitation of the chief of staff, I joined him and the major-general on board the *Seguranca*. At this meeting was arranged the position of the transports in the formation for landing and the time and place of debarkation. The naval vessels were at once put to work rearranging the formation and assigning the transports to their new stations. Owing to the trouble experienced in keeping stations when stopped the night before, I decided to keep the columns in motion during the night and gradually to change course until daylight. At daylight on the 22d the heads of the columns were in position off Daiquiri, and the naval vessels were sent to the rear to close up the lagging transports. As soon as the ships were in position and the debarkation about to begin, the *Indiana* hauled down the senior officer's pennant and stood to the westward to take station assigned in the blockading-line. It had been my hope to be allowed to complete this service by joining in the fire upon the beach at Daiquiri, but the orders received from the Commander-in-Chief, through the chief of staff, were imperative that I should leave Daiquiri as soon as the vessels of the convoy I had had charge of should arrive there.

On the afternoon of the 21st, while on board the *Seguranca*, I was handed a communication from General Shafter in regard to getting his generals on board his ship for consultation. No notice of the General's wishes had been communicated to me, either by signal or any other means, up to this time. I at once ordered the *Bancroft* to go around and collect the generals, as the quickest way. The transports were getting into their new positions, and it was with difficulty they could be induced to stop. Also, the sea was rough, and to get them in and out of the boats caused loss of time. However, the *Bancroft* did her work well, and continued it until midnight.

I regarded the placing of the ships at Daiquiri at daylight in proper order as of the utmost importance, and, had any time been lost in getting the columns again in motion, much delay would have resulted. Had General Shafter's wishes in this matter been made known to me in the forenoon or morning of the same day, all could have been arranged.

In bringing this duty to a successful conclusion, I desire to say that Commander Hunker turned over the convoy to me in excellent order at Dry Tortugas, and my thanks were due to him and to all the commanding officers of naval vessels for their vigilance and well-directed efforts, which made it possible for this large convoy to arrive at its destination without loss or accident.

LANDING COMMISSARY STORES THROUGH THE SURF

PREPARATIONS FOR LANDING THE TROOPS

As Told by Admiral Sampson

During the week ending June 22 we were actively engaged in examining the various points of landing possible, and on the 17th an attempt was made at early daylight to examine Cabañas Bay, the forces being under the charge of Lieutenant Harlow, and consisting of two steam-cutters, one from the *New York* in charge of Naval Cadet Powell, and one from the *Massachusetts* in charge of Naval Cadet Hart. The entrance is extremely narrow, leading into a small bay. The launches were, however, subjected to so heavy and continued a fire at short range that they were obliged to retreat. Much of the fire was from within fifty yards, and though the two boats were struck seventeen times, no one, fortunately, was injured. Lieutenant Harlow, in his report, particularly praised the conduct of Cadets Hart and Powell and Cockswains O'Donnell and Blom.

On the 19th General Garcia and his staff paid a visit to the ship, having arrived that morning at General Rabi's camp at Aserraderos. He had left 4000 of his men, whom he had advanced to within two days' march of Santiago, and had come to the coast for the purpose of consultation. Three thousand troops were left behind near Holguin, to observe some ten thousand Spanish troops which were concentrated there, and to prevent their passage in the direction of Santiago.

My impressions of General Garcia were of the most pleasant character. He was a large, handsome man, of most frank and engaging manners, and of most soldierly appearance. He remained some time on board, though, unfortunately, so sea-sick that he was obliged to lie down during the whole of his visit.

The fleet, by my direction, furnished arms, clothing, and food to the extent of its ability to the Cuban forces both east and west of Santiago. Much was done in this direction by our ships at Guantanamo, and Commander McCalla there was most energetic in rendering them all assistance possible. That the returns for the aid rendered would be good we had the best evidence in the activity and courage shown by the Cubans at Guantanamo, and Commander McCalla was most eulogistic in reference to their conduct.

The forces available were estimated as 600 under General Perez, near Guantanamo Bay; 600 under General Castillo, near Point Sigua, some few miles east of Daiquiri; 1100 under General Rabi, at Aserraderos, and 7000 under General Garcia, distributed as mentioned above.

On the morning of the 20th I received by the *Wompatuck* a letter from Captain Taylor, of the *Indiana*, stating that the transports conveying the army would arrive during the day. I sent Captain Chadwick, my chief of staff, on board the *Gloucester* to meet the fleet and convey my compliments to General Shafter, with the request that he would come in the *Segurança* to the blockade-line.

On the arrival of General Shafter, about noon, I went on board, and shortly after we steamed to Aserraderos, eighteen miles to the west, and we together paid a visit to Generals Garcia and Rabi. General Castillo had previously been sent for from Point Sigua. Arrangements were then made with reference to our future operations. It was regarded that the army should be debarked at Daiquiri on the morning of the 22d, that 500 of General Rabi's men should be transported from Aserraderos to a point (Cujababo) five miles west of La Sigua, to join there the forces under General Castillo, this whole force then to assist

SHELLING THE SPANIARDS OUT OF THE SHORE ROADS.—Drawn by Carlton T. Chapman

on the landing of the army by assaulting on the flank the Spanish force at Daiquiri, and that during the landing at Daiquiri a feint should be made to the westward of the entrance to the harbor of Santiago by men-of-war and transports, assisted by 500 men under General Rabi. This was all carried out. It was further arranged that General Garcia's forces, now two days from Santiago, should be diverted to Asserraderos, and should be there embarked on the 24th, to join our troops landed at Daiquiri.

The *Texas* engaged, or fired upon, the vicinity of the entrance to Cabañas Bay, and during the forenoon was more or less engaged with the western battery. She did excellent firing at some 4000 yards' range. She was struck by one shell, and one man was killed and eight wounded.

At 10.30 I left the blockade and went to the eastward to observe the progress of our attempt at disembarkation. Our vessels, stationed as per order of battle, were actively firing at Aguadores and Ensenada de los Altares, known locally as Siboney, and at Daiquiri. Our fire, however, at Daiquiri I found was simply preparatory to the actual landing of our troops, as practically no resistance was made. The Spaniards apparently at once retreated from this point, as also from Siboney.

The progress of disembarkation was rendered somewhat difficult by a heavy sea, the heaviest which we have had during the three weeks the fleet has been stationed here, owing to a stiff blow off the coast of Jamaica.

THE CONFERENCE AT ASERRADEROS

By Caspar Whitney

The entire meeting was exceedingly interesting and picturesque in setting. We left the transport fleet off Santiago and steamed west twelve miles, where we hove to about three miles off shore; then, in three small boats, General Shafter and the important members of his staff, and Davis, Bonsal, Remington, and I, rowed to the shore, the General's boat leading, and ours next. As we approached we discovered about one hundred Cubans on the beach; and as the General's boat got into shallow water two Cuban officers rode out

CHIEF-TRUMPETER C. W. PLATT, OF THE "ROUGH RIDERS," RAISING THE AMERICAN FLAG AT DAIQUIRI

on horseback to greet him, while a score of Cubans waded in, and, catching hold of the General's boat, hauled it on shore. The balance of us waded up to our middle.

As we reached dry land the Cubans gathered around; some shouted "Cuba libre! Viva Americanos!" and all seemed eager to show their appreciation of our efforts in their behalf. After a short audience given to the crowds which pressed upon us, we took up our march towards Garcia's camp. For a mile we followed a narrow winding trail, going up grade always, and at times steeply. The Cubans had fallen in behind us and acted as escort, and all along on the trail other Cubans stood here and there at present arms, or gravely saluted us as we went past.

Finally we reached the foot of a small eminence which crowned the mountains running down to the sea. From the foot to the top two lines of Cuban soldiers stretched, perhaps three hundred in all; and as we began the climb to the top, on which was Garcia's camp, or, rather, the hut in which a rendezvous had been agreed upon, they all presented arms, and a tiny bugle gave forth a most plaintive welcome.

The conference lasted an hour or thereabouts, and during it the Cubans filed past several times, evidently in an attempt to impress us—as on the stage twenty soldiers will parade in front and pass around behind the scenes to the front again, to give the appearance of a regiment.

They were all armed with rifles, some had machetes also, and all looked well nourished. None of the soldiers had shoes, and their clothes were ragged, but certainly seventy-five per cent. of them never had worn a shoe, and never would. General Garcia was a good-looking man of much dignity.

After the conference the Cubans formed a hollow square, and once again the plaintive sound of the bugle heralded our approach; we passed through the square under an escort of twenty men, and all the square fell in behind us.

On the 22d the troops began their landing at Daiquiri. The *New Orleans, Detroit, Castine*, and *Wasp* were directly in front of the harbor, and back and very near came our ship. Two miles back were the remainder of the transports. About 2000 troops were got into small boats towed by launches, and when they started towards shore the gunboats opened fire—and such a fire! They simply riddled the town, setting fire to what the Spaniards had not had time to fire before running away, and the marksmanship was splendid. It was great—the excitement of stealing up to shore under fire and the prospect of a fight made the blood course. The Spaniards cut and run, and gave no fight.

Simultaneously with the bombarding at this point, other points five and eight miles west of here were shelled and the settlements fired.

THE DISEMBARKATION

As Told by Captain Goodrich

At 4.30 A.M., June 22, the *St. Louis* was at her rendezvous at Daiquiri and within a mile and a half of the great pier. This position was taken in order to demonstrate to the transport captains that the approaches were perfectly safe. The steam-cutters, sailing-launches, cutters, and whale-boats detailed from certain other vessels of the fleet arrived about 6 to 6.30 A.M., in tow of the *Suwanee* and *Wompatuck*. Some steam-cutters came up under their own power. The *St. Louis* furnished a large number of boats, which could carry at one trip nearly 1000 men, or rather more than half the capacity of all the boats employed. About half of the boats of the *St. Louis* were manned by volunteers from the fire-room. The types of boats may be arranged in the following order of individual

CUBAN REINFORCEMENTS LANDING AT SIBONEY

GENERAL VIEW OF THE CAMP AT DAIQUIRI.—Photograph by James Burton

value for the work under consideration: First, navy sailing-launches; second, life-boats of the *St. Louis;* third, navy-cutters; fourth, collapsible boats of the *St. Louis;* fifth, navy whale-boats.

A great deal of delay was experienced in getting the first batch of troops in the boats—the causes being numerous and largely avoidable. Some confusion at the outset was occasioned in getting the steam-cutters and their tows in readiness, but this was as nothing in comparison with the hinderance caused by the remoteness of the transports from the shore. The *Knickerbocker,* a very important member of the fleet, with 600 men to be landed in advance of the army, had lost herself during the night and only appeared in the afternoon. In the meantime four steam-launches, with eleven boats in tow, were vainly seeking her far out at sea. My plans were also disarranged through the absence of certain steam-launches, and of the steam-barge *Laura,* all of which had been promised me. I may, in all frankness, add that neither the boats' crews nor the boats' officers were as familiar at first with the quickest method of getting a soldier into a boat, and of carrying on this special duty generally, as they soon became. However, shortly after 9 A.M. a sufficient number of boats were filled with troops to warrant the advance—the preconcerted signal to this effect was hoisted on board the *Wompatuck,* to which vessel I had transferred myself with my aids, Lieutenant Catlin, U. S. Marine Corps, and Mr. Richard S. Palmer.

The *New Orleans, Detroit, Castine,* and *Wasp* then opened a fire heavy enough to drive out the whole Spanish army in Cuba had it been there. So far as known no reply was made.

The *Suwanee,* which had been assigned to my particular assistance, kept close by on the port quarter of the *Wompatuck,* and shelled the low woods to the west of Daiquiri, the *Wompatuck,* in the advance, firing a few times also. Following the *Wompatuck* were the steam-cutters with their tows of boats laden with troops.

Happily, no opposition was encountered, and, also happily, the smaller or inner pier was found to be available for landing. Midshipman Halligan, of the *Brooklyn,* was the first man ashore, at a little before 10 A.M.

VIEW INLAND FROM THE CAMP AT DAIQUIRI.—Photograph by James Burton

THE HILL ON WHICH THE STARS AND STRIPES WERE RAISED AT DAIQUIRI.—PHOTOGRAPH BY JAMES BURTON

The troops landed as rapidly as the heavy swell alongside the pier would permit, and the landing, once begun, continued all day. By 6 P.M. some 6000 troops were ashore and the army abundantly capable of holding its own.

By the middle of the afternoon the boats' crews and officers had acquired the most expeditious and convenient methods of receiving and discharging troops, while the beach-master, Lieutenant F. K. Hill, had systematized the approach to and handling of boats at the dock, so that a continuous stream of men disembarking could be maintained. A larger number would have been scored had the transports not as a rule kept from two to five miles off.

The next morning, June 23, the landing began afresh. Profiting by our experience of the preceding day, the operation of landing reached and maintained a surprisingly high rate. As before, the only drawback was the remoteness of the transports from the dock. The *Osceola*, on the 22d, and the steam-lighter *Laura*, on the 23d, brought in, the former some 200 men, the latter some 330. As the *Laura* could and did go alongside the dock, she proved of notable assistance.

On the afternoon of the 23d the major-general in command of the Fifth Army Corps informed me that he had determined to land men at Siboney, or Ensenada de los Altares, about four miles to the westward of Daiquiri and that much nearer Santiago. Accordingly, the entire lot of boats was sent to Siboney, where the *St. Louis* followed them. Happily, a convenient and safe anchorage was found for the ship, encouraging the transports to come closer in. Moreover, General Shafter, in response to my request that the transports should be made to come nearer, had placed their captains unreservedly under my orders, so far as the landing was concerned. In consequence of this order I was enabled to go on board a transport as it came in, assure the captain that his responsibility for the safety of his ship ceased the moment he obeyed my instructions, take charge of her, and berth her near the shore. In this way but a small distance was covered by the boats in transit, and the landing went on most rapidly in spite of the surf, which at times was quite heavy. During the night the beach was illuminated by the *St. Louis*'s search-lights, so that the work went on almost as easily and quickly as in the daytime.

The disembarkation continued during the 24th, 25th, and 26th, an immense amount of ammunition, food, and forage being taken ashore by the navy, so that the troops and animals could be subsisted. The speed of landing at Los Altares was, normally, 600 Americans or 1000 Cubans per hour.

On the afternoon of Sunday, June 26, the *St. Louis* returned to the fleet off Santiago, bringing with her all the boats, except five steam-cutters, which had been already sent back on the 24th instant; also *Oregon's* boats.

The usefulness of a huge vessel like the *St. Louis*, possessing great resources in the shape of accommodations, supplies, and *personnel*, was amply demonstrated on the occasion just described. For four days and nights she acted as mother-ship, feeding and berthing nearly two hundred extra men and officers; coaling, watering, and repairing steam-cutters; furnishing voluntary relief-crews of machinists and firemen for the latter for night work; hoisting at her davits at sundown all navy pulling-boats not detailed for night duty; and all this without even taxing her facilities. There seemed to be room for everybody and the means to supply every want.

For the success of the undertaking, which, I had reason to believe, was generally considered to have reflected great credit on the naval service, I was deeply indebted to my subordinates, who manifested unflagging zeal and great ability in discharging an irksome, delicate, and, at times, dangerous duty.

At the earnest request of Colonel Weston,

GROUP OF THATCHED HOUSES AT SIBONEY

On the 27th the *St. Louis* accompanied the *Yale* to Siboney and landed 1300 troops from the latter ships, the *Yale* furnishing a whale-boat and a cutter to assist. The steam-cutters were from the *Indiana*, *Massachusetts*, and *Oregon*. On the *St. Louis's* return to Santiago that evening, the last of the boats detailed from other ships to take part in the landing—viz., the *Oregon's* steam-cutter and whale-boat—were sent back to their own ship. The usefulness of steam-cutters in towing empty boats off and full boats in cannot be exaggerated. The service was hard and continuous. I marvel only that breakdowns were so few and slight.

Of the navy boats, one *Brooklyn* cutter, beached at Daiquiri the first day, was the only one entirely lost; all, however, were more or less bruised and a few somewhat damaged, unavoidably.

The *St. Louis* received and cared for seven men on the 24th ultimo, wounded in the action of that day, Surgeon R. Lloyd Parker rendering valuable service. It was during this affair, when word came from shore that the Spaniards were driving back our troops, that the *St. Louis* fired a number of shells in the supposed direction of the enemy, some of which by good luck were reported to have fallen in his midst.

At the beginning much delay was caused by the timidity of the troops in getting into the boats; in other cases on account of orders not having arrived on board the transports to disembark their troops, causing much loss of time, the boats shoving off unloaded. In other cases delay was due to the efforts of company officers to make the landing by companies instead of filling the boats to their fullest capacity on each of their trips.

THE CAMP AT SIBONEY (ENSENADA DE LOS ALTARES)—TRANSPORTS IN HARBOR

of the Commissary Department, I left him two sailing-launches, with a man in charge of each, for the purpose of unloading the steam-lighter *Laura*. He expressed himself as able with the *Laura* and the launches to feed 30,000 men before Santiago; without the launches, as powerless. While it may be somewhat irregular to comment upon the actions of an officer of another branch of the service, I cannot refrain from mentioning my admiration of the energy, tact, and skill displayed by Colonel Weston, and of the results he achieved under my eyes.

Lighter with Stores.

THE CAMP AT ENSENADA DE LOS ALTARES.—("The *St. Louis* kept her search-light on the beach, and the soldiers went in swimming."—*From a Correspondent's Letter.*)

SIBONEY—THE HILL TO THE LEFT SHOWING TRAIL TO LAS GUASIMAS

GRIMES'S BATTERY GOING UP EL POZO HILL.—By Frederic Remington.

THE AMERICAN TROOPS LEAVING CAMP AT DAIQUIRI FOR THE ATTACK ON SANTIAGO.—Photograph by James Burton

THE INVESTMENT OF SANTIAGO

"THE landing of the Americans at Daiquiri," said the German Rear-Admiral Plüddemann in his *Comments*, already referred to, "was the largest landing effected since that of the Western powers at Balaklava. The voyage and the landing were effected in the most beautiful weather; the Americans had good luck, as they always did. The forces were landed unmolested." Of this landing Senator Lodge wrote: "It was a very excellent piece of work, thoroughly and punctually performed, exciting admiration among foreign onlookers, who had just beheld with amazement the performances connected with the embarkation at Tampa."

"On the 24th of June," said the President of the United States, "took place the first serious engagement, in which the First and Tenth Cavalry and the First United States Volunteer Cavalry, General Young's brigade of General Wheeler's division, participated, losing heavily. By nightfall, however, ground within five miles of Santiago was won. The advantage was steadily increased. On July 1st a severe battle took place, our forces gaining the outworks of Santiago; on the 2d El Caney and San Juan were taken after a desperate charge, and the investment of the city was completed. The navy co-operated by shelling the town and the coast forts."

Of the "first serious engagement" here mentioned by the President, and particularly of the First United States Volunteer Cavalry, popularly known as the "Rough Riders," Senator Lodge wrote in his article in HARPER'S MAGAZINE on "The Spanish-American War": "This regiment, enlisted, officered, disciplined, and equipped in fifty days, may well be considered for a moment as it moves forward to action only two days after its landing. It is a very typical American regiment. Most of the men come from Arizona, New Mexico, and Oklahoma, where the troops were chiefly raised. There are many cowboys, many men of the plains, hunters and pioneers and ranchmen, to whom the perils and exposure of frontier life are a twice-told tale. Among them can be found more than twoscore civilized but full-blooded Indians—Americans by an older lineage than any of those who were fighting for the domination of the New World. Then there are boys from the farms and towns of the far-western Territories. Then, again, strangest mingling of all, there are a hundred or more troopers from the East—graduates of Yale and Harvard, members of the New York and Boston clubs, men of wealth and leisure and large opportunities. They are men who have loved the chase of big game, fox-hunting, and football, and all the sports which require courage and strength and are spiced with danger. Some have been idlers, many more are workers, all have the spirit of adventure strong within them, and they are there in the Cuban chaparral because they seek perils, because they are patriotic, because, as some think, every gentleman owes a debt to his country, and this is the time to pay it. And all these men, drawn from so many sources, all so American, all so nearly soldiers in their life and habits, have been roughly, quickly, and effectively moulded and formed into a fighting regiment by the skilful discipline of Leonard Wood, their colonel, a surgeon of the line, who wears a medal of honor won in campaigns against the Apaches; and by the inspiration of Theodore Roosevelt, their lieutenant-colonel, who has laid down a high place in the administration at Washington and come hither to Cuba because thus only can he live up to his ideal of conduct by offering his life to his country when war comes.

"These 'Rough Riders,' as they have been popularly called, marched along the westerly trail, so shut in by the dense undergrowth that it was almost impossible to throw out flankers or deploy the line, and quite impossible to see. And then suddenly there were hostile volleys pouring through the brush, and a sound like the ringing of wires overhead. No enemy was to be seen. The smokeless powder gave no sign. The dense chaparral screened everything. Under the intense heat men had already given way. Now they began to drop, some wounded, some dead. The Rough Riders' fire and advance steadily, led onward by Colonel Wood and Lieutenant Colonel Roosevelt. A very trying place it was for perfectly new troops, with the burning tropical heat, the unseen enemy, the air filled with the thin noise of the Mauser bullet. But there was no flinching, and the march forward went on.

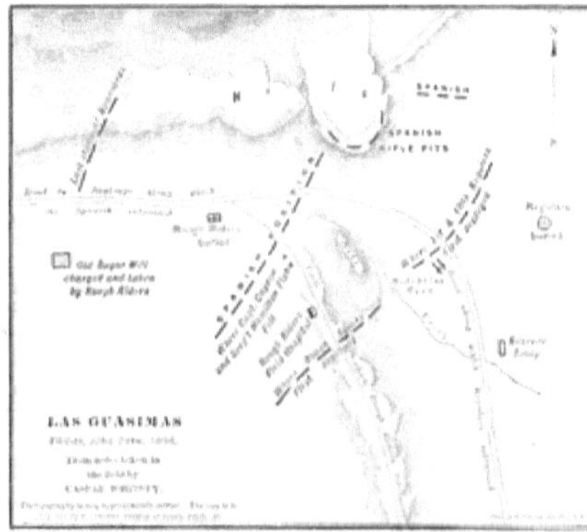

COLONEL THEODORE ROOSEVELT, OF THE "ROUGH RIDERS"

"Along the eastern road the regulars advanced with equal steadiness and perfect coolness. They do not draw the public attention as do the volunteers, for they act just as every one expected, and they are not new, but highly trained troops. But their work is done with great perfection, to be noted in history later, and at the time by all who admire men who perform their allotted task in the simple line of daily duty, bravely and efficiently. Thus the two lines moved forward constantly, along the trails and through the undergrowth, converging to the point at which they aimed, and Colonel Wood's right flank finds the anticipated support from the advancing regulars. The fire began to sweep the approaches and the strong rock forts on the ridge. Spaniards were seen at last, apparently without much desire to remain in view; the two columns pressed forward, the ridge was carried, the cross-road reached, and the fight of Las Guasimas had been won."

THE ADVANCE UPON SANTIAGO

General Shafter's Story

The orders for June 24 contemplated General Lawton's division taking a strong defensive position a short distance from Siboney, on the road to Santiago; Kent's division was to be held near Santiago, where he disembarked; Bates's brigade was to take position in support of Lawton, while Wheeler's division was to be somewhat to the rear on the road from Siboney to Daiquiri. It was intended to maintain this situation until the troops and transportation were disembarked and a reasonable quantity of necessary supplies landed. General Young's brigade, however, passed beyond Lawton on the night of the 23d–24th, thus taking the advance, and on the morning of the latter date became engaged with a Spanish force intrenched in a strong position at Las Guasimas, a point on the Santiago road about three miles from Siboney. General Young's

THE BATTLE OF LAS GUASIMAS, JUNE 24—THE HEROIC STAND OF THE "ROUGH RIDERS."—Drawn by W. A. Rogers

THE HOTCHKISS BATTERY IN ACTION AT LAS GUASIMAS.—DRAWN BY R. F. ZOGBAUM

force consisted of one squadron of the First Cavalry, one of the Tenth Cavalry, and two of the First United States Volunteer Cavalry; in all, 964 officers and men.

The enemy made an obstinate resistance, but were driven from the field with considerable loss. Our own loss was one officer and fifteen men killed; six officers and forty-six men wounded. The reported losses of the Spaniards were nine killed and twenty-seven wounded. The engagement had an inspiring effect upon our men, and, doubtless, correspondingly depressed the enemy, as it was now plainly demonstrated to them that they had a foe to meet who would advance upon them under a heavy fire delivered from intrenchments. General Wheeler, division commander, was present during the engagement, and reported that our troops, officers and men, fought with the greatest gallantry. This engagement gave us a well-watered country farther to the front on which to encamp our troops.

My efforts to unload transportation and subsistence stores, so that we might have several days' rations on shore, were continued during the remainder of the month. In this work I was ably seconded by Lieutenant-Colonel Charles F. Humphrey, deputy quartermaster-general U. S. A., chief quartermaster, and by Colonel John F. Weston, assistant commissary-general of subsistence, chief commissary; but, notwithstanding the utmost efforts, it was difficult to land supplies in excess of those required daily to feed the men and animals, and the loss of the scow, mentioned as having broken away during the voyage, as well as the loss at sea of lighters sent by the Quartermaster's Department, was greatly felt. Indeed, the lack of steam-launches, lighters, scows, and wharves could only be appreciated by those who were on the ground directing the disembarkation and landing of supplies. It was not until nearly two weeks after the army landed that it was possible to place on shore three days' supplies in excess of those required for the daily consumption.

After the engagement at Las Guasimas, and before the end of the month, the army, including General Garcia's command, which had been brought on transports to Siboney from Asserraderos, was mostly concentrated at Sevilla, with the exception of the necessary detachments at Daiquiri and Siboney.

On June 30 I reconnoitred the country about Santiago and made my plan of attack. From a high hill, from which the city was in plain view, I could see the San Juan Hill and the country about El Caney. The roads were very poor, and, indeed, little better than bridle-paths until the San Juan River and El Caney were reached.

The position of El Caney, to the northeast of Santiago, was of great importance to the enemy as holding the Guantanamo road, as well as furnishing shelter for a strong outpost that might be used to assail the right flank of any force operating against San Juan Hill.

In view of this I decided to begin the attack next day at El Caney with one division, while sending two divisions on the direct road to Santiago, passing by El Pozo House, and as a diversion to direct a small force against Aguadores, from Siboney along the railroad by the sea, with a view of attracting the attention of the Spaniards in the latter direction and of preventing them from attacking our left flank.

CAPTAIN ALLYN K. CAPRON

Troop L, "Rough Riders." Killed at Las Guasimas

During the afternoon I assembled the division commanders and explained to them my general plan of battle. Lawton's division, assisted by Capron's Light Battery, was ordered to move out during the afternoon towards El Caney, to begin the attack there early the next morning. After carrying El Caney, Lawton was to move by the Caney road towards Santiago, and take position on the right of the line. Wheeler's division of dismounted cavalry and Kent's division of infantry were directed on the Santiago road, the head of the column resting near El Pozo, towards which height Grimes's Battery moved on the afternoon of the 30th, with orders to take position thereon early the next morning and at the proper time prepare the way for the advance of Wheeler and Kent on San Juan Hill. The attack at this point was to be delayed until Lawton's guns were heard at El Caney and his infantry fire showed that he had become well engaged.

The remainder of the afternoon and night was devoted to cutting out and repairing the roads, and to other necessary preparations for battle. These preparations were far from what I desired them to be, but we were in a sickly climate; our supplies had to be brought forward by a narrow wagon-road, which the rains might at any time render impassable; fear was entertained that a storm might drive the vessels containing our stores to sea, thus separating us from our base of supplies; and, lastly, it was reported that General Pando, with 8000 reinforcements for the enemy, was *en route* from Manzanillo, and might be expected in a few days. Under these conditions I determined to give battle without delay.

Early on the morning of July 1, Lawton was

THE CAPTURE OF EL CANEY.—Drawn by Howard Chandler Christy

The Seventh Regular Infantry, charging through the fields at the north of El Caney, are cutting their way through the wire fence. Major Corliss, who is prominent in the foreground of the picture, was at this time pierced through the shoulder by a Mauser bullet

in position around El Caney. Chaffee's brigade on the right, across the Guantanamo road, Miles's brigade in the centre, and Ludlow's on the left. The duty of cutting off the enemy's retreat along the Santiago road was assigned to the latter brigade. The artillery opened on the town at 6.15 A.M. The battle here soon became general, and was hotly contested. The enemy's position was naturally strong, and was rendered more so by block-houses, a stone fort, and intrenchments cut in solid rock, and the loop-holing of a solidly built stone church. The opposition offered by the enemy was greater than had been anticipated, and prevented Lawton from joining the right of the main line during the day, as had been intended. After the battle had continued for some time Bates's brigade of two regiments reached my headquarters from Siboney. I directed him to move near El Caney, to give assistance, if necessary. He did so, and was put in position between Miles and Chaffee. The battle continued with varying intensity during most of the day and until the place was carried by assault about 4.30 P.M. As the Spaniards endeavored to retreat along the Santiago road, Ludlow's position enabled him to do very effective work, and practically to cut off all retreat in that direction.

After the battle at El Caney was well opened, and the sound of the small-arm fire caused us to believe that Lawton was driving the enemy before him, I directed Grimes's battery to open fire from the heights of El Pozo on the San Juan block-house, which could be seen situated in the enemy's intrenchments extending along the crest of San Juan Hill. This fire was effective, and the enemy could be seen running away from the vicinity of the block-house. The artillery fire from El Pozo was soon returned by the enemy's artillery. They evidently had the range of this hill, and their first shells killed and wounded several men. As the Spaniards used smokeless powder, it was very difficult to locate the position of their pieces, while, on the contrary, the smoke caused by our black powder plainly indicated the position of our battery.

At this time the cavalry division, under General Sumner, which was lying concealed in the general vicinity of the El Pozo House, was ordered forward with directions to cross the San Juan River and deploy to the right on the Santiago side, while Kent's division was to follow closely in its rear and deploy to the left.

These troops moved forward in compliance with orders, but the road was so narrow as to render it impracticable to retain the column-of-fours formation at all points, while the undergrowth on either side was so dense as to preclude the possibility of deploying skirmishers. It naturally resulted that the progress made was slow, and the long-range rifles of the enemy's infantry killed and wounded a number of our men while marching along this road, and before there was any opportunity to return their fire. At this time Generals Kent and Sumner were ordered to push forward with all possible haste and place their troops in position to engage the enemy. General Kent, with this end in view, forced the head of his column alongside of the cavalry column as far as the narrow trail permitted, and thus hurried his arrival at the San Juan and the formation beyond that stream. A few hundred yards before reaching the San Juan the road forks, a fact that was discovered by Lieutenant-Colonel Derby of my staff, who had approached well to the front in a war balloon. This information he furnished to the troops, resulting in Sumner moving on the right-hand road, while Kent was enabled to utilize the road to the left.

SAN JUAN AND CANEY

Artillery and Mortar Positions shown on San Juan Ridge—were not taken until after July 3

General Wheeler, the permanent commander of the cavalry division, who had been ill, came forward during the morning, and later returned to duty and rendered most gallant and efficient service during the remainder of the day.

After crossing the stream the cavalry moved to the right with a view of connecting with Lawton's left when he could come up, and with their left resting near the Santiago road.

SPANISH EARTH-WORKS AND TRENCHES AT EL CANEY

In the meantime Kent's division, with the exception of two regiments of Hawkins's brigade, being thus uncovered, moved rapidly to the front from the forks previously mentioned in the road, utilizing both trails, but more especially the one to the left, and, crossing the creek, formed for attack in the front of San Juan Hill. During this formation the Second Brigade suffered severely. While personally superintending this movement, its gallant commander, Colonel Wikoff, was killed. The command of the brigade then devolved upon Lieutenant-Colonel Worth, Thirteenth Infantry, who was soon severely wounded, and next upon Lieutenant-Colonel Liscum, Twenty-fourth Infantry, who, five minutes later, also fell under the terrible fire of the enemy, and the command of the brigade then devolved upon Lieutenant-Colonel Ewers, Ninth Infantry.

While the formation just described was taking place, General Kent took measures to hurry forward his rear brigade. The Tenth and Second Infantry were ordered to follow Wikoff's brigade, while the Twenty-first was sent on the right-hand road to support the First Brigade, under General Hawkins, who had crossed the stream and formed on the right of the division. The Second and Tenth Infantry, Colonel E. P. Pearson commanding, moved forward in good order on the left of the division, passed over a green knoll, and drove the enemy back towards his trenches.

After completing their formation under a destructive fire, and advancing a short distance, both divisions found in their front a wide bottom, in which had been placed a barbed-wire entanglement, and beyond which there was a high hill, along the crest of which the enemy was strongly posted. Nothing daunted, these gallant men pushed on to drive the enemy from his chosen position, both divisions losing heavily. In this assault Colonel Hamilton, Lieutenants Smith and Shipp were killed, and Colonel Carroll, Lieutenants Thayer and Myer, all in the cavalry, were wounded.

BLOCK-HOUSE

Great credit is due to Brigadier-General H. S. Hawkins, who, placing himself between his regiments, urged them on by voice and bugle-calls to the attack so brilliantly executed.

In this fierce encounter words fail to do justice to the gallant regimental commanders and their heroic men, for, while the generals indicated the formations and the points of attack, it was, after all, the intrepid bravery of the subordinate officers and men that planted our colors on the crest of San Juan Hill and drove the enemy from his trenches and block-houses, thus gaining a position which sealed the fate of Santiago.

In this action on this part of the field most efficient service was rendered by Lieutenant John H. Parker, Thirteenth Infantry, and the Gatling-gun detachment under his command. The fighting continued at intervals until nightfall, but our men held resolutely to the positions gained at the cost of so much blood and toil.

I was greatly indebted to General Wheeler, who, as previously stated, returned from the sick-list to duty during the afternoon. His cheerfulness and aggressiveness made itself felt on this part of the battle-field, and the information he furnished to me at various stages of the battle proved to be most useful.

My own health was impaired by overexertion in the sun and intense heat of the day before, which prevented me from participating as actively in the battle as I desired; but from a high hill near my headquarters I had a general view of the battle-field, extending from El Caney on the right to the left of our lines on San Juan Hill. My staff-officers were stationed at various points on the field, rendering frequent reports, and through them by the means of orderlies and the telephone I was enabled to transmit my orders. During the afternoon I visited the position of Grimes's battery on the heights of El Pozo, and saw Sumner and Kent in firm possession of San Juan Hill, which I directed should be intrenched during the night. My engineer officer, Lieutenant-Colonel Derby, collected and sent forward the necessary tools, and during the night trenches of very considerable strength were constructed.

During the afternoon Major Dillenback, by my order, brought forward the two remaining batteries of his battalion and put them in position at El Pozo, to the left of Grimes. Later in the afternoon all three batteries were moved forward to positions near the firing-line, but the nature of the country and the intensity of the enemy's small-arm fire was such that no substantial results were gained by our artillery in the new positions. The batteries were intrenched during the night. General Duffield, with the Thirty-third Michigan, attacked Aguadores, as ordered, but was unable to accomplish more than to detain the Spaniards in that vicinity.

After the brilliant and important victory gained at El Caney, Lawton started his tired troops, who had been fighting all day and marching much of the night before, to connect with the right of the cavalry division. Night came on before this movement could be accomplished. In the darkness the enemy's pickets were encountered, and the division commander, being uncertain of the ground and as to what might be in his front, halted his command and reported the situation to me. This information was received about 12.30 A.M., and I directed General Lawton to return by my headquarters and the El Pozo House as the only certain way of gaining his new position.

This was done, and the division took position on the right of the cavalry early next morning, Chaffee's brigade arriving first, about half past seven, and the other brigades before noon.

On the night of July 1 I ordered General Duffield, at Siboney, to send forward the Thirty-fourth Michigan and the Ninth Massachusetts, both of which had just arrived from the United States. These regiments reached the front the next morning. The Thirty-fourth was placed in rear of Kent, and the Ninth was assigned to Bates, who placed it on his left.

Soon after daylight on July 2 the enemy opened battle, but because of the intrenchments made during the night, the approach of Lawton's division, and the presence of Bates's brigade, which had taken position during the night on Kent's left, little apprehension was felt as to our ability to repel the Spaniards.

It is proper here to state that General Bates and his brigade had performed most arduous and efficient service, having marched much of the night of June 30-July 1, and a good part of the latter day, during which he also participated in the battle of El Caney, after which he proceeded, by way of El Pozo, to the left of the line at San Juan, reaching his new position about midnight.

All day on the 2d the battle raged with more or less fury, but such of our troops as were in position at daylight held their ground, and Lawton gained a strong and commanding position on the right.

About 10 P.M. the enemy made a vigorous assault to break through my lines, but he was repulsed at all points.

On the morning of the 3d the battle was renewed, but the enemy seemed to have expended his energy in the assault of the previous night, and the firing along the lines was desultory until stopped by my sending the following letter within the Spanish lines:

"Headquarters United States Forces,
"Near San Juan River, *July 3, 1898*. 8.30 A.M.

"Sir,—I shall be obliged, unless you surrender, to shell Santiago de Cuba. Please inform the citizens of foreign countries, and all women and children, that they should leave the city before ten o'clock to-morrow morning.

"Very respectfully, your obedient servant,
"William R. Shafter,
"Major-General United States Volunteers.

"*The Commanding General of the Spanish Forces, Santiago de Cuba.*"

To this letter I received the following reply:

"Santiago de Cuba, *July 3, 1898*.

"*His Excellency the General Commanding Forces of the United States near San Juan River:*

"Sir,—I have the honor to reply to your communication of to-day, written at 8.30 A.M. and received at 1 P.M., demanding the surrender of this city, or in the contrary case announcing to me that you will bombard this city, and that I advise the foreigners, women, and children that they must leave the city before ten o'clock to-morrow morning.

"It is my duty to say to you that this city will not surrender, and that I will inform the foreign consuls and inhabitants of the contents of your message.

"Very respectfully,
"José Toral,
"Commander-in-Chief Fourth Corps."

GENERAL HAWKINS AT SAN JUAN.—Drawn by R. F. Zogbaum

Several of the foreign consuls came into my lines and asked that the time given for them, the women, and children to depart from the city be extended until ten o'clock on July 5. This induced me to write a second letter, as follows:

"Santiago de Cuba, *July 3, 1898*.

"Sir,—In consideration of a request of the consular officers in your city for further delay in carrying out my intentions to fire on the city, and in the interests of the poor women and children who will suffer very greatly by their hasty and enforced departure from the city, I have the honor to announce that I will delay such action solely in their interests until noon of the 5th, provided that during the interim your forces make no demonstration whatever upon those of my own.

"I am, with great respect, your obedient servant,
"William R. Shafter,
"Major-General United States Army."

My first message went in under a flag of truce at 12.30 P.M. I was of the opinion that the Spaniards would surrender if given a little time, and I thought this result would be hastened if the men of their army could be made to understand that they would be well treated as prisoners of war. Acting upon this presumption, I determined to offer to return all the wounded Spanish officers at El Caney who were able to bear transportation, and who were willing to give their paroles not to serve against the forces of the United States until regularly exchanged. This offer was made and accepted. These officers, as well as several of the wounded Spanish privates, twenty-seven in all, were sent to their lines under the escort of some of our mounted cavalry. Our troops were received with honors, and I had every reason to believe that the return of the Spanish prisoners produced a good impression on their comrades.

The cessation of firing about noon on the 3d practically terminated the battle of Santiago; all that occurred after this time may properly be treated under the head of the siege which followed. After deducting the detachments retained at Siboney and Daiquiri to render those depots secure from attack, organizations held to protect our flanks, others acting as escorts and guards to light batteries, the members of the hospital corps, guards left in charge of blanket-rolls which the intense heat caused the men to cast aside before entering battle, orderlies, etc., it is doubtful if we had more than 12,000 men on the firing-line on July 1, when the battle was fiercest and when the important and strong positions of El Caney and San Juan were captured.

A few Cubans assisted in the attack at El Caney, and fought valiantly, but their numbers were too small to change materially the strength, as indicated above. The enemy confronted us with numbers about equal to our own; they fought obstinately, in strong and intrenched positions, and the results obtained clearly indicated the intrepid gallantry of the company officers and men, and the benefits derived from the careful training and instruction which had been given in the company in recent years in rifle practice and other battle exercises. Our losses in these battles were 22 officers and 208 men killed, and 81 officers and 1203 men wounded; missing, 79. The missing, with few exceptions, reported later.

LAS GUASIMAS

General Young's Account

I moved from my bivouac near the landing, with headquarters brigade, the First Volunteer Cavalry (Wood's), one squadron of the First United States Cavalry (Bell's), one squadron of the Tenth United States Cavalry (Norvell's), and the Hotchkiss mountain-gun battery (4 guns, Captain Watson, Tenth Cavalry, temporarily commanding), all dismounted. The remainder of the brigade was ordered to follow early the following morning on receiving its rations.

I arrived at Siboney with the head of the column at about 7 P.M., where I bivouacked for the night with the First Volunteer Cavalry, the two squadrons of the First and Tenth United States Cavalry and the battery being delayed by the crowded condition of the trail and the difficulty of following through the jungle after night.

THE STORMING OF SAN JUAN—THE HEAD OF THE CHARG

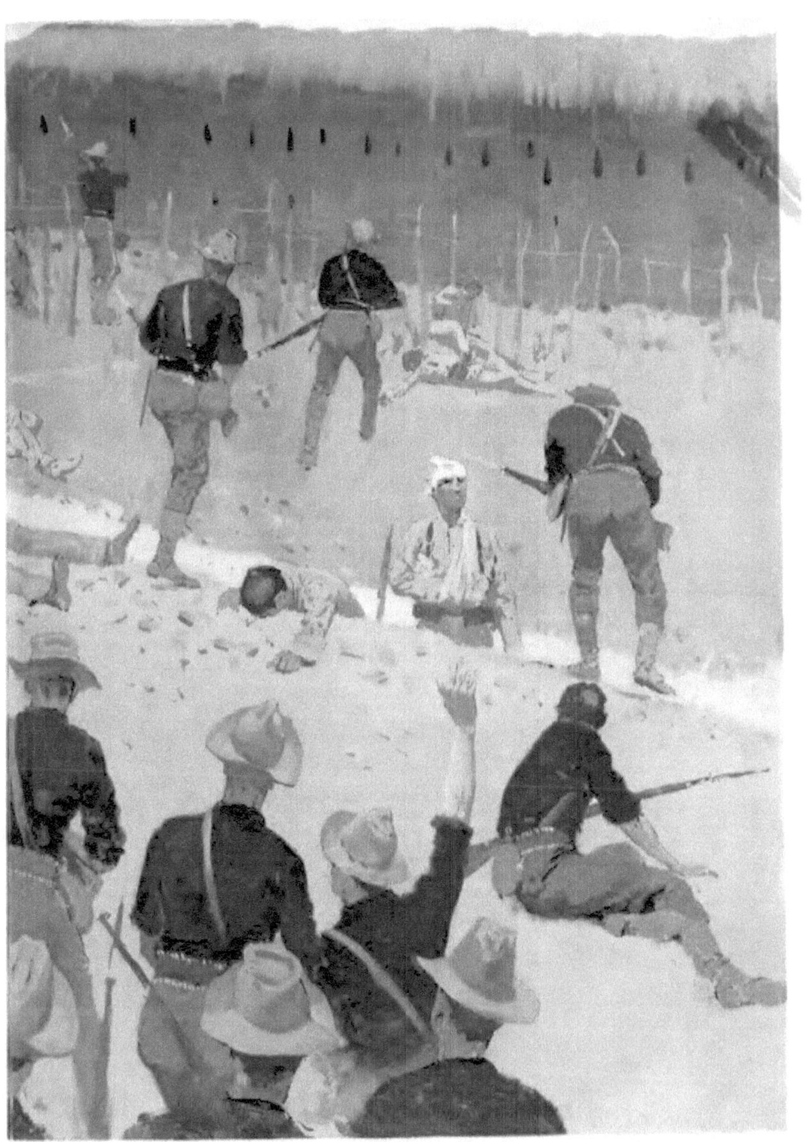

NTIAGO DE CUBA, JULY 1, 1898.—DRAWN BY FREDERIC REMINGTON

I reported to General Wheeler, and from him learned of an engagement between Cubans and Spaniards in that vicinity during the day, resulting in the repulse of the former with some loss. Later I met General Castillo, the commander of the Cuban forces, who gave me a full description of the topography of the country and much information regarding the Spanish troops, their manner of fighting, etc. General Castillo expressed the belief that although the Spaniards had successfully resisted his attack, they would fall back to Santiago during the night; but he also stated that he had received information that they were being reinforced.

Deeming it essential that positive information should be obtained as to the position and movements of the enemy in our front, I asked and obtained from General Wheeler authority to make a reconnaissance in force for this purpose, General Castillo having promised to assist and co-operate with me with a force of 800 effective Cubans.

Leading from Siboney there are two roads, or more properly trails, one to the eastward, the other to the westward of the little town, which unite about one mile before reaching Sevilla and a little in advance of the scene of the Cuban-Spanish engagement. The trails are at no point more than one and a half miles apart.

I concluded to move by the two trails, General Castillo having informed me that his outposts covered both. I consequently directed Colonel Wood to move with his regiment by the western route, cautioning him to keep a careful lookout and to attack any Spaniards he might encounter, connecting in the latter event by the right flank with the other column while trying to gain the enemy's right flank. Colonel Wood marched about 6 A.M. of the 24th, and I sent my personal aides, First Lieutenant T. R. Rivers, Third Cavalry, and Second Lieutenant W. R. Smedberg, Fourth Cavalry, to accompany his column.

The other, the right column, marched at 5.45 A.M. I moved with it, accompanied by Captain A. L. Mills, assistant adjutant-general. I proposed to attack the enemy in front and on his left if I found him in position.

SAN JUAN RIDGE AND BLOCK-HOUSE

At 7.20 A.M., the right column being masked in an open glade, Captain Mills with a patrol of two men advanced, and discovered the enemy located, as described by General Castillo, in a locality called Las Guasimas, from trees of that name in the vicinity. After having carefully examined the enemy's position, I prepared to develop his strength. Canteens were ordered filled, the Hotchkiss battery was placed in position in concealment at about nine hundred yards, and Bell's squadron was deployed, with Norvell's in support.

On discovering the enemy I had sent a Cuban guide to warn Colonel Wood, and, knowing that his column had a more difficult route, and would require a longer time to reach the position, I delayed the attack some time in order that the development on both flanks should begin simultaneously. During this delay General Wheeler arrived and was informed of my dispositions, plan of attack, and intentions. After an examination of the position by him, and his approval of my action, I ordered the attack, and it was executed in a manner winning the admiration of the division commander and all present who witnessed it.

The Spanish forces occupied a range of high hills in the form of an obtuse angle, with the salient towards Siboney, and with an advance party on the trail on which I had been moving. The attack of both wings was simultaneous, and the junction of the two lines occurred near the apex of the angle on the ridge, which had been fortified with stone breastworks flanked by block-houses.

The Spaniards were driven from their position and fled precipitately towards Santiago. The attacking force numbered 950 men, while that of the enemy, at first estimated at 2000, was afterwards learned from Spanish sources to have been 2500. The Cuban military authorities claimed the Spanish strength was 4000. It was also reported that Lieutenant-General Linares, commanding the Spanish forces in eastern Cuba, and two other general officers were present and witnessed the action. The fire of the enemy was almost entirely by volleys, executed with the precision of parade.

BARBED-WIRE ENTANGLEMENTS

The ground over which the right column advanced was a mass of jungle growth, with wire fences, not to be seen until encountered, and precipitous heights as the ridge was approached. It was impossible for the troops to keep touch along the front, and they could only judge of the enemy from the sound and direction of his fire. However, had it not been for this dense jungle, the attack would not have been made against an overwhelming force in such a position. Headway was so difficult that advance and support became merged and moved forward under a continuous volley-firing, supplemented by that of two rapid-fire guns. Return firing by my force was only made as here and there a small clear spot gave a sight of the enemy. The fire discipline of these particular troops was almost perfect. The ammunition expended by the two squadrons engaged in an incessant advance for one hour and fifteen minutes averaged less than ten rounds per man. The fine quality of these troops is also shown by the fact that there was not a single straggler, and in not one instance was an attempt made by any soldier to fall out in the advance to assist the wounded or carry back the dead. The fighting on the left flank was equally creditable and was remarkable, and I believe unprecedented in volunteer troops so quickly raised, armed, and equipped.

Our total losses were one officer and fifteen men killed; six officers and forty-four men wounded. Forty-two dead Spanish soldiers were found, the bodies of nearly all of whom had been thrown into the jungle for concealment. Spanish newspapers of Santiago the day after the battle gave their loss as seventy-seven killed. It was known that many wounded were carried to the city.

Every possible attention was given to the wounded, and the medical officers were unremitting in their efforts to alleviate their sufferings. Circumstances necessarily limited their appliances to the first-aid order. The wounded were carried on improvised litters to Siboney, and the dead were carefully buried on the battle-field, a proper record of their burial being kept.

Finding, when the ridge was carried, that many of my men had become exhausted by the excessive heat and exertion, I ordered a halt and occupation of the captured position. Had I had at hand at the time of the assault a force of mounted cavalry, the fruits of our victory would have been more apparent.

General Castillo did not appear on the field, nor did any of his troops come to the front until the firing had ceased. No other troops than those mentioned were engaged in the action. Three troops of the Ninth United States Cavalry arrived on the left after the firing had stopped, and were posted as pickets until relieved by General Chaffee's brigade of General Lawton's division, which then took the advance.

The action of all officers and men, so far as my personal observation extended, was superb. Captain Knox, after being shot through the abdomen, and seeing his lieutenant and first sergeant wounded, gave necessary orders to his troops and refused to allow a man in the firing-line to assist him to the rear; Lieutenant Byram, after having his scalp wound dressed, and knowing his captain (Knox) to be wounded, assumed command of his troop, but fell fainting while pushing to the front; Captain Mills, the only member of my staff present with me on this part of the field, was most conspicuous for his daring and unflagging energy in his efforts to keep troops in touch on the line, and in keeping me informed of the progress made in advancing through the jungle. Both Colonel Wood and Lieutenant-Colonel Roosevelt disdained to take advantage of shelter or cover from the enemy's fire while any of their men remained exposed to it—an error of judgment, but happily on the heroic side. The behavior of all men of the regular and volunteer forces engaged in this action was simply superb, and I felt highly honored in the command of such troops.

The chief results following from this action with the Spaniards were: a test of the valor of the opposing forces; the spirit of superiority it fixed in our own; the opening of the road to the gates of Santiago de Cuba; and the gaining of a beautiful camping-ground for our army on the heights overlooking that city, which could now easily be taken at our leisure.

THE ROUGH RIDERS AT LAS GUASIMAS

As Told by Colonel Wood

I LEFT camp at the sea-coast at 5.40, proceeding by trail in the direction of the town of Sevilla. On reaching the top of the mesa an advance-guard was thrown out and every precaution taken against surprise, as we had positive information that the enemy was ahead of us in force. The character of the country was such that reconnoitring was extremely difficult; the dense growth of underbrush rendered the rapid movement of flanking-parties practically impossible. At 7.10 our advanced point discovered what they believed to be signs of the immediate presence of the enemy. The command was halted and the troops deployed to the right and left in open skirmish order and the command ordered to advance carefully. The firing began almost immediately, and the extent of firing on each flank indicated that we had encountered a very heavy force. Two additional troops were deployed on the right and left, thus leaving only three troops in reserve. It was soon apparent that their lines were overlapping us on both flanks. Two other troops were rapidly deployed, one on the right and one on the left, which gave our line a length about equal to their own. The firing about this time was exceedingly heavy, much of it at very short range, but on account of the heavy undergrowth comparatively few men were injured at this time. It was about this time that Captain Capron was mortally wounded. The firing on his immediate front was terrific. The remaining troop was sent to the front and the order given to advance very slowly.

Men and officers behaved splendidly, and advanced, slowly forcing back the enemy on the right flank. We captured a small block-house and drove the enemy out of a very strong position in the rocks. We were now able to distinguish their line, which had taken a new position about 800 or 1000 yards in length and about 300 yards in front of us. The firing was exceedingly heavy here, and it was here also that we had a good many men and several officers wounded. Our men continued to advance in good order, and steadily forced the Spanish line back.

We now began to get a heavy fire from a ridge on our right, which enfiladed our line. This ridge was the position which was being attacked by two squadrons of the regular cavalry, and was held in very strong force by the Spanish in small rock forts along its entire length, supported by two machine-guns.

Having cleared our right flank, we were able to pay some attention to the Spanish on the above-mentioned ridge, and centred upon it the fire of two troops. This fire, with the attacking force on the other side, soon completed the evacuation of this end of the ridge, and the regular assault completed the evacuation along the entire length of the ridge. Of the Spaniards who retreated from the ridge some few fell into line, but apparently only remained there a moment, when large masses of them were seen to retreat rapidly, and we were able to distinguish parties carrying litters of wounded men.

At this time my detached troop had moved out to the left to take the right end of the Spanish line in flank. This was successfully accomplished, and as soon as this troop gained its position "Cease firing and advance" was ordered. Our men advanced within 300 yards of the enemy, when we again opened heavy fire. The Spanish broke under this fire and retreated rapidly. We advanced to the last position held by them and halted, having established before this a connection on our right with the regular troops, who had successfully carried the ridge before mentioned. This left us in complete possession of the entire Spanish position.

Our troops were too much exhausted and overcome with the heat and hard work of the two preceding days to continue the pursuit. Had we had any mounted men or even fresh foot-troops, I think we could have captured a large portion of their force, as they seemed completely disheartened and dispirited.

About thirty minutes after the firing had ceased three troops of the Ninth United States Cavalry, under Captain Dimmick, reported to me, and I advanced them, forming a heavy line of outposts covering our entire front, at a distance of about 800 yards from our line. About two hours after the fight was over a number of Cubans came up and made a short reconnaissance as far as Sevilla and reported that the Spanish had apparently fled into Santiago, as they found no evidence of them. They reported a quantity of blood along the trail and a quantity of abandoned equipments, and every evidence of a complete rout from the point of their break in our front to Sevilla.

In regard to the conduct of the officers and men, I can only say that one and all behaved splendidly. Captain Capron died shortly after the termination of the fight. I cannot say enough in commendation of the gallant conduct of this officer. His troop was in advance and met the enemy in very heavy force and resisted them and drove them back, and it was in the performance of this duty that the captain was mortally wounded. The service he performed prior to his death and the work of his troop subsequently to it were of the very greatest value in connection with the success of the engagement. Captain Capron's loss was an irreparable one to the regiment. Major Brodie was shot through the arm while on the firing-line. Captain McClintock, also, had both bones of his leg broken on the firing-line.

THE CAPTURE OF THE BLOCK-HOUSE, SAN JUAN.—Drawn by Howard Chandler Christy

Lieutenant Thomas, Captain Capron's first lieutenant, was shot shortly after the fall of Captain Capron.

We found no wounded Spaniards, but all along the line we found their abandoned equipments, and there was every evidence of a large number of wounded. We discovered about forty dead Spaniards. There might have been some mistake in the figures, owing to the jungle character of the country, and it seemed probable that a careful search might reveal many more. The First Squadron was under the command of Lieutenant-Colonel Theodore Roosevelt, and the Second under Major Alex. O. Brodie. Both of these officers deserve great credit for the intelligence and courage with which they handled their men. This remark would apply to all officers.

I desire to express my appreciation of the gallant and effective services of Captain McCormick, Seventh Cavalry, attached to my regiment, for any duty to which I assigned him; also of Captain Rivers and Lieutenant Smedberg, of General Young's staff, whose services were of the greatest value and performed under heavy fire.

THE WOUNDED, GOING TO THE REAR, CHEERING THE AMMUNITION-TRAIN.—Drawn by Frederic Remington

---

EL CANEY

General Lawton's Account

The town of El Caney is situated at an important point about four miles northeast of Santiago de Cuba, on the main road from Guantanamo to that city, where reinforcements for the Spanish garrison of Santiago de Cuba would probably concentrate. The town was strongly fortified with numerous block-houses within its limits and on the roads leading thence. On a prominent hill of the town was a stone fort, surrounded, as was afterwards known, by intrenchments cut in solid rock. The reduction of El Caney being determined upon, and being on the right flank of the general advance on Santiago de Cuba, the duty devolved on the Second Division, to which was attached Light Battery E, First Artillery, commanded by Captain Allyn Capron, First Artillery. After due reconnaissance by the division and brigade commanders, the movement began about 3 P.M. on June 30 from the division camp, about four miles east of Santiago, on the main road from Siboney through Sevilla.

The light battery first opened on a column of Spanish troops, which appeared to be cavalry moving westward from El Caney, and at about two miles' range, resulting, as was afterwards learned, in killing sixteen in the column. The battery remained during the action at its first position until about 2.30 P.M., when it was moved to a new position south of and about 1000 yards from certain block-houses in the town, where a few shots, all taking effect, were fired. This firing terminated the action, as the Spanish garrison were attempting to escape. General J. C. Bates, United States Volunteers, with two regiments of his Independent Brigade, the Third and Twentieth Infantry, having been sent by the major-general commanding the forces of the United States in Cuba to relieve the Second Brigade of the Second Division, these holding the main road from El Caney to Santiago, so as to permit it to join in the attack, also came forward, joined in the attack, taking position between the Second and Third brigades, and rendered material assistance, especially in the assault of the stone fort.

During the action I was accompanied most of the time by Major-General J. C. Breckinridge, Inspector-General United States Army, as a spectator, and had the advantage of his valuable suggestions and advice during the day. His horse was shot under him in the advance upon Santiago on the morning of the 2d instant.

EL CANEY

General Breckinridge's Account

The artillery opened fire about 7 A.M. The battery was entirely beyond the reach of small-arms fire, and the enemy had no artillery. The battery opened fire with shrapnel at what appeared to be a column of cavalry moving along the road from El Caney towards Santiago, then fired a few shots at the block-houses, then a few at hedges where the enemy's infantry seemed to be located, and then fired a few shots into the village. At about eleven o'clock the battery stopped firing; during all this time a continuous fire of musketry, partly firing at will and partly by volleys, was kept up in all parts of the lines. Our lines were drawing closer towards the enemy's works, and the brigade in reserve was brought up on the line. General Bates's Independent Brigade reached the position in the afternoon and also went into the line, all closing in towards the village. Between one and two o'clock the division commander directed the battery of artillery to concentrate its fire upon the stone fort, or block-houses, situated on the highest point in the village on the northern side, and which was the key-point to the village. This fort was built of brick, with walls about a foot thick, about 45 by 35 feet, with semicircular bastions diagonally opposite each other. The practice of the artillery against this was very effective, knocking great holes into the fort and rendering it untenable.

The infantry of Chaffee's, Bates's, and Miles's brigades then made an assault upon the work and carried it. There were a number of small block-houses on the other side of the village, from which a strong fire was kept up for some time after the stone fort had fallen. Word was sent to the commander of the artillery to bring his battery down so as to take these block-houses, but by the time the battery arrived the fire had ceased. But there was one block-house still occupied by the Spaniards, and at this the battery fired four shots, resulting in the loss of a number of Spaniards killed inside the block-house.

Orders having reached the division commander in the meantime to withdraw his forces as soon as possible and come into touch with the division on his left, our troops were not moved into the village, but were ordered to bivouac near the road leading into the city of Santiago. I was with General Lawton's command from daylight on July 1 until about seven o'clock on the morning of July 2.

SAN JUAN HILL—PORTION OF THE LINE HELD BY THE NINTH UNITED STATES INFANTRY

EL CANEY

Account by General Bates

My brigade left Siboney on the evening of June 30, at 8.30, and marched up over the hill trail. We followed this trail to its junction with the main road, and proceeded along the main road in the dark to the place just vacated by Wheeler's cavalry division as a camp. Here we found General Wheeler's headquarters tents still standing, and went into camp in the rear of them about midnight. We struck camp at 6.30 A.M., July 1, and marched to a point adjacent to General Shafter's headquarters, where I reported in person to General Shafter. At 10.5 A.M. I moved my brigade from this location to within about one and a half miles of El Caney and met General Lawton upon the road at this point.

After a consultation with him lasting some minutes, I halted my brigade upon the road in order to give an opportunity for the placing of a battery that General Lawton expected to put in position between Colonel Miles's right and General Chaffee's left. I waited some time for this to be done, but, the battery not putting in an appearance, I moved my brigade down the road in the direction of El Caney, crossed the San Juan River, and, taking the first cross-roads, moved to the right to a position upon this cross-road to the right of the brigade commanded by Colonel Miles and pushed rapidly to the front. After my brigade had remained in this road for some time under a heavy fire, we moved to the right to the assault of a small hill, occupied upon the top by a stone fort and well protected by rifle-pits. General Chaffee's brigade charged them from the right, and the two brigades, joining upon the crest, opened fire from this point of vantage, lately occupied by the Spaniards, upon the village of El Caney.

From this advantageous position the Spaniards were easily driven from place to place in the village proper, and as fast as they sought shelter in one building were driven out to seek shelter elsewhere. The sharp-shooters of my command were enabled to do effective work at this point. The town proper was soon pretty thoroughly cleaned out of Spaniards, though a couple of block-houses upon the hill to the right of the town offered shelter to a few, and some could be seen retreating along a mountain road leading to the northwest. A part of these made a stand in a field among some bowlders. The Third United States Infantry, under command of Colonel John H. Page, and the Twentieth United States Infantry, under command of Major W. S. McCaskey, performed most efficient and meritorious services in the engagement before the village of El Caney. At about 4.30 P.M. the firing from the village had practically ceased, and, as General Ludlow's brigade was then moving up the valley from the left upon the village, it was deemed unwise to charge El Caney, as our troops would have been subjected to the fire from this brigade.

After consultation with General Chaffee, I withdrew my brigade, hoping there was yet time to aid in the attack more to the left. My command having had a long, hard march, this withdrawal took more time than anticipated. Darkness was coming on. I therefore halted the command at the first water at which we arrived, and proceeded in person to report to the corps commander, and was then ordered to the extreme left. I immediately moved the command, and reached this position at midnight. My command had been then continuously marching or fighting for twenty-seven hours and a half, with the exception of six and one-half hours spent near General Wheeler's headquarters. On the morning of July 2 I placed the Twentieth Infantry on the left of the Second Infantry and in continuation of their line, and held the Third Infantry in reserve near the brigade of Colonel Pearson, of General Kent's division, as that part of the line seemed to need strengthening. The loss in action at El Caney suffered by my brigade was three killed and ten wounded; on the 2d of July it was one killed and eighteen wounded. The wounded included Captains Rodman and Moon, of the Twentieth Infantry.

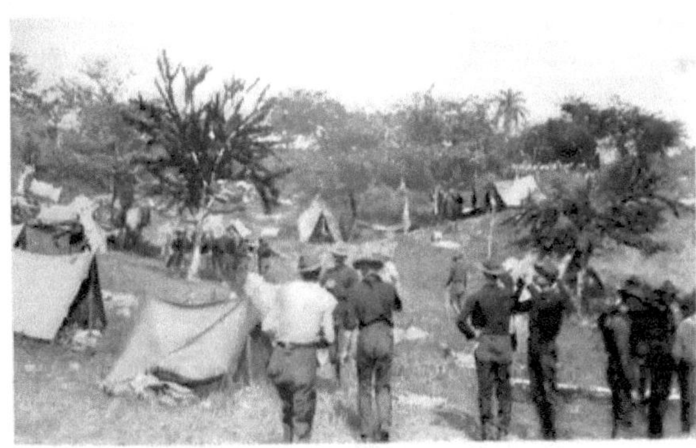

GENERAL WHEELER'S HEADQUARTERS, SAN JUAN

BRIG.-GENERAL H. W. LAWTON

SAN JUAN

General Wheeler's Account

After the engagement of June 24, I pushed forward my command through Sevilla into the valley, Lawton's and Kent's commands occupying the hills in the vicinity of that place. After two days' rest, Lawton was ordered forward, and on the night of the 30th instructions were given by Major-General Shafter to this officer to attack El Caney, while the cavalry division and Kent's division were ordered to move forward on the regular Santiago road. The movement commenced on the morning of July 1.

The cavalry division advanced and formed its line with its left near the Santiago road, while Kent's division formed its line with the right joining the left of the cavalry division. Colonel McClernand, of General Shafter's staff, directed me to give instructions to General Kent, which I complied with in person, at the same time personally directing General Sumner to move forward. The men were all compelled to wade the San Juan River to get into line. This was done under very heavy fire of both infantry and artillery. Our balloon having been sent up right by the main road, was made a mark of by the enemy. It was evident that we were as much under fire in forming the line as we would be by an advance, and I therefore pressed the command forward from the covering where it was formed. It merged into open space, in full view of the enemy, who occupied breastworks and batteries on the crest of the hill which overlooked Santiago, officers and men falling at every step. The troops advanced gallantly, soon reached the foot of the hill, and ascended, driving the enemy from their works and occupying them on the crest of the hill.

To accomplish this required courage and determination of a high order on the part of the officers and men, and the losses were very severe. Too much credit cannot be given to General Sumner and General Kent, and their gallant brigade commanders, Colonel Wood and Colonel Carroll of the cavalry, General Hamilton S. Hawkins, commanding First Brigade, Kent's division, and Colonel Pearson, commanding Second Brigade. Colonel Carroll and Major Wessels were both wounded during the charge, but Major Wessels was enabled to return and resume command. General Wikoff, commanding Kent's Third Brigade, was killed at 12.10. Lieutenant-Colonel Worth took command and was wounded at 12.15. Lieutenant-Colonel Liscum then took command and was wounded at 12.20, and the command then devolved upon Lieutenant-Colonel Ewers, Ninth Infantry.

Upon reaching the crest I ordered breastworks to be constructed, and sent to the rear for shovels, picks, spades, and axes. The enemy's retreat from the ridge was precipitate, but our men were so thoroughly exhausted that it was impossible for them to follow. Their shoes were soaked with water by wading the San Juan River, they had become drenched with rain, and when they reached the crest they were absolutely unable to proceed farther. Notwithstanding this condition these exhausted men labored during the night to erect breastworks, and furnished details to bury the dead and carry the wounded back in improvised litters. I sent word along the line that reinforcements would soon reach us, that Lawton would join our right, and that General Bates would come up and strengthen our left. After reaching the crest of the ridge General Kent sent the Thirteenth Regulars to assist in strengthening our right. At midnight General Bates reported, and I placed him in a strong position on the left of our line. General Lawton had attempted to join us from El Caney, but when very near our lines he was fired upon by the Spaniards and turned back, but joined us next day at noon by a circuitous route. During all the day, on July 2, the cavalry division, Kent's division, and Bates's brigade were engaged with the enemy, being subjected to a severe fire and incurring many casualties, and later in the day Lawton's division also became engaged.

SAN JUAN

General Kent's Account

On the afternoon of June 30 I moved my Second and Third brigades (Pearson's and Wikoff's) forward about two miles to a point on the Santiago road near corps headquarters. Here the troops bivouacked, the First Brigade (Hawkins's) remaining in its camp of the two preceding days, slightly in the rear of corps headquarters.

On the following morning (July 1), at seven o'clock, I rode forward to the hill where Captain Grimes's battery was in position. I here met Lieutenant-Colonel McClernand, assistant adjutant-general Fifth Corps, who pointed out to me a green hill in the distance which was to be my objective on my left, and either he or Lieutenant Miley, of Major-General Shafter's staff, gave me directions to keep my right on the main road leading to the city of Santiago. I had previously given the necessary orders for Hawkins's brigade to move early, to be followed in turn by Wikoff and Pearson. Shortly after Grimes's battery opened fire I rode down to the stream and there found General Hawkins at the head of his brigade at a point about two hundred and fifty yards from the El Pozo sugar-house. Here I gave him his orders.

The enemy's artillery was not replying to Grimes's battery. I rode forward with Hawkins about one hundred and fifty yards, closely followed by the Sixth Infantry, which was leading the First Brigade. At this point I received instructions to allow the cavalry the right of way, but for some unknown reason they moved up very slowly, thus causing a delay in my advance of fully forty minutes. Lieutenant Miley, of General Shafter's staff, was at this point, and understood how the division was delayed, and repeated several times that he understood I was making all the progress possible. General Hawkins went forward, and word came back in a few minutes that it would be possible to observe the enemy's position from the front.

I immediately rode forward with my staff. The fire of the enemy's sharp-shooters was being distinctly felt at this time. I crossed the main ford of the San Juan River, joined General Hawkins, and with him observed the enemy's position from a point some distance in advance of the ford. General Hawkins deemed it possible to turn the enemy's right at Fort San Juan, but later, under the heavy fire, this was found impracticable for the First Brigade, but was accomplished by the Third Brigade coming up later on General Hawkins's left. Having completed the observation with my staff, I proceeded to join the head of my division, just coming under heavy fire. Approaching the First Brigade, I directed them to move alongside the cavalry (which was halted). We were already suffering losses caused by the balloon near by attracting fire and disclosing our position.

The enemy's infantry fire, steadily increasing in intensity, now came from all directions, not only from the front and the dense tropical thickets on our flanks, but from sharp-shooters thickly posted in trees in our rear, and from shrapnel apparently aimed at the balloon. Lieutenant-Colonel Derby, of General Shafter's staff, met me about this time and informed me that a trail or narrow way had been discovered from the balloon a short distance back leading to the left to a ford lower down the stream. I hastened to the forks made by this road, and soon after the Seventy-first New York Regiment of Hawkins's brigade came up. I turned them into the by-path indicated by Lieutenant-Colonel Derby, leading to the lower ford, sending word to General Hawkins of this movement. This would have speedily delivered them in their proper place on the left of their brigade, but under the galling fire of the enemy the leading battalion of this regiment was thrown into confusion and recoiled in disorder on the troops in rear.

At this critical moment the officers of my

BRIG.-GENERAL JACOB F. KENT
Photograph by [illegible]

staff practically formed a cordon behind the panic-stricken men and urged them again to go forward. I finally ordered them to lie down in the thicket and clear the way for others of their own regiment who were coming up behind. This many of them did, and the Second and Third Battalions came forward in better order and moved along the road towards the fork. One of my staff-officers ran back, waving his hat to hurry forward the Third Brigade, who, upon approaching the forks, found the way blocked by men of the Seventy-first New York. There were other men of this regiment crouching in the bushes, many of whom were encouraged by the advance of the approaching column to rise and go forward. As already stated, I had received orders some time before to keep in rear of the cavalry division. Their advance was much delayed, resulting in frequent halts, presumably to drop their blanket rolls and due to the natural delay in fording a stream. These delays under such a hot fire grew exceedingly irksome, and I therefore pushed the head of my division as quickly as I could towards the river in column files of twos paralleled in the narrow way by the cavalry. This quickened the forward movement and enabled me to get into position as speedily as possible for the attack. Owing to the congested condition of the road, the progress of the narrow columns was, however, painfully slow. I again sent a staff-officer at a gallop to urge forward the troops in rear.

The head of Wikoff's brigade reached the forks at 12.20 P.M. and hurried on the left, stepping over prostrate forms of men of the Seventy-first. This heroic brigade, consisting of the Thirteenth, Ninth, and Twenty-fourth United States Infantry, speedily crossed the stream and were quickly deployed to the left of the lower ford. While personally superintending this movement Colonel Wikoff was killed; the command of the brigade then devolved upon Lieutenant-Colonel Worth, Thirteenth Infantry, who immediately fell severely wounded, and then Lieutenant-Colonel Liscum, Twenty-fourth Infantry, who five minutes later also fell under the withering fire of the enemy. The command of the brigade than devolved upon Lieutenant-Colonel E. P. Ewers, Ninth Infantry. Meanwhile I had again sent a staff-officer to hurry forward the Second Brigade, which was bringing up the rear. The Tenth and Second Infantry, soon arriving at the forks, were deflected to the left, to follow the Third Brigade, while the Twenty-first was directed along the main road to support Hawkins.

Crossing the lower ford a few minutes later, the Tenth and Second moved forward in column in good order towards the green knoll already referred to as my objective on the left. Approaching the knoll, the regiments deployed, passed over the knoll, and ascended the high ridge beyond, driving back the enemy in the direction of his trenches. I observed this movement from the Fort San Juan Hill. Colonel E. P. Pearson, Tenth Infantry, commanding the Second Brigade, and the officers and troops under his command, deserve great credit for the soldierly manner in which this movement was executed. Prior to this advance of the Second Brigade, the Third, connecting with Hawkins's gallant troops on the right, had moved towards Fort San Juan, sweeping through a zone of most destructive fire, scaling a steep and difficult hill, and assisting in capturing the enemy's strong position (Fort San Juan) at 1.30 P.M. This crest was about one hundred and twenty-five feet above the general level, and was defended by deep trenches and a loop-holed brick fort surrounded by barbed-wire entanglements.

For the capture of the hill, credit is almost equally due the Sixth, Ninth, Thirteenth, Sixteenth, and Twenty-fourth regiments of infantry. The Thirteenth captured the enemy's colors waving over the fort, but unfortunately destroyed them, distributing the fragments among the men, because, as was asserted, "It was a bad omen," two or three men having been shot while assisting the captor, private Arthur Agnew, Company H, Thirteenth Infantry. The greatest credit was due to the officers of my command, whether company, battalion, regimental, or brigade commanders, who so admirably directed the formation of their troops, unavoidably intermixed in the dense thicket, and made the desperate rush for the distant and strongly defended crest.

I have already mentioned the circumstances

MAJOR-GENERAL JOSEPH WHEELER

of my Third Brigade's advance across the ford, where in the brief space of ten minutes it lost its brave commander (killed) and the next two ranking officers by disabling wounds. Yet in spite of these confusing conditions the formations were effected without hesitation, although under a stinging fire, companies acting singly in some instances, and by battalion and regiments in others, rushing through the jungle, across the stream waist-deep, and over the wide bottom thickly set with barbed-wire entanglements. First Lieutenant Wendell L. Simpson, adjutant Ninth Infantry, acting assistant adjutant-general Third Brigade, was noticeably active and efficient in carrying out orders which I had given him to transmit to his brigade commander, who no longer existed.

The enemy having retired to a second line of rifle-pits, I directed my line to hold their positions and intrench. At ten minutes past 3 P.M. I received almost simultaneously two requests—one from Colonel Wood, commanding a cavalry brigade, and one from General Sumner—asking for assistance for the cavalry on my right, "as they were hard pressed." I immediately sent to their aid the Thirteenth Infantry, who promptly went on this further mission despite the heavy losses they had already sustained.

Great credit is due to that gallant officer and gentleman, Brigadier-General H. S. Hawkins, who, placing himself between the two regiments, leading his brigade, the Sixth and Sixteenth Infantry, urged and led them by voice and bugle calls to the attack so successfully accomplished. My earnest thanks are due to my staff-officers present at my side and under my personal observation on the field. General Wheeler, though ill and suffering, was so perfectly at home under fire that he inspired all of us with assurance.

At daylight on the morning of July 2 the enemy resumed the battle, and firing continued throughout the day, part of the time in a drenching rain. At nightfall the firing ceased, but at 9 P.M. a vigorous assault was made all along our lines. This was completely repulsed, the enemy again retiring to his trenches. The following morning firing was resumed and continued until near noon, when a white flag was displayed by the enemy and firing was ordered to cease.

SAN JUAN

Lieutenant-Colonel Roosevelt's Account

On July 1 the First Volunteer Cavalry Regiment, with myself in command, was moved out by order of Colonel Wood, commanding the Second Cavalry Brigade, directly following the First Brigade. Before leaving the camping-ground several of our men were wounded by shrapnel. After crossing the river at the ford we were moved along and up its right bank under fire, and were held in reserve at a sunken road. Here we lost a good many men, including Captain O'Neil, killed, and Lieutenant Haskell, wounded. We then received orders to advance and support the regular cavalry in the attack on the intrenchments and block-houses on the hills to the left. The regiment was deployed on both sides of the road, and moved forward until we came to the rearmost lines of the regulars. We continued to move forward until I ordered a charge, and the men rushed to the block-houses and rifle-pits on the hill to the right of our advance. They did the work in fine shape, though suffering severely. The guidons of Troops E and G were first planted on the summit, though the first men up were some A and B troopers, who were with me.

We then opened fire on the intrenchments on a hill to our left, which some of the other regiments were assailing and which they carried a few minutes later. Meanwhile we were under a heavy rifle fire from the intrenchments along the hills to our front, from whence the enemy also shelled us with a piece of field artillery until some of our marksmen silenced it. When the men got their wind we charged again and carried the second line of intrenchments with a rush. Swinging to the left, we then drove the Spaniards over the brow of the chain of hills fronting Santiago. By this time the regiments were much mixed, and we were under a very heavy fire, both of shrapnel and from rifles from the batteries, intrenchments, and forts immediately in front of the city. On the extreme front, I now found myself in command, with fragments of the six cavalry regiments of the two brigades under me. The Spaniards made one or two efforts to retake the line, but were promptly driven back.

Both General Sumner and Colonel Wood sent me word to hold the line at all hazards, and that night we dug a line of intrenchments across our front, using the captured Spaniards' intrenching tools. We had nothing to eat except what we captured from the Spaniards; but their dinners had fortunately been cooked, and we ate them with relish, having been fighting all day. We had no blankets or coats, and lay by the trenches all night. The Spaniards attacked us once in the night, and at dawn they opened a heavy artillery and rifle fire. Very great assistance was rendered us by Lieutenant Parker's Gatling-gun battery at critical moments; he fought his guns at the extreme front of the firing-line in a way that repeatedly called forth the cheers of my men. One of the Spanish batteries which was used against us was directly in front of the hospital, so that the Red Cross flag flew over the battery, saving it from our fire for a considerable period. The Spanish Mauser bullets made clean wounds; but they also used a copper-jacketed or brass-jacketed bullet which exploded, making very bad wounds indeed.

We continued to hold the ground; the food was short, and until the 4th we could not get our blankets, coats, or shelter-tents, while the men lay all day under the fire from the Spanish batteries, intrenchments, and guerillas in trees, and worked all night in the trenches, never even taking off their shoes. But they were in excellent spirits, and ready and anxious to carry out any orders they might receive. At the end of the first day the eight troops were commanded, two by captains, three by lieutenants, two by second lieutenants, and one by a sergeant who was made acting lieutenant.

We went into the fight about four hundred and ninety strong; eighty-six were killed or wounded, and there were about half a dozen missing. The great heat prostrated nearly forty men, some of them among the best in the regiment. Besides Captain O'Neil and Lieutenant Haskell, Lieutenants Leahy, Devereux, and Carr were wounded. All behaved with great gallantry. As for Captain O'Neil, his loss was one of the severest that could have befallen the regiment. He was a man of cool head, great executive capacity, and literally dauntless courage.

The guerillas in trees not only fired at our troops, but seemed to devote themselves especially to shooting at the surgeons, the hospital assistants with Red Cross bandages on their arms, the wounded who were being carried in litters, and the burying-parties. Many of these guerillas were dressed in green uniforms. We sent out a detail of sharp-shooters among those in our rear, along the line where they had been shooting the wounded, and killed thirteen.

To attempt to give a list of the men who showed signal valor would necessitate making up an almost complete roster of the regiment. Many of the cases which I mention stand merely as examples of the rest, not as exceptions. Captain Jenkins acted as major, and showed conspicuous gallantry and efficiency. Captains Lewellen, Muller, and Luna led their troops throughout the charges, handling them admirably. At the end of the battle Lieutenants Kane, Greenwood, and Goodrich were in charge of their troops, immediately under my eye, and I particularly commend their conduct throughout. Lieutenant Franz, who commanded his troop, also did well.

Corporals Waller and Fortesque and Trooper McKinley, of E; Corporal Rhoads, of Troop D; Troopers Allerton, Winter, MacGregor, and Ray Clark, of F; Troopers Bugbee, Jackson, and Waller, of A; Trumpeter Macdonald, of Troop L; Sergeant Hughes, of Troop B; and Trooper Geiven, of G, all continued to fight after being wounded, some severely. Most of them fought until the end of the day.

Trooper Oliver B. Norton, of B, who with his brother was by my side throughout the charging, was killed while fighting with marked gallantry. Sergeant Ferguson, Corporal Lee, and Troopers Bell and Carroll, of K; Sergeant Dame, of Troop E; Troopers Goodwin, Campbell, and Dudley Dean, and Trumpeter Foster, of B; and Troopers Greenwald and Bardelas, of A, were all worthy of special mention for coolness and gallantry. The most conspicuous gallantry was shown by Trooper Rowland. He was wounded in the side in our first fight, but kept in the firing-line. He was sent to the hospital next day, but left it and marched out to us, overtaking us, and fought all through this battle with such indifference to danger that I was forced again and again to rate and threaten him for running needless risk.

Great gallantry was shown by four troopers whom I could not identify, and by Trooper Winslow Clark. It was after we had taken the first hill. I had called out to rush the second, and, having by that time lost my horse, I climbed a wire fence and started towards it. After going a couple of hundred yards, under a heavy fire, I found that no one else had come; as I discovered later, it was simply because, in the confusion, with men shooting and being shot, they had not noticed me start. I told the five men to wait a moment, as it might be misunderstood if we all ran back, while I returned and started the regiment; and as soon as I did so the regiment came with a rush. Meanwhile the five men coolly lay down in the open, returning the fire from the trenches. It is to be wondered at that only Clark was seriously wounded; and he called out, as we paused again to lay his canteen where he could reach it, to continue the charge and leave him where he was. All the wounded had to be left until after the fight, for we could spare no men from the firing-line.

IN THE REAR OF THE BATTLE—WOUNDED ON THE SAN JUAN ROAD.—Drawn by Frederic Remington

Torpedo-Boat *Ariete* — Torpedo-Gunboat *Pluton* — Torpedo-Gunboat *Terror* — Converted Merchantman, *Ciudad de Cadiz*, as Convoy — Torpedo-Boat *Rayo* — Torpedo-Boat *Azor* — Torpedo-Gunboat *Furor*

SPAIN'S TORPEDO-BOAT FLOTILLA *EN ROUTE* FROM THE CANARIES TO PUERTO RICO.—BY W. LOUIS SONNTAG, JR.

COMBINED SEA AND LAND ATTACK AT AGUADORES, JULY 1.—Drawn by Carlton T. Chapman

THE NAVAL BATTLE OF SANTIAGO

ON July 3, immediately following the brilliant achievement of the American land forces in front of Santiago, occurred the decisive naval combat of the war. The Spanish fleet, attempting to leave the harbor of Santiago, was met by the American squadron under command of Admiral Sampson. In less than three hours all the Spanish ships were destroyed, the two torpedo-boats being sunk, and the *Maria Teresa*, *Almirante Oquendo*, *Vizcaya*, and *Cristobal Colon* driven ashore. The Spanish Admiral and over sixteen hundred men were taken prisoners, while the Spanish loss of life was deplorably large, some six hundred perishing. On the American side but one man was killed, on the *Brooklyn*, and one man seriously wounded. Although the American ships were repeatedly struck, not one was seriously injured. "Where all so conspicuously distinguished themselves," wrote the President of the United States, "from the commanders to the gunners and the unnamed heroes in the boiler-rooms, each and all contributing towards the achievement of this astounding victory, for which neither ancient nor modern history affords a parallel in the completeness of the event and the marvellous disproportion of casualties, it would be invidious to single out any for especial honor. Deserved promotion rewarded the more conspicuous actors—the nation's profoundest gratitude is due to all of these brave men who by their skill and devotion in a few short hours crushed the sea-power of Spain and wrought a triumph whose decisiveness and far-reaching consequences could scarcely be measured. Nor could we be unmindful of the achievements of our builders, mechanics, and artisans for their skill in the construction of our warships. With the catastrophe of Santiago, Spain's effort upon the ocean virtually ceased. A spasmodic effort towards the end of June to send her Mediterranean fleet under Admiral Camara to relieve Manila was abandoned, the expedition being recalled after it had passed through the Suez Canal."

MORRO CASTLE, SANTIAGO

THE SUCCESSION OF EVENTS

AS RELATED BY

THE SECRETARY OF THE NAVY

ALL the troops were successfully landed by the boats of the navy, and the joint operations of the army and navy began which finally resulted in the surrender of Santiago. On July 1, in accordance with a request from General Shafter of June 30, the forts at Aguadores were bombarded and a demonstration made at the entrance of the harbor of Santiago; and on July 2 the batteries at the entrance of the harbor were heavily bombarded, especially the Punta Gorda battery, by the *Oregon* and *Indiana*. A report of this bombardment was sent to General Shafter, and Admiral Sampson stated that it was impossible to force an entrance to the harbor until the channel could be cleared of mines, which could only be done after the forts at the entrance of the harbor were taken by our troops. General Shafter replied that it was not possible to say when he could take the batteries at the harbor's mouth, and urged that an effort be immediately made by the navy to force an entrance.

Admiral Sampson wrote to General Shafter that the forts which had been bombarded by the squadron could not inconvenience the army in capturing the city, as they could not fire except to seaward; that as the channel to the harbor was strewn with observation mines an effort to force an entrance would result in the sinking of one or more naval vessels and in closing the entrance to the harbor; but that if it was desired that the navy should attempt to force the entrance he would at once prepare to undertake it, although he had hoped that an attack by the army on the shore batteries from the rear would leave the navy at liberty to drag the channel for torpedoes.

On the morning of July 3, an interview having been prearranged between General Shafter and Admiral Sampson, the latter, in the flag-ship *New York*, left the fleet for Siboney. When the flag-ship was about four miles east of her blockading station, and about seven miles from the Morro, the Spanish squadron was seen steaming out of the harbor entrance. This was at 9.30 A.M. The vessels of the blockading squadron were, as usual, in their designated positions, making a semicircle about the harbor entrance, counting from the eastward in the following order: *Indiana*, *Oregon*—the *New York's* place being between these two—*Iowa*, *Texas*, and *Brooklyn*. The *Massachusetts* had gone that morning to Guantanamo for coal. The *Gloucester* and *Vixen* lay to the eastward and westward of the harbor entrance, close to the land. The torpedo-boat *Ericsson* was in company with the flag-ship.

DESTRUCTION OF THE FORT AT AGUADORES, JULY 1.—Drawn by Carlton T. Chapman

The *New York's* three splendid shots: the first tilted the flag-staff; the second tore the flag in two; the third carried it away

Admiral Cervera's squadron came out of the harbor in the following order: *Infanta Maria Teresa*, *Vizcaya*, *Cristobal Colon*, *Almirante Oquendo*, and the torpedo-boat destroyers *Pluton* and *Furor*. The *New York* turned and steamed for the escaping fleet, flying the signal to close in towards the harbor entrance and attack the vessels; but our ships had already, in accordance with standing orders, at once engaged the Spanish ships with the utmost spirit and vigor, and in the course of a running fight, which continued until 1.20 P.M., the latter were completely destroyed and sunk, and the famous victory, with its splendid credit to officers and men, was won. The casualties on our side were one man killed and ten wounded, most of them in the drum of the ear by the concussion caused by the guns. Our ships suffered no injury of any account. Admiral Cervera, about 70 officers, and 1600 men were made prisoners, while about 350 Spaniards were killed or drowned and 160 wounded. Many of the enemy were rescued from their sinking ships by our men. The prisoners, except the officers, who were sent to Annapolis, were brought to Portsmouth, New Hampshire, and kept in Camp Long, on Seavey's Island, in the harbor of that city, until they were released. During this time they were fed and clothed and comfortably cared for. There was little sickness, and the wounded and ailing soon recovered under good treatment.

On July 4, at night, the Spanish cruiser *Reina Mercedes*, which had not left Santiago with Cervera's squadron, was seen steaming out of the harbor. She was sunk just before reaching the narrow part of the entrance channel, presumably by the fire of the *Massachusetts* and *Texas*. The object of this manœuvre was doubtful, but it had the effect of further obstructing the channel.

On July 5 the department telegraphed to Admiral Sampson that the President had issued the following order: "General Shafter and Admiral Sampson should confer at once for co-operation in taking Santiago." General Shafter immediately requested Admiral Sampson to come to him for conference. On the next day Admiral Sampson, being ill, sent his chief of staff, who had a conference with General Shafter, in which it was arranged that, in case the Spanish commander refused the second demand for surrender, a continued bombardment of Santiago should be begun by the fleet on the 9th; that, if this were not sufficient, there should be an assault on the Socapa battery by the marines and Cuban forces, and an effort made by some of the smaller ships of the squadron to enter the harbor.

On July 10, the squadron, complying with the request of General Shafter, began a further bombardment of Santiago. This was continued on the 11th. At 12 M. General Shafter signalled: "Please continue firing with heavy guns until 1 o'clock, and then cease firing until further orders." At 4.45 P.M. the *Brooklyn* reported to the flag-ship: "General Shafter states that fire from ships is very accurate, shell falling in city; lines have been advanced. Flag of truce went forward to demand unconditional surrender. Will communicate with you fully directly to Aguadores as to time of firing and result of truce."

On July 12 the Admiral received a despatch from General Shafter stating: "My lines are now complete to the bay north of Santiago. Your shots can be observed from there perfectly, at least those that fall in the town. Flames followed several shots fired to-day." At 8.10 P.M. General Shafter signalled: "A truce now exists, and will probably continue all day to-morrow, the 13th."

On July 13, at 9.5 A.M., Admiral Sampson signalled to General Shafter: "As Commander-in-Chief of the naval forces engaged in joint operations, I expect to be represented in any conference held to arrange the terms of surrender of Santiago, including the surrender of the shipping and the harbor. Questions are involved of importance to both branches of the service." This was replied to at 2.40 P.M. by General Shafter, as follows: "I shall be glad to have you represented, but difficult to let you know. Conference may take place at any hour."

At 1.15 P.M., on the 14th, General Miles telegraphed to Admiral Sampson: "I will be glad if you will send to these headquarters an officer to represent you during negotiations for evacuation." At 1.38 P.M. General Miles was replied to: "When do you want Admiral Sampson's representative there?" At 2.23 P.M., before any arrangement could be made by which Admiral Sampson could send a representative to the headquarters of the army, General Miles telegraphed: "Enemy has surrendered."

On the next day, July 15, General Miles advised Admiral Sampson that the surrender had not actually been concluded, and then on the 16th wrote him that at the request of the Spanish officials delay had been granted to communicate with the

ADMIRAL SAMPSON'S ACCOUNT OF THE BATTLE

THE enemy's vessels came out of the harbor between 9.35 and 10 A.M., the head of the column appearing around Cay Smith at 9.31 and emerging from the channel five or six minutes later.

The positions of the vessels of my command off Santiago at that moment were as follows. The flagship *New York* was four miles east of interview with General Shafter, who had been suffering from heat prostration. I made arrangements to go to his headquarters, and my flag-ship was in the position mentioned above when the Spanish squadron appeared in the channel. The remaining vessels were in or near their usual blockading positions, distributed in a semicircle about the harbor entrance, counting from the eastward to the westward, in the following order: The *Indiana* about a mile and a half from shore, the *Oregon*

and *Vixen* lay close to the land and nearer the harbor entrance than the large vessels, the *Gloucester* to the eastward and the *Vixen* to the westward. The torpedo-boat *Ericsson* was in company with the flag-ship and remained with her during the chase until ordered to discontinue, when she rendered very efficient service in rescuing prisoners from the burning *Vizcaya*.

The Spanish vessels came rapidly out of the harbor, at a speed estimated at from eight to ten knots, and in the following order: *Infanta Maria Teresa* (flag-ship), *Vizcaya*, *Cristobal Colon*, and the *Almirante Oquendo*. The distance between these ships was about 800 yards, which means that from the time the first one became visible in the upper reach of the channel until the last one was out of the harbor an interval of only about twelve minutes elapsed. Following the *Oquendo*, at a distance of about 1200 yards, came the torpedo-boat destroyer *Pluton*, and after her the *Furor*. The armored cruisers, as rapidly as they could bring their guns to bear, opened a vigorous fire upon the blockading vessels, and emerged from the channel shrouded in the smoke from their guns.

The men of our ships in front of the port were at Sunday "quarters for inspection." The signal was made simultaneously from several vessels, "Enemy's ships escaping," and general quarters was sounded. The men cheered as they sprang to their guns, and fire was opened probably within eight minutes by the vessels whose guns commanded the entrance. The *New York* turned about and steamed for the escaping fleet, flying the signal, "Close in towards harbor entrance and attack vessels," and gradually increasing speed, until towards the end of the chase she was making sixteen and one-half knots, and was rapidly closing on the *Cristobal Colon*. She was not, at any time, within the range of the heavy Spanish ships, and her only part in the firing was to receive the undivided fire from the forts in passing the harbor entrance, and to fire a few shots at one of the destroyers, thought at the moment to be attempting to escape from the *Gloucester*.

The Spanish vessels, upon clearing the harbor, turned to the westward in column, increasing their speed to the full power of their engines. The heavy blockading vessels, which had closed in towards the Morro at the instant of the enemy's appearance, and at their best speed, delivered a rapid fire, well sustained and destructive, which speedily overwhelmed and silenced the Spanish fire. The initial speed of the Spaniards carried them rapidly past the blockading vessels, and the battle developed into a chase, in which the *Brooklyn* and *Texas* had, at the start, the advantage of position. The *Brooklyn* maintained the lead until the *Oregon*, steaming with amazing speed from the commencement of the action, took first place. The *Iowa* and the *Indiana* having done good work, and not having the speed of the other ships, were directed by me, in succession, at about the time the *Vizcaya* was beached, to drop out of the chase and resume blockading stations. These vessels rescued many prisoners. The *Vixen*, finding that the rush of the Spanish ships would put her between two fires, ran outside of our own column and remained there during the battle and chase.

The skilful handling and gallant fighting of the *Gloucester* excited the admiration of every one who witnessed it. She was a fast and entirely unprotected auxiliary vessel—the yacht *Corsair*—and had a good battery of light rapid-fire guns. She was lying about two miles from the harbor entrance, to the southward and eastward, and immediately steamed in, opening fire upon the large ships. Anticipating the appearance of the *Pluton* and *Furor*, the *Gloucester* was slowed, thereby gaining more rapidly a high pressure of steam, and when the destroyers came out she steamed for them at full speed, and was able to close to short range, while her fire was accurate, deadly, and of great volume. During this fight the *Gloucester* was under the fire of the Socapa battery. Within twenty minutes from the time they emerged from Santiago Harbor the careers of the *Furor* and the *Pluton* were ended, and two-thirds of their people killed. The *Furor* was beached, and sank in the surf; the *Pluton* sank in deep water a few minutes later. The destroyers probably suffered much injury from the fire of the secondary batteries of the battle-ships *Iowa*, *Indiana*, and the *Texas*, yet I think a very considerable factor in their speedy destruction was the fire, at close range, of the *Gloucester's* battery. After rescuing the survivors of the destroyers, the *Gloucester* did excellent service in landing and securing the crew of the *Infanta Maria Teresa*.

The method of escape attempted by the Spaniards, all steering in the same direction, and in formation, removed all tactical doubts or difficulties, and made plain the duty of every United States vessel to close in, immediately engage, and pursue. This was promptly and effectively done. As already stated, the first rush of the Spanish squadron carried it past a number of the blockading ships, which could not immediately work up to their best speed; but they suffered heavily in passing, and the *Infanta Maria Teresa* and the *Oquendo* were probably set on fire by shells fired during the first fifteen minutes of the engagement. It was afterwards learned that the *Infanta Maria Teresa's* fire-main had been cut by one of our first shots, and that she was unable to extinguish fire. With large volumes of smoke rising from their lower decks aft, these vessels gave up both fight and flight, and ran in on the beach—the *Infanta Maria Teresa* at about 10.15 A.M. at Nima Nima, six and a half miles from Santiago Harbor entrance, and the *Almirante Oquendo* at about 10.30 A.M. at Juan Gonzales, seven miles from the port.

The *Vizcaya* was still under the fire of the leading vessels; the *Cristobal Colon* had drawn ahead, leading the chase, and soon passed beyond the range of the guns of the leading American ships. The *Vizcaya* was soon set on fire, and, at 11.15, she turned inshore and was beached at Aserraderos, fifteen miles from Santiago, burning fiercely, and with her reserves of ammunition on deck already beginning to explode. When about ten miles west of Santiago the *Indiana* had been signalled to go back to the harbor entrance, and at Aserraderos the *Iowa* was signalled to "Resume blockading station." The *Iowa*, assisted by the *Ericsson* and the *Hist*, took off the crew of the *Vizcaya*, while the *Harvard* and the *Gloucester* rescued those of the *Infanta Maria Teresa* and the *Almirante Oquendo*. This rescue of prisoners, including the wounded, from the burning Spanish vessels was the occasion of some of the most daring and gallant conduct of the day. The ships were burning fore and aft, their guns and reserve ammunition were exploding, and it was not known at what moment the fire would reach the main magazines. In addition to this a heavy surf was running just inside of the Spanish ships. But no risk deterred our officers and men until their work of humanity was complete.

There remained now of the Spanish ships only the *Cristobal Colon*, but she was their best and fastest vessel. Forced by the situation to hug the Cuban coast, her only chance of escape was by superior and sustained speed. When the *Vizcaya* went ashore, the *Colon* was about six miles ahead of the *Brooklyn* and the *Oregon*; but her spurt was finished, and the American ships were now gaining upon her. Behind the *Brooklyn* and the *Oregon* came the *Texas*, *Vixen*, and *New York*. It was evident from the bridge of the *New York* that all the American ships were gradually overhauling the chase, and that she had no chance of escape. At 12.50 the *Brooklyn* and the *Oregon* opened fire and got her range—the *Oregon's* heavy shell striking beyond her—and at 1.20 she gave up without firing another shot, hauled down her colors, and ran ashore at Rio Tonguino, forty-eight miles from Santiago. Captain Cook, of the *Brooklyn*, went on board to receive the surrender. While his boat was alongside, I came up in the *New York*, received his report, and placed the *Oregon* in charge of the wreck, to save her, if possible, and directed the prisoners to be transferred to the *Resolute*, which had followed the chase. Commodore Schley, whose chief of staff had gone on board to receive the surrender, had directed that all their personal effects should be retained by the officers. This order I did not modify. The *Cristobal Colon* was not injured by our firing, and probably not much injured by beaching, though she ran ashore at high speed. The beach was so steep that she came off by the working of the sea. But her sea-valves were opened and broken, treacherously, I am sure, after her surrender; and despite all efforts she sank. When it became evident that she could not be kept afloat, she was pushed by the *New York* bodily up on the beach, the *New York's* stem being placed against her for this purpose—the ship being handled by Captain Chadwick with admirable judgment—and sank in shoal water, and, it was thought, might be saved. Had this not been done she would have gone down in deep water and would have been, to a certainty, a total loss.

I regarded this complete and important victory over the Spanish forces as the successful finish of several weeks of arduous and close blockade, so stringent and effective during the night that the enemy was deterred from making the attempt to escape at night, and deliberately elected to make the attempt in daylight. That this was the case I was informed by the commanding officer of the *Cristobal Colon*.

It seems proper to describe briefly here the manner in which this was accomplished. The harbor of Santiago is naturally easy to blockade, there being but one entrance, and that a narrow one, and the deep water extending close up to the shore-line, presenting no difficulties of navigation outside of the entrance. At the time of my arrival before the port—June 1—the moon was at its full, and there was sufficient light during the night to enable any movement outside of the entrance to be detected; but with the waning of the moon

Oregon wreathed in smoke — Socapa Battery — Iowa waiting off the entrance for the Spanish Fleet — Cay Smith — Fort Morro — Newark

NAVAL BOMBARDMENT OF SANTIAGO'S HARBOR DEFENCES, JULY 2.—DRAWN BY CARLTON T. CHAPMAN

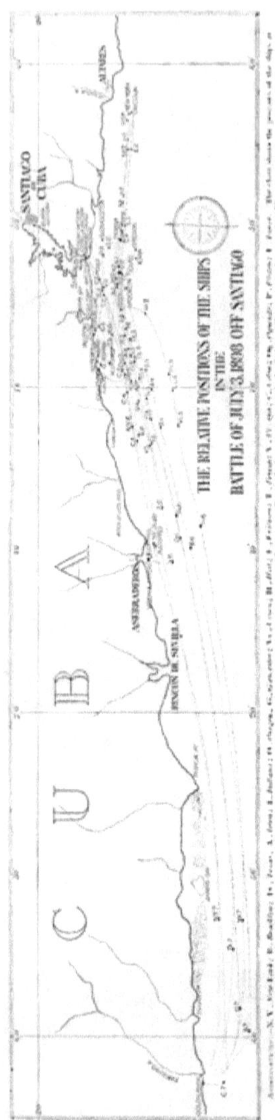

and the coming of dark nights there was opportunity for the enemy to escape, or for his torpedo-boats to make an attack upon the blockading vessels. It was ascertained with fair conclusiveness that the *Merrimac*, so gallantly taken into the channel on June 3, did not obstruct it. I therefore maintained the blockade as follows: To the battle-ships was assigned the duty, in turn, of lighting the channel. Moving up to the port, at a distance of from one to two miles from the Morro—dependent upon the condition of the atmosphere—they threw a search-light beam directly up the channel, and held it steadily there. This lighted up the entire breadth of the channel for half a mile inside of the entrance so brilliantly that the movement of small boats could be detected. Why the batteries never opened fire upon the search-light ship was always a matter of surprise to me; but they never did. Stationed close to the entrance of the port were three picket launches and, at a little distance farther out, three small picket vessels—usually converted yachts—and, when they were available, one or two of our torpedo-boats. With this arrangement there was at least a certainty that nothing could get out of the harbor undetected. After the arrival of the army, when the situation forced upon the Spanish Admiral a decision, our vigilance increased. The night-blockading distance was reduced to two miles for all vessels, and a battle-ship was placed alongside the search-light ship, with her broadside trained upon the channel, in readiness to fire the instant a Spanish ship should appear. The commanding officers merited the greatest praise for the perfect manner in which they entered into this plan and put it into execution. The *Massachusetts*, which, according to routine, was sent that morning to coal at Guantanamo, like the others had spent weary nights upon this work, and deserved a better fate than to be absent that morning.

When all the work was done so well it is difficult to discriminate in praise. The object of the blockade of Cervera's squadron was fully accomplished, and each individual bore well his part in it—the commodore in command of the second division, the captains of ships, their officers and men. The fire of the battle-ships was powerful and destructive, and the resistance of the Spanish squadron was, in great part, broken almost before they had got beyond the range of their own forts. The fine speed of the *Oregon* enabled her to take a front position in the chase, and the *Cristobal Colon* did not give up until the *Oregon* had thrown a 13-inch shell beyond her. This performance added to the already brilliant record of that fine battle-ship, and spoke highly of the skill and care with which her admirable efficiency had been maintained during a service unprecedented in the history of vessels of her class. The *Brooklyn's* westerly blockading position gave her an advantage in the chase which she maintained to the end, and she employed her fine battery with telling effect. The *Texas* and the *New York* were gaining on the chase during the last hour, and, had any accident befallen the *Brooklyn* or the *Oregon*, would have speedily overhauled the *Cristobal Colon*. From the moment the Spanish vessel exhausted her first burst of speed the result was never in doubt. She fell, in fact, far below what might reasonably have been expected of her. Careful measurements of time and distance gave her an average speed, from the time she cleared the harbor mouth until the time she was run on shore at Rio Tarquino, of 13.7 knots. Neither the *New York* nor the *Brooklyn* stopped to couple up their forward engines, but ran out the chase with one pair, getting steam, of course, as rapidly as possible on all boilers. To stop to couple up the forward engines would have meant a delay of fifteen minutes, or four miles in the chase.

Several of the ships were struck—the *Brooklyn* oftener than the others—but very slight material injury was done, the greatest being aboard the *Iowa*. Our loss was one man killed and one wounded, both on the *Brooklyn*. It is difficult to explain this immunity from loss of life or injury to ships in a combat with modern vessels of the best type, but Spanish gunnery was poor at the best, and the superior weight and accuracy of our fire speedily drove the men from their guns and silenced their fire. This is borne out by the statements of prisoners and by observation. The Spanish vessels, as they dashed out of the harbor, were covered by the smoke from their own guns, but this speedily diminished in volume and soon almost disappeared. The fire from the rapid-fire batteries of the battle-ships appeared to have been remarkably destructive. An examination of the stranded vessels showed that the *Almirante Oquendo* especially had suffered terribly from this fire. Her sides were everywhere pierced and her decks were strewn with the charred remains of those who had fallen.

COMMODORE SCHLEY'S REPORT

TO THE COMMANDER-IN-CHIEF

At 9.35 A.M., Admiral Cervera, with the *Infanta Maria Teresa*, *Vizcaya*, *Oquendo*, *Cristobal Colon*, and two torpedo-boat destroyers, came out of the harbor of Santiago de Cuba in column at distance and attempted to escape to the westward. Signal was made from the *Iowa* that the enemy was coming out, but his movement had been discovered from the *Brooklyn* at the same moment. The *Brooklyn* was the farthest west, except the *Vixen*, in the blockading line. Signal was made to the western division, as prescribed in your general orders, and there was immediate and rapid movement inward by your squadron and a general engagement at ranges beginning at 1100 yards and varying to 3000 yards until the *Vizcaya* was destroyed, about 10.50 A.M. The concentration of the fire of the squadron upon the ships coming out was most furious and terrific, and great damage was done them.

About twenty or twenty-five minutes after the engagement began, two vessels, thought to be the *Teresa* and *Oquendo*, and since verified as such, took fire from the effective shell-fire of the squadron, and were forced to run on the beach some six or seven miles west of the harbor entrance, where they burned and blew up later. The torpedo-boat destroyers were destroyed early in the action, but the smoke was so dense in their direction that I cannot say to which vessel or vessels the credit belongs. This, doubtless, was better seen from your flag-ship.

The *Vizcaya* and *Colon*, perceiving the disaster to their consorts, continued at full speed to the westward to escape, and were followed and engaged in a running fight with the *Brooklyn*, *Texas*, *Iowa*, and *Oregon* until 10.30, when the *Vizcaya* took fire from our shells. She put her helm to port, and, with a heavy list to port, stood inshore and ran aground at Aserraderos, about twenty-one miles west of Santiago, on fire fore and aft, and where she blew up during the night. Observing that she had struck her colors, and that several vessels were nearing her to capture and save her crew, signal was made to cease firing. The *Oregon* having proved vastly faster than the other battle-ships, she and the *Brooklyn*, together with the *Texas* and another vessel which proved to be your flag-ship, continued westward in pursuit of the *Colon*, which had run

lyn and the *Oregon*, was turned over to you as one of the trophies of this great victory of the squadron under your command.

During my official visit, a little later, Commander Eaton, of the *Resolute*, appeared and reported to you the presence of a Spanish battle-ship near Altares. Your orders to me were to take the *Oregon* and go eastward to meet her, and this was done by the *Brooklyn*, with the result that the vessel reported as an enemy was discovered to be the Austrian cruiser *Kaiserin Maria Theresia*, seeking the commander-in-chief.

The *Brooklyn* occupied the most westward blockading position, with the *Vixen*, and, being more directly in the route taken by the Spanish squadron, was exposed for some minutes, possibly ten, to the gun-fire of three of the Spanish ships and the west battery, at a range of 1500 yards from the ships and about 3000 yards from the batteries; but the vessels

acted with conspicuous courage; although unable to engage the heavier ships of the enemy with his light guns, nevertheless he was close in to the battle-line under heavy fire, and many of the enemy's shot passed beyond his vessel.

I beg to invite special attention to the conduct of my flag-lieutenant, James H. Sears, and Ensign Edward McCauley, Jr., aide, who were constantly at my side during the engagement, and who exposed themselves fearlessly in discharging their duties; and also to the splendid behavior of my secretary, Lieutenant B. W. Wells, Jr., who commanded and directed the fighting of the fourth division with splendid effect.

I would commend the highly meritorious conduct and courage in the engagement of Lieutenant Commander N. E. Mason, the executive officer, whose presence everywhere over the ship during its continuance did much

THE BATTLE OF SANTIAGO, JULY 3.—Drawn by Carlton T. Chapman

close inshore, evidently seeking some good spot to beach if she should fail to elude her pursuers.

This pursuit continued with increasing speed in the *Brooklyn*, *Oregon*, and other ships, and soon the *Brooklyn* and *Oregon* were within long range of the *Colon*, when the *Oregon* opened fire with her 13-inch guns, landing a shell close to the *Colon*. A moment afterwards the *Brooklyn* opened fire with her 8-inch guns, landing a shell just ahead of her. Several other shells were fired at the *Colon*, now in range of the *Brooklyn's* and *Oregon's* guns. Her commander, seeing all chances of escape cut off, and destruction awaiting his ship, fired a lee gun and struck her flag at 1.15 P.M., and ran ashore at a point some fifty miles west of Santiago Harbor. Your flag-ship was coming up rapidly at the time, as was also the *Texas* and *Vixen*. A little later, after your arrival, the *Cristobal Colon*, which had struck to the *Brook-*

of the entire squadron, closing in rapidly, soon diverted this fire and did magnificent work at close range. I have never before witnessed such deadly and fatally accurate shooting as was done by the ships of your command as they closed in on the Spanish squadron, and I deem it a high privilege to commend to you, for such action as you may deem proper, the gallantry and dashing courage, the prompt decision, and the skilful handling of their respective vessels of Captain Philip, Captain Evans, Captain Clark, and especially of my chief of staff, Captain Cook, who was directly under my personal observation, and whose coolness, promptness, and courage were of the highest order. The dense smoke of the combat shut out from my view the *Indiana* and the *Gloucester*, but as these vessels were closer to your flag-ship, no doubt their part in the conflict was under your immediate observation.

Lieutenant Sharp, commanding the *Vixen*,

to secure the good result of this ship's part in the victory.

The navigator, Lieutenant A. C. Hodgson, and the division officers, Lieutenant T. D. Griffin, Lieutenant W. R. Rush, Lieutenant Edward Simpson, Lieutenant J. G. Doyle, Ensign Charles Webster, and the junior divisional officers were most steady and conspicuous in every detail of duty contributing to the accurate firing of this ship in her part of the great victory of your forces.

The officers of the Medical, Pay, Engineer, and Marine corps responded to every demand of the occasion, and were fearless in exposing themselves. The warrant officers, Boatswain William L. Hill, Carpenter G. H. Warford, and Gunner F. T. Applegate, were everywhere exposed, in watching for damage, reports of which were promptly conveyed to me.

I have never in my life served with a braver, better, or worthier crew than that of

THE NAVAL BATTLE OF SANTIAGO—DESTRUCTION OF ADMIRAL C

RA'S FLEET, SUNDAY MORNING, JULY 3.—DRAWN BY CARLTON T. CHAPMAN

the *Brooklyn*. During the combat, lasting from 9.35 A.M. until 1.15 P.M., much of the time under fire, they never flagged for a moment, and were apparently undisturbed by the storm of projectiles passing ahead, astern, and over the ship.

The result of the engagement was the destruction of the Spanish squadron and the capture of the Admiral and some thirteen to fifteen hundred prisoners, with the loss of several hundred killed, estimated by Admiral Cervera at six hundred men.

The casualties on board the *Brooklyn* were: G. H. Ellis, chief yeoman, killed; J. Burns, fireman, first-class, severely wounded. The marks and scars show that the ship was struck about twenty-five times, and she bears in all forty-one scars as the result of her participation in the great victory of your force on July 3, 1898. The speed-cone halyards were shot away, and nearly all the signal halyards. The ensign at the main was so shattered that in hauling it down at the close of the action it fell in pieces.

I congratulate you most sincerely upon this great victory to the squadron under your command, and I am glad that I had an opportunity to contribute in the least to a victory that seems big enough for all of us.

From Captain Eulate, of the *Vizcaya*, and the second in command of the *Colon*, Commander Contreras, I learned that the Spanish Admiral's scheme was to concentrate all fire for a while on the *Brooklyn*, and the *Vizcaya* to ram her, in hopes that if they could destroy her the chance of escape would be increased, as it was supposed she was the swiftest ship of your squadron. This explains the heavy fire mentioned and the *Vizcaya's* action in the earlier moments of the engagement. The execution of this purpose was promptly defeated by the fact that all the ships of the squadron advanced into close range and opened an irresistibly furious and terrific fire upon the enemy's squadron as it was coming out of the harbor.

I cannot close this report without mentioning in high terms of praise the splendid conduct and support of Captain C. E. Clark, of the *Oregon*. Her speed was wonderful and her accurate fire splendidly destructive.

CAPTAIN CHADWICK'S ACCOUNT

THE *New York* had started at 8.30 for the army-landing at Siboney, the commander-in-chief having an appointment with the general commanding the army. A few minutes after the crew had been called to quarters for Sunday inspection, firing was heard and a ship was seen leaving the harbor entrance; the helm was at once put over, the crew called to general quarters, signal "Close in towards harbor entrance and attack vessels" made, orders given to spread all fires, and the ship headed back for the enemy, whose ships were seen successively coming out at a high speed. The flag-ship *Infanta Maria Teresa* was first, then another armored cruiser of the same class (which turned out to be the *Vizcaya*), followed by the *Cristobal Colon*, an armored cruiser (*Oquendo*), and the torpedo-boat destroyers *Furor* and *Pluton*.

The nearer ships had immediately engaged, and by the time we were off the entrance, one, the flag-ship, was already afire and was soon ashore. The *Indiana* and *Gloucester* were actively engaged with the torpedo-boats. The *New York* fired some 4-inch shell at the one nearer the port, towards which she was headed and to which she seemed attempting to return, but she was already practically out of the fight. The boiler of the more advanced one had blown up, showing a vast column of condensed steam. During this time the batteries, whose line of fire we had crossed close to, repeatedly fired upon us, but without effect. No return was made to this fire. A shell from the west battery fell within two hundred yards of the ship when we were over four miles to the westward and we had thought ourselves entirely out of range. We stood on, leaving the *Gloucester*, which had shown herself so capable, to look after the survivors in the torpedo-boats. By this time a second cruiser was ashore and burning (the *Almirante Oquendo*), while the third, the *Vizcaya*, and the *Cristobal Colon* were still steaming rapidly westward. The *Indiana* was now signalled (11.26 A.M.) to return to the blockading position to look after anything which might be there. Very shortly the *Vizcaya* turned shoreward, smoke began to issue from her after part, and by the time that she was ashore on the reef at Aserraderos (fifteen miles west of Santiago) she was ablaze. The *Iowa* had signalled a little before that she had surrendered, and stopped off this place, where she gave much assistance in the rescue of the *Vizcaya's* people.

The *New York* stood on in chase of the *Cristobal Colon*, with ahead of us the *Brooklyn*, *Oregon*, *Texas*, and *Vixen*—the *Oregon* being much nearer inshore of the two headmost ships, but not in gunshot. We were rapidly increasing our speed. It was evident, however, that the *Colon* would give us a lengthy chase, and at noon the crew left quarters and went to dinner.

About 12.30 the *Oregon* opened fire, and some of her shell were observed to strike beyond the *Colon*. This made her capture a foregone conclusion, and shortly after one o'clock she turned in towards shore and soon struck her colors. She had been beached at a small inlet known as Rio Tarquino. By the time we arrived a boat was alongside her from the *Brooklyn*, and Captain Cook, the boarding officer, came alongside the *New York* and reported. The *New York* then sent a boat to take possession, the commanding officer going in the boat. I was received by the commodore of the squadron, the captain, Captain de Navio Don Emilio Moreu, and Captain de Navio, of the first-class, Don José de Paredes y Chacon (which latter had been civil governor of Santiago and had only just been attached to the squadron). I arranged for the transfer of the crew and officers, a division to each ship present, and the engineer force to be left aboard. While aboard, however, the *Resolute* arrived, and it was arranged to transfer the whole number to her.

I had taken with me the fleet surgeon, an engineer officer, and the carpenter to examine and make secure everything necessary. The engineer officer reported to me that she was making water aft. I had previously had soundings taken and found eight feet at the bow and seventy at the stern, so that but a small portion of the ship was ashore. I returned as quickly as possible to the flagship to report the situation. The *Oregon* was signalled to take charge, and the men were hastened on board, a number being sent also from the *New York*. Our work of closing water-tight doors, etc., was of no avail. A large number of sea-valves had been treacherously opened and the valves so broken as to make it impossible to close them. The ship thus slowly settled. At 7.30 she came afloat and came out into deeper water. The officer in charge (Lieutenant-Commander Cogswell) had let go an anchor, but as it was clear that if she went down in water of the depth in which she was she could never be recovered, the *New York's* stem was placed against her quarter, and later, a line being taken from our own bow to hers, the *Colon* was forced inshore. It was by this time dark, but, using a search-light, we were enabled gradually to force the ship in on the beach, the chain being paid out at the same time. She thus sank in a very moderate depth of water, and it seemed very probable that she might be saved.

At 11 P.M. the flag-ship returned to Santiago, leaving the *Texas* and *Oregon* in charge of the prize.

Though the *New York* was not able to come to action with any of the larger ships on account of her distance to the eastward, every nerve was strained to do so, and all was done

Pluton *Furor*

THE *GLOUCESTER* AND THE SPANISH TORPEDO-BOATS

The *Furor* is in a sinking condition, and the *Pluton* is heading for shore

THE FORWARD TURRET OF THE BATTLE-SHIP *IOWA* IN ACTION.—Drawn by H. Reuterdahl.

THE *INFANTA MARIA TERESA* ASHORE AND AFIRE.—Drawn by Carlton T. Chapman

that could be done. Our speed had rapidly increased so that we were going not less than seventeen knots at the end. We were immediately astern while all others were considerably to seaward. We were thus in a position to prevent a possible doubling to the rear and escape to the southeast; and there can be no question that we would have quickly overhauled the *Colon* had she continued her flight, and would have insured her capture had there been an accident of any sort to the other ships in pursuit.

The officers and crew, as they always had done, acted in the most enthusiastic and commendable manner. They had worked into so complete a system that the ship was practically instantaneously ready for action, and while all were deserving of commendation and credit, I think it no derogation from the deserts of others to name particularly Lieutenant-Commander Potter, to whom as executive officer so much of the ship's efficiency was due, and Chief Engineer McConnell, who had kept the machinery in the admirable order which enabled us at all times to develop the ship's full speed.

CAPTAIN COOK'S ACCOUNT

At 9 A.M., July 3, I gave orders and arrangements were made on the *Brooklyn* for general muster at 9.30 A.M. At 9.30 A.M. the enemy were telegraphed by the *Iowa* as coming out. At the same time they were discovered by the quartermaster on watch, N. Anderson, of the *Brooklyn*, and reported to the officer of the deck. The executive officer, Lieutenant-Commander Mason, who was on deck about to execute the order for general muster, immediately gave the order, "Clear ship for action and general quarters." Signal was made at the same time, "Enemy coming out—action." I went immediately forward, stood for the enemy, and gave orders to get steam on all boilers. We started with steam on three boilers, at about twelve-knots speed.

The head of the Spanish squadron, in column, was just outside the entrance of the harbor of Santiago heading about southwest. The Spanish squadron consisted of the *Maria Teresa* (flag), *Vizcaya*, *Oquendo*, and *Colon*, and two torpedo-destroyers. We opened fire on the leading ship in five minutes from the discovery.

The port battery was first engaged as we stood with port helm to head off the leading ship, and giving them a raking fire at about 1500 yards range. The enemy turned to the westward to close into the land. We then wore around to starboard, bringing the starboard battery into action. The enemy hugged the shore to the westward.

The *Brooklyn*, leading, was followed by the *Texas*, *Iowa*, *Oregon*, *Indiana*, and *Gloucester*. The *Vixen*, which had been to the westward of us on the blockade, ran to the southward and eastward of us, and kept for some time off our port side, distant about 1000 yards, evidently intending to guard against torpedo attack upon our ship. The shell passing over us fell very thick about her, some passing over her. At this time the firing was very fast and the whistling of shell incessant, and our escape with so little injury was miraculous, and could only be attributed to bad marksmanship on the part of the enemy. The *Maria Teresa*, which had dropped astern while we were wearing, under the heavy fire of our fleet ran ashore, the *Vizcaya*, *Oquendo*, and *Colon* continuing on and gaining in distance.

The *Brooklyn* was engaged with the three leading ships of the enemy, which were forging ahead, the *Texas*, *Iowa*, and *Indiana* keeping up a heavy fire, but steadily dropping astern. The *Oregon* also was keeping up a steady fire and was coming up in the most glorious and gallant style, outstripping all others. It was an inspiring sight to see this battle-ship, with a large white wave before her, and her smoke-stacks belching forth continued puffs from her forced draught. We were making fourteen knots at the time, and the *Oregon* came up off our starboard quarter at about 600 yards, and maintained her position, though we soon after increased our speed to fifteen knots, and just before the *Colon* surrendered were making nearly sixteen.

The *Oquendo*, soon after the falling out of the *Teresa*, dropped astern, and, on fire, ran ashore. The *Vizcaya* and *Colon* continued on, under fire from the *Brooklyn* and *Oregon*. The other vessels of our fleet were well astern and out of range. The *Texas* was evidently coming up fast. At about 10.53 A.M. the *Vizcaya* was seen to be on fire, and the *Colon* passed inside of her with increased speed, took the lead, and gradually forged ahead. The *Vizcaya* soon after ran on the beach, ablaze with fire. We signalled the *Oregon* to cease firing on the *Vizcaya*, as her flag was down. Firing immediately ceased, and we both continued the chase of the *Colon*, now about 12,000 yards away. The ranges ran from 1500 to 3000 yards with the *Vizcaya* as she kept in and out from the coast. We steered straight for a distant point near Cape Cruz, while the *Colon* kept close to the land, running into all the bights. She could not have come out without crossing our bows, and we were steadily gaining on her. We were getting more steam all the time, and now had four and one-half boilers on, and the remaining one and one-half nearly ready.

After running for about fifty miles west from the entrance, the *Colon* ran into a bight of land, beached, fired a gun to leeward, and hauled down her flag. The *Oregon* and *Brooklyn* had just previously begun to fire upon the *Colon* and were landing shell close to her.

I was sent on board by Commodore Schley to receive the surrender. The captain spoke English, and received me pleasantly, though naturally much depressed. He surrendered unconditionally. He was polite, shook hands, and said that his case was hopeless, and that he saw that we were too much for him. I was on board about fifteen minutes. As we came from the *Colon* the flag-ship *New York* came in with the *Texas*. I reported on board the flag-ship to Rear-Admiral Sampson. I stated to him that I believed the *Colon* could be gotten off the beach.

During the entire action I was in constant communication with Commodore Schley, so that I was enabled promptly to execute his orders and instructions. The officers and crew behaved with great and unexceptionable coolness and bravery, so that it was difficult to discriminate. They were encouraged in their best efforts by Commodore Schley's enthusiasm, and by his cheery words, "Fire steady, boys, and give it to them."

The executive officer, N. E. Mason, with his usual zeal, was continually at the battery directing the firing and keeping me well informed of the exact condition of the ship, and in encouraging both officers and men by his example of coolness and courage.

Lieutenant Hodgson was on the bridge coolly and deliberately taking bearings, and measuring and giving ranges. He was assisted in getting ranges and noting time by Chief Yeoman George Ellis, with a stadiometer, until Ellis was killed by a passing shell.

The officers of the divisions, Lieutenants T. D. Griffin, W. R. Rush, E. Simpson, J. G. Doyle, B. W. Wells, and Ensign Webster, all performed their full duties deliberately and efficiently. The naval cadets in divisions were cool and efficient, Naval Cadets Halligan, Marble, Abele, and Cronan having especially been noticed for good service. Lieutenant B. W. Wells, secretary to Commodore Schley, volunteered for command of a division, and was given the fourth division, thus enabling me to station a commissioned officer in a turret.

Too much praise cannot be given to the engineer's department for the hard work done by all in steadily raising the steam until the speed rose from twelve to sixteen knots.

The marines did splendid service at the guns and at their stations. The orderlies carried messages quickly and effectively. Captain Murphy and Lieutenant Borden were constant in their visits to the different stations, to be assured of efficiency.

Medical Inspector Paul Fitzsimons and Past Assistant Surgeon De Valin were in constant attendance at the divisions and on deck to be ready for any emergency.

Flag-Lieutenant James H. Sears was particularly active, standing in the open, directing signals, reporting fall of shot and position of the enemy. He was cool and firm in his duty.

Ensign McCauley attended personally to signals while constantly under fire, at one time mounting the forward turret and making the wigwag himself. His coolness was conspicuous.

The boatswain, Mr. Hill, was continually about the forecastle, ready for any duty, and materially assisted in watching the fall of shots, and thus checked the ranges.

The gunner, F. T. Applegate, rendered very valuable and conspicuous service at the battery, making repairs wherever practicable during the action.

The carpenter, G. H. Warford, was on the alert, watching for effects of shell and in examining compartments, pipes, and valves.

The signalmen, under Chief Quartermaster O'Connell, all stood in the open and performed their duties courageously.

I call especial attention to the valuable and conspicuous services rendered during the ac-

THE *ALMIRANTE OQUENDO* ASHORE AND AFIRE.—Drawn by Carlton T. Chapman.

tion by B. Gaynor (gunner's mate, first-class). Gaynor was a natural mechanic and a very intelligent man, and he went from gun to gun repairing breaks, and was constant in his work keeping them in condition for use.

Chief Gunner's Mate D. F. Diggins was in all parts of the ship attending faithfully and coolly to the electric apparatus.

N. Anderson (quartermaster, first-class) was a particularly bright seaman. He was at the wheel and kept the ship steadily on her course. He had been particularly known in the ship as a valuable man.

N. Morrissey (landsman) twice got out on the muzzle of a forward 6-pounder and backed out a jammed shot. Private Macneal, U. S. M. C., also went out on the muzzle of the forecastle 6-pounder and cleared a jammed shot.

We had but two personal casualties, George H. Ellis (chief yeoman) killed, and J. Burns (fireman, first-class) wounded. The ship was struck twenty times by whole shot and many times by pieces of bursting shell and from small shot of machine-guns. No serious injury was done to the ship, and all repairs could be temporarily done by the ship's force, excepting to the 5-inch elevating gear. The smoke-stacks were hit in several places; the signal halyards, rigging, and flags were cut in many places. The flag at the main was destroyed, being much cut by shot and flying pieces of shell. The 8-inch guns worked satisfactorily; some trouble and delay was caused by jamming of locks. The turrets worked well. The 5-inch battery gave great trouble with the elevating gear. At the end several were rendered useless for battle. Two were bulged at the muzzle. We fired 100 rounds of 8-inch, 473 of 5-inch, 1200 of 6-pounder, and 200 of 1-pounder ammunition.

The splendid and efficient work done in the engine and fire rooms was largely due to the zeal and intelligence of P. A. Engineer Carter, who went immediately to his station in the engine-rooms and was unremitting throughout the action in his efforts to get the best speed.

CAPTAIN CLARK'S ACCOUNT

At 9.30 A.M. the Spanish fleet was discovered standing out of the harbor of Santiago de Cuba. They turned to the westward and opened fire, to which our ships replied vigorously. For a short time there was an almost continuous flight of projectiles over the *Oregon*, but when our line was fairly engaged, and the *Iowa* had made a swift advance as if to ram or close, the enemy's fire became defective in train as well as range. The *Oregon* was only struck three times, and at least two of these were by fragments of shells. We had no casualties.

As soon as it was evident that the enemy's ships were trying to break through and escape to the westward we went ahead at full speed, with the determination of carrying out to the utmost the order "If the enemy tries to escape, the ships must close and engage as soon as possible and endeavor to sink his vessels or force them to run ashore." We soon passed all of our ships except the *Brooklyn*, bearing the broad pennant of Commodore Schley. At first we only used our main battery, but when it was discovered that the enemy's torpedo-boats were following their ships we used our rapid-fire guns, as well as the 6-inch, upon them with telling effect. As we ranged up near the sternmost of the ships she headed for the beach, evidently on fire. We raked her as we passed, pushing on for the next ahead, using our starboard guns as they were brought to bear, and before we had her fairly abeam she too was making for the beach. The two remaining vessels were now some distance ahead, but our speed had increased to sixteen knots, and our fire, added to that of the *Brooklyn*, soon sent another, the *Vizcaya*, to the shore in flames. The *Brooklyn* signalled, "*Oregon*, well done." Only the *Cristobal Colon* was left, and for a time it seemed as if she might escape; but when we opened with our forward turret guns and the *Brooklyn* followed, she began to edge in towards the coast, and her capture or destruction was assured. As she struck the beach her flag came down and the *Brooklyn* signalled, "Cease firing," following it with "Congratulations for the grand victory, thanks for your splendid assistance."

The *Brooklyn* sent a boat to her, and when the Admiral came up with the *New York*, *Texas*, and *Vixen*, she was taken possession of. A prize crew was put on board from the *Oregon* under Lieutenant-Commander Cogswell, the executive officer, but before 11 P.M. the ship, which had been filling in spite of all efforts to stop leaks, was abandoned, and just as the crew left she went over on her side.

I cannot speak in too high terms of the bearing and conduct of all on board our ship. When they found the *Oregon* had pushed to the front, and was hurrying to a succession of conflicts with the enemy's vessels if they could be overtaken and would engage, the enthusiasm was intense.

As these vessels were so much more heavily armored than the *Brooklyn*, they might have concentrated upon and overpowered her, and consequently I am persuaded that, but for the way the officers and men of the *Oregon* steamed and steered the ship and fought and supplied her batteries, the *Colon*, and perhaps the *Vizcaya*, would have escaped.

LIEUTENANT USHER'S ACCOUNT

On the morning of July 3, 1898, the torpedo-boat *Ericsson* was proceeding under half-speed on the starboard quarter of the flag-ship *New York* towards Siboney when the enemy was sighted coming out of Santiago entrance, we being then five or six miles to the eastward of

Cristobal Colon *Oregon* *Brooklyn*

THE LAST OF CERVERA'S FLEET

THE *OREGON* OVERHAULING THE *VIZCAYA* AND *CRISTOBAL COLON* OFF SANTIAGO, JULY 3

Drawn by Carlton T. Chapman

the Morro. The vessels of our fleet were firing on the enemy. The helm was put hard aport at once and full power put on as speedily as possible, and the course directed towards the enemy's ships, the crew at quarters, and the vessel in all respects ready to deliver torpedo attack. By the time we had turned to westward two of the enemy's vessels were out in plain sight. They were followed at short intervals by the other two cruisers, and then, after a longer interval, by the two torpedo-boat destroyers. The fire of the shore batteries supported the enemy's fleet, and the fire of both fleets was rapid and continuous. The flagship *New York* had hoisted signal 250, "Close in towards harbor entrance and attack vessels." The *Ericsson* proceeded as fast as possible, the steam-pressure and speed gradually increasing. The shore batteries at entrance to Santiago were directing their fire on the *Gloucester* at this time, which was hotly engaged with the two torpedo-boat destroyers. At full speed we drew near the entrance, and as we passed, and afterwards, the fire of the shore batteries was directed on us. Several shell struck near us, short or beyond, and two burst overhead and over.

The *Ericsson* was not struck. The *Brooklyn*, *Texas*, *Oregon*, *Iowa*, and *Indiana* were closely engaged with the *Colon*, *Vizcaya*, *Oquendo*, and *Maria Teresa*; the firing was furious. As we drew near, the two torpedo-boat destroyers were seen to strike to the *Gloucester*, and the *Maria Teresa* and *Oquendo* to run ashore, strike their colors, and display white flags. They were both on fire, and clouds of steam were arising from their hatches and ports. The *Indiana* remained near them, the *Iowa* directed her fire on the *Vizcaya*, and the *Oregon* joined in the chase of the *Colon*. The course of the *Ericsson* was directed towards the *Vizcaya*, prepared to deliver torpedo attack, but before we could

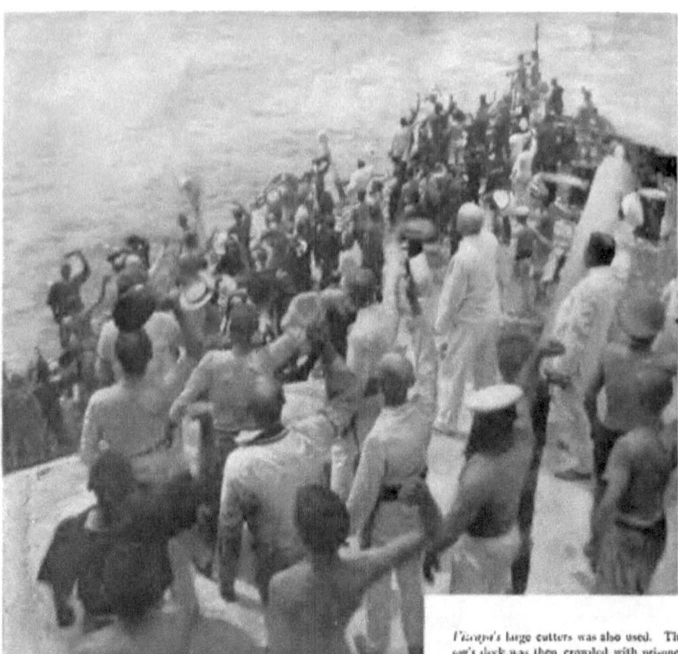

THE CREW OF THE *OREGON* CHEERING THE SURRENDER OF THE *COLON*

arrive within striking distance the *Vizcaya* was seen to strike to the *Iowa*, run ashore, and burst into flames, her engines being left running and clouds of steam issuing from all her openings on deck and in her sides. The course of the *Ericsson* was then set for the *Colon*, which was running very fast to the westward, pursued by the *Brooklyn*, *Texas*, and *Oregon*. As the *Ericsson* was hauling away from the *New York* in the chase, signal was made, interrogatory, 2872, "Request permission to continue the chase." The flag-ship hoisted negative, and by wigwag signal directed the *Ericsson* to pick up men in the water astern. Turned with port helm and found and picked up one man afloat on a piece of wreckage, and then returned to the chase, the *New York* in the meantime chasing fast after the *Colon*. As we came up with the *Iowa*, lying about two miles seaward of *Vizcaya*, the *Ericsson* was hailed and directed to go inshore and rescue the crew of the *Vizcaya* from the burning vessel. Ran close alongside the *Vizcaya* and sent small boat to her, boats from *Iowa* pulling in also at same time. Edward Ryan, gunner's mate, second-class, manned the small boat and brought off the officers and men from the stern of the *Vizcaya*, a duty of great danger. Explosions from the ammunition on board the *Vizcaya* began about this time, and her guns, which had been left loaded, were fired one after the other by the flames. The *Vizcaya* was on fire fore and aft, but the mass of the fire was aft, and the position of the *Ericsson* was perilous in the extreme, and only the urgency of the occasion caused her to remain. Rescued eleven officers and about ninety sailors and marines from the vessel, many of them sorely wounded. The Spanish were no sooner taken on board than they urged immediate withdrawal of the *Ericsson*, but this vessel remained until all alive had been taken from the *Vizcaya* by the *Ericsson's* small boat and the boats from the *Iowa*. One of the *Vizcaya's* large cutters was also used. The *Ericsson's* deck was then crowded with prisoners, most of them naked and many of them wounded, and she returned to the *Iowa*, towing the *Vizcaya's* cutter, also filled with prisoners. These were all put on board the *Iowa*, and the *Ericsson* was by her directed to verify the information given by the *Resolute*, which came up from eastward, and signalled, "Enemy's ships to eastward." Spoke *Resolute*, which reported that she had made out an enemy's battle-ship off Siboney; then spoke transport *Comal*, which had only seen the signal displayed by the *Resolute*; then spoke *Harvard*, which also reported having made out an enemy's battle-ship: requested *Harvard* to notify *Iowa*, and proceeded under full speed to eastward. Off vicinity of Siboney sighted *Indiana* and an Austrian battle-ship. The *Indiana* signalled *Ericsson* to come within hail, and directed that we proceed under full speed to westward to notify our vessels of presence of Austrian battle-ship *Kaiserin Maria Theresia*, which, desiring to go into Santiago, had been referred to the commander-in-chief in view of the existing conditions. Proceeded as directed until up with *Iowa*; reported to *Iowa*, and that our coal was almost gone, and that we were using salt feed in the boilers, the vessel only carrying two hours' fresh feed at full power, and the *Ericsson* then having been over four hours under full power. Received permission to return to eastward, and proceeded until signalled by *Harvard* to come within hail; by her was directed to tow her boats to and from the burning wrecks of the Spanish cruisers *Maria Teresa* and *Oquendo*. This was accordingly done until no more persons remained to be rescued from the two vessels, the remaining prisoners being all ashore on the beach. Received permission from the commander of the *Harvard* to proceed to eastward. About 6 P.M. spoke *Iowa*, and received permission to go to Guantanamo for coal and water, at which harbor the *Ericsson* arrived at 9.45 P.M., and reported the victory to commanding officer U.S.S. *Massachusetts*, the senior officer present.

There were no casualties on board the *Ericsson*.

THE ENTRANCE TO SANTIAGO HARBOR, JULY 7, 1898.—By Carleton T. Chapman

"A HOT TIME IN THE OLD TOWN."—Drawn by W. A. Rogers

The band of the battle-ship *Oregon*, on the forward 13-inch gun-turret, celebrating the surrender of the *Cristobal Colon*, July 3, immediately after the victory

THE NAVAL BATTLE OF SANTIAGO.—*Continued*

CAPTAIN PHILIP'S ACCOUNT

At daylight on the morning of the 3d the *Texas* stood out from the entrance to the harbor, taking day-blockading position, about three miles from the Morro (the Morro bearing north-northeast).

At 9.35, the Morro bearing N. by E. ½ E., distant 5100 yards, the enemy's ships were sighted standing out of the harbor. Immediately general signal 250 was made; this signal was followed by the *Iowa's* almost at the same time.

The ship, as per order, was heading in towards the entrance; went ahead full speed, putting helm hard astarboard, and ordering forced draught on all boilers. The officer of the deck, Lieutenant M. L. Bristol, had given the general alarm and beat to quarters for action at the same time.

As the leader, bearing the Admiral's flag, appeared in the entrance, she opened fire, which was, at 9.40, returned by the *Texas* at range of 4200 yards while closing in. The ship leading was of the *Vizcaya* class and the flag-ship.

Four ships came out, evidently the *Vizcaya*, *Oquendo*, *Maria Teresa*, and *Colon*, followed by two torpedo-boat destroyers. Upon seeing these two we immediately opened fire upon them with our secondary battery, the main battery at the time being engaged with the second and third ships in line. Owing to our secondary battery, together with the *Iowa* and *Gloucester*, these two destroyers were forced to beach and sink.

While warmly engaged with the third in line, which was abreast and engaging the *Texas*, our fire was blanketed for a short time by the *Oregon* forging ahead and engaging the second ship. This third ship, after a spirited fire, sheered inshore, and at 10.35 ran up a white flag. We then ceased fire on the third and opened fire with our forward guns at long range (6600 yards) on the second ship (which was then engaged with the *Oregon*) until 11.5, when she (the enemy's second ship) sheered in to the beach, on fire.

At 11.10 she struck her colors. We ceased fire and gave chase, with *Brooklyn* and *Oregon*, for the *Colon*, until 1.20, when she sheered in to beach and hauled down her colors, leaving them on deck at foot of her flag-staff. We shut off forced draught and proceeded at moderate speed to close up.

During this chase the *Texas* was holding her own with the *Colon*, she leading us about four miles at the start.

The entire battery of the *Texas* remained in a most excellent condition and ready for any service required by the commander-in-chief. The bearing and performance of duty of all officers met with my entire approval.

CAPTAIN TAYLOR'S ACCOUNT

AT 9.37 A.M., while the crew of the *Indiana* were at quarters preliminary to general muster, I noted two guns fired from the *Iowa* and general signal "Enemy's ships escaping" flying. I at once cleared ship for action, and the crew were at the guns in a remarkable short time, all officers and men showing an alacrity that indicated clearly their pleasure at the opportunity offered them.

The Spanish squadron was seen emerging from the harbor, and in a few moments a general action ensued. The leading ship, which proved to be the *Infanta Maria Teresa*, flying the flag of Vice-Admiral Cervera, was followed by the other vessels of the squadron as follows: *Vizcaya*, *Cristobal Colon*, *Oquendo*, and the torpedo-boat destroyers *Furor* and *Pluton*. The enemy's vessels headed to the westward and our ships headed in the same direction, keeping as nearly abreast of them as possible.

The *Indiana* fired on all of them as they came out one by one, and continued the action later by firing principally on the *Maria Teresa*, *Oquendo*, *Furor*, and *Pluton*. Several of our shells were seen to take effect on these vessels. Our secondary-battery guns were directed principally on the destroyers, as were the 6-inch guns. The destroyers were sunk through the agency of our guns and those of the *Gloucester*, which vessel had come up and engaged them close aboard.

The initial fire of the last two ships was directed at the *Indiana*, and, although falling very close, only striking the ship twice, did no injury to ship or crew.

Our ranges were obtained by stadiometer angles on Morro as the ships emerged, and then by angles on the tops of the rear ships. The ranges were from 4500 to 2000 yards, observed from the top. From the bridge I could see that our shooting was excellent and showed its effect. One of our 13-inch shells was seen to enter the *Maria Teresa* under the quarter-deck and explode, and that ship was observed on fire very shortly afterwards.

About 10.15 A.M. we observed the *Maria*

CAPTAIN H. C. TAYLOR
Of the *Indiana*

Teresa and *Oquendo* on fire and heading for the beach, the fire from their guns having ceased. We then devoted our special attention to prevent the escape of the destroyers, which appeared more than a match for the *Gloucester*, she being the only small vessel near to engage them. They were soon seen to blow up, apparently struck by our 6-inch and 6-pounders. We now fired our large guns at the *Vizcaya*, which was at long range. She made for the shore soon after, on fire and battery silenced. These ships hauled down their colors as they made for the beach. The Spanish flag-ship hoisted the white flag as she grounded.

We now ceased firing. The *Colon* was observed well over the western horizon, closely pursued by the *Brooklyn*, *Oregon*, and *Texas*, offshore of her. The flag-ship *New York*, steaming full speed to the westward, as soon as the *Vizcaya* surrendered, signalled us "Go back and guard entrance of harbor." Several explosions were observed on board the burning ships. At noon we turned and stood to the eastward for our station, in obedience to the above signal. Observed the *Harvard* and several transports standing to the westward.

About 12.30 the *Resolute* came within hail and informed us by megaphone that a Spanish battle-ship was sighted to the eastward, standing towards us. Later the *Harvard* passed, confirming the information, and adding that

CAPTAIN R. D. EVANS
Of the *Iowa*

the ship was painted white. We made out the vessel ahead and stood for her with our guns bearing. She proved to be the Austrian armored cruiser *Kaiserin Maria Theresia*. She sent an officer on board and requested permission to enter the harbor. I referred him to the commander-in-chief. She then stood on to the westward and we resumed our station.

During this action we used no armor-piercing shell except the smokeless-powder 6-pounders, and the good effect of the common shell is shown by the fires on the enemy's ships and the short time taken to disable them without piercing their armor, and with almost no injury to our ships.

The guns and mounts worked well; only two failures of electric primers noted.

During the afternoon I sent boats with surgeon on shore to the burning vessels to assist in caring for the wounded. The boats returned, bringing 1 wounded officer and 17 men as prisoners.

Received also during the afternoon and night prisoners from the *Gloucester* and *Hist*, in all 7 officers and 217 men, which were on the 4th transferred to the *St. Louis*.

The conduct of the officers and crew was in every respect commendable; coolness and good discipline prevailed, coupled with a marked enthusiasm. This desirable condition of affairs was largely due to the efforts of the officers, and I commended to the commander-in-chief the executive officer, Lieutenant Commander John A. Rodgers, and all the officers of the ship for the part taken by the *Indiana* in bringing about this great victory and the complete destruction of the enemy's squadron.

COMMANDER EATON'S

RELATION OF EVENTS

AS WITNESSED FROM THE *RESOLUTE*

THE *Resolute*, which I commanded, lay just east of the *Indiana*, distant from her 1000 feet, and about 2.6 miles from the Morro, when the *Maria Teresa* was sighted.

The *Indiana* had been nearer the Morro, but about nine o'clock circled to the eastward with a port helm, leaving the *Resolute* within the arc of the circle described by the fleet. The *Resolute* was then turned under a slow bell, and stopped when the *Indiana* was due west of us and just outside the circle of fighting ships. The *Gloucester* was to the northward and eastward, and nearly off Aguadores.

As the *Maria Teresa* appeared, the *Iowa* fired a 6-pounder and hoisted signal. Within a few seconds of this shot (not more than five or ten) all the Spanish batteries opened, and at the same instant the port broadside of the *Maria Teresa* was discharged. It seemed to me then that all, or nearly all, of these shot and shell were fired at the *Indiana*, and as the *Resolute* lay directly in line the water around the *Indiana* and the *Resolute* was alive with the fall of projectiles.

Before the *Vizcaya* appeared the *Indiana* opened fire with her heavy guns and, with screws whitening the water astern, was heading for the Morro.

As the *Vizcaya* came out, I distinctly saw one of the *Indiana's* heaviest shell strike her abaft the funnels, and the explosion of this shell was followed by a burst of flame which

CAPTAIN PHILIP GIVING THANKS ON THE DECK OF THE *TEXAS*.—Drawn by T. de Thulstrup

"I want to make public acknowledgment here that I believe in God, the Father Almighty. I want all you officers and men to lift your hats, and from your hearts offer silent thanks to the Almighty."

for the moment obscured the after part of the *Vizcaya*.

The *Vizcaya* fired her port battery apparently at the *Indiana*, for many of the shell struck about and beyond the *Resolute*, which was then heading east.

The *Cristobal Colon*, as soon as she was clear of Morro Point, fired her first broadside at the *Indiana*.

The *Oquendo*, in coming out, also fired her first broadside at the *Indiana*, and I could see some of the *Indiana's* shell strike the *Oquendo* as she steamed south.

Following close astern of the *Colon* and the *Oquendo* came the destroyer *Furor*, and I distinctly saw her struck by an 8-inch or 13-inch shell from the *Indiana*, which was followed by an explosion and flames on board the *Furor*.

During all this time the *Indiana* had been steaming ahead, and I roughly estimated that she was then about 3000 yards from the *Oquendo* and the *Furor*.

The *Resolute* was almost in line with the *Indiana*, and I could clearly follow the course of her projectiles.

The other ships engaged, except the *Oregon*, and occasionally the *Brooklyn*, which showed at times to the southward of the other vessels (the *Resolute* being by this time well to the eastward), were hidden in smoke.

From the position of the ships engaged it appeared to me that the *Indiana* was the first to close with the escaping enemy, and though I could see the *Teresa* and *Vizcaya* sweeping across her course, it was apparent that the *Indiana's* shells were the first to reach them.

This was due, first, to the *Indiana's* proximity, and, second, to the fact that the *Indiana* had a fair beam target on each ship as she came out.

The *Oregon* had this in a less degree, and

THE CUSTOM-HOUSE AT SANTIAGO

the other vessels engaged seemed to have fired their first shell when the Spanish ships were four points on.

In addition to the heavier shell noted as striking the enemy, we could count many lighter projectiles from the secondary battery exploding on board, and, as the *Indiana's* fire was incessant, I took these to be from her guns.

The Spanish officers who were prisoners from the *Colon* and the *Vizcaya* told me that the fire from the *Indiana* and the *Oregon* as they passed from the harbor was deadly in its destructiveness, and that although the *Colon* escaped with small injury, due to her greater speed and being in a measure covered by other ships, the *Vizcaya* was hopelessly crippled before she had gone a mile from the Morro.

CAPTAIN EVANS'S ACCOUNT

On the morning of the 3d of July, while the crew of the *Iowa* was at quarters for Sunday inspection, the leading vessel of the Spanish squadron was sighted at 9.31 coming out of the harbor at Santiago de Cuba. Signal "Enemy's ships coming out" was immediately hoisted and a gun fired to attract attention. The call to general quarters was sounded immediately, the battery made ready for firing, and the engines rung full speed ahead.

The position of the *Iowa* at the time of sighting the squadron was the usual blockading station off the entrance of the harbor, Morro Castle bearing about north and distant about three to four miles. The steam at this time in the boilers was sufficient for a speed of five knots.

After sighting the leading vessel, the *Infanta Maria Teresa* (Admiral Cervera's flag-ship), it was observed that she was followed in succession by the remaining three vessels of the Spanish squadron, the *Vizcaya*, *Cristobal Colon*, and *Almirante Oquendo*. The Spanish ships moved at a speed of about eight to ten knots, which was steadily increased as they cleared the harbor entrance and stood to the westward. They maintained a distance of about 800 yards between vessels. The squadron moved with precision and stations were well kept.

Immediately upon sighting the leading vessel fires were spread, and the *Iowa* headed towards her. About 9.40 the first shot was fired from the *Iowa*, at a distance of about 6000 yards.

The course of the *Iowa* was so laid that the range speedily diminished. A number of shots were fired at ranges varying between 6000 and 4000 yards. The range was rapidly reduced to 2500 yards, and subsequently to 2000 and to 1200 yards.

When it was certain that the *Maria Teresa* would pass ahead of us, the helm was put to starboard, and the starboard broadside delivered at a range of 2500 yards. The helm was then put to port and the ship headed across the bow of the second ship, and as she drew ahead the helm was again put to starboard and she received in turn the full weight of our starboard broadside at a range of about 1800 yards. The *Iowa* was again headed off with port helm for the third ship, and as she approached the helm was put to starboard until our course was approximately that of the Spanish ship. In this position, at a range of 1400 yards, the fire of the entire battery, including rapid-fire guns, was poured into the enemy's ship.

About ten o'clock the enemy's torpedo-boat destroyers *Furor* and *Pluton* were observed to have left the harbor and to be following the Spanish squadron. At the time that they were observed, and in fact most of the time that they were under fire, they were at a distance varying from 4500 to 4000 yards. As soon as they were discovered the secondary battery of the *Iowa* was turned upon them, while the main battery continued to engage the *Vizcaya*, *Oquendo*, and *Maria Teresa*.

The fire of the main battery of the *Iowa* when the range was below 2500 yards was most effective and destructive, and after a continuance of this fire for perhaps twenty minutes it was noticed that the *Maria Teresa* and *Oquendo* were in flames and were being headed for the beach. Their colors were struck about 10.20, and they were beached about eight miles west of Santiago.

About the same time (10.25) the fire of the *Iowa*, together with that of the *Gloucester* and another smaller vessel, proved so destructive that one of the torpedo-boat destroyers (*Pluton*) was sunk, and the *Furor* was so much damaged that she was run upon the rocks.

After having passed, at 10.35, the *Oquendo* and *Maria Teresa*, on fire and ashore, the *Iowa* continued to chase and fire upon the *Vizcaya* until 10.36, when signal to cease firing was sounded on board, it having been discovered that the *Vizcaya* had struck her colors.

At 11 the *Iowa* arrived in the vicinity of the *Vizcaya*, which had been run ashore, and, as it was evident that she could not catch the *Cristobal Colon*, and that the *Oregon*, *Brooklyn*, and *New York* would, five cutters—two steam—were immediately hoisted out and sent to the *Vizcaya* to rescue her crew. Our boats succeeded in bringing off a large number of officers and men of that ship's company, and in placing many of them on board the torpedo-boat *Ericsson* and the auxiliary despatch vessel *Hist*.

About 11.30 the *New York* passed, in chase of the *Cristobal Colon*, which was endeavoring to escape from the *Oregon*, *Brooklyn*, and *Texas*.

We received on board the *Iowa* from the *Vizcaya*, Captain Eulate (the commanding officer) and twenty-three officers, together with about two hundred and forty-eight petty officers and men, of whom thirty-two were wounded. There were also received on board five dead bodies, which were immediately buried with the honors due to their grade.

The battery behaved well in all respects. The ship was struck in the hull, on the starboard side, during the early part of the en-

THE *REINA MERCEDES*, SUNK IN THE HARBOR OF SANTIAGO BY SAMPSON'S GUNS

gagement, by two projectiles of about 6-inch caliber, one striking the hull two or three feet above the actual water-line and almost directly on the line of the berth deck, piercing the ship's side between frames 9 and 10, and the other piercing the side and the coffer-dam between frames 18 and 19. These two wounds, fortunately, were not of serious importance. Two or three other projectiles of small caliber struck about the upper bridge and smoke-stacks, inflicting trifling damage, and four other small projectiles struck the hammock nettings and the side aft.

There were no casualties among the ship's company to report. No officer or man was injured during the engagement.

After having received on board the rescued crew of the *Vizcaya*, the *Iowa* proceeded to the eastward and resumed the blockading station in obedience to the signal made by the commander-in-chief about 11.30.

Upon arriving on the blockading station, the *Gloucester* transferred to the *Iowa* Rear-Admiral Cervera, his flag-lieutenant, and the commanding officers of the torpedo-boat destroyers *Furor* and *Pluton*, and also one man of the *Oquendo's* crew, rescued by the *Gloucester*.

Naval cadets Frank Taylor Evans and John E. Lewis, and five men belonging to the *Massachusetts* were on board the *Iowa* when the enemy's ships came out. They were stationed at different points and rendered efficient service.

The officers and men of the *Iowa* behaved admirably. No set of men could have done more gallant service. I cannot express my admiration for my magnificent crew. So long as the enemy showed his flag they fought like American seamen; but when the flag came down they were as gentle and tender as American women.

LIEUTENANT-COMMANDER WAINWRIGHT'S ACCOUNT

At the battle of Santiago, on July 3, the officers and crew of the *Gloucester* were uninjured, and the vessel was not injured in hull or machinery, the battery only requiring some slight overhauling.

It was the plain duty of the *Gloucester* to look after the destroyers, and she was held back, gaining steam, until they appeared at the entrance. The *Indiana* poured in a hot fire from all her secondary battery upon the destroyers; but Captain Taylor's signal, "Gunboats close in," gave security that we would not be fired upon by our own ships. Until the leading destroyer was injured our course was converging, necessarily; but as soon as she slackened her speed we headed directly for both vessels, firing both port and starboard batteries, as the occasion offered.

All the officers and nearly all the men deserved my highest praise during the action. The escape of the *Gloucester* was due mainly to the accuracy and rapidity of the fire. The efficiency of this fire, as well as that of the ship generally, was largely due to the intelligent and unremitting efforts of the executive officer, Lieutenant Harry P. Huse. The result is more to his credit when it is remembered that a large proportion of the officers and men were untrained when the *Gloucester* was commissioned. Throughout the action he was on the bridge and carried out my orders with great coolness. That we were able to close in with the destroyers—and until we did so they were not seriously injured—was largely due to the skill and constant attention of Past Assistant Engineer George W. McElroy. The blowers were put on and the speed increased to seventeen knots without causing a tube to leak or a brass to heat. Lieutenant Thomas C. Wood, Lieutenant George H. Norman, Jr., and Ensign John T. Edson not only controlled the fire of the guns in their divisions and prevented waste of ammunition, but they also did some excellent shooting themselves. Acting Assistant Surgeon J. F. Bransford took charge of one of the guns and fired it himself occasionally. Acting Assistant Paymaster Alexander Brown had charge of the two Colt guns, firing one himself, and they did excellent work. Assistant Engineer A. M. Proctor carried my orders from the bridge and occasionally fired a gun when I found it was not being served quite satisfactorily. All were cool and active at a time when they could have had but little hope of escaping uninjured.

Lieutenants Wood and Norman, Ensign Edson, and Assistant Engineer Proctor were

SPANISH PRISONERS FROM ADMIRAL CERVERA'S FLEET AT SEAVEY'S ISLAND, PORTSMOUTH, NEW HAMPSHIRE

Captain Emilio Díaz Moreu, of the *Cristóbal Colón*, checking off the names of the men of the *Vizcaya* and *Colon* in charge of the boats engaged in saving life. They all risked their lives repeatedly in boarding and remaining near the two destroyers and the two armed cruisers when their guns were being discharged by the heat and their magazines and boilers were exploding. They also showed great skill in landing and taking off the prisoners through the surf.

Admiral Cervera and his officers and men were treated with all the care and consideration possible. They were fed and clothed as far as our limited means would permit.

ACCOUNT BY LIEUTENANT HUSE

EXECUTIVE OFFICER OF THE *GLOUCESTER*

AT 9.43 A.M., the *Gloucester* then being about 3000 yards southeast of Morro, the officer of the deck reported that the Spanish fleet was coming out of Santiago. All hands were called to general quarters, the captain came on the bridge, and I took the deck. Fire was opened at 3500 yards from the after guns (3-pounder rapid-fire); and, as they were brought to bear, from the bow gun (3-pounder rapid-fire) and the starboard guns forward (6-pounder rapid-fire). The fire-room blowers were started, and, turning to starboard, the range was decreased to 3000 yards. Four Spanish cruisers came out in column and stood to the westward close inshore. In the belief that the two torpedo destroyers known to be in the harbor would come out, the captain directed me to slow down and wait for them, keeping up a deliberate fire on the cruisers from the port battery. There was no other gunboat with the fleet at the time, and the battle-ships *Iowa*, *Indiana*, *Oregon*, and *Texas*, and the armored cruiser *Brooklyn* were engaged with the four Spanish vessels, *Cristobal Colon*, *Oquendo*, *Vizcaya*, and *Infanta Maria Teresa* (flag), all standing to the westward under full head of steam. The forts on shore kept up a slow fire throughout the action till it was evident to them that our boats were being used to rescue Spanish seamen, when their fire ceased.

When the larger vessels were well clear and the rear one about 1500 yards to the westward of the Morro, the destroyers *Pluton* and *Furor* came out and followed in their wake. At once we opened rapid fire on them from the starboard battery at a range of 2500 yards, and the engines were run at full speed, the ship heading about west-northwest. Presently signal was made from the *Indiana*, "Gunboats will advance." After this signal it appeared that the fight between the *Gloucester* and the two apparently uninjured destroyers was a thing apart from the battle in which the larger ships were engaged. The starboard forward guns (one 3-pounder and two 6-pounder rapid-fire) were turned on the leading vessel, the *Pluton*, while the starboard after gun and the stern gun (both 3-pounder rapid-fire) were aimed at the *Furor*. The speed of the *Gloucester* was gradually increased to over seventeen knots, and then we were slowly overhauling the torpedo destroyers and closing in towards them. The fire from both sides was vigorous, but, while many shots struck the water close alongside or went whistling over our heads, we were not hit once during the whole action. This was the more remarkable as the monotonous reports of an automatic gun could be heard after the 2500-yard range was passed, and the zone of fire could be distinctly traced by a line of splashes describing accurately the length of the ship and gradually approaching it. But at a distance variously estimated from ten to fifty yards, the automatic fire suddenly ceased. It was afterwards found to be from a 1-pounder Maxim, and the execution aboard would have been terrible during the few minutes that must have elapsed before the ship was sunk had the fire reached us. Meanwhile the service of our own guns was excellent, and at a range of 1200 yards the two 6-millimeter automatic Colt rifles opened on the enemy. The *Pluton* had now (about 10.15) slackened her speed, showing evident signs of distress, and our fire was concentrated on the *Furor*. The range was decreased to six hundred yards, and at this distance the majority of shots appeared to strike. The *Pluton* was run on the rocks about four miles west of Morro and blew up. Our crew cheered

CAPTAIN JOHN W. PHILIP
Of the *Texas*
Photograph by [illegible]

at the sight of the explosion. The *Furor* soon commenced to describe circles with a starboard helm, her fire ceased, and it became apparent that she was disabled. A white rag was waved from forward, and we stopped firing. Lieutenants Wood and Norman and Assistant Engineer Proctor were sent to rescue the crews and to see if the prizes could be saved. These found a horrible state of affairs on the *Furor*. The vessel was a perfect shambles. As she was on fire and burning rapidly, they took off the living and then rescued all they could find in the water and on the beach. The *Pluton* was among the rocks in the surf and could not be boarded, but her crew had made their way ashore or were adrift on life-buoys and wreckage. These were all taken on board. I afterwards learned that the *New York* passed a number of men in the water who had doubtless jumped overboard from the destroyers to escape our fire. All these were probably drowned.

While this work was going on several explosions took place on the *Furor*, and presently—at about 11.30—she threw her bows in the air, and, turning to port, slowly sank in deep water.

The following were rescued from the destroyers: *Furor*—Commander Carlier, Lieutenant Arderius (badly wounded), three petty officers, fourteen enlisted men; total, nineteen. *Pluton*—Commander Vazquez, Lieutenant Boado, four petty officers, twenty enlisted men; total, twenty-six.

While one of our boats was still ashore, seeing heavy clouds of smoke behind the next point the ship was moved in that direction, the men being at quarters and everything in readiness for further action. On rounding the point two men-of-war were found on the beach burning fiercely aft, the majority of the crew being crowded on the forecastle and unable apparently to reach land, only two hundred yards away. Our boats, under Lieutenant Norman and Ensign Edson, put off to the nearer vessel, which proved to be the flag-ship *Infanta Maria Teresa*, and rescued all on board by landing them on the beach through the surf. Lieutenant Norman formally received the surrender of the commander-in-chief and all his officers and men present, and, as soon as all hands had been transferred ashore, brought on board the *Gloucester* all the higher officers, including the Admiral. Lieutenant Wood meanwhile rescued the remaining survivors on board the *Oquendo*, the second of the burning vessels.

The Spanish officers not feeling that the prisoners on shore were secure from attack by Cuban partisans, by the captain's orders I directed Lieutenant Norman to land with a small force, establish a camp on shore, and hoist the United States flag over it. He took with him all the rations that could be spared from the stores aboard.

There were several incidents of interest which I will refer to briefly: The colors of the *Furor* and *Oquendo* were brought on board by Lieutenant Wood, and the colors of the *Pluton* by Mr. Proctor.

The flag-ship *New York*, while hastening from Siboney to join in the general action, saw the *Gloucester* close to her two disabled antagonists and cheered her as she went by.

The *Indiana* made the general signal to the *Gloucester*, "Congratulations."

During the night, the ship then being on the blockading station, the assistant chief of staff hailed from a torpedo-boat, and, after inquiring about our casualties, added, "The Admiral admired your splendid work."

By order of Captain Evans, the Admiral and his staff were transferred from the *Gloucester* to the *Iowa*, all other unwounded prisoners were sent to the *Indiana*, and the twenty-two wounded were taken to Siboney and put on board the army hospital-steamer *Olivette*. One wounded prisoner died on board and was buried at sea on the way back from Siboney.

A comparison of the armament of the contending vessels is interesting:

Furor.—Length, 220 feet; displacement, 370 tons; armament, two 14-pounder rapid-fire guns, two 6-pounder rapid-fire guns, two 1-pounder Maxim automatic, two 14-inch torpedo-tubes; complement of men, 67.

Pluton.—The same.

Gloucester (late the yacht *Corsair*, N.Y.Y.C.).—Length, 241 feet; displacement, 800 tons;

armament, four 6-pounder rapid-fire guns, four 3-pounder rapid-fire guns, two 6-millimeter Colt automatic; complement of men, 93.

The action was a remarkable one. The *matériel* of the enemy was superior in every respect; and yet, having destroyed two vessels, either one of which would have been a fair match for the *Gloucester*, and inflicted terrible loss to their *personnel*, I had to report not one casualty. This result I attributed wholly to the accuracy and rapidity of our fire, which made the proper service of the guns on board the Spanish ships utterly impossible. In this opinion I was borne out by the statements of our prisoners, who commented on the awful destructiveness of our fire, and spoke of their unsuccessful efforts to use their torpedoes, the crews being swept away repeatedly by bursting shell. They also referred to the deadly effect of the Colt automatic 6-millimeter guns, and said that the projectiles from these passed clean through the vessels.

Camp of [illegible] guarding stores — Camp of the Wounded

TWILIGHT AT SIBONEY, JULY 7.—Drawn by Carlton T. Chapman

LIEUTENANT SHARP'S ACCOUNT

BETWEEN 9.35 and 9.45 A.M. the *Vixen* was at a point about four miles to the westward of Morro, and at a distance of about one and a half miles south of the shore-line. At about 9.40 it was reported to me that an explosion had taken place in the entrance of Santiago Harbor. I went on deck and almost immediately sighted the leading vessel of the Spanish fleet standing out of the entrance. Some of the vessels of our fleet were closing in towards Morro and firing.

The *Vixen* was heading towards the Morro. The engines were ordered ahead at full speed and the helm put hard aport, the object being to cross ahead of the leading Spanish vessel, and thus not obstruct the gun-fire of our own fleet, the shells from which soon began to fall about the position we had just left.

The leading Spanish vessel opened fire on the *Vixen* with her starboard bow guns, the projectiles from which passed over us, all being aimed too high. I estimate the number of shots fired at us at this time to have been between five and ten.

As the *Vixen* gathered headway her head came to about south by east, opening the *Brooklyn* up about two points on our port bow; steadied her and steamed on about this course until we had reached a position about a mile to the southward and westward of the *Brooklyn*, which was now turning with port helm and firing her guns as they bore on the enemy's vessels. At 9.50 hoisted signal No. 252. The course was then ordered changed to west-southwest, the intention being to steer a parallel course to that of the Spanish fleet. By some mistake the quartermaster steadied the helm on southwest by south, which was soon discovered, but not until the *Vixen* had increased her distance offshore by perhaps another half-mile. The course west-southwest was again ordered, and when steadied on it we were at an estimated distance of about five miles from the shore. From about 10.15 the courses and times of changing were as follows: At 10.15 changed course to W. ½ S., at 10.36 to N.W. by N., at 11 W.N.W., at 11.5 W. by N., at 11.10 N.W. by W., at 11.15 W. by N., at 11.30 W. by S., at 1.30 W. by N. All these courses were by the steering compass, and the speed was estimated from twelve to thirteen and a half knots per hour.

Seeing that the Spanish vessels were out of range of our guns, while we were well within range of theirs, we reserved our fire.

About 11.6, having approached within range of the *Vizcaya*, we opened fire with our starboard battery at an elevation of 3000 yards for the 6-pounder guns, and extreme elevation for the 1-pounders; continued the fire for six minutes, when, seeing that the ensign of the *Vizcaya* was not flying, at 11.12 I ordered cease firing. We expended twenty-seven 6-pounder armor-piercing shells and eighteen 1-pounder common shells.

After passing Aserraderos the course was held at from west by north to west by south, heading for the point on the western horizon. Average speed, about twelve to thirteen and a half knots; average number of revolutions, 105 per minute; average steam pressure, 122½ pounds.

The *Brooklyn* and *Oregon* bore on the port and starboard bows respectively, and were

LIEUT.-COMMANDER RICHARD WAINWRIGHT
Of the *Gloucester*

gradually dropping the *Vixen* astern, as was the *Cristobal Colon*, which was running closer inshore. About 12.25 the *Oregon* opened fire on the *Colon*, as did also the *Brooklyn*, feeling their way up to the range, which was apparently obtained after the fourth or fifth shot. About 1.20 the *Oregon* and *Brooklyn* headed inshore about four points. About 1.28 the *Texas* hoisted signal, "Enemy has surrendered." This signal was repeated to the *New York* by the *Vixen*. At 2.30 the *Vixen* stopped off Rio Tarquino, in the vicinity of the *Oregon* and *Brooklyn*. The *Cristobal Colon* was close inshore, bows on the beach, her colors down, lying on the deck at the foot of her flag-staff.

The following notes were taken during the chase by my orders upon the suggestion of Lieutenant Harlow. These notes were written by Assistant Paymaster Doherty. The incidents and times were given by Lieutenant Harlow, whose watch was five minutes slow of deck-clock time. The times taken after 10.30 are accurate: those taken before that time were estimated.

NOTES BY LIEUTENANT HARLOW

EXECUTIVE OFFICER OF THE *VIXEN*

AT 9.45 A.M. reported tug coming out of harbor. Mr. Harlow examined it through a glass and discovered it to be a Spanish cruiser flying what was probably an Admiral's flag.

Notified commanding officer, called all hands to quarters, and stood to southward. *Brooklyn* hoisted signal No. 250. The leading vessel had about changed course to west when second vessel appeared, followed shortly afterwards by the *Colon*. The first two vessels were evidently the *Vizcaya* and *Oquendo* or *Maria Teresa*. Fleet closing in and opening fire. About 10 A.M. enemy's leading vessel had headed to west, full speed, followed by the others. The *Brooklyn*, at 10, was nearest vessel, and, standing to north, engaged two leading ships.

At this time the two leading ships were quite close together, with an interval of, perhaps, three-fourths of a mile between second ship and *Colon*. About 10.5 the *Brooklyn* began to turn with port helm and made a complete turn to eastward, coming around so that when again heading west the enemy's two leading ships bore well on her starboard bow and the *Colon* on her starboard quarter. For the next fifteen minutes the *Brooklyn* sustained and returned the fire of the two leading ships, with an occasional shot from the *Colon*.

The *Vixen* steered courses of various time intervals, of south, southwest by south, and about 10.15 was going ahead full speed W. ½ S. (steering compass). The shells that went over *Brooklyn* struck close ahead, astern, and on starboard beam of *Vixen*, and several passed directly over, a piece of bursting shell going through the flag at main-mast head.

At 10.32 A.M. *Colon* and first boat close together, just clear of *Brooklyn's* bow. *Colon* evidently passing ahead. The first ship that came out of harbor stopped off Juan Gonzales, undoubtedly on fire. *Oregon* forging ahead and firing ahead. Enemy's destroyers to westward of Cabañas, evidently engaged by *Iowa* and *Texas* and apparently on fire. *Indiana* a little to the westward of Morro.

At 10.34 *Colon* still gaining. Ship which led before rapidly dropping behind, and two on fire near Juan Gonzales. *Colon* reserving fire. *Colon* commenced firing again at 10.37. No other United States vessels in sight. *Texas*

LIEUTENANT ALEXANDER SHARP, JR.
Of the *Vixen*

and *Iowa* in rear of *Oregon* five to six miles. Distance between *Iowa* and *Indiana* about four miles. *Colon* slacking up.

At 10.40 second vessel just clear of stern of *Brooklyn*. *Vixen* distant about five miles. *Oregon* gaining rapidly. *Colon* using only smokeless powder.

At 10.46 *Brooklyn* forged ahead from our point of view. *Oregon* fired 13-inch from forward gun.

At 10.47 *Texas* considerably ahead of *Iowa* and gaining rapidly.

At 10.48 shell from *Brooklyn* burst apparently alongside of second vessel. *Texas* passed Juan Gonzales at 10.49. *Indiana* off Cabañas at 10.49. *Vixen* at 10.50 veered inshore, heading about north-northwest.

At 10.53 *Texas* gaining. *Iowa* off Gonzales. Yacht and *Indiana* off Guyacabon.

At 10.54 *Vizcaya* (?) evidently on fire and heading for beach, with a heavy list to port quarter.

At 10.56 *Vizcaya* heading for Aserraderos. *Texas* coming up five miles distant. *Vizcaya*, at 11, with colors flying, nearly ashore at Aserraderos.

At 11.1 *Vizcaya* ported helm and headed about east. *Texas* fired forward gun. *Iowa* and *New York* close offshore, and torpedo-boat astern of *New York* about one mile.

At 11.4 *Vizcaya* starboarded and stood close inshore.

At 11.5 *Vixen* opened fire on *Vizcaya*, and at 11.7 her colors came down and orders were given on board the *Vixen* to cease firing.

At 11.9 sudden burst of fire from her, and probably sinking.

At 11.15 *Texas* and other ships reserved their fire. *Iowa* gaining on *Texas*. Vessels in sight at 11.16, *Iowa* and *Indiana*; *Indiana* at least ten miles from *Colon*. Vessel ashore at Aserraderos probably flag-ship.

At 11.20 *Iowa* evidently had stopped.

At 11.24 flames were seen bursting from the *Vizcaya*.

At 11.26 the *Vizcaya* exploded, followed at 11.30 by another explosion, probably magazine, with large sheets of flame. Other explosions at 11.33, 11.35, 11.36, and 11.41.

At 11.42 the position of the ships as seen from the *Vixen* was as follows: The *Colon* close inshore, distant about seven miles from the *Vixen*; the *Oregon* about one point on the starboard bow, distant about one and a half miles; the *Brooklyn* one point on starboard bow, distant about three miles; the *Texas* on starboard quarter, distant about one mile; *Iowa* two points on starboard quarter, distant about eight miles; *New York* one point on starboard quarter, distant about ten miles; the two latter apparently off Boca del Rio. No other vessels in sight. Smoke of ships destroyed off Juan Gonzales in sight, but hulls invisible.

At 11.52 another explosion occurred on the *Vizcaya*.

Position at noon practically the same, except *Texas* gaining rapidly. *Vixen* abreast of Cevilla, thirty miles west of Santiago. *Texas* bearing three points on starboard quarter, distant one mile. *Oregon* and *Brooklyn* one point on starboard and port bows respectively, distant four and five miles. *Colon* two points on starboard bow, distant about ten miles, close under the hill Bayamita. *Vixen* shifted Nos. 2 and 3 1-pounder guns upon their mounts at 12.3, No. 3 1-pounder being disabled.

At 12.5 *New York* was in line with burning ship at Aserraderos, about nine miles distant.

At 12.15 *Texas* on starboard quarter, *Vixen* heading west by south. *New York* two points on starboard quarter and evidently gaining.

COMMANDER J. G. EATON
Of the *Resolute*

BOMBARDING THE CITY OF SANTIAGO FROM OFF AGUADORES, JULY 11.—Drawn by Carlton T. Chapman

The *Indiana*, listed to starboard by swinging out her big guns, is firing her 8-inch broadside

Oregon one-half point on starboard bow. *Brooklyn* one point on port bow, distant nine miles. *Colon* one point on starboard bow, distant ten miles, half-way between third and fourth hills. *Oregon* started firing at 12.20, her shot falling short. Fired only one shot from 13-inch gun.

At 12.23 *Oregon* fired again; shot struck a little ahead of *Colon*, and appeared to pass over her. *Colon* is almost hull down from the *Vixen*. *Brooklyn* started firing at 12.26; struck very short, about two thirds of distance to *Colon*; second shot at 12.26, about three-fourths distance to *Colon*; third shot at 12.27, about four-fifths distance to *Colon*; fourth shot about five-sixths of distance.

At 12.29 the *Oregon* fired again; shot went over. There were thirteen seconds between the flash of the *Brooklyn's* shot and the time the shell struck the water.

At 12.30 the *Texas* bore one point forward of the starboard beam.

At 1.13 the *Brooklyn* and *Oregon* headed in about four points.

At 1.23 the *Texas* hoisted signal, "Enemy has surrendered." The *Colon* lying at Rio Tarquino. Boat from the *Brooklyn* went alongside *Colon's* starboard side at two o'clock.

CAPTAIN COTTON'S ACCOUNT

On Sunday, the 3d of July, the *Harvard*, under my command, was at Altares, Cuba, discharging the military stores brought in the ship with the troops from Newport News. Nearly all of the boats and the majority of the officers of the ship were employed in this work. Some of the boats were away from the ship discharging their loads, and others were alongside loading.

At 10.45 A.M. the *Resolute* passed Altares at a considerable distance, standing to the eastward, sounding her whistle vigorously and flying a signal which announced that the Spanish fleet had "fled." With the utmost despatch I recalled the boats and officers to the ships, hoisted the former, sent the steam-launch on shore, got under way, and stood to the westward to join the Admiral. The ship was cleared for action.

I had previously observed that the fleet was firing, but supposed that it was a bombardment of the Morro and the neighboring batteries. The ships of the fleet had meantime disappeared to the westward, none being in sight when I came out from behind the land where I could command an uninterrupted view of the coast west of Morro.

I soon came up with the wrecks on shore of two of the smaller vessels and two of the cruisers of the Spanish fleet, and shortly afterwards with the wreck of a third cruiser, all of the cruisers burning fiercely.

I had meantime passed the *Indiana* and one of our torpedo-boats, standing to the eastward in search of the missing Spanish cruiser, and informed them that a large Spanish battle-ship or cruiser was in sight to the eastward of Daiquiri. They immediately stood on in chase, but the supposed enemy was ascertained later to be the Austrian cruiser *Kaiserin Maria Theresia*.

At the most westerly of the three wrecks of the Spanish cruisers, the *Vizcaya*, I found the battle-ship *Iowa* and communicated with her. Learning from Captain Evans that Admiral Sampson, in the *New York*, was in chase of the *Cristobal Colon* and was probably many miles to the westward, I decided not to go farther in that direction.

Shortly afterwards the *Iowa* and the *Harvard* stood to the eastward, and upon reaching the wrecks of the *Oquendo* and *Maria Teresa* Captain Evans informed me that the officers and crews of both vessels were on shore in great distress and suffering for want of food, and asked me if I would rescue them—a request with which I of course instantly complied, and which would have been unnecessary had I previously known the circumstances concerning them.

I took the *Harvard* in as near the wrecks as I deemed to be prudent, and at 4.40 P.M. lowered nine of our boats and sent them in to the shore to rescue the survivors. This work continued until 9.45 P.M., when the last boat-load of Spanish prisoners came alongside. During the greater part of the time the steam-cutter of the *Indiana* rendered valuable assistance in towing our boats to and from the shore. We had the good-fortune to rescue thirty-five officers and six hundred and thirty-seven men, without accident to them or to our boats, notwithstanding the fact that the landing was through the surf, and dangerous as well from the incessant explosion of ammunition on board the Spanish cruisers, both small and large, as from the surf. The boats were handled with skill and judgment by the officers in command of them, who were Lieutenants Beale, Roberts, Davis, and Bradshaw, Ensigns Turner and Cuming, and Cadets Nox and Bruff, whose conduct and that of the boats' crews was commendable.

Among the rescued were thirty-eight sick and wounded. At ten o'clock I steamed on to rejoin the ships off Santiago, reaching them at 10.55 P.M., with the junior medical officer of the *Indiana* and a lieutenant and a boat's crew of the *Gloucester*.

The Spanish officers and men received every attention that it was possible to bestow upon them for their comfort and welfare. Some of them came on board wholly nude, and many with only a shirt or trousers. As soon as possible after their arrival on board they were provided with food and necessary clothing. About three hundred working-suits and many shoes and canvas hats were issued to them. The sick and wounded were attended by our own medical staff, assisted by two of the Spanish medical officers, who were among those rescued.

Lieutenant Joseph Beale, of the *Harvard*, was the senior officer in charge of the transportation of the Spaniards to our ship, and I invite attention to the terms in which he speaks of the highly commendable conduct of the officers and men associated with him in the successful accomplishment of an important and humane duty, and one not without exposure to danger.

Sixteen of the most severely wounded men were transferred to the U. S. hospital-ship *Solace*. None of the Spanish officers on board of the *Harvard* was so seriously wounded as to require transfer to that vessel.

LIEUTENANT BEALE'S STORY

OF THE

RESCUE OF SURVIVORS

THE first two boats were sent at 4.40 P.M. to the *Oquendo*, then ashore in Juan Gonzales Bay and burning fiercely. Fifteen exhausted men were here saved, most of them hanging on lines from the bows to escape the fire, and all of them in the last extremity from heat, smoke, and fright. In the meantime six more of the heavy ship's boats proceeded to the adjoining bay, called Playa Nima Nima, where the *Maria Teresa* was ashore and afire, with her bow not more than seventy-five yards from the beach. The first boat in made fast to a small chain hanging from the bows of the ship and veered in through the surf close to the beach, sending a line ashore. The survivors were taken into the boat over this line and transferred to the next boat ahead, which, when loaded, shoved off and pulled straight for the *Harvard*, passing within a few yards of the burning ship.

In this way most of the survivors were taken off. Two boat-loads of the most seriously wounded were placed in a beached sixoared

CAPTAIN F. J. HIGGINSON
Of the *Massachusetts*

cutter of the *Gloucester* and taken off by her crew. The steam-cutter of the *Indiana* was most useful in towing our heavy boats, and in one instance pulled one of them off the beach.

A detail of officers and men from the *Indiana* and *Gloucester* was most useful in helping the Spaniards to the boats and succoring the wounded. For five hours the men worked close to a fiercely burning ship amid the incessant explosion of small-arm ammunition, at least one explosion of a more serious character taking place, and, although warned frequently by the Spanish officers that a great explosion forward might take place at any moment, worked coolly and steadily.

In five hours six hundred and thirty-seven Spanish officers and men, all of them worn out and many seriously wounded, were taken from the burning *Oquendo* or through the surf and transferred to the *Harvard*, without accident to man or boat, by crews of men, most of whom had been in the service only one month. Such a happy result under such trying surroundings could only have been brought about by the sustained courage of the men and their officers. I call attention particularly to the humane way the men handled and helped the Spaniards into the boats, treating them in all respects as comrades in distress. The humanity displayed by our men was fully equal to their courage.

CAPTAIN F. A. COOK
Of the *Brooklyn*

ACCOUNT BY LIEUTENANT HAZELTINE

COMMANDING THE *HIST* DURING THE EVENTS NARRATED

AT 9.35 A.M., while the *Hist* was immediately astern of the flag-ship *New York*, following her to Altares, and when about five miles to the eastward of Morro Castle, the enemy was discovered leaving the harbor.

Turned immediately with the port helm and steamed full speed to the westward, in wake of flag-ship. About 9.45 flag-ship made general signal "Close in to mouth of harbor and attack enemy." At 9.45 beat to general quarters. Speed at first seven knots, increasing gradually to eleven.

While running past the forts the *Hist* was fired at six times, several shells striking very near.

About 10.40 A.M. passed the *Gloucester* close inshore, and about three miles to the westward of Morro, standing by the wrecks of the Spanish destroyers *Pluton* and *Furor*.

Made out the two vessels ashore and burning in Juan Gonzales Bay to be the *Infanta Maria Teresa* and *Almirante Oquendo*, and the *Hist* was headed inshore towards them to pick up the survivors.

While thus standing in, the New York *Herald's* despatch-boat *Golden Rod* came up and hailed, requesting that we take Surgeon Simons, of the *Iowa*, who had been ashore with the army the previous day, and whom they had on board, to his ship, as he feared there had been many casualties.

Dr. Simons was sent on board, and the *Hist* was again headed to the westward, and steamed full speed the nine miles to Aserraderos, where the *Vizcaya* lay beached and in flames, and off which lay the *Iowa*. About five miles to the westward of Juan Gonzales Bay, passed the *Indiana* standing to the eastward.

About 11.45, after sending Surgeon Simons on board the *Iowa*, I was directed by Captain Evans to stand inshore to the wreck of the *Vizcaya*, and assist in the rescue of her crew.

The *Vizcaya* was reached at 11.55. Found the torpedo-boat *Ericsson* standing by her, also a number of the *Iowa's* boats. Immediately lowered our four boats and sent them to the rescue.

The first twenty-three picked up by our boats were placed on board the *Ericsson*, which shortly after steamed out to the *Iowa*, and thence to the eastward.

The *Iowa*, after taking on board a number of prisoners, recalled her boats, and also steamed off to the eastward.

During the next five hours the *Hist* lay close to the burning wreck, and rescued one hundred and forty-three more from the ship, water, and shore. Nearly all were nude and very hungry, claiming to have had no food for the previous twenty-four hours. They were immediately furnished with clothing, food, and drink.

Of the one hundred and sixty-six picked up, some twenty were wounded, five or six desperately. Several had been given first aid by Cubans on shore. All possible medical assistance was given them.

Lieutenant F. H. Hunicke and Assistant Engineer E. S. Kellogg had charge of the boats, and for an hour or more laid alongside the *Vizcaya*, taking men from her bow, side, and stern, and from the water, during all of which time she was on fire fore and aft and the explosions on board were almost incessant, thus making this work exceedingly hazardous. The petty officers and entire crew took turns in manning the boats for this dangerous duty.

About 2 P.M. the *Resolute* passed to the westward, displaying signal "Enemy's ship in sight"; and soon after made out a battle-ship flying the Austrian colors, and also an international signal, "D. C. J.," signifying "Austrian colors."

The Cubans on shore at Aserraderos did not fire on the Spaniards. In fact, when our boats were taking the Spaniards from the beach the Cubans rendered valuable assistance.

Lieutenant-Colonel Juan Vaillant, commanding Cuban camp at Aserraderos, paid a visit to the *Hist*.

About 5.30 P.M., after having taken on board the last survivor, the *Hist* was headed to the eastward, and steamed full speed for Santiago, arriving off there about seven o'clock. Reported to Captain Taylor, of the *Indiana*, and requested a surgeon, who was immediately sent. I was then directed to report to Captain Evans, of the *Iowa*, who ordered that the prisoners, including the wounded, be transferred to the *Indiana*. This was accomplished by 11.15.

At 11.45 P.M. the *Brooklyn* came up, and, after hailing, sent on board Flag-Lieutenant Sears, for immediate transportation to Altares, with despatches from Commodore Schley. Landed Lieutenant Sears at 2.30 A.M., and at 4.30 left Altares for Santiago. Placed Lieutenant Sears on the *Brooklyn* at 6 o'clock, and at 6.30 A.M., July 4, joined the flag-ship *New York* off Santiago.

COMMANDER EATON'S ACCOUNT

The *Resolute* having arrived off Santiago at 6 A.M., I reported in person on board the flag-ship to the chief of staff, and from him received orders to remain in the vicinity until further orders. While lying to the northeast of the line, just to the eastward of the *Indiana*, we sighted the leading vessel of the Spanish fleet coming out. At the same time the *Iowa* fired a shot.

We at once headed the ship to the eastward, but had not got her steady on her course before a 10-inch shell struck about forty feet from the starboard side of the ship abreast the pilot-house, and a minute later a 6-inch shell struck about seventy feet astern the ship. During the next five minutes a number of projectiles struck the water beyond and about her.

Making all the speed possible, I headed for Altares in order to communicate with the commander-in-chief. Before reaching Altares I met the flagship *New York* coming to the westward, and communicated to her that the Spanish fleet was coming out and standing to the western part of the line.

Having then received orders to proceed to Guantanamo, I headed in that direction, signalling to the *Harvard* as we passed Altares that the Spanish fleet was coming out.

At 10.20, when off Daiquiri, we sighted a large man-of-war, painted a dingy white, with two funnels and two military tops, standing to the westward. On proceeding nearer we made out what I took to be the Spanish flag, together with a signal which I could not read.

Heading the ship to the southward to pass around him, the stranger put his helm to starboard and apparently stood after us to sea. Being convinced by this manœuvre on his part that he was an enemy, I at once headed to the westward, and, running down to the fleet of army transports, warned them to sea.

In repassing Altares I also signalled to the *Harvard* that an enemy was coming from the eastward.

Continuing my course to the westward, I crossed the entrance to Santiago Harbor, and the Socapa battery fired two shots at us; the first, from a large gun, passed directly over the pilot-house, and the second, apparently a 6-inch shell, passed over the forecastle of the ship.

Shortly after passing the southern entrance I sighted a wreck burning on the beach, and a little later discovered the *Gloucester* standing by a second wreck, apparently to save her crew. These wrecks, together with three others that we sighted, were all blazing fiercely, and two of them blew up with a loud report and a large volume of smoke shortly after we passed them.

BURNING THE FEVER-INFECTED BUILDINGS AT SIBONEY.—STARTING THE BLAZE, JULY 11.—Drawn by Carlton T. Chapman

At 12.45 I communicated with the *Indiana* and told her of the man-of-war I had sighted off Daiquiri. Captain Taylor ordered me to proceed at once to the commander-in-chief with the information.

At 1.15 I communicated with the *Iowa* and notified Captain Evans that I had sighted a Spanish man-of-war off Daiquiri, and at his request assisted in recalling some of his boats from the wrecks near by.

I then proceeded to the westward and found the flag-ship with her consorts lying off the *Cristobal Colon*, which was aground at the mouth of a small stream. Here I received 508 Spanish prisoners, of whom 494 were enlisted men and 14 were officers. I also received a guard of 25 marines, and commissioned an officer to assist in guarding the prisoners.

At 11 P.M. I got under way and proceeded to Guantanamo Bay, where I arrived at 7.30 A.M. of the 4th.

At the time action began, and during action, while the *Resolute* was under fire from the enemy, she carried in one of the upper staterooms on the hurricane deck 240 pounds of dry gun-cotton with detonators, and on the lower deck 23,000 pounds of wet gun-cotton in mines. The destruction of the ship might have resulted from the explosion of a single shell, especially in the dry gun-cotton. As many shells struck around, about, and beyond the ship, she was during two epochs of the day in serious danger.

THE STORY OF CERVERA'S PILOT

I WAS in the forward tower of the *Infanta Maria Teresa*, by the side of Admiral Cervera, who was as calm as though he had been at anchor in his own cabin. He was observing the channel and the hostile ships, and only said these words:

"Pilot, when may we shift our helm?" He had reference to turning to starboard, which could only be done after we had passed the Diamante Bank. After a few seconds he said:

"Pilot, advise me when we may shift our helm."

"I will advise you, Admiral," I answered.

A few moments later I said: "Admiral, our helm may be shifted now."

In a moment the Admiral, without shouting, without becoming excited, as calm as usual, said: "To starboard," and, the next minute, "Fire!" At the same moment, simultaneously, the two guns of the turret and those of the port battery fired on a ship which seemed to me to be the *Indiana*. I thought the ship was sinking. I cannot tell you all that passed. By this time there were already many dead and wounded in the battery, because they had been firing on us for some time, and I believe that in spite of the water that was in the ship she was already on fire then. The Admiral said to me:

"Good-bye, pilot: go now—go, and be sure you let them pay you, because you have earned it well." And he continued to give his orders.

THE RESCUE OF THE SPANISH ADMIRAL

[A Contemporary Account from Harper's Magazine]

INTRODUCTORY

THE following article is a verbatim account, now put in print for the first time, of one Peter Keller's experiences at the rescue of the Admiral and the crew of the flag-ship of the Spanish fleet at Santiago, July 3. The story was dictated to a stenographer by Keller, and is told in his own language. Keller is an old man-of-war's man, but for many years he has followed the occupation of ship-rigger. At the breaking-out of hostilities he volunteered, and served his country as boat-swain's mate on board the U. S. S. *Gloucester*. The incident in which Keller took part is thus described in the official report of Dr. John Tracy Edson, acting ensign, U. S. N., of the *Gloucester*:

"After the *Furor* had been sunk and the *Pluton* had exploded, I was sent with my division in command of the ship's cutter, with instructions to rescue the crew of the *Infanta Maria Teresa*. As we approached the vessel, which was in flames, I saw the crew crowded forward on the forecastle, and I noted that the vessel lay nearly broadside on to a sandy beach, distant about two hundred yards. As we neared her I held up a rope's end to indicate my purpose. A line which they gave me I took to the beach, and called for a good swimmer to take it through the surf. Otto Brown responded so manfully to my call that it was easily seen that he was the right man for the work. With the line about his neck, he fought against the breakers for twenty minutes. He returned once to the boat for a rest. The line was more carefully tended after this by William G. Bee, and, after another struggle, the cutter being closer in this time, he made the beach. I sent Keller also through the surf to secure the line ashore. The cutter was hauled to and from the ship along this line, carrying each time eight or ten men from the burning wreck. As we neared the beach each time, I found it necessary to throw one or more of the Spaniards into the water in order to expedite the work. The men were immediately grabbed by Keller or Brown, and passed along the line to the beach. In this manner the cutter landed about two hundred officers and men, and I believe that Admiral Cervera was among the number.

"The only other boat engaged in this rescue was the gig from the *Gloucester*, in charge of Lieutenant Norman. We worked frequently in association, and succeeded in rescuing every soul on board without losing a single life. Among the rescued were many wounded who required much assistance. This was ably rendered by Keller and Brown, who remained in the water for about two hours.

"During the whole time that the men were engaged in the work there were occasional reports on board, as from exploding ammunition. As we left the wreck for the *Gloucester*, the fire had reached the forward turrets, so that nearly the whole ship was aflame. One of the 11-inch guns was discharged, sending a shot into the water close alongside of us."

THE NARRATIVE OF PETER KELLER

Keller's account of his part in the rescue is as follows:

When the whale-boat was called away from the *Gloucester*, I stood forward, alongside of my gun, looking towards the Spanish destroyers. When the orders came to lower the cutter, we lowered the cutter with all the crew. Mr. Ensign Edson, who was in charge, ordered me to steer for one of the burning ships, which we didn't know by name. After we neared the boat we found out there was a heavy surf. The ship was lying broadside towards the beach. We crossed her bow, and I passed the remark to Mr. Edson that the surf was so heavy that we could not land through it. I told him we should have to go around the bow and try to get a line. Mr. Ensign Edson told me: "Damn it, keep your mouth shut. I'm in charge of this boat." After that I thought it was advisable for me to keep quiet, as I was told by the officer in charge.

We rounded the bow of the boat, which we found out was the *Maria Teresa*, the flag-ship of the Spanish fleet. Mr. Edson took the painter of the cutter in his hand and lifted it up towards the forecastle of the Spanish man-of-war, to make them understand, I suppose, that they were to give us a rope, which we intended to make fast ashore, so that we could haul our boat to and fro off the beach. They gave us a line, and we headed for the shore, about two hundred yards.

When we reached the surf Mr. Edson called for a volunteer to take the line ashore. Seaman Brown responded. He took the line round his neck, and jumped overboard without the order of Ensign Edson. He hesitated a little before he jumped, because he had no orders. After he had fought in the water about ten minutes he was getting exhausted. Our officer in charge saw that he could not make the beach, so he backed the boat in and picked him up. "Brown," said he, "you were a little too hasty. I didn't mean you to jump overboard at the present time. I was getting the boat a little nearer before I sent you off."

Mr. Edson gave me the orders to go in a little nearer to the beach. As we neared the beach, Mr. Edson thought that Brown could make the beach in safety. He ordered him to go ahead. At that I asked permission to help Brown out. Mr. Edson said, "Can you swim?" I told him, "Yes, sir." He said, "Well, Keller, go ahead."

I tore my clothes from my body, and I jumped overboard and swam towards Brown, and helped him to carry the line ashore. When we got there I saw about forty-five Spaniards, and their boats, which had been smashed to pieces on the rocks. As soon as we could, I and Brown ran up to a tree. I took half a turn with the line around the tree, and then turned round and called upon the Spaniards the best way I could, "Wiene qui!" That means, "Come here." Those addressed came to us, and I told them to give us a pull, so that we could stretch the line.

After the line was made fast I sang out to Ensign Edson, the officer in charge: "The line is fast, sir. Go ahead." He responded, "All right." While Mr. Edson was hauling his boat towards the *Maria Teresa* to save the officers and men, I remarks to Otto Brown, seaman, "By gosh! that line is very poor, Otto." Brown said, "It looks very poor, Keller." I took the line in my hands, and rubbed it and smelt it. It smelt to me like the rope was pretty bad—that is, an old rope.

I turned round and asked one of the Spaniards if there was any Spanish officer ashore. The man told me, "Yes." I said, "Where?" and he pointed out with his finger an officer clad in undershirt and drawers, with a white cap on, and told me in Spanish, "Almiranto"; that means as much as "There is the Admiral."

I went up to Admiral Cervera, who had

half a cigarette in his fingers, and told him, "Admiral, be so kind and tell one of your officers aboard they should give us a better line if they want us to save all his people, because I found out that the line was very poor." Admiral Cervera turned round and told one of his officers, in Spanish, to hail the *Maria Teresa* and tell them to give us a better rope. The answer he got from the *Maria Teresa*, from one of the officers, was that they could not give us any better rope, because everything was afire.

Then I asked Admiral Cervera if his magazines—powder-magazines—were under water. Admiral Cervera told me the after magazine was under water, but the forward one he was not sure of. I passed the remark to Otto "Hombre no massa!" That means, "Don't kill." It seemed to me he understood. Then I asked him in Spanish, "Dicen Vds. oficiales Cubanos?" He responded, "Si, señor." He turned around and pointed the captain out to me, and told me, "El capitan." That means, "He is the captain of the company."

I went to him and said, "I am an American petty officer, and my officer in charge is in the boat, and as he cannot speak to you, I make it my business to tell you that these Spaniards are United States prisoners of war, and they cannot be touched by your people"—that means, by the Cubans—"and I will make it my business, when I go back, to tell my division officer, Mr. Ensign Edson." He responded to me, "I will take care of them, Lieutenant Norman, hove in sight, and I saw Lieutenant Norman talking to Mr. Edson. After that I saw the gig and cutter working frequently to and fro from the beach.

There were some men on the davit-falls of the burning ship, and I told Mr. Edson, "Those men hanging on the davits, it would be good to go around there and save them." As we had been rescuing these people the small ammunition and the big ammunition was being exploded right and left, so that the boats' crews in charge of Mr. Edson and Mr. Norman were in danger of being destroyed any moment. After the officers and crew had been rescued from the forecastle, Mr. Edson, with the cutter, went astern of the *Maria Teresa*. There was a couple of men hanging on a boat's fall; he

BURNING THE FEVER-INFECTED BUILDINGS AT SIBONEY.—VIEW OF HARBOR WITH TRANSPORTS, JULY 11. Drawn by Carlton T. Chapman.

Brown: "My God! if we don't get other help we can't save those people! That rope is very poor."

By this time Mr. Edson came back from the *Maria Teresa* with the first load of Spaniards. As he neared the beach—we will say about seventy-five yards—he threw the Spaniards overboard, and I and Brown received them and brought them ashore in safety.

When Mr. Edson went back for another load, I noticed some Cubans coming down. I knew they were Cubans, because they had their rifles, ammunition, and machetes. They were running towards the Spaniards. I could see that the Spaniards were trembling, and that the Cubans were preparing to fire at them. I jumped towards the first one I met, and told him in Spanish, the best way I could, and they won't be touched." Then I told him that I thought it would be a good thing to draw a cordon around them, so that they don't run away from us, because I thought if they did they might get shot by the Cubans.

The work of rescuing went on, to my best knowledge, for about two hours. Amongst those rescued from the *Maria Teresa* were many wounded, and wounded very heavy. As I remember, one man was shot all to pieces. Ensign Edson and one of the boat's crew lifted him up carefully out of the cutter, lowered him in the water, and I and Brown had to take him ashore through the surf more dead than alive. As far as I understood afterwards, that man died on the beach.

After we had about three or four loads put safe ashore by the cutter, the gig, in charge of picked up those men, put them in the gig, and left for the *Gloucester*. Mr. Norman, with the *Gloucester's* gig, brought the last load of Spaniards ashore. After I and Brown had taken them through the surf, and Brown had returned to the gig, Mr. Norman, who was in a hurry to return to the *Gloucester*, hollered to me, where I was on shore, and said: "Keller, you better hurry up, else you get left."

I jumped in the surf, and as I swam to the stern-post of the gig, I told him, "Mr. Norman, the Admiral is ashore." Mr. Norman told me, "Hell! is he ashore?" I said, "Yes, sir. Don't you want him aboard?" He said, "Yes; go and get him."

I jumped in the surf again, swam ashore, went towards the Admiral, and I told him: "Admiral, will you be so kind and come along with me? The officer in charge of the gig would like to have you to come aboard the *Gloucester*." The Admiral extended his right hand, patting me on my shoulder, and said, "Yes, boy." He turned around and asked me if he could take his officers along with him. I told him, "Yes, sir." Then he called on his son, and the captain of the *Maria Teresa*, and his whole staff, and we proceeded towards the boat. As we proceeded towards the boat Brown was waiting for us.

The Admiral, Brown, and I jumped in the surf. I told the Admiral to get his hand around my neck and the other hand around Brown, and he did it, and we swam towards the gig. When we reached the gig, the Admiral put his hand on the toll-board of the gig. Mr. Norman extended his hands and got hold of his both hands, while I and Brown lifted him up and put him in the gig. Then we went back and went after the captain. As the captain was wounded and was helpless, I and Brown had to carry him through the surf. When we came to the gig he extended his right hand, as his left hand was wounded. Mr. Norman extended his hands, grabbed his right hand, and I and Brown took him by the legs and lifted him up carefully. By this time he was taken by Boatswain's Mate Thompson and let down in the gig.

Then we went back again and got the doctor, and some of the junior officers, and Cervera's son, and brought them to the gig. Then we left and proceeded towards the *Gloucester*.

As we rounded the bow of the *Maria Teresa* the Admiral told us not to go too close, because there is some of the 11-inch guns elevated and loaded, and they might explode any minute. At this time I was sitting on the tiller, and Lieutenant Norman told me to keep her off. I hardly did keep her off, when one of the guns exploded, and the shell dropped right in front of us, about ten yards, into the water.

We proceeded towards the *Gloucester*. During the voyage Admiral Cervera told Mr. Norman, "I surrender to you American people, but I don't recognize the Cubans; I don't surrender to the Cubans. And please, for Heaven's sake, send some of your men to watch my men, as I am afraid that those men will be killed by the Cubans."

As we came alongside the *Gloucester* on the starboard gangway, I saw Captain Wainwright and Lieutenant Huse receiving Admiral Cervera and his staff. There were side-boys, and he was given the full honor of Admiral, and the chief boatswain's mate piped him over the side. Then I saw Admiral Cervera hand in hand with Captain Wainwright, and they all went aft to the quarter-deck, where he and his staff went down in the officers' cabin.

I got out of the boat and jumped aboard the ship. As I went forward I saw the prisoners from the *Pluton* and *Furor* underneath the awnings, and I saw the two Colt automatic rapid-fire guns trained on them. I tried to get forward and talk to some of those prisoners, but there were guards stationed, and I was not allowed to do so.

I turned around and I saw lots of coffee—three or four coffee-cans standing around the deck—and some hard bread. I was very tired, and thought that a little coffee would strengthen me up. I went to get a cup of coffee, when I met Dr. Bransford. I told him: "I feel weak. I have been in the water, I and Brown, for a considerable time." He said, "Come down and I will give you something." I called Brown, and we went together down below. The doctor give us a tumbler of whiskey each, and told us to keep quiet, because we had been working too hard.

On the berth-deck, where the sick-bay was, I saw the wounded Spaniards and the heavy wounded laying around on the deck, and Dr. Bransford and the sick-nurse attending to them. As I returned I met Ensign Edson on the steps going down to the sick-bay to attend to the wounded, for he had been a doctor before he entered the service. I passed the remarks to Brown: "That's very nice, ain't it, Otto? Mr. Edson is going to help Dr. Bransford now." I and Brown stopped at the skylight and looked down on the berth-deck, and saw Mr. Edson attending to the lieutenant of the *Pluton*. Then I felt kind of dizzy. I tried to lay down for a few minutes, but I could not rest. When the cutter was called away the second time, I tried to go in it, but Mr. Norman told me not to go, as I had done good work and was too tired, and he was afraid I might get sick. I turned around and went forward; then I saw Mr. Edson attending to one of the wounded. That same fellow died about five o'clock in the afternoon, and was buried at sea.

CAPTAIN CHARLES S. COTTON
Of the *Harvard*

After we had everything straightened up aboard the *Gloucester*, and the wounded was pretty well attended to, with the best comfort we had to give them, we transferred our prisoners to the *Iowa*. I saw that some of those prisoners did not want to leave us. Ensign Edson got hold of them and coaxed them to get in the boat, giving them to understand, the best way he could, that nothing would happen to them. They obeyed his orders and went in the boat, while I stood on the gangway and assisted them.

After all these prisoners were transferred from the *Gloucester*, they sent boats from the *Olivette* for the wounded, for we did not have places for them on board, and no comforts. Amongst these wounded were some very heavy wounded, and it was very difficult to get them out of the berth-deck. Mr. Edson come to me and told me to rig some kind of gangway to get them into the boat out of the hold. I understood what Mr. Edson wanted me to do, but we did not have much lumber aboard, only a few boards, and I could not rig the thing Mr. Edson wanted, so I suggested that we use boards, and send them up on the boards. Mr. Edson misunderstood me, and thought the plan would not work. After I explained to him, he came to the conclusion that it would work, and told me, "Go ahead, Keller."

We took each a badly wounded man, laid him on a board, with the hammock he was in, lifted the board up from below, and two men on deck hauled the board with the wounded man and hammock and laid him on the deck. Then Mr. Edson told me to do the same way in getting them over the side into the *Olivette's* boats. In this way we hauled out three heavy-wounded men and put them in the boats. The light-wounded were assisted partly by me and by Mr. Edson, and in this way we brought them all into the boat.

After the wounded were all gone, and the prisoners all gone, there was one dead man to be buried. Mr. Huse gave orders to Otto Brown to sew the body up in a hammock, put some ballast on his feet, and get him ready. After everything was done, Mr. Huse called me and told me to call all hands to quarters. I called all hands to quarters, and we laid the dead man on a board, covered him with a captured flag from the *Pluton*, and brought him aft. Mr. Huse called the master-at-arms, Mr. P. A. Mehan, to read a couple of chapters out of the Bible, while the whole ship's crew was present, captain and all. After this was done we took the dead man, marched around the ship, put him on a rail, and Mr. Huse told me to pipe him over the side. Piping over the side is the greatest honor a man can get aboard a ship, and these honors are given only to an officer or a dead man. So we buried the man with full honors.

After this was done Mr. Huse told me to "pipe down"—which means to disband. Then we went back to Santiago and resumed our station for the night on the blockade.

A SPANISH ACCOUNT

FROM *EL IMPARCIAL*, OF MADRID

THE Admiral went out at 9.30 A.M., knowing, he says, what must necessarily happen, and what he had so many times foretold.

"The first ships," he says, "that went out was the flag-ship *Maria Teresa*, followed by the *Vizcaya*, *Colon*, *Oquendo*, and finally the destroyers, all under full steam.

"When the ships went out the engines were under such high pressure that the enemy was surprised, and subsequently expressed great admiration on that account.

"At 9.35 A.M. the *Maria Teresa* attacked and opened fire on a hostile battle-ship of the type of the *Indiana*, and on the *Iowa*, then rushed upon the *Brooklyn*, which, on account of her greater speed, offered for us the greatest danger."

Admiral Cervera then enumerates the ships composing the hostile fleet, among which special mention should be made of the *New*

York, Admiral Sampson's flag-ship, the *Brooklyn*, Commodore Schley's flag-ship, and the battle-ships *Iowa*, *Texas*, *Oregon*, and *Indiana*, besides armed transatlantic liners.

Our fleet followed the course prescribed beforehand, and, the American ships coming alongside, the battle soon became general. "There could be no doubt as to the outcome," says Cervera, "but I should never have believed that our ships would be destroyed so rapidly."

The first injuries which the *Infanta Maria Teresa* had the misfortune to sustain consisted in the bursting of an auxiliary steam-pipe and of the water-mains.

Early in the battle Commander Concas, who was fighting with the greatest bravery, fell, wounded. Cervera then took command, intending that the second commander should take the place of the first; but this could not be carried out on account of the heat of the battle.

The dead and wounded were falling incessantly.

Admiral Cervera's apartments had taken fire through the explosion of some 57-mm. shells. There was not sufficient water to be had to extinguish the fire, which soon spread.

Cervera gave orders to an adjutant to flood the after compartments.

In view of the absolute impossibility of defending the ship any longer in that position, she was directed, with the greatest possible speed, towards the beach west of Punta Cabrera, where she ran ashore just at the moment when the engine stopped.

The second and third commanders agreed with the Admiral that it was altogether impossible to continue the fight, and the *Maria Teresa* hauled down her flag, which did not fall into the hands of the enemy, the flames having destroyed it. The compartments were then flooded.

The fire invaded the forward deck without giving the crew time to escape: they were saved with the assistance of two American boats.

Among the wounded were Lieutenant Lopez Ceron and Ensign Carrasa. The following were missing: Captain of Infantry H. Rodriguez, who, according to Admiral Cervera, was killed by a projectile; Ensign Francisco Linares, Second Surgeon Julio Diaz, First-class Machinist Juan Montero, and Second-class Machinist José Melgares. The body of the latter afterwards drifted to the shore.

Those who knew how to swim jumped into the water; finally a rope was thrown to the shore.

A Spanish boat was lowered, but sank, owing to the injuries it had received; a steam-launch had the same fate.

Cervera jumped into the water, followed by his son and two seamen.

Many reached the shore swimming, most of them arriving there naked.

The American officer who was in command of the life-saving boats invited Admiral Cervera to go to the yacht *Gloucester*, which he did, together with his flag-officer, who had been wounded, and his adjutant and the second commander of the *Teresa*, who was the last one to leave the ship.

The *Oquendo* stranded half a league from the *Maria Teresa*, and the *Vizcaya* and *Colon*, pursued by hostile ships, were lost from sight.

According to the purser of the *Oquendo*, the history of this ill-fated ship was as follows:

"The unequal battle became more so when a hostile projectile entered the forward turret, killing the whole *personnel*, with the exception of one gunner, who was badly wounded. Of the 14-cm. battery two guns only remained in action, and these fought with incomparable energy. The after turret was soon without a commanding officer; he had been killed as he opened the door, being almost asphyxiated inside of the turret. There were two fires on board the *Oquendo*, one in the orlop deck forward, which was soon gotten under control, and the other in the stern, which could not be suppressed, the pumps failing to give water. From the very beginning of the battle the 14-cm. ammunition hoists failed to work. When our commander, Mr. Lazaga, saw that the fire could not be controlled and that all the guns were out of action, he prepared to beach the ship, first giving orders to discharge all the torpedoes in order to prevent the enemy from approaching. Driven to the last extreme, and after consulting with all the officers present, he ordered the flag to be hauled down. The second and third commanders and three

VICE-ADMIRAL CÁMARA

lieutenants had already been killed, and while Mr. Lazaga was directing the rescue of the crew he gave his own life for his country. The men of the *Oquendo* witnessed calmly and without becoming terrified the constant explosions on board, determined above all things that the enemy should not set foot on the ship."

"When the American officer invited me to go to the *Gloucester*," says Mr. Cervera, "I gave instructions to the third commander of the *Teresa*, Mr. Aznar, for the re-embarkation, and I heard nothing further from him.

"On board the *Gloucester* were twenty wounded from the destroyers, the commanders and three officers of the *Teresa* and the purser of the *Oquendo*, and about ninety-three men of the crews of the ships. We were the object of the greatest solicitation, all being anxious to administer to our needs, nearly all of us having arrived there naked.

"The commander of the *Gloucester* said: 'The vessel is small to receive so many people. I will try to find a larger one.'

"The insurgents had about two hundred men of the fleet, among them five or six wounded. I spoke with some of them, and they said if we would go with the rebels they would assist us. I thanked them and added: 'We have surrendered to the Americans. If you have surgeons I should be grateful if they would attend the wounded on the shore, some of whom are in a serious condition.'"

The commander of the *Gloucester* offered Admiral Cervera that he would ask the insurgents for the men they were holding from the fleet.

Mr. Cervera, proceeding with his narrative, says:

"We proceeded westward until we met the nucleus of the fleet; some of us were transferred to the *Iowa*, others to the hospital-ship.

"On board the *Gloucester* I asked the commander of the destroyers for news, and learned the disastrous fate of these two ships.

"Villamil found a glorious death in the battle, and the best proof of how the *Furor* fought is found in the great number of casualties she had. The commander of the *Pluton* was wounded in one foot."

On board the *Iowa* Admiral Cervera was received with military honors.

"On the gangway," he says, "I saw the commander of the *Vizcaya* wearing his sword, which the commander of the *Iowa* did not wish to take from him on account of the valor the former had displayed in the battle."

From the *Iowa*, where he remained until 4 P.M., Admiral Cervera was transferred to the cruiser *St. Louis*, where he found the second commander of the fleet, Mr. Paredes, and the commander of the *Colon*, Mr. Diaz Moreu.

The hostile forces were three times as large as ours.

The Admiral produced a telegram which he sent to our government immediately after the battle, and in which it was stated that there had been six hundred killed and many wounded.

The *Pluton* was not sunk, but succeeded in running ashore.

Cervera's account devotes a long paragraph to the eulogy of the chivalry and courtesy of the enemy. They clothed the naked, giving them everything they needed; they suppressed their shouts of joy in order not to increase the suffering of the defeated, and all vied in making their captivity as easy as possible.

Among the prisoners there were with Admiral Cervera the second commander, one chief, four officers, and thirty-two men of the *Maria Teresa*; the purser and thirty-five men of the *Oquendo*; three commanders, eleven officers, seven midshipmen, and three hundred and forty-seven men of the *Vizcaya*; the three commanders, fourteen officers, and one hundred and ninety-one men of the *Colon*; the commander, the first machinist, and ten men of the *Furor*; and the commander, one officer, and nineteen men of the *Pluton*; also Lieutenant Enrique Capriles, who was on board the *Vizcaya*, but did not belong to her crew. Most of the prisoners were taken to the steamer *Solace*.

Cervera's narrative concludes with the following words:

"The 3d day of July has been one of terrible disaster, as I had foreseen. Nevertheless, the number of dead is less than I had feared.

"The country has been defended with honor, and we have the consciousness of duty well done, but with the bitterness of knowing the losses suffered and our country's misfortunes."

TROOP C, NINTH U. S. CAVALRY, CAPTAIN TAYLOR, LEADING THE CHARGE AT SAN JUAN.—By Fletcher C. Ransom

AMERICAN TROOPS GOING TO THE FRONT PASSING THE SCENE OF THE BATTLE OF LAS GUASIMAS

THE CAPITULATION OF SANTIAGO

FOLLOWING the victories of Las Guasimas, El Caney, and San Juan, and the destruction of Cervera's fleet, the city of Santiago was closely besieged by land, while the American ships guarding the entrance to the harbor cut off all relief on that side. After a truce to allow of the removal of non-combatants, protracted negotiations continued from July 3d until July 15th, when, under menace of immediate assault, the preliminaries of surrender were agreed upon. On the 17th General Shafter occupied the city. The capitulation embraced the entire eastern end of Cuba. The number of Spanish soldiers surrendering was 22,000, all of whom were subsequently conveyed to Spain at the expense of the United States. "The individual valor of officers and soldiers," said the President in his annual message, "was never more strikingly shown than in the several engagements leading to the surrender of Santiago, while the prompt movements and successive victories won instant and universal applause. To those who gained this complete triumph, which established the ascendency of the United States upon land as the fight off Santiago had fixed our supremacy on the seas, the earnest and lasting gratitude of the nation is unsparingly due. Nor should we alone remember the gallantry of the living: the dead claim our tears, and our losses by battle and disease must cloud any exultation at the result and teach us to weigh the awful cost of war, however rightful the cause or signal the victory."

The situation during the investment and negotiations for surrender was described by Inspector-General Breckinridge in the following words: "On the 3d there was comparatively little firing on either side. In the morning the Spanish fleet left the harbor and attempted to escape to sea, but was destroyed by our navy lying in wait for it outside the harbor. General Shafter sent in a demand for the surrender of the Spanish forces and city of Santiago.

"From this time until the surrender of the army and the city there was no firing except on the afternoon of the 10th, when a desultory bombardment of the lines and city was made by our artillery, beginning about half past four and lasting until nearly dark, accompanied by very little small-arms firing on either side, and resulting in few casualties and probably not a very great amount of damage. The navy took part in this bombardment from a point outside of the entrance to the harbor.

"In demanding the surrender of the town we notified the enemy of a bombardment in case the city were not surrendered. Permission was given for the non-combatants to leave the city. They did leave in the following days to the number of perhaps 20,000, filling the neighboring villages and roads with destitute people, mostly women and children. It then seemed to fall to our lot to see that these people did not starve in a desolate country, and to be as much our duty to take care of these people, whom our policy had driven from their homes, as it was for Spain to feed the *reconcentrados*, whom they drove from their homes under their war policy. The task was not insignificant.

"From the 1st of July on we continued to extend our lines on both flanks, but especially around towards our right, until the city was completely invested on the eastern and northern sides. Spanish reinforcements had been expected from the north, and, besides that, the city was not so strongly defended on this side as on the east. Our lines of intrenchments were occupied as follows:

"On the extreme right, the Cubans under General Garcia, next, Lawton's division, next, Wheeler's division of dismounted cavalry, next, Kent's division, and, on the left, Bates's Independent Brigade. A brigade of volunteers, under General Duffield, was left at Siboney and vicinity.

"There was a heavy rain on the afternoon of July 10, heavy rain that night and nearly all day of the 11th, with very heavy rain at night. The water supply of the city of Santiago was cut on the 8th of July. This, it is thought, had very little effect, on account of the heavy rains that followed and the ample cisterns which the city of Santiago contains.

"The light batteries, which arrived with our other troops on the 9th of July, began to unload as soon as possible, but the roads were rendered so bad by the rains, which followed almost immediately, that it was next to impossible to get them up to the front. Two batteries, however, did arrive before the close of hostilities. The others were stopped on the way.

"General Miles, commanding the army, reached headquarters in the field on the afternoon of July 12, and held a conference with the Spanish commander on the 13th. He was present at the capitulation on the 14th, and returned to his ship in the port of Siboney on the same day."

Somewhat more in detail, the Secretary of War of the United States thus described the course of events connected with the close of the Santiago campaign: "After the cessation of firing about noon on the 3d, the surrender of the Spanish forces was demanded by General Shafter. This being refused, the commanding general of the Spanish forces was notified that the bombardment of Santiago would begin at noon of the 5th, thus giving two days to enable the women and children to leave the city.

"On July 3 the Spanish fleet fled from the harbor and was destroyed by our navy. The surrender being again demanded on July 4, negotiations were renewed. No engagement, however, took place until July 10, when at 4 P.M. the Spaniards opened fire, which was soon silenced. On the morning of the next day the bombardment was renewed, and continued until 2 P.M., when upon another demand for the surrender of the enemy the firing ceased and was not again renewed.

"Major-General Miles arrived off Santiago July 11, and that evening communicated with General Shafter by telephone, and on the 12th arrived at General Shafter's headquarters. On July 13 and 14 he, with General Shafter, met the Spanish commander under flag of truce between the lines, to discuss the surrender of the Spanish forces. On the afternoon of July 14 General Miles left General Shafter's head-

ON THE BATTLE-GROUND OF LAS GUASIMAS—AMERICANS GOING TO THE FRONT

quarters and soon thereafter went on board ship, preparatory to sailing for Puerto Rico. On July 17 the Spanish commander, General Toral, surrendered the city, including the troops in Santiago and the surrendered district, upon our terms, and at noon of that date the American flag was, by order of General Shafter, hoisted over the Governor's palace.

"The shipment of the Spanish prisoners to Spain, under the agreement, commenced August 9 and ended September 17. Total number of people shipped was 22,864.

"On August 4 General Shafter received orders to embark his command for Montauk Point, New York. The movement continued until August 25, when he sailed with the last of his troops, except a few left in hospital, sick, turning over the command of the department to Major-General Lawton."

GENERAL SHAFTER'S ACCOUNT

The arrival of General Escario on the night of July 2, and his entrance into the city, were not anticipated, for although it was known, as previously stated, that General Pando had left Manzanillo with reinforcements for the garrison of Santiago, it was not believed that his troops could arrive so soon. General Garcia, with between 4000 and 5000 Cubans, was intrusted with the duty of watching for and intercepting the reinforcement expected. This, however, he failed to do, and General Escario passed into the city along on my extreme right and near the bay. Up to this time I had been unable to complete the investment of the town with my own men; but to prevent any more reinforcements from coming in or the enemy from escaping, I extended my lines as rapidly as possible to the extreme right, and completed the investment of the place, leaving General Garcia's forces in the rear of my right flank to scout the country for any approaching Spanish reinforcements, a duty which his forces were very competent to perform.

It had been reported that 8000 Spanish troops had left Holguin for Santiago. It was also known that there was a considerable force at San Luis, twenty miles to the north.

In the battle of Santiago the Spanish navy endeavored to shell our troops on the extreme right, but the latter were concealed by the inequalities of the ground, and the shells did little, if any, harm. Their naval forces also assisted in the trenches, having 1000 on shore, and I was informed that they had sustained considerable loss; among others, Admiral Cervera's chief of staff was killed. Being convinced that the city would fall, Admiral Cervera determined to put to sea, informing the French consul it was better to die fighting than to sink his ships. The news of the great naval victory which followed was enthusiastically received by the army.

BRIGADIER-GENERAL WILLIAM LUDLOW
DRAWN BY FREDERIC REMINGTON

The information of our naval victory was transmitted under flag of truce to the Spanish commander in Santiago on July 4, and the suggestion again made that he surrender to save needless effusion of blood.

On the same date I informed Admiral Sampson that if he would force his way into the harbor the city would surrender without any further sacrifice of life. Commodore Watson replied that Admiral Sampson was temporarily absent, but that in his (Watson's) opinion the navy should not enter the harbor.

In the meanwhile letters passing between General Toral and myself prevented the resumption of hostilities. Each army, however, continued to strengthen its intrenchments. I was still of the opinion that the Spaniards would surrender without much more fighting, and on July 6 called General Toral's attention to the changed conditions, and at his request gave him time to consult his home government. This he did, asking that the British consul, with the employés of the cable company, be permitted to return from El Caney to the city. This I granted.

The strength of the enemy's position was such that I did not wish to assault if it could be avoided.

An examination of the enemy's works, made after the surrender, fully justified the wisdom of the course adopted. The intrenchments could only have been carried with very great loss of life, probably with not less than 3000 killed and wounded.

On July 8 General Toral offered to march out of the city with arms and baggage, provided he would not be molested before reaching Holguin, and to surrender to the American forces the territory then occupied by him. I replied that while I would submit his proposition to my home government, I did not think it would be accepted.

In the meanwhile arrangements were made with Admiral Sampson that when the army again engaged the enemy the navy would assist by shelling the city from ships stationed off Aguadores, dropping a shell every few minutes.

On July 10 the First Illinois and the First District of Columbia arrived and were placed on the line to the right of the cavalry division. This enabled me to push Lawton farther to the right and practically to command the Cobra road.

On the afternoon of the date last mentioned the truce was broken off at 4 P.M., and I determined to open with four batteries of artillery, and went forward in person to the trenches to give the necessary orders, but the enemy anticipated us by opening fire with his artillery a few minutes after the hour stated. His batteries were apparently silenced before night, while ours continued playing upon his trenches until dark. During this firing the navy fired from Aguadores, most of the shells falling in

BRIGADIER GENERAL ADNA R. CHAFFEE
Drawn by Frederic Remington

BRIGADIER-GENERAL SAMUEL S. SUMNER
Drawn by Frederic Remington

the city. There was also some small-arms firing. On this afternoon and the next morning we lost Captain Charles W. Rowell, Second Infantry, and one man killed, and Lieutenant Lutz, Second Infantry, and ten men wounded.

On the morning of July 11 the bombardment by the navy and my field-guns was renewed, and continued until nearly noon, and on the same day I reported to the Adjutant-General of the army that the right of Ludlow's brigade of Lawton's division rested on the bay. Thus our hold upon the enemy was complete.

At 2 P.M. on this date (the 11th) the surrender of the city was again demanded. The firing ceased, and was not again renewed. By this date the sickness in the army was increasing very rapidly, as a result of exposure in the trenches to the intense heat of the sun and the heavy rains. Moreover, the dews in Cuba are almost equal to rains. The weakness of the troops was becoming so apparent that I was anxious to bring the siege to an end, but, in common with most of the officers of the army, I did not think an assault would be justifiable, especially as the enemy seemed to be acting in good faith in their preliminary propositions to surrender.

On July 11 I wrote General Toral as follows: "With the largely increased forces which have come to me, and the fact that I have your line of retreat securely in my hands, the time seems fitting that I should again demand of your Excellency the surrender of Santiago and of your Excellency's army. I am authorized to state that, should your Excellency so desire, the government of the United States will transport the entire command of your Excellency to Spain."

General Toral replied that he had communicated my proposition to his general-in-chief, General Bianco.

On July 12 I informed the Spanish commander that Major-General Miles, commander-in-chief of the American army, had just arrived in my camp, and requested him to grant us a personal interview on the following day. He replied that he would be pleased to meet us. The interview took place on the 13th, and I informed him that his surrender only could be considered, and that, as he was without hope of escape, he had no right to continue the fight.

On the 14th another interview took place, during which General Toral agreed to surrender, upon the basis of his army, the Fourth Army Corps, being returned to Spain, the capitulation embracing all of eastern Cuba

GENERAL VIEW OF THE TOWN OF EL CANEY.—Photograph by James Burton

east of a line passing from Ascraderos, on the south, to Sagua de Tanamo, on the north, *via* Palma Soriano. It was agreed that commissioners should meet during the afternoon definitely to arrange the terms of surrender, and I appointed Major-Generals Wheeler and Lawton and Lieutenant Miley to represent the United States.

The Spanish commissioners raised many points, and were especially desirous of retaining their arms. The discussion lasted until late at night and was renewed at 9.30 o'clock next morning. The terms of surrender finally agreed upon included about 12,000 Spanish troops in the city and as many more in the surrendered district.

It was arranged that the formal surrender should take place between the lines, on the morning of July 17, each army being represented by one hundred armed men. At the time appointed I appeared at the place agreed upon, with my general officers, staff, and one hundred troopers of the Second Cavalry, under Captain Brett. General Toral also arrived, with a number of his officers and one hundred infantry. We met midway between the representatives of our two armies, and the Spanish commander formally consummated the surrender of the city and the 24,000 troops in Santiago and the surrendered district.

TAKING WOUNDED TO DIVISION HOSPITAL

SECOND-DIVISION HOSPITAL IN THE FIELD AT EL CANEY

After this ceremony I entered the city with my staff and escort, and at twelve o'clock noon the American flag was raised over the Governor's palace with appropriate ceremonies.

The Ninth Infantry immediately took possession of the city, and perfect order was maintained. The surrender included a small gunboat and about two hundred seamen, together with five merchant ships in the harbor. One of these vessels, the *Mexico*, had been used as a war vessel, and had four guns mounted on it.

In taking charge of the civil government all officials who were willing to serve were retained in office, and the established order of government was preserved as far as consistent with the necessities of military rule.

I soon found the number of officials was excessive, and I greatly reduced the list, and some departments were entirely abolished.

A collector of customs, Mr. Donaldson, arrived soon after the surrender, and, due to his energy and efficiency, this department was soon working satisfactorily. The total receipts had, up to my departure, been $102,000.

On August 4 I received orders to begin the embarkation of my command and ship them to Montauk Point, Long Island, New York. The movement continued without interruption until August 25, when I sailed for Montauk with the last troops in my command, turning over the command of the district to Major-General Lawton.

Before closing, I wish to dwell upon the natural obstacles I had to encounter and which no foresight could have overcome or obviated. The rocky and precipitous coast afforded no sheltered landing-places, the roads were mere bridle-paths, the effect of the tropical sun and rains upon unacclimated troops was deadly, and a dread of strange and unknown diseases had its effect on the army.

At Daiquiri the landing of the troops and stores was made at a small wooden wharf which the Spaniards had tried to burn, but unsuccessfully, and the animals were pushed into the water and guided to a sandy beach about two hundred yards in extent. At Siboney the landing was made on the beach and at a small wharf erected by the engineers.

I had neither the time nor the men to spare to construct permanent wharves.

In spite of the fact that I had nearly 1000 men continuously at work on the roads, they were at times impassable for wagons.

The San Juan and Aguadores rivers would often suddenly rise so as to prevent the passage of wagons, and then the eight pack-trains with the command had to be depended upon for the victualling of my army, as well as the 20,000 refugees, who could not in the interests of humanity be left to starve while we had rations.

Often for days nothing could be moved except on pack-trains.

THE OLD CHURCH AT EL CANEY—REFUGEES FROM SANTIAGO LINED UP FOR DISTRIBUTION OF FOOD

GENERAL VIEW OF THE BATTLE-GROUND OVER WHICH THE AMERICANS FOUGHT THEIR WAY ON JULY 1

After the great physical strain and exposure of July 1 and 2, the malarial and other fevers began rapidly to advance throughout the command, and on July 4 the yellow-fever appeared at Siboney. Though efforts were made to keep this fact from the army, it soon became known.

The supply of quartermaster and commissary stores during the campaign was abundant, and, notwithstanding the difficulties in landing and transporting the ration, the troops on the firing-line were at all times supplied with its coarser components—namely, of bread, meat, sugar, and coffee. There was no lack of transportation, for at no time up to the surrender could all the wagons I had be used.

The sick and wounded received every attention that it was possible to give them. The medical officers without exception worked night and day to alleviate the suffering, which was no greater than invariably accompanies a campaign. It would have been better if we had had more ambulances, but as many were taken as was thought necessary, judging from previous campaigns.

The discipline of the command was superb. Not an officer was brought to trial by court-martial, and, as far as I know, no enlisted men. This speaks volumes for an army of this size and in a campaign of such duration.

A CORRESPONDENT'S ACCOUNT

By John Fox, Jr.

Chaffee's Headquarters, July 10—Sunday at the trenches. A truce is on. The band that helped the wounded in the wake of Chaffee's charging brigade is playing "Calvary."

"Hosanna!"

It is the most cheerful spot on a battle-field—the trenches—and a comparatively safe spot for the non-combatant even during action. Men at the front see their comrades drop, usually without an outcry, and pass on, if advancing, under an excitement of conflict that quickly makes them callous. At the trenches, and after sharp action is over, the dead are buried, the wounded and the sick are carried to the rear—to be seen no more, unless they come back to take a place in the ranks again. The firing dies down to the popping duel of sharp-shooters and the uncanny whistle of a vagrant shell. A short peace of reaction follows, which quiets the strained nerves, but does not last long; the men get restless and impatient quickly. But while they may sit in the sun by day and sleep in the mud at night, as they did here before Santiago, they are saved contact with that ghastly road of choking odors and choking memories that leads through the rear, and

THE GROUND OVER WHICH THE AMERICANS CHARGED TO TAKE THE BLOCK-HOUSE ON THE SAN JUAN HILL

SCENE FROM SAN JUAN FORT, WHERE THE BATTLE TOOK PLACE.—Photograph by James Burton

to the still pitiful pictures under the hospital tents at Siboney. Moreover, during action the Spanish fire sweeps that same road between the base of the hill under the trenches and the woods, and makes the zone of just getting to the front or just getting away more dangerous even than the front itself; and then to the man who must go to the rear there has always been the inglorious and enraging possibility of being potted in the back by a sharp-shooter from a royal palm or a mango-tree. Lastly, the bands play up and down the lines, and, especially when a truce comes, a curious spirit of holiday pervades the air. There is nothing more incongruous, nothing more grotesque, on the field after a battle than the sight of a bass-drum or a big bass-horn lying, as I saw several on the afternoon of July 1, just under the conquered Spanish trenches. But it is very fine and inspiriting next morning to hear both booming to a Sousa march or a jolly negro melody; and it is moving beyond words just now to hear "Calvary" swelling reverently overhead and breaking gently against the still, green spires that far up the valley thrust themselves now and then into cloudland.

"Hosanna! Glory to God!"

The wind is gentle and cool, the air is clear and brilliant, the sun shines, the mountains are divine in majesty and peace, but it is glory to the God of Battles that band is playing now, for the memories of El Caney still bleed, and with more than half a circle of bayonets we invest Santiago: a truce is on, and we are expecting the Spaniard to give up his plucky fight.

Last night Major-General Lawton, who is never to be caught napping, for the reason that he never seems to sleep (I believe he never went to his cot the first week except to have the shirt in which he came ashore restored to its original color), shot out his right flank a mile and a half, so that, with the Cubans, out of whom he can get more work than any other general in the army, he holds El Cobre road—the last avenue of escape for the Spaniards to the hills.

General Ludlow is next to the Cubans, and keen, watchful, untiring Chaffee—a major-general, too, since his reckless courage and strong fight at El Caney—touches Ludlow's left flank on one side, and, on the other, the right flank of that nimble old veteran, who scales trees for personal reconnaissance and mounts his horse for battle from an ambulance—General Wheeler. Of this division, and of the whole line, indeed, Colonel Roosevelt, of course, has the shortest air-line from his rifle-pits to the Spanish trenches. Kent's division starts from Wheeler, following ever the throttling sweep of a circle.

So that the wings of the army are more than half shut, like the wings of our bird of freedom when he drops through the air for prey. Therefore we have sent the Spaniard word that unless he gives up the fight this day the awful rending of beak and claws shall begin again, and the iron wings shall be folded closer. Meanwhile the little men in light blue sit calmly on the edge of their trenches and smoke cigarettes, while the big men in dark blue sit on the edge of theirs and good-humoredly cast tobacco juice towards Santiago. Down in the hollows midway between the lines are Spanish soldiers and American soldiers gathering yams and mangoes, with only a narrow cocoanut grove between them. For half an hour I watched two of the Americans trying to round up and drive into our lines half a dozen horses that were running loose in a field and belonged to Spanish officers, until a major, fearing that the mischievous dare-devils might bring on an engagement during a truce, sent a lieutenant down to stop them. The lieutenant rode a gray mule as a flag of truce, and I rode down with him, but the Spaniards paid as little attention to us as they paid to the men we were after, and the lieutenant rebuked these men with a stern severity in his voice that was not, I'm sure, in his heart, and they let the horses alone. At one point along the line two Spanish officers came towards our trenches and signalled for our officers to approach, which they did. The Spaniards said they had been trying to get over for two days, and I am told they were good fellows; that they brought along a little rum, and Spaniard and American drank mutual healths, and swore with equal heartiness at the Cuban, and declared that motive of the war a wicked shame. And by-and-by, when peace was come, they would have a dinner at the Waldorf, and talk it all over, and be decorously merry.

However, the rumor now is that the Spaniards are not going to surrender to-day, and

FIRST VIEW OF SANTIAGO FROM THE HILLS—ABOUT FIVE MILES DISTANT

THE CITY AND HARBOR FROM THE RESIDENCE OF THE BRITISH CONSUL.

we begin firing at noon. Meanwhile we have given the enemy nine round days of fair weather in which to recover his spirits, gather yams, and make good and ready for his fight in the last ditch.

There are many others besides us who are anxious to get into Santiago—eighteen thousand others, indeed—the half-starved refugees who came out of Santiago when we announced that we meant to shell the town, and are waiting at the little conquered town of El Caney for the time when they may go home again. I was there yesterday afternoon, under the guidance of the Major, with whom I came down on the *Iroquois*, and it is a distressing scene. The town is built about a plaza, and the houses—those that are not thatched hovels—are low, and have blue walls and red-tiled roofs. At the head of the plaza stands a big and very old cathedral, which is a storehouse just now for Uncle Sam, whose generous right hand reaches daily from the door to give rations to his enemy as to himself, while the left stays under his coat-tails unknowing. They are mostly women and children, the refugees—white women, yellow women, brown women, and black women; and babies black, babies brown, babies yellow, and white babies, ludicrous mites, some of them, and nearly all as naked as they were at birth. Some of the women were the wives and widows of Spanish officers, and the few men in the crowd were sick or aged or straggling Cubans. Most of the refugees expected to be out of Santiago for only a day or two, so even the well-to-do were hungry, and the poor and the *reconcentrados* were nearly starved. The distribution of rations, in spite of priest and soldiers, was in consequence little more than a mob-like fight for hardtack. It is such a town as would have about one thousand inhabitants in our States. Imagine, then, how these refugees are crowded! The plaza is a swarm of women and children; the streets, the curbstones, the narrow sidewalks are massed with women and children; so are the porches, door-steps, doorways, hallways; the back yards and side yards are full, and so is the little creek that runs between the town and the shattered stone fort which Chaffee stormed. And always the cry is, "Mucha hambre! mucha hambre!" But when they are not hungry they are as laughing and light-hearted as though they had

LIGHT ARTILLERY MOVING TO A NEW POSITION.

CONFERENCE OF FOREIGN CONSULS FROM SANTIAGO WITH GENERAL WHEELER CONCERNING THE BOMBARDMENT

not a care in the world and would never get hungry again. Not one over five years of age and under sixty but knew the Major—who had been playing the part of a summer Santa Claus in the town—and had a smile for him; and for each the Major had a smile, while the fat little priest who gave out the bread called him his brother, and embraced him as such. And how the dusky groups of roguish girls in the porches flashed dark eyes and white teeth at him as he rode by, and how the Major smiled back and loved it all!

The Major has done his work well. During the fight around El Caney his duties led him several times into the "jaws of hell," as he says, and he went in—not without flinching, for the Major is frank, but he went in. Once he was sent with a guard of five troopers to find General Ludlow.

"The bullets in one lane were like hail," said the Major. "'Don't go down there, sir,' said a soldier. 'You'll be killed. General Ludlow is back there.' I rode back through that awful lane. 'Where is General Ludlow?' I said to a soldier. 'General Ludlow—' he said, and a bullet caught him in the forehead, and he fell dead. I was sent to another place, and another, and I couldn't find him. Finally I went to an old officer. 'Colonel,' I said, 'I've been looking for General Ludlow for two hours, and can't find him. I've got five troopers here. I'm not married myself, and of course I don't care for myself, but they're all married men, and I've got to think of them. I don't want to risk their lives any more. Now, I'm a tenderfoot, and I ask you frankly what ought I to do?' 'Don't you report to your superior officer,' said the colonel, 'until you have found General Ludlow.' That was enough for me, and off I started; but I said to the troopers, 'You needn't come, not a one of you.' But every one came. Once I got ahead of our own line. I heard a click, looked up, and there was a Spanish picket-post not fifty yards away, with their guns levelled. I lay down on my horse and skipped. The bullets whistled, but I wasn't touched. Finally I did find him. 'This way, Webb, my boy,' he called from the woods. It was hot in there. 'Stoop, sir; stoop,' said a soldier; and as I stooped the poor fellow himself got a bullet in the breast. 'Here you are,' called the general, who was standing straight, with his shoulders squared. I straightened up my backbone too, though I never felt so humble in my life, and I gave my message and started away. When I had got off fifty yards the general called me back through that death-hole. I left again, and if he didn't call me back *again!* 'General,' I said, 'for God's sake, don't call me back any more.' He laughed, and didn't; and here I am."

So, now that promotions rustle the Cuban air, the Major says frankly, and with logic and justice: "If I am a staff-officer, put me back in the rear and let me be ornamental. If I am to have duties steadily on the firing-line and ahead of it, as I had, and do them, as I did—here's So-and-so and So-and-so being made colonel, brigadier-general, and major-general—what do I get?"

Noon now, and the Spaniards decline to surrender. We shall begin bombarding at four. Meanwhile here is the story of the day's advance towards Santiago, brought up by a croaker from the rear: The correspondent's hammock swung, at corps headquarters, from the limb of a mango-tree. The siege-guns were behind because the roads were bad; the pack-mules tramped through mud; the wagons creaked through mire; and men on foot—even the wounded, one day—waded the bridgeless creek four or five times between front and the rear, and yet a body of volunteers and an engineer or two were busy all morning cutting a wagon-road through thick brush to the top of a low hill about three-quarters of a mile away. At noon, while staff-officers, aides, and attachés were at lunch, came the order to move camps. Lunch stopped short, off bustled aide and attaché, the big wagons rolled in, and there was a great falling of tents and a mighty bustle for fear the wagons might roll out again before each man had his outfit tossed in. Such was the hurry that even the solemn and elegant attachés hurriedly helped to fold their own things. Out came the guard of mounted troopers, out the guard of infantry, out the Spanish prisoners, and out the correspondents, who sought to keep in touch with the source of the done, the doing, and the undone; out came the commanding general, mounted, and with his left foot swathed; out the very tall aide and the courtly inspector-general and other members of the staff; out the attachés and their orderlies and servants—all mounted—everybody mounted except the infantry, the Spanish prisoners, and the correspondents, whose horses were left behind at Tampa. The general led the way, followed by the very tall aide, the courtly inspector-general, the other staff-officers, the attachés, the troopers, the three big army-wagons with their six-mule teams, the infantry, the Spanish prisoners, and the correspondents—and the long train wound laboriously along and up the wagon-road cut that morning through thick brush by engineer and volunteer, when the one road from front to rear was muddy and bridgeless, and the siege-guns were still where they stayed till the end—behind. Now and then the procession halted for axe-men to clean out a bush and broaden the road here and there, but in time it crawled slowly to the top of the

SAN JUAN HILL TERRACED FOR TENTS OF UNITED STATES TROOPS

hill. There the general swept horizon and hill with his eye for perhaps three minutes. Then he turned his horse. The very tall aide turned his horse. The courtly inspector-general, the aides, and attachés turned theirs. Turned, too, the heavy wagons, creaking, and the six mules each; turned troopers, infantry, Spanish prisoners; turned correspondents — aside into the grass to laugh: and as the long train wound up, so wound it down — down the trail that engineer and volunteer had laboriously cut through thick brush that morning, and back to the same still smoking camp. There the general swept the scene with his eye, rode to a fresh spot a little way off, and halted. And there, one hundred yards from where it sat before, sits the general's camp to-day. The hammock of the correspondent swings from the same limb of the mango-tree.

The poor wounded have had a hard time. Apparently the powers thought there were not going to be any wounded; and, without doubt, few on Cuban soil dreamed there would be so many. The wounded at Las Guasimas were carried three miles to Siboney by hand, for when that fight was over not a wagon for ammunition, supplies, or hospital needs was on shore.

Especially at El Caney, men not seriously wounded lay for hours awaiting their turn after the men who were worse hurt. Nowhere were hospital preparations complete enough in tents, medicine, nurses, or surgeons—on the field, in the rear, or at Siboney. At Siboney the surgeons had not time to get the names, or even to count the number brought in. If you wanted to see a wounded friend, you had to walk the aisle between the row of bandaged soldiers until you found him.

BOMB-PROOFS

And the way those brave fellows took their suffering! Sometimes the jolting ambulances were too much, and soldiers would pray for the driver, when he stopped, not to start again. One man groaned. "Grit yer teeth," said another, an old Irish sergeant, sternly—"grit yer teeth; there's others that's hurt here except you."

The sergeant himself was shot through the head, and thereafter no man in that ambulance uttered a sound. It was the slightly hurt, the men who were wounded in the leg or arm, who made the most noise.

Three men were brought into a hospital from San Juan. The surgeon took the one who was groaning. He had a mere scratch on one leg. Another was dressed; and as the third sat silently on a chair, still another was attended, and another, before the surgeon turned to the man who was so patiently awaiting his turn.

"Where are you hurt?"

The man pointed to his left side.

"Through?"

"Yes, sir."

That wounded courtier Cosby, feverish, trembling, with a scraped temple, a badly wounded hand, and a bullet in his chest, staggered painfully some ten miles, waving off all assistance, and confessing at last, as he sat on the beach in the broiling sun, waiting to be taken to a hospital-ship, that if it were handy, and could be got without too much trouble, he thought he would like a canned peach.

Out from the firing line at El Caney staggered a soldier with half his face shot away, and went staggering to the rear without aid. On the way he met a mounted staff-officer, and he raised his hand to his hatless, bleeding forehead in a stern salute, and, without a gesture for aid, staggered on. The officer's eyes filled with tears.

SPANISH FORT AND TRENCH, SANTIAGO

"Lieutenant," said a trooper, "I'm wounded."

"Can you get to the rear without help?"

"I think I can, sir," and he started. After twenty paces he pitched forward—dead. His wound was through the heart.

Such are the men who sleep in Cuban soil, who lie in the hospitals and on the transports at Siboney and on the big white relief-ship, that was as grateful a gift from home as though it had come from the Almighty Himself.

It is now half past three, and firing will begin at four. An army buckboard, drawn by a mule and driven by a large gentleman in a pith helmet, is moving along the base of the hill. Here and there a major or colonel, or perhaps a brigadier-general, looks stern. Some of the captains smile. A lieutenant or two grins broadly, and the sarcastic private in the trenches curses bitterly. Our commanding general is passing by.

I have just come down from the trenches to Roosevelt's tent. The hill under the firing-line looks like the abode of cave-dwellers, so burrowed is it with bomb-proofs, which are merely shallow earth caves dug into the side of a hill with the point of a bayonet, and covered with flat, projecting roofs of planks and layers of dirt. The men dug bomb-proofs and trenches most willingly, especially the negro troopers. "Foh God," said one, as he swung his pick at dusk after the fight of San Juan, "I never thought I'd git to love a pick befoh!"

The men up at the trenches are ready. Their cartridges are piled along the edge of the pits—in the tops of corned-beef cans, on pieces of boards, in little hollows scooped from the dirt—and everybody is eager and expectant. Sergeant Borrowe, bronzed and grimy, is at the breech of his long dynamite-gun, as keen for an experiment as a child with a Christmas toy that he has not fully mastered. A young German stands at a machine-gun not far away.

"It iss nervous at first," he says, "just waiting. But after the shooting begins it iss all right. I hear no bullets nutting—the gun makes

"A TRUCE IS ON!"

GENERAL MILES BEFORE SANTIAGO DURING THE NEGOTIATIONS FOR SURRENDER.—Photograph by James Burton

so much noise. Two of my men were killed the odder day, and I shoot on for two hours and not know it."

Across the air-line from Roosevelt's outermost trench I could see a group of Spanish officers ride hastily to the little house opposite and then gallop along the line. Those fellows seem to do things with great ceremony across there. The officers were evidently giving orders when to begin fire, for, as they passed, the straw hats began to drop out of sight in the Spanish trenches. Pretty soon the Spanish flag went up, about one hundred yards from the still flying flag of truce. Then down came the white flag, and up it went again—whimsically. Then a Spaniard seized it, shook it across at the Americans, and pulled it down permanently. But no Spaniard fired. He rarely does first; he is too polite, I suppose.

So we are waiting in Roosevelt's tent for our signal-gun, which is to thunder out on the right flank. A storm is coming. There is vertical lightning up and down the big black mountains in the east. The wind is high, and blowing the plumes of the palm towards Santiago. After it comes a thick gray mist of rain from the mountains, and the drops strike the tent overhead. It is three minutes after four, and no signal-gun yet. I suppose we are waiting for the storm to pass.

"Have you read *Salammbô?*" asks a voice outside, with an intonation that one hears in a Harvard class-room; "and do you remember Hanno, the fat general, who lay in the shade and scratched himself with a golden spatula?"

Nobody answers; that first shot comes!

An hour and a half later, and the firing has quieted down to the popping duel of the sharpshooters. We are in the tent again, and an occasional Mauser ball whistles overhead. It is curious, but even the tent-flaps seem to be some sort of protection against those nasty little insects. The bombardment was, after all, very mild, and this is how it seemed: When the first gun roared to the right, a rattling ran down the line towards us, and the Mausers began to pop and sing. Everybody sprang to his feet and followed Colonel Roosevelt up the hill, each man bending low to lessen the danger surface that his anatomy presented to the bullets coming over the hill. Davis forgot his glasses, and coolly went back for them. I waited for him awhile—a very little while—but when several bullets spat around me rather viciously and rather near, I accepted the hospitable invitation of two Rough Riders and crawled under a bomb-proof, between Lieutenant Greenway and Captain Llewellyn. There were about twenty of us in there. The planks overhead were thin, the cracks between them were wide, and the dirt on top was shallow—very shallow. "We're all right except for the shrapnel," said the captain several times. Every now and then a soldier would stick his head outside, or go out to light his

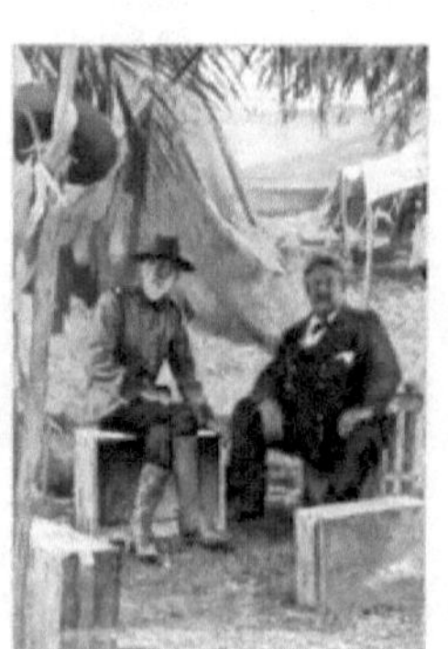

GENERALS WHEELER AND SHAFTER

pipe or for some other reason, and the captain would call him down sharply:

"Get down there! We don't want to be bothered with wounded men now. Get down!"

We could hear the steady flutter of the machine-gun, the rapid-fire Colt's going like an old-fashioned mowing-machine in a meadow, and now and then a shell.

"All right," repeated the captain, "except for the shrapnel."

And the shrapnel were friendly; I could not tell that a ball touched the bomb-proof. The Spaniards were not firing heavily. They were evidently saving their ammunition and waiting for another wild American charge—which never came; and so the bombardment ended in about an hour, as the rain had ended—in a slow patter, an occasional drop, and then in stillness. Indeed, I can almost liken an action of this sort at the trenches to an expected rain-storm in which there is a good deal of lightning. It thunders, the drops begin to patter, and you run for shelter, and you lie in comfort and in safety, except for the chance of being struck by lightning, which flashes sometimes uncomfortably near. By-and-by the storm passes, the rain quiets down to random drops, and you come out into the air, look around at the heavens, and stretch yourself.

Loud cheering rose at the trenches as we turned away, and somebody said that Sergeant Borrowe had tossed a Spanish cannon, a tree, and a mass of mingled breastwork and Spaniards into the air with one charge from his terrible gun. At General Wheeler's headquarters, farther down, the report was that the Rough Riders, without orders, had charged along their air-line and had captured the Spanish trenches. Somebody said the one rumor was not true, but nobody seemed to think the other at all improbable.

There was but one fatality on our side that afternoon, and that was a tragedy. On the left flank Captain Rowell, of the Second Infantry, was instantly killed by a Spanish shell.

As a first lieutenant he had waited twenty years for promotion, and his promotion outran his death but a few days.

Next morning, after the Sunday bombardment, we sent word over to ask the Spaniard if now he would be good. General Toral replied that he would at least be better if the home government would let him. So we gave him time until the following Thursday in which to communicate with Madrid. In the beginning he declined any and all terms of surrender; then an unconditional surrender; then he was willing to march out with the full honors of war, bearing his arms, with his flag flying, and the American soldier doing it homage, to march into another province, and thus be ready to fight us again some day. Now he was considering any terms that did not involve humiliation to Spanish honor and Spanish pride. Meanwhile the heroic figure of General Miles had appeared one fine morning, superbly mounted, and a reverent "Praise God!" ran along the lines. And General Randolph, too, of the artillery. I saw the latter at the front but once. He disappeared then, but I noticed that guns began to roll up from the rear as though they had wings, and I knew the siege-guns, if needed, would follow, even if they had mountains to climb. There was nobody who did not have a cheerful eye on General Randolph.

THE TREE UNDER WHICH THE FINAL CONFERENCE WAS HELD

Thursday came, and the word went round that the Spaniard had come down from his high horse. He would stack his arms, march out, evacuate the province, surrender all the troops in it—some 20,000—and in return we should feed them and carry them back to Spain. The sunny air straightway was rent with cheers. The sickest man in one regiment sprang from his blanket and led all his comrades in a foot-race for the trenches, there to join in the hallelujahs. Still, the doubting were suspicious. The wily Spaniard must be up to some game. Perhaps he was contemplating general peace at Madrid, and perhaps he was merely "working" our opulent government for the transportation of as many of his troops as possible, where sooner or later they would have to go—home. Maybe he really thought we were 50,000 strong—a French refugee had brought out word that such was the Spanish belief at Santiago—and on this supposition not one of the men who loved our commanding general least but gave him full credit for his bull-dog persistency and for the stark audacity of his first demands. But the Spaniard, whatever his reason, was this time in earnest, and out under the peace tree between the lines a commission was appointed on each side to draw up the terms. The surrender was sure, and a courteous Englishman raised his hat to the victorious general, and asked if he would be permitted to enter Santiago and witness the raising of the flag. Rasping oaths form the chief part of the general's vocabulary.

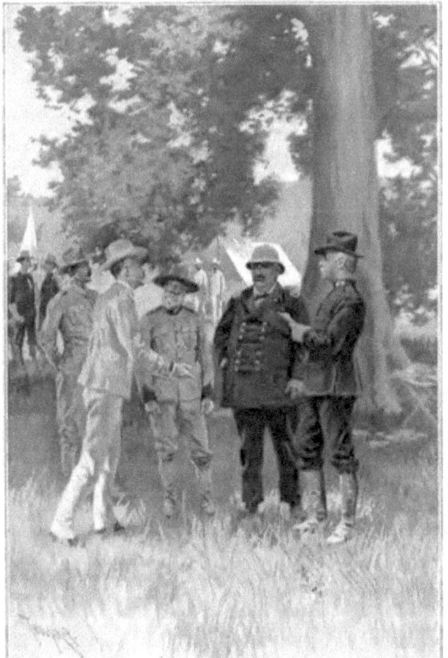

MEETING OF THE GENERALS TO ARRANGE THE SURRENDER OF SANTIAGO

"Not a —— —— rod," the Englishman was told, violently. "If any newspaper man goes into that town I'll have him shot, —— ——."

Therefore the obedient and the orderly went quietly back to their transports at Siboney, while the disobedient or the disbelieving remained on the field and marched into Santiago and saw the colors raised.

It happened at noon on Sunday, the 17th. The soldiers were drawn up at parade rest along the great ten-mile circle of the trenches and stood facing Santiago. They could see nothing—only the red roofs of the town—but the batteries were to thunder word when the red-and-yellow flag of defeat went down and the victorious Stars and Stripes rose up. While they waited, men in straw hats and blue clothes appeared in an open field towards Santiago and began swinging hammocks and tethering horses, while men in Panama hats advanced to the American trenches, saluting courteously. The Americans sprang across the trenches to meet them, and while they were shaking hands, and on the stroke of twelve, the thunder of twoscore and one salutes began. The Spaniards looked rather startled, but the cheers rose and they understood. From the right rose the cheers, gathering volume as they came, swinging through the centre far to the left, and swinging through the centre back again, until they broke in a wild storm against the big green hills. Then to the rear the storm ran, over Las Guasimas, and down the foothills to be mingled with the surf at Siboney, and swung by the rocking transports out to sea. Under the sea too it sang, along the cables—to ring through the white corridors of the great Capitol, and spread like a hurricane through our own waiting land. Already the bands were playing when the force of it broke at the trenches—playing the "Star-spangled Banner"—and the soldiers cheered again. Then they grew quiet—the bands were playing hymns: old, old hymns that the soldier had heard, with bowed head and at his mother's side, in some little old country church at home; and what hardship, privations, wounds, death of comrades, had rarely done, those old hymns did now—they brought the tears. Then some thoughtful soldier pulled a box of hardtack across the trenches, and the little Spanish soldiers fell upon it like school-boys, and scrambled like pickaninnies for a penny.

AMERICAN TROOPS CHEERING UPON RECEIVING THE NEWS OF SANTIAGO'S FALL.—Photograph by James Burton

THE SPANISH ACCOUNT

By Lieutenant José Müller y Tejeiro

At night the chiefs of the army assembled in the apartments occupied by the staff of the division, and as a result of the meeting the following memorandum was drawn up:

"On the 13th day of July, 1898, in the city of Santiago de Cuba, the following-named persons assembled, previous notice having been given of such meeting: General of Division José Toral y Velázquez, for the time being commander-in-chief of the Fourth Army Corps, as president; General of Brigade Federico Escario; Colonel Francisco Oliveros Jiménez, of the Civil Guard; the following lieutenant-colonels of the different battalions: José Cotrina Gelabert, of the Asiatic Battalion; Juan Puñet, of the battalion 'Constitucion'; Pedro Rodríguez, of the Talavera Battalion; Ventura Fontán, of the staff; Baldomero Barbón, of the Alcántara Battalion; Segundo Pérez, of the San Fernando Battalion; José Escudero, of the Provisional Battalion of Puerto Rico, No. 1; Luis Melgar, of the Artillery; and Ramón Arana, of the Puerto Rico Chasseurs; Julio Cuevas, commissary of war; Pedro Martin, sub-inspector of the medical department of the army, and Juan Diaz Muelas, captain of engineers, all as voting members, and the last named as secretary.

"The president stated that although he did not consider Santiago de Cuba a stronghold of war, and though he was in direct communication with the commander-in-chief, from whom he received precise instructions, so that it was not necessary to proceed to the convocation of the Council of Defence referred to in Article 683 of the Regulation of Campaign, he desired, nevertheless, to learn the opinion of said council, constituted in accordance with the provisions of the regulation referred to, and of the lieutenant-colonels of the battalions, as to whether, in view of the condition of the forces defending the city, it would be advisable to prolong the defence, or, on the contrary, to capitulate on the most favorable terms obtainable.

"The junta, considering that Santiago has no other works of defence of a permanent nature than a castle without artillery at the mouth of the harbor and a few forts in the precinct, none of them substantial, so that its only real defence consists in the trenches which have been dug in suitable positions in the circuit of the city, and other earthworks in said circuit and in more advanced positions, all effected hurriedly and with scant resources;

"Considering, further, that for the defence of this line of trenches, about 14 kilometers long, not continuous, there are available only about 7000 infantry and 1000 guerillas, all of whom have been doing constant service in the trenches, with hardly any troops to support them and without any reserves of any kind, the rest of the forces (the total forces consisting of about 11,500 men), belonging to other arms and garrisoning the Morro and the batteries of Socapa and Punta Gorda, or being assigned to other services, such as supplying all the posts with water, patrolling the city, etc., which services would have been rendered by the inhabitants if the city had remained loyal, but which must now be performed by the army, the inhabitants having abandoned the city;

"Considering, further, that, in view of the great extent of the line referred to, the position of the forces on the same, the difficulty of communication, and the proximity of the hostile positions to ours, it is difficult for the troops stationed at one part of the line to render prompt assistance to those stationed at another part which might be more seriously threatened;

"Considering, further, that at the present time the only available artillery of the precinct consists of four 16-cm. rifled bronze guns, one 12-cm., one 9-cm. bronze gun, two long 8-cm. rifled bronze guns, four short ones of the same caliber, two 8-cm. Plasencia, and two 75-mm. Krupp guns: that the 12 and 16 cm. guns, according to reliable information, are about to give out and will admit of only a few more shots, and that the 75-mm. Krupp guns have hardly any ammunition, and that the above is all the artillery we have to oppose to the enemy's numerous modern guns;

"Considering, further, that the million Spanish Mauser cartridges, being the total available, counting those at the artillery park and the spare cartridges of the troops, will be used up in two or three attacks made by the enemy; that the Argentine Mauser cartridges can hardly be used, and the Remington only by the irregular forces;

"Considering, further, that, owing to the failure of the commercial element to lay in supplies prior to the blockade which had long been foreseen, there is a great scarcity of meat and of all other articles of food for the troops, it being necessary to reserve for the military hospital the few heads of cattle now on hand, so that the only available food for the soldiers consists of rice, salt, oil, coffee, sugar, and whiskey, and this only for about ten days longer;

GENERALS MILES, SHAFTER AND WHEELER RETURNING FROM THE CONFERENCE

"Considering, further, that, if the food of the 1700 sick at the hospital is inadequate, the food furnished the soldiers is still more so, and yet they have to spend night and day in the trenches, after three years of campaign, the last three months without meat except on rare days, and for some time past reduced to the rations above enumerated;

"Considering, further, that with such inadequate rations the soldiers, whose physical strength is already considerably shaken, far from being able to repair their strength, must necessarily become weaker every minute, especially since, in spite of their poor nourishment, the greatest fatigues are required of them;

RAISING THE AMERICAN FLAG ON THE CITY HALL AT SANTIAGO

"Considering, further, that there is an ever-growing contingent of soldiers among the troops who, though not in hospitals, are sick,

GENERAL VIEW OF SANTIAGO, SHOWING THE CATHEDRAL ON THE TOP OF THE HILL

and who are enabled to remain at their posts only by their superior courage, which circumstances, however, cannot fail to weaken the resistance of the only line of defence we have;

"Considering, further, that, since the cutting of the aqueduct, great difficulties are experienced by the small forces available for furnishing water to the majority of the forces in the trenches of the precinct, especially those near the coast, which difficulties must naturally increase when the city is bombarded by sea and by land, so that there is well-founded fear that the soldiers who are unable to leave the trenches may find themselves without the water of which they are so much in need;

"Considering, further, that, in view of the location of the hostile positions, mostly in the immediate vicinity of ours, completely surrounding the city and in control of all the avenues, there is no possibility of abandoning the city without a fierce battle under the most unfavorable circumstances for us, owing to the impoverished condition of the soldiers and the fact that it would be necessary to effect the concentration of the forces in sight of the enemy;

"Considering, further, the great superiority of the enemy, who, besides a contingent of men said to exceed 40,000, possesses seventy pieces of modern artillery and a powerful fleet;

"Considering, further, that no supplies can reach the city except by sea, and that there is no prospect of receiving any as long as a powerful hostile fleet completely closes the entrance of the harbor;

"Considering, further, that, under these circumstances, to continue so unequal a fight would lead to nothing except the sacrifice of a large number of lives;

"And considering, finally, that the honor of our arms has been completely vindicated by these troops, who have fought so nobly and whose behavior has been lauded by our own and other nations, and that by an immediate capitulation terms could be obtained which it would not be possible to obtain after hostilities have again broken out,

"The junta is of unanimous opinion that the necessity for capitulation has arrived."

Negotiations for the capitulation having been opened, I think it proper to give the following important document:

"NEUTRAL CAMP, NEAR SANTIAGO DE CUBA,

"Under the Flag of Truce, *July 14, 1898*.

"Recognizing the nobleness, valor, and bravery of Generals Linares and Toral, and of the Spanish troops who took part in the actions that have recently occurred in the vicinity of Santiago de Cuba, as shown in said battles, we, the undersigned, officers of the United States army, who had the honor of taking part in the actions referred to, and who now constitute a committee, duly authorized, treating with a similar committee of officers of the Spanish army for the capitulation of Santiago de Cuba, unanimously join in asking the proper authorities that these brave and gallant soldiers may be granted the privilege of returning to their country carrying the arms which they have so nobly defended.

"(Signed)

"JOSEPH WHEELER,
"*Major-General U. S. V.*

"W. H. LAWTON,
"*Major-General U. S. V.*

"J. D. MILEY,
"*First Lieutenant, Second Artillery, Aide.*"

THE PLAZA DE ARMAS, SANTIAGO

SPANISH SOLDIERS IN SANTIAGO AFTER THE SURRENDER

Under a giant cotton-tree the following capitulation was signed on the 16th of July by Generals Wheeler and Lawton and Lieutenant Miley for the Americans, and General Escario and Lieutenant-Colonel Ventura Fontán for the Spaniards, commissioners acting under instructions of their respective commanders-in-chief and with the approval of their respective governments; Robert Mason signing as interpreter:

"1st. The hostilities between the Spanish and American forces shall cease absolutely and finally.

"2d. The capitulation shall include all the forces and war material in said territory (territory of the division of Santiago).

"3d. The United States agree to transport all the Spanish forces in said territory to the Kingdom of Spain with the least delay possible, the troops to be embarked, as early as can be done, at the nearest ports they occupy.

"4th. The officers of the Spanish army shall be permitted to carry their arms with them, and officers as well as men shall retain their private property.

"5th. The Spanish authorities agree to raise, or assist the American navy in raising, all the mines and other obstructions to navigation now existing in the bay of Santiago de Cuba and its entrance.

"6th. The commander of the Spanish forces shall deliver, without delay, to the commander of the American forces, a complete inventory of the arms and munitions of war in the district above referred to, as also a statement of the number of troops in the same.

"7th. The commander of the Spanish forces, upon leaving said district, shall be authorized to take with him all the military archives and documents belonging to the Spanish army now in said district.

"8th. All that portion of the Spanish forces known as volunteers, mobilized troops, and guerillas who may desire to remain in the island of Cuba shall be allowed to do so, on condition that they will deliver up their arms and give their word of honor not again to take up arms against the United States during the continuation of the present war with Spain.

"9th. The Spanish forces shall leave Santiago de Cuba with honors of war, afterwards depositing their arms at a place mutually agreed upon, to await the disposition which the government of the United States shall make of them, it being understood that the United States commissioners shall recommend that the Spanish soldiers be permitted to return to Spain with the arms which they have so gallantly defended.

"10th. The clauses of the foregoing document shall go into effect immediately after having been signed."

In conformity with the terms of this capitulation, the surrender of the city to the American army took place on the 17th of July.

At 9 A.M. the Spanish flag was hoisted on Punta Blanca Fort and saluted by twenty-one guns; shortly after it was lowered.

At 9.30 Generals Toral and Shafter, commanders-in-chief of the Spanish and American forces, respectively, the latter accompanied by his staff and many of the commanders and officers of the American fleet, witnessed the marching by, under arms, of a company of the former, representing all the Spanish forces, as it was difficult to assemble them. The American forces presented arms and beat a march.

The heights of Conosa was the theatre of this sad scene. The morning was very beautiful, and the clearness of the sky formed a singular contrast with the gloom that enwrapped the spirits of our troops.

When the march was ended, the American forces remained at their posts, while ours left the trenches and proceeded to the city for the purpose of depositing their arms.

The forces of the Socapa and Punta Gorda were taken by sea, in the steamer *Reina de Los Angeles*, to Las Cruces pier, and from there they marched to the Artillery Park, where they delivered arms and ammunition. Without them, they proceeded to the camp outside of the city, where all the forces were to assemble until the arrival of the vessels which, as agreed upon, were to convey them to Spanish soil. The other troops did the same, after depositing their arms at the points designated beforehand.

The troops having evacuated the city, one thousand men of the United States army entered it, hoisting the flag of that nation at the

A STREET VIEW IN SANTIAGO

AMERICAN FLAG FLYING OVER CITY HALL AND GOVERNOR'S RESIDENCE

Palace and Morro Castle. It was the only flag raised in the city. No insurgent forces, nor individuals belonging to the same, entered the city with arms. The situation remained the same till the day when the army embarked for Spain.

As the operations at the Park lasted several hours, it was curious to see the avidity with which the Americans were looking for numbers worn by the 29th battalion (Constitucion), sabres, buttons, and decorations of our officers and soldiers. It was noticed with what satisfaction they kept whatever articles and arms they could gather. Some of them put on the crosses, covered with dirt and blood, that had adorned the breasts of the Spaniards. There were so many incidents of the same order that it would be tedious to enumerate them. They showed the high conception which the American forces had of the valor of our army.

At 10 A.M. an officer of the American army, delegated for that purpose, took possession of the Comandancia de Marina and the office of the captain of the port, which were surrendered to him after we had gathered up such documents and communications as should be preserved, and destroyed the others or made them useless.

The forces deposited arms and ammunition, preserving excellent order, which was not disturbed for a moment. Then they marched to the camp outside of the city. The arms were all deposited at the Park, and not surrendered to the enemy.

CONTEMPORARY NOTES

By Inspector-General Breckinridge

It is not known that the Spaniards have taken a single prisoner from the army during this campaign. We have taken several hundred Spanish officers and soldiers, some of whom were wounded. These Spanish prisoners, from their conduct, apparently expected to receive harsh treatment, if not immediate execution; but they were, of course, well treated, and seemed to be surprised at it. The wounded prisoners were sent into the Spanish lines. Some of those not wounded were exchanged for some of our sailors who were held prisoners by the Spaniards, and one wounded Spanish officer was exchanged for Lieutenant Hobson, of the navy, though General Shafter was ready, if necessary, to give three of equal rank for him.

There were a number of deserters from the Spanish lines into ours, the reason of their desertion being given by them as ill treatment on the part of their officers and government.

Experience has shown that there can be no doubt as to the bravery of the Spanish soldier when fighting behind intrenchments. As to their qualities for fighting in the open, we have had no opportunity to judge, as they have been wholly on the defensive and far from aggressive or enterprising in this campaign.

The Mauser rifle seems an excellent and rapid weapon, and its smokeless cartridge adds to its special efficiency, whether or not equal to our own or better. It is a magazine-rifle, and is loaded with five cartridges at a time. These cartridges are held in a clip, and are detached from the belt and placed in the rifle in one motion.

The uniform worn by the Spanish soldier consists of blouse and trousers of a light-blue drilling, with fine white vertical stripes, a good, serviceable straw hat, and rather light-weight shoes. They seem to use no tentage, their protection from the weather being by means of their block-houses or other houses or sheds in the vicinity, and by such covering as they can get by putting up temporary

SPANISH PRISONERS MARCHING TO TRANSPORTS

SANTIAGO—WHERE AN AMERICAN SHELL STRUCK

structures of palm leaves. Their food, so far as can be judged from what was found in intrenchments after they had left, consisted mostly of rice and hard bread of a brownish color.

In the beginning the Cuban soldiers were largely used as outposts on our front and flanks. There has been a great deal of discussion among officers of this expedition concerning the Cuban soldiers and the aid they have rendered. They seem to have very little organization or discipline, and they do not, of course, fight in the battle-line with our troops. Yet in every skirmish or fight where they are present they seem to have a fair proportion of killed and wounded. They were of undoubted assistance in our first landing, and in scouting our front and flanks. It is not safe, however, to rely upon their fully performing any specific duty, according to our expectation and understanding, unless they are under the constant supervision and direction of one of our own officers, as our methods and views are so different and misunderstanding or failure so easy.

Our troops seem to have been reduced to a minimum of protection from the weather that they could have by means of clothing and tentage, and from the nature of the case they often suffered a great deal from unavoidable exposure, both from the heat and tropical rains. Many days and nights it was necessary for them to bivouac without putting up their shelter-tents. In other cases the ground has been so wet that it was impossible to be protected from it, and so they have been obliged to remain for days and nights together in their wet clothing. The same is true of the officers as of the men, the officers in no case having greater protection than the men.

It is difficult, perhaps impossible, to give adequate impression of the straits and discomforts, even suffering, to which individuals were driven, which may seem remarkable, as we were never beyond a day's march from the base of supplies. In the trenches it was either very hot on clear days, with the sun beating down upon them, or very wet on rainy days, with the trenches partly filled with water. As a result, considerable sickness was to be expected among the men, the trouble being mostly in the nature of fever, not always malarial, but a fever that was quite high and lasted from three to six days.

That there should be any suffering or ill-health along the firing-line for lack of food, clothing, modern arms, or other supplies, may either appear temporarily necessary or hardly credited, according to the point of view. Especially during the days it seemed that no tents and but little eating, and no animals, were possible on the advance or fighting lines. The need of witnesses from every corps and bureau of the army may not have been appreciated, if indeed any were needed. What the army cheerfully endured and accomplished with its valor deserves and has doubtless received the clearest appreciation, and protection against unnecessary deprivations is of course always assured.

Some men, notably among the volunteers, started out carrying overcoats. These were left on the transports or quickly abandoned. In some cases even blankets, blouses, and underclothing were thrown away. Knapsacks were strewn along the roadsides; and yet it is almost as difficult in this climate to keep warm at night as it is to keep cool in the daytime, as there is hardly a night when a covering is not needed in addition to the usual clothing worn, and never a day when the usual clothing is not uncomfortably warm.

What became of personal property wherever left will possibly prove a problem to some to solve. The khaki uniform worn by many officers quickly loses its shape and dandy color, and is not strong enough to withstand the thorns constantly met with beside the road and in the underbrush through which it is often necessary to pass. Many wear workmen's suits or the brown canvas uniform, as more suitable in this sort of country, service, and climate, than the blue.

It is perhaps but little cooler, but it is cheaper, and stands the wear and tear. The blue-flannel or black shirt, campaign hat, brown canvas leggings, shelter-tents, haversacks, canteen with leather strap, meat-can, knife, fork, and spoon, however, seem to give fair satisfaction. The knapsack, or pack of whatever nature, seems to disappear, and all come down naturally to plain blanket-roll. The tin cup is of proper size and material, but is still unsatisfactory on account of its being so unhandy for the purpose of boiling coffee. What it requires is a bail, in addition to the handle which it now has, and nesting qualities, and a model for patent has been seen.

A serious question that seems ever to return for sufficient consideration is, What shall be done with the soldier's heavy pack when he goes into action? Shall he carry it with him, weighing him down in the charge and pursuit, or shall he throw it aside, never to see it again, perhaps? In the battle of July 1 and 2 it became in most cases a physical necessity to throw the pack aside. In some cases regiments deposited their packs by the roadside and marched some miles after the battle to recover them again. In others, packs were thrown haphazard into the bushes, and in many cases were never recovered by their proper owners. Apparently the Cubans and sick found some comfort from the owners' loss.

SANTIAGO—DISCUSSING THE SURRENDER ON A STREET CORNER

THE RELIEF-SHIPS AT THE DOCKS IN SANTIAGO

FIELD ARTILLERY IN ACTION.—By T. de Thulstrup.

THE PUERTO RICAN CAMPAIGN

WITH the fall of Santiago the occupation of Puerto Rico became the next strategic necessity on the part of the United States. General Miles, the major-general commanding the army, had previously

MAJOR-GENERAL JOHN M. WILSON

been assigned to organize an expedition for that purpose. As has been seen, he was already at Santiago, where he had arrived on the 11th of July with reinforcements for General Shafter's army. The same day he went on shore, communicated with General Shafter, and arrived at the latter's headquarters on the following day, July 12. On July 14 he returned to Siboney, moved all the troops then on transports to Guantanamo, about forty miles east of Santiago, and with these troops, consisting of 3415 infantry and artillery, two companies of engineers, and one company of the Signal Corps, he left Guantanamo on July 21, having nine transports convoyed by the fleet under Captain Higginson, with the *Massachusetts* (flag-ship), *Dixie*, *Gloucester*, *Columbia*, and *Yale*, the two latter carrying troops. The expedition landed at Guanica, July 25, which port was entered with little opposition, and the flag of the United States was raised on the island. Here the fleet was joined by the *Annapolis* and the *Wasp*, while the *Puritan* and *Amphitrite* went to San Juan and joined the *New Orleans*, which was engaged in blockading that port. General Miles was subsequently reinforced by General Schwan's brigade of the Third Army Corps, by General Wilson with a part of his division, and also by General Brooke with a part of his corps, numbering in all 16,973 officers and men.

On the 26th, in an engagement at Yauco, the Spaniards were defeated. On July 27 the naval vessels of the United States entered the harbor of Ponce, and the next day the army took possession of the city, the troops being pushed well forward on the San Juan road, whence the Spaniards had withdrawn.

August 5 the troops under General Brooke had an engagement with the Spaniards at Guayama, which was finally occupied by the Americans. August 8 there was an action near Guayama, the Spaniards being driven in the direction of Cayey. August 9 the Americans advanced from Yauco, occupying, successively, Sabana Grande, San German, Lares, and Arecibo, entering Mayaguez, after an engagement, August 10, near Hormigueros. At Coamo an engagement took place August 9, the Spaniards being defeated and one hundred and sixty-seven prisoners being taken. At Assomanten, August 12, the Spanish position was shelled, and on August 13, the American command being ready to move forward, orders were received suspending hostilities.

Prior to the signing of a protocol on the 12th of August, the forces under General Miles in Puerto Rico had participated in six engagements, and had occupied a large portion of the island.

On August 30 General Miles sailed for the United States, turning over the command of the troops in Puerto Rico to Major-General Brooke. The final evacuation of Puerto Rico by the Spanish troops occurred October 18, and on that date the American flag was hoisted over the public buildings and forts at San Juan.

"This campaign," said the President, "was prosecuted with great vigor, and by the 12th of August much of the island was in our possession and the acquisition of the remainder was only a matter of a short time. At most of the points in the island our troops were enthusiastically welcomed. Protestations of loyalty to the flag and gratitude for delivery from Spanish rule met our commanders at every stage. As a potent influence towards peace the outcome of the Puerto Rican expedition was of great consequence, and generous commendation is due to those who participated in it."

BRIGADIER-GENERAL THEODORE SCHWAN

ACCOUNT BY GENERAL MILES

I WAS anxious to proceed as quickly as possible to the island of Puerto Rico, and so telegraphed the authorities in Washington. After some delay authority was granted, and I started from Guantanamo on July 21 with 3415 infantry and artillery, together with two companies of engineers and one company of the Signal Corps, on nine transports, convoyed by Captain Higginson's fleet, consisting of the battle-ship *Massachusetts* (flag-ship) and two smaller vessels. The *Yale* and *Columbia* were armed ships, but, being loaded with troops, they were practically only available as transports. The above

BRIGADIER-GENERAL GUY V. HENRY

number includes the men who were sick, of which there were nearly a hundred, which reduced our effective force to about 3300 men, and with that number we moved on the island of Puerto Rico, at that time occupied by 8233 Spanish regulars and 9107 volunteers.

For several days I had been anxiously looking for the arrival of tugs, launches, and lighters that had been ordered from Santiago, Washington, and Tampa, but none arrived prior to our departure, although I still hoped to meet them as we moved north through the Windward Passage. As all cablegrams concerning our landing-place had passed over foreign cables, and as it was important to deceive the enemy (who, I afterwards learned, were marching to and intrenching the ground we were expected to occupy at the very time we were taking possession of the southern coast of Puerto Rico), and owing to the non-arrival of launches, lighters, etc., the question of successfully disembarking the command became somewhat serious; and, after all hope of receiving any appliances of this kind had disappeared, I considered the advisability of finding a safe harbor and capturing necessary appliances from the enemy. I therefore wrote the following letter to Captain Higginson while at sea:

"Our objective point has been Pt. Fajardo or Cape San Juan, but so much time has occurred since the movement was decided in that direction, and such publicity has been given the enterprise, that the enemy has undoubtedly become apprised of our purpose. While it is advisable to make a demonstration near the harbor of San Juan near Pt. Fajardo or Pt.

BRIGADIER-GENERAL OSWALD H. ERNST

Figueroa, I am not decided as to the advisability of landing at either of these places, as we may find them well occupied by strong Spanish forces. If we draw them to that vicinity, we might find it judicious to move quickly to Puerto Guanica, where there is deep water near the shore—4½ fathoms—and good facilities for landing. We can move from Cape San Juan to that point in twelve hours (one night), and it would be impossible for the Spaniards to concentrate their forces there before we will be reinforced. I am also informed that there are a large number of strong lighters in the harbors at Ponce and Guanica, as well as several sailing-vessels, which would be useful. As it is always advisable not to do what your enemy expects you to do, I think it advisable, after going around the northeast corner of Puerto Rico, to go immediately to Guanica and land this force and move on Ponce, which is the largest city in Puerto Rico. After, or before, this is accomplished we will receive large reinforcements, which will enable us to move in any direction or occupy any portion of the island of Puerto Rico.

THE LANDING AT GUANICA.—Drawn by Howard Chandler Christy

"Your strong vessels can cover our landing and capture any vessels in the harbor of Ponce, Guanica, or the ports on the southern coast; one light vessel can remain at Cape San Juan to notify transports that will arrive where we have landed, and another could scout off the northwest corner of Puerto Rico to intercept others and direct them where to find us."

The following messages will further explain the circumstances and the final decision to change our course:

[Flag Message for Captain Higginson.]

"General Miles desires, if possible, you send in advance any naval vessels you can spare to the Port Guanica, reported to be without fortifications or torpedoes. If secured, hold, and report quickly to us, Cape San Juan.

"It is more important to land at Guanica than at Cape San Juan. If we can land there, he has troops enough to take the harbor of Ponce and let your fleet into that port.

"Possibly all of this can be accomplished by going by the south side. Can send Captain Whitney, who was at Ponce in June, to you, if desired. Answer."

[Signal from *Massachusetts*.]

"All right. Guanica it is. Shall I send

TROOP-SHIPS AND CONVOY AT PLAYA DE PONCE.—Drawn by T. Dart Walker

THE OCCUPATION OF PONCE.—DRAWN BY CARLTON T. CHAPMAN

orders to transport at Cape San Juan to join at Guanica?"

[Answer sent by General Miles.]

"Better be sure we can land at Guanica, then send for the transports. You can notify all vessels accordingly. Do you want Whitney?"

Captain Whitney was sent to report to Captain Higginson on the *Massachusetts*, with his maps and reports.

[Flag Message for Captain Higginson.]

"I would call your attention to the railroad between Ponce and Yauco, which I was informed passes right by the sea at one point, El Peñon, about eight miles west of Ponce. A vessel carrying a gun or two despatched to this point could prevent reinforcements from being sent by rail from there to Yauco, or detachment of troops, rolling-stock supplies, etc., from being brought into Ponce from Yauco."

[Flag Message for Captain Higginson.]

"Railroad from Ponce to Yauco runs close to sea, six to eight miles west of Ponce. Shell or destroy this and prevent Spanish troops moving."

Instead of making a demonstration at Pt. Fajardo, it was finally decided to go direct to Guanica. We arrived off that point near daylight on July 25, and the harbor was entered without opposition. The guns of the *Gloucester*, Commander Wainwright commanding, fired several shots at some Spanish troops on shore. The landing of the marines, sailors, and our troops immediately commenced, and after a short skirmish the Spanish troops were driven from the place and the flag of the United States was raised on the island.

In this, and in subsequent movements, I was very ably and cordially assisted by the navy, which rendered invaluable aid in disembarking troops and supplies from the transports, using their steam-launches to tow the lighters loaded with men and animals from the transports to the shore. Ten lighters were captured at Guanica and seventy at Ponce.

In the subsequent military operations in the interior, I found Captain Whitney's knowledge of the country and the information gained by him in his perilous journey through Puerto

Rico to be in every respect thoroughly accurate and of great value to me in the conduct of the campaign.

At daylight on the 26th of July, with six companies of the Sixth Massachusetts and one of the Sixth Illinois Volunteer Infantry, under command of Brigadier-General Garretson, an attack was made upon a strong force of Spaniards near Yauco, and after a spirited and decisive engagement the enemy was defeated and driven back, giving us possession of the railroad and the highway to the city of Ponce, and leaving them open for the march of General Henry's command to that place.

THE MILITARY ROAD LEADING INTO YAUCO

On the 27th of July Major-General Wilson arrived in the harbor of Guanica with General Ernst's brigade. The same day Commander Davis, of the *Dixie*, entered Port Ponce and found that it was neither fortified nor mined. The next morning the fleet and transports, with General Wilson's command, moved into the harbor of Port Ponce. The troops disembarked and marched to the city of Ponce, a distance of two miles, and we took formal possession of the city and adjacent country, the Spanish troops withdrawing on the military road to San Juan, and our troops being pushed well forward in that direction. In the meantime General Henry's command had been directed to proceed to Ponce, where he arrived shortly afterwards, joining General Wilson's command.

Before landing I was aware of the fact that there existed considerable disaffection among the people in the southern portion of the island, and as our force was so much inferior to the Spanish I deemed it advisable, if possible, to encourage this feeling, and also to impress the people of the island with the good intentions of the American forces, and for this and other reasons I issued the following proclamation to the inhabitants of Puerto Rico:

"In the prosecution of the war against the Kingdom of Spain by the people of the United States, in the cause of liberty, justice, and humanity, its military forces have come to occupy the island of Puerto Rico. They come bearing the banner of freedom, inspired by a noble purpose to seek the enemies of our country and yours, and to destroy or capture all who are in armed resistance. They bring you the fostering arm of a nation of free people, whose greatest power is in its justice and humanity to all those living within its fold. Hence, the first effect of this occupation will be the immediate release from your former political relations, and it is hoped a cheerful acceptance of the government of the United States. The chief object of the American military forces will be to overthrow the armed authority of Spain and to give to the people of your beautiful island the largest measure of liberty consistent with this military occupation. We have not come to make war upon the people of a country that for centuries has been oppressed, but, on the contrary, to bring protection, not only to yourselves but to your property, to promote your prosperity, and bestow upon you the immunities and blessings of the liberal institutions of our government. It is not our purpose to interfere with any existing laws and customs that are wholesome and beneficial to your people so long as they conform to the rules of military administration of order and justice. This is not a war of devastation, but one to give to all within the control of its military and naval forces the advantages and blessings of enlightened civilization."

And the following letter of instructions to General Wilson was published for the information and guidance of all concerned:

"The following instructions will govern you or your successor in the discharge of your duties relating to the military government of the territory now occupied, or hereafter to be occupied, by the United States forces under your command:

"The effect of the military occupation of the enemy's territory is the severance of the former political relations of the inhabitants, and it becomes their duty to yield obedience to the authority of the United States, the power of the military occupant being absolute and supreme and immediately operating upon the political conditions of the inhabitants. But generally, as long as they yield obedience to their new condition, security in their person and property and in all other

THE LANDING AT ARROYO.—Drawn by Carlton T. Chapman

General Miles and Staff — Fourth Ohio Volunteers

SKIRMISH NORTH OF GUAYAMA, AUGUST 8.—Drawn by Lucius Hitchcock, from Sketches made by Lieutenant J. M. A. Darrach and T. Dart Walker

SKETCH MAP OF GUAYAMA AND VICINITY

private rights and relations will be duly respected.

"The municipal laws, in so far as they affect the private rights of persons and property and provide for the punishment of crime, should be continued in force as far as they are compatible with the new order of things, and should not be suspended unless absolutely necessary to accomplish the objects of the present military occupation. These laws should be administered by the ordinary tribunals substantially as they were before the occupation. For this purpose the judges and other officials connected with the administration of justice may, if they accept the authority of the United States, continue to administer the ordinary laws of the land as between man and man, under the supervision of the commander of the United States forces. Should it, however, become necessary to the maintenance of law and order, you have the power to replace or expel the present officials, in part or altogether, and to substitute others, and to create such new and supplementary tribunals as may be necessary. In this regard you must be guided by your judgment and a high sense of justice.

"It is to be understood that under no circumstances shall the criminal courts exercise jurisdiction over any crime or offence committed by any person belonging to the army of the United States, or any retainer of the army, or person serving with it, or any persons furnishing or transporting supplies for the army; nor over any crime or offence committed on either of the same by any inhabitant or temporary resident of the occupied territory. In such cases, except when courts-martial have jurisdiction, jurisdiction to try and punish is vested in military commissions and such provost courts as you may find necessary to establish. The native constabulary, or police force, will, so far as may be practicable, be preserved. The freedom of the people to pursue their accustomed occupations will be abridged only when it may be necessary to do so.

"All public funds and securities belonging to the Spanish government in its own right, and all movable property, arms, supplies, etc., of such government, should be seized and held for such uses as proper authority may direct. And whatever real property the Spanish government may have held should be taken charge of and administered; the revenues thereof to be collected and reported for such disposition as may be made of the same, under instructions from these headquarters.

"All public means of transportation, such as telegraph lines, cables, railways, telephone lines, and boats, belonging to the Spanish government, should be taken possession of and appropriated to such use as may be deemed expedient.

"Churches and buildings devoted to religious worship, and all school-houses, should be protected.

"Private property, whether belonging to individuals or corporations, is to be respected, and can be confiscated only as hereafter indicated. Means of transportation, such as telegraph lines and cables, railways and boats, may, although they belong to private individuals or corporations, be seized by the military occupant, but, unless destroyed under military necessity, are not to be retained.

"As a result of military occupation of this country, the taxes and duties payable by the inhabitants to the former government become payable to the military occupant. The money so collected to be used for the purpose of paying the necessary and proper expenses under military government.

"Private property will not be taken except upon the order of brigade and division commanders in cases of absolute military necessity, and when so taken for the public use of the army will be paid for in cash at a fair valuation.

"All ports and places in actual possession of our forces will be opened to the commerce of all neutral nations, as well as our own, in articles not contraband of war, upon payment of the prescribed rates of duty which may be in force at the time of the importation.

"A memorandum in respect to the jurisdiction of military commissions and provost courts is herewith enclosed."

Enclosure I

"I. Except as hereinafter restricted, and subject to the supervision and control of the commanding general, the jurisdiction of the municipal government and of the civil and criminal courts remain in force.

"II. The said criminal courts shall not exercise jurisdiction over any crime or offence committed by any person belonging to the army of the United States, or any retainer of the army, or person serving with it, or any person furnishing or transporting supplies for the army; nor over any crime or offence committed on either of the same by any inhabitant or temporary resident of said territory. In such cases, except when courts-martial have jurisdiction, jurisdiction to try and punish is vested in military commissions and the provost court, as hereinafter set forth.

"III. The crimes and offences triable by military commission are murder, manslaughter, assault and battery with intent to kill, robbery, rape, assault and battery with intent to commit rape, and such other crimes, offences, or violations of the laws of war as may be referred to it for trial by the commanding general. The punishment awarded by military commission shall conform, as far as possible, to the laws of the United States or the custom of war. Its sentence is subject to the approval of the commanding general.

"IV. The provost court has jurisdiction to try all other crimes and offences referred to in section II. of this order, not exclusively triable by court-martial or military commission, including violations of orders of the laws of war, and such cases as may be referred to it by the commanding general. It shall have power to punish with confinement, with or without hard labor, for not more than . . ., or with fine not exceeding . . . . or both. Its sentence does not require the approval of the commanding general, but may be mitigated or remitted by him.

"V. The judge of the provost court is appointed by the commanding general. When, in the opinion of the provost court, its power of punishment is inadequate, it shall certify the case to the commanding general for his consideration and action."

Brigadier-General Schwan arrived July 31, and was subsequently instructed to disembark part of the Eleventh Infantry, under Colonel De Russey, at Guanica, and march to Yauco, and thence west with an additional force of two batteries of artillery and one troop of cavalry. The following letter of instructions was addressed to General Schwan:

"You will proceed from Ponce with the six companies of the Eleventh Infantry to Yauco, moving by rail if desirable. You will also move by wagon-road Troop A, Fifth Cavalry, and two batteries of light artillery. At Yauco you will take the remainder of the Eleventh Infantry and two companies of the Nineteenth and proceed to Sabana Grande, San German, Mayaguez, thence to Lares and Arecibo.

"At Yauco you will take with you all the wagon transportation brought from Guanica.

"You will drive out or capture all Spanish troops in the western portion of Puerto Rico. You will take all necessary precautions and exercise great care against being surprised or ambushed by the enemy, and make the movement as rapidly as possible, at the same time exercising your best judgment in the care of your command to accomplish the object of your expedition.

"It is expected that at Arecibo you will be joined by the balance of your brigade. Such rations and supplies will be taken as you decide to be proper and necessary.

"Report frequently by telegraph."

Major-General Brooke arrived July 31, and was directed to disembark his command at Arroyo, and move thence to Cayey. On August 5 he had a sharp engagement with the Spanish troops at Guayama, which was finally occupied by our forces. An action took place near Guayama on August 8, the Spaniards being driven from their position farther in the direction of Cayey. Arrangements for investing and attacking that place, both directly and in the rear, were promptly made, and were about to be consummated when the order for cessation of hostilities arrived.

On August 9 General Schwan's command advanced from Yauco westward, occupying successively the important towns of Sabana Grande, San German, Lajas, Cabo Rojo, and Hormigueros, finally entering the city of Mayaguez, after a sharp engagement on August 10 near Hormigueros, in which a strong force of the enemy was engaged. In this action, in which artillery, infantry, and cavalry were

GENERAL HAINS'S FLANK MOVEMENT, AUGUST 13—SCENE NEAR THE POINT WHERE THE GENERAL RECEIVED THE MESSAGE ANNOUNCING THE CESSATION OF HOSTILITIES.—Drawn by Lucius Hitchcock from Sketches by F. [illegible]

THE DRAMATIC ENDING OF HOSTILITIES IN PUERTO RICO—DELIVERY OF THE PRESIDENT'S MESS

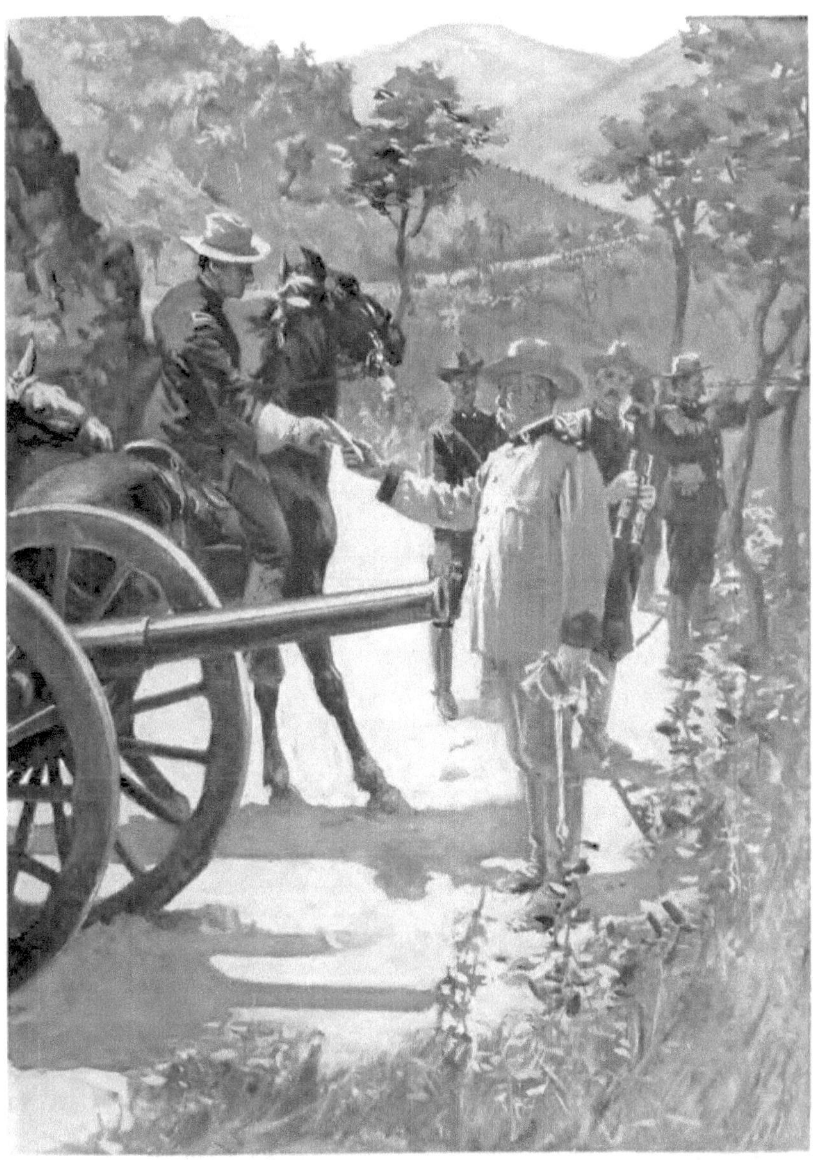

TO GENERAL BROOKE ON AUGUST 13, AS HE WAS ABOUT TO OPEN FIRE. DRAWN BY F. DART WALKER

THE FOURTH OHIO VOLUNTEERS IN A SKIRMISH ON THE ROAD TO CAYEY

DRAWN BY T. DE THULSTRUP, FROM A SKETCH BY T. DART WALKER

admirably employed, the Spanish forces, although strongly posted on ground of their own selection, and skilfully disposed, and being equal in strength to our own, were routed with severe loss, while our own loss was but one killed and sixteen wounded. The enemy was pursued towards Lares, which town would have been occupied August 13 by our troops had not the order to suspend hostilities been received. Near this place, at the crossing of the Rio Prieto, the advance, under Colonel Burke, overtook the enemy, inflicting upon him a heavy loss in killed, wounded, and drowned.

From August 7 to August 15 General Schwan's troops marched ninety-two miles, occupied nine towns, made prisoners of war of one hundred and sixty-two regulars (including the commander of the military department of Mayaguez), captured and paroled two hundred volunteers, captured much valuable material, and cleared the western part of the island of the enemy.

Great credit was due to the troops who composed and the general who commanded the expedition for well-sustained and vigorous action in the face of most trying conditions.

In the meantime General Stone had made a practicable road over what had been considered an impassable trail, by way of Adjuntas and Utuado, through the centre of the territory; and General Henry moved his command over that road with the object of intercepting the enemy retreating before General Schwan, and later of effecting a junction with him at Arecibo, his advance troops having already reached the immediate vicinity of that place. This operation would have formed a strong division on the line of retreat of the Spanish troops occupying the western portion of the island.

At Coamo a sharp engagement took place on August 9 between the troops of Major-General Wilson's command, under the personal direction of Brigadier-General Ernst, and the Spanish forces at that place. The United States

THE NEWS OF THE PEACE PROTOCOL—GENERAL BROOKE STOPPING THE ARTILLERY IN ITS ADVANCE UPON ABONITO

troops, guided by Lieutenant-Colonel Biddle, of the Engineers, made a skilful flank movement at Coamo, which was admirably executed by the Sixteenth Pennsylvania Regiment of Volunteer Infantry, under Colonel Hulings. Passing over a mountain trail, they made a wide detour, coming in rear of the Spanish troops under cover of night, without being discovered, and, striking the military road to San Juan, cut off the enemy's retreat. In this engagement the commanding officer of the Spanish troops and the second in command were killed, and one hundred and sixty-seven prisoners taken.

The road to Aibonito was thus cleared and our troops were advanced and well disposed for the capture of the Spanish forces that had taken positions near that place.

At Assomante, on the 12th of August, the artillery of General Wilson's command began shelling the enemy's position preparatory to an advance in front, while a rear attack was to be made by General Ernst's brigade. This command was under arms and ready to move August 13, when orders were received suspending hostilities.

During the nineteen days of active campaign on the island of Puerto Rico a large portion of the island was captured by the United States forces and brought under our control. Our

SPANISH AND AMERICAN TROOPS EXCHANGING SOUVENIRS IN THE STREETS OF GUAYAMA

Drawn by Lucius Hitchcock, after a Sketch by F. Dake W[illegible]

forces were in such a position as to make the positions of the Spanish forces, outside of the garrison at San Juan, utterly untenable. The Spaniards had been defeated or captured in the six different engagements which took place, and in every position they had occupied up to that time. The volunteers had deserted their colors, and many of them had surrendered to our forces and taken the oath of allegiance. This had a demoralizing effect upon the regular Spanish troops.

The success of the enterprise was largely due to the skill and good generalship of the officers in command of the different divisions and brigades. Strategy and skilful tactics accomplished what might have occasioned serious loss to achieve in any other way. The loss of the enemy in killed, wounded, and captured was nearly ten times our own, which was only three killed and forty wounded. Thus the island of Puerto Rico became a part of the United States. It embraces nearly 3700 square miles, and had a population of nearly a million souls. It no longer afforded a base of operations for any foreign government, thereby being a menace to ours. Under the rule of nations, which required troops to remain during a truce in exactly the positions they occupied at the time of cessation of hostilities, the commands were obliged to stay where they were, without regard to the suitability of the camping-grounds; and as hostilities ceased during the rainy season in Puerto Rico, this requirement had an injurious effect upon the health of the troops. They therefore suffered to some extent on account of exposure and the unusual climatic effects incident to the country. As soon as practicable, however, a large portion of the troops were returned in good condition to the United States.

THE EXPEDITION AGAINST LARES AND ARECIBO—THE ELEVENTH INFANTRY DRAWING THE ENEMY

The artillery was well organized and equipped, under the direction of Brigadier-General John I. Rodgers, and rendered efficient service wherever used.

The bureau of military information, under charge of Lieutenant-Colonel Wagner, was exceedingly useful, and furnished valuable and important information obtained by it regarding the nature of the enemy's country and the position of their forces.

The Signal Corps, under Colonel James Allen, rendered very excellent service, especially in the use of ocean cables; and the field-telegraph and signal detachment, under charge of Major Reber, rendered most important service. Telegraph and telephone lines were extended hundreds of miles and followed close to the picket and skirmish lines.

While *en route* to the United States from Puerto Rico, Lieutenant-Colonel Rowan and Lieutenant Charles F. Parker made a journey of nearly 2000 miles through the territory of Cuba, and obtained most valuable information concerning that country and the condition of its inhabitants, which was both of political and military interest.

THE ACTION NEAR YAUCO

As Told by General Garretson

At about 6 P.M. of the 25th a report was sent in from the outpost, consisting of Company G of the Sixth Illinois, that the enemy in considerable numbers had been observed. I sent out two companies of the Sixth Massachusetts as a reserve.

During the night the enemy opened fire on the outposts, and their commander sent in a report, which arrived in camp at 2 A.M., July 26, that an attack on the outpost was expected. At 3 A.M., I, with my staff and Major W. C. Hayes, First Ohio Cavalry, and five companies of the Sixth Massachusetts, left camp for the outposts on the Yauco road. The command

THE OCCUPATION OF MAYAGUEZ

The Spaniards evacuated hurriedly. General Schwan pursued, and, after a sharp fight near Las Marias, captured a number of Spaniards and marched them back to Mayaguez

SPANISH INFANTRY LEAVING MAYAGUEZ, AUGUST 10, TO MEET THE ELEVENTH UNITED STATES INFANTRY

arrived there shortly before daylight, at about 4.30 o'clock. From the reports of the outposts the enemy were supposed to be in the field to the right of the road to Yauco. Packs were thrown off and the command formed for attack. The company of the Sixth Illinois remained on the hill on which the house of Ventura Quiñones was situated, and protected our right flank. The remaining companies were collected, two as support and three as reserve. After advancing to within two hundred yards of the plain of the hacienda Santa Decideria, the advance-guard of our attacking force was discovered by the enemy, who opened fire from a position on the hill to the west. The north and east slopes of this hill intersect each other, forming a solid angle. It was along this angle that the enemy were posted. Their reserve, posted in a road leading from the hacienda to the east, also opened a strong fire on the road. A body of the enemy moved against the company on our right (Company G, Sixth Illinois), stationed on the hill of Ventura Quiñones. This company had intrenched themselves during the night, and, after repulsing the attacking force, directed their fire against the enemy on the hill to the west.

The conformation of the ground was such that the fire of the enemy's reserves and party on the left was effective in the seemingly secure hollow in which our reserves were posted. The heavy volume of fire, the noise of shots striking the trees and on the ground, and the wounding of two men among the reserves caused a momentary confusion among the troops. They were quickly rallied and placed under cover. The fire of the advance party and supports was directed against the party of the enemy on the hill, and temporarily silenced their fire from that direction.

Our advance-guard of two companies, ignoring the enemy on the hill, then deployed mainly to the right of the road, and were led with quick and accurate military judgment and great personal gallantry by Lieutenant Langhorne, First Cavalry, aide, against the reserves of the enemy. The supports and one company of the reserves, under direction of Captain L. G. Berry, charged against the party on the west of the hill, through the barbed-wire fence and chaparral. The reserves were deployed along the barbed-wire fence running at right angles to the road, conducted through the fence, and brought up in rear and to the left of the attacking party conducted by Lieutenant B. Ames, adjutant, Sixth Massachusetts. The enemy were driven from the hill and retired to the valley, disappearing behind the hacienda. The reserves of the enemy ceased firing and retired. It was supposed that they had retired to the hacienda, as this house was surrounded on the sides presented to our view with loop-holed walls. The troops on the hill were collected along the road, and a reserve of three companies was established at its intersection with the main road to Yauco. The two companies in advance, which were deployed, wheeled to the left and advanced through the corn-field on our right. The remainder of the command deployed and advanced to the hacienda, enveloping it on the left. It was then discovered that the enemy had retired from the hacienda in the direction of Yauco, along cleverly concealed lines of retreat.

As the object of the expedition was considered accomplished, and in obedience to instructions received from Major-General Miles, no further pursuit was undertaken.

GUAYAMA

General Brooke's Account

On August 5 I directed an advance on the town of Guayama, and at 1 P.M. the Fourth Ohio, Colonel Coit commanding, supported

SPANISH INFANTRY ENTERING MAYAGUEZ AS PRISONERS, AUGUST 11

by the Third Illinois, Colonel Bennitt commanding, and dynamite-guns, commanded by Captain Potter, Fourth Ohio Volunteer Infantry, all under the immediate command of General Hains, entered and took possession of Guayama. The enemy made slight resistance about one mile from town. We had four men wounded slightly.

On Wednesday, August 8, a reconnaissance for the purpose of developing the enemy's position and to clear the way for the engineers to correctly map the country was made by order of General Hains during my absence at Ponce, where I had been summoned by the commanding general. It was found that the enemy had taken position on a crest commanding the road, from six to eight miles from Guayama. Our loss was five enlisted men wounded, none seriously.

On the 12th I made preparations to move Hains's brigade, consisting of the Third Illinois, Fourth Pennsylvania, and the Fourth Ohio; the cavalry, consisting of Troop H, Sixth Cavalry, and the Philadelphia City Troop; the artillery, consisting of light batteries B, Pennsylvania; the Twenty-seventh Indiana Battery; Battery A, Missouri, and Battery A, Illinois, against the Spanish position on the road between Guayama and Cayey. General Hains was directed to take one regiment of his command and to move on the westward slope of the mountains bordering the valley through which the Cayey road runs, and, moving at an early hour, to get in the rear of the Spanish position at or near the buildings of Pablo Vasquez. One battalion of the Fourth Pennsylvania Regiment was left at Arroyo; one was stopped at Guayama, and one was moved up the Cayey road. The Third Illinois was pushed up the Cayey road to within sight of, and within artillery range of, the position occupied by the Spaniards. Two batteries of artillery were then brought forward and placed in position, and two were parked on the north side of Guayama. Two dynamite-guns were also brought forward. All this, as far as the movement on the Cayey road was concerned, was very deliberate—slow, in fact—in order to enable General Hains to get to the rear of the Spanish position, the design being to capture the Spaniards. The road General Hains marched over was a mountain trail, and in places quite difficult.

SPANIARDS SURPRISED BY COLONEL HULINGS'S REGIMENT IN THEIR FLIGHT FROM COAMO

After waiting until it was believed that General Hains was at or near the position he was to take, the artillery was unmasked and everything was ready to shell the enemy, when a message was received as follows:

"PORT PONCE, *August 13, 1898.*

"MAJOR-GENERAL BROOKE, Arroyo:

"By direction of the President all military operations against the enemy are suspended. Negotiations are nearing completion, a protocol having just been signed by representatives of the two countries. All commanders will be governed accordingly.

"By command of Major-General Miles.

"GILMORE, Brigadier-General."

Withdrawing the troops from their advanced position, I placed them in as healthful camps as I could find; established outposts, and moved my own headquarters to Guayama. On August 14 I sent to the commanding officer of the Spanish troops in my front, and to Governor-General Macias, under flag of truce, copies of the President's orders, and on August 15 General Macias, under flag of truce, acknowledged receipt. After that date nothing of importance occurred in my front.

THE TAKING OF GUAYAMA

COLONEL COIT'S ACCOUNT

I REPORTED with nine companies of infantry and part of one company in charge of five Sims-Dudley dynamite-guns (33 officers and 925 enlisted men) to General Hains, on the road to Guayama, at 8.30 A.M., August 5.

The ammunition for the Sims-Dudley dynamite-guns and subsistence was transported in two ox-carts, an additional cart being used to draw the guns. The dynamite-guns were in charge of Captain John D. Potter, Company F, Fourth Ohio Volunteer Infantry.

Major Speaks was placed in command of the advance, consisting of three companies, A, B, and C, of the First Battalion.

Information obtained from residents along the line of march indicated that the enemy would be found on the outskirts of Guayama. Our advance-guard struck their outposts in a cut about two miles west of Arroyo, on the road leading to Guayama.

Companies A, B, and C were immediately deployed as a line of skirmishers and were pushed forward over the road and along on the high ground, the firing becoming general within a half-mile of Guayama; our lines advanced, the enemy retreating within the city, and passed on to the north, continuing the firing before entering the city. Companies C and I, under the command of Major Baker, were used to reinforce the skirmish-line.

The Third Battalion, under Major Sellars, advanced on the main road, entering at the same time as the skirmish-lines on the right and left. After entering the city, several shots were fired. The Third Battalion was immediately taken, by my instruction, to the city building, and the chief municipal officer was sent for. Upon his reporting, I notified him that I had taken his city in the name of the United States of America. He announced by an interpreter publicly to the citizens that he welcomed the representatives of the United States.

The regimental colors were placed on the top of the city building at 1 P.M. The city officers proffered the keys of the city to me, and I directed them to exercise their several functions, and promised them that no interference whatever would be made in the city government. General Hains, arriving at this time, assumed military control.

The Third Battalion, under Major Sellars, was sent out to establish outposts on the main road to Cayey. Major Baker, with Companies E and I, was sent to the northwest of the city to establish outposts; a detachment from Company A, under Sergeant Andrus, was sent to protect the city waterworks, and the First Battalion was held in the city for a reserve and for police duty. The advance and skirmish line was under the immediate direction of Major John C. Speaks, who, with Captain MacLee Wilson, regimental adjutant, Lieutenant Harry Krumm, adjutant of the First Battalion, and Regimental Sergeant-Major Frank C. Radcliffe, deserved special commendation for their services and bravery throughout the march.

The band was of inestimable value in caring for the wounded and those overcome by heat and fatigue.

Captain Curtis, of the Indiana Battery — Major Rodney as Adjutant

MARCH OF UNITED STATES ARTILLERY OVER ALMOST IMPASSABLE ROADS.— FROM SKETCH MADE ON THE SPOT BY T. DART WALKER

THE ENGAGEMENT NEAR HORMIGUEROS

GENERAL SCHWAN'S ACCOUNT

NEAR a point on the main road where it is flanked by sugar-mills, our cavalry was fired into, though without effect, by the enemy's scouts, who were concealed behind a hedge lining the Hormigueros road. They were easily dispersed. The infantry advance-guard having passed this point, the cavalry took the latter road, and, crossing the Rosario, turned westward and advanced under cover of the railroad embankment until, taking advantage of every opportunity to damage the enemy by its fire action, it reached a position beyond the covered wooden bridge along the road.

The brigade commander had left San German at the head of the main body. When he heard the firing in his front he sent word to commanding officers to advance without further halt and to keep their commands closed up. Similar orders were sent to the train. He was informed and approved of the route taken by the cavalry before reaching the bridge. He crossed the latter about 3.30 P.M., being at that time about five hundred yards in advance of the main body.

A staff-officer, who had been sent ahead to select camp, reported at this time the ground west of the Cabo Rojo road as suitable for this purpose; but owing to the suspected proximity of the enemy, whose position had not yet been determined, it was decided to push ahead and beyond the iron bridge. This, despite the fact that the men had now marched thirteen miles and were quite tired. Once in possession of the iron bridge and the high ground to the north of it, the command would occupy a strong position which would make it hard to check its advance on Mayaguez. Accordingly the advance-guard, under Captain Hoyt, moved forward, deploying its advance party as skirmishers and its supports into a line of squads. In this formation it continued until it had approached the bridge within about four hundred yards. At this juncture the enemy opened fire—at first individual fire. The firing aimed at the advance-guard accelerated the march of the Eleventh Infantry, which had crossed the wooden bridge in column of fours and reported to the brigade commander, whose staff had already commenced the demolition of the wire fences enclosing the road. About the time that the brigade commander caused the deployment of two companies to reinforce the advance-guard, Major Gilbreath in command, the enemy from his position in the hills to the right front fired volleys at the main body through the interval separating the infantry advance-guard from the cavalry, wounding a number of men, also an officer and several horses of the brigade staff. Meanwhile the artillery battalion, under the authority of the brigade commander, had taken up position to the left of the road. As the powder used by the enemy was absolutely smokeless, and his position being, moreover, screened for the most part by the trees along the Rio Grande, the question of the exact direction to be given Major Gilbreath's detachment and to the lines of battle about to be formed from the main column became a most perplexing one. Luckily this uncertainty did not last long, those of the enemy's bullets that struck the ground near us solving the problem. Some slight confusion was caused by a premature and hurried deployment of the remaining companies, which interfered somewhat with the brigade commander's intention of forming two additional lines, one to support the fighting-line and the other to act as a reserve or as the changing conditions of the combat might render expedient. But under his supervision this defective formation was soon rectified; three companies being placed on the right and four companies on the left of the road, the former under Lieutenant-Colonel Burke moving forward in support of Major Gilbreath, and the latter being held back for a time. Major Gilbreath's and Colonel Burke's troops being unable to cross the creek, passed over the bridge that spans it by the left flank, the former's companies having previously occupied a sheltered place in a ditch parallel to and to the right of the main road. About this time the advance-guard, one of the companies of which (Penrose's) had previously held for a short time a knoll on the left of the road, moved forward and crossed the iron bridge, the advance sections of the companies being led by Lieutenants Alexander and Wells, respectively. After the latter had occupied the knoll for a time the entire advance-guard, including the two Gatling guns, was concentrated on the right of the railroad. It dislodged the enemy, and, with the cavalry troop on the right—which arrived about this time, after doing effective work in threatening the enemy's flank—and the companies of Major Gilbreath pushed forward in the centre, took up a position on the northern line of hills. Here they were joined by the remainder of the infantry and by two pieces of artillery under First Lieutenant Archibald Campbell, which the brigade commander had ordered forward, and which by their fire added to the discomfiture of the enemy. The two Gatling guns under Lieutenant Maginnis with the advance did good work, at first near the creek, where the gunners had a good view of the enemy, and later on at the various positions of the advance-guard. The two guns with the main body were also operated from the crest of the hill during the latter stage of the combat.

The affair ended about six o'clock, and the troops, including all the artillery, bivouacked on or near the position occupied by the enemy. About an hour previously the brigade commander had ordered the wagon-train, which had been halted east of the wooden bridge, to a point north of the northern iron bridge, there to be drawn up in double column. The train afterwards went into park between the railroad and the Rio Grande, near enough to the bivouacs to enable the men to get what was necessary to their comfort for the night.

THE ENCOUNTER NEAR COAMO

Account by General Ernst

With a view to capturing the Spanish garrison, the division commander directed that one regiment be sent by the mountain trail to the rear of the town, and that the front attack be deferred until this regiment could reach its position.

The Sixteenth Pennsylvania Infantry was selected for the turning movement. It left its camp, 650 strong, at 4.15 P.M., August 8, and, under the guidance of Lieutenant-Colonel Biddle, marched six miles and then went into bivouac. At 6 A.M., August 9, the two other regiments of the brigade and four guns of Captain Anderson's battery left their camps to take position for the front advance upon the town.

The Third Wisconsin Infantry, 788 strong, was sent to the right, with orders to cross the Coamo River and advance on the Santa Isabel road until the latter should reach the river, then to leave the road and advance up the left bank of the river. While it was moving to its position fire was opened upon the block-house with the four guns of Captain Anderson's battery. A feeble infantry fire was returned from the block-house for a few minutes, but it was soon silenced and the block-house destroyed, leaving the Third Wisconsin without opposition at that point.

The Second Wisconsin Infantry, 824 strong, was then formed for attack, with orders to advance along the main military road. These movements were well under way when heavy infantry fire was heard from the opposite side of the town, indicating that the Sixteenth Pennsylvania was engaged with the enemy. A battalion of the Second Wisconsin was formed in column and hurried forward on the main road, with a view to reaching the scene of action more quickly than it could be done by the advancing line, but it found the bridge destroyed and the gorge impassable, and was compelled to turn back and seek a crossing elsewhere. About this time the sound of infantry fire ceased. The troops engaged in the front attack entered the town about 9.40 A.M. without opposition, finding all intrenchments deserted. The regularity and steadiness of this advance seemed to have made an impression.

In the meantime the Sixteenth Pennsylvania had resumed its march at 4.30 A.M. on the 9th, being somewhat delayed in starting by a guide losing his way. After an extremely arduous march of seven miles, they reached the road at which they were aiming at about 8 A.M., and found the Spanish forces in full retreat. They immediately attacked the enemy in flank, but the latter, finding excellent intrenchments in the ditches bordering the road, made a stout resistance. It was not until after a sharp engagement of an hour, and the death of their commanding officer, that the enemy surrendered.

ASSOMANTE

General Wilson's Account

At a point about five and one-half miles from Coamo the advance of the troop was stopped by the fire of the batteries on El Peñon and Assomante Hill. I directed it to take position here as an outpost until it could be relieved by the infantry.

The enemy's position for the defence of Aibonito, as was evident from the inspection of it that I could then make, and confirmed by reconnaissances during the 10th and 11th, was one of unusual natural strength. The military road leading up from Coamo runs for about four miles in a direction a little east of north on the left bank of the cañon of the Coamo River; thence it runs northeast to Aibonito. Upon its left is the main divide of the mountain chain crossing the island from east to west. Aibonito is situated in a pocket in the hills on the northern slope. About two and one-half miles northwest of the town and on the main divide is the Assomante Hill and El Peñon, constituting a position of great natural strength. Upon the summit of El Peñon and Assomante batteries had been erected, and on the slope below them infantry intrenchments, completely sweeping the highway with a plunging fire for several miles.

From the point where this position comes in sight to one moving up the steep grade of the military road, the latter, except for very short distances at a few points, was swept by the fire from the enemy's position. The two points from which artillery could be brought to bear on our side were respectively about 1200 and 800 feet below the Spanish batteries and completely exposed to the enemy's fire. Deep and precipitous ravines were encountered the moment one left the road, and the exposure of the latter evidently made a direct attack impracticable without very great loss.

On the evening of the 9th I moved my headquarters camp to a point on the river north of and immediately outside the town of Coamo. General Ernst's brigade encamped along the valley in advance, its outposts about five and one-half miles to the front, with pickets well out on all approaches and both flanks.

Careful reconnaissances of all approaches having been made on the 10th and 11th, under direction of Colonel Biddle, I decided that it was practicable again to turn the enemy by his right, moving the main body of the brigade to Barranquitas, and thence to Aibonito *via* Honduras, or to Cayey *via* Comocir and Cidra, or to Las Cruces, on the main highway to San Juan, as circumstances might determine, and leaving one battalion to hold the line then occupied by our outposts in front of Aibonito. I therefore directed General Ernst to be prepared to move his troops on the Barranquitas trail at daylight on the morning of the 13th. Meanwhile, for the purpose of diverting the enemy's attention from this movement and still further developing his position, I ordered an artillery reconnaissance to be made at 1 P.M. on the 12th instant. Accordingly, Captain Potts's light battery, F, Third United States Artillery, advanced from its camp at Coamo, and four guns came into position on the reverse side of a low ridge to the left of the road, at a range of 2130 yards from the batteries on Assomante Hill and about 1200 feet below them. One piece, subsequently joined by an additional gun, was placed by Major Lancaster on the road some distance farther to the front.

The guns opened fire at 1.25 P.M., and at 2.15 the enemy's guns were silenced and the infantry apparently driven from their trenches. They returned, however, as soon as our fire slackened—the ammunition being nearly exhausted—and opened a well-aimed fire. Lieutenant Hains, Third Artillery, was seriously wounded by a rifle bullet which passed through his body from side to side below the arms. Captain F. T. Lee, Company F, Third Wisconsin, was slightly wounded in the right arm. Corporal Oscar Swanson, Company L, Third Wisconsin, was killed by a bursting shell. The same shell wounded Private Frederick Vought mortally; Corporal August Yank, left arm; Private George J. Bunce, chest, all of the Third Wisconsin. Private Delos Sizer, also of the Third Wisconsin, received a bullet wound in the left leg.

Farther advance towards San Juan on this line required the dislodgement of the enemy from this position. Before beginning the turning movement I decided to send a flag of truce to the enemy, demanding the surrender of the place. I was influenced in this by the belief that the rumors universally current in the public press as to the near completion of peace negotiations, and of which it was possible that the Spanish officers at San Juan were not informed, had some foundation. In the event of a refusal to surrender, and in the absence of official information from proper authority, I had no course but to continue my advance.

Lieutenant-Colonel Bliss, of my staff, who carried the flag, was informed that my demand would be telegraphed to the captain-general at San Juan, and that his reply might make it necessary to send an officer to confer with me. I accordingly sent an officer at 6 A.M. to the Spanish lines, who received the reply telegraphed by the captain-general. This was a curt refusal to surrender, though from its terms I suspected that General Macias was well informed as to the progress of peace negotiations. Pending the receipt of this reply, I suspended General Ernst's movement for a few hours. It was about to be resumed when I received from Major-General Miles the telegraphic orders of the President suspending all future operations against the enemy.

MANILA AND THE SEAT OF WAR

ADMIRAL DEWEY AND GENERAL MERRITT IN ADMIRAL DEWEY'S CABIN ON THE FLAG-SHIP *OLYMPIA*

DRAWN BY T. DE THULSTRUP, FROM A PHOTOGRAPH BY F. D. MILLET

THE FALL OF MANILA

"THE last scene of the war," wrote the President to the American Congress, "was enacted at Manila, its starting-place." The movement of General Merritt's command to the Philippines commenced, as already related, on the 25th of May, the first expedition arriving off Manila June 30. Other troops arrived July 17, 25, 31, August 21, 24, and 31.

General Merritt arrived off Manila July 25, and immediately visited the troops in camp which had preceded him under command of Brigadier-General Anderson. Preparations were at once commenced to attack the Spanish forces holding the city.

On July 31 the Spaniards made a sharp attack on the American forces on the Calla Real. August 7 the Spanish commander was notified to remove all non-combatants from Manila within forty-eight hours. On the same date he replied that the Spanish forces were without places of refuge for the wounded and the sick women and children then lodged within the walls.

August 9 a joint demand was made for the surrender of the city, signed by General Merritt and Admiral Dewey. The Captain-General offered to consult his government, if time were allowed in which to communicate by way of Hong-Kong. This was refused, on account of the time required, the urgent need of relieving the American troops from the trenches, and the great exposure to unhealthy conditions in a bivouac during the rainy season.

August 12 orders were issued for the advance, and on the 13th the combined attack by the army and navy occurred, resulting in the capture of Manila the same day. Immediately after the surrender the Spanish colors

27

on the sea front were hauled down and the American flag raised. The prisoners captured at Manila were nearly 13,000; also 22,000 stand of arms.

The cablegram sent August 12 to General Merritt, containing the text of the President's proclamation directing a cessation of hostilities, was not received by him until August 16.

The casualties were: 17 enlisted men killed, 10 officers and 96 enlisted men wounded.

GENERAL MERRITT'S ACCOUNT

In obedience to the order assigning me to the command of the Department of the Pacific, and the special instructions from the President, furnished me by the Secretary of War, under date of May 28, 1898, I embarked with my staff from San Francisco on the steamer *Newport* June 29, and arrived at Cavité, Manila Bay, July 25, 1898. The military situation in Manila Bay I found to be as follows:

First California, First Nebraska, Tenth Pennsylvania, and Batteries A and B of the Utah Artillery, along the line of the bay shore near the village of Paranaque, about five miles by water and twenty-five miles by the roads from Cavité.

Immediately after my arrival I visited General Greene's camp and made a reconnaissance of the position held by the Spaniards, and also the opposing lines of the insurgent forces, hereafter to be described. I found General Greene's command encamped on a strip of sandy land running parallel to the shore of the bay and not far distant from the beach, but, owing to the great difficulties of landing supplies, the greater portion of the force had shelter-tents only, and were suffering many discomforts, the camp being situated in a low, flat place, without shelter from the heat of the tropical sun or adequate protection during the terrific downpours of rain so frequent at this season. I was at once struck by the exemplary spirit of patient, even cheerful, endurance shown by the officers and men under such circumstances, and

warfare with the Spaniards for several months, and were at the time of my arrival in considerable force, variously estimated and never accurately ascertained, but probably not far from 12,000 men. These troops, well supplied with small-arms, with plenty of ammunition and several field-guns, had obtained positions of investment opposite to the Spanish line of detached works throughout their entire extent; and on the particular road called the Calle Real, passing along the front of General Greene's brigade camp and running through Malate to Manila, the insurgents had established an earthwork or trench within eight hundred yards of the powder-magazine fort. They also occupied as well the road to the right, leading from the village of Pasay, and the approach by the beach was also in their possession. This anomalous state of affairs—namely, having a line of quasi-hostile native troops between our forces and the Spanish position—was, of course, very objectionable, but it was difficult to deal with, owing to the peculiar condition of our relations with the

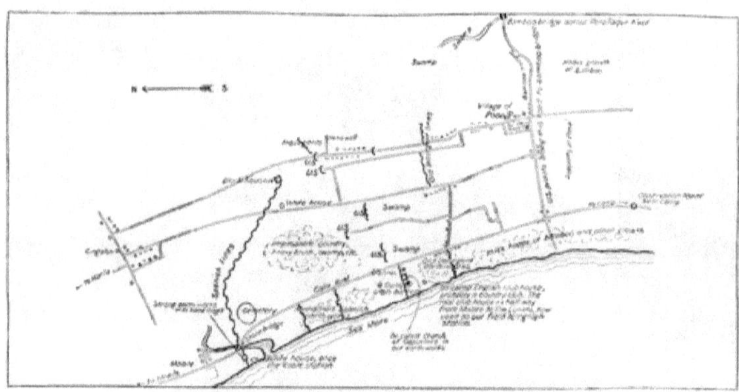

POSITIONS OF AMERICAN, SPANISH, AND INSURGENT FORCES.—FROM A SKETCH-MAP BY F. D. MILLET

The American fleet of warships, commanded by Rear-Admiral George Dewey, was anchored in line off Cavité and just outside of the transports and supply vessels engaged in the military service. The distinguished Admiral above mentioned was in full control of the navigation of the bay, and his vessels passed and repassed within range of the water batteries of the town of Manila without drawing the fire of the enemy.

Brigadier-General Thomas M. Anderson, United States Volunteers, was in command of the military forces prior to my arrival, and from his report I learned that his headquarters were in Cavité, and that the troops were disposed as follows:

The Second Oregon, detachments of California Heavy Artillery, Twenty-third Infantry, and Fourteenth Infantry occupied the town of Cavité; while Brigadier-General F. V. Greene, United States Volunteers, was encamped with his brigade, consisting of the Eighteenth Infantry, Third United States Artillery, Company A, Engineer Battalion, First Colorado,

this feeling of admiration for the manner in which the American soldier, volunteer and regular alike, accepted the necessary hardships of the work they had undertaken to do grew and increased with every phase of the difficult and trying campaign which the troops of the Philippine expedition brought to such a brilliant and successful conclusion.

I discovered during my visit to General Greene that the left or north flank of his brigade camp extended to a point on the Calle Real about 3200 yards from the outer line of Spanish defences of the city of Manila. This Spanish line began at the powder magazine, or old Fort San Antonio, within a hundred yards of the beach and just south of the Malate suburb of Manila, and stretched away to the Spanish left in more or less detached works, eastward, through swamps and rice-fields, covering all the avenues of approach to the town and encircling the city completely.

The Filipinos, or insurgent forces at war with Spain, had, prior to the arrival of the American land forces, been waging a desultory

insurgents, which may be briefly stated as follows:

Shortly after the naval battle of Manila Bay, the principal leader of the insurgents, General Emilio Aguinaldo, came to Cavité from Hong-Kong, and, with the consent of our naval authorities, began active work in raising troops and pushing the Spaniards in the direction of the city of Manila. Having met with some success, and the natives flocking to his assistance, he proclaimed an independent government of republican form, with himself as president, and at the time of my arrival in the islands the entire edifice of executive and legislative departments and subdivision of territory for administrative purposes had been accomplished, at least on paper, and the Filipinos held military possession of many points in the islands other than those in the vicinity of Manila.

As General Aguinaldo did not visit me on my arrival, nor offer his services as a subordinate military leader, and as my instructions from the President fully contemplated the

BRIGADIER-GENERAL ARTHUR MACARTHUR

occupation of the islands by the American land forces, and stated that "the powers of the military occupant are absolute and supreme and immediately operate upon the political condition of the inhabitants," I did not consider it wise to hold any direct communication with the insurgent leader until I should be in possession of the city of Manila, especially as I would not until then be in a position to issue a proclamation and enforce my authority, in the event that his pretensions should clash with my designs.

For these reasons the preparations for the attack on the city were pressed and military operations conducted without reference to the situation of the insurgent forces. The wisdom of this course was subsequently fully established by the fact that when the troops of my command carried the Spanish intrenchments, extending from the sea to the Pasay road on the extreme Spanish right, we were under no obligations, by prearranged plans of mutual attack, to turn to the right and clear the front still held against the insurgents, but were able to move forward at once and occupy the city and suburbs.

To return to the situation of General Greene's brigade as I found it on my arrival, it will be seen that the difficulty in gaining an avenue of approach to the Spanish line lay in the fact of my disinclination to ask General Aguinaldo to withdraw from the beach and the Calle Real, so that Greene could move forward. This was overcome by instructions to General Greene to arrange, if possible, with the insurgent brigade commander in his immediate vicinity to move to the right and allow the American forces unobstructed control of the roads in their immediate front. No objection was made, and accordingly General Greene's brigade threw forward a heavy outpost line on the Calle Real and the beach, and constructed a trench in which a portion of the guns of the Utah batteries was placed.

The Spaniards, observing this activity on our part, made a very sharp attack with infantry and artillery on the night of July 31. The behavior of our troops during this night attack was all that could be desired. Our position was extended and strengthened after this, and resisted successfully repeated night attacks, our forces suffering, however, considerable loss in wounded and killed, while the losses of the enemy, owing to the darkness, could not be ascertained.

The strain of the night fighting and the heavy details for outpost duty made it imperative to reinforce General Greene's troops with General MacArthur's brigade, which had arrived in transports on the 31st of July. The difficulties of this operation can hardly be overestimated. The transports were at anchor off Cavité, five miles from a point on the beach where it was desired to disembark the men. Several squalls, accompanied by floods of rain, raged day after day, and the only way to get the troops and supplies ashore was to load them from the ship's side into native lighters (called *cascos*) or small steamboats, move them to a point opposite the camp, and then disembark them through the surf in small boats, or by running the lighters head on to the beach. The landing was finally accomplished, after days of hard work and hardship; and I desire here to express again my admiration for the fortitude and cheerful willingness of the men of all commands engaged in this operation.

Upon the assembly of MacArthur's brigade in support of Greene's, I had about 8500 men in position to attack, and I deemed the time had come for final action. During the time of the night attacks I had communicated my desire to Admiral Dewey that he would allow his ships to open fire on the right of the Spanish line of intrenchments, believing that such action would stop the night firing and loss of life; but the Admiral had declined to order it unless we were in danger of losing our position by the assaults of the Spaniards, for the reason that, in his opinion, it would precipitate a general engagement, for which he was not ready. Now, however, the brigade of General MacArthur was in position and the *Monterey* had arrived, and under date of August 6 Admiral Dewey agreed to my suggestion that we should send a joint letter to the captain-general notifying him that he should remove from the city all non-combatants within forty-eight hours, and that operations against the defences of Manila might begin at any time after the expiration of that period.

This letter was sent August 7, and a reply was received the same date, to the effect that the Spaniards were without places of refuge for the increased numbers of wounded, sick women, and children lodged within the walls. On the 9th a formal joint demand for the surrender of the city was sent in. This demand was based upon the hopelessness of the struggle on the part of the Spaniards, and that every consideration of humanity demanded that the city should not be subjected to bombardment under such circumstances. The captain-general's reply, of same date, stated that the council of defence had declared that the demand could not be granted; but the captain-general offered to consult his government if we would allow him the time strictly necessary for the communications by way of Hong Kong.

This was declined on our part for the reason that it could, in the opinion of the Admiral and myself, lead only to a continuance of the situation, with no immediate result favorable to us, and the necessity was apparent and very urgent that decisive action should be taken at once to compel the enemy to give up the town, in order to relieve our troops from the trenches and from the great exposure to unhealthy conditions which were unavoidable in a bivouac during the rainy season. The sea-coast batteries in defence of Manila were so situated that it was impossible for ships to engage them without firing into the town; and as the bombardment of a city filled with women and children, sick and wounded, and containing a large amount of neutral property, could only be justified as a last resort, it was agreed between Admiral Dewey and myself that an attempt should be made to carry the extreme right of the Spanish line of intrenchments in front of the positions at that time occupied by our troops, which, with its flank on the sea-shore, was entirely open to the fire of the navy.

It was not my intention to press the assault at this point, in case the enemy should hold it in strong force, until after the navy had made practicable breaches in the works and shaken the troops holding them, which could not be done by the army alone, owing to the absence of siege guns. It was believed, however, as most desirable, and in accordance with the principles of civilized warfare, that the attempt should be made to drive the enemy out of his intrenchments before resorting to the bombardment of the city.

By orders issued some time previously MacArthur's and Greene's brigades were organized as the Second Division of the Eighth Army Corps, Brigadier-General Thomas M. Anderson commanding; and in anticipation of the attack General Anderson moved his headquarters from Cavité to the brigade camps and assumed direct command in the field. Copies of the written and verbal instructions referred to above were given to the division and brigade commanders on the 12th, and all the troops were in position on the 13th at an early hour in the morning.

About 9 A.M. on that day our fleet steamed forward from Cavité, and before 10 A.M. opened a hot and accurate fire of heavy shells and rapid-fire projectiles on the sea-flank of the Spanish intrenchments at the powder-magazine fort, and at the same time the Utah batteries, in position in our trenches near the Calle Real, began firing with great accuracy. At 10.25, on a prearranged signal from our trenches that it was believed our troops could advance, the navy ceased firing, and immediately a light line of skirmishers from the Colorado regiment of Greene's brigade passed over our trenches

OLD MONASTERY, NEAR MALATE, GENERAL GREENE'S HEADQUARTERS

and deployed rapidly forward, another line from the same regiment from the left flank of our earthworks advancing swiftly up the beach in open order. Both these lines found the powder-magazine fort and the trenches flanking it deserted, but as they passed over the Spanish works they were met by a sharp fire from a second line situated in the streets of Malate, by which a number of men were killed and wounded, among others the soldier who pulled down the Spanish colors still flying on the fort and raised our own.

LOOKING DOWN THE AMERICAN TRENCHES.—Drawn by Lucius Hitchcock

The works of the second line soon gave way to the determined advance of Greene's troops, and that officer pushed his brigade rapidly through Malate and over the bridges to occupy Binondo and San Miguel, as contemplated in his instructions. In the meantime the brigade of General MacArthur, advancing simultaneously on the Pasay road, encountered a very sharp fire, coming from the block-houses, trenches, and woods in his front, positions which it was very difficult to carry, owing to the swampy condition of the ground on both sides of the road and the heavy undergrowth concealing the enemy. With much gallantry and excellent judgment on the part of the brigade commander and the troops engaged, these difficulties were overcome with a minimum loss, and MacArthur advanced and held the bridges and the town of Malate, as was contemplated in his instructions.

The city of Manila was now in our possession, excepting the walled town; but shortly after the entry of our troops into Malate a white flag was displayed on the walls, whereupon Lieutenant-Colonel C. A. Whittier, United States Volunteers, of my staff, and Lieutenant Bromlay, United States Navy, representing Admiral Dewey, were sent ashore to communicate with the captain-general. I soon personally followed these officers into the town, going at once to the palace of the governor-general, and there, after a conversation with the Spanish authorities, a preliminary agreement of the terms of capitulation was signed by the captain-general and myself. This agreement was subsequently incorporated into the formal terms of capitulation, as arranged by the officers representing the two forces.

Immediately after the surrender the Spanish colors on the sea-front were hauled down and the American flag displayed and saluted by the guns of the navy. The Second Oregon Regiment, which had proceeded by sea from Cavité, was disembarked, and entered the walled town as a provost-guard; and the colonel was directed to receive the Spanish arms and deposit them in places of security. The town was filled with the troops of the enemy, driven in from the intrenchments, regiments formed and standing in line in the streets; but the work of disarming proceeded quietly, and nothing unpleasant occurred.

In leaving the subject of the operations of the 13th, I desire to record my appreciation of the admirable manner in which the orders for attack and the plan for occupation of the city were carried out by the troops exactly as contemplated. For troops to enter under fire a town covering a wide area, to deploy rapidly and guard all principal points in the extensive suburbs, to keep out the insurgent forces pressing for admission, to disarm quietly an army of Spaniards more than equal in numbers to the American troops, and, finally, by all this to prevent entirely all rapine, pillage, and disorder, and gain entire and complete possession of a city of 300,000 people filled with natives hostile to European interests, and stirred up by the knowledge that their own people were fighting in the outside trenches, was an act which only the law-abiding, temperate, resolute American soldier, well and skilfully handled by his regimental and brigade commanders, could accomplish.

Prior to the action on the 13th, a general order was issued, and a copy sent to Aguinaldo's representative, as an indication of the conduct that would be expected of them in the event that any bands of the insurgents should effect an entrance to the city.

The trophies of Manila were nearly $900,000, 13,000 prisoners, and 22,000 arms.

Immediately after the surrender my headquarters were established in the *ayuntamiento*, or city office of the governor-general, where steps were at once inaugurated to set up the government of military occupancy. A proclamation was issued and published in all the newspapers of the city in English, Spanish, and native dialect; and one of my two very efficient brigade commanders, General MacArthur, was appointed provost-marshal-general and civil governor of the town, while the other, General Greene, was selected for the duties of intendente-general de hacienda, or director of financial affairs, the collectors of customs and internal revenue reporting to him. Lieutenant-Colonel Whittier, an efficient business man of long experience, was appointed collector of the customs; and a bonded officer, Major Whipple, of the pay department, was announced as custodian of the public funds, to whom all Spanish money derived from any source was to be transmitted for safe-keeping and disbursement under orders.

On the 16th a cablegram containing the text of the President's proclamation directing a cessation of hostilities was received by me, and at the same time an order to make the fact known to the Spanish authorities, which was done at once. This resulted in a formal protest from the governor-general in regard to the transfer of public funds then taking place, on the ground that the proclamation was dated prior to the surrender. To this I replied that the *status quo* in which we were left with the cessation of hostilities was that existing at the time of the receipt by me of the official notice, and that I must insist upon the delivery of the funds. The delivery was made under protest.

After the issue of my proclamation and the establishment of my office as military governor, I had direct written communication with General Aguinaldo on several occasions. He recognized my authority as military governor of the city of Manila and suburbs, and made professions of his willingness to withdraw his troops to a line which I might indicate, but at the same time asking certain favors for himself. The matters in this connection had not been settled at the date of my departure. Much dissatisfaction was felt by the rank and file of the insurgents that they were not permitted to enjoy the occupancy of Manila, and there was some ground for trouble with them owing to that fact; but, notwithstanding many rumors to the contrary, I was of the opinion that the leaders would be able to prevent serious disturbances, as they are sufficiently intelligent and educated to know that to antagonize the United States would be to destroy their only chance of future political improvement.

On the 28th of August I received a cablegram directing me to transfer my command to Major-General Otis, United States Volunteers, and to proceed to Paris, France, for conference with the peace commissioners. I embarked on the steamer *China* on the 30th in obedience to these instructions.

GENERAL ANDERSON'S ACCOUNT

THE first expeditionary force reached Manila Bay June 30, and the disembarkation of men and material began the next day. Cavité was selected as the landing-place and base of operations. Rear-Admiral Dewey gave every possible assistance and favored me with a clear statement of the situation.

On the first day of July I had an interview with the insurgent chief, Aguinaldo, and learned from him that the Spanish forces had withdrawn, driven back by his army, as he claimed, to a line of defence immediately around the city and its suburbs. He estimated the Spanish forces at about 14,000 men, and his own at about the same number. He did not seem pleased at the incoming of our land forces, hoping, as I believed, that he could take the city with his own army, with the coöperation of the American fleet.

Believing that, however successful the insurgents might have been in guerilla warfare against the Spaniards, they could not carry their lines by assault or reduce the city by siege, and suspecting, further, that a hearty and effective coöperation could not be expected, I had at once a series of reconnaissances made exactly to locate the enemy's lines of defence and to ascertain their strength.

Both outer and inner lines were located and profiles obtained of their walls and parapets.

The results of my investigations led to the conclusion that while siege operations, if necessary, could best be conducted from the east and north, an assault with the coöperation of the navy could best be made from the south, along the bay and the line of the Cavité-Parañaque-Manila road.

On July 15 one battalion of the First California Volunteers was sent over and encamped on the west shore of Manila Bay, at the hamlet of Tambo, about three miles from the south suburb of Manila, called Malate. This was done to secure this line of advance, if it should meet the approval of the major-general commanding, on his arrival, and also to guard there a depot of transportation, which the chief quartermaster of the expedition was ordered to establish at that point. The two remaining battalions of the California regiment were sent over from Cavité two days later, and the cantonment was named Camp Dewey, in honor of the hero of Manila Bay.

The second expeditionary force, under Brigadier-General F. V. Greene, arrived here July 17, and the third, under Brigadier-General Arthur MacArthur, on July 30. The several military organizations of these expeditions were transferred to Camp Dewey at various dates from July 17 to August 9. This task was at once dangerous and difficult on account of tropical rains, sudden severe squalls on the bay, and a heavy surf beating on the shore during nearly the whole time the transfers were being made from transports in the harbor and at Cavité. The landings of men and material, the latter including camp and garrison equipage, ammunition, and subsistence, had to be made from native lighters, called *cascos*, and small boats. Not a man was lost, and only a small amount of stores.

While selecting the camp and fixing the location of the several commands in it, I remained at Cavité and gave my personal attention to the landing of the troops and the forwarding of supplies.

Major-General Merritt having arrived in the harbor on July 27, I at once called on him and stated what had been done and reported for orders.

On the 1st of August General Orders No. 2, from the Headquarters, Department of the Pacific, was issued, by which the military forces present in the harbor were organized into a division of two brigades, the first under Brigadier-General Arthur MacArthur, and the second under Brigadier-General F. V. Greene. Under this order I was assigned to the command of the division which was designated as the Second Division, Eighth Army Corps.

As I did not go in person to Camp Dewey until 11 A.M. on the 10th of August, I will not attempt to detail the operations in the trenches and the several combats between our troops and the enemy after our occupation, by mutual agreement, of the left section of the insurgents' line, extending from the Pasay road to the beach. These conflicts began on the night of July 31, as soon as the enemy had realized that we had taken the places of the Filipinos and had begun a system of earthworks to the front of their old line.

It may have been merely coincident, but these attacks and sorties began at the time the captain-general of Manila was relieved by his second in command.

A NIGHT BATTLE IN THE RAIN—THE ENGAGEMENT OF JULY 31, NEAR MALATE.—DRAWN BY LUCIUS HITCHCOCK, FROM SKETCH BY JOHN McCUTCHEON

For more than six weeks the insurgents had kept up a bickering infantry fire on the Spanish trenches, firing occasionally some old siege pieces captured by Admiral Dewey at Cavité and given to Aguinaldo. These combats were never serious, and the Spaniards, so far as I know, made no sorties upon them. But there

RESISTANCE FROM THE HOUSES IN MALATE—VOLUNTEERS FROM THE FIRST CALIFORNIA IN CONFLICT WITH THE RESISTANTS

is no doubt of the fact that the Spaniards attacked our lines with force and vindictiveness, until they were informed that the bringing on of a general engagement would lead to a bombardment of the city. After this there was for several days a tacit suspension of hostilities.

On the 9th the foreign war vessels left their anchorage in front of Manila and our own fleet cleared for action. The next morning I went to Camp Dewey, and, finding the adjutant-general there, was told by him that the general commanding wished me to issue a tactical order for a projected attack on the enemy's lines.

I had before studied the ground, but I went over the whole field again with the brigade commanders. Instructions had been received from the major-general commanding to extend our line to the right, if the consent of the insurgents could be obtained to our taking that part of their line fronting the Spanish block-house No. 14; but this was not to be attempted if it was likely to bring on a partial engagement before the general assault. The next day, General Aguinaldo's consent having been given that we should replace the gun he had in an advanced position on the Pasay road with one of our own, I issued a tactical order of battle conforming to the general instructions I had received from the major-general commanding.

I had previously instructed the engineer company to prepare portable bamboo bridges, and had distributed wire-cutters, which I had purchased before leaving San Francisco, to pioneer parties to enable them to cut wire entanglements in front of the enemy's works. Half of these wire-cutters, with insulated handles, were given to the Colorado regiment, which had been designated to make the attack on the right of the enemy's works, and the other half were sent to General MacArthur. One-half of the engineer company, acting as pioneers, in conformity with the order, operated with each brigade.

The ground in front of General Greene's brigade was comparatively open, and roads were cut through the low bushes and briars quite close up to the enemy's first line by Colonel Hale of the First Colorado. The night before the attack wire entanglements were found and cut. This was a very useful and creditable performance.

I had learned from natives, and also from a field reconnaissance of Major Bell's, that the water in the little stream emptying into the bay at the angle of the Polvorin was very shallow. No very stout resistance was anticipated to an advance of the left of our line if the naval guns silenced the guns of the Polvorin and Malate batteries.

The outlook for General MacArthur's brigade was discouraging. Its advance was hampered and intersected in all directions by swamps and paddy fields; the bush was thick, and the enemy's line particularly strong at this point. It was a crenellated line of earthworks, faced with sand-bags. Pieces of field artillery were known to be on the line west of block-house No. 14. The problem was made difficult—first, from the fact that we could not be sure whether our first attack was to be tentative or serious, this depending on action of the navy; second, from our orders not to displace the insurgents, without their consent, from their position to the right of their gun on the Pasay road. This to the very last the insurgent leaders positively refused to give. Yet, if we could not go far enough to the right to silence their field-guns and carry that part of their line, they would have a fatal cross-fire on troops attacking block-house No. 14. I therefore directed General MacArthur to put the three 2.10-inch guns of Battery B, Utah Volunteer Artillery, in the emplacement of the insurgent gun and to place the Astor Battery behind a high garden wall to the right of the Pasay road, to be held there subject to orders.

I assumed that when the action became hot at this point, as I knew it would be, the insurgents would voluntarily fall back from their advanced position, and that the Astor Battery and its supports could take position without opposition.

Major-General Merritt came to division headquarters on the 11th. I at once summoned the brigade commanders, and, upon their reporting, we were asked when we would be ready to attack. I replied that the assault could be made the next morning (August 12). But we were informed that the naval bombardment would take place on Saturday, the 13th instant, probably at 10 A.M. I understood from the general commanding that he would be personally present on the day of battle. I therefore only deemed it necessary to make such tactical disposition as would put my division in the best position for the commanding general's personal directions.

General Babcock came to my headquarters on the morning of the 13th, and informed me that the major-general commanding would remain on a despatch-boat, and that he would accompany me and communicate any orders he might receive from his chief.

On this same morning all parts of the division were in the positions designated in my order, except that the leading battalion of the reserve, instead of taking post five hundred yards in rear of the cross-roads from the Calle Real to Pasay, had taken post in the open

MAP OF THE BATTLE OF MANILA

field abreast of the cross-road. The other battalions of the reserve moved up proportionally, and thus the whole reserve was under the fire zone, but as neither shells nor bullets fell among them I did not move them back.

Field-telegraph stations were established at General MacArthur's headquarters, at the left of the intrenchments of the Second Brigade on the beach, at the reserve near the Pasay road, and near the hospital in the camp.

The fleet opened fire at 9.30 A.M. The first shots fell short; but the range was soon found, and then the fire became evidently effective. I at once telegraphed General MacArthur to open on block-house No. 14 and begin his attack. At the same time seven of the guns of the Utah batteries opened fire on the enemy's works in front of the Second Brigade, and two guns on the right of this brigade opened an oblique fire towards block-house No. 14.

Riding down to the beach, I saw two of our lighter-draught vessels approach and open on the Polvorin with rapid-fire guns, and observed at the same time some men of the Second Brigade start up the beach. I ordered the First California, which was the leading regiment of the reserve, to go forward and report to General Greene. Going to the reserve telegraph, I received a message from MacArthur that his fire on the block-house was effective, but that he was enfiladed from the right. I knew from this that he wished to push the insurgents aside and put in the Astor Battery. I then authorized him to attack, which he did, and, soon after, the Twenty-third Infantry and the Thirteenth Minnesota carried the advance line of the enemy in the most gallant manner, the one gun of the Utah Battery and the Astor Battery lending most effective assistance.

In the meantime the Colorado regiment had charged and carried the right of the enemy's line, and the Eighteenth Regular Infantry and the Third Heavy (Regular) Artillery, acting as infantry, had advanced and passed over the enemy's works in their front without

THE ATTACK ON FORT SAN ANTONIO—Drawn by T. de Thulstrup

UNITED STATES TROOPS MARCHING ALONG THE BE

...NTO MANILA, AUGUST 13, 1898. DRAWN BY G. W. PETERS

IN THE AMERICAN TRENCHES

opposition. The reserve was ordered forward to follow the Second Brigade and a battery of Hotchkiss guns was directed to follow the Eighteenth Infantry. Going to the telegraph station on the left of our line on the beach, I found the operator starting forward in the rear of the First California, and I moved forward until the instrument was established in the first house in Malate. The first ticking of the sounder informed me that General MacArthur was heavily engaged at a second line of defence near Singalong.

It was evident that the best way to assist him was to press our success on the left. I therefore directed General Greene to connect, if possible, with General MacArthur by sending a regiment to the right. But the enemy seemed determined for a time to give us a street fight, and the Colorado and California regiments were the only ones available. At this juncture the Eighteenth Infantry and the Hotchkiss battery appeared to be stopped by a broken pier of a bridge, but the engineer company brought forward a portable bridge, and in a few minutes these organizations pressed forward through the Malata-Ermita redoubts. Soon the men from Nebraska and Wyoming came on shouting, for the white flag could now be seen on the sea-front, yet the firing did not cease, and the Spanish soldiers at the front did not seem to be notified of the surrender. In the meantime the reserve had been ordered forward, except one regiment, which was ordered to remain in the Second Brigade trenches. The seven Utah guns were also ordered to the front, one infantry battalion being directed to assist the men of the batteries in hauling the guns by hand.

The field-telegraph wires, extending in a wide circuit to the extreme right, for a time gave discouraging reports. The front was contracted, the enemy intrenched, and the timber thick on both sides of the road. Only two regiments could be put on the firing-line. The Fourteenth Infantry was brought forward, but could not fire a shot. Under these circumstances I telegraphed MacArthur to countermarch and come to Malate by way of Greene's intrenchments and the beach. This was at 1.25 P.M., but soon after I learned that MacArthur was too far committed to retire. The guns of the Astor Battery had been dragged to the front only after the utmost exertions, and were about being put into battery. At the same time I received a telegram stating that the insurgents were threatening to cross the bamboo bridge on our right; and to prevent this and guard our ammunition at Pasay, I ordered an Idaho battalion to that point. It was evidently injudicious under these circumstances to withdraw the First Brigade, so the order was countermanded and a despatch sent announcing our success on the left.

In answer, the report came that Singalong had been carried, and that the brigade was advancing on Paco.

At this point it was subsequently met by one of my aides, and marched down to the Cuartel de Malata by the Calzada de Paca. I had gone in the meantime to the south bridge of the walled city, and, learning that the Second Oregon was within the walls, and that Colonel Whittier was in conference with the Spanish commandant, I directed General Greene to proceed at once with his brigade to the north side of the Pasig, retaining only the Wyoming battalion to remain with me to keep up the connection between the two brigades.

A remarkable incident of the day was the experience of Captain Stephen O'Connor, of the Twenty-third Infantry. With a detachment of fifteen skirmishers he separated from his regiment and brigade at block-house No. 14, and, striking a road, probably in the rear of the enemy, marched into the city without opposition until he came to the Calle Real in Malata. Along this street he had some unimportant street fighting until he came to the Paseo de la Calzada, where, learning that negotiations were going on for a surrender, he took post at the bridge of the north sally-port, and the whole outlying Spanish force south of the Pasig passed by his small detachment in hurrying in *intramuros*.

Our loss in the First Brigade was three officers wounded, four enlisted men killed, and thirty-five wounded. The loss in the Second Brigade was one enlisted man killed and five wounded, making a total of five killed and forty-three wounded.

The antecedent loss in the trenches was fourteen killed and sixty wounded, making a total of one hundred and twenty-two casualties in the taking of Manila. This was only part of the price we paid for this success, for men died daily in our hospitals from disease contracted from exposure in camp and trenches. All hardships and privations have been borne by our soldiers with remarkable patience and cheerfulness. The opposition we met in battle was not sufficient to test the bravery of our soldiers, but all showed bravery and dash. The losses showed that the leading regiments of the First Brigade—Thirteenth Minnesota, Twenty-third Infantry, and the Astor Battery—met the most serious opposition and deserved credit for their success. The Colorado, California, and Oregon regiments, the Regulars, and all the batteries of the Second Brigade showed such zeal that it seemed a pity they did not meet foemen worthy of their steel.

My staff officers were active, zealous, and intelligent in the performance of their duties, and the men and officers of the entire division showed the best qualities of American soldiers.

GENERAL MacARTHUR'S ACCOUNT

SEVERAL hours before the operations of the 13th were intended to commence, there was considerable desultory firing from the Spanish line, both of cannon and small-arms, provoked no doubt by Philippine soldiers, who insisted upon maintaining a general fusillade along their lines, with which the American line connected just east of the Pasay road. The fire was not returned by our troops, and when the formation of the day was commenced things at the front were comparatively quiet. By eight o'clock the position was occupied; about 9.35 the naval attack commenced, and some twenty minutes thereafter the gun of Battery B, Utah Artillery, opened on block-house No. 14, the guns of the Astor Battery having engaged an opposing battery some minutes after the opening of the naval attack. There was no reply from the block-house or contiguous lines, either by guns or small-arms. The opposition to the Astor fire, however, was quite energetic; but after a spirited contest the opposition, consisting probably of two pieces, was silenced.

This contest was the only notable feature of the first stage of the action, and was especially creditable to the organization engaged. The position, selected by Lieutenant March after careful personal reconnaissance, was, perhaps, the only one possible in the vicinity, and it was occupied with great skill and held with commendable firmness, the battery losing three men wounded, one of whom afterwards died. The Utah gun on the road fired fourteen shots at block-house No. 14 with good effect, as was subsequently ascertained upon inspection of the work. Lieutenant Grow and detachment deserved great credit for the commendable manner in which the piece was served and pulled through the mud without the assistance of horses.

Some time about eleven o'clock concentrated infantry fire was heard in front of the Second Brigade, and not long thereafter an exultant shout indicated sub-

THE *MONTEREY* IN ACTION

BOMBARDMENT OF FORT SAN ANTONIO, AUGUST 13, 1898.—As seen from a Newspaper Despatch-boat by G. W. Peters

stantial success for our arms on the left. It was therefore assumed that the enemy had been so shaken as to make the advance practicable without a serious disadvantage to our troops.

Sergeant Mahoney, with a squad of Company D, Twenty-third United States Infantry, by a well-conducted scout, soon ascertained that the Spanish line was abandoned, and a general advance was immediately ordered. At about 11.20 a United States flag was placed upon block-house No. 14, thus concluding the second stage of the action without opposition and without loss.

A battalion of the Twenty-third Infantry, under Lieutenant-Colonel French, was stationed at this point to prevent armed bodies other than American troops crossing the trenches in the direction of Manila. The general advance was soon resumed, the Thirteenth Minnesota leading, with Company K as advance-guard, then the Astor Battery, a battalion of the Twenty-third Infantry, the battalion, Fourteenth Infantry, and the North Dakota Regiment, following in the order named.

At a point just south of Singalong, a block-house was found burning, causing a continuous explosion of small-arms ammunition, which, together with a scattering fire from the enemy, retarded the advance for a time. All difficulties were soon overcome, however, including the passage of the Astor Battery, by the determined efforts of Lieutenant March and his men, assisted by the infantry of the Minnesota regiment, over a gun emplacement which obstructed the road.

In the village of Singalong the advance fell under a loose fire, the intensity of which increased as the forward movement was pressed, and very soon the command was committed to a fierce combat. This strong opposition arose at block-house No. 20 of the Spanish defences, a detached work with emplacements for six guns, which fortunately were not filled on the 13th, but the work was occupied by a detachment of infantry, probably a strong rear-guard.

The advance party, consisting of men of the Minnesota regiment, reinforced by volunteers from the Astor Battery, led by Lieutenant March, and by Captain Sawtelle, of the brigade staff, as an individual volunteer, reached a point within less than eighty yards of the block-house, but was obliged to retire to the intersecting road in the village, at which point a hasty work was improvised and occupied by a firing-line of about fifteen men. Aside from conspicuous individual actions in the first rush, the well-regulated conduct of this firing-line was the marked feature of the contest.

The main body of the fighting-line, consisting of Company C, Twenty-third Infantry, Companies C, E, G, H, K, and L, Thirteenth Minnesota, and the Astor Battery, were well screened behind the village church and stone walls of adjacent gardens. In the early stage of the contest it seemed possible that an offensive return might be attempted, accordingly the position was secured by detached posts east and west on the intersecting road, and the construction of a succession of hasty intrenchments in the village street, and the occupancy of a strong defensive position by the main body in the rear. It soon became apparent, however, that the enemy was making a paroxysmal effort, and would soon yield to steady pressure.

Lieutenant-Colonel French, commanding a battalion of the Twenty-third Infantry, composed of Companies D, F, G, and H, acting on his own initiative, advanced without orders to the sound of the combat, and placed his battalion in position on the intersecting road to the west of the village, in precisely the position where, in the event of a crisis, he would have been most useful.

At about 1.30 P.M. all firing had ceased, and two scouting-parties, voluntarily led by Captain Sawtelle and Lieutenant March, soon thereafter reported the retreat of the adversary. The city was entered, without further incident, through the Paco district, detachments being placed at the bridges. The contact was made about twelve o'clock and the contest continued with great ferocity until 1.35—that is to say, about an hour and a half. The loss in the combat was three officers wounded, four enlisted men killed, and thirty-three wounded, including one man of the North Dakota regiment wounded far in the rear of the fighting-line; making the total casualties for the day forty-three killed and wounded.

The character of the ground absolutely precluded the possibility of any regular deployment, and as a consequence most of the troops present were unable to participate in the actual conflict, a fact much to be regretted, as all were eager to be at the front, and from the well-known character of the officers and men there can be no doubt that all would have displayed the same excellent qualities shown by their comrades in the village.

The combat of Singalong can hardly be classified as a great military event, but the involved terrain and the prolonged resistance created a very trying situation and afforded an unusual scope for the display of military qualities by a large number of individuals.

The invincible composure of Colonel Ovenshine, during an exposure in dangerous space for more than an hour, was conspicuous and very inspiring to the troops, and the efficient manner in which he took advantage of opportunities as they arose during the varying aspects of the fight was of great practical value in determining the result.

The cool, determined, and sustained efforts of Colonel Reeve, of the Thirteenth Minnesota, contributed very materially to the maintenance of the discipline and marked efficiency of his regiment.

The brilliant manner in which Lieutenant March accepted and discharged the responsible and dangerous duties of the day, and the pertinacity with which, assisted by his officers and men, he carried his guns over all obstacles to the very front of the firing-line, was an exceptional display of warlike skill and good judgment, indicating the existence of many of the best qualifications for high command in battle.

The gallant manner in which Captain Sawtelle, brigade quartermaster, volunteered to join the advance party in the rush, volunteered to command a firing-line, for a time without an officer, and again volunteered to lead a scout to ascertain the presence or absence of the enemy in the block-house, was a fine display of personal intrepidity.

The efficient, fearless, and intelligent manner in which Lieutenant Kernan, Twenty-first United States Infantry, acting assistant adjutant-general of the brigade, and Second Lieutenant Whitworth, Eighteenth United States Infantry, aide, executed a series of dangerous and difficult orders, was a fine exemplification of staff work under fire.

The splendid bravery of Captains Bjornstad and Seebach, and Lieutenant Lackore, of the Thirteenth Minnesota, all wounded, and, finally, the work of the soldiers of the first firing-line, as previously referred to, all went to make up a rapid succession of individual actions of unusual merit.

AMERICAN TROOPS GUARDING THE BRIDGE OVER THE RIVER PASIG ON THE AFTERNOON OF THE SURRENDER

GENERAL GREENE'S ACCOUNT

THE brigade left San Francisco, June 15, on the four transports *China*, *Colon*, *Zealandia*, and *Senator*, and arrived at Cavité on July 17, where I reported for duty to Brigadier-General T. M. Anderson. On leaving San Francisco the brigade consisted of the following: First Colorado Infantry, Colonel Irving Hale; First Nebraska Infantry, Colonel John P. Bratt; Tenth Pennsylvania Infantry, Colonel A. L. Hawkins; First Battalion Eighteenth United States Infantry, Lieutenant-Colonel C. M. Bailey; First Battalion Twenty-third United States Infantry, Lieutenant-Colonel John W. French; Battery A, Utah Artillery, Captain R. W. Young; Battery B, Utah Artillery, Captain F. A. Grant; detachment of Company A, Engineer Battalion, Second Lieutenant William D. Connor.

The battalion of the Twenty-third Infantry was detached and landed at Cavité. The other troops were landed on the beach about three miles south of Manila on July 18, 20, and 21, without loss or accident. Camp was established near the beach and named Camp Dewey, in honor of the distinguished Admiral commanding the United States squadron in these waters. The insurgent forces under General Aguinaldo then occupied a thin line of trenches and barricades about three thousand yards in front of us, facing the Spanish works at distances varying from two hundred to one thousand yards. Our outposts were immediately posted in rear of the insurgents, to guard against

RAISING THE AMERICAN FLAG OVER FORT SANTIAGO, MANILA, ON THE EVENING OF AUGUST 13, 1898.—DRAWN BY G. W. PETERS

any surprise in case the latter should be driven in by the Spaniards.

August 1 the Second Division was organized by the major-general commanding, and I was assigned to the command of the Second Brigade. It consisted of the troops above named, except the Twenty-third Infantry, and of the following: First California Infantry, Colonel James F. Smith; Second Battalion Eighteenth United States Infantry, Major Charles Kellar; both battalions of this regiment under command of Colonel D. D. Van Valzah; First Battalion Third United States Artillery, Captain James O'Hara; Second Battalion, Third United States Artillery, Captain W. E. Birkhimer; Company A, Engineer Battalion, Lieutenant W. D. Connor.

These troops were landed on July 27 and August 4, partly on the beach and partly on the Paranaque River, about one mile in the rear. The landing was effected under great difficulties, during a heavy southwest gale, which lasted for nearly two weeks, and was accompanied by high surf and downpour of rain. Considerable damage was done to rations and other property, but no lives were lost.

On the morning of July 29, in compliance with verbal instructions received the previous day from the adjutant-general of the Eighth Army Corps, I occupied the insurgent trenches, from the beach to the Calle Real, with one battalion Eighteenth United States Infantry, one battalion First Colorado Infantry, and four guns, two from each of the Utah batteries, these trenches being vacated at my request by the insurgent forces under Brigadier-General Noriel. As these trenches were badly located and insufficient in size and strength, I ordered another line constructed about one hundred yards in advance of them, and this work was completed, mainly by the First Colorado, during the night of July 29-30. The length of this line was only 270 yards, and on its right were a few barricades, not continuous, occupied by the insurgents, extending over to the large rice-swamp just east of the road from Pasay to Paco. Facing these was a strong Spanish line, consisting of a stone fort (San Antonio de Abad) near the beach, intrenchments of sand-bags and earth about seven feet high and ten feet thick, extending in a curved direction for about 1200 yards and terminating in a fortified block-house, known as No. 14, beyond our right on the Pasay road. It faced our front and enveloped our right flank. Mounted in and near the stone fort were seven guns in all—viz., three bronze field-guns of 3⅗ inches caliber, four bronze mountain-guns of 3.2 inches caliber, and in the vicinity of block-house No. 14 were two steel mountain-guns of 3.2 inches caliber. The line was manned throughout its length by infantry, with strong reserves at Malate and at the walled city in its rear.

Shortly before midnight of July 31-August 1 the Spaniards opened a heavy and continuous fire, with both artillery and infantry, from their entire line. Our trenches were occupied that day by the two battalions of the Tenth Pennsylvania Infantry, one foot battery (H), nearly two hundred strong, of the Third Artillery, and four guns, two of Battery A and two of Battery B, Utah Artillery.

All the troops in camp were under arms within fifteen minutes after the firing began. Captain Hobbs, with Battery K, Third Artillery, proceeded to the trenches at once, without waiting for orders.

I then ordered one battalion of the First California Infantry to move forward to the trenches, the second battalion of the same regiment to move forward as far as the cross-road to Pasay, about 1200 yards in rear of the trenches, the third battalion of the same regiment and the three battalions of the First Colorado Infantry to move forward to a line just out of range of the Spanish infantry fire and there await orders. The First Nebraska Infantry and the battalion of Eighteenth United States Infantry were held under arms in camp. The Third Artillery and First California met with considerable loss in advancing through the infantry fire in rear of our trenches. Captain Hobbs, of the Third Artillery, was slightly wounded, and Captain Richter, of the First California, mortally wounded. One sergeant was killed, and eight men of these two commands were also wounded before reaching the trenches. When they reached there the fire of the Spaniards had practically ceased. Meanwhile the attack had been sustained by the Tenth Pennsylvania Infantry, Battery H of the Third Artillery, and the four guns of the Utah Artillery. For about an hour and a half the firing on both sides, with artillery and infantry, was very heavy and continuous, our expenditure of ammunition being 160 rounds of artillery and about 60,000 rounds of infantry. That of the Spaniards was nearly twice as much.

The heaviest losses were sustained by the second battalion of the Tenth Pennsylvania, under Major Cuthbertson, which was posted on the right of our intrenchments and without cover. Major Cuthbertson reported that the Spaniards left their trenches in force and attempted to turn our right flank, coming within two hundred yards of his position. But as the night was intensely dark, with incessant and heavy rain, and as no dead or wounded were found in front of his position at daylight, it is possible that he was mistaken and that the heavy fire to which he was subjected came from the trenches near block-house No. 14, beyond his right flank, at a distance of about seven hundred yards. The Spaniards used smokeless powder, the thickets obscured the flash of their guns, and the sound of a Mauser bullet penetrating a bamboo pole is very similar to the crack of the rifle itself.

As the firing slackened I ordered the First Colorado and the third battalion of the First California to return to camp, and then proceeded to the trenches and remained there till nearly daylight. The firing ceased about 2 A.M. and was renewed for a short period about 9 A.M. The losses of the night were as follows:

	Killed or died of wounds.	Wounded.
Tenth Pennsylvania	6	29
Third Artillery	2	5
First California	2	8
Battery B, Utah Artillery		1
Total	10	43

This attack demonstrated the immediate necessity of extending our intrenchments to the right, and, although not covered by my instructions (which were to occupy the trenches from the bay to Calle Real, and to avoid precipitating an engagement), I ordered the First Colorado and one battalion of the First California, which occupied the trenches at 9 A.M., August 1, to extend the line of trenches to the Pasay road. The work was begun by these troops, and continued every day by the troops occupying the trenches in turn, until a strong line was completed by August 12, about twelve hundred yards in length, extending from the bay to the east side of the Pasay road. Its left rested on the bay and its right on an extensive rice-swamp, practically impassable. The right flank was refused, because the only way to cross a smaller rice-swamp, crossing the line about seven hundred yards from the beach, was along a cross-road in rear of the general line. As finally completed the works were very strong in profile, being from five to six feet in height and eight to ten feet in thickness at the base, strengthened by bags filled with earth.

PUERTA REAL, OR THE KING'S GATE, IN THE OLD WALL OF MANILA

The only material available was black soil saturated with water, and without the bags this was washed down and ruined in a day by the heavy and almost incessant rains. The construction of these trenches was constantly interrupted by the enemy's fire. They were occupied by the troops in succession, four battalions being usually sent out for a service of twenty-four hours, and posted with three battalions in the trenches, and one battalion in reserve along the cross-road to Pasay; Cossack posts being sent out from the latter to guard the camp against any possible surprise from the northeast and east. The service in the trenches was of the most arduous character, the rain being almost incessant and the men having no protection against it. They were wet during the entire twenty-four hours, and the mud was so deep that the shoes were ruined and a considerable number of men rendered barefooted. Until the notice of bombardment was given on August 7 any exposure above or behind the trenches promptly brought the enemy's fire, so that the men had to sit in the mud under cover, and keep awake, prepared to resist an attack, during the entire tour of twenty-four hours. After one particularly heavy rain a portion of the trench contained two feet of water, in which the men had to remain. It could not be drained, as it was lower than an adjoining rice-swamp in which the water had risen nearly two feet, the rainfall being more than four inches in twenty-four hours. These hardships were all endured by the men of the different regiments in turn with the finest possible spirit and without a murmur of complaint.

August 7 the notice of bombardment after forty-eight hours, or sooner if the Spanish fire continued, was served, and after that date not a shot was fired on either side until the assault was made on August 13. It was with great difficulty, and in some cases not without force, that the insurgents were restrained from opening fire, and thus drawing the fire of the Spaniards during this period.

THE OFFICIAL RESIDENCE OF THE GOVERNOR-GENERAL, MANILA

Owing to the heavy storm and high surf it was impossible to communicate promptly with the division commander at Cavité, and I received my instructions direct from the major-general commanding, or his staff-officers, one of whom visited my camp every day, and I reported direct to him in the same manner. My instructions were to occupy the insurgent trenches near the beach, so as to be in a good position to advance on Manila when ordered, but meanwhile to avoid precipitating an engagement; not to waste ammunition, and (after August 1) not to return the enemy's fire unless convinced that he had left his trenches and was making an attack in force. These instructions were given daily in the most positive terms to the officer commanding in the trenches, and in the main they were faithfully carried out.

More ammunition than necessary was expended on the nights of August 2 and 5, but in both cases the trenches were occupied by troops under fire for the first time, and in the darkness and rain there was ground to believe that the heavy fire indicated a real attack from outside the enemy's trenches. The total expenditure of ammunition on our side in the four engagements was about 130,000 rounds, and by the enemy very much more.

After the attack of July 31–August 1, I communicated by signal with the captain of the U. S. S. *Raleigh*, anchored about three thousand yards southwest of my camp, asking if he had received orders in regard to the action of his ship in case of another attack on my troops. He replied: "Both Admiral Dewey and General Merritt desire to avoid general action at present. If attack too strong for you, we will assist you, and another vessel will come and offer help."

In repeating this message, Lieutenant Tappan, commanding U. S. S. *Callao*, anchored nearer the beach, sent me a box of blue-lights, and it was agreed that if I burned one of these on the beach the *Raleigh* would at once open fire on the Spanish fort.

On the 2d and again on the 3d I reported to General Merritt that I was perfectly confident of being able to hold the trenches against any force that could be brought against them, and that, as the losses in sending forward supports were so heavy before they could reach the trenches, I had increased the force posted in them so that they could probably hold them without assistance from camp. On both days General Merritt replied, approving what I had done, but repeating the caution against bringing on an engagement or wasting ammunition in reply to the Spanish fire. On the 4th the *Monterey* arrived about noon, and as we had then lost nearly sixty men in killed and wounded without being permitted to make a counter-attack, I reported to General Merritt, requesting that the *Monterey* be anchored off Fort San Antonio de Abad, and, that she demolish it the instant the Spanish artillery again opened fire. On the morning of the 5th General Merritt telegraphed for me to meet him at Bakoor, opposite Cavité, and on arriving there I accompanied him to the *Newport*, and later, at his request, visited Admiral Dewey on the *Olympia*.

I explained the situation fully to both—viz., that I was perfectly able to hold the trenches against any possible attack, but that nearly every night my men were being killed or wounded by Spanish shells or bullets; that my own artillery was not sufficient to silence that of the enemy, but that the larger guns of the navy could destroy their fort in half an hour. I considered it my duty to make known these facts to them. The Admiral explained his plans in detail and stated the reasons why he desired to avoid engaging his ships at that time, but said positively that, if I burned the blue-light any night, the *Raleigh* would instantly open fire and would be followed by three other ships, all of which were under steam. I reported this to General Merritt, and was by him instructed to continue the passive defence in accordance with previous instructions, and not give the signal for the navy unless in imminent danger of being driven out of the trenches—a contingency which I considered most improbable.

On the evening of August 6th, Brigadier General MacArthur, commanding First Brigade, whose troops had been arriving during the last two days, arrived in camp. Our commissions were of the same date, but he was senior to me by length of service, and on the morning of the 7th I reported to him and asked his instructions. In reply he desired me to continue in command of the trenches and the supervision of the landing of troops and stores until the arrival of the division commander or the establishment of his own headquarters. At 3 P.M. he received a telegram from the division commander, directing him to assume command, which he did. He continued, however, until the arrival of the division commander, to direct the officers commanding his troops detailed for trench duty to report to me for instructions.

On the 9th the foreign fleet of war vessels which had been anchored in front of Manila withdrew, and was followed by a number of private launches bringing persons and property out of Manila; this in consequence of the forty-eight hours' notice of bombardment, which expired at noon of that date.

General MacArthur and myself were in perfect accord as to the proper method of attacking the Spanish position, and in compliance with General Merritt's instructions we sent him during the afternoon, by Captain Mott, of his staff, a joint memorandum.

On August 10 General Babcock, adjutant general, arrived in camp at 1 P.M., bringing instructions from General Merritt in reply to the memorandum of the previous day and asking for further information, both of which were contained in a memorandum which I handed to General Babcock. While we were talking with General Babcock the division commander arrived in camp, and all further instructions were received from him.

On August 11 General Merritt was in camp, and summoned the two brigade commanders to division headquarters, and notified them that the bombardment would take place on Saturday, August 13, and that it would depend on the result whether it was to be followed by an immediate assault or whether this would be deferred until the insurgent trenches on the right had been secured.

On August 12 the orders of the division commander were received at 5 P.M., and the brigade orders for the attack were immediately issued. These orders were carried out in every particular.

During the twenty-five days that I was at Camp Dewey daily reconnaissances were made by officers and men of the volunteer regiments under my command, supplemented by Company A of the Engineer Battalion, after it was assigned to me, and fairly accurate maps of the country in our front had been prepared. Captain Grove and Lieutenant Means, of the First Colorado, had been particularly active in this work and fearless in penetrating beyond our lines and close to those of the enemy. As the time for attack approached, these officers made a careful examination of the ground between our trenches and Fort San Antonio de Abad, and finally, on August 11, Major J. F. Bell, United States Volunteer Engineers, tested the creek in front of this fort and ascertained not only that it was fordable, but the exact width of the ford at the beach, and actually swam in the bay to a point from which he could examine the Spanish line from the rear. With the information thus obtained it was possible to plan the attack intelligently.

The position assigned to my brigade extended from the beach to the small rice-swamp, a front of about seven hundred yards. I placed three additional guns, making seven in all, in the trenches between the beach and the Calle Real. Seven battalions—viz., First Colorado Infantry, Eighteenth United States Infantry, and Third United States Artillery—were placed in the trenches, and eight battalions—viz., First California, First Nebraska, and Tenth Pennsylvania—were in reserve. Two navy boat guns, 3-inch caliber, manned by detachments from Batteries A and B, Utah Artillery, were placed on the right, near the swamp, facing the Spanish trenches near block-house No. 14, at six hundred yards. Three Hotchkiss revolving cannon, 1-inch caliber, manned by a detachment of the Third United States Artillery, were with the reserve. The troops were in the trenches at 8 A.M. and the reserve in position at 10 A.M. The day opened with heavy rain, which continued at intervals until nearly noon.

The navy opened fire at 9.30 A.M. and the guns in the trenches at 9.35. The firing was deliberate and careful, and nearly every shot took effect in San Antonio de Abad, which was silenced at the first round and made no response. Only twenty-seven shots were fired in fifty-five minutes. General Babcock, adjutant-general, was present with me in the trenches and brought instructions from General Merritt to advance with infantry as soon as the artillery was silenced, and to make this a demonstration or a real attack according to the amount of resistance encountered. At 10.15 I sent forward the first battalion of the First Colorado along the beach and in the field on its right, and followed this up with the second and then the third battalion of the same regiment, at distances of about two hundred yards. They met a light fire from the woods on their right flank, in rear of the Spanish trenches and in the direction of Cingalon and Paco. They replied to this with volleys, and the companies nearest the beach forded the creek, advanced through the water on the beach, turned the right flank of the trenches, and entered Fort San Antonio de Abad from the rear, hauling down the Spanish flag and hoisting the American flag about 11 A.M. The fort was found empty, except two dead and one wounded; four guns were in it, two field pieces of 3.6 inches, and two mountain-guns of 3.2 inches, from which the breech-blocks had been removed.

Seeing the fort captured without resistance, I ordered the Eighteenth United States Infantry to move by the left flank over the trenches and along the road to Manila in column of fours, not anticipating any resistance. As they showed themselves, however, a sharp fire was met from the woods near Cingalon, and the second battalion deployed to the right of the road in the formation for attack. Although the enemy could not be accurately located, on account of his using smokeless powder, this fire was replied to by volleys, which had the effect of subduing it. The battalion then moved forward by rushes, followed by the first battalion, until it reached the Spanish trenches, which had been abandoned, leaving three dead. When the Eighteenth United States Infantry advanced, I sent orders to the Third United States Artillery to advance to the front from its position on the right, and their advance was made in the formation for attack at the same time as the Eighteenth United States Infantry. They were subject to the same fire from their right and front near the Cingalon woods, to which they replied, subduing it, and then advancing to the Spanish trenches, which they found deserted.

Just as the advance of the Eighteenth Infantry and Third Artillery began, the commanding officers of the reserve, which had been ordered up by the division commander, reported to me, and I directed them to follow by the beach, and ordered the artillery to follow on to Manila as soon as they could get the assistance of the infantry to haul their guns. As the bridge near the fort appeared to be broken by artillery fire, I directed the engineer company to carry forward some large trestles and flooring of bamboo, which had been prepared the previous day, and this was done under fire.

Having made these dispositions, I rode rapidly forward by the beach and through the creek to the fort. A portion of the First Colorado was in the Spanish trenches replying to a fire from a second line of defence running along the road from Malate to Cingalon. The rest of the Colorado regiment and all of the California were in the houses, a few hundred yards in our front, replying to this same fire from the flank. The engagement here lasted about fifteen minutes before the enemy's fire was subdued, and resulted in the loss of one killed and one wounded in the Colorado regiment. The First Nebraska and Eighteenth United States Infantry having now come up, I directed them to move forward, the former along the beach and the latter along Calle Real. The Colorado regiment was directed to protect the right flank from any possible attack from Cingalon and Paco. The California regiment was already in advance on Calle Real. In this way the brigade moved through Malate, from street to street, meeting a straggling fire from the direction of Paco, but no serious resistance. The U. S. S. *Callao*, commanded by Lieutenant Tappan, and carrying several machine-guns and one 3-inch gun, kept abreast or slightly in advance of the head of the column and within two hundred yards of shore all the way to the walled city, and was always in position to render most valuable assistance had determined resistance been met.

After advancing through Malate and Ermita, the open space at the Luneta, just south of the walled city, was reached about 1 P.M. A white flag was flying at the southwest bastion, and I rode forward to meet it under a heavy fire from our right and rear on the Paco road. At the bastion I was informed that officers representing General Merritt and Admiral Dewey were on their way ashore to receive the surrender, and I therefore turned east to the Paco road. The firing ceased at this time, and on reaching this road I found nearly one thousand Spanish troops who had retreated from Santa Ana through Paco, and, coming up the Paco road, had been firing on our flank. I held the commanding officers, but ordered these troops to march into the walled city. At this point the California regiment a short time before had met some insurgents who had fired at the Spaniards on the walls, and the latter, in returning the fire, had caused a loss in the California regiment of one killed and two wounded.

My instructions were to march past the walled city on its surrender, cross the bridge, occupy the city on the north side of the Pasig, and protect lives and property there. While the white flag was flying on the walls, yet very sharp firing had just taken place outside, and there were from 5000 to 6000 men on the walls, with arms in their hands, only a few yards from us. I did not feel justified in leaving this force in my rear until the surrender was clearly established, and I therefore halted and assembled my force, prepared to force the gates if there were any more firing. The Eighteenth Infantry and First California were sent forward to hold the bridges a few yards ahead, but the second battalion, of the Third Artillery, First Nebraska, Tenth Pennsylvania, and First Colorado were all assembled at this point. While this was being done I received a note from Lieutenant-Colonel Whittier, of General Merritt's staff, written from the captain-general's office within the walls, asking me to stop the firing outside, as negotiations for surrender were in progress.

I returned within the walls with the messenger and found the late Governor-General Augustin, the Acting Governor-General Jaudenes, Admiral Montojo, Lieutenant-Colonel Whittier, and Lieutenant Brumby, of the navy. The Spaniards had drawn up terms of surrender, which Colonel Whittier informed me would probably be accepted by General Merritt, who was now on his way ashore from the *Newport*. I then returned to the troops outside the walls and sent Captain Birkhimer's battalion of the Third Artillery down the Paco road to prevent any insurgents from entering. Feeling satisfied that there would be no attack from the Spanish troops lining the walls, I put the regiments in motion towards the bridges, brushing aside a considerable force of insurgents who had penetrated the city from the direction of Paco, and were in the main street with their flag, expecting to march into the walled city and plant it on the walls. After crossing the bridges, the Eighteenth United States Infantry was posted to patrol the principal streets near the bridge, the First California was sent up the Pasig to occupy Quiapo, San Miguel, and Malacanan, and with the First Nebraska I marched down the river to the captain of the port's office, where I ordered the Spanish flag hauled down and the American flag raised in its place.

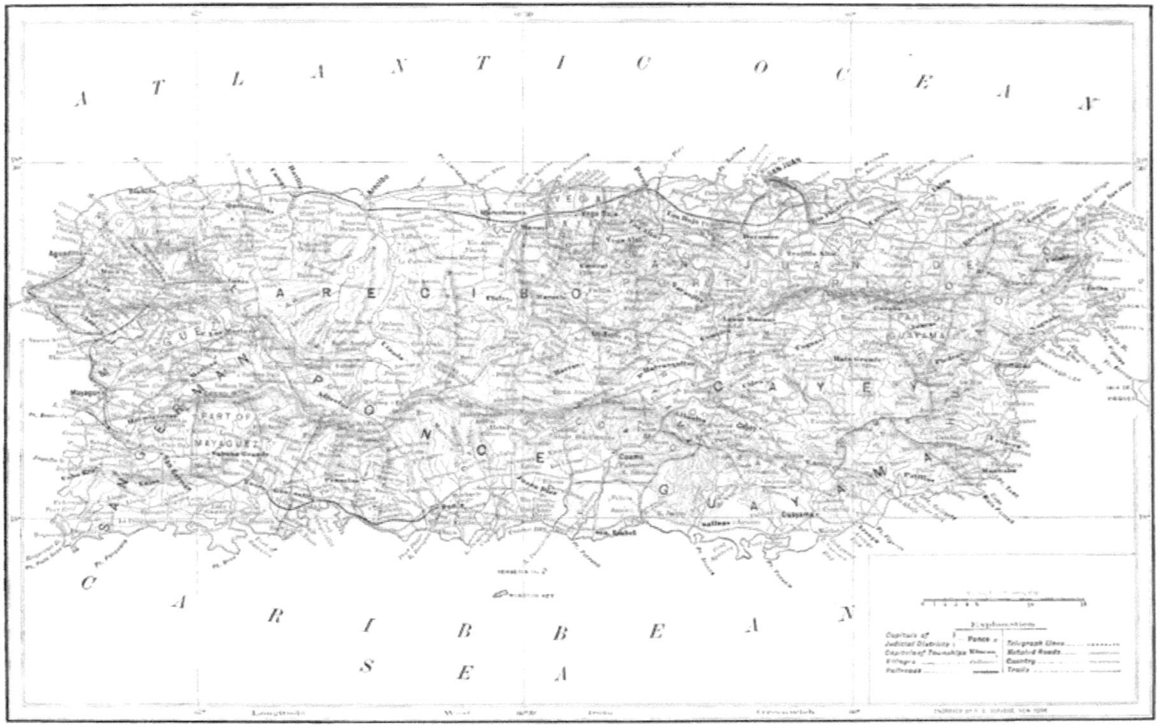
ATLANTIC OCEAN
CARIBBEAN SEA
ARECIBO
SAN JUAN DE PORTO RICO
VEGA BAJA
AGUADILLA
SAN GERMAN
PART OF MAYAGUEZ
PONCE
GUAYAMA
CAYEY
PART OF GUAYAMA
SAN JUAN
Ponce
Mayaguez
Aguadilla
Arecibo
Guayama
Explanation
Capitals of Judicial Districts
Capitals of Townships
Villages
Railroads
Telegraph Lines
Metaled Roads
Country
Trails
Longitude West from Greenwich

PUERTO RICO

THE RETURN TO PEACE

THE general situation at the time of the issuance of the order suspending hostilities was described in the following words by Senator Lodge:

"More fortunate than the generals and the troops in Puerto Rico, Admiral Dewey and General Merritt, thanks to distance and a severed cable, were able to complete their work and set the final crown upon their labors by taking Manila before the order reached them to cease hostilities. That order, when it came, found them masters of the great Eastern city they had fought to win. In Puerto Rico the news stayed Schwan's cavalry in pursuit of the Spaniards, Brooke's gunners with the lanyards in their hands, and halted the other columns in their march over the island. In Cuba it saved Manzanillo, just falling before the guns of Goodrich and his little squadron, and checked the movements which were bringing port after port into American possession. It stopped also the departure of a fleet which, by its existence and intention, was a potent cause of the coming of peace. Even before the battle of the 3d of July, the department at Washington was making ready to send a fleet consisting of the *Iowa*, *Oregon*, *Yankee*, *Yosemite*, and *Dixie*, under Commodore Watson, in the flag-ship *Newark*, direct to Spain, primarily to fight the fleet of Admiral Camara, which had wandered helplessly across the Mediterranean with vague outgivings about going to Manila, but which merely went through the Suez Canal, and then turned round and came back again. But after the battle of July 3 the preparations of Commodore Watson's squadron were pushed more energetically than ever, reinforcements were prepared, and it was known that it was to cross the Atlantic in any event, and carry war to the very doors of Spain's coast cities. This fact was soon as well known in Europe as in America. Presently it became clear that Watson's fleet was no pretence, but a very grim reality; that it was nearly in readiness; and, finally, that it was on the very eve of departure. What American ships and seamen could do had just been shown at Manila and Santiago, and there was no reason to suppose that they would be less effective on the Spanish coasts. Spain did not like the prospect, and some of her neighbors were as averse as she to the sound of American guns in the Mediterranean, not heard in those waters now for nearly a century. It would be something new, something which might disturb concerts and *Bands* and other excellent arrangements, and must not be permitted. It became clear to the diplomatic mind that Spain must make peace, and make it at once, on any terms. Hence arose what is politely called pressure, although poor Spain did not need much pressing. The war which she had forced—no one knows exactly for what reason—for what she called her pride or her point of honor, had resulted in a series of rapid, crushing, and unbroken defeats. She had expected, perhaps, to make a stand, to win a fight, somewhere; but her whole system, her entire body politic, was rottener than any one dreamed, and the whole fabric went to pieces like an egg-shell when struck by the hand of a vigorous, enterprising enemy. Her sea-power was shattered and entirely gone in the Pacific and in American waters. Manila Bay was in the hands of Dewey, and the surrender of the city waited only for his demand. Cuba could not be relieved; Santiago province was in American hands, and the rest of the island would go the same way as fast as the United States could land troops and capture ports. Puerto Rico was half gone, and the American columns were marching as rapidly as possible to complete the conquest of the island. And then there in the background was Watson's fleet, very imminent now, and likely to be off Cadiz or Barcelona in a fortnight. Clearly it was high time for peace."

M. JULES CAMBON

The bombardment of Manzanillo, here referred to by Senator Lodge, occurred on the 12th of August; and the official report of the event gave occasion for the expression of the keen disappointment felt throughout the army and navy of the United States upon the receipt of the President's order suspending hostilities.

"Yesterday morning, the 12th instant," said Captain Goodrich, writing on the 13th of August, "my little flotilla got under way at half past four, and proceeded to the vicinity of Manzanillo. The *Resolute*, *Suwanee*, *Hist*, and *Osceola* anchored well outside of the northern entrance. I hoisted a flag of truce on the *Newark*, and proceeded to an anchorage about three miles distant from the town, whence I sent the *Alvarado*, also bearing a flag of truce, to present to the military commandant a demand for surrender. This demand was placed in his hands by Lieutenant Blue at thirty-five minutes past noon. The reply was to the effect that the Spanish military code forbade a surrender, except as the sequence of a siege or other military operation.

"The town, being fortified, was exempt from the privileges and immunities attached to defenceless places. Nevertheless, sufficient time was given to permit non-combatants to leave the city. At three o'clock I signalled to the outlying vessels to take the stations off the town which had been assigned, and at 3.35 hauled down the flag of truce on the *Newark* and proceeded towards Manzanillo until the shoalness of the water forbade her nearer approach. At 3.40 fire was opened from the *Newark* on the batteries, and was maintained with tolerable steadiness until 4.15 with an accuracy surprising in view of the short time during which she had been commissioned. The other vessels followed shortly after.

"At 4.15 P.M., having seen supposed white flags hoisted on the Spanish gunboat *Cuba Española* and the commandant's quarters, I made signal "Cease firing," and sent the *Alvarado* in under flag of truce. At the same time the *Suwanee*, *Hist*, and *Osceola*, all under the immediate orders of Lieutenant-Commander Delehanty, were approaching the town from the southward through the middle channel. When these vessels were within one thousand to fifteen hundred yards of the batteries the Spanish authorities opened fire on them at 4.35, paying no attention to the flag of truce on the *Alvarado*, which (as I was afterwards informed) they failed to perceive. The *Alvarado* hauled down her flag of truce and joined the other gunboats in returning the fire. At 4.50 I opened fire again from the *Newark*. The Cuban forces at this time appeared to the northward of the town and began discharging volleys, which were returned apparently by Spanish artillery. The *Newark* threw a number of 6-inch shells in this direction in order to assist the Cubans. The *Suwanee*, *Osceola*, *Hist*, and *Alvarado* soon returned to the neighborhood of the flag-ship, and we all anchored at about 5.30 P.M. for the night. From that time until daylight this morning [August 13] one 6-inch shell was fired from the *Newark* at the batteries at irregular intervals, one shot being fired during each half-hour. Daylight revealed a large number of white flags flying over the block-houses and batteries of Manzanillo and the approach of a boat from shore bearing a flag of truce. The captain of the port came off and delivered to me a cipher despatch from the Secretary of the Navy, reading as follows: 'Protocol of peace signed by the President; armistice proclaimed.' My disappointment was, as may be imagined, very great, for I had every reason to believe that the garrison was entirely ready to surrender. I had hoped that the fleet might have won one more laurel and gained one more important victory before the conclusion of peace."

In the same hope of "one more laurel, one more victory before the conclusion of peace," General Wilson writes, as has been seen in his account of the shelling of Assomante: "I was influenced in my demand for the surrender of the place by the belief that the rumors universally current in the public press as to the near completion of peace negotiations, and of which it was possible that the Spanish officers at San Juan were not informed, had some foundation. In the event of a refusal to surrender, and in the absence of official information from proper authority, I had no course but to continue my advance."

THE CESSATION OF HOSTILITIES

President McKinley's Account

The total casualties in killed and wounded in the army during the war with Spain were: Officers killed, 23; enlisted men killed, 257; total, 280; officers wounded, 113; enlisted men wounded, 1464; total, 1577. Of the navy: Killed, 17; wounded, 67; died as result of wounds, 1; invalided from service, 6; total, 91.

It will be observed that while our navy was engaged in two great battles and in numerous perilous undertakings in blockade and bombardment, and more than 50,000 of our troops were transported to distant lands and were engaged in assault and siege and battle and many skirmishes in unfamiliar territory, we lost in both arms of the service a total of 1668 killed and wounded; and in the entire campaign by land and sea we did not lose a gun or a flag or a transport or a ship, and, with the exception of the crew of the *Merrimac*, not a soldier or sailor was taken prisoner.

On August 7, forty-six days from the date of the landing of General Shafter's army in Cuba and twenty-one days from the surrender of Santiago, the United States troops commenced embarkation for home, and our entire force was returned to the United States as early as August 24. They were absent from the United States only two months.

It is fitting that I should bear testimony to the patriotism and devotion of that large portion of our army which, although eager to be ordered to the post of greatest exposure, fortunately was not required outside of the United States. They did their whole duty, and, like their comrades at the front, earned the gratitude of the nation. In like manner, the officers and men of the army and of the navy who remained in their departments and stations faithfully performing most important duties connected with the war, and whose requests for assignment in the field and at sea I was compelled to refuse because their services were indispensable here, were entitled to the highest commendation. It was my regret that there seemed to be no provision for their suitable recognition.

In this connection it is a pleasure for me to mention in terms of cordial appreciation the timely and useful work of the American National Red Cross, both in relief measures preparatory to the campaigns, in sanitary assistance at several of the camps of assemblage, and,

HON. WILLIAM R. DAY

later, under the able and experienced leadership of the president of the society, Miss Clara Barton, on the fields of battle and in the hospitals at the front in Cuba. Working in conjunction with the governmental authorities and under their sanction and approval, and with the enthusiastic co-operation of many patriotic women and societies in the various States, the Red Cross fully maintained its already high reputation for intense earnestness and ability to exercise the noble purposes of its international organization, thus justifying the confidence and support which it received at the hands of the American people. To the members and officers of this society, and all who aided them in their philanthropic work, the sincere and lasting gratitude of the soldiers and the public was due and was freely accorded.

In tracing these events we are constantly reminded of our obligations to the Divine Master for His watchful care over us and His safe guidance, for which the nation made reverent acknowledgment and offered humble prayer for the continuance of His favor.

The annihilation of Admiral Cervera's fleet, followed by the capitulation of Santiago, having brought to the Spanish government a realizing sense of the hopelessness of continuing a struggle now become wholly unequal, it made overtures of peace through the French Ambassador, who with the assent of his government had acted as the friendly representative of Spanish interests during the war. On the 26th of July M. Cambon presented a communication signed by the Duke of Almodovar, the Spanish Minister of State, inviting the United States to state the terms upon which it would be willing to make peace. On the 30th of July, by a communication addressed to the Duke of Almodovar and handed to M. Cambon, the terms of the United States government were announced, substantially as in the protocol afterwards signed. On the 10th of August the Spanish reply, dated August 7, was handed by M. Cambon to the Secretary of State. It accepted unconditionally the terms imposed as to Cuba, Puerto Rico, and an island of the Ladrones group, but appeared to seek to introduce inadmissible reservations in regard to the demand of the United States as to the Philippine Islands. Conceiving that discussion on this point could neither be practical nor profitable, I directed that in order to avoid misunderstanding the matter should be forthwith closed by proposing the embodiment in a formal protocol of the terms upon which the negotiations for peace were to be undertaken. The vague and inexplicit suggestions of the Spanish note could not be accepted, the only reply being to present as a virtual ultimatum a draft of protocol embodying the precise terms tendered to Spain in the note of the United States of July 30, with added stipulations of detail as to the appointment of commissioners to arrange for the evacuation of the Spanish Antilles. On August 12 M. Cambon announced his receipt of full powers to sign the protocol so submitted. Accordingly, on the afternoon of August 12, M. Cambon, as the Plenipotentiary of Spain, and the Secretary of State, as the Plenipotentiary of the United States, signed a protocol providing that Spain relinquish all claim of sovereignty over and title to Cuba; that Spain cede to the United States the island of Puerto Rico and other islands under Spanish sovereignty in the West Indies, and also an island in the Ladrones to be selected by the United States; and that the United States occupy and hold the city, bay, and harbor of Manila pending the conclusion of a treaty of peace which should determine the control, disposition, and government of the Philippines.

The protocol provided also for the appointment of joint commissions on the part of the United States and Spain, to meet in Havana and San Juan, respectively, for the purpose of arranging and carrying out the details of the stipulated evacuation of Cuba, Puerto Rico, and other Spanish islands in the West Indies; for the appointment of not more than five commissioners on each side, to meet at Paris not later than October 1, and to proceed to the negotiation and conclusion of a treaty of peace, subject to ratification according to the respective constitutional forms of the two countries. It also provided that upon the signature of the protocol hostilities between the two countries should be suspended, and that notice to that effect should be given as soon as possible by each government to the commanders of its military and naval forces.

Immediately upon the conclusion of the protocol, I issued a proclamation of August 12 suspending hostilities on the part of the United States. The necessary orders to that end were at once given by telegraph. The

THE DUKE OF ALMODOVAR

M. JULES CAMBON, THE FRENCH AMBASSADOR, SIGNING THE PEACE PROTOCOL ON BEHALF OF SPAIN.—Drawn by T. de Thulstrup

blockade of the ports of Cuba and San Juan de Puerto Rico was in like manner raised. On the 18th of August the muster-out of 100,000 volunteers, or as near that number as was found to be practicable, was ordered.

On the 1st of December 101,165 officers and men had been mustered out and discharged from the service, and 9002 more were mustered out by the 10th of the same month. Also a corresponding number of general and general staff officers were honorably discharged the service.

The military commissions to superintend the evacuation of Cuba, Puerto Rico, and the adjacent islands were forthwith appointed: for Cuba, Major-General James F. Wade, Rear-Admiral William T. Sampson, Major-General Matthew C. Butler; for Puerto Rico, Major-General John R. Brooke, Rear-Admiral Winfield S. Schley, Brigadier-General William W. Gordon, who soon afterwards met the Spanish Commissioners at Havana and San Juan, respectively. The Puerto Rican Joint Commission speedily accomplished its task, and by the 18th of October the evacuation of the island was completed. The United States flag was raised over the island at noon on that day. The administration of its affairs was provisionally intrusted to a military governor until Congress should otherwise provide. Owing to the difficulties in the way of removing the large numbers of Spanish troops still in Cuba, the evacuation was not completed before the beginning of 1899.

Pursuant to the fifth article of the protocol, I appointed William R. Day, former Secretary of State, Cushman K. Davis, William P. Frye, and George Gray, Senators of the United States, and Whitelaw Reid, to be the Peace Commissioners on the part of the United States. Proceeding in due season to Paris, they there met on the 1st of October five commissioners, similarly appointed on the part of Spain. Their negotiations made hopeful progress, so that I was soon able to lay a definitive treaty of peace before the Senate.

RATIFICATION OF THE TREATY

By Henry Cabot Lodge

The signing of the protocol took place at Washington on August 12, and hostilities ceased. This was the practical end of active war, but it was only a truce or an armistice. The war was not ended or over, and could not be until a treaty was concluded. For this work, under the provisions of the protocol, the President appointed Mr. Day, who resigned the Secretaryship of State, Senator Davis, of Minnesota, Senator Frye, of Maine, Senator Grey, of Delaware, and the Honorable Whitelaw Reid commissioners on the part of the United States, to negotiate a treaty of peace at Paris. The Spanish government appointed a like commission, headed by Don Eugenio Montero Rios, the President of the Senate, and a very learned and able lawyer of high distinction. The commissioners of both governments met in Paris on October 1, and exchanged their powers. The negotiations then began, and lasted until December 10, when the treaty was signed. The Spaniards struggled hard and resisted stoutly. All Europe was with them in sympathy, and especially France and Germany. The Americans were doing their work in a hostile atmosphere, with no friendly nation near except England, and they did it in a way which added another triumph to the annals of American diplomacy. They were all men of the highest distinction, of experience, and tried ability, and they not only met the Spanish arguments strongly and thoroughly, but they conducted their difficult task without stumbling or error. There was a contest over the Cuban and other debts, which called forth much discussion, and a most successful parrying of all the Spanish efforts to secure for those debts some recognition or some acceptance by the United States. There was also discussion on some minor points, but the question upon which the real conflict turned, and which soon overshadowed everything else, was the Philippines. Dewey's victory had come with the shock of a great surprise as well as the splendor of a great glory. No one had dreamed that the war meant the entrance of the United States into the Orient. But there the flag was, there it fluttered victorious, and the stream of events, so much more powerful than human plannings when they are the outcome of world forces, moved relentlessly on. Dewey must be supported and relieved. So a ship and some troops went to him. Then it was clear that they were inadequate, and more ships and more troops followed across the Pacific. They could not be there for nothing. Manila must be taken, and so it was taken before news of the protocol could reach that distant place with its cut cable. Hostilities ceased, and we held Manila in our grasp. No one would have consented to give up that city and its noble harbor—the prize and pearl of the Orient. But if we were to retain Manila, the scene of Dewey's victory, which the American people would never surrender, were we to hold it alone and nothing else, surrounded by territory in other hands, with all the burdens and perils which such a situation implied? We must hold Manila, and, if Manila, then the only possible thing was to hold the island of Luzon as well. That was as far as the President or the mass of the American people had gone when the commissioners sailed for Paris in September. Some members of the commission were utterly opposed to the retention of the Philippines or any considerable portion of any one of them. But when they settled down to work, when the inexorable demand for action came upon them, when they could no longer speculate upon possibilities without responsibility, as their fellow-citizens at home could do, then the question broadened and deepened, and began to settle itself and burn away all doubts, as great questions have a way of doing. The stream of events was running on in the same inevitable fashion. Those who had rejoiced in the rush of the current

THE AMERICAN PEACE COMMISSION AT A CONFERENCE IN THEIR COUNCIL-ROOM AT THE CONTINENTAL HOTEL, PARIS

THE LAST SESSION OF THE AMERICAN AND SPANISH PEACE COMMISSIONERS.—Drawn by F. Luis Mora from a Photograph

and those who tried to stem it alike went with it. The forces which had been let loose by the Spanish war were world forces, and they presented their arguments with the grim silence and the unforgiving certainty of fate. Will you go away and leave the Filipinos to Spain? they asked; leave them to a tyranny and oppression tenfold worse than that in Cuba which carried you into the war? Clearly impossible. Will you force Spain out of the islands, and then, having destroyed the only government and the only sovereignty which has ever existed there, will you depart yourselves and leave the islands to anarchy and bloodshed, to sanguinary dictatorship, and to the quick seizure of European powers and a possible world-wide war over the spoils? Again clearly impossible. Again no thoroughfare. Again a proposition which no strong, high-spirited people could entertain. Will you, then, call in the other powers of the earth to help you settle the question of these islands, determine their destiny, and establish a government for their people? Once more, no. Such a solution is incompatible with decent pride and honest self-respect, and could lead only to mischief and confusion, to wars and rumors of wars. What, then, will you do? Is there aught you can do but replace the sovereignty you have dashed down, and with your own sovereignty meet the responsibilities which have come to you in the evolution of the time, and take yourselves the islands you have won? Quite clearly now the answer comes that no other course is possible. The American commissioners heard in all this, as the great master of music heard in the first bars of his immortal symphony, "the hand of Fate knocking at the door." Some of them had always believed in this outcome, some had not, but all became absolutely convinced that there was but one road possible, and so they demanded all the Philippines from Spain, and made the demand an ultimatum. The Spaniards struggled hard. They disputed our right to make the demand under the terms of the protocol; they argued and resisted; they threatened to break off the negotiations; and then they yielded, because they could do nothing else. This done, the treaty was soon made, and it was an admirable instrument, a masterpiece in every respect. No loop-hole was left for any claim for debts or aught else; no words could be found which could be strained to bind the United States

HON. JOHN HAY, SECRETARY OF STATE, SIGNING THE MEMORANDUM OF RATIFICATION ON BEHALF OF THE UNITED STATES

in any way in the future. The American commissioners came home with a triumphant treaty, a very fit result of an entirely victorious war.

Much dispute and opposition has arisen among people successful in war in times past, and will arise again, over treaties of peace, but such opposition has always proceeded on the ground that the victor nation received too little. The treaty of the United States with Spain, signed in Paris on December 10, 1898, has the unique distinction of having excited opposition and attack among the victors because it secured too much and was too triumphant. An organization called by the strange name of the Anti-Imperialist League was formed in the Eastern States. Some men who had once been eminent in politics gave their names to its support, and others who felt that they ought to be eminent in politics gave their services. A vigorous crusade was begun, but the popular response in the way of the easily signed petition was surprisingly small, for the good sense of the American people made two points clear to them. One was that a peace treaty ought to be ratified, the other that they had won these new possessions, and had no doubt that they could trust themselves to deal with them honestly, ably, and for their own truest and best interests, as well as those of the people of all the islands. A failure in the field of popular discussion before the people and in the newspapers, the fight against the treaty was transferred to the Senate of the United States.

The constitutional provision which requires a vote of two-thirds of the Senate to ratify a treaty simplifies the work of opposition to ratification. It seemed incredible at first that a treaty of peace could possibly be defeated. Party lines were not drawn on the question, and it was at first supposed that resistance to the ratification of the treaty would be confined to a very few Senators, who had been opposed to the movement in favor of the Cubans, as well as to the entrance into war, and were now consistently opposed to its results. But as time went on the necessities of factions in the Democratic party developed an opposition which included a majority of the Democratic Senators, and this made the minority formidably large—nearly one-third of the Senate, if not in excess of it. It is not needful to trace in detail the course of the debate, which from the side of opposition proceeded on three lines—lack of constitutional power to acquire and hold the Philippines, the violation of the principles of the Declaration of Independence involved in doing so, and sympathy and admiration for the Filipinos, feelings as profound as they were rapid in growth. The friends of ratification took the very simple ground that the treaty committed the United States to no policy, but left it free to do exactly as seemed best with all the islands, that the American people could be safely intrusted with this grave responsibility, and that patriotism and common-sense alike demanded the end of war and the re-establishment of peace, which could only be effected by the adoption of the treaty. The contest was earnest and bitter, the canvass energetic to a degree never seen in the Senate, and the result close. When the Senate went into executive session on Monday, February 6, with the time for the vote fixed for three o'clock, the treaty had only 58 sure votes, 60 being needed for ratification; the opposition had 29 sure votes, and the remaining 3 were doubtful. At half-past two one of the doubtful voters was declared to be for the treaty, making 59. Just before three o'clock another vote was promised, and the third doubtful vote was given to the treaty after the roll had been called. The final vote stood 57 to 27—including the pairs, 61 to 29, just two-thirds and one vote to spare. Opinion as to the outcome had fluctuated, even among those best informed, down to the last moment. Yet as one looks back when all is done, it seems clear that no other result was possible. The responsibility which had come to the American people with the flash of Dewey's guns on May 1 could not be avoided, and the American people were too strong, too high-spirited, too confident, to run away from it. The hand of Fate was knocking at the door of the Senate as it had knocked at the door of the American commissioners in Paris. To that knock all doors fly open, and to the stern visitant without but one answer could be given.

Nothing remained after the end of the conflict in the Senate but the exchange of ratifications, which took place on the 11th of April, 1899, and so the war ended.

THE PROTOCOL

William R. Day, Secretary of State of the United States, and His Excellency Jules Cambon, Ambassador Extraordinary and Plenipotentiary of the Republic of France at Washington, respectively possessing for this purpose full authority from the Government of the United States and the Government of Spain, have concluded and signed the following articles, embodying the terms on which the two governments have agreed in respect to the matters hereinafter set forth, having in view the establishment of peace between the two countries, that is to say:

Article I.

Spain will relinquish all claim of sovereignty over and title to Cuba.

Article II.

Spain will cede to the United States the island of Puerto Rico and other islands now under Spanish sovereignty in the West Indies, and also an island in the Ladrones to be selected by the United States.

Article III.

The United States will occupy and hold the city, bay, and harbor of Manila pending the conclusion of a treaty of peace which shall determine the control, disposition, and government of the Philippines.

Article IV.

Spain will immediately evacuate Cuba, Puerto Rico, and other islands now under Spanish sovereignty in the West Indies; and to this end each government will, within ten days after the signing of this protocol, appoint commissioners, and the commissioners so appointed shall, within thirty days after the signing of this protocol, meet at Havana for the purpose of arranging and carrying out the details of the aforesaid evacuation of Cuba and the adjacent Spanish islands; and each government will, within ten days after the signing of this protocol, also appoint other commissioners, who shall, within thirty days after the signing of this protocol, meet at San Juan, in Puerto Rico, for the purpose of arranging and carrying out the details of the aforesaid evacuation of Puerto Rico and other islands now under Spanish sovereignty in the West Indies.

Article V.

The United States and Spain will each appoint not more than five commissioners to treat of peace, and the commissioners so appointed shall meet at Paris not later than October 1, 1898, and proceed to the negotiation and conclusion of a treaty of peace, which treaty shall be subject to ratification according to the respective constitutional forms of the two countries.

Article VI.

Upon the conclusion and signing of this protocol, hostilities between the two countries

M. JULES CAMBON, THE FRENCH AMBASSADOR, SIGNING THE MEMORANDUM OF RATIFICATION ON BEHALF OF SPAIN

MARINE PARADE, AUGUST 20, IN NEW YORK HARBOR—FIVE BATTLE-SHIPS AND TWO ARMORED CRUISERS IN LINE

DRAWN BY H. REUTERDAHL

shall be suspended, and notice to that effect shall be given as soon as possible by each government to the commanders of its military and naval forces.

Done at Washington in duplicate, in English and in French, by the undersigned, who have hereunto set their hands and seals, the 12th day of August, 1898.

[SEAL] WILLIAM R. DAY

[SEAL] JULES CAMBON

THE TREATY OF PEACE

THE United States of America and Her Majesty the Queen Regent of Spain, in the name of her august son Don Alfonso XIII., desiring to end the state of war now existing between the two countries, have for that purpose appointed as plenipotentiaries:

The President of the United States,

William R. Day, Cushman K. Davis, William P. Frye, George Gray, and Whitelaw Reid, citizens of the United States:

And Her Majesty the Queen Regent of Spain,

Don Eugenio Montero Rios, President of the Senate; Don Buenaventura de Abarzuza, Senator of the Kingdom and ex-Minister of the Crown; Don José de Garnica, Deputy to the Cortes and Associate Justice of the Supreme Court; Don Wenceslao Ramirez de Villa-urrutia, Envoy Extraordinary and Minister Plenipotentiary at Brussels; and Don Rafael Cerero, General of Division;

Who, having assembled in Paris, and having exchanged their full powers, which were found to be in due and proper form, have, after discussion of the matters before them, agreed upon the following articles:

ARTICLE I.

Spain relinquishes all claim of sovereignty over and title to Cuba.

And as the island is, upon its evacuation by Spain, to be occupied by the United States, the United States will, so long as such occupation shall last, assume and discharge the obligations that may under international law result from the fact of its occupation, for the protection of life and property.

ARTICLE II.

Spain cedes to the United States the island of Puerto Rico and other islands now under Spanish sovereignty in the West Indies, and the island of Guam in the Marianas or Ladrones.

ARTICLE III.

Spain cedes to the United States the archipelago known as the Philippine Islands, and comprehending the islands lying within the following line:

A line running from west to east along or near the twentieth parallel of north latitude, and through the middle of the navigable channel of Bachi, from the one hundred and eighteenth (118th) to the one hundred and twenty-seventh (127th) degree meridian of longitude east of Greenwich, thence along the one hundred and twenty-seventh (127th) degree meridian of longitude east of Greenwich to the parallel of four degrees and forty-five minutes (4° 45') north latitude, thence along the parallel of four degrees and forty-five minutes (4° 45') north latitude to its intersection with the meridian of longitude one hundred and nineteen degrees and thirty-five minutes (119° 35') east of Greenwich, thence along the meridian of longitude one hundred and nineteen degrees and thirty-five minutes (119° 35') east of Greenwich to the parallel of latitude seven degrees and forty minutes (7° 40') north, thence along the parallel of latitude of seven degrees and forty minutes (7° 40') north to its intersection with the one hundred and sixteenth (116th) degree meridian of longitude east of Greenwich, thence by a direct line to the intersection of the tenth (10th) degree parallel of north latitude with the one hundred and eighteenth (118th) degree meridian of longitude east of Greenwich, and thence along the one hundred and eighteenth (118th) degree meridian of longitude east of Greenwich to the point of beginning.

The United States will pay to Spain the sum of twenty million dollars ($20,000,000) within three months after the exchange of the ratifications of the present treaty.

ARTICLE IV.

The United States will, for the term of ten years from the date of the exchange of the ratifications of the present treaty, admit Spanish ships and merchandise to the ports of the Philippine Islands on the same terms as ships and merchandise of the United States.

ARTICLE V.

The United States will, upon the signature of the present treaty, send back to Spain, at its own cost, the Spanish soldiers taken as prisoners of war on the capture of Manila by the American forces. The arms of the soldiers in question shall be restored to them.

Spain will, upon the exchange of the ratifications of the present treaty, proceed to evacuate the Philippines, as well as the island of Guam, on terms similar to those agreed upon by the commissioners appointed to arrange for the evacuation of Puerto Rico and other islands in the West Indies, under the Protocol of August 12, 1898, which is to continue in force till its provisions are completely executed.

The time within which the evacuation of the Philippine Islands and Guam shall be completed shall be fixed by the two governments. Stands of colors, uncaptured war vessels, small-arms, guns of all calibers, with their carriages and accessories, powder, ammunition, live-stock, and materials and supplies of all kinds, belonging to the land and naval forces of Spain in the Philippines and Guam, remain the property of Spain. Pieces of heavy ordnance, exclusive of field artillery, in the fortifications and coast defences shall remain in their emplacements for the term of six months, to be reckoned from the exchange of ratifications of the treaty; and the United States may, in the meantime, purchase such material from Spain, if a satisfactory agreement between the two governments on the subject shall be reached.

HON. JOHN HAY, SECRETARY OF STATE, HANDING TO M. JULES CAMBON, THE FRENCH AMBASSADOR, THE $20,000,000 DUE TO SPAIN UNDER THE TREATY OF PEACE, AT THE STATE DEPARTMENT, MAY 1, 1899.—PHOTOGRAPH BY WILBERT MELVILLE

GENERAL MACIAS RECEIVING THE AMERICAN COMMISSIONERS AT THE PALACE, SAN JUAN, PUERTO RICO

DRAWN BY T. DART WALKER

THE JOINT AMERICAN AND SPANISH COMMISSION FOR THE EVACUATION OF CUBA

Article VI.

Spain will, upon the signature of the present treaty, release all prisoners of war, and all persons detained or imprisoned for political offences, in connection with the insurrections in Cuba and the Philippines and the war with the United States.

Reciprocally, the United States will release all persons made prisoners of war by the American forces, and will undertake to obtain the release of all Spanish prisoners in the hands of the insurgents in Cuba and the Philippines.

The Government of the United States will at its own cost return to Spain, and the Government of Spain will at its own cost return to the United States, Cuba, Puerto Rico, and the Philippines, according to the situation of their respective homes, prisoners released or caused to be released by them, respectively, under this article.

Article VII.

The United States and Spain mutually relinquish all claims for indemnity, national and individual, of every kind, of either government, or of its citizens or subjects, against the other government, that may have arisen since the beginning of the late insurrection in Cuba and prior to the exchange of ratifications of the present treaty, including all claims for indemnity for the cost of the war.

The United States will adjudicate and settle the claims of its citizens against Spain relinquished in this article.

Article VIII.

In conformity with the provisions of Articles I., II., and III. of this treaty, Spain relinquishes in Cuba, and cedes in Puerto Rico and other islands in the West Indies, in the island of Guam, and in the Philippine Archipelago, all the buildings, wharves, barracks, forts, structures, public highways, and other immovable property which, in conformity with law, belong to the public domain, and as such belong to the Crown of Spain.

And it is hereby declared that the relinquishment or cession, as the case may be, to which the preceding paragraph refers, cannot in any respect impair the property or rights which by law belong to the peaceful possession of property of all kinds, of provinces, municipalities, public or private establishments, ecclesiastical or civic bodies, or any other associations having legal capacity to acquire and possess property in the aforesaid territories renounced or ceded, or of private individuals, of whatsoever nationality such individuals may be.

The aforesaid relinquishment or cession, as the case may be, includes all documents exclusively referring to the sovereignty relinquished or ceded that may exist in the archives of the Peninsula. Where any document in such archives only in part relates to said sovereignty, a copy of such part will be furnished whenever it shall be requested. Like rules shall be reciprocally observed in favor of Spain in respect of documents in the archives of the islands above referred to.

In the aforesaid relinquishment or cession, as the case may be, are also included such rights as the Crown of Spain and its authorities possess in respect of the official archives and records, executive as well as judicial, in the islands above referred to, which relate to said islands or the rights and property of their inhabitants. Such archives and records shall be carefully preserved, and private persons shall without distinction have the right to require, in accordance with law, authenticated copies of the contracts, wills, and other instruments forming part of notarial protocols or files, or which may be contained in the executive or judicial archives, be the latter in Spain or in the islands aforesaid.

Article IX.

Spanish subjects, natives of the Peninsula, residing in the territory over which Spain by the present treaty relinquishes or cedes her sovereignty, may remain in such territory or may remove therefrom, retaining in either event all their rights of property, including the right to sell or dispose of such property or of its proceeds; and they shall also have the right to carry on their industry, commerce, and professions, being subject in respect thereof to such laws as are applicable to other foreigners. In case they remain in the territory they may preserve their allegiance to the Crown of Spain by making, before a court of record, within a year from the date of the exchange of ratifications of this treaty, a declaration of their decision to preserve such allegiance; in default of which declaration they shall be held to have renounced it and to have adopted the nationality of the territory in which they may reside.

The civil rights and political status of the native inhabitants of the territories hereby ceded to the United States shall be determined by the Congress.

ARTICLE X.

The inhabitants of the territories over which Spain relinquishes or cedes her sovereignty shall be secured in the free exercise of their religion.

ARTICLE XI.

The Spaniards residing in the territories over which Spain by this treaty cedes or relinquishes her sovereignty shall be subject in matters civil as well as criminal to the jurisdiction of the courts of the country wherein they reside, pursuant to the ordinary laws governing the same; and they shall have the right to appear before such courts, and to pursue the same course as citizens of the country to which the courts belong.

ARTICLE XII.

Judicial proceedings pending at the time of the exchange of ratifications of this treaty in the territories over which Spain relinquishes or cedes her sovereignty shall be determined according to the following rules:

1. Judgments rendered either in civil suits between private individuals, or in criminal matters, before the date mentioned, and with respect to which there is no recourse or right of review under the Spanish law, shall be deemed to be final, and shall be executed in due form by competent authority in the territory within which such judgments should be carried out.

2. Civil suits between private individuals which may on the date mentioned be undetermined shall be prosecuted to judgment before the court in which they may then be pending or in the court that may be substituted therefor.

3. Criminal actions pending on the date mentioned before the Supreme Court of Spain

THE EVACUATION OF HAVANA—FAREWELL COURTESIES BETWEEN SPANISH AND AMERICAN OFFICERS IN THE PALACE AS TWELVE O'CLOCK STRUCK.—Drawn by T. Dart Walker

against citizens of the territory which by this treaty ceases to be Spanish shall continue under its jurisdiction until final judgment; but, such judgment having been rendered, the execution thereof shall be committed to the competent authority of the place in which the case arose.

ARTICLE XIII.

The rights of property secured by copyrights and patents acquired by Spaniards in the island of Cuba and in Puerto Rico, the Philippines, and other ceded territories, at the time of the exchange of the ratifications of this treaty, shall continue to be respected. Spanish scientific, literary, and artistic works, not subversive of public order in the territories in question, shall continue to be admitted free of duty into such territories for the period of ten years, to be reckoned from the date of the exchange of the ratifications of this treaty.

ARTICLE XIV.

Spain will have the power to establish consular officers in the ports and places of the territories, the sovereignty over which has been either relinquished or ceded by the present treaty.

ARTICLE XV.

The government of each country will, for the term of ten years, accord to the merchant vessels of the other country the same treatment in respect of all port charges, including entrance and clearance dues, light dues, and tonnage duties, as it accords to its own merchant vessels not engaged in the coastwise trade.

This article may at any time be terminated on six months' notice given by either government to the other.

PEACE JUBILEE AT PHILADELPHIA—LIEUTENANT HOBSON AND THE *MERRIMAC'S* CREW PASSING THROUGH THE COURT OF HONOR.—DRAWN BY T. DART WALKER

PEACE JUBILEE IN CHICAGO—PRESIDENT McKINLEY REVIEWING THE PROCESSION.—Sketch by H. Reuterdahl

Article XVI.

It is understood that any obligations assumed in this treaty by the United States with respect to Cuba are limited to the time of its occupancy thereof; but it will, upon the termination of such occupancy, advise any government established in the island to assume the same obligations.

Article XVII.

The present treaty shall be ratified by the President of the United States, by and with the advice and consent of the Senate thereof, and by her Majesty the Queen Regent of Spain; and the ratifications shall be exchanged at Washington within six months from the date hereof, or earlier if possible.

In faith whereof, we, the respective plenipotentiaries, have signed this treaty and have hereunto affixed our seals.

Done in duplicate at Paris, the tenth day of December, in the year of our Lord one thousand eight hundred and ninety-eight.

[SEAL] William R. Day
[SEAL] Cushman K. Davis
[SEAL] William P. Frye
[SEAL] George Gray
[SEAL] Whitelaw Reid
[SEAL] Eugenio Montero Rios
[SEAL] B. de Abarzuza
[SEAL] J. de Garnica
[SEAL] W. R. de Villaurrutia
[SEAL] Rafael Cerero

RATIFICATION

The message to Congress in which President McKinley said, "In the name of humanity, in the name of civilization, in behalf of endangered American interests, which give us the right and the duty to speak and to act, *the war in Cuba must stop*," was dated April 11, 1898. The American and Spanish ratifications of the treaty of Paris were exchanged at Washington on April 11, 1899. At three o'clock in the afternoon, M. Cambon, accompanied by the first secretary of the French embassy, M. Thiébaut, arrived at the White House. Mr. Hay, Secretary of State, and Mr. Sidney Smith, chief of the Diplomatic Bureau of the State Department, were on hand to receive them, and the party proceeded without delay to the President's office. The various branches of the government were represented, and a few other persons were present by permission. All remained standing while a memorandum, done in duplicate in English and French, was being read. This was a formal statement to the effect that the Secretary of State, authorized by the President, and the French ambassador, "especially authorized for this purpose" by the Queen Regent, met at the White House for the purpose of effecting the exchange of the ratifications of the treaty of peace concluded at Paris, December 10, 1898, compared the original instruments of those ratifications, and then proceeded to their exchange. After the reading of this document the two copies were sealed, and M. Cambon and Mr. Hay affixed their signatures. President McKinley then handed to M. Cambon the American copy of this memorandum, or protocol, together with the copy of the treaty which bore his signature, receiving from the French ambassador the Spanish copy of the memorandum, and that copy of the treaty which Cristina of Austria, Queen Regent of Spain, had signed on March 17. President McKinley then issued the proclamation of peace, in which the full text of the treaty was embodied. "And whereas the said convention has been duly ratified on both parts"—thus the proclamation continued—"and the ratifications were exchanged in the city of Washington on the 11th day of April, 1899: now, therefore, be it known that I, William McKinley, President of the United States of America, have caused the said convention to be made public, to the end that the same and every article thereof may be observed and fulfilled with good faith in the United States and by the citizens thereof."

SPECIAL COMMISSIONER ROBERT P. PORTER ARRANGING WITH GENERAL GOMEZ AT REMEDIOS FOR THE DISBANDMENT OF THE CUBAN ARMY.—Drawn from Life by T. Dart Walker

UNITED STATES WAR-SHIPS IN A BLOW—SQUALLY WEATHER OFF THE CUBAN COAST.—By Carlton T. Chapman

WOMAN'S PART IN THE WAR

GENERAL ACCOUNT

By Clara Bewick Colby

It is often said that the history of the world is the history of its progress. Certain it is that all the way from the primitive contests of savage tribes, which forced woman to be the agriculturist and the artisan, down to our own Civil War, which for the first time placed the women of this country in responsible government positions, every war has broken down barriers which have surrounded woman, made her independent of conventional restrictions, developed her resources, and placed her on a better footing for the further use of her powers. Since time began woman has done her part in standing beside the warrior—although the strife was often against her will—as comrade, adviser, physician, nurse, and succoring ministrant. Woman has always done for her country in the person of its defenders all she has been allowed to do, and a cruel fate she has often considered it which kept her from a more complete expression of her loyalty and courage.

The facilities for recording and reporting the aid which women gave in the war with Spain made so splendid a presentation of it that it was recognized and praised by witnesses before an investigating commission, by officials in their reports, and by the Congress of the United States.

The great lack in the war management was the not sufficiently utilizing the intelligent, trained, patriotic womanhood of the nation. When the Civil War was in progress, women were untrained in working under leadership and ignorant of their own powers. Yet with all this lack of preparation they did a magnificent work.

When the Spanish-American war broke out, there were a million women trained to work in organization, and just as zealous to serve their country as were the men who enlisted to fight its battles. This great force ought to have been recognized and utilized and the whole sanitary and commissary departments placed under their control. Some women of great experience and executive qualities should have had their official position at the War Department, where they could have administered the housekeeping branches of the service, and in every village and hamlet women would have rallied to their support and organized to carry out their commands. It is one of the most pitiful things in all history that American women, with all their equipment for good service, have been forced to be idle or allowed only after the harm had been done to ameliorate suffering that was needless and ought not to have been possible; and the National Council of Women spoke with no uncertain sound on this point, passing a resolution asking the government to consider how it might most largely avail itself of woman's assistance in matters relating to the food, sanitation, nursing, and medical attendance of the army and navy.

The channels through which woman's patriotism was directed to the aid of the government were the American Red Cross, the D.A.R., the Woman's National War Relief Association, the Woman's Relief Corps, numerous other organizations, and individual volunteer effort. The full story can never be told, for it was an outburst of patriotism on the part of women fully commensurate with that of the men who responded to their country's call, knowing it meant self-sacrifice, perhaps to the death.

The Red Cross work included not only that immediately directed by Miss Barton and her associates, but that of the American National Red Cross Committee and its more than two thousand auxiliaries, which sprang up all over the country. The committee had headquarters in New York, distributing-points in various cities, and branches in all the camps in the Southern States. Hospital and supply ships were fitted out. The *Solace* was sent out in May, and several others in June. The yacht *Red Cross* was fitted up as a medical supply-boat and offered to the government. The reason given for its refusal is a good illustration of the technicalities by which military authorities are governed, and which, strictly construed, often prove a rule "how not to do it."

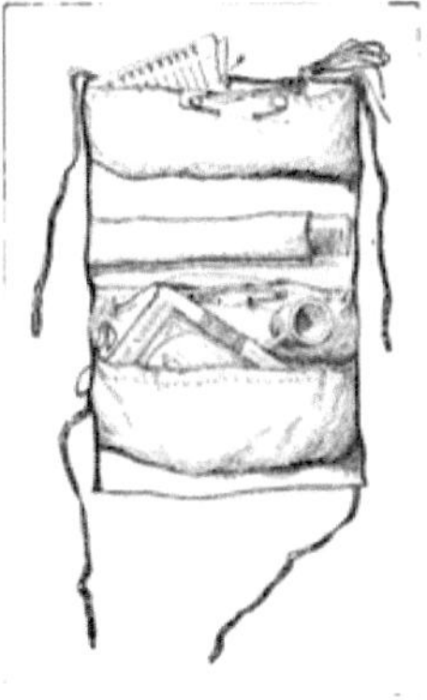

A SOLDIER'S HOUSEWIFE

A government, under the Geneva Constitution, could accept a hospital-ship built and fitted out under its supervision, and to be used for no other purpose. But this boat contained also medical supplies, and this prevented it coming under the rule. Permission for the *Red Cross* to take coal from any naval coaling-station or boat, receipts to be given by the Red Cross representative, and bills to be paid by the committee, was refused, and in various ways the Red Cross was made to feel that its assistance was not desired.

Early in the year Miss Barton had gone to Cuba and worked there with the Red Cross, ameliorating the suffering of the *reconcentrados* until about the time war was declared, when she returned and offered the services of the Red Cross to the government. They were declined with the statement that the government would be abundantly able to provide for the needs of its soldiers. Miss Barton, in the latter part of April, went South in the *Texas*, watching for the first opportunity which would land her in Cuba and put her in a position where she could help the *reconcentrados*, for whose assistance the supplies with which the *Texas* was loaded had been contributed. The opportunity came with the sailing of Sampson's fleet, and Miss Barton landed at Guantanamo shortly after our marines. Reaching Siboney June 26, Dr. Lesser and others of the Red Cross officials immediately went to the hospital of the United States troops, where the wounded and dying lay on the bare floor, many even without a blanket under them, and lacking every comfort. The surgeon in charge, carrying out the policy of the surgeon-general, declined assistance. Not allowed to minister to our own soldiers, they went to General Garcia, who welcomed their aid with tears of gratitude, but begged them to wait a few hours until the hospital could be made fit for them to enter. Miss Barton says graphically: "The Red Cross nurses are not accustomed to wait when there is something that needs to be done to alleviate suffering, and they went to work, scrubbed the floor, washed the patients and put clean night-shirts on them, and before nightfall the place was a little heaven." This hospital was just across from where our own wounded lay suffering, and some of our soldiers, going by, noticed the transformation and began to inquire how it was that the Red Cross gave them the go-by and lavished its attention on the Cubans. Their vigorous protest and the awful exigencies of that fearful period of waiting for government supplies broke through all formalities and led the army surgeons to solicit Red Cross co-operation, which was gladly given. The Red Cross followed the army into Santiago and into other ports as soon as they were opened, remaining in Cuba until November, when the surgeon-general thanked it for its aid and notified it that the government was now abundantly able to care for its sick soldiers.

In Puerto Rico the Red Cross received the most cordial co-operation. General Henry's report, forwarded to the War Department, stated that the Red Cross provided ice until the government supply reached Ponce, erected ten hospital tents, supplied with suitable diet for the whole voyage all transports conveying the sick and convalescent, gave first aid to many injured men, secured medical reports, and daily performed numerous offices of personal kindness for the soldiers.

The work of the Red Cross National War Relief Committee continued from May 9 to December 1, 1898, and covered an outlay of $277,604.28. It is estimated that the total value of gifts for the army from this source alone was over three million dollars, including supplies and transportation. Foremost among all the auxiliaries which helped to make the sum total of this magnificent work was Auxiliary No. 3, which had charge of nurses. This not only cared entirely for the many nurses which were under the Red Cross, and who gave their services without pay, but contributed very largely to the comfort of the government contract nurses. At Sternberg Hospital, in Chickamauga Park, for instance, where Miss Cromlein, a Red Cross nurse, had, after weeks of almost hopeless entreaties and efforts, induced the authorities to place the nursing wholly in charge of women, the Red Cross

ADELAIDE WORTH BAGLEY
Mother of Lieutenant Bagley

Auxiliary had the entire supervision of the nurses, furnished a hall and a special kitchen for them, and, later in their work, lest heart and flesh should fail in their vigils in that fever-stricken camp, paid the expense of little outings on Lookout Mountain for parties of nurses in turn. Red Cross Auxiliary No. 3 not only won the confidence and gratitude of the entire nation, but the thanks of the surgeon-general, who, in a letter, said: "I desire to express my high appreciation of the valuable services rendered to the medical department by this organization."

The Daughters of the American Revolution organized a committee known as the D. A. R. Hospital Corps, which had headquarters in Washington to receive and distribute the contributions of the chapters. Dr. Anita Newcomb McGee, committee director, on April 27 wrote to the Surgeon-General of the War Department and to the Bureau of Medicine and Surgery of the Navy Department offering to furnish trained women nurses. General W. K. Van Reypen, on behalf of the latter, responded with hearty approval. General Sternberg, in his reply, dated April 28, stated that no trained nurses were needed at present, and he did not intend to send any women with the troops to Cuba. He expected, he wrote, to rely principally on trained men in the hospital corps for service in the wards. It is quite probable that the offer of the D. A. R. determined the surgeon-general to employ women nurses, as in a subsequent letter reviewing the matter he says that on April 28 he applied to Congress for authority to employ, by contract, at the rate of thirty dollars a month, as many women nurses as might be required, since he foresaw the necessity for a large force of trained nurses. To use his own language: "The want of a sufficient body of trained hospital-corps men necessitated the detail of enlisted men from the regiments for hospital duty in several of the camps and the employment of trained nurses at the general hospital."

Over 1700 women nurses were employed during the war with Spain, of which number about 1000 were contracted for through the D. A. R. Hospital Corps; the others were unpaid volunteers, either individually taking up the work or going under the Red Cross Auxiliary or the sisterhoods.

According to the statement of Mrs. Daniel Manney, President-General of the D. A. R.: "During the five months of the existence of the Hospital Corps, 5821 sets of pajamas, 1027 shirts, 3233 pillow-cases, 3436 towels, 6401 handkerchiefs, 11,432 flannel bands, 360 sets of underwear, 1718 pairs of slippers, and 993 pairs of hose, in all 45,349 garments, have been distributed, together with tons of food supplies and medical supplies of various sorts, from 197 chapters in the United States. The smaller gifts were accompanied by as much self-sacrifice and actuated by as pure patriotism as the larger ones. The money sent by the various chapters was $3,320.79."

Much State and local chapter work was done direct. For instance, the New York City Chapter contributed to Camp Wikoff and the Brooklyn hospitals and aided in relief of New York soldiers in the various camps, besides giving $850 to the Red Cross work. The Connecticut Chapter sent to hospitals fifty-two consignments of goods, each consisting of from six to twelve packing-cases, and in the purchase of clothing and food they expended over $1000. The Chicago Chapter made over two thousand garments. Philadelphia threw open its hospitals to sick soldiers and brought all their sick men from the various camps in thoroughly equipped hospital trains. At one time they had over three thousand sick soldiers in their hospitals, volunteer women aiding in their care. The Mary Washington Chapter of the District of Columbia took up the task of caring for the families of the District Volunteers, who were not paid for more than three months. Many of them had enlisted because they had been long out of work and their families, "a class of persons whom it was a privilege and pleasure to help," would have suffered but for this timely aid.

On no city was there such long-continued demand for sympathy and aid as the presence in its vicinity of between 40,000 and 50,000 soldiers made on Chattanooga; and nobly the women rose to the occasion. The Northern boys will especially have tender memories of the loving ministration of Southern women, to whom mainly came the opportunity of succoring the camps and of caring for the needs of soldiers; and if Southern women had been the bitterest opponents in the Civil War by reason of their fierce espousal of the cause that stood to them for home and country, by their patriotic and tender care of the boys in blue during the war with Spain they cemented forever the ties which now bind all sections of our country.

SALLIE C. HOBSON
Mother of Lieutenant Hobson

ANNIE EVANS BLUE
Mother of Lieutenant Blue

The Chattanooga Chapter held a meeting in June to receive reports of members who had been investigating the needs of the camp. One stated that a surgeon had said: "You ladies can do nothing. We need everything before our government supplies come. We need cots; we have typhoid patients on the ground. We need fifty blankets before night for the soldiers sick with pneumonia." Before night all these needs were supplied by this little band, and with the same energy the committee appointed for mid-summer work kept up its efforts during the season. A circular was sent out asking assistance from those States which had troops at Camp Thomas, and it was suggested that the responses be forwarded to Dr. I. W. Trimble, president of the relief commission. Each morning the relief wagon went out carrying supplies to Dr. Trimble at the distribution depot at the camp. Here the surgeons in charge of the tent hospitals sent their requisitions, and as far as possible all the demands were filled. This chapter donated nearly $2000 in money for milk, butter, ice, and other things that had to be purchased, besides sending out a large number of miscellaneous supplies.

All organizations of women worked in unison. The W.C.T.U. kept a "Soldiers' Rest." The Young People's Baptist Union and the Epworth League each maintained free hospitals. Citizens cared for soldiers in their homes, and when troops marched the long distance from Chickamauga Park to Lookout Mountain, unable to stop to eat by the way,

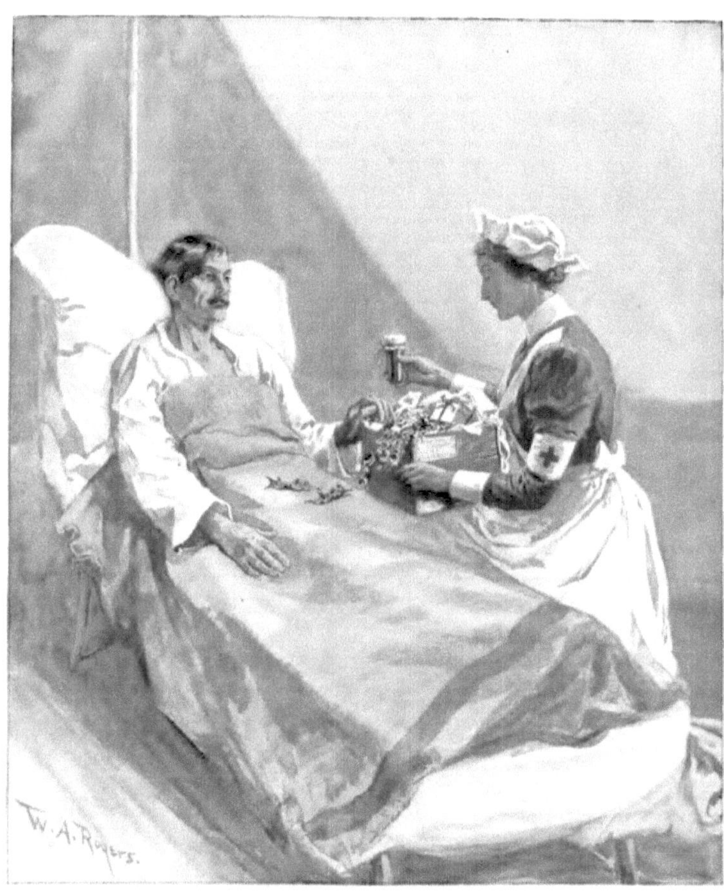

A BOX FROM HOME.—Drawn by W. A. Rogers

women would come out of their doors and hand a glass of milk, an apple, or a sandwich to each soldier, receiving in return thanks that were a benediction. Surely "the cup of cold water" brought its reward to the giver in a consciousness of being in some measure a co-worker for their country.

In several Southern cities—notably in Atlanta, Knoxville, Nashville, and Chattanooga—the young ladies formed Girls' Relief Societies, raising funds in a hundred ways to help the work.

The Woman Suffrage Associations in various places directed their efforts during the summer mainly to relief work. This was especially notable in Iowa. In the county of the State president, Mrs. Ballard, eight per cent. of the voters were at Chickamauga. A letter was sent out to the clubs in every county urging that they take the initiative in the patriotic work of ministering to the needs of the soldiers. They responded heartily, and liberal donations from all sides were sent in under the banner of equal rights. The cottage belonging to the State Association was made Chaplain's headquarters and post-office at Camp McKinley, and there the boys wrote their letters and read the magazines with the mother faces of Lucy Stone and Mrs. Stanton beaming down upon them.

The National Society of New England Women, under the presidency of Mrs. Slade, was represented on the board of the New York Soldiers' and Sailors' Families Protective Association by six members. One hundred and fifty families were cared for by the women, the men furnishing the rentals. A cottage was maintained at Lake Mohegan all summer, where wives and children of soldiers were given an outing. Each of the twenty-five members of the executive committee undertook to give personal care to twenty families. With these were also united the Women's War Relief Commission and the Women's Patriotic League.

The Women's National War Relief Association was incorporated at Albany May 31, with Mrs. U. S. Grant, president; Mrs. Ellen Hardin Walworth, director-general; Helen Miller Gould, assistant director. Its object, as stated, was to give expression in a practical way to the patriotic sentiments of the

MISS CLARA BARTON

women of the nation by finding means to supplement with material aid the sacrifices of time, strength, and life made by the men of the nation in the war. Large numbers of auxiliaries formed and volunteered assistance with money and supplies. This association fitted out the ships *Relief* and *Solar* with carbonating plants, electric fans, food, and medicine. It sustained Mrs. Walworth in her work at Fortress Monroe, where she was ready to care for the sick and wounded as soon as they returned from Santiago. Special food for sick and convalescent was prepared at a cost of $100 a week, and eighteen trained cooks were kept here three months by the association. A steam-launch was fitted out at a cost of $1600 as a yellow-fever hospital near Santiago. Nearly two thousand men were placed in county hospitals and in homes for special care, and of each of these cases a careful record was sent to the War Department. In such work, including that at Montauk Point, the association expended $46,479.58.

The International Brotherhood League, Mrs. Katherine A. Tingley, president, conceiving that practical patriotism was in the line of its spiritual philosophy, issued a "war relief call" early in August, which was liberally responded to, and this body assumed the duty of providing nurses for Montauk Point.

The Soldiers' Rests must not be forgotten. They furnished a cool, pleasant resort for the soldier where he could find stationery and a comfortable place to write, something to read, ice-water, the acceptable fruit, nourishing food, and often—alas for the necessity!—the special care which was required to sober up the man for whom the city temptations had been too strong, thus enabling him to return to camp without arrest and disgrace and with the strongest incentive to keep straight thereafter, that he might show the women that their confidence had not been misplaced. At Chattanooga the women not only welcomed those who came to them, but when sick soldiers were sent in from Camp Thomas, as they were until the latter part of August, without food, transportation, or furloughs, to lie in the depot until those things should be furnished, sometimes during a delay of thirty hours, they went *en masse*, carrying pillows and everything for the men's comfort, and fed and nursed them until arrangements were completed for their departure. In the Washington Rest there was the special feature of a "woman doctor," one of the best physicians in the city, who gave part of every day to caring for the ailments of those who visited the Rest. The soldiers had all been vaccinated, and many a sore arm did this physician dress, bringing comfort and relief. In the cities near camps where these Rests were established there was no lack of flowers, supplies, and assistance. Women who could help in no other way spent a portion of their time there as a reception committee, making the one bit of home atmosphere that the boys had in their long summer of enforced waiting. Many were the letters of gratitude that came from mothers far away for the care of their loved ones, and many a link was welded in the chain that binds humanity into a brotherhood, the only basis on which the conception of the fatherhood of God is possible.

While every woman who assisted the organized effort felt grateful for the privilege of having been as a grain of sand in the mortar that made solid the wall of patriotism which stood for the nation's honor and the freedom of the oppressed, especially fortunate were some in being able to render conspicuous service.

Miss Helen Miller Gould followed up a large donation to the government at the outset of the war by unremitting personal work. At Montauk Point she gathered up the sick soldiers that were without friends and sent them to convalesce at her beautiful home on the Hudson, which she fitted up as a hospital. But the greatest of her many benefactions was that of which least has been told. When the soldiers at Montauk Point were mustered out or furloughed they usually went direct to New York, where they often fell victims to the snares of the metropolis and were soon penniless in some low lodging-house. Miss Gould, learning these facts, hired the Salvation Army headquarters and fitted them up as a hotel, where all soldiers were kept without charge. The Salvation Army people were placed in charge; agents were placed on all the trains running to the city from Montauk Point to notify the soldier where a good bed and wholesome food awaited him. The police were requested to take all drunken soldiers and sailors to "Fort Gould," as they called it, rather than to the police-station. The hospitality was accepted by hundreds, and when the soldier was ready to leave, if he had no money, his railroad ticket was purchased for him. And not only this, but headquarters were opened for the assistance of all who wished to find employment.

Miss Jeannette Jennings, a Washington correspondent of the *New York Tribune*, went to Cuba as a Red Cross volunteer nurse on the *Texas*, and when the *Seneca* was about to leave Siboney with a hundred sick and wounded soldiers on board without a nurse to care for them, Miss Jennings prevailed on the captain to disregard his orders and delay sailing long enough for her to go back to the *Texas* for some necessary supplies and then take her with him. The ministrations of Miss Jennings were the only bright feature of the voyage in that crowded, filthy boat, which lacked every comfort save that which she had been able to supply. For weary days and nights she nursed the fever-stricken patients and helped them to feel that God had not forgotten them, since a woman was there to soothe and aid.

When General Wheeler announced his determination to go to the war, his daughter Anna applied to the War Department for a commission as nurse, but was notified that none but trained nurses were accepted. Nothing daunted, she managed to be enrolled with the Red Cross nurses. Her youth, beauty, and social position made conspicuous the service which was gladly performed by a thousand others. Of her five months' hard work she said, in an interview, that for the first time she knew what it was to be perfectly satisfied. Her work engrossed every thought; she was never tired or conscious of heat or discomfort, being so profoundly possessed by a sense of the need there was of help and joy that she could give it.

Miss Delia Weeks, of Des Moines, had had ten years' experience as a nurse, and many of the soldiers who were gathering in that city for their journey to San Francisco were personally known to her. She determined to accompany them, and her application to the authorities at Washington for a commission as nurse was signed by the Governor of Iowa and many leading citizens and physicians in Des Moines. When, after much delay, it came back unsigned the day the troops left for the coast, the city of Des Moines took the matter up, raised $500 in twelve hours, and sent Miss Weeks off the next day. The Iowa volunteers received her royally at Camp Merritt; and they were thereafter the envied of all the other regiments, for Miss Weeks was the only woman nurse in the camp for a long time. When the troops went to Manila she accompanied them. She was joined later by others; about thirty women cared for the United States troops in the Philippines.

But, as Governor Wolcott, of Massachusetts, said, in a tribute to the relief work done by women: "It is not alone these women, it is the thousands of women in every city and town, who by work, by thought, and by prayer aided and encouraged the soldiers at the front." How cold and inadequate must be any review of the work which represents the toils, the tears, and the sacred joys of the women of the nation.

With all this duplication of machinery and lack of centralization it is wonderful that there

MRS. JOHN A. LOGAN

was so little waste of resources; that each effort should seem to fit into its right place. The lesson of it all was that there should be a national relief association recognized by the government and responsible to it, which should in peace and war be the nation's arm of beneficence. The Red Cross, with its new achievements and home triumphs, and the expressed intention of the Executive to invite the auxiliaries to become a part of the national body, might thus unite the people of America for concentrated action, and, while giving full scope to the brain and heart of woman, might coordinate the work of all citizens to the great purposes of patriotism in its widest sense.

WOMAN AND THE WAR

By Mrs. John A. Logan

Women from time immemorial have shared in the joys and sorrows of mankind. In all ages the gentler sex have borne their part of the burdens of life. Loyal to the stronger sex, they have followed their fate, whether in war or in peace. In all wars American women have been foremost in sacrifice and potent service for their country. The heroines of the Revolution have been as much revered as the greatest heroes of that immortal strife for liberty; "1812," the war with Mexico, and the rebellion of 1861 had their heroines, whose courage and endurance of hardships at home, in the hospitals, and on the field rivalled that of the "Joans" of other ages.

In the years of sweet peace since Appomattox, American women, North and South, had been busy binding up the wounds, effacing the scars, and smoothing the pathway of progress and unity. They had wrought incessantly in all the fields of civilization. They had trampled down prejudice and ignorance, and had kept abreast with the advancement of the times. Christianity, education, and philanthropy had occupied them constantly, whetting to the keenest edge their finer sensibilities; a wail of anguish from any source had received a prompt response. Local and national calamities had enlisted their indefatigable efforts for relief.

Following upon the appeal of the Armenians for help came the reports of the desperate suffering and persecution of the *reconcentrados* in Cuba, day by day their condition becoming more appalling, until all Christian people were horrified at the ghastly pictures presented by the press. Miss Clara Barton, as the chief executive of the Red Cross, applied for permission to visit the afflicted isle with relief for those who were in need of succor. After much delay, General Blanco granted her the privilege of succoring them — his permit, of course, including Spanish soldiers and subjects alike. Humanitarians from all over the country offered money and services to Miss Barton to be used in the prosecution of her work.

Undaunted by the shocking conditions and the insincerity of Spanish officials through whom she had to operate, she accomplished wonders and rescued many lives; but as horrors multiplied with each receding day, she was forced to lay the facts before the government. Public sympathy becoming universal, Congress was at last aroused, and, at the solicitation of a metropolitan journal, distinguished Senators and Representatives, accompanied by their wives, made a visit to Cuba. Beyond question, the appeal of Mrs. Thurston, reiterated by her husband on the floor of the United States Senate in obedience to her dying injunction, did more to touch the heart of the whole nation than anything that had hitherto been uttered.

From that hour women all over the land began earnest systematic efforts for the suffering Cubans. When eventually war was declared in humanity's name, women from Maine to California, and from the Lakes to the Gulf of Mexico, joined in the patriotic work of sending husbands, sons, and brothers to the front, while they offered their services as volunteers for any duty they might do inside or outside the hospital corps.

MISS ANNA WHEELER

Those with means at their command vied with the rich men of the nation in their generous tender of money to the government, to be used as deemed best by those at the head of affairs. From Miss Helen Gould's one-hundred-thousand-dollar check down to the widow's mite, money and everything else was given freely to the government, the Surgeon-General's Department, and to the various patriotic societies for war relief. The Red Cross Society, under Miss Clara Barton's leadership, bonded the *State of Texas*, which lay in the harbor of Tampa Bay many days awaiting the sailing of the expedition to Cuba, determined to accompany that expedition, though then ignored by the Surgeon-General's Department. She was the first to enter Santiago Harbor with unlimited supplies for suffering sailors, soldiers, Spaniards, and Cubans, which were distributed at the critical moment to save many lives. The fearlessness of Miss Barton and her efficient corps in venturing into fever-stricken districts with medicines and stores for all classes and conditions has no parallel in history. Testimonials continually given by the beneficiaries of the Red Cross, through her provident, intelligent, and far-seeing executive ability, can no more be expunged from the records of the American-Spanish war than can the heroic work in the war of 1861–65 and that of the Franco-Prussian war of 1870–71.

At every camp in the United States where troops were being mobilized women could be seen daily in their visits of ministration to the soldiers. Every hospital in the land was the recipient of bounties, the result of women's work. It is not too much to say that the women of the nation furnished a large percentage of the hospital supplies, and that, too, after making a hard fight to be allowed to do so, after becoming impatient at the tardy and incomplete provision by the government for the rapidly multiplying patients. Days and weeks were spent in importuning the authorities for admission before the indispensable trained female nurses or saintly Sisters of Mercy and Charity were allowed in the hospitals. The inadequate corps of nurses of the regular army of twenty-five thousand men were deemed sufficient in the face of the increase to two hundred thousand, including the volunteer regiments, not one of which brought a man fitted or desiring to be detailed in the hospital service, and this with a register of thousands of names of efficient, eligible women impatient to enlist for any field.

Finally, the department, because of the alarming fatalities and a threatened epidemic of typhoid and other fevers, yielded, and placed in the hands of the executive committee of the Daughters of the American Revolution the power to appoint trained nurses in the various army hospitals. In the meantime, fortunately for the sailors and soldiers of the nation, through the Red Cross Society and in the private and public hospitals of the cities, many of our sick and wounded were receiving the best of care and the benefit of modern appliances and methods of treating medical and surgical patients. Women — God bless them! — from the highest to the lowest walks of life, were everywhere busy with their labors of love and mercy. Hospital-ships shared in the contributions of women and societies of women. Mrs. L. Z. Leiter's munificent gift of a hospital at Chickamauga was the greatest boon to the army stationed on that historical ground.

And not alone were the nation's defenders the objects of their humanity and tenderness. Their families came in for a large share on the score of their dependence upon those who had gone in the service of their country.

Scarcely had the sound of Dewey's guns died away, when women from every part of the country begged to be allowed to go to the Philippines to nurse the sick of his command. They were willing to enter the service, though they knew they must serve within range of the frowning forts of Manila. Neither cannon-balls, disease, nor distance had any terrors for these noble women. They only knew our men were there and might need their tender care, and they begged to go. Failing to secure permission, the women of San Francisco organized a war relief and sent out tons of supplies with the troops who went to Dewey's relief.

Wealth and position served as an inspiration to many of the fairest in the land. Fewer graced the social functions at summer resorts, many preferring the daily drudgery of the work they felt called to do for their country's defenders. The organization of the National War Relief in New York brought to the front some of the ablest, most influential, and wealthy women of the whole country. Mrs. Ellen Hardin Walworth, as president, assumed charge of the distributions at Fortress Monroe, establishing the diet-kitchen at that post, greatly relieving the sick, and reforming hospital provisions. Later she took charge of the distribution at Montauk Point, where, assisted by Mrs. Washington A. Roebling and Miss Helen Gould, she contributed largely to the comfort of the army landed there from Cuba.

The writer was at Montauk Point, awaiting the return of a loved one, soon after its occupation as a resort for the recuperation of our fever-stricken army. When the first hospital tents were erected and the first patients received, the Red Cross Society, under the direction of Mr. Howard Townsend and his able corps of male and female assistants, made its appearance with abundant supplies simultaneously with the government, and was established beside the distribution-tent at the general hospital. It secured the first trained nurses and provided for their accommodation. Under the inimitable direction of Miss Quintard, these nurses worked heroically, later ably assisted by the Catholic Sisters, all of whom slept in tents, caught their meals when they could, and nursed, night and day, the hundreds of desperately sick men, who but for these faithful, skilful nurses would soon have slept the sleep that knows no waking. Others, notably Mrs. Mott, wife of a well-known physician of East Hampton, Long Island, spent every day after the arrival of the first transport handing milk, sandwiches, and other refreshments to the men debarking from the transports, so ill that they would have fallen but for Mrs. Mott's timely thoughtfulness. Again she would, with others, drive through the camps distributing to the sick there. Mrs. Livingston Mason came with a yacht well equipped with all the appliances—nurses, physicians, and supplies—for the treatment of very sick men, and took them to Newport to nurse them back to health. Mrs. Scheppe, Mrs. Carroll, and others of the Patriotic League of New York, were tireless in their labors and generosity.

Innumerable names could be given of individual women who devoted their whole time to such patriotic work during our war with Spain. One family, however, it would be ungracious not to mention. General Joseph Wheeler was among the very first to offer his services to the President, and, though beyond his threescore years, was allowed as eligible to military service. He was so persistent that the President commissioned and assigned him to an important command. One son accompanied him as a member of his staff. He had four lovely young daughters. Anna insisted upon going, and succeeded in getting into the hospital service with Miss Clara Barton. The other three—one a school-girl—did what they could in the local efforts for the soldiers near their home. The moment their father and sister Anna reached Montauk, they came to visit them and to join in the hospital work, all three going into the detention-camp hospital, where they were exposed hourly to whatever of contagion there might be. No regular soldier was more punctual at his post than were these lovable girls day after day. Finally, the youngest son, a cadet at Annapolis, arrived, not having seen his father or sisters for months. The tenderness with which he was greeted by his doting father and sisters was beautiful, but they would not leave their self-imposed duty to the suffering and dying soldiers to go to some resort to spend the holidays. Fond of the sea, the dear boy lost his life while bathing in the surf of the treacherous ocean beach at Montauk.

SISTER BETTINA (MRS. A. M. LESSER)

Overwhelmed by this cruel blow, they laid down their work to follow the remains of their idolized boy to his last resting-place beside their mother, who died some years ago. Who can estimate the good those four girls did, or the anguish of their patriotic hearts?

Misfortunes, sickness, and death touch the hearts of women; but to say that women are governed altogether by their emotions is most unjust. Intuition, tact, and good judgment enable them to accomplish much more than men with the same amount of money. They have no contempt for small things, and will spend hours in attending to details and the study of economy in small things that aggregate large savings which would be overlooked by men. They have no hesitancy to do what a man would consider undignified, and would delegate to subordinates. The product of Miss Willard's diet-kitchens at Camp Wikoff probably did as much towards the restoration of the invalids as the medicines administered by the physicians. The wives of army officers, conspicuously Mrs. Johnson, Mrs. Tate, Mrs. Guilfoyle, and others, who hurried to Montauk to greet their husbands on their arrival at Camp Wikoff, soon joined the patriotic women they found engaged in relieving the suffering; and they proved efficient recruits, because most of them had had experience in camp life and knew what to do. To estimate the good result of woman's work would require volumes instead of columns. We had reason to be proud that women's part in the war with Spain was for good and not for evil. Had some bright woman been chosen as special ambassador to Spain, I have no doubt that she could have so ably seconded General Woodford's efforts for peace that the Queen Regent might have been influenced to accept some of the peace propositions that were made. One woman can approach another more effectively when the fate of a child is at stake, because of the sympathy of motherhood, which is the same in mothers no matter what their race or station in life. The most loyal women in America could not but sympathize with the Queen Regent of Spain, who, uninfluenced by ambitious men, would perhaps have secured to Cuba life, protection, and the pursuit of prosperity and happiness, thereby averting war and saving for her son the territory now lost to him forever.

THE STATUS OF THE RED CROSS

By Clara Barton

At the time of the outbreak of the Three Years' War in Cuba, some forty governments in all were bound together by the compact known as the Red Cross, or the International Convention of Geneva of 1864.

The one word *neutral* signifies the whole essence of this treaty: it defines the condition of all sick and wounded soldiers, all surgeons, nurses, and attendants, all hospitals, ambulances, and other appliances while they display the Red Cross arm-badge or flag duly authorized and inscribed by the military power of the army to which they are attached; and, furthermore, all inhabitants of a country in the vicinity of where a battle is raging, as well as their buildings, are sacredly regarded as neutral while they are administering to the wants of the wounded and disabled, or being employed for hospital purposes.

Wounded soldiers falling into the enemy's hands are *neutral*, and *must* be sent to the frontier for delivery to their own army as soon as possible, provided, of course, that the country to which they belong is an adherent to the Red Cross treaty.

The reason why Japan at this time was doing such effective and commendable work as a humanitarian nation was apparent. She was carrying out to the letter the spirit and the obligations of the Geneva Red Cross Treaty, to which she gave her adhesion in 1886, while her Emperor was standing at the head of her civil Red Cross Society.

In six great wars the Red Cross had been conspicuous. Written history records the beneficent work it had done, but only unwritten history can relate the prevention of untold misery and suffering on every field.

Japan, as a Red Cross nation, met difficulties and dangers unknown in any former war where the Red Cross had worked, from the fact that her enemy, China, was not a nation signatory to the Treaty of Geneva; hence humanity was shown on one side in the treatment of sick and wounded, while inhumanity ran riot on the other.

Great injustice was done to the Red Cross internationally and to Japan by the sensational announcement in newspaper reports to the effect that Japan had refused the Red Cross—had turned it back at Port Arthur.

The facts were as follows: A number of humane and worthy gentlemen—Americans, Englishmen, Germans, and citizens of other nations, clergymen, physicians, and government officials residing in China—formed a Red Cross Society and obtained the sanction of Li Hung Chang to go to the relief of the Chinese wounded. They procured the steamship *Tosmen*, entered Port Arthur, announced themselves as belonging to a private Red Cross Society, and asked the Japanese commandant for the Chinese wounded, for the purpose of taking them back to Tien-Tsin, whence the steamer had come. The duty of the Japanese commandant was plain. China was not a party to the Red Cross treaty, consequently the Tien-Tsin Red Cross Society, however praiseworthy its object, had no governmental identity or authorized existence. While its intentions were noble and laudable, it was unfortunately irresponsible, from the fact that it had no government to become responsible for and to authorize its action.

REFUGEES AT EL CANEY WAITING FOR A DISTRIBUTION OF FOOD BY THE RED CROSS.—FROM A PHOTOGRAPH BY JAMES BURTON

The society was courteously received, and its good intentions acknowledged and appreciated, but its request was properly declined, and it was requested to leave the harbor. The Chinese wounded in the hands of the Japanese were prisoners of war, and while they were receiving merciful treatment in the Japanese Red Cross hospitals, there was no authority for delivering them to a private society, even though it had come with the countenance and sanction of consuls of neutral nations. The national responsibility that attaches to a member of the treaty was entirely absent.

Had China's civilization reached the point where she could appreciate and recognize the humanity of the Red Cross and had she joined the treaty, her wounded, as soon as they were in a condition to be removed, would have been delivered to her by the Japanese.

The above incident is thus specifically dealt with in order to explain the difficulties in the way of correct judgment on the action of the Red Cross. The public and press generally referred to it as an ordinary charitable society for good works, free to make its own conditions, and to follow the judgment of its own private officials, like societies in general; forgetting, or rather never knowing, the fact that it was a treaty, bound by stringent and delicate laws, the disregard of which would impair its validity as materially as any other treaty, and consequently it was not the will or desires of individuals that must control or become responsible for its actions, but the law of nations, framed and confirmed by the highest authorities of the countries of the world.

When this fact became better known or more fully realized the reports of our well-intentioned press were less misleading, more reliable, instructive, and satisfactory.

THE RED CROSS BEFORE SANTIAGO

SIBONEY was parching under the rays of the late June sun. In the improvised hospital seventy sick soldiers were lying. They lay on the floor, because there were no beds; in the clothes which they wore when they fell from exhaustion and weakness, because there were no night-clothes; and they ate army rations or none at all, because there were no hospital supplies. The building of five bare rooms where they were quartered was ramshackle, leaky, filthy, and infected with the multiform insect life of that clime. Any day the fighting might begin at the front, where the American army lay on its arms, ten miles away. That meant that there would be many wounded to add to the sick. What was to be done with them nobody knew.

Out in the bay the *State of Texas*, laden with Red Cross supplies, rode at anchor. A force of her nurses had come to the hospital, offering their services, only to have them promptly declined. The fiction had been promulgated at Washington that the surgical department of the army was thoroughly equipped; that it wanted nothing; that any organization tendering its services would simply put itself in the position of a meddler. The Red Cross people had been made to understand this, so the nurses went on to the Cuban hospital, where the sick had no official fictions to live up to and knew when they were badly off. Such was the condition of affairs when the American hospital was visited by a woman who had come to Cuba to help American soldiers, and who proposed to do it despite obstacles. Dr. Harvard, the surgeon in charge, saw her standing in the doorway, a slender woman of early middle age, with an eager, kindly, resolute face. It was Miss Jeanette Jennings, afterwards known as the heroine of the *Seneca's* terrible trip from Cuba with one hundred wounded soldiers and no hospital appliances or supplies. She asked Dr. Harvard why the offers of the Red Cross nurses had been refused. When she afterwards spoke of what followed Miss Jennings smiled.

"I asked him if the condition of affairs in the hospital was such as he would wish to be reported at home. I talked a great deal. Most women do when they are stirred up, and I was stirred up. After a long time I think it was the first chance he had—he said it was his assistant who had done the declining, and that he was ready to accept the proffered services."

Shortly after, Surgeon-Major Lagarde had come in from the front, and having observed the condition of affairs, promptly sent a formal request to Miss Clara Barton, in charge of the *State of Texas*, for the services of all her nurses. Within an hour the force was at work upon a building near the hospital selected for the purpose, cleaned it out thoroughly, put up cots fitted out with clean bedding, flew the Red Cross flag over it, and transferred the sick to the new quarters. The old hospital was not used thereafter, and eventually was included in the purifying flames that were set to sweep the town after yellow-fever had broken out.

None too soon were the arrangements made, for on Friday, July 1, the wounded began to come in from the front. Across the roadway

THE *RELIEF*.—WARD NUMBER ONE—FORE UPPER DECK

from the new hospital was a row of deserted tents, of which the flooring was hay. Blankets thrown over this hay furnished the beds for the wounded. One tent was used for the operations, and in this three of the trained nurses worked for twenty-four hours without intermission, during which time the wounds of four hundred and seventy-five men were dressed. The sufferers bore the weary waiting for treatment and the tortures of the knife alike with uncomplaining courage.

All the next day and night the wounded came trailing in, some on foot, dragging themselves step by step, others supported by comrades who themselves were perhaps only less severely hurt, but by far the greatest number in the jolting army wagons, which ran back and forth unceasingly from the front to Siboney, making their constant grim additions to the population of the hospital hamlet. A wagon-load was ten or a dozen men, who, as they were lifted out, lay in line, waiting each his turn with the surgeons, whether it was a leg to be amputated, or only a weakening flesh wound to be bound up before the soldier could go back into the hail of bullets. The desperate cases were kept in the field hospital, while those who could be moved were sent to Siboney.

At the front there was a desperate dearth of supplies, relieved only when General Shafter sent an authorization to Miss Barton to seize any vehicles of whatever kind in which to send necessaries for the wounded to the front. Major Legarde, who delivered the authorization, said: "God knows what we should have done without the Red Cross! We have nothing. We are helpless. Supplies were sent on here for the army, they say. If they were they are packed away in the hold of some ship, and nobody knows where they are. They might as well be back in Washington."

Whatever could be spared was sent forward to equip the emergency hospital, but the pressure in Siboney was growing all the time, as many cases treated at the front were despatched to the hospital, nearly twelve miles away, over the weariest road that ever misery limped upon. Many fell by the way and were picked up fainting by the wagons. Some few wandered in delirium from the fairway into the fields and fell in the rank grass. Perhaps some comrade passing in the road would catch a glimpse of a uniform as the grass waved, and drag the body out for burial; perhaps no human eye saw the man more. But the vultures and the land-crabs are keener of sight, and where the discovery was theirs the body must go to an unnamed sepulture.

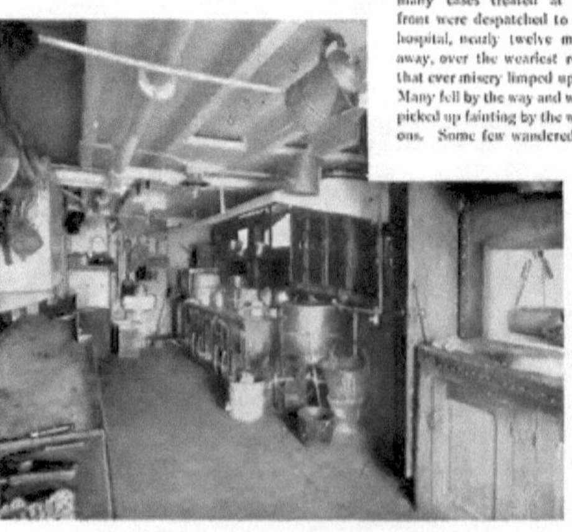

THE GALLEY OF THE *RELIEF*

These crabs were the terror of the nurses. They are a singularly repulsive reptile, often beautiful of hue, but invariably hideous in shape and ridiculously unwieldy in movement —which is not to say that they cannot move undesirably fast when they wish. Their passage across a wooden floor—and they are very partial to wooden floors—produces an amount of racket entirely disproportionate to the cause. They made sleep unpleasant for the wounded lying on the straw by insisting on sharing their warm blankets. One night, when Miss Jennings was on duty in the Red Cross hospital, the place was invaded by a gigantic specimen, which hoisted itself up on the step, waddled across the floor, and, to the extreme horror of the nurse, appeared to menace her with waving claws. To call for help would have been to wake the entire room, so she was fain to stand and tremble, until a soldier passing the door saw her signals of distress in the glaringly bright moonlight and came to her assistance. With a broom he chased the reptile under a cot, where it fixed itself and could not be moved. The remainder of that night was a period of misery for Miss Jennings. The big raw-necked vultures that hung about the place were not popular with the Americans, but they were not dreaded as were their fellow-scavengers the crabs.

Meantime life in Siboney was not all hospital life by any means. Far and wide it had become known that the "Americanos" were feeding all good Cubans, and it was surprising what a number of good Cubans materialized from an apparently deserted country-side every morning at the hour of apportionment. Signs of famine were not prevalent, unless enormous appetites can be regarded in that light. Hundreds of refugees of all ages, in all varieties of picturesque disarray, would collect within the roped space to wait for Uncle Sam's bacon and hardtack, and, having received it, would vanish

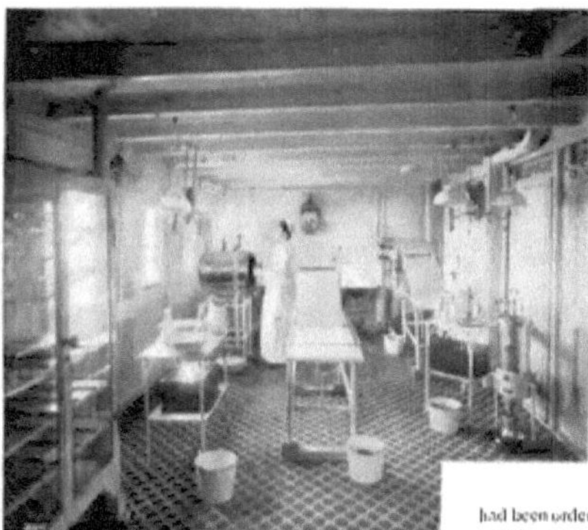

THE OPERATING-ROOM OF THE *RELIEF*

into the chaparral. These people camped in the surrounding country, and got along pretty comfortably on what was given to them, eked out with what they could procure from nature. A wandering American came upon a refugee family camping in a shaded spot near where a stream plunged over a miniature precipice to form a deep pool, whence the Cubans took fish with hook and line. Farther up the stream were other camps, and this form of gypsy life looked to the American to be far from unattractive. With the coming of the rains, however, there was a general scuttling for the town. Great was the wretchedness that the rains brought to the hospital sufferers, particularly the wounded who had to sleep on the ground; for their straw was wet through every day, and the miasmatic vapor that rose after each furious rain-burst sickened and poisoned them into the lassitude that is its peculiar effect.

There came a day when they brought Brewer, the post-office clerk, in from the front, where he had been wearing himself out carrying and tending the wounded. It was fever, but a fever different from that which had been filling the cots. In two days everybody in Siboney knew that Yellow Jack had come. Brewer made a gallant fight against the fever; but he had wasted himself in overwork, and so he died, having done something more than his duty. The same courage that had inspired them to face Spanish bullets was with the soldiers now that they lay helpless to the scourge. There was none of that panic that spreads and makes tenfold more deadly an epidemic. It spread, but not swiftly, nor was it a virulent type of the disease. Most of the buildings in the town were burned down, and sanitary measures which would have been regarded as almost a waste of time a week earlier were minutely enforced. A plague-camp, no matter how mild the disease, is the grewsomest place where men are gathered together; yet, when her duty called Miss Jennings away, it was to a harder trial than any she had undergone in the hospital.

At the last moment the *Seneca*, a transport, had been ordered to take nearly one hundred wounded soldiers to the North. She was absolutely without facilities to act as a hospital-ship—devoid of appliances, short of medicines, scant of ice, over-crowded, and entirely without the necessary devices of surgery or suitable food for the sick. No sooner had Miss Jennings heard of this than she decided to go with the *Seneca*, on the ground that she could do more good there than anywhere else. Taking a supply of malted milk, beef tea, whiskey, and a few other simple necessaries for the sick-room from the *State of Texas*, the nurse cast her lot in with the foreign military attachés and the newspaper correspondents who made up the passenger-list. These gentlemen cheerfully gave up their state-rooms to the wounded soldiers, but there were far too few to go around, and the sufferers tossed on the decks during the rough weather of the early part of the trip. There were on board two young contract surgeons, who did the best they could under the circumstances; but they had no instruments or bandages, and one of them was deathly seasick half the time. By far the greatest part of the care devolved upon Miss Jennings, and during the entire trip until the ship reached Fort Monroe she did not take off her clothes or get more sleep than she could snatch sitting up in her chair. The captain and crew were indefatigable in their efforts; all the passengers did what they could to help; but the handicap was too great, and there was terrible and useless suffering. The sanitary condition of the *Seneca* became indescribable; the air was pestilent between-decks, the water turned bad, and a case of fever developed that looked like yellow-fever. If it had been, Miss Jennings thought, the *Seneca* would have shown a death record, before the fever had run itself out, that would have made it historical in the statistics of pest-ships. But it was not the dreaded disease. The ship came to New York, the patients were taken to Bellevue, and the courageous nurse, taking with her as a remembrance a letter of gratitude signed by all her fellow-passengers, went on to her home in Washington to rest, and restore herself for a return to Cuba if her services should be needed there again. This is one woman's simple record of duty bravely done.

THE RED CROSS IN CALIFORNIA

By Blanche Partington

"God bless the women of the Red Cross!" said General Merritt, the day before he sailed for Manila. "We shall never forget the splendid kindness and hospitality without end that San Francisco has accorded us during our stay here."

"Tell all the world for us," a member of the general's staff said to me, "that every officer and man in the service blesses the noble women of the Red Cross. Their work is priceless; we have met with nothing like it." And certainly one of the most remarkable and unique developments consequent upon the military movements in San Francisco was the singularly varied and useful activity of the Red Cross Society of California—an auxiliary of the national association.

In the heat and bustle of hurried preparation for an unexpected war, here as elsewhere, the overtaxed government had left undone many of those things it ought to have done; and, to begin with, it had never reckoned to do for the soldier what his mother, for example, had always considered as indispensable to his well-being. Here was where the Red Cross Society came in. The women just "mothered" the boys in blue, bridging over rough places, feeding the hungry, tending the sick—generally

LOADING STORES ON THE *RELIEF*

preventing much needless suffering from unavoidable governmental hitches.

From the moment when the soldier set foot on Californian soil it was brought vividly to his remembrance that the famous "Sanitary Commission" of the Civil War—a worthy forerunner of the Red Cross Association—was indebted for one-fourth of its funds, something over a million dollars, to the miners of far California.

And the son of his father was finely faithful to the ancient traditions of the State, though it was towards the "native daughter of the golden West" that soldier-worship most inclined—and reasonably.

Hers was the gentle hospitality that met the incoming hero at all hours with hearty greetings, and with wholesome food not less welcome. Hers was the gracious kindliness that filled his hands with the wonderful blossoms of California, that he might know he had fallen among friends; and hers, too, the wise thoughtfulness that, as soon as he had eaten, found pencil and postal-cards for willing fingers to tell those left behind of safe arrival in this far city of the Golden Gate.

This was the work of the Red Cross Society at the ferry depot, through which all soldiers coming into the city must pass; and to say that it was appreciated were much to understate the case. To many of them the atmosphere of friendliness was simply overpowering. Strong men choked back their tears. They could not eat, but just looked helplessly at the kind faces of the women whose goodness had brought the first touch of that most terrible of the sufferings of a soldier's life—homesickness. And the kindness followed to camp. Where the overworked authorities had failed to furnish necessary food, blankets, underwear, shoes, stockings, etc., the Red Cross Society came forward and supplied the temporary deficiency, and the government, recognizing the work as a worthy outlet for the pent-up sympathies of the women, gladly accepted their service.

Every small town in California had its Red Cross Society: every creed and nationality subscribed to its support. Thum Shu, the editor of a Chinese newspaper published in San Francisco, one day turned in $100 to the Red Cross that he had collected in a few hours among his wealthy countrymen, and promised further immediate and considerable help if it would be accepted from that source. Gifts came pouring in hourly to the San Francisco headquarters in the most wonderful variety and quantity. Fresh and dried fruit by the ton, flannel for bandages and calico by the 1000 yards, eggs by the hundred dozen, beef-tea by the gallon, and pies by the million. Fish came in by the hundred-weight, and ham and beef and cheese and fresh vegetables. Then there were "comfort-bags," sleeping-caps, palm-leaf fans, literature and writing materials, and much tobacco.

As was befitting the essential purpose of the Red Cross Society, the sick soldier was kept in tender remembrance, and we found for him good gifts in plenty—wine in abundance, flowers, ices, jelly, milk, chickens, delicate puddings, besides the before-mentioned beef-tea and eggs; also sheets, pillows, and mattresses. Outside of the efforts of the Red Cross in this direction, the French and German hospitals took many soldiers into their wards, and the homœopaths treated all of their kind free of charge.

There were writing-tents at the camps, where all materials were furnished free to soldiers, where there was quiet, and where reading-matter was to be had also. These tents were appreciated to the extent of between 1500 and 2000 letters per day.

It will readily be seen from all this that the ideal of the Red Cross work at first—until more serious service should perhaps be required of it—was not the supplying of governmental deficiencies, though, as I have before said, much was done in this direction, but it was an attempt, however inadequate, to show the boys in blue that every inch of American ground was home to them, that every American woman loved every man of them as she loved her own son and brother, and that so long as they were with us they should lack none of the loving service that every woman in America was longing to render them.

A GROUP OF NURSES

It made the heart born with new belief in love of country, heroism, and self-sacrifice to hear the story of the resources of the Red Cross Society, and of the splendid kindness outside of it.

Little children emptied their savings-banks; the school-children subscribed—and put up lunches for the soldiers. Poor women took in plain sewing and gave the proceeds. A crippled woman sent 1800 yards of bandaging that she had pieced together of 1-inch to 18-inch strips of the left-over unsoiled flannel from the press in one of the press-rooms of the big dailies, where her son was employed. An old Grand Army soldier invited the boys to a free cherry lunch on his fruit ranch; the Chutes—a favorite place of entertainment—was free to any man in uniform; and a steamship company placed its boats at their disposal, that two thousand at least of the strangers might see our beautiful bay. Sutro's baths—the largest in the world—were given up to them for a day; several street-car lines were free to them, and on those that were not, women and men both would pay the fares of these honored guests of San Francisco.

Artists gave pictures to sell, singers sang, musicians played, actors acted, and jockeys raced to swell the funds.

The Mint employés set aside a day's salary, employés of all kinds made collections, the church gave a collection, the stores gave ten per cent. off to all purchasers in uniform—none were unrepresented in this monument of service.

And those whom they served! Ancient enemies the most deadly! The foes of a man's own household! It was an infinitely touching sight to see the deep gladness with which North and South joined hands, inexpressibly rejoiced that they were at last, in very deed and truth—a Union.

Perhaps no warmer welcome was accorded to any of San Francisco's soldier guests than was given the gallant Southerners from Tennessee, and certainly no heartier response greeted the Red Cross ladies of the welcoming committee than the grateful cheers of the boys in blue from Tennessee. There were colored citizens in our Californian regiments, and Mexicans who had sworn fealty to the Stars and Stripes, and even an occasional Spaniard.

War, the great engine of hatred, had come like an angel of peace, welding men's hearts into a wonderful unity. So strange are the ways of wisdom!

THE RELIEF-WORK OF THE WOMEN OF NEW YORK

By Anna Wheeler

"There is nothing so precious as the sight that is quick to see the sorrows of others, unless it be the heart that hurries to help them."

This beautiful sentiment, expressed by Lew. Wallace in *The Fair God*, was most thoroughly and exquisitely exemplified in the relief-work of the women of New York during the summer of the war. They were not only quick to see the sorrows and sufferings of our gallant soldiers, but with loving hearts, and willing hands, and open purses hurried to help them and relieve their suffering in every way in the world that these very potent factors can be of assistance.

As organizations and as individuals they left nothing undone that wealth and power and love could accomplish to combat and conquer the fearful fevers which, assisted by hardships and privations, had made such pitiable inroads in our army. They went to work in such a genuine, practical, earnest way as to leave no possibility of anything but the most wonderful results.

Of course the relief-work was by no means confined to New York, but it is of that work we speak at present. When our country's heroes came home, sick with fever, and weakened and worn out in body and soul, homesick and heartsick, they were met by our country's heroines with every delicacy and hospital comfort that the wealth of New York could procure.

It is not for me here to dwell upon the work of the Red Cross. The limitless good it did was too widespread and is too well known over the length and breadth of our land. Many a nurse at Montauk Point remembered with pleasure and pride the great comfort the suffering patients found in the quantities of pajamas, sheets, pillow-cases, towels, slippers, champagne, ice-cream, milk, fruit, and, indeed, every other imaginable comfort and luxury sent by the women of New York. Besides the things they sent they also gave *carte blanche* to be drawn upon without limit for any need that might possibly arise, and they sent money to be given to soldiers starting home, to make their journey more comfortable.

Many a dainty belle who had never fastened her own shoes came and offered assistance to do anything the hour required—wash dishes, sweep floors, or anything else that could in any way add to the comfort or welfare of the patients. They brought many a ray of sunshine writing letters for the patients, fanning the fevered brows, and sitting beside the convalescents in cheerful conversation, brightening a tedious hour, doing so many little things which the very busy nurses, having every moment filled with more important duties, had no time to do.

Too much praise cannot be given to the trained nurses at Montauk. They made just as gallant soldiers in the service of our country as those who fought on the battle-field. They were all women who had their living to make, and by hard work had achieved a position which commanded for them $25 a week and a comfortable living.

In the hospital they were getting a dollar a day, which was almost giving their time, and there was hardly one among the whole of them who would not have gladly volunteered her services free had it been necessary; and, indeed, I know of many cases where the services were volunteered after the required quota was filled by the government, and many were bitterly disappointed at not being able to give their services to the country.

I saw not one instance of carelessness or callousness or time-serving, but all the nurses were conscientiously devoted to their duty, and considered no hard work or fatigue or loss of rest worthy of the slightest consideration if they could by any possibility further the interest or comfort of those who were sick and suffering. Their conscientious devotion to duty was all the more beautiful in that they could look forward to no promotion, or shoulder-straps, or public recognition, or honorable mention, or any glory except that beautiful light which shines in one's heart from a knowledge of duty well done and honors well deserved.

I saw so much heart-breaking sorrow and suffering among my countrywomen that summer, and so much sweet unselfishness. Every mother or sister or wife whose own loved one had passed into his new home beyond the stars, where no sickness or pain could touch him further, was so willing to hide in her heart her grief, and serve in any way the son or brother or husband of some other woman, who could still live and feel and suffer.

One poor young girl, who had been trying for three days to have her brother's body sent home, said to a nurse who had offered her assistance:

"No, don't trouble about me; I shall get on somehow. You can't help the dead. Go back and help the living."

One of the sweetest individual instances of the many that came under my observation was that of the mother of one of our soldiers who was the first to lose his life on the blood-stained battle-fields of Cuba, who sent a trained nurse down to the hospital, at her own expense, to nurse the comrades of her son, so that though he were dead he could still help his fellow-soldiers. What a beautiful, practical memorial!

In addition to all these deeds a number of New York ladies offered their elegant country-houses and grounds at Newport and scattered along the coast for the use of the sick and convalescent soldiers. And others came in their yachts to take any number from time to time, from five to thirty-five soldiers, and give entire care to them until they had recovered health and strength.

The actions of both the men and women of our country in this war accentuated and deepened that feeling in our hearts which made each one of us reverently echo the words of George Washington:

"I thank God that I, too, am an American."

The following winter, in the whirl of the social season of New York, many a heart throbbed more happily underneath an elegant opera-cloak or in the brilliant glare of a ball-room at the memory of the pain and suffering relieved by a dainty, delicate hand that summer, and the sounding of the depth and sweetness of that beautiful message, "Inasmuch as ye did it unto one of the least of these, ye did it unto Me."

A GROUP OF VOLUNTEER NURSES WHO HAVE TAKEN THE OATH OF ALLEGIANCE TO THE RED CROSS SOCIETY.—The flag on the table is the one carried by Clara Barton through Armenia

THE WORK OF THE RELIGIOUS ORDERS

By Alice Worthington Winthrop

All students of national events must realize that it is a fact, as well as an epigram, that history repeats itself. As an evidence of this, it is well to reread, in Kinglake's *Crimean War*, the experiences of the allied armies before Sebastopol in the autumn and winter of 1854–55, and to compare them with those of the American army during the war with Spain. The allies were spared the heat from which the United States troops suffered in Cuba, but there were the same deficiencies in the quartermaster and commissary departments, the same bad cooking, affecting the health of the men (who also slept on the bare ground), the same absence of laundry and other facilities, and a far greater lack of medical supplies; while the allied armies had, in addition, the sufferings and perils incident to intense cold. In terms which seem prophetic of American experience, Kinglake shows how unprepared England was for the war. Though she had maintained a career of conquest for the previous forty years, because she had met no antagonist worthy of her steel, she had not that efficient "mainspring of military operations which men call a War Department." "The bellicose name, Secretary of War," he adds, "was deceptive. The males at that time in England suffered from a curious lameness in the use of brain power."

The hospital service was, as a consequence, seriously impaired. "The internal administration of our hospitals," says Kinglake, "was cursed by frightful overcrowding, by want of due ventilation, by an appalling lack of cleanliness, by want of sufficient attendance, by want of hospital comforts, and, finally, by want of proper food rightly cooked and supplied at right times. Therefore what the stricken soldier encountered, when entering the haven provided for him by rich, clumsy, improvident England, was not only a fresh access of misery, too often followed by death, but misery and death brought about by causes which his country, if acting with prudence and unhampered by its system of polity, could hardly have failed to arrest. How angels descended upon these scenes of wretchedness and—within the sphere of their mission—turned evil into good, we shall by-and-by not fail to see."

These "angels" were women "who were stirred with a heavenly thought impelling them to offer and say that—if only the State were consenting—they would go out to tend our poor soldiers laid low on their hospital pallets by sickness or wounds." Mary Stanley, the sister of Dean Stanley, and Florence Nightingale, "in gentle, almost humble guise, brought to the State a new power." Under their guidance, ten Catholic Sisters, eight Protestant Sisters, and twenty trained nurses landed at Scutari on the 5th of November, 1854, the very day of the battle of Inkerman. "Woman brought to the rescue," says Kinglake, "in an hour of gloom and need, that forethought, that agile brain-power, that organizing and governing faculty, of which our country had need."

This was the origin of woman's part in the modern English and American military hospital. If space permitted, the present writer, whose part it is to present the services of the religious orders, would gladly take up the story of what women accomplished, from the initiation of the hospital system in the United States during its Civil War until the time of the war with Spain. Above all, she would dwell on the labors of that noble, patriotic woman of letters, Anna Hanson Dorsey, through whose inspiration Edwin L. Stanton, in 1862, brought the Sisters of Mercy and the Sisters of Charity to the front, and enabled them to carry on the magnificent work which they performed during the Civil War.

Passing, however, to the war with Spain, the present writer labors under two difficulties in relating the work of the religious orders—lack of space, and the modesty of the Sisters, who could not be prevailed on to speak of themselves in connection with the events in which they took part. It is largely through the courtesy of the surgeon-general of the army, of the surgeons under whom the Sisters served, of Dr. Anita Newcomb McGee, who officially selected and employed them, and of Ella Loraine Dorsey, through whose instrumentality the Sisters took part in the war, that this account has been written.

A word must be said of the labors of these two women, who voluntarily endured the heat of a Washington summer, the thraldom of official life, and onerous fatigue, in order to examine, equip, and transport these nurses; the total number examined approaching 6600. These women contributed their time, their strength, and their intelligence to this object; and, as Daughters of the American Revolution and patriotic American citizens, gave of their best to the service of their country. "Too much cannot be said," stated the annual report of the association named, "in praise of Miss Ella Loraine Dorsey, ex-Vice-President of the D. A. R., for her valuable assistance in all matters relating to the Roman Catholic Sisters, as well as for her constant and unvarying interest in all matters pertaining to the corps, and her earnest co-operation in every project which had for its object help for the soldiers."

The religious orders in the United States which furnished contract nurses in the late war, and the number furnished, were as follows: The Sisters of Charity, 196; the Sisters of Mercy, 13; the Sisters of the Holy Cross, 11; the Sisters of St. Joseph, 11; the Congregation of American Sisters, 4. To these should be added four Sisters of Charity who served without contracts at the Naval Hospital, Norfolk, Virginia; five Sisters of Charity without contracts at Camp Wikoff, Montauk, New York; and twelve Sisters of Charity serving without contracts at San Francisco, California. Also one Sister of the Holy Cross, without contract, at Lexington, Kentucky.

Of these, the Sisters of Charity formed one of the largest organizations in the United States, numbering in one "province" 1517 Sisters. The order was instituted in Paris, in 1633, by St. Vincent de Paul, for work among the poor; to whom, for more than two hundred and fifty years, the cornet (originally the cap of the Breton peasant) was the symbol of simple, tender, and loving service towards the sick and suffering. For a considerable period previous to the war between the United States and Spain these Sisters had been in charge of the French military hospitals, and had ministered to the soldiers on the field of battle. It is related that when, in the Algerian campaign, an army corps was ordered to the front without them, the soldiers positively refused to obey the order. "We won't fight without our Sisters," they said; and a halt was actually called until a detachment of Sisters could be formed to join them. This was no difficult undertaking, for it was a part of their rule that the Sisters should always be ready for marching orders.

DEPARTURE OF RED CROSS RELIEF-SHIP *STATE OF TEXAS* FOR CUBA ON APRIL 23

Dr. A. M. Lesser, of the Red Cross Hospital, bidding farewell to Dr. J. B. Hubbell, Field Agent of the Central Cuban Relief

The Order of the Sisters of Mercy was founded in Ireland, in 1827, and was one of the first introduced into the United States. No act of charity was foreign to this noble body of women; they cared for children, for the aged, for unprotected women, and for the sick and suffering poor in hospitals and in their own homes. They even added, as a special work of mercy, "visiting the sick rich."

In the busy secular life of to-day few dream of the quiet heroism and self-sacrifice of the Sisters of Mercy, many of whom devote their lives to the inmates of prisons, administering to their spiritual and temporal needs, comforting the condemned criminal, walking with him even to the foot of the gallows and exhorting him to repentance, that, like the thief on the cross, he may be saved at the last. At the time of the war with Spain this order probably ranked, numerically, next to the Sisters of Charity in the United States.

The Sisters of St. Joseph belong to an order founded in France in 1650, but practically wiped out by the French Revolution. It was revived later, principally as a teaching order, but a certain number qualified as nurses, and were found satisfactory in the Civil War and in the war with Spain by the surgeons under whom they served.

The Sisters of the Holy Cross belong to an essentially modern order, founded in France in 1841 and introduced into the United States in the same year. It is generally diffused throughout the West. These Sisters were admirably equipped for teaching and for nursing—the objects for which they were instituted.

The service of the Congregation of American Sisters constitutes, for the sociologist and the general reader, one of the picturesque features of the American-Spanish War. This order, sanctioned by the Pope in 1888, was instituted at Fort Pierre, South Dakota, by Mother Catherine Sacred White Buffalo, a full-blooded Sioux Indian, born in the war-camp of the Dakotas, a grand specimen of her race, to whose advancement in civilization she devoted her life. She went to her reward

CONVALESCENT SOLDIERS LUNCHING ON THE DECK OF THE *MISSOURI*

in 1893, worn out by her heroic efforts in teaching and caring for the sick and destitute of her tribe, dying before the altar of the chapel of St. Berthold, which her zeal had erected, at the early age of twenty-six. She left behind her five Sisters, of whom one, Josephine Two Bears—in religion, Sister Mary Joseph—was a full-blooded Indian of high lineage. The prioress of the order was Mother Bridget, the granddaughter of Cloud Eagle, the great Sioux chief.

From the establishment of the order these Sisters conducted a hospital at Fort Pierre, having as their chaplain and physician Father Craft, a former professor in the New York Medical College, who became a priest and devoted himself to work among the Indians. He was one of the few white men who, living among them, become enthusiastic admirers of the Indian character. He was with the Seventh Cavalry in the battle at Wounded Knee, where he himself was severely wounded.

When war was declared, Father Craft telegraphed to the War Department, offering his own services and those of the community to the government for the war. "We are all ready to come immediately," he declared, "and are competent to undertake any services that Sisters can do. We would prefer to work among the wounded on the field of battle. We are ready to proceed at once to any place where we are needed—to Cuba, Puerto Rico, Manila, or any of the camps in the United States, and to attend to either white or colored soldiers. As we are accustomed to attending the sick under conditions much harder and more trying to health and strength than any existing in military camps, we thought we might be of service where others would break down. If we are needed, please send for us." Father Craft referred to Senator Proctor, to Generals Schofield, Miles, and Brooke, and to officers and surgeons at Pine Ridge Agency during the Indian War of 1890-91 "who remember my services with the army at that time."

As soon as the offer of their services was accepted, this intrepid band, inspired by the noblest zeal and by "a love of our native land—I don't know that you would call it patriotism, since our people are not citizens of the United States," as the prioress pathetically remarks—took the long journey from Dakota to the South, and was attached to the Seventh Army Corps. Father Craft was unable to obtain a position as chaplain, and, determined to serve his country and to remain with his beloved Sisters, enlisted for the war as a hospital steward. They were attached to the hospitals at Jacksonville and Savannah, and, just before the close of the war, went with the Seventh Corps to Cuba.

On the 21st of April, 1898, the day on which war was declared, the Sisters of Mercy telegraphed, offering their services to the President as nurses for the war. Two days later, Sister Beatrice, of the Providence Hospital, Washington, made the same offer for the Sisters of Charity in that "province." From all parts of the country came similar applications from various branches of this order, and from the Sisters of the Holy Cross, and the Sisters of St. Joseph. The religious orders all over the land—in Boston, Omaha, Iowa, Montana, Oregon—were eager to show their love of their country, by serving it in its hour of need.

At the beginning of the war, grave doubts existed in Washington as to the desirability, or even the possibility, of the employment of female nurses in the new conditions by which the army was confronted. It was partly, of course, a sense of chivalry towards women which forbade the very idea of their facing the unknown dangers which the troops so bravely marched to meet; of any woman sharing in the perils of war and treading with her brothers that crimson trail "which leads to dusty death." If there was also an idea on the part of the American man that he could, for once, accomplish some great work without the help of his sister woman, shall we question his wisdom, or, rather, shall we not admire his temerity? At any rate, to all the appeals of the Sisters, as well as to those of other organizations, the same answer was at first returned: "The surgeon-general has no authority for the employment of female nurses." This authority was afterwards conferred on him by Congress.

On the 20th of May the Military Hospital at Key West was established; and here, for the first time during the war, the Sisters were allowed to prove their patriotism. Sister Mary Théophile, Superior of the Order of the Holy Name (a teaching order founded in 1843, and better known on the Pacific than the Atlantic coast), seeing that the quarters intended for the hospital service were inadequate, offered to Major William R. Hall, the surgeon in charge, the use of the convent of the order. Major Hall, from whom the present writer obtained many facts in connection with this act of patriotism, bore witness to the generosity and self-devotion of these Sisters. Not only was their beautiful convent placed absolutely at his disposal, but everything was done for the comfort of the sick inmates. The Sisters of the same order at Tampa gave themselves up to the care of the soldiers who reached that great railway terminus after long journeys, under inexperienced officers, without any of the comforts of life, and even without food. "Often the rations gave out"—the men complained—"before we were half way." Between the end of May and first of August, these Sisters, without thought of remuneration, prepared, cooked, and served no less than three thousand meals to soldiers of all conditions and creeds. "While we had anything in the pantry," wrote Sister Theophile, "the poor boys did not suffer."

"You refer to our feeding the soldiers," she writes. "Is it possible this news has reached Washington? We always admired the gentlemanly conduct of the men; no matter how great their hunger, they never deviated an iota from the manliness that goes to make a true soldier. This is the note I would like to have mentioned: the behavior of those men was worthy of admiration." Sister Théophile adds an earnest request, with which the present writer reluctantly complies, that the names and work of individual Sisters be not mentioned.

Events which have already been recorded in this history followed in rapid succession; the departure of the troops from Key West, their landing in Cuba, and the fights at El Caney and San Juan. Official reports bear sufficient testimony to the distresses of the wounded after the assault. Then, and during the whole campaign, our troops suffered from insufficient surgical aid and appliances, from bad food and bad water, and from intense heat and malarial and other fevers. Already the surgeon had begun to realize that the "pestilence which walketh in the noonday" is more to be dreaded in southern countries than even the bullets of the enemy. General Sternberg had foreseen this and endeavored to avert it, and gradually the War Department perceived the necessity for the employment of women; above all, of immunes who could care for the rapidly increasing number of sufferers from yellow and pernicious malarial fevers. It recognized, also, the necessity of some centre of authority to examine, organize, and be in a measure responsible for the nurses thus employed. At this juncture the Daughters of the American Revolution patriotically offered to supply the existing demand, to examine and make contracts with female nurses, and to arrange all the details with regard to their employment, as well as their transportation to their respective destinations. This offer was accepted, and Dr. Anita Newcomb McGee, Vice-President of the D. A. R., was enrolled as an acting assistant surgeon in the army and placed in charge of the work. With her was associated Ella Loraine Dorsey, a former vice-president of the D. A. R., who undertook to make all arrangements with and for the religious orders. The task of these two ladies was rendered more difficult by the fact that, excluding all volunteer aid, and all communities or organizations, the government would make contracts only with individuals. This system must be held responsible for any confusion which detracted, however slightly, from the value, at first, of the Sisters' services. Accustomed to the rule of community life, which accepts the decision of the Superior as final, only such discipline and conscientiousness as theirs could at once have transferred this obedience to the surgeons in charge. Their vows, however, recognized submission to the authority of the physician as their first duty in nursing the sick; and, when they were once incorporated in the organization of nurses, his right to command was accepted by the Sisters without question.

On the 17th of July, Dr. Cleborne, of the Naval Hospital, Norfolk, Virginia, applied to the mother-house at Emmittsburg, Maryland, for Sisters of Charity to aid in the care of the wounded men—Americans and Spanish prisoners—at the hospital. He asked especially for four or six Sisters to act as night nurses, and for one who could speak Spanish. Four were sent, one of whom spoke Spanish. These Sisters served as volunteers before the contract system was established. They remained until their services were no longer necessary, the wounded having recovered and the prisoners having returned to Spain.

On the 4th of August, the offer of the immune Sisters of Charity was accepted. Five of these from the Maryland province and seven from New Orleans took the oath of allegiance, signed the required contract, and sailed on the transports *Yale* and *Yucatan*, on August 8, for Santiago de Cuba. Upon their arrival, the commanding general and the chief surgeons, believing that the sick should be removed as rapidly as possible to a temperate climate, and on account of the inadequate accommodation for the Sisters, and for other reasons, strongly advised that the latter should return on the *Yale*. They sailed, therefore, with eight hundred men (of whom two hundred and fifty were already sick), *en route* for Montauk. The writer has before her a letter from General Wood (who, as a physician as well as a general officer, was especially qualified to decide as to the wisdom of this course), in which he states that the Sisters came back "through no fault of their own," and that this step was taken in the interests of the sick soldiers. At Montauk they joined the thirty Sisters of Charity who, under the superintendence of Sister Adelaide d'Aulnoy, had been ordered there on the 18th of August.

THE WOMEN OF THE RED CROSS AUXILIARY GOING DOWN SAN FRANCISCO BAY TO TAKE LEAVE OF THE TROOP-SHIPS FOR MANILA

TROOPS LANDING AT MONTAUK—MRS. MOTT FEEDING THE HUNGRY SOLDIERS.—Drawn by W. A. Rogers

She had already brought order out of chaos and had created, according to the testimony of Dr. Leonard B. Almy, surgeon in charge, a "model hospital." He writes: "When I was first given charge of the Annex Hospital (which was then only a hospital in our prospective vision), I was told that the 'Sisters' were to do my nursing. At first I was prejudiced, not in their favor; but I found that, certainly for a military hospital at least, they are a great success. They were disciplined themselves, and obeyed orders promptly and without a murmur of discontent at any hardships or overwork, or any of the vicissitudes of camp-life. I do not remember to have had a complaint from any one of them, and I had one hundred and four of them at one time. Their wards were models of neatness. I can certify to their faithfulness, skill, and unvarying thoughtfulness, and am very glad to do so. The statements I have made were not only from my own observation, but from the reports of the ward surgeons (contract doctors)." The personal experience of the present writer corroborates all the facts stated by Dr. Almy as to what is described by Mrs. Cowdin as the "beautiful and gracious work of the Sisters" at Montauk.

Altogether one hundred and eleven Sisters of Charity served at Montauk, and they remained there in numbers varying according to the needs of the service, until the dissolution of that hospital-camp, late in September.

On the 10th of August, ten Sisters of Charity, under Sister Lucia, were detailed to the hospital at Fort Thomas, Newport, Kentucky, where the surgeon in charge was Major William R. Hall, who testified to the "magnificent service" which they rendered, nursing 2500 men with great skill and with an exceedingly small death rate. The Sisters, afterwards increased to fifteen, remained at Fort Thomas until the hospital was closed.

On August 20th, eleven Sisters of Mercy, principally typhoid-fever expert nurses, and nine Sisters of Charity, were ordered to the Sanger-Hoff general hospital at Chickamauga, Georgia. It is unnecessary here to dwell on the miseries of that camp, where, before the Sisters' arrival, amid dirt indescribable, untrained soldiers had attempted in vain to bring any semblance of comfort to the patients. "Speak to me, Sister—just one word," said one poor fellow as the Sister entered the ward. "It is the first time I have heard a woman's voice for four months."

The difficulties which the Sisters had to contend with at Chickamauga were nearly insurmountable. Even after they had succeeded, notwithstanding the deficiency of water, in cleaning the overcrowded wards, the heat and dust and flies were almost unendurable. But there was never a word of complaint; they were merry in spite of their discomforts and privations. The Superior, Sister Mary Bernard, wrote: "We manage to get along delightfully. We are bright and happy; and I might add that the almost total absence of conveniences is a great source of amusement. Perhaps fortune may favor us with a few tables. At present we can boast of one chair only, and our tent furniture consists of a cot without a mattress, sheets, or pillows." Major Brechemin, surgeon in charge at Chickamauga, wrote of his appreciation of the "noble and devoted work done by these glorious women," and was "proud to have been associated with them."

Fifty-five more Sisters of Charity were asked for at Chickamauga, and remained there until the camp was closed, late in September—going thence to the hospitals at Knoxville, Lexington, Huntsville, and Columbus, Georgia. These hospitals closed in November, when the Sisters attached to the Seventh Army Corps went to Jacksonville and Savannah, and thence to Cuba. There they were attached to the hospital at Matanzas, where the Sisters of St. Joseph remained. The Sisters of the Holy Cross returned home from Matanzas, their services being no longer required.

On August 22d, ten Sisters of Charity, under Sister Elizabeth, were ordered to report for duty at Camp Alger. Though in the immediate neighborhood of Washington, it was here, perhaps, that the hardships and privations of the Sisters were most severe. And yet the only comment of Sister Elizabeth was this: "We had our trials." The Sisters remained at Camp Alger until the troops left in September.

On August 29th, ten Sisters of Charity were applied for, for the military hospital at Ponce, Puerto Rico. Nine more were added, to remain until their services were no longer required. Eleven Sisters of the Order of St. Joseph, and the same number of the Holy Cross, were detailed to the John Blair Gibbs Hospital at Lexington, Kentucky, under Major Edgar Mearns, surgeon in charge. Here a little over a hundred nurses were employed, of whom forty-eight, including the above, were Catholic Sisters, under Sister Lydia. It is a source of regret that Major Mearns's tribute to the Sisters is too long to be quoted in full. "I am certain," he writes, "that the moral effect of the presence of the Sisters had a most salutary influence upon the rough men who were detailed from the regiments to serve the sick. The mixture of Sisters with nurses gave a dignity and decorum to our wards which they would not otherwise have had. The professional nurses loved them and begged to be sent where they were; all wanted to be under 'Captain Lydia.' Our contract nurses saw hard service, and they bore hardships, privations, and straining exertions with unflinching courage. Fidelity and perfect discipline were unfailing characteristics of the Catholic Sisters. Their good faces were an inspiration, and will ever be a happy memory to me."

Thirty-three Sisters of Charity were detailed to Camp Cuba Libre, Jacksonville, where they served in the hospital until the close of the camp.

The Sisters of the Order of St. Joseph, after leaving Camp Hamilton, went to Matanzas, Cuba, where they were attached to the Second Brigade Hospital. "We are happy to say," wrote Sister Mary Liguori, the Superior, "that we have been shown the greatest consideration by all. Our dear Lord is richly repaying us for the little we are doing or trying to do for Him. May He give us grace to accomplish much during our stay here in this His most neglected field. We see a great deal of poverty, but I think our government is nobly supplying the poor people with food and with the means of earning a living. No wonder the nation is blessed."

Many of the soldiers ordered to the Philippines were compelled by illness to remain in California. The Archbishop of San Francisco stated that twelve Sisters of Charity were engaged in nursing them at the Presidio Hospital, San Francisco.

Except as employed at the Sisters' own hospitals, where the sick soldiers were everywhere generously and hospitably cared for, this enumeration completes the list of the Sisters employed in the United States. In addition, Father Roma, of San Juan, Puerto Rico, in November, offered the services of fifteen Sisters of Charity, if required, on the island. The surgeon-general, with his invariable courtesy, replied that, while their services were not required at present, "they would form a valuable reserve from which to draw in case of emergency."

It was stated by a Spanish authority that of 700 Sisters sent by Spain to the war, 100 perished by "bullets and illness," 300 remained in the hospital service, and 300 returned with sick soldiers to the mother-country.

The mortality among the Sisters was greater, in proportion, than among the trained nurses. The latter lost seven out of a total of 1250, while five of the 250 Sisters employed died in the service.

The reports at the War Department were an evidence of the high average character of the Sisters' work, and to many of these were added the personal approval of the surgeons in charge. One surgeon in charge wrote to Miss Dorsey: "You should not thank me, dear madame, for the little I can do for these gentle, sweet women, for somehow or other they breathe peace and hope to us worldly and selfish creatures, whose lives are so absorbed in the hopes and cares of our narrow world." Colonel John V. R. Hoff wrote as follows: "No words can express my sense of obligation to the kind Sisters for their admirable work with, and tender care for, our sick."

The Sisters indeed carried with them an atmosphere of serenity and peace. The high motive which animated their work, their forgetfulness of self, and their patient and tender ministrations were, to many of the soldiers confided to their care, a revelation of womanly nobility and sweetness; while their crowning virtue, to the surgeons, was the fact that they never complained. In all their sufferings from the heat and dirt at Camp Alger and Chickamauga, from the many discomforts and privations of Montauk, not a murmur of discontent was heard. As they passed through the hospital wards, all bad language, all blasphemy was stilled. The roughest men learned to be patient and gentle, with such examples before them. The Sisters gave a certain dignity to the rudest surroundings; and the trained nurses, many of them young women who had never before left the shelter of home, felt that its sanctity still surrounded them when under the protection of the Sisters.

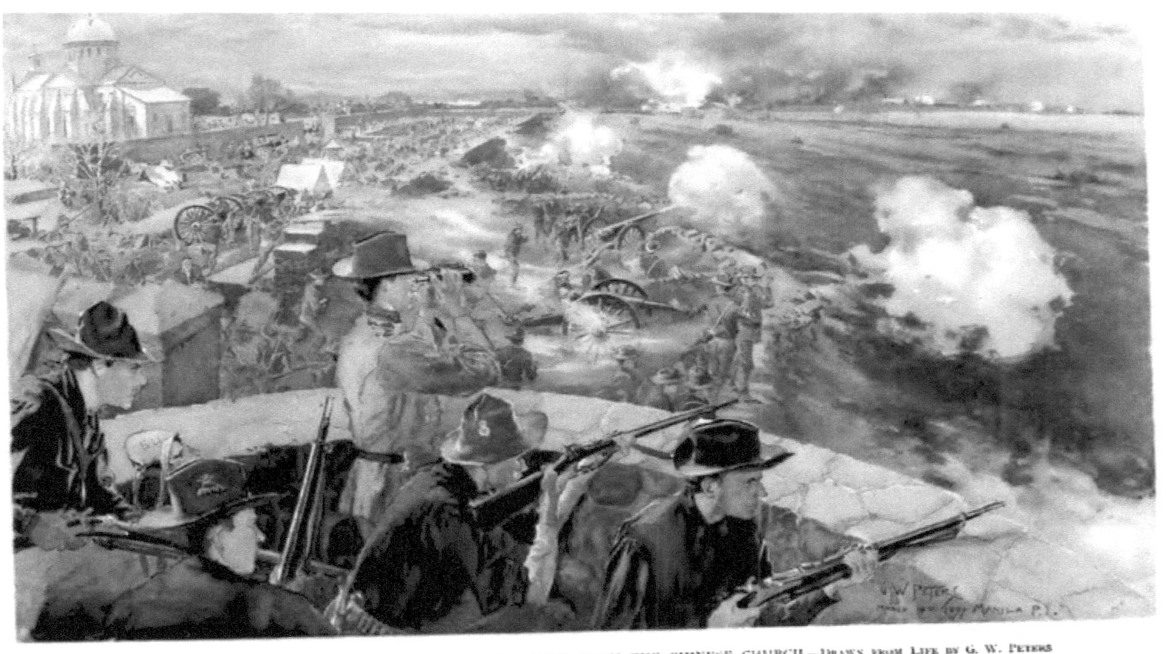

THE BATTLE BEFORE CALOOCAN, FEBRUARY 10, 1899—VIEW FROM THE CHINESE CHURCH.—Drawn from Life by G. W. Peters

Battery of Utah Artillery in the Middle Foreground; the Tenth Pennsylvania Volunteers, of General MacArthur's Division, behind the Wall

THE REVOLT OF THE FILIPINOS

THE United States having by the Treaty of Paris succeeded to the sovereignty of Spain in the Philippines, the President instructed Major-General Elwell S. Otis, commanding the American forces in the archipelago, to issue a proclamation to the inhabitants announcing and outlining a humane policy of government, and appointed a commission, consisting of President Schurman of Cornell University, Admiral Dewey, Major-General Otis, Professor Dean Worcester of the University of Michigan, and Colonel Charles Denby, formerly minister to China, to make a personal study of conditions in the islands for the guidance of the supreme executive in the conduct of affairs.

Emilio Aguinaldo, the young native leader of the Filipinos, having kept himself fully informed, through his representative at Washington, Felipe Agoncillo, of the progress of negotiations, and being thus enabled to anticipate the slow movement of diplomacy, issued protests and counter proclamations innumerable against the new order of things, and, on the 4th of February, 1899, two days before the ratification by Congress of the treaty of peace, declared war and began hostilities against the United States.

The situation, the change of attitude on the part of the Filipinos, and the events characteristic of the revolt and its suppression are described in the following accounts and reports of eye-witnesses and principal participants.

ELWELL S. OTIS

Major-General in Command of the American Forces in the Philippines

---

THE INSURGENTS

General Greene's Account as Laid Before the American Peace Commissioners, October 4, 1898.

AGUINALDO, in a message to foreign governments of August 6, 1898, asking for recognition of belligerency and independence, claimed to have a force of 30,000 men, organized into a regular army. This included the force in the provinces of Luzon outside of Manila. What was in evidence around Manila varied from 10,000 to 15,000. It was composed of young men and boys, some as young as fifteen years of age, recruited in the rural districts, having no property and nothing to lose in a civil war. They had received no pay, and, although Aguinaldo speaks in his proclamation of his intention and ability to maintain order wherever his forces penetrate, yet the feeling is practically universal among the rank and file that they are to be compensated for their time and services and hardships by being allowed to loot Manila.

Their equipment consists of a gun, bayonet, and cartridge-box; their uniform, of a straw hat, gingham shirt, trousers, and bare feet; their transportation, of a few ponies and carts, impressed for a day or a week at a time; for quarters they have taken the public building in each village or pueblo, locally known as the Tribunal, and the churches and convents; from these, details are sent out to man the trenches. Their food while on duty consists of rice and banana leaves, cooked at the quarters and sent out to the trenches. After a few days or a week of active service they return to their homes to feed up or to work on their farms, their places being taken by others, to whom they turn over their guns and cartridges.

Their arms have been obtained from various sources—from purchases in Hong-Kong; from the supply which Admiral Dewey found in the arsenal at Cavité; from capture made from the Spaniards. They are partly Mausers and partly Remingtons. Their ammunition was obtained in the same way. They have used it freely, and the supply is now rather short. To replenish it they have established a cartridge factory at the village of Imus, about ten miles south of Cavité, where they have four hundred people engaged in reloading cartridges with powder and lead found at Cavité or purchased abroad. They have no artillery, except a few antique columbiads obtained from Cavité, and no cavalry. Their method of warfare is to dig a trench in front of the Spanish position, cover it with mats as a protection against the sun and rain, and during the night put their guns on top of the trench above their heads and fire in the general direction of the enemy. When their ammunition is exhausted, they go off in a body to get a fresh supply in baskets, and then return to the trenches.

The men are of small stature, from 5 feet to 5 feet 6 inches in height, and weigh from 110 to 130 pounds. Compared with them, our men from Colorado and California seem like a race of giants. One afternoon, just after we entered Manila, a battalion of the insurgents fired upon the outposts of the Colorado regiment, mistaking them, as they claimed, for Spaniards. The outpost retreated to their support and the Filipinos followed; they easily fell into an ambush, and the support, numbering about eighty men, surrounded the two hundred and fifty Filipinos, wrenched the guns out of their hands, and marched them off as unarmed prisoners, all in the space of a few minutes. Such a force can hardly be called an army, and yet the service which it has rendered should not be underestimated. Between two thousand and three thousand Spanish native troops surrendered to it during the months of June and July; it constantly annoyed and harassed the Spaniards in the trenches, keeping them up at night and wearing them out with fatigue; and it invested Manila early in July so completely that all supplies were cut off and the inhabitants, as well as the Spanish troops, were forced to live on horse and buffalo meat, and the Chinese population on cats and dogs. It captured the waterworks of Manila and cut off the water supply, and if it had been in the dry season would have inflicted great suffering on the inhabitants for lack of water.

These results, it is true, were obtained against a dispirited army containing a considerable number of native troops of doubtful loyalty. Yet from August, 1896, to April, 1897, they fought 25,000 of the best regular troops sent out from Spain, inflicting on them a loss of over 150 officers and 2500 men killed and wounded, and they suffered still greater losses themselves. Nevertheless, from daily contact with them for six weeks, I am very confident that no such results could have been obtained against an American army, which would have driven them back to the hills and reduced them to a petty guerilla warfare. If they attack the American army this will certainly be the result; and while these guerilla bands might give some trouble so long as their ammunition lasted, yet with our navy guarding the coasts and our army pursuing them on land, it would not be long before they were reduced to subjection.

In August, 1896, an insurrection broke out in Cavite under the leadership of Emilio Aguinaldo, and soon spread to other provinces on both sides of Manila. It continued with varying successes on both sides, and the trial and execution of numerous insurgents, until December, 1897, when the Governor-General, Primo de Rivera, entered into written agreement with Aguinaldo. The document is in possession of Señor Felipe Agoncillo. In brief, it required that Aguinaldo and the other insurgent leaders should leave the country, the government agreeing to pay them $800,000 in silver and promising to introduce numerous reforms, including representation in the Spanish Cortes, freedom of the press, general amnesty for all insurgents, and the expulsion or secularization of the monastic orders.

Aguinaldo and his associates went to Hong Kong and Singapore. A portion of the money, $400,000, was deposited in banks at Hong Kong, and a lawsuit soon arose between Aguinaldo and one of his subordinate chiefs named Artacho, which is interesting on account of the very honorable position taken by Aguinaldo. Artacho sued for a division of the money among the insurgents according to rank. Aguinaldo claimed that the money was a trust fund, and was to remain on deposit until it was seen whether the Spaniards would carry out their promised reforms, and if they failed to do so it was to be used to defray the expenses of a new insurrection. The suit was settled out of court by paying Artacho $5000.

No steps have been taken to introduce the reforms; more than 2000 insurgents, who had been deported to Fernando Po and other places, are still in confinement, and Aguinaldo is now using the money to carry on the operations of the present insurrection.

On the 24th day of April Aguinaldo met the United States consul and others at Singapore and offered to begin a new insurrection in conjunction with the operations of the United States navy at Manila. This was telegraphed to Admiral Dewey, and by his consent, or at his request, Aguinaldo left Singapore for Hong-Kong on April 26; and when the *McCulloch* went to Hong-Kong early in May to carry the news of Admiral Dewey's victory, it took Aguinaldo and seventeen other revolutionary chiefs on board and brought them to Manila Bay. They soon after landed at Cavité, and the Admiral allowed them to take such guns, ammunition, and stores as he did not require for himself. With these, and some other arms he had brought from Hong-Kong, Aguinaldo armed his followers, who rapidly assembled at Cavité, and in a few weeks he began moving against the Spaniards. Part of them surrendered, giving him more arms, and the others retreated to Manila.

Soon afterwards two ships which were the private property of Señor Agoncillo and other insurgent sympathizers were converted into cruisers and sent with insurgent troops to Subig Bay and other places to capture provinces outside of Manila. They were very successful, the native militia in Spanish service capitulating with their arms in nearly every case without serious resistance. On the 18th of June Aguinaldo issued a proclamation from Cavité establishing a dictatorial government, with himself as dictator. In each village or pueblo a chief (*jefe*) was to be elected, and in each ward a headman (*cabeza*); also in each pueblo three delegates—one of police, one of justice, and one of taxes. These were to constitute the junta, or assembly, and after consulting the junta the chiefs of pueblos were to elect a chief of province and three councillors—one of police, one of justice, and one of taxes. They were also to elect one or more representatives from each province to form the revolutionary congress.

AGUINALDO IN DECEMBER, 1897

This was followed on June 20 by a decree giving more detailed instructions in regard to the elections. On June 23 another decree followed changing the title of the government from dictatorial to revolutionary, and of the chief officer from dictator to president; announcing a cabinet, with a minister of foreign affairs, marine, and commerce, another of war and public works, another of police and internal order, justice, instruction, and hygiene, and another of taxes, agriculture, and manufactures; the powers of the president and congress were defined, and a code of military justice was formulated.

On the same day a manifesto was issued to the world explaining the reasons and purposes of the revolution. On June 27 another decree was issued containing instructions in regard to elections. On August 6 an address was issued to foreign governments stating that the revolutionary government was in operation and control in fifteen provinces, and that in response to the petition of the duly elected chiefs of these provinces an appeal is made for recognition of belligerency and independence.

The scheme of government is set forth in the decree of June 23. It provides a dictatorship of the familiar South American type. All power is centred in the president, and he is not responsible to any one for his acts. He is declared to be "the personification of the Philippine public, and in this view cannot be held responsible while he holds office. His term will last until the revolution triumphs." He appoints not only the heads of departments, but all their subordinates, and without reference to congress. This body is composed of a single chamber of representatives from each province. The election is to be con-

THE LEADERS OF THE INSURRECTION GATHERED AT AGUINALDO'S HOUSE

FILIPINOS IN ACTION.—"FIRE AT WILL."

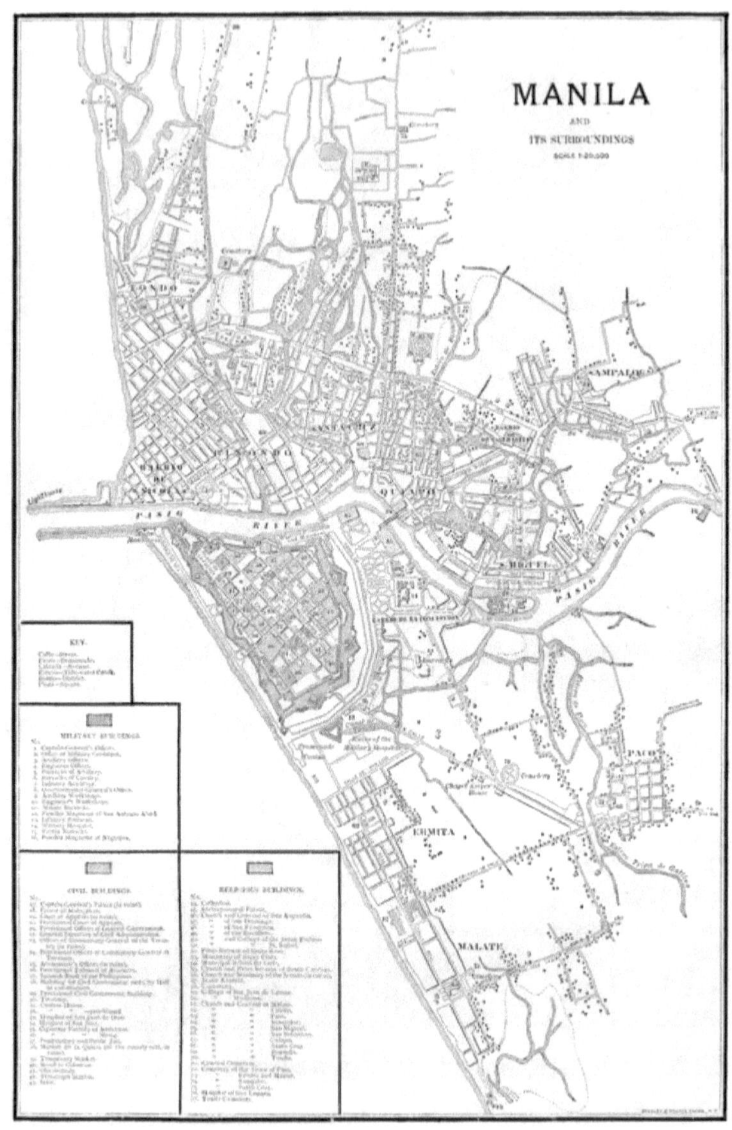

MANILA AND VICINITY—FROM AN ACCURATE AND VERY RARE SPANISH MAP, OBTAINED BY F. D. MILLET

THE MONTANA REGIMENT WAITING THE ORDER TO ADVANCE ON CALOOCAN

ducted by an agent of the president, and the qualifications of electors are "those inhabitants most distinguished for high character, social position, and honorable conduct."

If any province is still under Spanish rule its representative is to be appointed by the president. Congress is to deliberate on "all grave and transcendental questions whose decision admits of delay and adjournment, but the president may decide questions of urgent character, giving the reasons for his decision in a message to congress." The acts of congress are not binding until approved by the president, and he has power of absolute veto. Congress held its first session at Malolos in September, 1898.

While this scheme of government is a pure despotism, yet it claims to be only temporary, and intended to "prepare the country so that a true republic may be established." It also provides a rude form of governmental machinery for managing the affairs of the provinces. Aguinaldo claims in his address of August 6 that it is in force in fifteen provinces whose aggregate population is about 2,000,000.

In the province of Cavité and that portion of the province of Manila outside of the city and its suburbs which was occupied by the insurgent troops, as well as those of the United States, their military forces, military headquarters, etc., were very much in evidence, occupying the principal houses and churches in every village and hamlet, but there were no signs of civil government or administration. It was reported, however, that Aguinaldo's agents were levying taxes or forced contributions not only in the outside villages, but (after we entered Manila) by means of secret agents in the market-places of the city itself. At Aguinaldo's headquarters, in Bacoor, there were signs of activity and business, and it was reported that his cabinet officers were in constant session there. Aguinaldo himself never failed to claim all the prerogatives due to his alleged position as the *de facto* ruler of the country.

The only general officer who saw him or had any direct communication with him was General Anderson. He did much to thwart this officer in organizing a native wagon-train and otherwise providing for his troops, and he went so far in a letter of July 23 to warn General Anderson not to land American troops on Philippine soil without his consent—a notice which it is hardly necessary to say was ignored. The day before the attack on Manila he sent staff-officers to the same general asking for our plans of attack, so that their troops could enter Manila with us. The same request had previously been made to me by one of his brigade commanders, to which I replied that I was not authorized to give the information desired.

Aguinaldo did not call upon General Merritt on his arrival, and this enabled the latter to avoid any communication with him, either direct or indirect, until after Manila had been taken. General Merritt then received one of Aguinaldo's staff-officers in his office as military governor. The interview lasted more than an hour. General Merritt referred to his proclamation as showing the conditions under which the American troops had come to Manila and the nature of the military government which would be maintained until further orders from

THE ADVANCE ON CALOOCAN—ON THE FIRING-LINE OF THE KANSAS VOLUNTEERS

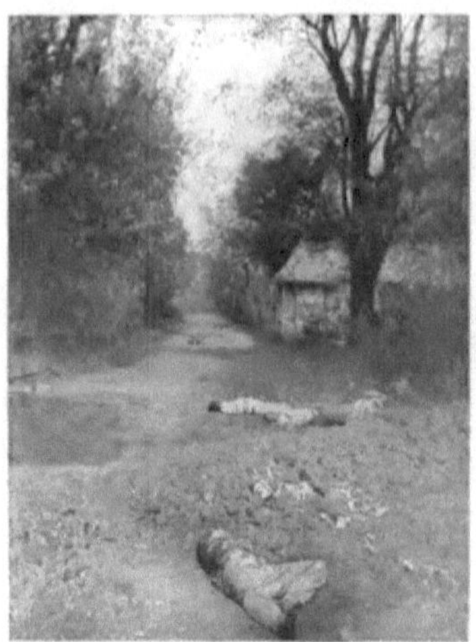

ON THE ROAD TO CALOOCAN, FEBRUARY 10

PHOTOGRAPH BY LIEUT. C. F. O'KEEFE, U. S. A.

Washington. He agreed upon the lines outside of the city of Manila up to which the insurgent troops could come, but no farther, with arms in their hands; he asked for possession of the water-works, which was given; and while expressing our friendship and sympathy for the Philippine people, he stated very positively that the United States government had placed at his disposal an ample force for carrying out his instructions, and even if the services of Aguinaldo's forces had been needed as allies he should not have felt at liberty to accept them.

The problem of how to deal with Aguinaldo's government and troops will necessarily be accompanied with embarrassment and difficulty, and will require much tact and skill in its solution. The United States government, through its naval commander, has to some extent made use of them for a distinct military purpose, viz., to harass and annoy the Spanish troops, to wear them out in the trenches, to blockade Manila on the land side, and to do as much damage as possible to the Spanish government prior to the arrival of our troops; and for this purpose the Admiral allowed them to take arms and munitions which he had captured at Cavité and their ships to pass in and out of Manila Bay in their expeditions against other provinces. But the Admiral has been very careful to give Aguinaldo no assurances of recognition and no pledges or promises of any description. The services which Aguinaldo and his adherents rendered in preparing the way for attack on Manila are certainly entitled to consideration; but, after all, they were small in comparison with what was done by our own fleet and army.

There is no reason to believe that Aguinaldo's government has any elements of stability. In the first place, Aguinaldo is a young man of 28 years; prior to the insurrection of 1896 he had been a schoolmaster and afterwards gobernadorcillo and municipal captain in one of the pueblos of the province of Cavité. He is not devoid of ability, and he is surrounded by clever writers. But the educated and intelligent Filipinos of Manila say that not only is he lacking in ability to be at the head of affairs, but if an election for president were held he would not even be a candidate. He is a successful leader of insurgents, has the confidence of young men in the country districts, prides himself on his military ability, and if a republic could be established the post he would probably choose for himself would be general-in-chief of the army.

In the next place, Aguinaldo's government, or any entirely independent government, does not command the hearty support of the large body of the Filipinos, both in Manila and outside, who have property, education, and intelligence. Their hatred of Spanish rule is very keen, and they will co-operate with Aguinaldo or any one else to destroy it. But after that is done they fully realize that they must have the support of some strong nation for many years before they will be in a position to manage their own affairs alone. The nation to which they all turn is America, and their ideal is a Philippine republic under American protection, such as they have heard is to be granted to Cuba. But when it comes to defining their ideas of protection and the respective rights and duties of each under it—what portion of the government is to be administered by them and what portion by us; how the revenues are to be collected, and in what proportion the expenses are to be divided—they have no clearly defined ideas at all; nor is it to be expected that they should have, after generations of Spanish rule, without any experience in self-government. This class—the educated natives with property at stake—look upon the prospect of Aguinaldo's government and forces entering Manila with almost as much dread as the foreign merchants or the Spaniards themselves.

Finally, it must be remembered that this is purely a Tagalo insurrection. There are upwards of thirty races in the Philippines, each speaking a different dialect; but five-sixths of the entire Christian population is composed of the Tagalos and Visayas. The former live in Mindoro and the southern half of Luzon, and the latter in Cebu, Iloilo, and other islands in the centre of the group. The Tagalos are more numerous than the Visayas, but both races are about equal in civilization, intelligence, and wealth. It is claimed by Aguinaldo's partisans that the Visayas are in sympathy with his insurrection and intend to send representatives to the congress. But it is a fact that the Visayas have taken no active part in the present insurrection, nor in that of 1896; that the Spanish government is still in full control at Cebu and Iloilo and in the Visayas' islands, and that Aguinaldo has as yet made no effort to attack them. The Visayas number nearly 2,000,000, or about as many as the population of all the Tagalo provinces which Aguinaldo claims to have captured. There is no evidence to show that they will support his pretensions, and many reasons to believe that, on account of racial prejudices and jealousies and other causes, they will oppose him.

Upon one point all are agreed, except possibly Aguinaldo and his immediate adherents, and that is that no native government can maintain itself without the active support and protection of a strong foreign government. This being admitted, it is difficult to see how any foreign government can give this protection without taking such an active part in the management of affairs as is practically equivalent to governing in its own name and for its own account.

DISAFFECTION OF THE FILIPINOS

ACCOUNT BY MAJOR-GENERAL OTIS

A SMALL band of men, natives of Luzon and leaders of the rebellion of 1896 against Spain, were induced by the latter country,

ON THE ROAD TO CALOOCAN—THE AFTERMATH

PHOTOGRAPH BY LIEUT. C. F. O'KEEFE, U. S. A.

DEAD FILIPINOS IN TRENCH OF BASTION FORT BEFORE SANTA ANA.—PHOTOGRAPH BY LIEUT. C. F. O'KEEFE, U. S. A.

through a money consideration, to remove permanently from the islands. After the destruction of the Spanish fleet in the harbor of Manila and the blockade of that city by the United States naval forces, a number of these men returned to the vicinity of Manila. They were doubtless encouraged without authority to attempt the organization of what they were pleased to denominate an independent government for the Filipino people — they themselves to become its controlling element. The widespread animosity which a great majority of the inhabitants of southern Luzon entertained against the continuance of Spanish domination made these people eager to assist any demonstration which promised deliverance. Aguinaldo and his associates landed from American vessels in Cavité (the province of his nativity), supplied by United States agents with arms and ammunition in small quantities for the purpose of raising a native force to assist the American troops to keep back from the shore of Manila Bay the scattered Spanish troops giving annoyance in that vicinity. Availing themselves of the zealous co-operation of the people of the southern provinces to terminate Spanish supremacy, they took advantage of the active hostilities then existing between the United States and Spain, by which the great bulk of the Spanish army was held at Manila, to drive out or capture the Spanish army detachments stationed at southern points, thus increasing their war munitions and being enabled thereby to add numerical strength to their forces. In May, shortly after landing at Cavité, Aguinaldo issued a proclamation forecasting an independent Filipino government, with himself as its chief executive. Early in August the establishment of the independence of the insurgent government was officially proclaimed by him to the world, and as early as June he warned the United States authorities against the landing of its military forces on Philippine soil without first obtaining his consent, because, as he expressed it, "The Filipino people might consider the occupation of Philippine territory by North American troops a violation of their rights."

When the United States forces landed from their transports near and to the south of Manila for the purpose of attacking the city, the fiction that they were acting as allies of the insurgents and in furtherance of Philippine independence appears to have been conveyed by insurgent leaders, and thus when the city was surrendered by Spanish authorities the insurgent troops entered the city to the number of several thousand at the same time the United States was securing possession.

The subsequent efforts on the part of the United States to comply with the articles of capitulation with Spain, by occupying the city of Manila and its defences, and the demands of Aguinaldo to be placed in possession of public buildings and to nominate for office all city functionaries, has been fully shown. He released his hold of such portions of the city as were in possession of his troops, thereby permitting the United States to carry out its agreement with Spain, only after he had peremptory commands to do so; and then he established his military lines in close contact with the city limits—this on the plea that should Manila revert to Spain he desired to be in position to take the offensive; and he even asked that his troops might be permitted to return to the positions evacuated by them in case Spanish authority should be re-established. Not yet prepared to declare hostility against the United States, he busied himself with strengthening his lines about the city, confining our forces strictly within its limits, while he and other rebellious subjects of Spain busied themselves with the formation of what they were pleased to call a republican form of government for the Philippine Islands.

In the absence of Spanish authority with adequate power forcibly to assert itself, many able and conservative men gave adherence to this seemingly *de facto* government and continued to co-operate with it until the latter part of November, when the determination of Aguinaldo and his confidential advisers for absolute political independence, and their declared hostility against the United States, caused them to withdraw their adherence. Affairs thereafter were controlled by that radical element which, from the first, had manifested an unfriendly disposition, and which, securing additional arms and ammunition from the Asiatic coast, organized, equipped, and partially uniformed a military force, strengthened its lines around Manila, and boasted of its ability to place eighty thousand armed men in the field. Its established newspapers, printed in Manila, indulged freely in falsehood and abuse of American authority, insulting officers and men. The condition of affairs continued to grow more threatening daily, aided possibly by the quiet, undemonstrative attitude which the United States troops had assumed, and their apparent disregard of the disparaging remarks of insurgent officers, both military and civil, who were permitted full freedom to circulate throughout the city at their pleasure.

Finally, early in January a few of the leading conservative Filipinos of the section, marking the critical condition of affairs and fearing war, which appeared inevitable unless some pacific measures could be adopted, waited upon me and desired that I appoint a committee of army officers to meet a committee appointed by the insurgent government for the purpose of effecting some compromise by which peace might be maintained. These gentlemen were informed that I was ready at any time to open negotiations with the general of the insurgent army, but could not recognize in word or deed an insurgent government; that I would be pleased to appoint a commission to confer with one which General Aguinaldo, as chief of the insurgent forces, might be pleased to name. This reply, made in written memoranda, was conveyed to Malolos and elicited the following response:

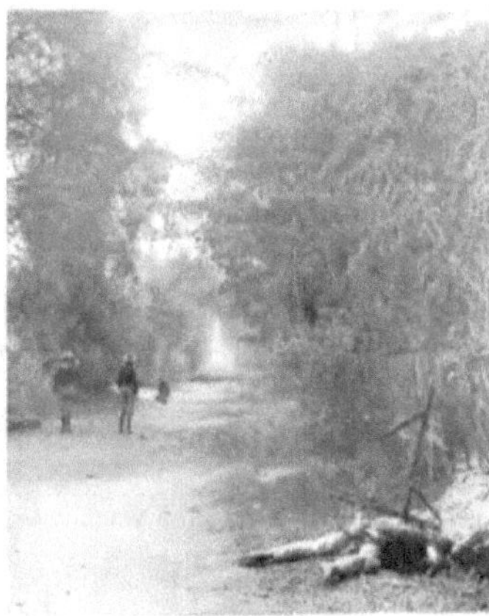

"BLOODY LANE" WHERE THE FOURTEENTH INFANTRY CHARGED.—PHOTOGRAPH BY LIEUT. C. F. O'KEEFE, U. S. A.

(Translation.) MALOLOS, *January 9, 1899.*

Major-General E. S. Otis, General of the American Forces of Occupation in Manila:

GENERAL, I have been informed, after the interview between the commissioners of my government and Mr. Carman, that there will be no inconvenience on your part in naming, as commanding general, representatives who will confer with those whom I will name for the same object.

Although it is not being explained to me the reason why you could not treat with the commissioners of my government, I have the faculty of doing the same with those of the commanding general, "who cannot be recognized." Nevertheless, for the sake of peace, I have considered it advisable to name, as "commanding general," a commission composed of the following gentlemen: Mr. Florentino Torres, Ambrosio Flores, and Manuel Arguelles, that they may together represent me and arrive at an accord with those whom you will name, with the object of using such methods as will normalize the actual situation created by the attitude of your government and troops.

If you will deign to attend to said commissioners, and through these methods come to some understanding, "if only temporary," that will insure the peace and harmony among ourselves, the Filipino public would reach a grateful glory.

I am yours, General, with the highest consideration.

Your most respectful servant,

EMILIO AGUINALDO.

To this letter I replied as follows:

HEADQUARTERS DEPARTMENT OF THE PACIFIC AND EIGHTH ARMY CORPS,

MANILA, P. I., *January 9, 1899.*

General Emilio Aguinaldo, Commanding Revolutionary Forces, Malolos, P. I.:

GENERAL, I have the honor to acknowledge the receipt of your communication of to-day, and am much pleased at the action you have taken. I greatly regret that you have not a clear understanding of my position and motives, and trust that my explanation, assisted by the conference I have invited, will make them clear to you.

In my official capacity I am merely the agent of the United States government to conduct its affairs under the limits which its constitution, laws, precedents, and specific instructions prescribe. I have not the authority to recognize any national or civil power not already formally recognized by my government, unless specifically authorized so to do by the instructions of the Executive of the United States. For this reason I was unable to receive officially the representatives of the revolutionary government, and endeavored to make that inability clear to the distinguished gentlemen with whom I had the pleasure to converse a few evenings since. You will bear witness that my course throughout my entire official connection with affairs here has been consistent, and it has pained me that I have not been able to receive and answer communications of the cabinet officers of the government at Malolos, fearing that I might be erroneously charged with lack of courtesy.

Permit me now, briefly, General, to speak of the serious misunderstanding which exists between the Filipino people and the representatives of the United States government, and which I hope that our commissioners, by a thorough discussion, may be able to dispel. I sincerely believe that all desire peace and harmony, and yet by the machinations of evil-disposed persons we have been influenced to think that we occupy the position of adversaries. The Filipinos appear to be of the opinion that we meditate attack, while I am under the strict orders of the President of the United States to avoid conflict in every way possible. My troops, witnessing the earnestness, the comparatively disturbed and unfriendly attitude of the revolutionary troops and many of the citizens of Manila, conclude that actual hostilities have been determined upon, although it must be clearly within the comprehension of unprejudiced and reflecting minds that the welfare and happiness of the Filipino people depend upon the friendly protection of the United States. The hand of Spain was forced, and she has acknowledged before the world that all her claimed rights in this country have departed by due process of law. This treaty acknowledgment, with the conditions which accompany it, awaits ratification by the Senate of the United States; and the action of its Congress must also be secured before the Executive of that government can proclaim a definite policy. That policy must conform to the will of the people of the United States expressed through its Representatives in Congress. For that action the Filipino people should wait, at least, before severing the existing friendly relations. I am governed by a desire to further the interests of the Filipino people, and shall continue to labor with that end in view. There shall be no conflict of forces if I am able to avoid it; and still I shall endeavor to maintain a position to meet all emergencies that may arise.

Permit me to subscribe myself, General,

With the highest respect,

Your most obedient servant,

E. S. OTIS,

Major-General U. S. Volunteers, Commanding.

Two members of the commission appointed by Aguinaldo were officers of his army, the third being a distinguished lawyer not a member of the Malolos government. On behalf of the United States, General R. P. Hughes, Colonel J. F. Smith of the California Volunteers, and Lieutenant-Colonel E. H. Crowder, Judge-Advocate of the Department, were detailed. The joint commission had several sessions, extending over a period of some three weeks; but no conclusions were reached, as the insurgent members could not submit any formulated statement which they were able to maintain. They presented as the desire of the insurgents absolute independence under the protection of the United States; but the nature and scope of the protection wished for they could not explain, and the conferences resulted in failure.

During the latter part of January the insurgents along their established lines and within the city exhibited increased aggressiveness, assuming a defiant attitude; so much so that our troops were gathered well in hand to meet any demonstrations which might be attempted. Insurgent armed parties entered far within our lines and defied our troops to resist their approaches. To arrest these proceedings, our officers, and citizens of Manila connected with the insurgent government, were sent to insurgent general officers at various places along their lines to request that they keep their men in check, which the latter invariably promised to do, paying, however, little heed

THE BURNING OF TONDO AND PART OF NEW MANILA DURING THE INSURGENT OUTBREAK, FEBRUARY 22

DRAWN FROM LIFE BY G. W. PETERS

INSURGENT ATTACK ON THE BARRACKS OF COMPANY C, THIRTEENTH MINNESOTA VOLUNTEERS, DURING THE TONDO FIRE.—Drawn from Life by G. W. Peters

to their promises. On February 1st a small detachment belonging to our Engineer Company was arrested within our territory and sent to Maiolos. This act brought on the following correspondence:

Headquarters Department of the Pacific and Eighth Army Corps,
Manila, P. I., *February 2, 1899.*

General Emilio Aguinaldo, Commanding Filipino Revolutionary Forces, Malolos:

General.—I have the honor to inform you that a small party of engineers, consisting of a sergeant and four privates, who were engaged in making surveys for the completion of the map of Manila, which the engineer corps is now busy in perfecting, has been missing for two or three days and is reported to be confined in Malolos. The detachment was sent out to do work within the city, with directions to confine itself to the city and suburban lines. Why they were arrested I do not understand, nor can I imagine for what reason they are held at Malolos. I am also informed that a citizen connected with Harper's Weekly newspaper of New York, engaged in taking views for that paper, has also been arrested and held as a prisoner. I know nothing of this except from report, nor do I know who the man is. [The artist referred to was G. W. Peters.] I am also informed that a private soldier who went beyond the lines without authority, with what motive I do not know, is also held as a prisoner.

I send my staff-officer, Lieutenant Haan, of the Engineer Corps, to make inquiry and request your action in this matter.

I am doing everything possible to preserve the peace and avoid all friction until the Filipino people can be made fully acquainted with the sentiments and intentions of the American government, when I am confident that they will appreciate the endeavors of the United States and will again look upon that country as their friend and protector. I also fully believe that the present unrest is the result of machinations of evil-disposed persons.

I am, General, most respectfully,

Your obedient servant,

E. S. Otis,

Major-General U. S. Volunteers, Commanding.

(Translation.) Malolos, *February 4, 1899.*

Major-General Otis, Chief of the Forces of Occupation of Manila and Cavite:

General.—In reply to your letter of February 2d, I have the honor to state that the sergeant and the four American soldiers of the Engineer Corps, to-day liberated, were detained within our territory, beyond our advanced lines on Solis Street, examining our intrenchments and defences at a distance of less than 300 metres.

The said individuals carried a revolver, knives, a compass, plans of Manila and its suburbs, a book with topographical notes, a measuring tape, a machete, two penknives, scales, etc.

INSURGENT HEADQUARTERS AT CALOOCAN, SHOWING EFFECT OF AMERICAN ARTILLERY FIRE.—From a Sketch by G. W. Peters

I deeply regret that these soldiers have been taken within our lines, according to the testimony of our officers, witnesses of their detention, inasmuch as there exists a decree, dated October 20th, which prohibits all foreigners from approaching our defensive works, taking photographic views of the same, drawing plans, or entering our territory with arms, although free transit is permitted all who are unarmed.

The correspondent of Harper's Weekly has been detained in San Juan del Monte taking photographic views; and the proof of this is that in care of Colonel Miguel he has been sent his camera and his horse.

I must state that in consideration of the friendship of the Filipino people for the Americans, the said soldiers have not been imprisoned, but detained, in accordance with the spirit of the decree of October 20th last. They have been lodged in the Gobierno Militar, and have been issued the daily rations of our officers. If they have been uncomfortable, it is due to the excessive sobriety of our race and of our soldiers, who are accustomed to eat but little and to sleep on the hard ground.

With these explanations I believe, General, you will understand the motive for the detention of your soldiers, today liberated, and who have been treated with all due consideration.

I therefore hope that your determination may be another motive on which to base our friendly relations with the great American Republic; and in consideration of this I also decree the liberty of the correspondent referred to.

I am, General, as ever,

Your obedient servant,

Emilio Aguinaldo.

It will be observed that the insurgent government insisted that this engineer party was arrested outside of our small field of operations, which I am confident was not the fact; but the correspondence is given to show the efforts of the American authorities to maintain the peace. During all this time our officers and men were insulted and openly proclaimed to be cowards; our outposts were attacked at night; and the impression became general that the insurgents, notwithstanding our efforts, would indulge soon in open attack; and in the belief apparently entertained by them that they would meet with feeble resistance, during the entire month of January they had labored incessantly to intrench strongly their lines and place their artillery in position, and boasted freely of their intentions soon to drive the American forces out of Manila. On the night of February 2d they sent in a strong detachment to draw the fire of our outpost, which took up a position immediately in front of and within a few yards of the same. The outpost was strengthened by a few of our men, who silently bore their taunts and abuse the entire night. This was reported to me by General MacArthur, whom I directed to communicate with the officer in command of the insurgent troops concerned. His prepared letter was shown to me and approved, and the reply received was all that could be desired. However, the agreement was ignored by the insurgents, and on the evening of February 4th another demonstration was made on one of our small outposts which occupied a retired position at least one hundred and fifty yards within the line which had been mutually agreed upon—an insurgent approaching the picket and refusing to halt or answer when challenged. The result was that our picket discharged his piece, when the insurgent troops near Santa Mesa opened a spirited fire on our troops there stationed.

The insurgent army had thus succeeded in drawing the fire of a small outpost, which they had evidently labored with all their ingenuity to accomplish in order to justify in some way their premeditated attack. It is not believed that the chief insurgent leaders wished to open hostilities at this time, as they were not completely prepared to assume the initiative. They desired two or three days more to perfect their arrangements; but the zeal of their army brought on the crisis which anticipated their action. They could not have delayed long, however, for it was their object to force an issue before American troops then *en route* could arrive at Manila.

The movements of troops during the protracted engagement which followed, and their success at every point, are described in the accounts by the commanding generals of division. I cannot speak too highly of the efficiency displayed by the troops under the most trying ordeals; and where all organizations engaged conducted themselves so courageously it would be difficult to undertake special mention. My adjutant-general, my aides, and other members of my staff conveyed many verbal instructions during the day to points most hotly contested, and assisted materially in the repeated successes of the battle.

During the night of February 4th and the

AMERICAN NAVAL AND LAND FORCES EXCHANGING SIGNALS AT NIGHT

BRIGADIER-GENERAL FREDERICK FUNSTON, U.S.V., THE COLONEL OF THE TWENTIETH KANSAS VOLUNTEERS PROMOTED FOR BRAVERY

following day the insurgents of the city were greatly agitated, fearing for their personal safety. A portion, to the number of about eight thousand, had been enrolled in a secret society for the purpose of attacking our troops within the city and performing incendiary work while the insurgents pressed us from without. This purpose was well known, and an attack upon our forces both in front and rear was anticipated. So admirably, however, had General Hughes, the Provost Marshal-General, disposed of three thousand troops of his command that the rising was suppressed wherever attempted. His action was quick and decisive. Early on the morning of the 5th the police companies so effectively delivered their fire upon these assembling organizations that they were dispersed and discouraged. Their loss in killed and wounded could not have been above fifty or sixty. They made no further very dangerous demonstrations until the night of February 23d, when they suffered a most severe punishment.

A movement on Caloocan, February 10th, was made with the intention of placing our northern line in better tactical condition, and consisted in swinging the left of General MacArthur's division to the front. That officer had requested to be allowed to do this shortly after the 5th, but was informed that we would await an anticipated concentration of the enemy on our left, where their activity was daily increasing. It was expected that if we remained quiet for a short time the enemy would collect his routed forces, which we could not pursue, and would place them in position

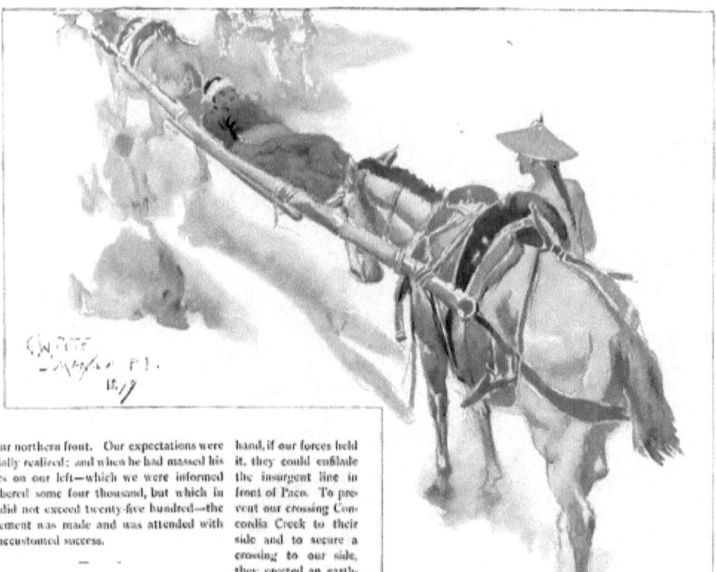

POLO—REMOVING THE AMERICAN WOUNDED FROM THE FIRING-LINE

on our northern front. Our expectations were partially realized; and when he had massed his forces on our left—which we were informed numbered some four thousand, but which in fact did not exceed twenty-five hundred—the movement was made and was attended with our accustomed success.

OPERATIONS OF THE FIRST DIVISION

General Anderson's Account

A line of delimitation had been agreed on between the department commander and the insurgent Filipino authorities, extending from the confluence of the Concordia Creek on the left of my line to the mouth of the *estero* San Antonio into Manila Bay, just below Fort Malate, an approximate distance of four miles. On the left of my line the American and Filipino pickets confronted each other on either side of Concordia Creek. At the Concordia bridge, near block-house 11, they were only a few paces apart. On the right of our line, our picket-line was established some distance back from the line of delimitation, following closely the old Spanish lines of defence, except that the important position of block-house 14 was not occupied, our advance post being at the site of block-house 13, some distance back in a thick growth of bamboo.

Finding that we did not hold our line of delimitation, the Filipino military forces advanced beyond this line and began to throw up a formidable line of intrenchments. They also constructed a number of detached earthworks along the left of our line, and prepared a number of strong stone houses and churches in Santa Ana and San Pedro Macati for defence. On the extreme left of our line, between block-house 11, occupied by our advance on the Paco-Macati road and the Pasig River, lies the suburb of Pandacan, which is on an island made by a number of tidal estuaries and the river. By occupying this position the insurgents could bring a flank fire on our forces in the suburb of Paco. On the other hand, if our forces held it, they could enfilade the insurgent line in front of Paco. To prevent our crossing Concordia Creek to their side and to secure a crossing to our side, they erected an earthwork on the east side of the creek on a bit of high ground. As the Pasig River makes a sharp re-entering bend just above Pandacan and below Santa Ana, a sudden and successful advance of our line from Paco would force their troops stationed on their extreme right into this bend as a *cul-de-sac*.

To prevent this, the insurgents constructed an enclosed bastioned earthwork on the neck of this peninsula, the fire from which would also sweep the plain between Paco and Santa Ana. All these preparations we witnessed without authority to prevent them—as Sumter was surrounded by batteries thirty-eight years previously.

As the insurgents saw their formidable works approaching completion they became more insolent day by day, and finally did everything they could in insolence and insults to provoke us to begin the conflict. As they were permitted to go and come through our lines at will, they knew just what troops we had, where they were located, and that we were making no visible preparations for defence. It seems proper to make these statements in order to justify the assertion that no troops ever behaved better under intense provocation, showing excellent discipline and self-control.

The first brigade of the first division, under Brigadier-General Charles King, was made up of the First California Volunteer Infantry, under Colonel James F. Smith, three battalions; the First Washington Volunteer Infantry, under Colonel J. H. Wholley, three battalions; and the First Idaho Volunteer Infantry, two battalions, under Major Daniel W. Figgins. To this force was added, during the progress of the battle, one battalion of Wyoming Volunteer Infantry under Major Frank M. Foote.

Two companies of the California regiment and one company of each of the other regiments were left in Manila to combat insurrection in the city, if that should be attempted. This brigade held the left of our line south of the Pasig, and faced in a general way to the eastward.

The second brigade, under Brigadier-General Samuel Ovenshine, was made up of the Fourteenth Regular Infantry, ten companies, under Major C. H. Potter; eight companies of the First North Dakota Volunteer Infantry; and six troops of the Fourth Regular Cavalry, acting as infantry, under Major Louis H. Rucker. This brigade held the right of the line from block-house 12, on Tripa de Gallina, to Fort Malate on the bay, and faced south.

There were in the division two batteries of artillery, one of six 3.2 breech-loading guns, under Captain A. B. Dyer, Sixth Artillery, and four mountain-guns, left by the Astor Battery, under Lieutenant H. L. Hawthorne. Dyer's Battery had no horses. The artillery was under the orders of the division commander, and under the general direction of Captain Dyer. Besides these, there was one company of regular engineers, acting as infantry, under Lieutenant W. G. Haan, United States Artillery.

The only preparations which could be made for battle, in view of orders to stand on the defensive, were the assignment of the different organizations to places on the firing-line and the selection of positions for the artillery. Apparently, nothing more could be done, as our government had to preserve a waiting policy until the treaty of peace with Spain was signed. Nevertheless, as an attack from the front might be followed by an uprising in the city, this procrastination placed the army under a great disadvantage. The only preparation I could make was to select a point I considered the key-point of the battle-field, on a slight knoll on the right of King's line beyond Paco bridge. To this point I had approaches prepared and sand-bags provided for protection for the guns. I also had two of Dyer's guns placed on Fort Malate, and arranged signals with the monitor *Monadnock* to direct its fire.

On February 4 hostilities began on the north side, but no firing took place on our front that day or the succeeding night. At 3.40 A.M. on the morning of the 5th the insurgents opened fire on block-house 11 with Mauser rifles. I had just ridden up to my headquarters in the city, from which I had telegraphic communication with every part of my command. I first telegraphed corps headquarters for permission to take the offensive when it became light enough to do so.

At seven o'clock I directed General Ovenshine to open artillery fire on block-house 14 and the wood near by, and to be prepared to drive the enemy from the Malate front; and, if they yielded easily, to turn to the left with part of his command and sweep the enemy from his entire front. If successful, he was to be ready to reinforce King's right and turn the left of the insurgent force operating from Santa Ana. This project was not carried out until later in the day, as permission was not given to assume the offensive until eight o'clock.

In the meantime the firing on King's line became heavier as the day advanced. The Washingtonians, the Idahoans, six companies of the California regiment, and Hawthorne's mountain battery were put on the firing-line on the Paco front. Four guns of Dyer's battery and four companies of Californians were sent to Battery Knoll on the right. A battalion of Wyoming volunteers, which had reported the night before, was brought up to the intersection of the Paco and Singalon roads, so that it could reinforce either brigade as occasion might require. The troops of the Fourth Cavalry were also kept in reserve. The artillery soon began to do effective service, and drove the insurgents from several strong positions near our line. Towards eight o'clock I learned that neither the fire from the navy nor from our guns on Malate had shaken the hold of the enemy on Ovenshine's front, and the volume of fire beyond Singalon and the demand for ambulances showed that a desperate battle was being waged there.

At last, at eight o'clock, a telegram came from Major-General Otis authorizing an advance if not made too far. I went at once to Battery Knoll, taking with me the Wyoming battalion. Finding there three companies of Californians, I placed these seven companies under the command of Colonel Smith, of the First California, and directed him to deploy and advance in line with the rest of King's brigade, substituting this for the intended co-operation of Ovenshine. Smith's right was a little later reinforced by Company A, Battalion of Engineers, under Lieutenant Haan.

General King was present, and was ordered to advance as soon as Smith deployed. These officers received this order with delight and their troops with enthusiasm. The movement began at 8.20 A.M. with a rush over the creek in our front; a cheer and rattling volleys as the whole line advanced—not by rushes, but with a rush. The insurgent line fell back before our advance, fighting, however, with spirit. The rice-fields in our front were intersected by little irrigating dikes, and behind each of these a stand was attempted, the Filipinos firing from behind them. Our men disdained these shelters and moved steadily on until a raking fire was opened on them from the redoubt on the neck of the bend between Pandacan and Santa Ana.

The Idaho regiment then made a turn to the left, charging the redoubt, carrying it at the point of the bayonet, and driving a regiment of insurgents to the bank of the river. The California companies in Pandacan at the same time crossed Concordia Creek and captured the smaller earthwork on the farther bank. On the lower side of Santa Ana, on the river, was another earthwork, in which two Krupp guns had been placed, bearing on the river, but with embrasures also on the land side; and to one of these one of the Krupp guns was transferred when an advance was made. To its fire Hawthorne's battery replied with good effect, until its fire was masked by the advance of our line. This earthwork was also carried, and both Krupp guns were captured. At the redoubt the Filipinos made a brave defence. As the Scotch Guard at Flodden Field formed an unbroken line around their king, so these misguided insurgents fell where they fought, filling the trenches with an unbroken line of killed and wounded. Apparently a whole battalion was driven to the bank of the river. They attempted to cross in boats and by swimming; but not a man was seen to gain the opposite bank, and for many days their bodies were seen floating down the stream. Major Figgins, commanding the Idahoans, estimated the enemy's loss in this movement at seven hundred killed, captured, wounded, and drowned.

At the same time the California battalion charged and drove the enemy out of Santa Ana, driving them from stone walls and convents, churches and houses, and fighting their way through blazing bamboo huts from which the natives were firing. This could not have been accomplished had not Colonel Smith's command broken the left of the insurgent line and carried the English cemetery, which was enclosed with a strong stone wall. The regular Engineer Company, under Lieutenant Haan, volunteered for this service and did yeoman work. The Wyoming battalion on the right of the line did not advance with the energy of the rest of the line. Had they done so, the enemy's forces might have been captured in Santa Ana. Retreating on San Pedro Macati, they attempted to make a stand. A number attempted to hold the church and cemetery of San Pedro Macati. Then the Wyomings came up at last, and did good service. By a skilful, tactical movement of the Engineer Company, this strong position was taken in reverse and carried. The insurgents finally broke and ran, and our forces advanced and captured the church and monastery of Guadalupe, a mile beyond. Many prisoners were taken in San Pedro Macati, and a well-supplied arsenal.

Brigadier-General Ovenshine, commanding the Second Brigade, had the North Dakota regiment, under Lieutenant-Colonel Treumann, occupying the old Spanish trenches from Fort Malate on the bay to an almost impassable swamp, which divided his line into

COLONEL OWEN SUMMERS, U. S. V., FIRST OREGON VOLUNTEERS

Brevetted Brigadier-General for Gallantry

two sections. From the farther east side of this swamp to block-house 12, on the Tripa de Gallina, his line was held by nine companies of the Fourteenth Infantry, under Major C. H. Potter, and three dismounted troops of the Fourth Cavalry, under Captain F. Wheeler, on the extreme left. There our men had to fight in dense woods and bamboo thickets. The enemy had strong intrenchments, and fired on us also from ditches and tree-tops. The fight raged here more fiercely than elsewhere. The left of our line could not advance, because the enemy had a flank fire upon it. When I sent Smith's improvised command echeloned to the left of King's line, I kept only one company in reserve in support for the artillery at Battery Knoll; but, finding that two companies which had been out on outpost duty during the night had been left behind in the advance, I ordered them over to the right to support Wheeler. This gave him advanced from block-house 13, but, after coming in view of the enemy's trenches, fell back. A gun of Dyer's battery was sent to him, but on account of the dense bamboo thickets that masked the enemy's line it could not do satisfactory service. Shortly after 2 P.M. Major Rucker, Fourth Cavalry, joined the cavalry battalion and relieved Captain Wheeler of command.

Hearing of the successful advance of the North Dakotans, I telegraphed General Ovenshine to carry out the project I had arranged with him, to attempt to roll up the enemy by a movement from right to left. As there was a long delay in carrying out this order, I repeated it several times by telegraph and aides sent with oral orders. It was at last found that he was under a false impression that he had received other orders from the corps commander. When this misapprehension was removed he made the movement with complete success.

under Lieutenant-Colonel Debose. For a time there was a lively contest in the town. The insurgents were so persistent that nearly all their *nipa* houses in the town had to be burned to dislodge them. Fifty-three prisoners were taken, all in ordinary clothing, but unquestionably participants in the savage warfare. While this was going on in the town a sharp musketry fire was opened on us from a large stone church near the Paco bridge. I directed Dyer's battery on the knoll to reverse its guns and open on the church. It was soon in flames, yet a number of desperate men took refuge in the church tower. It was several hours before they could be dislodged, and they kept up their resistance to the last.

During this engagement the telegraph men of the signal corps did effective service, carrying their lines to the extreme front at San Pedro Macati, Fort Malate, and Pasai. Lieutenant Kilbourne, who was with my head-

THE FIRST NEBRASKA VOLUNTEERS NEAR THEIR QUARTERS IN BINONDO—"RETREAT"

one battalion of the Fourteenth Infantry, his three troops of cavalry, and one company each of Washingtonians and Californians.

At about ten o'clock Ovenshine ordered an advance. The North Dakotans drove the enemy from their front back to the Carmelite convent.

Major Potter, with Matile's battalion of the Fourteenth Infantry, advanced through the woods to the right of block-house 14, and Captain John Murphy, with his battalion of the Fourteenth Infantry, charged block-house 14 and the adjoining trenches. After a desperate fight the enemy were driven out, but not without inflicting serious loss upon us. Captain Mitchell was mortally wounded leading his company. Lieutenant Miles, of the Fourteenth Infantry, was first in the enemy's trenches, and, followed by only six men, charged into the smoking ruins of the block-house. This was a daring and brilliant feat of arms. At the same time Captain Wheeler

In the meantime I had sent a battalion of the First Tennessee, under Lieutenant-Colonel Gracey Childers, to the Singalon front. They reached that point just as the North Dakotans were clearing the front and driving the enemy into the woods beyond the Tripa. The Tennessee battalion, crossing the same stream, opened on them, as did also Dyer's guns on Battery Knoll. Ovenshine then advanced with his brigade to Pasai, which he found abandoned. Leaving part of his command there, he marched with the rest up the Pasai-Macati road, and opened communication with General King at San Pedro Macati, and, returning, picketed the road.

This ended the fighting at the front, but soon after King's brigade had advanced beyond Paco a number of insurgents who had lain concealed in the town began to fire on the ammunition carts and hospital ambulances going to the front. Anticipating the possibility of this treachery, a small force had been left in Paco

quarters party, did a brave act in climbing a telegraph-pole at the Paco bridge to string a broken wire, under a cross-fire between desperadoes in the tower and our artillery.

New troops are generally demoralized by firing from flanks and rear. In this contest bullets seemed to come from all directions, but our men continued unconcerned. When I had my headquarters on Artillery Knoll, the artillery men and my staff officers and orderlies were subject to this cross-fire during the entire engagement, and, as the enemy used smokeless powder, it could only be surmised from what direction the fire came.

At two o'clock I rode to King's front and found his lines satisfactorily established. I then went to the Singalon front and found everything satisfactory there.

In this engagement we lost two officers and twenty-six men killed and four officers and ninety-five soldiers wounded; one enlisted man injured. We could only estimate the

ON THE ADVANCED FIRING-LINE

enemy's loss. Our burial parties interred in their own trenches 238 insurgent dead. We took about 306 prisoners and two very fine Krupp guns, besides a large number of small-arms, ammunition, and ordnance stores.

The coolness, energy, bravery, and *élan* of the officers and men of my division were worthy of the highest commendation. Beginning on the left, the Idaho regiment, under Major Figgins, did splendid service. Major McConville, who had served under my command in the War of the Rebellion, was killed leading his battalion, like the brave and faithful officer that he was. Captain Whittington was especially commended by his brigade commander.

The Washington regiment, under Colonel Wholley, received its baptism of fire. Its men fought like veterans. From the California regiment I expected excellent service. Colonel James F. Smith showed the very best qualities of a Volunteer officer. His services in every position in which he was placed were most valuable and efficient. Major Sime, of the same regiment, proved a natural-born soldier. He was not only brave, but cool and discreet.

Captain Haan, Lieutenant Third Artillery, in command of the Engineer Company, showed especial efficiency. The Wyoming battalion, although not well handled at first, when it got into action showed the bravery I had seen before in Wyoming men.

In the second brigade the North Dakotans made a dashing charge. The part of the Fourth Cavalry under fire fought as well as they always had in their many battles. The fighting of the Fourteenth Infantry under the trying surroundings in which they were placed was little less than heroic; certainly it was most effective. They were well led by Major Potter, Captain John Murphy, a well-tried veteran, and other efficient company officers—Matile, Eastman, Hasbrouck, Lassiegne, Biddle, and, in fact, all present, including Captains Martin and Kranthoff—who, although on staff duty, went to the front with their own regiment, performing excellent service.

Captain Dyer, Sixth Artillery, directed the artillery operations for me with rare skill and judgment. The platoon of Battery D, Sixth Artillery, placed in Fort Malate, was most effective, and Lieutenant Scott managed the platoon under his command in a most satisfactory manner. In fact, the work of this battery made victory certain. Lieutenant Hawthorne, in command of the battery of mountain guns (Astor Battery), gave proof of rare ability. From Paco to San Pedro Macati this battery was far to the front and did really splendid service.

To the skill, energy, and bravery of our two brigade commanders, Brigadier-General Charles King and Brigadier-General Samuel Ovenshine, the credit of success was largely due. I was grateful to them for their energetic and loyal support.

The medical department of the division, in its chief surgeon, Major H. W. Cardwell, did everything that skill and energy could do in the care of the wounded, extending their aid also to the wounded Filipinos.

The entire division staff was with me at the front, and I was indebted to its members for patient, energetic, and most efficient service. Captain H. C. Cabell, Adjutant-General, and Captain C. C. Walcutt, Chief Quartermaster and Acting Ordnance Officer, performed their important duties most effectively. Captain W. E. Birkhimer, Third Artillery, Inspector and Judge Advocate, gave valuable assistance by his untiring energy and marked ability. My personal aides were Lieutenants R. H. Allen and Thomas M. Anderson, Jr. Lieutenant A. P. Hayne, California Heavy Artillery, was with me as a volunteer aide, and Major Samuel Jones, Quartermaster's Department, also gave his assistance. These officers carried orders and made observations on all parts of the firing-line, in a number of instances correcting misapprehensions and leading organizations to their proper positions. Lieutenant Anderson, although ill from fever contracted at Santiago, insisted on performing his share of duty. The division clerks and orderlies also deserved high commendation.

The division had on the firing-line in the battle of the 5th about 3850 officers and men. We were opposed, as I believed, by about 5000 insurgent Filipinos. Of these I estimated that 2000 were killed, wounded, captured, or scattered. Within two days we had captured Pasig and Pateros, and our scouting-parties had gone to the Laguna de Bay.

THE TWENTIETH KANSAS

ACCOUNT BY COLONEL FREDERICK FUNSTON

THE outpost of the Twentieth Kansas Infantry in the car-station of the road to Caloocan was fired upon about 10 P.M., February 4, by insurgent patrols. Before this time the outposts of various other regiments had been fired upon and the general alarm had been given. The whole regiment was under arms in a few moments; and, leaving Companies A, B, F, and L, under Captain Buchan, to guard the quarters, the remaining companies, constituting the Second and Third Battalions, under Majors Whitman and Metcalf, marched to the relief of our outpost, now fighting valiantly under Captain A. G. Clark.

We were joined on the way by a detachment from the Utah Light Artillery, with one gun, under Lieutenant Seaman.

Upon arrival at the outpost I found that our men were making a stand in the road four hundred yards north of the car-station. The gun was placed in position in the middle of the road, and the four companies of the Second Battalion deployed in the gardens to the left and right, and an occasional reply was made to the enemy's fire, which appeared to come from the woods about eight hundred yards on our front. With the coming of daylight another gun of the Utah battery which had arrived was placed in position, and two companies of the Third Battalion were placed in the firing-line.

During the day Major Whitman was taken ill and returned to the city. At noon I received orders from the brigade commander, who was on the ground, to advance the line five hundred yards. This was done without difficulty, the woods being first cleared of the enemy by a dozen well-directed volleys. The two field-pieces were placed in the road in front of the small church and from them were fired a few well-directed shots. The insurgent barricades and trenches were distant only five hundred yards, and the fire from them was so galling that an advance was imperative. Major Metcalf had gone to protect our left flank with Companies C, D, and K, and did excellent service. Companies F and L had come out from the city under Captain Buchan, and with these two, and companies E, H, I, L, and M, I ordered a charge up the road and through the gardens and bamboo thickets that flanked it. This charge, which I led in person, was most gallantly made, the men firing as they advanced. The insurgents stood until we were within sixty yards, when they gave way. We occupied both lines of barricades, and were

A GUN OF THE UTAH ARTILLERY ABOUT TO BE FIRED IN THE ADVANCE ON THE WATER-WORKS

DRILLING AMERICAN TROOPS AT CAMP DEWEY

preparing to assault the small block-house, when Major Strong, adjutant-general of the division, arrived, and ordered me to retire for the night to the position that we had just left. This was done, and the night was passed without incident.

Our casualties in the desultory fighting of the day were one enlisted man killed and six enlisted men wounded.

On the morning of the 6th I received orders to advance to the insurgent barricades that we had taken the previous evening, and to occupy them. This was done without difficulty, as the enemy had fled. During the day we found and buried the bodies of thirty-one insurgents killed in our charge of the previous day.

The regiment was intrenched facing the north, the right resting on the railway, where it joined with the First Montana, and the left on the impassable bayous from the sea.

The day and night passed without incident, except for an occasional exchange of shots with the enemy.

On the afternoon of the 7th the enemy became so bold, firing from behind a dike five hundred yards in front of our line, that it became imperative to dislodge them; so, after obtaining permission from the brigade commander, I led three and one-half companies in an attack on this position, carrying it at the point of the bayonet. Our loss was First Lieutenant A. C. Alford, of Company B, a most bright and promising young officer, killed, and six enlisted men severely wounded.

I counted twenty-six dead insurgents on the ground where they had made their stand. In accordance with our original orders, we fell back to the trenches before dark, and remained there during the whole night undisturbed.

There were no further incidents of note until the 10th, when, in conjunction with the First Montana and Third Artillery, we were ordered to advance on the town of Caloocan. The attack, so far as the Twentieth was concerned, was made through dense woods and in the face of a hot though badly directed fire from the enemy, our loss being two enlisted men killed and one officer and eight enlisted men wounded. We were soon intrenched on the north side of the town of Caloocan, with our left on the water and our right, as before, on the First Montana.

Where everybody did so well it is impossible to make distinctions, but I note especially the splendid conduct of Major Wilder S. Metcalf, who was my right hand during the trying operations of these ten days.

Our entire losses in this time were five killed and twenty-seven wounded.

SCENE AT THE COMMISSARY DEPARTMENT IN MANILA.—155,000 RATIONS ABOUT TO BE ISSUED

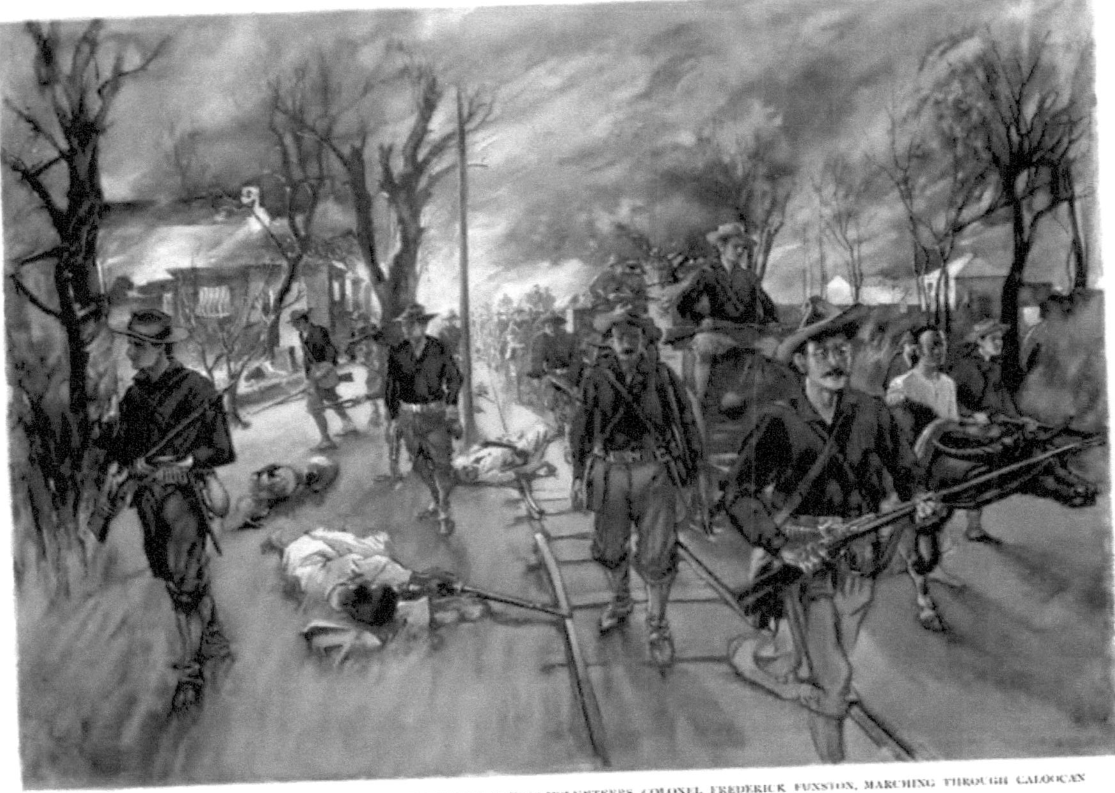

THE AMMUNITION-TRAIN AND RESERVES OF THE TWENTIETH KANSAS VOLUNTEERS, COLONEL FREDERICK FUNSTON, MARCHING THROUGH CALOOCAN AT NIGHT AFTER THE BATTLE OF FEBRUARY 10.—DRAWN FROM LIFE BY G. W. PETERS

SANTA MESA, NEAR MANILA, WHERE THE FIGHTING BEGAN

THE REVOLT OF THE FILIPINOS.—*Continued*

OPERATIONS OF THE SECOND DIVISION

General MacArthur's Account

At the commencement of hostilities the division was organized as follows: Artillery—Battalion Utah Artillery, Major R. W. Young, Cuartel de Meisic, 8 officers, 302 men.

First Brigade, Brigadier-General H. G. Otis commanding—Third United States Artillery, Major W. A. Kobbe, Cuartel de Meisic, 14 officers, 630 men; First Montana Infantry, Colonel H. C. Kessler, 1 Gunnao Street, 6 San Miguel Street, 48 officers, 846 men; Tenth Pennsylvania Infantry, Colonel A. L. Hawkins, Corregidor Island, 22, 42, and 44 Calle de Isis, Plaza Santa Cruz, 28 officers, 713 men; Twentieth Kansas Infantry, Colonel F. Funston, La Rosa tobacco warehouse, Aldecoa & Co.'s godown, and Administracion de Hacienda, 37 officers, 976 men; total, First Brigade, 127 officers, 3185 men.

Second Brigade, Brigadier-General Irving Hale commanding—First Colorado Infantry, Colonel H. B. McCoy, 86, 46, 1, 20, and 66 Calle Alix, 25 San Sebastian Street, San Sebastian Convent, 12 Plaza Santa Ana, 41 officers, 1033 men; First South Dakota Infantry, Colonel A. S. Frost, 2 and 10 Malacanan, 1 Conception, 5 Conception, 40 officers, 793 men; First Nebraska Infantry, Colonel J. M. Stotsenburg, Camp Santa Mesa, 37 officers, 886 men; total, Second Brigade, 118 officers, 2713 men; aggregate of division, 253 officers, 6200 men.

In addition to the foregoing, the river gunboat *Laguna de Bay* was attached to the division, the *personnel* and armament being as follows: Captain B. H. Randolph, Third United States Artillery, commanding, with a detachment of 2 non-commissioned officers and 27 privates of Battery G, Third United States Artillery; Second Lieutenant R. C. Naylor, 2 non-commissioned officers and 3 privates of the Utah Light Artillery, United States Volunteers, and First Lieutenant Edwin A. Harting and Second Lieutenant Samuel G. Larson, 5 non-commissioned officers and 20 privates of the First South Dakota Infantry, United States Volunteer Engineers and deck force, 5 non-commissioned officers and 12 privates. The armament of the gunboat consisted of two 3-inch naval rifles, two 1.65-inch Hotchkiss rifles and four Gatling guns. The infantry detachment was armed with Springfield rifles.

On February 27 the navy furnished a Colt's automatic gun, taken from the United States war-ship *Helena*, in charge of Lieutenant Cleland Davis, United States Navy, and three enlisted men of the Marine Corps. One battalion of three companies of the Second Oregon Infantry, United States Volunteers, under command of Major Eastwick, joined the division on February 7th, and was attached to the Second Brigade. The First Battalion, Wyoming Volunteer Infantry, joined the division on February 8th, and was attached to the Second Brigade. A squadron of three troops of the Fourth United States Cavalry, under command of Major Rucker, joined the division on February 9th, and remained on duty with it until February 18th, part of the time under the immediate orders of the division commander, and part of the time attached to the First Brigade. A platoon of the Sixth United States Artillery, under command of Second Lieutenant A. S. Fleming, joined the division on February 10.

The outpost line of each regiment in the city, by a general understanding in the premises, was to be occupied as a fighting-line by the respective organizations, upon signal by wire from division headquarters, through brigade commanders, to "carry out the pre-arranged plan."

The pertinacity of the insurgents, in passing armed parties over the line of delimitation into American territory, at a point nearly opposite the pipe-line outpost of the Nebraska regiment, induced a correspondence which, in the light of subsequent events, is interesting, as indicating with considerable precision a premeditated purpose on the part of somebody in the insurgent army to force a collision at that point. The original note from my headquarters, which was prepared after conference with the department commander, was carried by Major Strong, who entered the insurgent lines and placed the paper in the hands of Colonel San Miguel. The answer of Colonel San Miguel was communicated in an autograph note, which was written in the presence of Major Strong, who also saw Colonel San Miguel write an order to his officer at the outpost in question, directing him to withdraw from the American side of the line. This order Major Strong saw delivered to the officer on the outpost. The correspondence referred to is as follows; the original of Colonel San Miguel's note was written in the Spanish language:

MAJOR-GENERAL MacARTHUR'S HEADQUARTERS AT CALOOCAN

Headquarters Second Division,
Eighth Army Corps,

Manila, P. I., *February 2, 1899.*

Commanding General, Philippine Troops in Third Zone.

Sir: The line between your command and my command has been long established, and is well understood by yourself and myself. It is quite necessary under present conditions that this line should not be passed by armed men of either command. An armed party from your command now occupies the village in front of blockhouse No. 7, at a point considerably more than one hundred yards on my side of the line, and is very active in exhibiting hostile intentions. This party must be withdrawn to your side of the line at once. From this date, if the line is crossed by your men with arms in their hands, they must be regarded as subject to such action as I may deem necessary. Very respectfully,

ARTHUR MACARTHUR,
Major-General, United States Volunteers,
Commanding.

SAN JUAN DEL MONTE, *February 2.*

Major-General MacArthur:

MY VERY DEAR SIR,—In reply to yours dated this day, in which you inform me that my soldiers have been passing the line of demarcation fixed by agreement, I desire to say that this is foreign to my wishes, and I shall give immediate orders in the premises that they retire. Truly yours,

L. F. SAN MIGUEL,
Colonel and First Chief.

At about 8.30 P.M., February 4, an insurgent patrol, consisting of four armed soldiers, entered our territory at block-house No. 7, and advanced to the little village of Santol, which was occupied from the pipe-line outpost of the Nebraska regiment. This, it will be observed, was precisely the point referred to in the correspondence above quoted. The American sentinel challenged twice, and then, as the insurgent patrol continued to advance, he fired, whereupon the patrol retired to block-house 7, from whence fire was immediately opened by the entire insurgent outpost at that point.

At 9 P.M. Colonel Stotsenburg, First Nebraska Infantry, United States Volunteers, reported considerable firing at his outposts, which extended gradually along the entire front of the division. At 10.10 P.M. it was evident that hostilities had been commenced in earnest by the insurgents, and accordingly an order issued from division headquarters to put everything on the firing-line, according to a programme which had been prearranged for such an emergency.

The fire fight continued throughout the night with great ferocity, but no contact was made at any point on the line until daylight of the 5th, when a series of combats occurred along the entire division front, which, by twelve o'clock noon, resulted in the possession, by the Second Brigade, of the entire insurgent line from block-house 4, through 5, 6, and 7, San Juan bridge, Polvorin, Deposito, San Juan del Monte Church, San Felipe Convent, and Mandaloya, to the Pasig opposite Santa Ana. About 11 A.M. of the 5th a battalion of the Tennessee regiment joined the Second Brigade as a reinforcement, and thereafter rendered efficient service in connection with the occupation of all positions to the east of the Deposito.

In consequence of the decided success on the right, it seemed expedient to conform thereto by a general advance of the First Brigade. Accordingly, orders issued to the Montana regiment to occupy the Chinese Hospital and Lico, and to the Third Artillery and Kansas regiments to occupy the road west from Lico, crossing the Caloocan road and as far to the left thereof as necessary.

BRIGADIER-GENERAL CHARLES KING.—DRAWN BY G. W. PETERS.

The movement commenced about two o'clock, and was conducted with great spirit. The momentum of the advance, however, carried the several regiments beyond their designated objectives, and resulted in an impetuous rush to the front, in which the Kansas regiment and two guns of the Utah Light Artillery operated directly along the Caloocan road, and the Third Artillery, two guns of the Utah Light Artillery, and the regiments of Montana, Pennsylvania, and South Dakota converged upon the Chinese Hospital. The South Dakota regiment belonged to the Second Brigade, and was brought into the fight through the presence of mind and good judgment of Captain Lockett, Fourth United States Cavalry, Acting Inspector-General of the division, who, being on the ground and seeing the manifest importance of supporting the First Brigade, assumed the necessary authority to order the regiment to advance and connect with the Pennsylvania regiment and join in the action.

The combat was characterized by a fine display of initiative on the part of the troops engaged, all of whom were essential to the final success achieved, as it is probable that none of the regiments would have reached the hospital had it not been for the co-operation of all concerned.

By reason of a general tendency arising from the character of the ground, the First Brigade inclined somewhat towards the bay, and the Second Brigade, in like manner, inclined towards the Pasig River; that is to say, one inclined to the west and the other to the east, the effect of which was to create a gap between the two. It therefore became very important to arrest the forward movement, and to concentrate and connect the division line before dark. The connection between the two brigades was successfully accomplished at block-house No. 4, and the line established. The Third Artillery and the Montana regiments changed relative positions, so as to place the artillery on the right instead of the left of the Montana regiment, which position it occupied at the commencement of hostilities.

By signal during the night, connection was established with the United States warship *Charleston*, and, by arrangement, fire from the fleet commenced at daylight and continued with apparently excellent effect until about 11 A.M., when it was suspended on request from division headquarters, as the rapid advance from the right had placed it in the line of fire. At about 8.30 P.M. of the evening of the 5th a battalion of three companies of the Tennessee regiment, under Major McGuire, reported for duty with the division. One company was stationed as a guard at the Chinese Hospital, which was being used as a dressing station for our wounded, the other two companies being placed as a reserve at the corner of Dulumbayan Street and the Calle de Iris. Early on the morning of the 6th Major McGuire's battalion was relieved and returned to duty with the regiment.

On February 6 General Hale supervised the capture of the pumping-station of the water-works in the vicinity of Mariquina, the details of which operation were successfully carried out by Colonel Stotsenburg, of the First Nebraska Infantry, United States Volunteers. The tactical work was accomplished in the most inspiring manner.

Aside from the foregoing and the rectification of alignments at several points on the division front, nothing further of note occurred on this day.

The event of the 7th was an outpost affair on the front of the Kansas regiment, which originated in a wrangle between the opposing sentinels, successively supported from our side until Colonel Funston, with the sanction of the brigade commander, personally advanced with three and a half companies, under the command of Major Metcalf, and engaged an insurgent force of something more than two hundred men. The insurgents stood firmly, and the combat terminated in a hand-to-hand fight, in which bayonets and clubbed muskets were freely used, the result being the complete routing of the enemy, with a very considerable loss to them, twenty-six of their dead being counted within a space of about seventy-five square yards. The Kansas regiment lost First Lieutenant Alfred C. Alford, killed, and six soldiers wounded.

The various positions, which had been protected by hasty intrenchments, were maintained until the afternoon of the 10th, when the town of Caloocan was occupied by a premeditated movement, in which the Third United States Artillery and the regiments of Montana and Kansas, reinforced by the Idaho regiment under Major Figgins, three troops of the Fourth United States Cavalry under Major Rucker, seven guns of the Utah Light Artillery under Major Young, and a platoon of Battery D, Sixth United States Artillery, under Lieutenant Fleming, from the First Division, were employed.

The tactical scheme, which was carefully explained to the brigade and regimental commanders, was to the following effect: An artillery preparation of thirty minutes by the combined action of the navy and field guns, to be followed by the infantry advance, which involved a wheel to the right on block-house No. 2, as a pivot, until the left reached a point in front of the town. The troops advanced as posted in the trenches, a battalion of Idaho supporting Montana and Kansas, respectively. The Fourth Cavalry was deployed, facing the rear, to insure protection in the event of an uprising in the city.

The combined artillery preparation commenced at 3.09 P.M., and the infantry advance at 3.50 P.M., after which the programme, as prescribed, was executed with almost exact precision, and the American flag was raised in the town at 5.15 P.M. The tactical execution of the necessary movements was exemplary, and the resistance was such as to require the best efforts of all concerned.

In connection with the occupation of Caloocan, Company M of the Montana regiment, Captain Hallahan commanding, was placed under the orders of Major Bell, United States Volunteer Engineers, in charge of the office of Military Information, Headquarters Department of the Pacific, with a view to utilizing a ravine for a concealed advance, in the hope of deriving advantage from the sudden and unexpected appearance of troops on that part of the field. This duty, which was special in its nature, and also involved the possibility of extra hazard, was well performed.

From the 10th, the lines of the opposing armies were in close contact, which afforded scope for the characteristic sharp-shooting methods of the natives, and resulted in considerable loss to us, especially in the Kansas and Montana regiments. The disposition of the natives in this respect was considerably abated and very effectually controlled by the skilful placing of shrapnel from the guns of the Sixth Artillery and the Utah batteries.

In consequence of its advanced position at the pumping station, the Nebraska regiment engaged, from the first occupancy thereof, in a series of minor operations, which resulted in a large amount of arduous and dangerous work, all of which was cordially and well performed by this excellent regiment.

On the 23d a formidable uprising was undertaken in the city by the combined efforts of the natives, assisted by insurgent soldiers, who apparently passed our lines for the purpose of encouraging their friends in the city. Information of a successful attack by natives on the Tondo car-shed of the tramway line connecting Manila and Malabon was reported at my headquarters at the Caloocan church by a member of the guard of the Twentieth Kansas, who had been stationed thereat, and who had, with his party, been driven therefrom. The situation, thus disclosed, was quite embarrassing, and all the more so as it was not clearly elucidated by the meagre report of the soldier referred to; but it was quite apparent that the enemy, in some numbers, had successfully occupied ground between the city and the troops in the trenches—that is to say, the enemy had occupied a position directly in the rear of, and about three miles distant from, the left of the division.

Under these circumstances a company of the Montana regiment was directed towards the city by rail, utilizing that part of the Manila and Dagupan Railway within our lines. Major Mallory, Inspector-General of the Division, accompanied the command, and, under advice from division headquarters, conducted the operations thereof, and thereby materially aided in suppressing the demonstration.

The Volunteer Signal Corps detachment, under Captain Edgar Russel, from the commencement of hostilities, rendered not only important but indispensable services.

From the report of Captain Russel, the following extract is quoted at length, as illustrating the possibilities of developing a system of cooperation, whereby the fire of ships can be effectually controlled for the purpose of land operations:

"On February 10 Admiral Dewey's courtesy made it possible to arrange a complete scheme of firing by aid of signals, whereby points inshore, whether visible from the ship or not, could be reached by the guns of the navy when appropriate signals from shore were given. Caloocan church tower had been successfully experimented with as a point for signalling to the navy. The system adopted required a good map and an angle-measuring instrument. In this case use was made of the sextant loaned by the captain of the *Monadnock*. By observations from ship and church tower, and the angle signalled from ship, the position of the ship is accurately determined on the map, and a north and south line drawn through it. Having selected the point which it is desired to strike on shore, the scale of the map at once gives the range, and a small protractor gives the bearing from north and south line. Thus complete firing directions, either by day or night, would be given by such a message as this from shore: 'Thirty-eight degrees; six thousand two hundred yards.' This message was the one sent February 21, and the effect of the *Monadnock's* ten-inch shells on the village selected as the point, about one mile in front of the Kansas regiment, was terribly impressive. Three other shots, varying from 5000 to 6300 yards, were equally successful, thoroughly convincing all of the efficiency of this method of fire control."

The enthusiasm and military spirit of the enlisted force and subordinate officers of the division were a constant source of inspiration and confidence. Hurried from one state of danger and exertion to another, these splendid men responded in every instance with alacrity and that soldierly simplicity and directness of action which have always been the best characteristics of the profession.

The difficulties attending the execution of tactical operations on an extended line, such as that occupied by the division during the month, involve great presence of mind and endless exertion on the part of brigade and regimental commanders. The decision and sustained vigor of these officers insured such unity and strength throughout the command that every obstacle was quickly overcome, and every prearranged scheme carried out precisely as planned.

The force and effect of command depend largely upon the assistance of staff officers who, to natural ability and experience, join the spirit of enterprise. In respect of these essential qualifications, the staff service at my headquarters was greatly favored, and the highest appreciation of the zealous and intelligent work of these officers is cordially expressed.

VIEW OF SAN PEDRO MACATI FROM GENERAL KING'S HEADQUARTERS.—Drawn by G. W. Peters

GUN MOUNTED BY INSURGENTS TO CONTROL THE RAILROAD NEAR CALOOCAN

OPERATIONS OF KING'S BRIGADE

As Described by Himself

After several nights of promised attack I was riding to our night station at East Paco when overtaken by the division commander's despatch directing me to have my brigade in readiness for action. Orders were instantly sent to the First Idaho and First California to move up to the points designated in event of attack. On arriving at Paco I found the general's letter, and the usual night supports at block-house 11 were reinforced by the full battalion (First Washington) called for in his order. Lively firing was heard across the Pasig, but up to midnight not a shot was heard on our front. Just at 2.40, Sunday morning, February 5, the rattle of rifle-fire broke out along my line. All had been so quiet that the Californians had been sent back to their quarters; the Idahoans were also taking a rest; but now both commands were marched well forward. The line of the Washingtonians extended from Captain Fortson's position along the bend of the Concordia on our left to Battery Knoll on our extreme right, and the eastern (opposite) bank of the Tripa de Gallina was thickly covered by insurgents, visible only by the incessant flash of their Mausers, many of the bullets of which flew high and spattered into both East and West Paco, wounding two men of the First Idaho halted on the Calle Real.

A reconnaissance along the line, just after Captain Dyer reached the knoll with his guns, convinced me that the sooner I could get the order to advance the quicker we could sweep the front and wind up the entire business. This led to my appeal to be permitted to attack at dawn, which was necessarily refused; but, omitting minor incidents, such as the firing on our officers and men from many a Nipa hut and from Paco church itself, I at last, at about 8.30, received from General Anderson in person the long-prayed-for order, and he added to this the caution to advance no farther than Santa Ana.

While the division commander himself supervised the advance from Battery Knoll, which was made by several companies of Californians, supported by the Wyoming battalion, I hastened over to Paco and led the Idaho regiment to the front. Two companies of the California regiment had been thrown in on Wholley's right, near block-house 11, owing to the heavy fire the Washingtonians were receiving and the many casualties. These swept, with the Washingtonians, with eager impetuosity waist-deep through the boggy Tripa, and were speedily deployed in long line, continuing to the left the advance of Colonel Smith's line from Battery Knoll. Here it was comparatively plain sailing, but to our left of the Santa Ana road it was hard pounding indeed. Hawthorne, with his little "Astor" guns, had reached Concordia Bridge, and was replying with calm precision to the enemy's Krupps over towards the river, while the bridge was heavily swept by a fierce fire that seemed to come from every direction on our left and front. Fortson had earlier reported that his two companies were outflanked and galled by sharp fire, which I felt convinced must come from the redoubt in front of Pandacan. This, the Krupps, and the hostile trenches between the Pasig and the Santa Ana road became the objects of solicitude to me. Many of the Washingtonians were lying down behind the road firing coolly to our left front; and directing Major Figgins, with his first three companies, to support the right attack, I sent everything else, including the "University" company of the First California, in to the assault of the village and the trenches on the river side, giving orders to Major McConville to take the remaining three companies of the First Idaho and attack the redoubt from the south. It was his last order; this gallant old soldier fell leading his men.

But that redoubt lasted only a short time longer. Fortson dashed in across the Concordia from Pandacan, and, aided by one company of the Idahoans (the other two having had to change a sharply firing line to their right), they completely carried it, leaving the insurgents lying in heaps in the trenches, and whirling their survivors into the river, where many were drowned or shot.

By this time, fearful that the right advance under Colonel Wholley was going straight east instead of wheeling to half left to "round up" insurgents who were attempting to escape, I quit the left attack and joined his line. There was no time to be lost; so I personally ordered the left to halt, and, galloping along the line, by dint of much shouting swung it around, pivoting on the left until our right centre broke through the native huts and entered the town to the south of the old church. It was between ten and eleven when Santa Ana was won. Meantime, Colonel Smith had pushed on eastward.

Though our losses in killed and wounded were greater than those of any brigade in the corps, the damage inflicted on the enemy far exceeded that to which any other laid claim. This in itself is evidence of our severe and stubborn fight. The two Krupps we had the honor to send in cost us the life of Major McConville and the loss by wounds of many a gallant man.

I had already reported 110 of the enemy's dead as buried on the field in front of our left wing, when, in reaching out towards San Pedro Macati, Colonel Wholley found many more and gave them burial, making a total of 153. Even such of their wounded as could not be carried away fought hard; and many of them, in uniform, were taken in charge by our surgeons.

Though the First Brigade of the First Division was the only exclusively Volunteer brigade in the corps, it fought with all the steadiness, dash, and discipline of their comrades, the regulars.

I saw no instance of shirking; I saw many of daring leadership on the part of the officers and of devoted following on the part of the men. My regimental commanders, Colonel Smith, First California, Colonel Wholley, First Washington, and Major Figgins, First Idaho, bore themselves with marked bravery and ability, Wholley being under the heaviest fire for the longest time—his maiden fight at that. Major McConville died proudly, heading his men in the dash on a dangerous line. Major Weisenburger, First Washington, was an example of soldierly bearing throughout. Captain Fortson was in command on Pandacan Island, constantly exposed; and he and Captain Whittington, First Idaho, won my admiration for their daring assault on a fiercely defended position—the redoubt across the Concordia. Captain Otis, First Washington, with his cheek and ear scored by a Mauser, led his company from start to finish. Their loss of twenty-five killed and wounded in one company showed what they had to fight through. Lieutenants Erwin and Lohn, First Washington, the former severely wounded, were notably cool. Captain Dyer and Lieutenant Hawthorne, of the artillery, won the

BLOCK-HOUSE No. 11, LOOKING TOWARDS SAN PEDRO MACATI

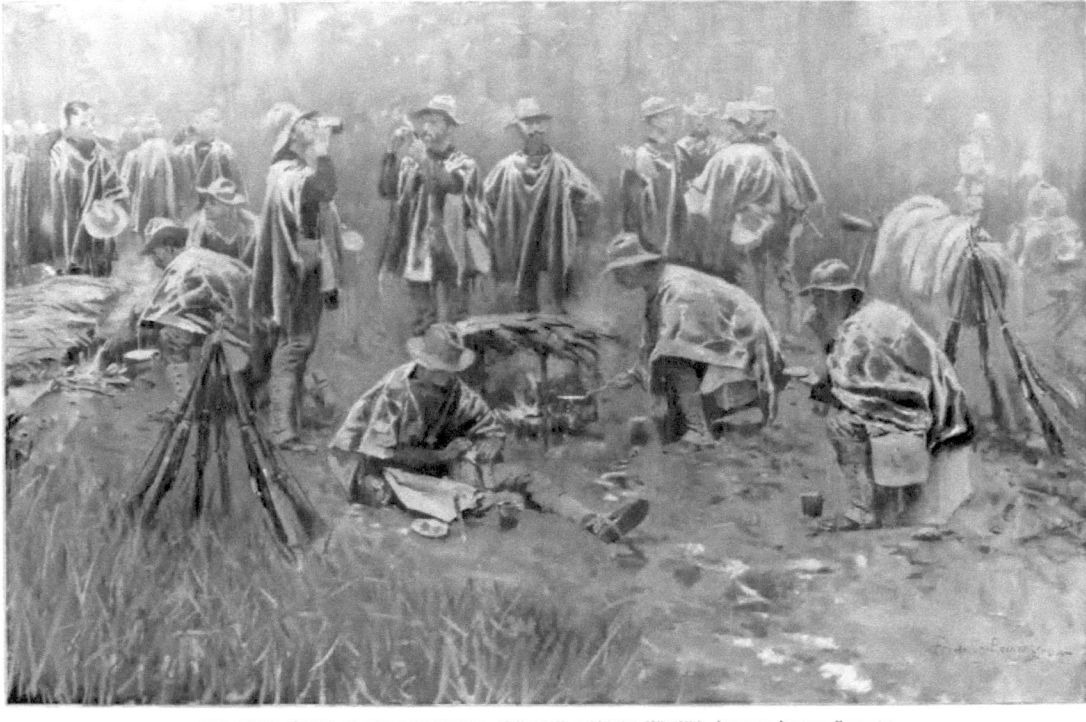

THE RAINY SEASON IN THE PHILIPPINES—AMERICAN SOLDIERS MESSING.—Drawn by Frederic Remington

BRIGADIER-GENERAL LOYD WHEATON ORDERING THE ADVANCE AT STONE QUARRY HILL, MARCH 13

DRAWN BY FREDERIC REMINGTON AFTER PHOTOGRAPHS

plaudits of the men for consummate skill and coolness.

Every man on my staff from the senior in rank, Brigade Surgeon Major Shiels, down to our mounted orderlies, won my thanks and admiration. Major Shiels was constant in his attendance on the wounded at the extreme front and under heavy fire. Lieutenants Merriam, Third United States Artillery, and Hutton, First California, were time and again compelled to risk their lives in carrying orders along the line. Captain Saxton, A. A. G., was systematic in the field office. His horse and that of Lieutenant Merriam's gave out at Concordia bridge, but they followed me afoot across the field. Captain Handy, brigade commissary, performed his duties under the fire of the enemy instead of the roof of his office; and the three orderlies, Privates Clay G. Mills, Company D, First Washington, Edward C. Hanford, Company K, First Washington, and Spencer G. Lane, First California, were constantly under heavy fire, and were soldiers their States might well be proud of.

One more name—that of Lieutenant-Colonel Duboce, First California—must not be omitted. He had a difficult and hazardous task in wiping out the cowardly gang that, under the sanctity of a church roof and from within the walls of apparently peaceful homesteads, for a time kept up a treacherous fire on officers and men hurrying by with orders or messages. I saw his work long hours after it was finished, and it was well done.

One feature of that Sunday's fight deserves special mention. Captain Cunningham, First

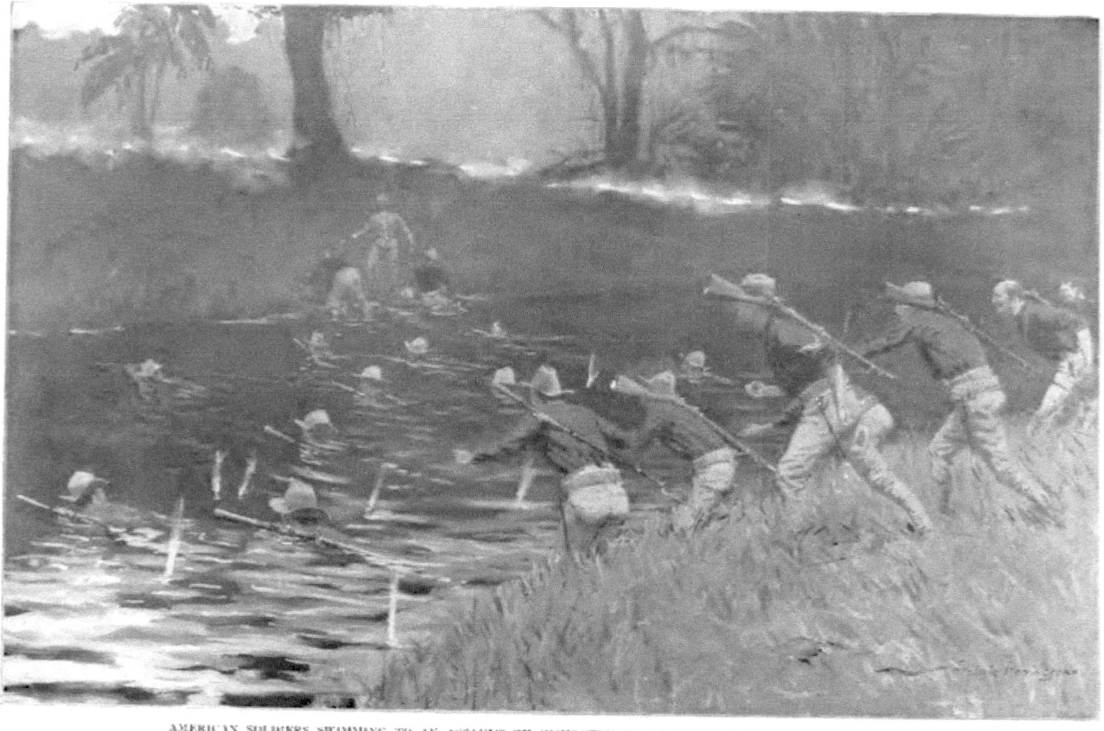

AMERICAN SOLDIERS SWIMMING TO AN ASSAULT ON INSURGENT INTRENCHMENTS.—Drawn by Frederic Remington

IN THE PHILIPPINES—A BAYONET RUSH OF UN

STATES TROOPS.—Drawn by Frederic Remington

California, with his fine company, had pushed forward under my personal direction to get a cross-fire on the trenches to the left of the Santa Ana road, from which so sharp a fire assailed us. After the trenches were outflanked he pushed on through the so-called convent, heading off fugitives from the captured redoubts down stream. He found himself assailed by a fire from across the Pasig. There was a large house apparently filled with insurgents; but this was close range, where the Springfield outweighed the Mauser, and five minutes' vigorous work resulted in the hoisting of the white flag across the river. Ferrying in Cascos, he found an insurgent captain dead, with a dozen others beside him. He brought back seventeen wounded, buried the dead, and strove to do whatever was possible for certain mortally wounded of the enemy.

OPERATIONS OF OVENSHINE'S BRIGADE

As Described by Himself

On February 4, 1899, the following organizations were on outpost duty at Singalong: Troop E, Fourth Cavalry; Company I, Fourteenth Infantry; Company I, First North Dakota Infantry, United States Volunteers.

On the night of February 4 heavy firing was heard on the north side of the city. As the firing continued and seemed to increase, I ordered the Second Brigade of the First Division to move to the positions assigned to it in case of hostilities with the insurgents, and went with the brigade staff-officers to Singalong.

Early on the morning of February 5 I received orders from division headquarters to open with the guns on block-house 14 and to make the attack on the insurgents in front of the brigade. At this time the Fourteenth Infantry, Companies A, C, D, E, F, G, I, K, and M, under Major C. H. Potter, Fourteenth Infantry, was on the Singalong road. Company C, Fourteenth Infantry, at block-house 12, half of Troop E, Fourth Cavalry, in block-house 12, and half of Troop E, Fourth Cavalry, in block-house 13, were under Captain Wheeler. Company I, First North Dakota, was in the old trench south of the church and between block-houses 12 and 13. The First North Dakota Infantry, Companies B, G, and H, were in the old Spanish trenches near and at the Malate Fort. Lieutenant D. L. Fleming, Sixth Artillery, with two guns of Dyer's Battery D, Sixth Artillery, were at Malate Fort. After sending word to Lieutenant Fleming to commence firing, I ordered the Fourteenth Infantry, then on the Singalong road, to advance to the trenches, and went with them. Captain Murphy's battalion, Companies F and M, and part of I, Fourteenth Infantry, being on the left, and the other companies, D, G, and K, Fourteenth Infantry, under Major Potter, on the right. This connected the left of this line towards block-house 13 and the right of it with the North Dakota regiment already in the trenches.

On the way into the trenches Captain Murphy, Fourteenth Infantry, with his battalion of that regiment, Companies F, M, and part of I, met with strong resistance from the insurgents and with heavy loss. A detachment of Company I, Fourteenth Infantry, under Lieutenant Miles, Fourteenth Infantry, on the left of the battalion, did most gallant service and suffered severely from the enemy.

After the firing from the Sixth Artillery had ceased, and also the firing from the *Monadnock* in the bay, Major Frank White, First North Dakota Infantry, with a battalion of his regiment, Companies G, H, and part of Company D, left the trenches and made a gallant and effective charge on the insurgents entrenched and concealed in thickets in front of his position, killing many insurgents and suffering no loss. As soon as this North Dakota battalion left the trenches a general fire from insurgents, also entrenched and in the jungle, in front of the part of the line held by the Fourteenth Infantry, except Captain Murphy's battalion, opened on our men. At this the Fourteenth Infantry, Companies D, G, and K, left the Spanish trenches and also charged the insurgents in their front in most gallant style, silencing them and driving them from their position in front.

During this time there was continuous firing in Captain Murphy's front. I sent several times to him to find out if he needed assistance, and each time received reply that though he had suffered many casualties he needed no more troops.

After the Fourteenth Infantry under Major Potter, and the North Dakota Battalion under Major White, had cleared their front, I sent a telegram from Fort Malate to the Division Commander asking for instructions.

Here I consider an explanation necessary. Lieutenant-Colonel E. H. Crowder, of the corps commander's staff, was on the firing line; and in conversation with him about the situation he said he knew that Major-General Otis wished the troops—I understood those in my brigade—to go and occupy Pasay as soon as the situation in front of Captain Murphy was cleared up; but that I would soon get detailed instructions through the division commander. This I misunderstood, and imagined I was to get some detailed instruction from Major-General Otis. Very soon Captain W. E. Birkhimer, Third Artillery, of the division commander's staff, came on the line and stated that General Anderson wished me to clear the trenches in front of Captain Murphy. I do not remember the exact words of Captain Birkhimer. I replied that I felt myself between two fires, as I was awaiting instructions from Major-General Otis and hardly knew just what was wanted of me. I believe Captain Birkhimer then left to see Major-General Anderson. Soon Lieutenant-Colonel Crowder again came on the line, and I explained to him how I stood. He regretted that I misunderstood him, and said my instructions were to come from Major-General Anderson and not direct from Major-General Otis. Believing I knew what the division commander wished, I advanced the Fourteenth Infantry under Major Potter, and the North Dakota Regiment, Lieutenant-Colonel Treumann, changed front to the left, thus clearing the jungle in front of us, and connecting the left of the line with Captain Murphy's battalion of the Fourteenth Infantry. The men moved in fine style through swamp and jungle, perfectly in hand and under control of their officers, and charged and cleared the insurgent trenches that were holding the troops at Singalong in check. This accomplished, I received an order from the division commander to move on to Pasay, and, if possible, occupy the road from there to connect with our troops at San Pedro Macati, but not to advance beyond the San Pedro Macati Road. The

DRIVING INSURGENTS THROUGH THE JUNGLE.—Photograph by Captain J. F. Case, First Oregon Volunteers

CHARGING INSURGENT EARTHWORKS BEYOND THE BAGBAG RIVER, APRIL 25—SKIRMISHERS SUPPORTING ARMORED TRAIN

brigade present with one company First Washington Infantry, one company First California Infantry, Troops C and L, Fourth Cavalry (Captain Gale), and one gun under Lieutenant Scott, Sixth Artillery, was reformed and took up the march to Pasay. On reaching Pasay it was found the insurgents had evacuated it. Captain Murphy's Battalion of the Fourteenth Infantry was left at this point, and the rest of the brigade marched to San Pedro Macati. Finding Colonel Smith, First California Infantry, there, I placed outposts along the road and returned with such part of the brigade as had not been left on the road to Pasay, and there took post.

All troops under my command were in excellent discipline and readily handled, firing being stopped at command in several instances. Brigade Quartermaster Lieutenant F. W. Hunt, First Idaho Infantry, rendered excellent service under fire. Much responsibility rested on Captain Sage, of the Twenty-third United States Infantry, and he met the requirements of his position.

Lieutenant M. C. Kerth, Twenty-third United States Infantry, aide-de-camp, twice placed himself in charge in advanced and dangerous positions, setting a splendid example to the men; his services as an aide were most valuable.

On the field, Second Lieutenant W. D. Connor, Corps of Engineers, United States Army, reported to me and volunteered his services as aide. His services were most acceptable and valuable, and he did gallant duty under fire.

Lieutenant A. S. Fleming, Sixth United States Artillery, with his guns and detachment, did excellent service.

The work of the vessels of our fleet was valuable on my front.

Lieutenant W. G. Haan, Third United States Artillery, with his company, A, United States Engineers, reported for duty with the brigade at Singalong Church on the morning of February 5. The Wyoming battalion was held in reserve, but was sent for duty early on the same day with the First Brigade, First Division, and was not under my command.

Except Captain Wheeler's troop, E, Fourth Cavalry, which was on outpost duty, the Fourth Cavalry Squadron was held in reserve in Manila, but part of it afterwards came on the line.

———

OPERATIONS OF H. G. OTIS'S BRIGADE

As Described by Himself

The general advance on Sunday, February 5, was participated in by all the regiments of the brigade, namely: the Twentieth Kansas, Colonel Frederick Funston; the First Montana, Colonel Harry C. Kessler; the Third United States Artillery (serving as infantry), Major W. A. Kobbé; and the Tenth Pennsylvania, Colonel A. L. Hawkins, posted from left to right in the order named. The forward movement was conducted with skill and gal-

Colonel Funston

COLONEL FUNSTON'S PASSAGE OVER THE RIO GRANDE UNDER A HOT FIRE, APRIL 27

The two white figures on the extreme left are Privates White and Trembly, who swam the river and fastened the ferry-rope to the shore

fantry, and was successful at every point. By night the new positions had been reached, the whole line having been carried forward several hundred yards.

During the forward movement of that afternoon the Twentieth Kansas Infantry had impetuously advanced, under a severe fire, nearly five hundred yards in advance of the position intended for it by the division commander, and had gallantly captured the two strong earthworks built by the enemy months before across the Caloocan road, besides taking two adjacent block-houses, losing several men in the operation, but punishing the enemy severely.

On Monday another advance was made and a new line established. This line was held without any considerable resistance from the enemy until late in the afternoon of Tuesday, the 7th, when a sharp fight was suddenly brought on by one of the Kansas captains in front of block-house 1. Acting upon his own motion, he had advanced with half his company into a thick wood to the left of the railway line, where a body of insurgents was concealed and was firing upon our outposts. I directed Colonel Funston to go forward, in person, with three companies to the support of the detachment engaged in the wood. This he proceeded to do with alacrity, with the result that the enemy's fire was completely silenced, after a furious combat of twenty minutes, in which the Kansas regiment lost one officer killed and six enlisted men wounded, while the enemy's loss was vastly out of proportion, nearly thirty dead Filipinos having been counted at the close of the combat there.

On the 8th and 9th comparative quiet reigned along the entire line, both day and night. On both days, however, there was some shelling of the town of Caloocan from both the ships and the land batteries, the town being in full view from the high open ground in front of the stone block-house, where five guns of the Utah Artillery were concentrated.

On the 10th, a general advance upon the insurgent position in and about Caloocan was ordered by the division commander. The execution of the forward movement was begun at 3.30 P.M., after thirty minutes of rather desultory shelling of the insurgent position by the land batteries and the guns of the *Charleston*, *Concord*, and *Callao*.

Upon the conclusion of the preliminary artillery bombardment, the signal for the infantry advance was given, and the forward movement was begun by the Kansas regiment on the extreme left, followed, respectively, by the First Montana and the Third Artillery to the right in quick succession, each command advancing from its own position, according to the well-understood plan.

The onset of the entire line was superb; the advance of the left was concealed from view by woods, but the centre and right—part of the Montana regiment and all of the Third Artillery—was in the open and made an inspiring battle picture. The resistance of the enemy in the wood, in numerous intrenchments on both sides of the railway track leading northward, and in the edge of the town of Caloocan, was determined, and the firing was spirited along the entire front; but the impetuous advance of our victorious troops could not be stayed, and the demoralized enemy was steadily driven before us at every point.

Caloocan was entered just before dark, the enemy driven out on the run, and the railway shops, round-house, warehouses, two engines, and one cannon captured, together with considerable other material of various sorts.

The left of our line, in its impetuosity and enthusiasm, had advanced beyond Caloocan in the direction of Malolos, in pursuit of the fleeing insurgents, until it had exceeded somewhat the limits prescribed in the orders of the day. The ardent volunteers were halted with some difficulty and brought back to the new line which had been determined upon in advance. It was found impossible, however, completely to establish the new position before night closed down, and for that reason the line, as first established, was only approximately true, though it was rendered secure for the night, and I prepared to correct the alignment with the coming of daylight.

I made my headquarters for the night in the Higgins house at Caloocan, and on the following day removed them to the wooded ravine in the rear of the centre of the brigade line.

The night passed without further fighting or serious incident; but early on the following morning an annoying fire from insurgent sharp-shooters was opened upon our left flank, coming from the direction of Malabon, a mile away towards the bay, and separated from Caloocan by wide lagoons and marshes, crossed by a single line of road. To support the troops who were meeting this flank fire, I ordered up two companies of the First Idaho, with good results; but the incident had delayed me somewhat in the more essential work of re-establishing the new general alignment.

In the meantime the division commander had arrived upon the field, and the work of reforming the new line was carried out under his own eye.

AMERICAN TROOPS ADVANCING OVER HALF-DESTROYED RAILROAD BRIDGE NEAR SANTO TOMAS, MAY 4

Drawn by Fletcher C. Ransom from Sketches made from Life by J. B. McCutcheon

COLONEL SUMMERS AND STAFF LEAVING BALINAG WITH SIX BATTALIONS.—Photograph by William Dinwiddie

OPERATIONS OF HALE'S BRIGADE

As Described by Himself

About 4 A.M. of Sunday, February 5, a telegram came from Colonel Stotsenburg, First Nebraska, requesting reinforcements, as the insurgents were closing in on him. There being none available in the city, I sent Lieutenant Perry to order Major Grove, with the two Colorado companies, D and I, just sent out, to move across the country in rear of line to Santa Mesa road and thence towards block-house 8 (the only place where the insurgents could possibly get in), to catch them if they had succeeded in getting around the Nebraska's right flank; and if he found nothing there, to move up behind camp and report to Colonel Stotsenburg. There was considerable firing down by San Juan bridge, and the Filipinos were cheering, but scouts sent to companies there and along the pipe-line reported that they had had no trouble and needed no support.

At 8.10 A.M., the enemy's infantry fire being about silenced, the force on Sampaloc Hill, under Major Anderson, with Colonel McCoy in general command, was ordered to charge block-house 5, the earthworks, and the village, halting and advancing by alternate rushes in case the enemy's fire should become too strong. They made the charge in fine style, and when half-way to the block-house the insurgents broke from the earthworks, bushes, and houses in surprising numbers and ran for the hills, the Americans picking them off as they ran. Thirty-five were gathered up in the immediate vicinity, twenty-four dead and eleven wounded. This movement broke their centre and showed that they could not stand a charge.

Colonel Frost and the South Dakota regiment, after five artillery shots each at block-house 4 and the earthwork between 4 and 5, as specified in the message sent to him, attacked and charged in excellent form, capturing this part of the line. In the afternoon, in compliance with instructions from the division commander, he also co-operated with the Tenth Pennsylvania in the capture of the Chinese cemetery and church, one and a quarter miles northwest of block-house 4, and the South Dakota troops were the first inside the church enclosure.

Thus, by 9.30 A.M., we were in possession of the entire insurgent line in front of the Second Brigade, from block-house 4 to San Juan bridge, a distance of two miles.

Every organization in the brigade, including those temporarily attached, drove the enemy in its front from intrenched positions, and did all the work set before it energetically and gallantly. The operations of the 5th resulted in the capture of the insurgent positions and the establishment of our line through block-houses 4, 5, 6, 7, San Juan bridge, Polverin, Deposito, San Juan del Monte church, San Felipe convent, and Mandaloyo, to the Pasig opposite Santa Ana. By the 10th the brigade covered the following lines: Front of block-houses 3, 4, 5, 6, 7, to San Juan bridge, 2½ miles; San Juan bridge to Deposito, 1 mile; Deposito south to Mandaloyo, on Pasig River, 2 miles; Deposito east to water-works on Mariquina River, 3¼ miles—a total of 8¾ miles.

— —

OPERATIONS OF THE PROVISIONAL BRIGADE

Account by General Loyd Wheaton

I was assigned to the command of a "Provisional Brigade," composed of the Twentieth and Twenty-second regiments United States Infantry, two battalions of the First Washington Volunteer Infantry, seven companies of the Second Oregon Volunteer Infantry, a platoon of the Sixth United States Artillery, and a squadron of three troops Fourth United States Cavalry.

My instructions were to clear the enemy from the country to Pasig and to strike him wherever found. The brigade was formed on the night of the 12th of March, and bivouacked in line in rear of the intrenched position extending from San Pedro Macati, on the Pasig, one mile and a half in the direction of Pasay from right to left in the following order: Squadron Fourth United States Cavalry, Major Rucker; Twenty-second United States Infantry, Colonel Egbert; Twentieth United States Infantry, Colonel McCaskey; seven companies Second Oregon Volunteer Infantry, Colonel Summers; one platoon (two guns) Sixth United States Artillery, Lieutenant Scott; two battalions First Washington Volunteer Infantry, Colonel Wholly. Soon after daylight on the morning of March 13 the brigade moved under my instructions, by *échelon*, from the right, the Fourth United States Cavalry and Twenty-second United States Infantry moving first, then the Twentieth United States Infantry, followed by the Second Oregon Volunteer Infantry. The right of the Twenty-second United States Infantry struck the enemy as he was retreating in the direction of Pasig, inflicting heavy loss. The whole line moved on and occupied the Pasig road, and then, marching east along the road, soon came under the fire of the enemy from his intrenched position at Pasig, on the north side of the river. We opened fire upon his intrenchments from one gun on the road and placed the other upon a cliff or ridge extending at

COLONEL SUMMERS'S COMMAND ADVANCING TO THE BATTLE OF MAASIN.—Photograph by William Dinwiddie

right angle to the Pasig. We occupied the ridge with infantry, and extended the Twentieth and Twenty-second United States Infantry to the right on the high ground in the direction of Pateros. One battalion of the Twenty-second United States Infantry, under Captain Lockwood, and the squadron of the Fourth United States Cavalry, under Major Rucker, attacked a force of the enemy in the direction of Pateros and drove him beyond Taghuig. The gunboat *Laguna de Bay*, under command of Captain Grant, came up, and night closed with the enemy driven to the north side of the Pasig.

March 15 I sent one battalion of the Twentieth United States Infantry, under Major Rogers, across the river at Pasig, brought up a gun, and shelled the intrenchments in front of Pasig and to the left. The battalion of the Twentieth United States Infantry carried the city by storm. I crossed a part of the Second Oregon Volunteer Infantry below Pasig, and when the rebels fled from Pasig they were exposed to a heavy flank-fire from this detachment. I sent the whole of the Twentieth United States Infantry over to Pasig, the regiment being taken across upon the steam-launch *Maritime*. I advanced the First Washington Volunteer Infantry on my right to Taghuig and captured about 500 prisoners. Night came on with the enemy in my front and on my right killed, captured, or dispersed. The enemy lost at least one thousand men this day.

March 16th I instructed Lieutenant-Colonel McCaskey, commanding the Twentieth United States Infantry at Pasig, to clear the country in his immediate vicinity of any of the insurgents who might be lurking near, and soon after received a despatch from him that he had sent out two battalions to be deployed as skirmishers to clear the island of Pasig. Soon after, heavy and long-continued firing was heard to the east and north of Pasig. At 12 M. I learned that Major William P. Rogers, commanding third battalion Twentieth United States Infantry, had come upon the enemy intrenched, one thousand strong, at the village of Cainta, and that he had carried the intrenchments and burned the town, the enemy flying in the direction of Tuy-tuy. Major Rogers returned with his battalion to Pasig. In this affair he lost two killed and fourteen wounded.

On the 17th of March, by direction of the corps commander, I returned the Twentieth United States Infantry to Manila, relieving the regiment at Pasig by a part of the First Washington Volunteer Infantry. On the afternoon of March 18, a force of the enemy appeared in the vicinity of Taghuig, which was held by one company of the First Washington Volunteer Infantry. I reinforced the place with two companies of infantry, and directed the Colonel of the Twenty-second United States Infantry to send one battalion of his regiment south of the position held by his regiment and to the west of Taghuig to ascertain the force of the enemy. The enemy was found about eight hundred strong, occupying the crests of the ridges, and a spirited combat ensued, which was terminated by darkness. The Twenty-second had twenty men killed and wounded in this affair. Among the wounded was Captain Frank B. Jones, Twenty-second Infantry, commanding the battalion. The enemy fell back towards the south.

On the morning of the 19th, soon after daylight, I formed lines and deployed in the extended order, facing to the south, as follows: Twenty-second United States Infantry and one gun Sixth Artillery on the right; Second Oregon Volunteer Infantry, five companies, centre; First Washington Volunteer Infantry, five companies, left. Advanced the line and struck the enemy four miles south of Taghuig. My line, wheeling to the left, partly enclosed him towards the lake, and he was completely routed with great loss. My left pursued him down the lake, fifteen miles from Taghuig, as far as San Pedro Tamisan, all the houses along the lake to that point being burned. The enemy's intrenchments on our left and in front of the First Washington Volunteer Infantry were carried, the enemy leaving more than two hundred dead upon the field. I returned to the vicinity of Pateros and there bivouacked, receiving orders to return the command to its former encampments near Manila, excepting that the First Washington Volunteer Infantry was designated to hold Pasig, Pateros, Taghuig, and adjacent country.

This ended the operations of the Provisional Brigade. In one week all the enemy's positions that were attacked were taken and his troops killed, captured, or dispersed. The towns from which he brought over troops or in which he resisted us were burned or destroyed. He burned them himself. His loss in killed, wounded, and captured was not less than 2500 men. I was ably supported and assisted by the several regimental commanders through the series of operations.

FURTHER OPERATIONS

THE first and second divisions, under Generals Anderson and MacArthur, aided by the war-ships of Admiral Dewey's fleet, had now cleared a zone of safety about the capital: and the provisional brigade, known as Wheaton's flying co'umn, had established a line of separation to divide the forces of Aguinaldo north and south. Meanwhile, February 11th, Ilo Ilo, second city in importance in the archipelago, which had been turned over by the Spanish military to the civil authorities, and by them to the insurgents, was shelled by the *Boston* and *Petrel*, and occupied by a detachment of the army under Brigadier-General Marcus P. Miller; and on March 19 cable communication was perfected between that city and Manila. The battle-ship *Oregon* arrived from New York, by way of San Francisco and Honolulu, on the 18th of March, "in fit condition," said the official despatch, "for any duty." On this date, also, the American land forces were reorganized for an aggressive movement against the insurgents. Two divisions of three brigades each were formed. General Lawton was assigned to the first division, consisting of the Washington, North Dakota, and California Volunteers, under General King; six troops of the Fourth Cavalry, the Fourteenth Regulars, the Idaho Volunteers, and a battalion of the Iowa troops, under General Ovenshine; the Third and Twenty-second Regular Infantry and the Oregon regiment, under General Wheaton; and Dyer's and Hawthorne's light batteries. The second division, under General MacArthur, comprised two batteries of the Third Artillery, the Kansas and Montana Volunteers, under General H. G. Otis; the Colorado, Nebraska, and South Dakota regiments, and six companies of the Pennsylvania regiment, under General Hale; the Fourth and Seventeenth Regulars, the Minnesota and Wyoming Volunteers, and the Utah Artillery.

On the 25th of March, General MacArthur led a forward movement towards Novaliches, northeast of Manila. The troops engaged were the Third Artillery, as infantry; the Montana, Kansas, Pennsylvania, Nebraska, Wyoming, Colorado, South Dakota, Minnesota, and Oregon Volunteers; the Third, Fourth, Seventeenth, Twenty-second, and Twenty-third Infantry; and the Utah battalion of artillery. The insurgents retired before the American advance, contesting every point, however, with courage and skill. Dense undergrowth, deep streams, and a rough country opposed the advance; and after a day's hard fighting the brigades of Otis and Hale had made only six miles. Wheaton's brigade, at Caloocan, had driven the insurgents a mile and a half northward across the Tuliahan River, and Brigadier-General Hall, on the right, had routed a considerable force of the Filipinos. The casualties on the American side were 176; 26 were reported killed. The insurgent loss was much greater. On the following day, the 26th, Wheaton's brigade took Malinta; Malabon was burned and evacuated; and an attempt to enclose the insurgents between two lines of Americans having failed, MacArthur's advance-guard, the Twentieth Kansas and the Third Artillery, joined Wheaton's brigade, and the forces combined to push the insurgents back upon Malolos, their capital. The brigades of Otis and Hale were now well on their way towards Marilao, which was taken on the 27th, when the South Dakota Volunteers, led by Colonel Frost, executed a brilliant charge upon a body of Filipinos commanded by Aguinaldo in person. On the 29th MacArthur advanced to Bocave, and thence to Guiguinto, three and one-half miles from Malolos. Here the Filipinos made a stand to resist the American advance across the river; and the artillery had to be got into position "by working it over the railroad bridge by hand and swimming the mules." Malolos was occupied on the 31st, after a slight show of resistance, Aguinaldo having removed his seat of government to San Fernando. A reconnaissance in force was made on the 4th of April by Lieutenant-Colonel Wallace, commanding the Montana regiment, with two field-pieces and a detachment of cavalry. About one thousand insurgents were engaged near Calumpit and dispersed. The casualties among the American troops during the two months of hostilities, including February 4 and April 4, as reported to the Adjutant-General at Washington, were 184 killed and 976 wounded.

On this latter date, April 4, the American commissioners to the Philippines issued their proclamation to the inhabitants announcing the intentions of the President in dealing with the islands. The proclamation was translated into the Spanish and Tagalog languages, and was widely distributed. Its statement of the policy of the Administration was in effect as follows: 1. The supremacy of the United States must and will be enforced throughout every part of the archipelago, and those who resist it can accomplish no end other than their own ruin. 2. Ample liberty and self-government will be granted. 3. The civil rights of the Philippine people will be guaranteed, and religious freedom assured. 4. Honor, justice, and friendship forbid the exploitation of the Philippines or Filipinos. 5. There shall be an honest and effective civil service in which natives shall be employed. 6. Honesty and economy shall be studied in levying taxes and applying the proceeds to public improvements and expenses of the government, and taxation may be lighter than in the past. 7. A pure, speedy, and effective administration of justice will be guaranteed. 8. Construction of roads and railways will be promoted. 9. Domestic and foreign trade will be fostered. 10. Schools will be established. 11. Reforms will be effected in all branches of the government.

General Lawton, with a force of 1500 men, consisting of eight companies of the Fourteenth Infantry, three companies of the Fourth Cavalry, four companies each of the First North Dakota and First Idaho, two mountain-guns, and two hundred sharp-shooters from various regiments, set out on the 8th on an expedition against Santa Cruz, on the southeastern shore of the Laguna de Bay. The force was transported in fifteen native lighters towed by seven tugs, and was convoyed by the gunboats *Laguna de Bay*, *Napidan*, and *Oeste*. The woods were shelled; the insurgents, after a determined resistance, were driven back eastward with heavy loss; and the town, after a running fight from house to house, was taken on the morning of the 10th.

North of Manila, the Filipinos, having on the night of the 10th attempted to cut off MacArthur's communication between Malolos and the capital, were driven inland on the 12th by General Wheaton, and on the 13th an insurgent attack on the American lines near Malolos was successfully repulsed. On the eastern or Pacific shore of Luzon, Lieutenant Gillmore and fourteen men from the United States gunboat *Yorktown*, while trying to rescue a besieged Spanish garrison near Baler, were ambushed and captured by the Filipinos.

The expedition to Santa Cruz having been withdrawn, General Lawton, on the morning of the 22d, advanced in a northeasterly direction from Manila, and with the North Dakota Volunteers, two battalions of the Third Infantry, the Twenty-second Infantry, three troops of the Fourth Cavalry, and Gale's squadron, cleared the country of hostiles in the vicinity of Novaliches. After a skirmish near the Tuliahan River, Lawton's column reached Novaliches at ten o'clock in the morning. Meanwhile, MacArthur strengthened his position before Calumpit, intending to drive the insurgents back on Lawton, who was to swing in westward from Novaliches, San José, and Norzagaray. Near Malolos, the Fourth Cavalry and the Nebraska Volunteers encountered a strong force of insurgents on the 23d. Colonel John M. Stotsenburg and Lieutenant Lester E. Sisson, of the Nebraska regiment, were killed; two privates of the same regiment and one trooper of the Fourth Cavalry were killed, and many were wounded. The Iowa and Utah Volunteers also had a number of men wounded.

The siege of Calumpit was begun by MacArthur's division on the 24th; the Fourth Cavalry and the Nebraska and Iowa Volunteers, under General Hale, took position near Calumpit, commanding the ford in the river; Generals MacArthur and Wheaton, with the Montana Volunteers, advanced to the left of the railroad, and the Kansas Volunteers moved forward to the right, north of Malolos. On the 25th the division advanced through the jungle across the Bagbag River, with a loss of six killed and twenty-eight wounded; the South Dakota Volunteers pursued the Filipinos to the outskirts of Calumpit.

On the following day, the 26th, Colonel Funston, with volunteers from his regiment, crossed the Bagbag River by crawling along the iron girders of the bridge, and dispersed the Filipinos at that point; General Hale's troops approached on the right, following the north bank of the river nearest the town from the east, with the First Nebraska Volunteers on the left and the First South Dakota and Fifty-first Iowa beyond; General Hale's right joined General Wheaton's left soon after noon; the insurgent losses were 70 killed and 350 prisoners; in the defence of Calumpit the Filipinos made use of artillery for the first time; just before noon the Utah Battery shelled the town; General Hale's brigade appearing on the right, the rebels retreated and the Americans entered the town. On the 27th, Colonel Funston, with 120 men of the Twentieth Kansas, crossed the Rio Grande under a galling fire from the insurgents, and, reinforced by General Wheaton's brigade, drove back the entire insurgent forces with a loss of two killed and twelve wounded; thirty-seven prisoners were taken. Referring afterwards to the heroic feat of swimming the river under fire, Colonel Funston said: "It wasn't much to do. We knew they couldn't shoot straight; and our boys would attend to them while we were crossing."

Colonel Manuel Arguelles and Lieutenant José Bernal, envoys of the Filipinos, entered the American lines April 28 to ask for a cessation of hostilities until their Congress could act on terms of peace. General Otis declined to recognize the Filipino government, demanding of the Filipinos an unconditional surrender. The commissioners returned to the insurgent lines on the 29th. Colonel Arguelles re-entered the American lines on the 2d of May with further propositions for a

THE TWENTY-FIVE SCOUTS IN GENERAL LAWTON'S COMMAND—THEIR LEADER, WILLIAM H. YOUNG, DIED OF WOUNDS MAY 16

cessation of hostilities; but was told that an armistice was out of the question.

Lawton, with part of his command, had reached Nozagaray on the 25th of April, and was there joined by the centre column from Bocave, a station on the railroad east of Bulacan; Colonel Summers, with two battalions each from the Oregon and Minnesota regiments, three troops of cavalry, and two guns, having marched across from Bocave and effected this junction successfully. Swinging now to the westward, Lawton's united force captured Baliuag on the 5th of May, after hard fighting. On the 8th, a reconnoitering party, consisting of two companies from the Minnesota Volunteers and two companies from the Oregon Volunteers, advanced to a point near San Miguel, about twelve miles north of Baliuag; and on the 14th San Miguel was taken by Lawton's scouts. Three days later the advance-guard, consisting of the Minnesota, Oregon, and North Dakota Volunteers and the Twenty-second Infantry, captured the town of San Isidora with slight opposition, the Filipinos being pursued to the mountains north of the town. The advance was resumed on the 18th, and on the 23d the expedition arrived at Malolos, having marched 120 miles in 20 days, engaged in 22 fights, captured 28 towns, destroyed 300,000 bushels of rice, killed 400 insurgents, wounded double that number, and lost only 6 men killed and 31 wounded.

Meanwhile, on the 4th of May, MacArthur's division began another forward movement. Hale's brigade, consisting of two battalions of the Fifty-first Iowa Volunteers, the First Nebraska, and the First South Dakota Volunteers, with a Gatling gun detachment under command of Major Young, of the Sixth Artillery, and Wheaton, with Hotchkiss and Gatling guns mounted on hand-cars, and the Twentieth Kansas and First Montana Volunteers deploying to the right and left, traversed a marshy country and met with resistance near San Tomas. The insurgents retreated after burning the villages of San Tomas and Minalin. Continuing the advance, Wheaton's troops met with a hot fire near San Fernando. The Filipinos retreated towards San Isidro. On the 8th the Filipinos attacked San Fernando, but were repulsed by the Montana Volunteers. On the 23d, Generals MacArthur and Funston—the latter having been promoted for bravery—with the Kansas and Montana Volunteer Infantry and the Utah Battery, dispersed 800 insurgents intrenched on the railroad beyond San Fernando, near Santa Anita. The insurgent loss was heavy, many prisoners being taken by the Americans.

On the 1st of June, General Lawton took command of the American troops forming the lines east and south of Manila, General MacArthur remaining in command of those on the north; and on the 3d, a force commanded by Brigadier-General Hall and consisting of eleven companies of the Oregon regiment, six companies of the Colorado regiment, four troops of the Fourth Cavalry, eight companies of the Fourth Infantry, four companies of the Ninth Infantry, four companies of the Wyoming regiment, and four mountain-guns, advanced from the pumping station, near Manila, while the Washington and North Dakota regiments and one battalion of the Twelfth Infantry, under Colonel Wholley, advanced from Pasig, in the resumption of active operations against the insurgents to the east and southeast of the capital. General Hall occupied Antipolo on the 4th, and continued his advance down the Morong peninsula, taking the town of Morong on the 5th without resistance, the Filipinos escaping to the northeast. General Lawton, in person, led the advance against the insurgents in the province of Cavité, south of Manila; and on the 10th of June, with a brigade consisting of six companies of the Colorado regiment, two battalions of the Ninth and two battalions of the Twenty-first Infantry, a troop of the Navada Cavalry, dismounted, and Scott's Battery, with four mountain guns, commanded by General Wheaton; a brigade made up of the Second, Thirteenth, and Fourteenth Infantry, two companies of the Twelfth Infantry, and a detachment of light artillery, commanded by General Ovenshine; and an escort composed of Russell's detachment of the Signal Corps and Stewart's troop of the Fourth Cavalry, he marched south from San Pedro Macati, on the Pasig River, and then towards Bacoor. After several sharp skirmishes the insurgents retreated southward along the shore. Several of the Americans were wounded and many were prostrated by the heat. Two officers were killed. Las Pinas and Paranaque, former strongholds of the insurgents, were occupied on the 11th; and on the 13th a lively engagement was fought on the banks of the Zapote, south of Las Pinas. American field-guns were engaged against a Filipino battery concealed in the jungle; the American gunboats bombarded the insurgents along the shore in the vicinity of Bacoor; the Fourteenth and Twenty-first Infantry crossed the Zapote River, carrying the trenches, while the insurgents were attacked in the rear by the Ninth and Twelfth Infantry and retreated to the fortified town of Imus, about four miles south of Bacoor. One hundred Filipinos were believed to have been killed and three hundred wounded in the engagement. On the 15th, Lawton captured the town of Imus. On the 19th, a battalion of the Fourth Infantry, leaving Imus to reconnoitre towards Perez das Marinas, was attacked in the rear by natives at first appearing friendly. Two Americans were killed and twenty-three wounded. The insurgent loss was heavy. General Wheaton and staff, with another battalion, reinforced the troops attacked, and later a third battalion was ordered to the front. On the following day, however, the town was taken without opposition; and on the 21st General Wheaton returned to Imus.

North of Manila, MacArthur's command was attacked in force near San Fernando on the 16th of June; and the hostiles were repulsed with heavy loss by the brigades of Generals Hale and Funston. The demonstration on the part of the Filipinos, led by Aguinaldo in person, was preceded by an attempt to cut off communication between San Fernando and Manila.

The largest force so far mobilized by the Filipinos, and under the personal command of Aguinaldo, was now confronting MacArthur near San Fernando. In the United States, rumors of a call for volunteers led individuals and organizations in various parts of the country to tender their services to the War Department. Governor Roosevelt telegraphed to President McKinley that, in the event of such a call, New York was prepared to furnish all the men the government might ask for. Major-General Elwell S. Otis, in a despatch to the Adjutant-General of the army, outlined the situation and conditions in the Philippines, in substance as follows: "During the rainy season little inland campaigning will be possible in Luzon. The insurgent armies have suffered great losses, and are scattered; the only large force held together (about 4000) is in Tarlac province and northern Pampanga; their scattered forces, in bands of fifty to five hundred, are in other portions of Luzon; in Cavité and Batangas provinces they could assemble possibly 2000, though demoralized by recent defeat. The mass of the people, terrorized by insurgent soldiers, desire peace and American protection; no longer flee on approach of our troops, unless forced by insurgents, but gladly welcome them; no recent burning of towns. The population within our lines is becoming dense, and is taking up land cultivation extensively. City population is becoming too great to be cared for; natives in southeast Luzon combining to drive out insurgents. The only hope of the insurgent leaders is in United States aid. They proclaim the near overthrow of the present administration, to be followed by their independence and recognition by the United States. This is the influence which enables them to hold out. Much contention prevails among them, and no civil government remains. Trade with ports not in our possession, former source of insurgent revenue, is now interdicted. I am not certain of the wisdom of this policy, as people in those ports are without supply of food and merchants are suffering losses; meditate restoring trade privileges, although insurgents reap benefits. Courts here in successful operation under direction of able Filipinos. Affairs in other islands are comparatively quiet, awaiting results in Luzon; all are anxious for trade, and repeated calls for American troops are received. Am giving attention to the Sulu Archipelago and Palawan Island. Our troops have worked to the limit of endurance. Volunteer organizations have been called in; replaced by regulars, who now occupy salient positions. Nebraska, Pennsylvania, and Utah now taking transports, and Sixth Infantry sent to Negros to relieve California. These troops are in good physical condition. Sickness among troops has increased lately, due mostly to arduous service and climatic influences. Nothing alarming. Of the 12 per cent. of the command reported sick, nearly 6 per cent. are in the general hospital. Many officers and men who served in Cuba break down under recurrence of Cuban fever, and regular regiments lately received are inadequately officered."

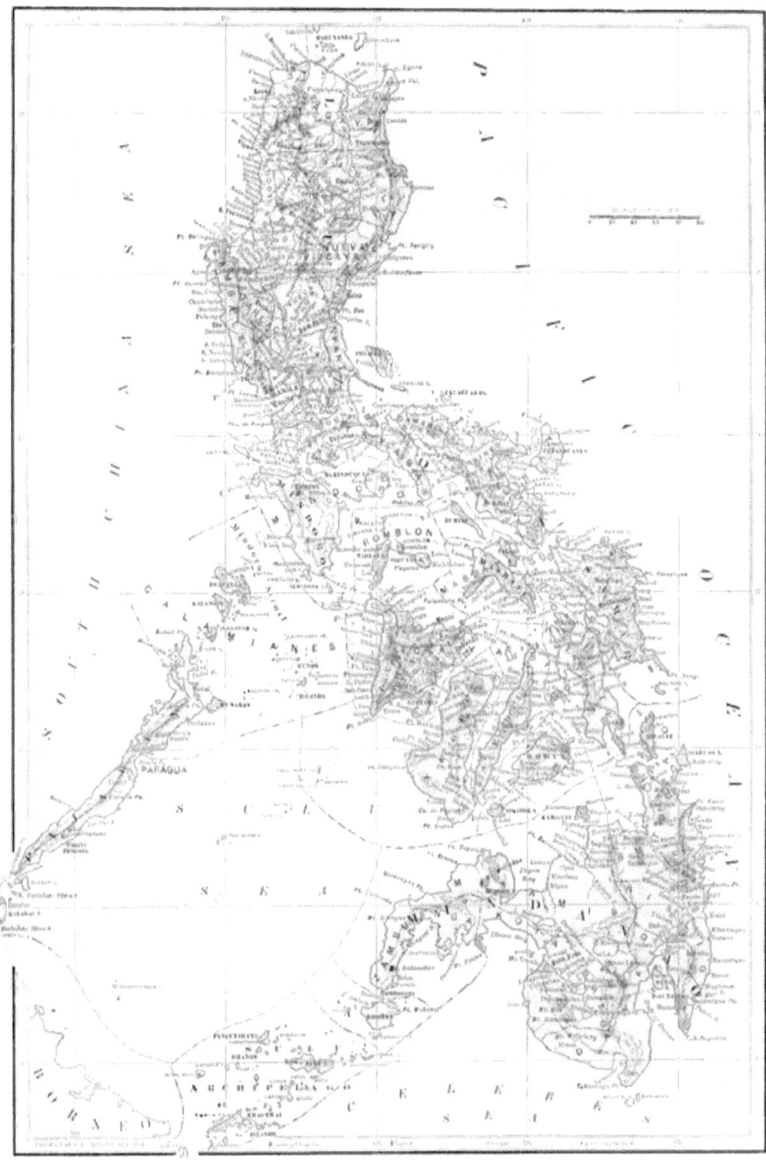

THE PHILIPPINE ISLANDS

THE COMMERCE OF MANILA—SCENE ALONG THE WATER-FRONT

THE RESULTS OF THE WAR

ASIDE from the emancipation of Cuba, the results of the Spanish-American War were almost wholly unforeseen. The more direct results, as indicated in the Treaty of Paris, were the cession to the United States of the island of Porto Rico "and other islands now under Spanish sovereignty in the West Indies," of the island of Guam in the Marianas or Ladrones, and of the vast archipelago known as the Philippine Islands. The raising of the American flag on Wake Island was incidental to the expedition to the Philippines. An indirect, though momentous, result of the war was the annexation to the United States, August 6, 1898, of the Republic of Hawaii. Instead of issuing a proclamation of neutrality, the Hawaiian government had virtually assumed the position of an ally of the United States, and had maintained it, in opposition to European governments and European individuals resident in the islands. Coal and other supplies were furnished to American war-ships and transports on their way to the Philippines, and the transfer was made in order that the Hawaiians might be in position to supply coal, provisions, and munitions of war without the possibility of international complications.

The interests of populations aggregating many millions were suddenly identified with those of the Americans; and the responsibilities so unexpectedly thrown upon the conquering nation called for a high order of statesmanship and constructive ability. What these interests were is told in the ensuing articles on the islands and their people.

THE PHILIPPINE ISLANDS

STATEMENT OF GENERAL CHARLES A. WHITTIER BEFORE THE UNITED STATES PEACE COMMISSION.

THE Philippine Islands are estimated to be in number between 600 and 1000—the latter, if we include the Sulu Archipelago and Paragua, extending over about twelve degrees of latitude, including the Protectorate, extreme south of the Sultanate of Sulu (Jolo)—with an area of about 114,500 square miles and a population estimated from 3,500,000 to 8,000,000. About twenty-five islands are of commercial importance, from practically all of which supplies of produce are collected and sent to Manila for baling, pressing, classification, and shipment to foreign ports. The principal islands are Luzon, Panay (of which Iloilo, the second port of the Philippines, is the important town), Negros, Samar, Leyte, Cebu, and Mindanao.

There are large tracts of unexplored country, occupied by various tribes, regarding which there are many rumors about their habits, ferocity, etc. This is particularly the case with the mountainous country in the central part of the northern portion of Luzon. It will require the intelligent, systematic work of years to open, develop, and govern these places. For ages it has been the Spanish official system to declare territories to be under their rule, without taking steps to make their possessions manifest to the rest of the world—or to themselves.

The Spaniards have apparently never known the number of the islands owned by them for all these years, or the population.

The products of the islands are: Sugar, rice, hemp, coffee (reduced of late years), tobacco, cocoa (small), cocoanuts (large and increasing), nipa palms, bamboo for rafts, furniture, carts, baskets, boats, bridges, carrying-poles, floats, etc., hardwoods of great variety. Fruits: Mangoes, bananas, pomelo (larger than our grape fruit, of same family), oranges, citrons, chicos, guavas, lemons, pineapples (not of best quality, cultivated for the leaves to make pina and jusi, dress and fine handkerchiefs, etc., fabrics), tamarinds, vanilla, sago (small products). No doubt it will be a great field for cotton. In fact, no country has such diversified possibilities.

Account of four products exported to different countries, and all imported from the interior of the Philippine Archipelago during the year 1897:

Products	Where Raised	Amount paid for export duties	Destination
Hemp	Provinces of Sorsogon (Albay), Legaspi, Leyte, Camarines, S. and N. Marinduque, Mindoro, Calbayoc, Cebu, Iloilo, and other southern provinces.	[illegible]	Spain, Australia, China, the United States, France, England, Japan, Singapore, and other foreign ports.
Sugar	Batangas, La Laguna, Cebu, Iloilo (small quantities), N. Ilocos, S. Ilocos, Pangasinan, Negros.	75,884	America, Australia, China, Japan, Spain, England.
Coffee	Batangas, La Laguna, Cavite (province of Mariñas), Zamboanga, both Ilocos, Camarines.	Free	Spain, China, Japan, Singapore.
Tobacco	This article is produced in almost all the provinces of the archipelago, and especially in Cagayan, Isabella de Luzon, Ilocos (S. and N.), and in all the southern provinces and in the Visayas.	553,605	Dutch possessions, England, France, Saigon, Singapore, English possessions, Australia, Spain, China, Egypt, France.

Products	Quantity	Value of same
	Kilos	
Hemp, raw and manufactured	[illegible]	[illegible]
Sugar	[illegible]	[illegible]
Coffee	[illegible]	[illegible]
Tobacco, raw and manufactured	[illegible]	[illegible]

Manilla hemp has a world-wide reputation, and is used for cordage, bonnets, hats, tapestry, carpets, hammocks, and other network, etc.

The sugar product is enormous. More capital and the combination of the producers, with modern machinery and improved roads, are required. It seems strange, entering the harbor of Hong-Kong, to see the magnificent plant of a sugar refinery there, which has made great profits, while at the Philippines practically the old rude methods prevail.

The growth of the cocoanut palm, a most profitable industry, may be greatly increased, and the use of the nut for domestic purposes, in desiccated form (a new method), and in the manufacture of oil and soap, is enormous. Of this product in Ceylon, Sir J. West Ridgway, Governor, after giving surprising figures as to its development, naming the value of the local consumption then at 20,000,000 rupees (say $6,600,000 in gold), adds:

> That the cultivation of the cocoanut palm is rapidly increasing is a matter of congratulation, but should not be the cause of surprise. There is no cultivation so simple, so cheap, and of which the returns are so certain.

There is an enormous production of tobacco and a ready market for all of the cigars and cigarettes made in the large factories of Manila.

Railways built to the mountains—distances from 20 to 250 miles—will give a new climate, where one can find at night a temperature of from 40 to 60 instead of the monotonous all-night 82 of Manila, and where vegetables and fruits in variety may be raised. The country to be opened by well-considered new lines will populate and develop fine sections. All this, of course, will take time.

Field-Marshal Roberts says:

> It (the Mutiny) hastened on the construction of the roads, railways, and telegraphs, which have done more than anything to increase the prosperity of the people and preserve order throughout the country.

This, true of India, will be most effectively the case of the Philippines. I quote a portion of an article by Mr. John Foreman, in the *Contemporary Review* for June, 1898:

> The islands are extremely fertile, and will produce almost anything to be found in the tropics. I estimate that barely one-fourth of the tillable land is now under cultivation. There is at present only one railway, of 120 miles. A number of lines would have to be constructed in Luzon, Panay, Negros, Cebu, and Mindanao islands. Companies would probably take up the contracts on ninety years' working concession and ninety-nine years' lease of acreage in lieu of guaranteed interest. The lands would become immensely valuable to the railway companies, and an enormous source of taxable wealth to the protectorate. Road-making should be taken up on Treasury account and bridge construction on contract, to be paid for by toll concessions. The port of Iloilo should be improved, the custom-houses abolished, and about ten more free ports opened to the world.
>
> Under the protectorate undoubtedly capital would flow into the Philippines. The coal-beds in Luzon and Cebu islands would be opened out; the marble deposits of Montalban and the stone-quarries of Angono (both near Manila) would surely be worked. The possibilities of development under a free, liberal government are so great that the next generation would look back with astonishment at the statistics of the present day.

If we compare Egypt under British control (in fact, if not in name), Mr. Edward Dicey says:

> The British occupation has now lasted for over fifteen years. During the first five comparatively little was accomplished, owing to the uncertain and provisional character of our tenure.

In this time (fifteen years) the population increased from a little under 7,000,000 to close upon 10,000,000. This is not due to foreign immigration—"and can only be accounted for by the fact that conditions of life amid the mass of population are more favorable, marriages more frequent, families larger, infant mortality, which before kept the population at dead-level, is less frequent, and the general health of the people has improved. To put the same idea in plainer words, the natives are better fed, better paid, better housed, better clothed," etc.

That, I think, is rather pertinent to our probable status in the Philippines.

I made the following jottings of a trip over the line of the only railroad in the islands:

A CANAL IN MANILA

> On Saturday, September 3, upon the invitation of Mr. Higgins, manager of the Manila Railroad, who furnished his private observation-car, and of Mr. Wood, of the firm of Smith, Bell & Co., who was our host, the party, consisting of Major Bement, Messrs. Miller, Wood, Price, Higgins, and myself, made a trip over the line of the railroad, leaving at about ten in the morning. One hundred and twenty-three miles of railroad in fair order, telegraphic communications destroyed in many places, probably requiring a month for their restoration.
>
> The line runs through a country of most extraordinary fertility. Rice is the principal product, much sugar, possibilities of cotton, coffee, or almost anything. A small amount of indigo is grown on the northern part of the line. The stations are at short intervals, in accordance with orders from the Spanish government. It is a country of splendid productive power; almost all of it is at present under cultivation.
>
> The following extensions and new lines are under consideration by the railroad company, and would be most valuable in the development of the island of Luzon: First, Manila to Batangas, south; second, Dagupan to Laoag, north; third, a branch, Gerona to Aliaga, 18 miles; fourth, a branch from Guiginto to the Cagayan Valley for the tobacco district.

Manila is naturally a healthy place, and the sanitary reforms necessary are very easy, especially as compared with much of the work in the east, particularly at Rangoon, the chief town of Lower Burma.

The islands have a small population when their area is considered. Luzon, larger than England, has only about 3,500,000, or a little over one-tenth of England's; Panay, 2,000,000; Negros and Cebu, 1,500,000; Mindanao, 2,000,000.

If any sensible nation governs these islands for purposes of development, a bureau of science, with the ablest chief and staff to be obtained, should at once be established, this to comprehend departments of geology, zoology, botany, and ethnology. The results obtained will be great and surprising. Also a land and forestry commission or a department of lands, surveys, and works. There are immense tracts of land to fall into the hands of the government which could be sold or leased. All of these possibilities have received no attention from the Spaniards.

I went to Manila without prejudice against the Spaniards there, perhaps a little doubtful, on account of the *Maine* massacre, for which, up to the time of the finding of the Court of Inquiry, I had been unwilling to believe that Spain was responsible; but testimony from all classes of people, English merchants, the general manager of the railway, also the general manager of the cable company—both of the last married Spanish women—a Frenchman and his wife, the advertisements in the papers, their treatment of their dead, their actions in battle and in civil administration, all convince me that they are without principle or courage, and brutally, wickedly cruel, showing no improvement of the character they had three hundred and twenty-five years ago, in the days of Philip II. The bones (skulls, arms, legs) of their dead lie without the honor of a covering of earth, exposed in their fashionable cemetery, exhumed on account of a failure by their descendants to pay rent for the tombs. The shooting in the Luneta (their favorite driveway) of dozens of so-called "rebels" and conspirators, notably Dr. Rizal, a man of literary merit, with no trial, under vague charges of belonging to secret societies, with the hope of making their victims confess to what, in many cases, did not exist, was made a *fête*, the papers advertising that their would be music, and I have been frequently told that women and children attended in their carriages. The tortures inflicted with the same view of eliciting confessions are too brutal to commit the narrative to paper.

I have brought from Manila, for the inspection of the Commissioners, four carvings in wood representing tortures inflicted by the Spaniards upon the natives. They were executed by Bonifacio Arevalo, who is now practising as a dentist in Manila. He is a man of fine presence, benevolent aspect, not sensational at all in his utterances, and in submitting them to me he wrote the wish that upon reaching Paris I would not forget that the Filipinos begged me to use my efforts to convince all concerned of the utter impossibility of their return to Spanish domination. He also gives a description of the models:

Figure No. 1 represents the chastisement which one of the municipal authorities of Jaen (Nueva Ecija) suffered in the prison of that town, the Spanish employés of the prison entertaining themselves by applying the most horrible tortures.

Figure No. 2 represents an honorably and peaceably inclined resident in a village of the province of Nueva Ecija, taken prisoner, brutally treated for being suspected, without cause, of belonging to the Katipunan, and afterwards shot.

Figure No. 3 represents one of the many natives of the Philippines whom, during the late insurrection, the Spaniards shot without previous trial, in the outskirts of the village, leaving their corpses without burial.

Figure No. 4 represents Mr. Moses Salvador, a young Tagalo, who studied several years in Europe. He is a native of Manila, and was imprisoned in September, 1896, for being a Freemason, was horribly martyrized in the headquarters of the police, and, after many months of imprisonment, was shot by order of the Spanish General Polavieja in the Luneta, in company with several of his countrymen, all condemned on the same charge, of which several were absolutely innocent.

A CORNER IN A MANILA CIGAR-FACTORY

The opinion of Alexandre Dumas, Sr., in regard to the Spaniards, was often quoted in the Philippines—that they possess "honor without honesty, religion without morality, pride with nothing to be proud of."

The rapacity, stealing, and immoralities of the priests are beyond question, and the bitterness of the natives against them has been caused and aggravated by years of iniquity. To demand a wife or daughter from a native has been a common occurrence. Failing to obtain acquiescence, the husband's or father's goods have been seized, he deported or thrown into jail under an order easily obtained from the government in Manila. The priests' influence is paramount: they are rich, and (fathers not only of the church) despised and hated by the people.

The skill of the Filipinos in trades, occupations, and professions is very great. Critics will call this skill imitation, but imitation of good things is not reprehensible. I refer now to the common people, and so will omit very able lawyers (one or two having ranked as the best of all nationalities in the Philippines) and the higher professions.

As accountants, they are excellent. In the custom-house sixty (more before) were employed during my administration. Any information desired, say the amount of imports and exports of last year, kind of articles, whence obtained, and where going, duties, etc., was sought from them, and the reply was always given in writing in a neat, satisfactory manner. All the cash was received by a native—$1,020,000, from August 22 to October 21, much of this in silver—all counterfeits and filled dollars were detected at once by his skill, and only $1 was returned to us from the banks. His neighbor, who kept the record of receipts, was most systematic and able. The Spaniards depended absolutely on them for the clerical work of the office, and the same in the other departments.

I visited three factories for the manufacture of cigars and cigarettes: First, that of H. J. Andrews & Co., where 150 to 200 natives were employed; second, the Alhambra, which had 300 in April, now 600; third, the Insular, with 2000. The Tabacallera, largely owned in Paris, I was unable to see; it has 4000. These working people seemed to me of the best—quiet, diligent, skilful. The same qualities were apparent in the one cotton-mill of the place, where at least 200 were employed.

As mariners, quartermasters of large boats, and managers of small ones, their skill has been proverbial over the East for years, and we had great opportunities during our three weeks in the bay of proving their ability and cleverness.

Manila straw hats have been famous for years; also pina cloth and jusi cloth, the former made of pineapple fibre and the latter made of pineapple fibre and hemp.

The station-masters and employés of the Manila Railway compare favorably with any I have ever seen at ordinary way-stations. Clean, neat, prompt, well-disciplined, their superiority is largely due to excellence of the general manager, Mr. Higgins, a man of great ability. Still, the quality is in the men. The three servants in his house (on the line) have all learned telegraphy by observation and imitation.

I have also some fine samples of their embroidery.

They are admittedly extraordinary musicians, and their orchestras and bands have found places all over the East, playing without notes with great harmony and sweetness. It seems to be instinct, and is all instrumental, with little or no vocal talent. All these accomplishments do not argue greatness, but they do show that they are something more than ignorant and brutal savages. I do not mean to ascribe to them all the virtues—they may be liars and thieves, it is a wonder they are not worse after the environment and example of centuries—but to my mind they are the best of any barbaric or uncivilized race I have ever seen, and open, I trust, to a wonderful development.

And now comes the vital question, What is to be done with these islands, and, if we hold them, what form of government is to prevail? Whatever grave doubts one may have as to colonial extension on the part of America, we have gone too far, either by design or chance, to recede. It cannot be denied that we owe it as a duty to the natives and to humanity that the islands should not be restored to Spain (even if they were they could not be held for a year). Any division of them is absolutely impracticable. This would induce constant friction, and the ruin of Manila as the great com-

SUGAR-MILL AND PLANTATION LABORERS' HOUSES IN HAWAII

mercial centre; the important products would be shipped direct from the southern islands and goods sent directly there in exchange. One owner must hold the whole country and prescribe uniform duties and government.

Many methods of government, with the natives as allies or subjects, are possible. I had often thought that it might be expedient at first to admit them to some of the minor offices in army and civil government, and if they show capacity, to enlarge their powers and opportunities, until finally they should have entire control, after proper compensation or an agreed subjection to us for our work and assistance to them. But—and I hope that I shall not be considered English-mad in my deference to their practice, the result of so many years of successful colonial government—I was told by a governor of one of the British colonies, Sir William McGregor, when I suggested such a course, that they have never thought it safe or expedient, when they have a colony of so many (in this case millions) of blacks, and so few white men, to intrust the government to the former. If of whites, as in Australia, yes, after trial trust the government to them, with what are practically supervising, or perhaps honorary governors, who maintain the connection with the mother or controlling country.

It will be admitted that England has been the only successful administrator of colonial government in the world. Holland has had a great career, but possibly things are not so well with it just now in Java and Sumatra; at any rate, it is not comparable to England. "The British colonial empire comprises forty distinct and independent governments, besides a number of scattered dependencies under the dominion or protection of the Queen." "Of the forty, eleven have elected assemblies and responsible governments." The other twenty-nine are divided into three classes: (1) No legislative council; legislative power delegated to officer administering the government, with, in most cases, power reserved by crown of legislating by order in council. (2) Legislative council nominated by the crown, with some power reserved, as in No. 1. (3) Legislative council partly elected, with reserve power in three countries, no general power reserved in five.

The different conditions of country, races, traditions, etc., have made absolutely different laws necessary—one country a gold currency, others silver; free-trade, open ports, tariffs, duties, internal and personal taxation prevail without following any precedents or existing laws of England, varying throughout the colonies.

The condition exists in very many colonies, that hundreds of thousands of natives are governed with a handful of soldiers—in many cases with none. The moral influence, justice, and fair dealing rule.

With strength, firmness, justice, and fair dealing, we can do anything with the native, and make a happy and prosperous country beyond any present expectations.

HAWAII

By Sanford P. Dole, Ex-President of the Republic

The native Hawaiians, including part-whites, form more than a third out of a population of 109,020, according to the census of 1896. There is a steady increase of the part-whites, with an equal division of the sexes. The pure natives are slowly decreasing in numbers, with men preponderating over women in the ratio of 53 to 47 per cent.

Naturally the part-whites have a hereditary superiority over the pure Hawaiians, and are, as a rule, more progressive.

The Anglo-Saxon element, made up of settlers from America, England, and Germany, and their descendants, while they represent but a small proportion of the aggregate population, form an influential part, taking the lead in religious, social, political, and business enterprises, and being the main factor in the formation of public sentiment.

Portuguese immigrants and their descendants, making an approximate seventh of the population, are an important addition to the community, with their characteristic qualities of thrift and order. While the percentage of illiteracy was large among the original immigrants, their children, under the peremptory school system of Hawaii, are making a promising advance in education.

The rest of the population is mainly Chinese and Japanese, with a scattering of other nationalities. The greater part of the Chinese and Japanese are temporarily in the country as laborers, without families, making a floating population constantly moving about in search of wages, and contributing largely to the passenger travel westward across the Pacific.

The majority of native Hawaiians have opposed annexation—some from political reasons based upon the hope of an eventual restoration of the monarchy; others from traditional familiarity with nominal native rule involving their feeling and prejudices; others from an undefined anxiety lest the annexation of Hawaii to the United States would injure them through loss of civil rights, political privileges, social standing, or in some other way which they could not forecast; and many on all of these grounds, with all of which race sentiment was an element of more or less force.

The average Hawaiian feels more than he thinks. He has never been able to analyze the political situation very thoroughly or to carry out any line of thought relating to Hawaiian affairs very far; and he is unable now to think out the question of annexation and how he is to be affected by it.

Many Hawaiians cheerfully accepted the abrogation of the monarchy, having lost confidence in it. These, as a rule, would have preferred the continuance of the republic of Hawaii to annexation, but, with confidence in the judgment of the annexationists and in the friendship and justice of the United States, they have bravely faced the—to them serious—new departure.

The Portuguese are good annexationists.

The Chinese were loyal to the republic of Hawaii, and would have preferred the continuance of its independence. Annexation has brought them grave anxieties.

The Japanese were not pleased with the extension of American sovereignty to Hawaii, but have accepted the situation with good grace.

The immediate effect of annexation is a rise in the values of real estate and sugar stock, and a general upward tendency in all kinds of business. There is excitement among speculators. Although these circumstances tend to support the theory of the existence of a boom, it is probable that, with the limited amount of land in the group, the new land values will rather increase than fall as time goes on, while values of sugar stocks will be affected favorably or otherwise mainly by the price of sugar and the state of the labor market, although it is evident that there is now a slight inflation of values.

Local politicians are considerably excited over the consummation of annexation, even to the extent of taking measures to influence the

SUGAR-PLANTATION PUMPING-STATION IN HAWAII

selection of local officials by the government at Washington.

There is some discontent among this class with the civil service status of the government of the republic of Hawaii, as it is and has been, on account of the absence of the political spoils system. Although annexation has inspired these with hopes in this direction, there is impatience at the slow and uncertain progress of events towards a permanent form of government on American lines.

Speculators are discontented with the Hawaiian land system, which intentionally excludes them from all participation in its benefits, and are looking hopefully to Washington for legislation that shall open the public lands to their manipulation, and are discussing means to promote such legislation.

The intermediate period in the programme of annexation is of value in giving the community time to adjust itself to the new relations. It is most important that the political development of Hawaii shall be a growth from former conditions, rather than that the present political plant shall be uprooted and another started in its place. It was fortunate that there was no sudden change of the civil system upon the transfer of sovereignty. That in itself was shock enough for the time being. All legitimate interests were conserved by the delay in the organization of the permanent government. Time was obtained for a deliberate study of the situation by the Hawaiian Commission and by Congress. That the government has continued much as before, except as to diplomatic relations, has undoubtedly promoted confidence in the field of business enterprise, and it has had a quieting effect upon the political situation, with its enthusiastic annexationists, its enthusiastic anti-annexationists, its royalists, and its great mass of puzzled and anxious people without definite views.

THE GOVERNMENT BUILDING, HONOLULU

That all important changes in the system of government or its administration should be gradual, and with due notice to all concerned, has always been a recognized feature of the policy of the republic of Hawaii. The Hawaiian Commissioners, in reporting an organic act for the territorial government of Hawaii, have been influenced by similar views. They recognized the fitness of the Hawaiian civil system for the local conditions, and were loath to introduce radical changes outside of the executive power. They felt that interference in the judicial or legislative function would tend to embarrass the administration of affairs and create a period of troublesome readjustment, causing worry, suspense, and uncertainty in all directions.

It is probably for the best that a territorial form of government, instead of immediate statehood, has been recommended. It cannot be doubted that the responsibilities and experiences of five and a half years of self-government as an independent power, with the serious obstacles and difficult questions which have beset the administration of affairs under the republic, have formed an effective school of preparation for the political union of the Hawaiian community with the United States. In like manner the experience of the nation under a territorial system will be educational in the line of American methods. Although the Anglo-Saxon element is probably as competent for the organization and maintenance of State government as the population of any American State, the Hawaiians and Portuguese need further opportunities of studying political principles and of putting them in practice. These a territorial government will furnish to some extent, and it will thus, in a measure, prepare the way for State government. Such a period of preparation will be in the interest of business prosperity, good government, and success in statehood when it comes.

It may be that some of the experiences under the territorial system will be bitter ones, and they may be all the more valuable on that account. If the Hawaiian distribution of official patronage is abolished for the more American but less scientific system, it is inevitable that the spoils feature of American politics will obtain a foothold in Hawaii. And if, in addition, the advisory feature of the Hawaiian administrative system is swept away, good government may become as difficult as it was under the decadence of the monarchy. Such retrogressions—temporarily disastrous though they may be—can be calmly endured, in the confidence that their reactions shall tend to keep alive that Hawaiian spirit of insistence on good government which has heretofore carried the insistors successfully through a period of difficulty and danger on the way to the accomplishment of their object.

Hawaii, as a civilized community, is older than any part of the United States west of the Rocky Mountains. There is much misconception on this point. Americans are arriving every day imbued with the idea that this is a new country, and that the mere fact of being on the ground is an advantage of great value, regardless of the want of capital, tools, or professional or mechanical skill. When gold was discovered in California, Hawaii was successfully administering its own affairs under a constitution and good laws, a legislature, and a supreme and subordinate courts. Life, liberty, and property were protected; schools existed in all parts of the country; churches were numerous and well attended.

For more than two generations enterprise has been developing and branching out in many directions. Local firms now have the business of the country well in hand. Annexation, by its stimulus to production and immigration, has already increased the traffic in lumber, machinery, tools, dry-goods, and groceries, and perhaps luxuries. The hotel and lodging-house business is very favorably affected, while the growing demand for rented houses, and for ground on which to build, has stimulated land values.

This business development makes room for new capital and new men. The new man with capital may find room in the established lines of business. He can hardly develop a new line of enterprise until American laws are extended to the islands, except perhaps in the field of agriculture, where it is extremely probable that products now not thought of may be profitably cultivated, and in the development of water-power.

During the intermediate period business growth will closely depend on the increase of the white population and the development of sugar production, but upon the extension of the American tariff to Hawaii there will be new opportunities for enterprise, such as canning of various kinds of fruit, the manufacture of textile fabrics, the production of tobacco, the cultivation of fruits and vegetables for American consumers, and raising flowers for the manufacture of perfumes.

The natural resources of the group are a fertile and well-watered soil, a considerable water-power, climate, and geographical position. Besides these there are no others to be seriously considered in forecasting its future development.

The geographical position of the Hawaiian Islands confers large business advantages, and promises much for the future. During the year 1898 there were one hundred and thirteen arrivals at Honolulu of large steamships going and coming between the Pacific coast and the Orient and the British colonies of the south seas. These vessels contributed greatly to the business of that port through their freight and passenger traffic, and by their requirements for coal, provisions, water, and repairs.

The commerce of the Pacific is in its beginning. Its growth will in the near future test the harbor facilities of the Hawaiian group to the utmost. Extensive wharf and dock improvements must be promptly made to meet the new requirements. All this means an increased demand for labor and capital.

The construction of the Nicaragua ship-canal, which may be regarded as a feature of that new American departure that includes the assumption of the control of the Spanish East and West Indies and Hawaii, will most materially add to the commanding commercial position of the Hawaiian Islands.

Upon the consummation of annexation, the cultivation of sugar under the conditions of rainfall and irrigation by gravitation had materially reached its limit. Stability, as a feature both of the government and of the sugar market, caused by that measure, has greatly promoted enterprise in the direction of irrigation by means of water artificially raised. This forecasts a considerable addition to the sugar product within the next few years, if the labor market proves to be reliable.

For a generation or more wild coffee-trees have furnished the local supply. Within seven or eight years the cultivation of this crop has been taken up and carried on with much energy. As three or four years from the nursery are required for the trees to reach full bearing, it is as yet early to speak with certainty in regard to the prospects for success. There is no doubt, however, that in suitable localities it will be a reliable and profitable crop. Further data are required as to soils, weather, elevation, and other matters of environment in relation to its successful cultivation. This product is not materially affected by annexation, except as that event raises land values and promotes the immigration of persons who want to plant coffee, thus casting both favorable and unfavorable influences over the prospects of this industry.

Tobacco has long been raised by the natives in small quantities for their own use. Both soil and climate favor its growth in sheltered and elevated localities in many parts of the group. It freely grows wild in such places. Plants from foreign seed flourish. What place Hawaiian tobacco is entitled to in the markets of the world is as yet unknown, as it has never yet been properly cured. We may expect that tobacco will be produced in Hawaii of good, if not first-class, quality, and that the extension of the American tariff to these islands will be the signal for exhaustive experiments in its culture and preparation.

A considerable part of the grazing area of the islands is fair arable land, and under annexation will be in demand for the cultivation of some crop or other. This will reduce the extent of grazing-lands, and will diminish stock-raising in the old Hawaiian way, which will be a direct benefit, as it will tend to promote a more intelligent and scientific system of stock-farming than has been the case heretofore. Quality will take the place of quantity as the paramount object, because it will pay better with the diminished pastures and the necessity of relying to a large extent on forage crops.

The land system of the republic of Hawaii, which encourages the settlement of individuals on small farms, has been very successful. The number of small landholders is constantly increasing, thus adding materially to the taxable value of the real estate affected, and developing a prosperous and conservative class of citizens. Although these farmers, for the most part, cultivate coffee and Indian corn, they are in a favorable position to take up the cultivation of such other crops as the new conditions under the extension of American laws and tariff shall encourage.

A RESIDENCE STREET IN HONOLULU

The continuation of this policy under annexation is vital to a successful settlement of the public land by a class which by its industry and its interest in public affairs shall favorably affect the future politics of the country.

The Hawaiian climate has been mentioned as one of the natural resources. The inhabited islands are within 154° 30′ and 160° 30′ west longitude and 19° and 22° 30′ north latitude. They are within the trade-wind belts, are surrounded in every direction by thousands of miles of ocean, unbroken by any shores save the smallest islets. The air currents that come to them are pure and full of the tonic of the sea. The temperature is hardly tropical, yet entices all of every age into the open air all the year round. Sunstroke is practically unknown. No one is debilitated except by his own inactivity. Out-of-door athletics prevail much as they do in America. Men from northern climates work freely and comfortably under the sun's direct rays. There is no deterioration of Anglo-Saxon families from generation to generation, either physically or mentally, but there are indications of a contrary tendency.

A climate of this quality is a resource, because it attracts tourists who are running away from cold weather and settlers who are tired of the struggle with nature in higher latitudes. It affects national prosperity as it promotes the general health. The tops of the highest mountains have heavy falls of snow in the rainy season. From these to the sea-shore is a large variety for one to choose from, with an environment of scenery everywhere—land and sea, forest and meadow and silver stream—which is beyond the anticipations of every visitor.

I do not know that anywhere else is there a civilized community whose social life is more natural and unconventional, without loss of refinement, than that existing in the Hawaiian Islands. There is no aristocracy, nor any "four hundred." There is no social color-line, and no definite social lines of any nature. There may be said to be loosely defined social sets, but there are no lines between them; they merge into each other. Education, refinement, polish—these have more to do with social position than any other circumstances. Wealth has its weight, but has hardly come to be regarded as a social circumstance, although it is a strong ally where the more important qualifications exist. Family is an important consideration.

There is no color prejudice affecting the Hawaiian, the Chinese, or the Japanese; or if there is, it is discoverable only in marital considerations. None of these races, if otherwise socially acceptable, are barred by color. The Hawaiians, and part Hawaiians in particular, are specially in demand socially.

A charm of Hawaiian society is its cosmopolitan quality. Every large social gathering has representatives from the great world races—Polynesian, Anglo-Saxon, Celt, Scandinavian, Frank, Mongolian.

A large part of the opposition to annexation among Hawaiians was due to anxiety lest they should be socially prejudiced by its consummation. Conscious that both the monarchy and the republic fostered their social advancement, they were afraid that, as a part of the great, eager American nation, they would be gradually ignored until their position should have become intolerable.

There is a good deal to say on the side of these fears. A large part of the white population is Hawaiian by birth and environment through the susceptible time of childhood. Another large part has sifted in slowly, one or two at a time, never in sufficient numbers to dominate in any line of influence, always absorbed, so to speak, by the Hawaiian community, and quickly converted to its sentiment and taste and likes and dislikes, and, among other things, to its recognition of the native Hawaiian as a social equal.

What will be the result when white men come in as they are coming now, and faster? Will the Hawaiian community still continue to dominate the situation and assimilate the arrivals as fast as they come, or will the new-comers, before they become Hawaiian, assert themselves and be a law unto themselves and the old society, making their social sentiment and indifference towards the native Hawaiian to be the paramount, unwritten code?

If this take place it will be unpleasant and

prejudicial for the Hawaiians and part Hawaiians, not only socially, but commercially as well. But it will not take place. The social community as it exists is strongly intrenched, and Hawaiian families are an essential part of it. Some of these have wealth as well as social prestige. There is a kindly sentiment in America towards the whole native element. They are civilized enough to escape being regarded as Indians are regarded by Americans. Their civilization is mainly an American product. Individuals may be indifferent or patronizing, but the American people are proud of the results of this educational enterprise of theirs, and will ever be disposed to foster the due blossoming and fruitage of this vine of their own planting and culture.

The industrious Hawaiian will be benefited by the larger horizon which annexation brings to him, and by the power and prestige of the great nation in which he may claim citizenship. The new environment will be educational; he will continue to be a man and brother, but in a larger sense than before. Competition in all lines will increase somewhat, but he will stand it, and will find the place to which his competency entitles him.

Especially will those who own the lands which they live on and cultivate be able to hold their own with new-comers. Some, indeed, will be led into mortgaging their homes and eventually losing them, but the many will learn, as they are learning now, to resist such temptations, and will come more and more to prize the independence which home-ownership confers.

The Chinese and Japanese element of the population, forming about forty-two per cent. at the census of 1896, must be considered in the social and political outlook. How will our future be affected by them: and does their presence constitute a menace to Hawaiian civilization?

There is one feature of the movements of these people which aids materially in the solution of these questions, and that is the fact that the great majority are here temporarily in search of wages, and that but few of these show any tendency to settle permanently. The rest return home—some to stay, others to return eventually, if they can. If the supply is cut off, the constant migration homewards rapidly diminishes the local colony.

In 1886, in consequence of understandings with the Japanese government at the inauguration of the immigration of Japanese laborers under treaty provisions, the influx of Chinese was substantially shut off. At that time their number in the islands was approximately 19,500. For eight years the doors were closed against them, and in that time their numbers fell off approximately to 15,300. The same result will be reached again in regard to them, now that restrictions have been placed upon their entrance into the country. Restrictions on the entry of Japanese would produce similar results.

Many of the Chinese in the country are employed on rice plantations, generally owned and managed by their countrymen. It is safe to say that white men will never be willing to do the work required in the cultivation of rice, as in all of it, except the harvesting, the laborer is compelled to work in water and mud. Chinese labor employed in raising rice may be left out of the consideration of the prospects of white labor.

In regard to raising sugar, it is not probable that white men will work in gangs under the direction of an overseer, according to the system generally in vogue at the present time. Experiments are now in operation to employ white men in sugar-plantation field-work under profit-sharing conditions. There seems to be no reason why the application of this principle should not be completely successful. If this be accomplished, it may be expected that systems of profit-sharing in a considerable variety will be gradually developed throughout the sugar plantations of the islands because of the greater liability of labor under such conditions. Such a change in the labor status will give the white laborer the most favorable conditions possible in relation to the most important crop of the country. The change cannot be made at once, but must have time for its effective accomplishment.

The temporary nature of the Chinese and Japanese stay in the country is further shown by the fact that those who take up agriculture as proprietors generally acquire leaseholds rather than actual ownership of land. While in 1896 seventy-four per cent. of the land-owners of the country were Hawaiians and part Hawaiians, and seven per cent. Portuguese, only three per cent. were Chinese, and one and a half per cent. Japanese, and at the same time the Chinese and Japanese, the great majority of whom were adult males, numbered forty-two per cent. of the whole population. It is true that opportunities of acquiring holdings in public lands are not open, as a rule, to the Chinese and Japanese under the special systems of the present land laws, but under the homestead law under the monarchy, which was put in operation in 1887, no distinctions were made, and none have existed for many years in the ordinary sales of public lands at auction.

From these facts and figures it will, I think, be clear that the Oriental element of the Hawaiian population is under easy control, and is not likely to become a menace to Anglo-Saxon civilization, unless, indeed, the enterprise of establishing families from other races upon the public lands, with ownership in the soil, should be neglected.

While the Chinese conduct all the rice plantations, and were the pioneers in sugar-culture, they do not at the present time manage a single sugar plantation, and the amount of sugar stock they hold is insignificant.

If the settlement of small farmers on the public lands continue, and especially if it should be carried out on a larger scale than at present, and if they should be, as a rule, men with families, content to make their permanent homes on their holdings, and looking to the cultivation of the soil instead of speculation in land for a living, the political and social future of the country will be secure.

Many native Hawaiians have refrained on political grounds from voting during the past few years. It is probable that in the future all will vote who can. All political parties will seek their support. This will give them a standing politically, and will be helpful to them. The natives will be numerically strong enough for a while to elect their own candidates on race lines, should they so desire, and they will probably do so in some cases; but it is not likely that this will generally happen. Such results will be reached by them more often in the politics of the local municipal corporations which will be inaugurated than in elections for the territorial legislature; for, while they are able sometimes to organize within the limits of a district, they have never succeeded in extending a political organization effectively over the group.

Without doubt the union of little Hawaii with great America lifts the curtain before a future full of great possibilities to Hawaii. To America the union is of great importance, but to that great country, with its manifold interests, it is but a ripple in the onward flow of its resistless energies—a rivulet joining the river.

To us of Hawaii it is present loss for a future and greater good, sovereignty and independence, and some heartfelt associations for participation in a greater sovereignty and a more effective independence represented by a government of incalculable strength.

We shall undoubtedly have our disappointments. There will be some bad mixed with the good. But there will be growth beyond all our precedents. Our local world will be larger, and we shall be more in touch with the great communities of the rest of the world. We are Americans now for better or worse. We have placed our fortunes and our future in the hands of the United States. We shall prosper or suffer as they shall deal with us.

THE GOVERNOR'S PALACE, SAN JUAN, PUERTO RICO

THE RESOURCES OF PUERTO RICO

FROM "THE FARMER'S YEAR BOOK, 1899"

PUERTO RICO may be described as having a mean latitude of 17° 56′ north, and longitude 67° 10′ west from Greenwich.

It is about 70 miles east of Hayti, 1025 miles from Key West, 400 miles from the east coast of Cuba, 1300 miles from New York, 2460 miles from Cape Verde, and about 3000 miles from Cadiz.

In area it is 3670 square miles, or about four times as big as Rhode Island. It is mountainous in the centre, with a belt of low lands on the coast, ranging from five to ten miles in width. The average height of the mountains is 1500 feet; the highest peak, El Yunque, is about 3600 feet above sea-level. It is exceedingly well-watered, having about 1300 streams, of which about forty are considerable rivers, navigable for small vessels to some extent.

The climate is hot, but not unhealthful; the temperature seldom exceeding 97° Fahrenheit, in the shade, and sinking at night to about 68°. The seasons are about equally divided between wet and dry; but the annual rainfall is not excessive (considering the long duration of the rainy season), averaging about 64 inches.

TYPICAL SUGAR-MILL NEAR PONCE—ANTIQUATED AND MODERN MACHINERY COMBINED

The soil of the cultivable portions is exceedingly fertile. The products are sugar, coffee, cotton, tobacco, potatoes, plantains, rice (of which there is a highland variety that requires no flooding), bananas, pineapples, oranges, and other fruits. The coffee raised in the western part is said to be without an equal. The rivers and the adjacent seas abound with the finest fish. There are said to be 500 varieties of trees, and timber and timber products may eventually become an industry of some importance. There are great herds of excellent cattle, that find abundant pasturage in the lowland districts and the foot-hills. Cattle-raising is a considerable industry.

Animal life is abundant and varied, but there are no beasts of prey.

There are mines of gold, coal, copper, iron, and salt, in general undeveloped, except as to salt, and a considerable variety of marble, limestone, and other building-stones, as yet but little developed.

The population in 1890, which had not been materially increased when the United States assumed control, was something over 800,000, of whom about 490,000 are white, the rest of mixed blood and negroes. Of the whites at that time, only 96,867 could read and write, and the total illiterate population is stated to have been 695,328. Of the mixed population, 300,000 are the Jebaros, an uncommon people, said to be of Spanish stock, with drops of native Indian blood in them. They are small farmers and laborers. The race is a fine one, showing the regular features and small feet of the Europeans.

The people have the qualities of an industrious and highly civilized race, and yet the island's resources remain mostly undeveloped. The prevailing religion is the Roman Catholic. More than one-seventh of the population are residents of the four principal towns—as, San Juan (the capital), 24,000; Ponce, 40,000; San Germain, 30,000; Mayaguez, 27,000.

The island had, in 1898, 137 miles of railroad and considerable additional lines under construction, and 470 miles of telegraph. There are a number of good harbors—as, at San Juan, on the north; Ponce, on the south; Mayaguez, on the west; and Maquado, on the east. The largest anchorage-ground on the southern coast is at Guanica, but one of the best in the West Indies is that at San Juan. It has a comparatively unobstructed entrance, with a depth at wharves of ten to thirteen feet, low water, and eleven to fifteen feet, high water.

Puerto Rico was discovered on November 15, 1493, by Columbus. In 1509 Ponce de Leon was appointed Governor by the King of Spain, and founded the first settlement on the island, now known as Puerto Viejo. The original name of the island was Boriquen, or Burenquen. Columbus called it Isla de San Juan Bautista. The natives whose number was put at the extravagant figure of 600,000, were treated so cruelly in the mines that bloody uprisings resulted, as a consequence of which they were gradually exterminated. Interesting relics of them are preserved in the Smithsonian Institution at Washington and in the Berlin Ethnological Museum. For a long time the island was used chiefly as a penal colony, and was subject to frequent attacks by the English and French navies and by pirates. In 1763 Spain first began to pay greater attention to the island, which first rose to prosperity under the rule of Captain-General Miguel de la Torre, in 1823. An unsuccessful attempt at a declaration of independence had been made three years before. Slavery was entirely abolished in 1873.

Spanish rule in Puerto Rico has been, of course, as elsewhere in Spanish colonies. The people have had no voice in their government. Their representatives in the Cortes have wielded no influence. The so-called Puerto Rican budget for 1894–95 (which is a fair sample of the tax burdens the people have had to bear) was 5,454,958 pesos. It was estimated that customs produced 2,300,000 pesos, which left much to be wrung from the islanders, though the expenditures did not reach the amount estimated. Under a free government all this would have been devoted to the use of the people. Under monarchical rule most of it was devoted to the support of about 35,000 Spaniards (including the soldiery), kept there to administer the government and hold the island in subjection. The regular military force numbered, under ordinary conditions, 4500 men, infantry, artillery, and cavalry. There was also a corps of more than 500 police and 14 battalions (6000 men) of Spanish volunteers.

Taking the latest reliable statistics, we find that the trade of the United States with Puerto Rico, for five years preceding the beginning of the trouble with Spain, was as follows:

	Exports to U. S.	Imports from U. S.
1893	$4,008,623	$2,510,007
1894	3,135,631	2,720,508
1895	1,506,512	1,833,544
1896	2,296,653	2,102,094
1897	2,181,024	1,988,888

The principal exports from the United States are flour, pork, lard, lumber, and staves for making hogsheads and other casks. The leading imports to the United States are coffee, sugar, and molasses, though there has been considerable trade in non-agricultural products, as cosmetics, chemicals, drugs, dyes, etc.

In recent years the annual export of coffee, sugar, molasses, and tobacco from the island amounted to more than $15,000,000, of which more than one-third went to Spain.

A TYPICAL SCENE IN THE MARKET, PONCE

INDEX TO ILLUSTRATIONS

INDEX

INDEX

INDEX

PORTRAITS

GENERAL INDEX

INDEX

INDEX

INDEX

www.ingramcontent.com/pod-product-compliance
Lightning Source LLC
Chambersburg PA
CBHW031329230426
43670CB00006B/286
* 9 7 8 3 7 4 4 7 4 8 2 3 0 *